EGYPT ALMANAC

SPONSORED BY

Cairo Barclays
Daimler-Chrysler Egypt
Glaxo
Siemens Egypt
Talaat Mostafa Group
Unilever Mashreq

Egypto-*file*

EDITORIAL STAFF

Project Manager Paul Ayoub-Geday

Managing Editor Mandy McClure

Business Editor Sarah Vellozzi

Concept, Iconography and Art Direction Paul Ayoub-Geday

Chief Editorial Adviser Max Rodenbeck

Graphic Designer Remon Hakim

Advertising and Sales Tom Olson and Robert Youssef

Proof Readers Robin Moger

Marketing assistant Tania Hamilton

Office Manager Salih Yassin Ali

Accountant Samir Haroun

Editorial Assistants Lorraine Miltgen, Dina Ramadan, Yasmine Ramadan, Sarah Rifky, Sarah Sirgani

Cover Design Berangere Dastarac and the Egypt Almanac

CAIRO REPRESENTATIVE OFFICE

3 Khadrawi Street, Downtown, Cairo

Telephone/Fax: (202) 575-4679

email: almanac@egyptofile.net

MARKETING & SALES OFFICE

Satellite Guide: 32 Zahraa St., Doqqi, Giza, Cairo

Telephone: (202) 336-0106 / Fax: 749-0491

email: satgolf@link.net

ACKNOWLEDGEMENTS

The publishers would like to thank the following for their help, advice and invaluable support, moral or professional, during the creation and production of the *Egypt Almanac 2003*: Naguib Amin, Nasser Amin, Tarek Atia, Mindy and Sherif Bahaeddin, Fatiha Bouzidi, Eric Denis and François Ireton of the Centre d'Etudes et de Documentation Economique, Juridique et Sociale (CEDEJ), Issandr Elamrani, Jean-Yves Empereur, Mai Ezzeldeen, Nevine Fathy, Anne Fianni, Mona El-Ghobashy, Amani Ghoneim, Barbara Ibrahim and the Population Council, John Iskander, Hisham Kassem and the *Cairo Times*, Marianne Khoury, Chris Larter, Mark Linz, Neil MacDonald, Bridget McKinney, Samia Mehrez, Robin Moger, Mohammed Mursi, Amgad Nagib, Tom Olson, Nina Prochazka, Lamia Radi, Sally Sabet, Amal Sabri, Reem Saad, David Sims, Cosimo Tendi, Chris Toensing, Patrick Werr, Richard Woffenden, Mona Zaki, and Michael Zaug.

2003 EDITION

Published by Egypto-*file* Ltd., LLC, Wilmington, DE, USA
Printed by Sahara Printing Company, Free zone
Scans & color separation by Virgin Graphics

The *Egypt Almanac* is published by Egypto-*file* Ltd.

ISBN: 977-5893-02-X

One inspired person
can make a difference.
450,000 can change the world.

SIEMENS

Global network of innovation

Infinite possibilities.

... to anywhere. As a leading car manufacturer, DaimlerChrysler offers countless solutions
for mobility. From small city coupés to heavy-duty buses. From 4-wheel drives to 18-wheel trucks.
Whatever your needs, we have vehicles that can take you from here ...
Find out more at www.daimlerchrysler.com.

DAIMLERCHRYSLER

Answers for questions to come.

cks manufactured by Freightliner LLC, Setra manufactured by EvoBus GmbH.

CONTENTS

The Land

The Land of Egypt

The Capital

The Provinces

A world of banking services

As well as being part of the local community, we're also part of a global banking network. For further details on all our services, come and see us at:

Head Office & Garden City Branch
12 Midan El Sheikh Youssef
P.O.Box 110 Maglis El Shaab
Cairo, Egypt
Tel.: (202) 3662600

Mohandseen Branch
51 El Hegaz street
P.O.Box 453 Embaba
Cairo, Egypt
Tel.: (202) 3033810/3033820

Alexandria Branch
10 El Fawatem street
P.O.Box 1097
Alexandria, Egypt
Tel.: (203) 4861307/4861308

Nasr City Branch
50 Abbas El Akkad street
P.O.Box 7026 6th Zone
Cairo, Egypt
Tel.: (202) 2754536

Prestige Banking Centres

Maadi Prestige Banking Centre
67 Road 9,
Cairo, Egypt
Tel.: (202) 3586158/3686187

Roushdy Prstige Banking Centre
Horreya Avenue,
Imperial Plaza
Alex., Egypt
Tel.: (203) 5232566/68

Cairo
BARCLAYS

Culture

Curtain Call

Performing Arts

Literature & Art

The Built Heritage

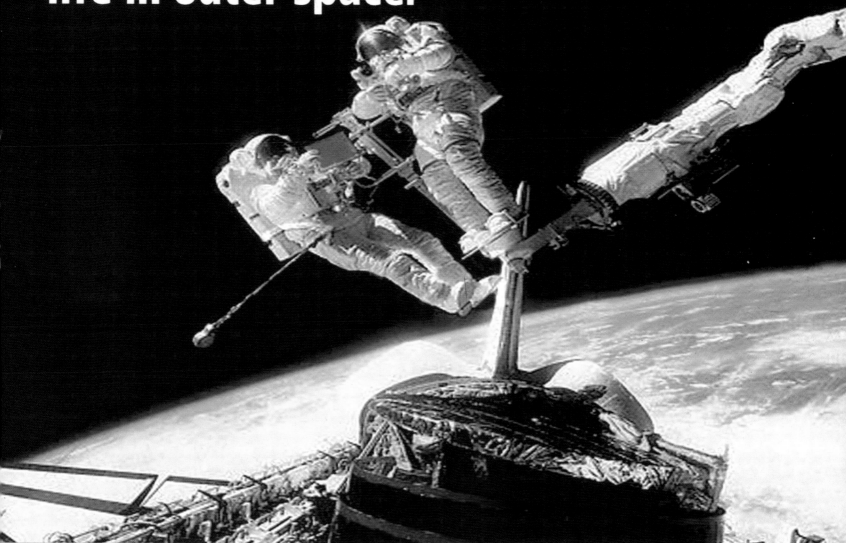

Let the Astronauts worry about life in outer space.

Our job is to improve life on Earth

Society

Roll Call

Living

Civil Society

Sport

Politics

The Art of Governance

The Game of Politics

Other Power Bases

Economy

The Big Picture

New Horizons Everyday

Through an unwavering commitment to coverage, as well as months of hard work, MobiNil is becoming a river that runs through the heart of Egypt. With its powerful GSM network reaching more cities everyday, improved quality and widespread coverage continues to be our main goal.

All this is aimed at providing you with a service that sets global standards for excellence, meeting your everyday communication needs.

المحمول فى يد الجميع

CONTENTS

Trade Challenges

Microeconomy

Finance

Industry

Agriculture

Energy

Services

Telecommunications

Transport

The back of the book

Porsche insists on Mobil 1.
Shouldn't you?

Mobil 1®

List of Maps

List of Graphs and Tables

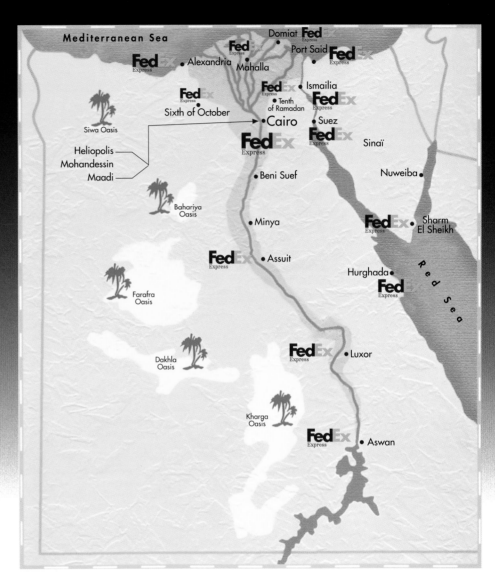

CONTENTS

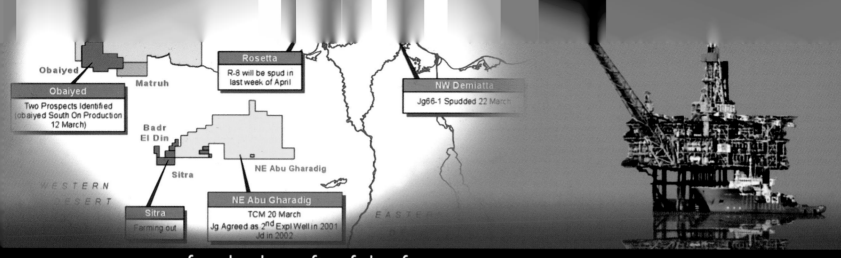

for the benefit of the future generation.

Shell Egypt is one of the oldest oil companies in Egypt, starting its activities in 1911. In 1979 it restarted its operations in the upstream and invested $3 billions; at least $300 millions will be invested over the next five years.

We produce 600 Mmscfld gas and 40,000 b/d oil from Badr El Din and Obaiyed fields in the Western Desert. Recently the Rosetta field, offshore Nile Delta, started production.

Our exploration concessions extend from the Western Desert to the Nile Delta. Our North East Mediterranean Deepwater Block covers depths from 800 to 3000m.

We have also started work to increase local gas usage through Fayum Gas, and our recent acquisition of an 18% stake in NATGAS. As a further commitment to invest in Egypt's future, Shell also has plans to invest $1.7 billions in a gas to liquid plant.

For our mutually rewarding relationship to continue, our investments and business culture must evolve in close harmony with the communities in which we are privileged to operate. Shell is particularly interested in the country's youth, sincerely believing that the key to a successful future is held in our children's hands.

www.shell.com
www.egyptart.org.eg

The Land

The Land of Egypt

The Capital

The Provinces

The Land of Egypt

The Face of Egypt at 2003

IN 1882, EGYPT HAD JUST SLIGHTLY MORE INHABITANTS THAN THE NETHERLANDS. EVEN THEN, HOWEVER, THESE TWO countries were the most densely populated areas of Africa and Europe. Though many things changed in Egypt during the 20th century, this basic fact did not: 130 years later, it is still the most densely populated area of Africa. Over the last hundred years, Egypt's population has increased more than five fold without any notable expansion of its inhabitable area. Today, about 98% of the population is packed into about 35,000 km², an area equivalent to the Netherlands—but with eight times the population. With an average of 1,700 people per inhabited km², Egypt is the most densely populated country in the world.

It is this growing demographic pressure that has and will continue to shape the broad contours of Egypt's future. In 2002, the population passed 66 million. By 2025, it is expected to reach 90 million, moving up to 100 million by 2040, and 140 million by the end of the century—and it is entirely possible that Egyptians will still be living in more or less the same space. Since the 1950s, the government has embarked on a series of grandiose land reclamation schemes to enlarge Egypt's cultivated land and, more importantly, relieve pressure in the Nile Valley. Thus far, however, they have had little demographic impact. Over the last 150 years, the 4,000 km² of reclaimed land in the Delta, on the lakes, and in the desert fringes have only absorbed 7% of population growth. The most recent attempts to conquer the desert, Toshka and the Salam Canal, look set to follow in the footsteps of their predecessors. With the focus on capital-intensive, rather than labor-intensive farming, there is little job incentive to attract the millions of Egyptians the government hopes to settle in such far-flung desert areas.

Even with a declining growth rate, increasing density in the Nile Valley represents the biggest challenge Egypt faces in the 21st century, touching on virtually every aspect of national development, whether economic, social, or environmental. The population today is growing at less than 2% a year, a far cry from the 2.8% rate of the 1970s. While this is overall good news, it translates into an increase in the working age population, creating higher job stress as more and more young people come of age and start looking for jobs. By 2025, the economy will need to generate 450,000 new jobs each year simply to absorb new entrants to the labor market. Add to that another 250,000 jobs needed annually over the next ten years to eliminate existing unemployment. Taking into account the actual capacity of the Egyptian economy to create jobs, annual GDP growth needs to reach 44% to create the required number of jobs by 2010.

Poverty and increasing impoverishment are the inevitable outcome. The richest 10% of society consume as much as the bottom 50%. Using a poverty line based on minimum access to food and shelter, 44% of families were poor in 1995 and 50% in 2000. After 20 years of restructuring and 10 years of adjustment, urban Egyptians are in general poorer than they were in 1958,

the date of the first Household Income and Expenditure Sample Survey. In 1996, Cairo, by far the largest urban center, registered a GDP of $12 billion, about the same level as Izmir, with a population of 2 million, or Nice, with only 500,000 inhabitants. Though the life of rural Egyptians has undoubtedly improved with the spread of basic infrastructure, it is worse today than it was at the beginning of the 1980s.

Growing inequalities—between rich and poor, rural and urban—have taken a heavy toll on human capital. Overall, 18% of kids under five years old suffer from malnutrition; in Upper Egypt, the number is more than 27%. Over half the population of Upper Egypt was illiterate in 1996, and in rural Fayyoum and Assyout, less than 40% were literate. The same goes for newer regions in the Delta, like Beheira and Kafr al-Sheikh, which were only reclaimed 150 years ago by migrant laborers, most of them coming from Upper Egypt.

But perhaps the greatest challenge represented by increasing population density—and one that has literally transformed the landscape—is the difficulty Egyptians have in finding homes. Nowhere is this more apparent than in the capital. With more than 25,000 inhabitants per km², Cairo is one of the densest urban agglomerations in the world. This explains why people often think the city has more people than it really does. Cairo is the 15th largest metropolis in the world, about the same in terms of population as Paris, but with a surface area that is nine times smaller. Situated at the heart of three governorates that contain 16 million inhabitants, the city itself holds 12 million souls.

In the quest for housing, desperate Cairenes have turned to informal housing, mostly illegally built settlements, often constructed on farmland. Every year for the last ten years, informal housing has gobbled up 3.7 km² of agricultural land around Cairo. With this type of housing growing at a rate of more than 3% annually, the city will have grown willy-nilly, with no de-

densification or urban planning, about 70 km² by 2020.

Though Cairo continues to burst at its seams, over the last two decades new patterns in urbanization and population distribution have emerged. In 1907, Cairo held 5.5% of the total population; by 1986, the number had reached 19.3%. By the last census in 1996, however, the number had shrunk to 17%, giving further evidence of a trend that started in the 1970s: the waning of Cairo as an attractive place to live. Since the 1990s, Cairo has been growing more slowly than the rest of Egypt, at a rate of 1.9% annually, compared to 2.1%. Simply put, the capital no longer attracts migrants from the provinces: 35% of Cairenes were not born in the city in 1960, while in 1996, only 12% were non-natives.

Yet, if Cairo's star is on the decline, the areas immediately surrounding it are increasingly popular. In the peripheral governorates of Giza and Qalyoubia, the percentage of non-natives is still important (about 25%). More than half of these are young families who cannot find lodging in Cairo and must resort to the new informal suburbs. These districts house about half of all

Cairenes, whereas the center of Cairo, the old city, and Boulaq have been losing their inhabitants for about 20 years. Thus, Cairo's slower rate of growth should not be taken as evidence of a move towards decentralization, but simply as a change in the scale of urbanization. Centralization around the capital continues, but the selectivity of access to the metropolis itself has increased. For all intents and purposes, greater Cairo is spreading to include large swathes of the Delta, all of it being incorporated into one big city.

More than one economic indicator confirms the trend. Even since 1917, Cairo has claimed 25% of jobs in chemistry, 30% in leather, 24% in metallurgy, 34% of jobs in finance, and 31% of legal and hotel sector activity. By 1996, greater Cairo claimed 40% of all industrial employment, and 46% of jobs in the financial and hotel sectors. The capital's weight has increased with the establishment of industrial zones in new cities like the Sixth of October and the Tenth of Ramadan, which are slowly replacing the traditional job centers like Helwan-Tibbin and Shubra al-Kheima. As joint ventures have been established in the desert, the older public sector enterprises have declined. Industry is thus progressively moving away from the center of Cairo to the fringes, the real magnet for jobs and growth.

All told, the Nile Valley to the south of Giza generates less than 5% of industrial value added, while the top

Infrastructure Inroads	1982	2001
Length of rail lines (km)	4,935	9,400
Length of metro (km)	-	63
Roads (km)	15,298	44,000
Bridges over the Nile	12	22
Telephone line capacity (millions)	0.51	8.8
Public-service telephones	250	36,048
Towns with auto-dialing	7	965
Port capacity (million tons)	26.6	58.8
Container terminals	-	5
Container capacity (million tons)	-	1.56
Commercial fleet (ships)	70	125
Fleet tonnage (million tons)	0.53	2
Civil airports	n/a	20
Water treatment capacity (m³/day)	850,000	7.3 million
Irrigation canals (km)	21,000	34,200

Source: State Information Service yearbook, MCIT

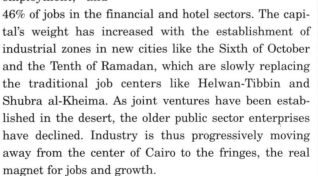

Already, 50% of Egypt's population lives and works within less than 100 km of Cairo, and 70% within 150 km

ten industrial cities, all north of Cairo, and the metropolitan industrial pole produce about 90%. That is, almost the whole totality of Egypt's potential for economic development is concentrated within less than three hours from Cairo, between the Mediterranean, Alexandria, and the Suez Canal. Already, 50% of Egypt's population lives and works within less than 100 km of Cairo, and 70% within 150 km.

As distances have become easily manageable and the cost of living in the city has become unbearable, migration has been replaced by a very high increase in daily commuting, especially among young rural Egyptians, many of whom find work in the city. Growing at 5.4% annually, the level of job creation in transport is higher than either industry or construction. In consequence, the countryside is urbanizing at breakneck speed. Right now, there are more than 600 villages with a population of more than 10,000, compared to only 40 in 1947. Close to 70% of Egyptians live in urban centers of more than 10,000 inhabitants. From 1990 to 1995, 700,000 agricultural jobs were lost in Egypt, accelerating the urbanization of economic activity, but they have not been replaced by sufficient job opportunities in other spheres. The collective urban accoutrements needed to make a smooth transition from rural to urban society and to create non-agricultural jobs have not kept pace with growth.

The most dynamic demographics are concentrated in these provincial agro-towns, while the importance of big cities diminish, their centers losing inhabitants and growth being concentrated in the peripheral villages. But despite population growth, most remain villages in terms of infrastructure, even though they may be home to more than 50,000 people. Only 3% of village households are connected to sewage disposal systems, as opposed to half in settlements officially recognized as cities. Here again, Upper Egypt is particularly under-equipped, with terrible health and environmental consequences for the population.

This is the new face of Egypt at the turn of the 21st century. Once the breadbasket of the ancient world, the increasing merging of the city with the countryside is leading Egypt inexorably towards urban agriculture. With better management of its limited water resources, Egypt may be able to follow the lead of densely populated countries like Japan or the Netherlands, which have successfully integrated agriculture with urban economies. In the long term, this is no less vital than land reclamation efforts. *ED*

Taming the Desert
Land reclamation threatens water resources

With more than 95% of the population living on less than 5% of the country's land, Egypt is under severe demographic pressure. To relieve it, the nation is once again having visions of enlarging its arable and habitable land by an intensive, systematic occupation of the desert. Land reclamation is nothing new—over the last 50 years, the construction of the Lake Nasser reservoir has allowed the reclamation of hundreds of millions of hectares. CAPMAS figures put the amount of land reclaimed between 1952 and 1990 at 2.261 million feddans (a feddan is approximately an acre). The current plans to conquer the desert, however, are limited in their ambitions by the difficulty of acquiring water resources.

Egypt, the "gift of the Nile" according to Herodotus, is under increasing stress due to the disparity between its water resources and demographics. It already uses about 63 billion m^3 of water every year, of which 55.5 billion comes from the Nile and the rest from aquifers and recycled wastewater. But the Egyptian population continues to grow at a rate of 1.9% per year, which translates into 20 million additional souls by 2015.

Egypt's attempts to create a new Nile Valley are

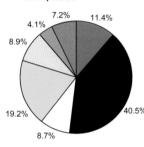

Land Reclamation 1999/2000

7.2%
4.1%
11.4%
8.9%
19.2%
40.5%
8.7%

- Suez
- Beheira
- Fayyoum
- Aswan
- New Valley
- Sharqiya
- Other

Source: CAPMAS

Most recently reclaimed land is on the fringes of the Delta, rather than the desert

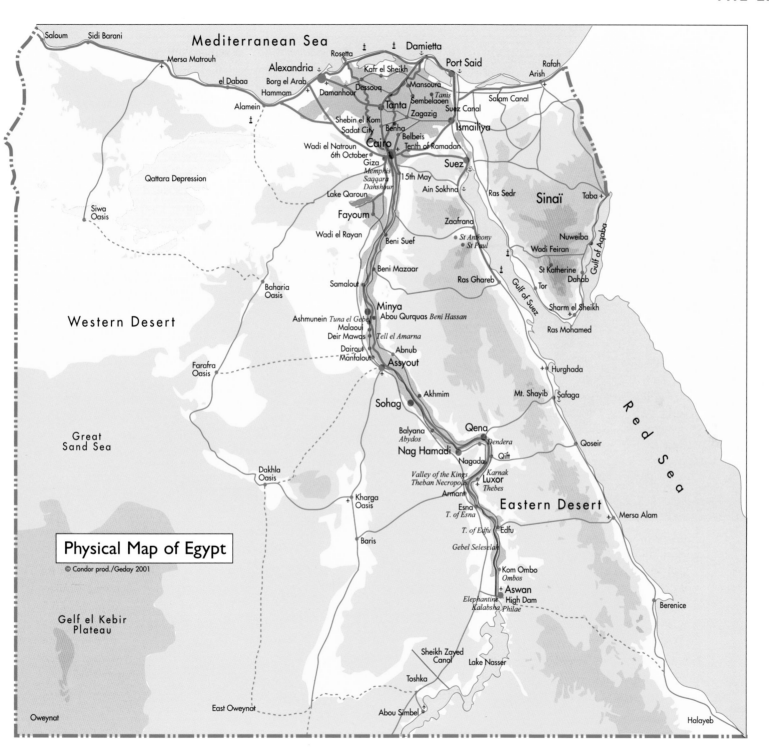

Physical Map of Egypt

© Condor prod./Geday 2001

Mediterranean Sea

Saloum · Sidi Barani
Mersa Matrouh
el Dabaa
Alexandria
Borg el Arab
Hammam
Alamein
Damanhour
Rosetta
Kafr el Sheikh
Dessouq
Damietta
Port Said
Rafah
Arish
Mansoura
Tanis
Sembelaoen
Salam Canal
Suez Canal
Tanta
Zagazig
Benha
Shebin el Kom
Sadat City
Belbeis
Tenth of Ramadan
Ismailiya
Wadi el Natroun
6th October
Cairo
Suez
Giza
Memphis
Saqqara
Dahshour
15th May
Ain Sokhna
Ras Sedr
Sinaï
Taba
Lake Qaroun
Qattara Depression
Fayoum
Zaafrana
Nuweiba
Wadi Feiran
Gulf of Aqaba
Siwa Oasis
Wadi el Rayan
Beni Suef
St Anthony
St Paul
St Katherine
Dahab
Tor
Gulf of Suez
Beni Mazaar
Ras Ghareb
Sharm el Sheikh
Samalout
Ras Mohamed
Baharia Oasis
Western Desert
Minya
Ashmunein Tuna el Gebel
Abou Qurquas Beni Hassan
Malaoui
Deir Mawas Tell el Amarna
Dairout
Manfalout
Abnub
Assyout
Hurghada
Mt. Shayib
Safaga
Farafra Oasis
Sohag
Akhmim
Great Sand Sea
Balyana
Abydos
Qena
Dendera
Qoseir
Nag Hamadi
Nagada
Qift
Dakhla Oasis
Valley of the Kings
Theban Necropolis
Karnak
Luxor
Thebes
Armant
Kharga Oasis
Esna
T. of Esna
Eastern Desert
T. of Edfu Edfu
Mersa Alam
Baris
Gebel Seleselah
Red Sea
Kom Ombo
Ombos
Aswan
High Dam
Elephantine
Kalabsha Philae
Gelf el Kebir Plateau
Berenice
Sheikh Zayed Canal
Lake Nasser
Toshka
East Oweynat
Abou Simbel
Oweynat
Halayeb

centered around two megaprojects: the Salam Canal and Toshka. The stated objective of the Salam Canal project is to settle the Sinai Peninsula with about three million people (currently about 340,000 people live there). The plan is based on the reclamation of 400,000

feddans fed by the waters of the Nile (approximately four billion m³ per year), which the canal will carry to North Sinai. The project was conceived around an already important communications route stretching along the coast to Rafah. With a railroad in the works, basic infrastructure in place, and burgeoning industrial development around al-Arish, the area is likely to witness rapid growth in the future; if a permanent peace in the region is ever reached, it could become a transit hotspot. The amounts of water required for the project, while large, are not so problematic: the canal will not drain water from the system at the top, but will take what is left at the end of its course through the Nile Valley. But the project is principally aimed at large investors, who will introduce mechanized agriculture rather than labor-intensive methods. Thus, it will employ only a limited number of workers from the Nile Valley or the Delta.

Much more problematic is the Toshka project, initiated in 1996 as grandest of the megaprojects. It is based on a massive exploitation of Nile water and underground aquifers in the Western Desert. In the first stage, the new canal (the Sheikh Zayed Canal) should allow the reclamation of 500,000 feddans. The five billion m³ of water necessary to irrigate this first slice of land will be pumped directly from Lake Nasser. In the long term, the government envisions irrigating a total surface area of 1.5 to 2 million feddans. Like the Salam Canal, the Sheikh Zayed Canal has created a vast irrigated perimeter assigned to large investors who will rely essentially on mechanized agriculture. In both cases, the demographic objective has been forgotten.

Toshka has been criticized for sucking huge amounts of money out of the economy—the cost of the first phase of the project is estimated at LE5.5 billion. But the biggest question to present itself is how the state will compensate downstream of the High Dam for the quantities of water it will need to pump to see Toshka profit. In July 1995, in a lecture at Cairo University, Mahmoud Abu Zeid (currently the minister of Public Works and Water Resources, and then the head of the Water Research Unit at the ministry) stated that Egypt was facing a water shortage, and he stressed the need to consider the feasibility of current land reclamation projects in light of this reality. In September of the same year, Abu Zeid gave the green light to the incipient

Parting the Waters

The most recent accord governing use of the Nile water was the Nile Waters Agreement of 1959. It essentially divided up the Nile flow between Egypt and Sudan and no other country bordering the Nile was consulted or allocated a share. The water was divided as follows:

Average Annual Nile Flow: 84 bn m³
Reservoir Losses from Evaporation/Seepage: 10 bn m³
Net Water Availability per year: 74 bn m³
Allotment to Sudan: 18.5 bn m³
Allotment to Egypt: 55.5 bn m³
Total Water Usage per year: 74 bn m³

Source: Egypt Almanac

Toshka project. So far, no convincing explanation has been supplied for the turnaround.

In order to find the five billion m³ of Nile water needed for the first stage of the project, officials have suggested reducing water consumption in the Nile Valley by limiting the areas cultivated with rice (in the northern Delta) and sugar cane (in Upper Egypt), both of which require large quantities of water. This solution poses serious ecological, economic, and social problems. While reducing the area of rice cultivation will reduce the quantity of Nile water needed for irrigation, this will translate into a drop in groundwater levels. In the northern Delta, an influx of salt water from the sea will filter in to compensate for the drop, increasing salinity levels in aquifers and the soil. Nor does the solution make sense from a pure water conservation standpoint. A feddan in the Delta planted with rice will still use less water than any crop will need in Toshka, due to extremely high evaporation levels. In Upper Egypt, substantially reducing the planting of sugar cane will not only penalize farmers, but will spark a head-on collision with the sugar industry, which sustains millions.

In the water system as a whole, diverting such amounts from the normal system of transport and distribution will reduce the quality of the water left to flow downstream. Recycled water cannot compensate for the quantities that will eventually be taken from Lake Nasser. Thus, the water left to flow downstream will carry higher concentrations of pollutants and salts.

The irony in Toshka is that in designing this most modern of megaprojects, state planners seem to have reverted to the days when Egypt depended on the annual floods for its agricultural livelihood. In years of high floods, there may well be "extra" water left to sit in Lake Nasser. (Conversely, a drought like that of the mid-1980s could require the use of the present reserves.) To base state water policy on such uncertainties and possible windfalls, however, undermines the logic of the High Dam itself. *HA*

Gift of the Nile

Over the last 30 years, the Aswan High Dam has assured Egyptians total protection from drought and flood. The same year it was built, in 1964, it blocked the southern frontier of the country from the strongest floods of the century. The flood of 1996, with its exceptional load of 130 billion m³ of water, would have been catastrophic if the Aswan Dam had not existed. Between 1984 and 1988, while Sudan and other African countries were living through the longest and most catastrophic drought of the last 50 years, the dam's embankment acted as a protective barrier against the same thing happening in Egypt. By 1988, the water reserves in Lake Nasser had been reduced almost to the strategic reserve level. If the floods had not returned that year, much of Egypt's farmland would have gone without water.

The construction of the High Dam was a turning point for Egyptian agriculture. Extending perennial irrigation to the whole of arable lands considerably enlarged the country's total irrigated surface and intensified production and efficiency, doubling the harvest. Today, on 7 million cultivated feddans about 12 million feddans worth of crops are harvested. *HA*

Sources of Water Pollution

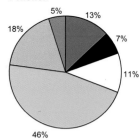

- ■ Primary Metals
- ■ Paper & Pulp
- ☐ Chemicals
- ▨ Food & Beverages
- ▨ Textiles
- ■ Other

Source: World Development Indicators 2000 (World Bank)

Food and beverage industries pollute the Nile the most

The Green Agenda

To conserve or to develop?

As a developing country with scarce natural resources, an exploding population, and widespread poverty, Egypt's environmental efforts over the last ten years have tended to give precedence to issues on the so-called "brown agenda," like wastewater treatment and pollution abatement. Although the importance of biodiversity, nature conservation, and habitat protection have been officially acknowedged, efforts to promote Egypt's green agenda have centered primarily on the country's protected areas. Just this year, in summer 2002, the government officially declared the creation of the Siwa and White Desert reserves, bringing the total number of protectorates to 23. A number of these sites, such as Ras Mohammed, are gaining international recognition and becoming important tourist attractions that contribute to the national and local economies. The parks are being promoted as ecotourism destinations, as a means to encourage environmentally friendly tourism of benefit to local communities.

Red Sea mangroves are threatened by uncontrolled tourist development along the coast

But cutting out swathes of land and calling them protected is not in itself enough to preserve them. The management authority—the Egyptian Environmental Affairs Agency (EEAA), under the Ministry of State for Environmental Affairs (MSEA)—has neither the resources, the trained manpower, nor the high level support to develop self-sustaining management and financial structures for the protectorates. However, technical and management capacities are gradually being enhanced through donor-funded projects at Wadi al-Rayan (the Italians), Saint Katherine's and the Gulf of Aqaba reserves (the EU), the Mediterranean coastal protectorates of Zaranik, Burullus, and al-Omayad (GEF-UNDP), and the Red Sea coast and islands (USAID). The Siwa and White Desert protectorates as yet have no management programs in place, but in Siwa, the Italians have been supporting the training of community guards for more than a year. They are planning to invest in the protectorate's infrastructure in the second phase of their support program, set to come on line next year. Institutionally, the EEAA is also slowly growing stronger. The appointment of Mostafa Fouda in 2000 as the head of the Nature Conservation Sector brought in much needed experience. It is hoped that the Natural Resource Management Training Center, which opened in last year in Sharm al-Sheikh, will eventually help to fill the gap in trained personnel, but the effect will take some time to trickle down.

Perhaps more important to ensuring the success of the EEAA's conservation efforts is greater commitment from other government agencies and officials. On paper, Law 102 of 1983 provides a legal framework for the status of protected areas, banning things like hunting and inappropriate development such as land reclamation. In practice, however, enforcement of the law varies, depending on the willingness of local authorities and government ministries to implement its provisions. In the past this has meant that illegal hunting within protected areas has been disregarded—and even permitted—by local governors. Last year, a prime ministerial decree was issued that would open up two small Nile islands, Dahab and al-Warraq, to development, though both are theoretically part of the Nile Islands Protected Area that runs from Aswan to the Mediterranean. The home of about 60,000 informal residents, the two islands are also some of the last remaining spots of green in Cairo, providing a rich haven for aquatic flora and fauna. Although the decree was eventually tabled following vocal objections from both parliament and the public, the move highlighted the still fragile status of Egypt's protected areas.

Outside of protected areas, new resorts are springing up almost daily along Egypt's coasts, providing more beds for legions of tourists even as they destroy some of the splendors that attract visitors in the first place. The hotel growth rate itself tells a frightening story: in 1982, the Red Sea mainland boasted only 327 hotel rooms, while South Sinai had only 312. There are now more than 34,000 rooms on the Red Sea coast alone. To try to alleviate the negative impact of such rapid development, in 2000 the Tourism Development Authority (TDA) introduced a system of basic environmental management in its Red Sea hotels, aiming to decrease solid waste, improve economic efficiency, and make greater use of renewable energy. USAID, which is assisting in the project, expects that by the end of 2003, almost 60% of TDA-owned hotel rooms will be participating in the program. By the same time, 65% of the TDA's tourism facilities will have received approval through environmental impact assessments (EIAs) prior to construction. These steps come as welcome news, but it still leaves many projects out of the loop. Though Law 4 of 1994—known as the "environment law"—stipulates that EIAs must be performed for any new development, projects continue without EIAs, particularly in the public sector.

In the Sinai, uncontrolled development continues to imperil wildlife and coral reefs. Hundreds, if not thousands, of White Storks die every year during migration, landing in Sharm al-Sheikh where they are attracted by the rubbish dumps, sewage farms, and green areas. The coastal lakes along the Mediterranean Sea are biodiversity hotspots, containing some of Egypt's most diverse ecosystems. Despite some laudable conservation projects—such as the Egyptian Tortoise conservation project and the three-year effort to save endangered marine turtles—severe pollution, urban encroachments, land reclamation schemes, and eroding coasts are taking their toll on these habitats. In desert environments, quarrying continues to deface the landscape and break up vital topsoil. Already by 1997, the MSEA stated that quarrying had completely demolished the limestone ridge formation that once extended from Alexandria to Alamein, its stone used to build holiday villages along the North Coast.

In addition to habitat loss, unauthorized hunting also represents a danger to wildlife. Excessive and illegal hunting has already decimated the local population of gazelle and ibex and several species of falcon. Birds are especially vulnerable, as hunting along the Mediterranean coast during the autumn migratory months is widespread. It is estimated that a quarter of a million quail are caught every year. Hunters catch everything that flies, including globally threatened species. In an effort to boost bird conservation efforts, BirdLife International released its Directory of Important Bird Areas in Egypt in 2000, identifying 34 sites of global importance for birds in the country.

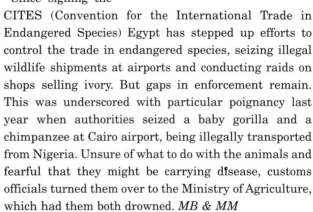

Since signing the CITES (Convention for the International Trade in Endangered Species) Egypt has stepped up efforts to control the trade in endangered species, seizing illegal wildlife shipments at airports and conducting raids on shops selling ivory. But gaps in enforcement remain. This was underscored with particular poignancy last year when authorities seized a baby gorilla and a chimpanzee at Cairo airport, being illegally transported from Nigeria. Unsure of what to do with the animals and fearful that they might be carrying disease, customs officials turned them over to the Ministry of Agriculture, which had them both drowned. *MB & MM*

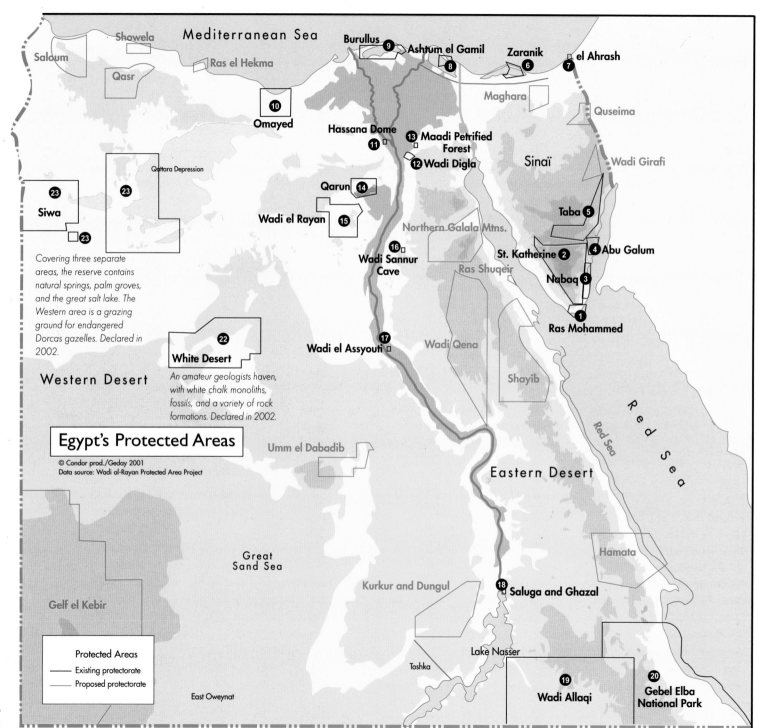

Mediterranean Sea

Showela

Saloum

Qasr

Ras el Hekma

Burullus **9**

Ashtum el Gamil **8**

Zaranik **6**

el Ahrash **7**

Maghara

Quseima

Omayed **10**

Sinaï

Hassana Dome **11** **13** Maadi Petrified Forest

Wadi Girafi

Qattara Depression

12 Wadi Digla

23

23

Siwa

Qarun **14**

Taba **5**

Northern Galala Mtns.

St. Katherine **2** **4** Abu Galum

23

Wadi el Rayan **15**

Covering three separate areas, the reserve contains natural springs, palm groves, and the great salt lake. The Western area is a grazing ground for endangered Dorcas gazelles. Declared in 2002.

16

Ras Shuqeir

Nabaq **3**

Wadi Sannur Cave

1

Ras Mohammed

22

White Desert

An amateur geologists haven, with white chalk monoliths, fossils, and a variety of rock formations. Declared in 2002.

Wadi el Assyouti **17**

Wadi Qena

Egypt's Protected Areas

© Condor prod./Geday 2001
Data source: Wadi al-Rayan Protected Area Project

Western Desert

Shayib

Red Sea

Red Sea

Umm el Dabadib

Eastern Desert

Great Sand Sea

Gelf el Kebir

Hamata

Kurkur and Dungul

18 Saluga and Ghazal

Lake Nasser

Toshka

Protected Areas

— Existing protectorate
— Proposed protectorate

East Oweynat

19

Wadi Allaqi

20

Gebel Elba National Park

Egypt's Protected Areas

1. Ras Mohammed National Park. Egypt's best-known protected area boasts some of the most spectacular reefs in the world with sheer cliffs of coral. Also an important bottleneck for migrating White Stork in the autumn.

2. St. Katherine Protectorate. High mountains rich in plant and animal life, including endemic species of plants and butterflies. Other attractions include Mt. Sinai, St. Katherine's Monastery, and traditional Bedouin communities.

3. Nabaq Protected Area. Includes the most northerly mangrove in the world, beautiful beaches and an eerie shipwreck. Wadi Kid contains one of the only populations of gazelle in Sinai.

4. Abu Galum Protected Area. A remote and attractive stretch of coastline fringed by coral reefs. The adjacent desert areas are of interest for wildlife and scenery.

5. Taba National Monument. Desert wilderness with stunning geological formations, such as the Colored Canyon, oases and cultural heritage sites, including *nawamis*, stone buildings that are the world's oldest roofed structures.

6. Zaranik Protected Area. A lagoon on Lake Bardawil that is a bottleneck for migrating waterbirds in the autumn. The adjacent desert boasts endangered wildlife and the pristine Mediterranean beach is a nesting site for sea turtles.

7. al-Ahrash Reserve. Contains sand dunes fixed with exotic vegetation.

8. Ashtum al-Gamil Protected Area. Comprises the degraded, polluted eastern portion of Lake Manzala. Possibly has importance for wintering waterbirds. Tinnis Island contains the ruins of a Roman and early Islamic city.

9. Lake Burullus Protected Area. This lake and sandbar along the Mediterranean coast is one of the last areas of wilderness in the Delta, though the new coastal highway is bringing change. Of global importance for wintering waterbirds.

10. al-Omayyed Biosphere Reserve. This Mediterranean coastal desert is a biodiversity hotspot. Man-made activities, including land reclamation, quarrying, and overgrazing are degrading this site making it one of Egypt's most threatened natural areas.

11. Hassana Dome Protected Area. A hill on the outskirts of Cairo of geological interest, but only to geologists. Most people drive by without realizing it is protected.

12. Wadi Digla Protected Area. A desert wadi on the doorstep of Maadi and a wonderful location for outdoor recreation, though it has a garbage problem.

13. Maadi Petrified Forest Protected Area. Contains some of the last remains of petrified wood in the Qattamiya area. Now surrounded by buildings, so has lost much of its charm.

14. Lake Qaroun Protected Area. Scenic lake, important for wintering waterbirds. Boasts neolithic sites, Roman cities, and temples and fossils in the surrounding desert.

15. Wadi al-Rayan Protected Area. Two man-made lakes linked by waterfalls, plus an uninhabited Saharan oasis with endangered wildlife and 40 million-year-old fossilized remains of primitive whales.

16. Sannour Cave National Monument. A cave with stalactites and stalagmites. Not open to the public.

17. Wadi al-Asyouti Protected Area. Part of a wadi in the Eastern Desert near Assyout.

18. Saluga and Ghazal Protected Area. Beautiful islands containing some of the last vestiges of indigenous flora in the Nile Valley. Unfortunately not open to tourists.

19. Wadi Allaqi Protected Area. Part of the largest *khor*—a *khor* is a long bay—on Lake Nasser and a huge tract of southern Eastern Desert, containing abandoned gold mines, Neolithic sites, and endangered wildlife. Visitors require permits.

20. Elba National Park. This mountain outcrop in the southeast corner of the Eastern Desert is an outpost of sub-Saharan flora and fauna in Egypt, but closed to the public. The decree protecting the area also covers all mangroves along the Red Sea coast and all islands from Hurghada southward. These are important sites for coral reefs, nesting marine turtles, and seabird colonies.

21. Nile Islands Protected Area. This runs from Cairo to Aswan. It is not clear which islands are included. Most are inhabited and cultivated although patches of nature remain. *MB & SB*

Egypt's Endangered Species

The National Biodiversity Country Study estimates that there are some 18,000 species occuring in Egypt, with more being discovered all the time. A number of plant and animal species occuring in Egypt are considered globally threatened.

Dugong (*Dugong dugon*): This marine mammal feeds on sea grass beds; it has become extremely rare with isolated populations scattered around the Egyptian Red Sea. Vulnerable.

White-eyed Gull (*Larus leucophthalmus*): Over 30% of the world population of this Red Sea endemic seabird breeds on Egypt's northern islands. Near-threatened.

Green Sea Turtle: One of five globally threatened sea turtles occurring in Egyptian waters, this species breeds on the Mediterranean coast and along the Red Sea coasts and islands. Endangered.

Ferruginous Duck (*Aythya nyroca*): Egypt has global importance for this waterbird, with a high proportion of the world population wintering in Egyptian wetlands. Near-threatened.

Corncrake (*Crex crex*): Large numbers of this globally threatened migrant pass through Egypt in the autumn and are illegally netted by hunters along the Mediterranean coast. Vulnerable.

African Skimmer (*Rynchops flavirostris*): Egypt is the northernmost distribution for this African wader, which breeds on islands in Lake Nasser and is irregularly reported along the Nile in Upper Egypt. Near-threatened.

Dorcas Gazelle (*Gazella dorcas*): Gazelles are found in all desert regions in Egypt, but over-hunting has decimated the populations with only small, scattered pockets remaining. Vulnerable.

Nubian Ibex (*Capra nubiana*): Illegally hunted, this animal is found in inaccessible mountainous regions in the Sinai and Eastern Deserts, which has helped to save it. Endangered.

Barbary Sheep (*Ammotragus lervia*): Recently rediscovered, small populations of this species persist in the mountains of the Eastern and Western Deserts, but are seriously threatened by

hunting. Endangered.

Stripped Hyena (*Hyaena hyaena*): This scavenger inhabiting the deserts of Egypt has become very scarce as a result of persecution by man. Near-threatened.

Fennec Fox (*Vulpes zerda*): This attractive fox is a widespread resident of sandy deserts and is illegally collected for the pet trade. Data deficient.

Houbara Bustard (*Chlamydotis undulata*): Recently split into two separate species east and west of the Nile, this desert bird is a favorite quarry of Arab falconers. As a result of hunting resident populations have dwindled. Near-threatened.

Egyptian Tortoise (*Testudo klienmanni*): One of the world's smallest tortoises, a near endemic species restricted to the Mediterranean coastal desert, threatened by habitat destruction and collection. Endangered.

Lappet-faced Vulture (*Torgos tracheliotus*): This large vulture was a former widespread resident of desert regions, but has declined throughout Egypt. Good numbers still can be found in the southern Eastern Desert. Vulnerable.

Origanum isthmicum: One of the 33 endemic plants occurring in the Sinai. A wild oregano confined to a mountain in North Sinai, like other endemics, it is little known. Rare.

Medemia argun: A near endemic palm tree that was previously thought to be extinct in Egypt; a small stand remains in the Dungul Oasis in the southern Western Desert. Endangered.

Grass-Loving Lizard (*Philochortus zollii*): Restricted in Egypt to Wadi al-Natrun, this lizard is highly endangered due to habitat destruction and should be listed as globally threatened. Not currently listed.

Greater Spotted Eagle (*Aquila clanga*): Significant numbers of this endangered bird of prey migrate biannually through Egypt, with small numbers wintering. Vulnerable. *MB*

Fennec fox (top); Medemia argun (middle); Egyptian tortoise (above); Barbary sheep (right inset photo)

The Brown Agenda

Water pollution is the biggest threat

In 2001, the World Economic Forum issued its first environmental sustainability index. Based on 22 indicators that measure things ranging from water quality to biodiversity to environmental regulatory frameworks, the index ranked 155 countries from best to worst. The good news is that Egypt made it into the top half at number 67, higher than some countries with much greater financial resources and better than most other countries in the region. For some key areas, however, it fared considerably worse. On air quality, for example, it came in very near the bottom at number 147.

For those who have experienced Cairo's annual "black cloud" phenomenon, the rating will come as no surprise. An oft-cited USAID study of environmental health risks in greater Cairo concluded that the high levels of particulate matter and lead in the city's air—some of the highest in the world—cause 10,000 to 25,000 deaths annually, cost Cairenes at least 90 million days a year of reduced activity due to sickness, and put kids growing up in the city in danger of losing up to 4.25 IQ points.

Outside of Cairo, where air pollution is less severe, water pollution constitutes the number one environmental health risk. Even though Egypt now boasts that 95% of its population is using improved water sources, the numbers do not account for informal housing areas, poorly installed or maintained piping systems, or inadequate water treatment plants. In a 2001 report on water quality across Egypt, the People's Assembly found that the drinking water in seven governorates contained levels of bacteria exceeding internationally accepted safe guidelines.

While large urban centers have centralized sewage and waste disposal systems, rural areas often do not. As a result, a substantial amount of the country's municipal and household waste is dumped untreated directly into the Nile or irrigation canals. Egypt is stepping up construction of new wastewater treatment plants—more than 100 are currently being built or planned—but demand far outstrips treatment capacity and is expected to do so for some years to come. It is estimated that by the year 2017, there will still be a gap, leaving about 800 million m^3 of untreated sewage (about 25% of the projected total) to flow down towards the Delta basin and ultimately into the soil and sea.

Industrial pollution is an even more serious threat to Egypt's scarce water resources, contributing the bulk of contaminants and toxic substances to the nation's water supply. Cairo's industries alone discharge about three-quarters of a ton of heavy metals every day. Even when

industrial waste is treated, these elements can make their way into irrigation water and permeate the soil, which in turn can translate into trace elements in food crops. In 1997, the World Bank estimated that bringing Egypt's industrial sector in line with world environmental safety regulations would cost about $1.3 billion and take about ten years.

Egypt is taking steps to address these most basic of environmental and health concerns. Former environment minister Nadia Makram Ebeid actively pursued an industrial clean-up crusade during her four years in office. Although her own assessment of the campaign's success tended to be a bit overstated—she was fond of officially declaring the Nile "a clean river"—about 300 factories had stopped releasing industrial waste into the Nile by the time she left the ministry in 2001. Incentives for industries to adopt environmentally friendly practices are also coming from the World Bank, which is overseeing a $48-million project that offers soft loans to enterprises that want to upgrade their production facilities to reduce air and water pollution.

Though the black cloud continues to make its annual autumn appearance, Cairo's air has received a boost from the USAID-funded Cairo Air Improvement Project (CAIP). Now in its fourth year, CAIP is addressing the city's air pollution problem by moving heavily polluting lead smelters out of the city, sponsoring vehicle emissions testing and tune-ups, and promoting the use of compressed natural gas (CNG) in private and public transport. Not only is CNG cleaner-burning than oil-based fuels, it is an economically savvy choice given Egypt's hefty gas reserves. With about 37,000 CNG cars and buses plying the roads, Egypt is now the world's sixth biggest user of CNG vehicles. CAIP has also established 39 air-quality monitoring stations across the country, with 12 in Cairo, and the stations have already shown an improvement in air quality in some areas. In Shubra al-Kheima—one of the most seriously affected areas in the city—lead levels dropped from 25 micrograms/m³ in 1999 to about 11/m³ in 2000—still 11 times WHO recommended levels, but a great improvement nonetheless.

Outside of the capital, last year Alexandria became the site of the first municipal garbage collection program in Egypt, a private venture run by the French firm Onyx, and similar programs are being designed for southern Cairo and Qalyubiya. Alexandrians may be pleased that no matter where they live in the city, for a few pounds a month, their garbage will magically disappear. How this will affect the livelihood of the city's traditional garbage collectors, the *zebbalin*, is still unclear. And although the city will be cleaner, the company has said that efforts to implement greener waste disposal measures, like recycling, are still a long way off. For now, Alexandria's garbage will be dumped in a newly created landfill 40 km outside the city—admittedly a better option than the old dumpsite on the shores of Lake Maryut.

With a population of 66 million crowded into the slender Nile Valley, stress on the system is inevitable. Fortunately, environmental awareness is on the rise, as is international environmental assistance, now pouring in to the tune of $60 million a year. But money isn't everything. Critics point to a lack of any integrated environmental management on the statewide level, as well as a stark gap between strict environmental laws and their considerably looser application. It is still too early to tell if Makram Ebeid's replacement, Mamdouh Riyad Tadros, will be able to rally his fellow ministers in support of any major initiatives. But as Egypt struggles to improve its economy and better the standard of living for its citizens, the degree to which it can implement environmentally sustainable policies will have a direct impact on the success of its efforts. *MM & NM*

The Capital
The big city is bursting at the seams

Cairo

Like all great cities, Egypt's capital is in a state of perpetual change. It swells, it mutates, it decays and reinvents itself at the same time. To full-time residents caught up in the city's ceaseless bustle, the change can pass unnoticed, like the slow branching of a giant tree. Allow for a lapse of time, though, and the change is striking. Whole new suburbs, as big as cities in themselves, spring out of the desert. Hallowed landmarks disappear, and new ones sprout in their place. The scale of things alters. The familiar ratio of streets to buildings, of people to space, of noise to silence is suddenly different.

Despite the economic slump, the last two years brought notable changes to the Cairo skyline. Those great shop windows of the city, the Corniches along the Nile, filled up with more flashy merchandise as the 40-story Royal Meridien Hotel opened, and the equally extravagant Four Seasons in Garden City neared completion. The riverfront at Boulaq, now perhaps the most dramatic architectural interface between old and new, sprouted its third pair of giant office blocks. The 35 floors of yet another commercial complex, called Nile City, seemed to cock a snook at the world's sudden wariness of twin towered structures. Far to the south in Maadi, the neo-Pharaonic Supreme Constitutional Court, one of the more notable new buildings in a city not noted for daring modern architecture, opened for business.

Embellishments to the Corniche reached down to street level, too. On the Cairo side, neat new sidewalks, wooden benches, and cast iron railings with a swirling design replaced the venerable Nasser-era decorative scheme so familiar from the soft focus of classic Egyptian cinema. The Giza side won a similarly drastic makeover. Not only is its riverside walkway now navigable without danger of injury, all the western governorate's streets have been labeled with snappy blue signs so that you stand a good chance of knowing where you are.

Nile lovers will also celebrate the refurbishment of the old Monasterly Palace on the island of Roda. Converted into a long-awaited museum devoted to the greatest of all Egyptian singers, Umm Kulthoum, it serves now as an elegant venue for evening concerts. Luckily, too, the modest, late-Ottoman palace by the Nilometer still enjoys a pleasant view of Gezirat al-Dahab, one of the few remaining patches of pre-urban pastoral verdure in the dusty metropolis. In 2001, inhabitants of the island's real villages successfully protested plans to evict them in favor of "tourist" villages. The disgruntled investors in the scheme seem to have had the last word, however. A brand new, wholly artificial island is being created opposite Maadi's Military Hospital, presumably with the aim of housing homeless tourists.

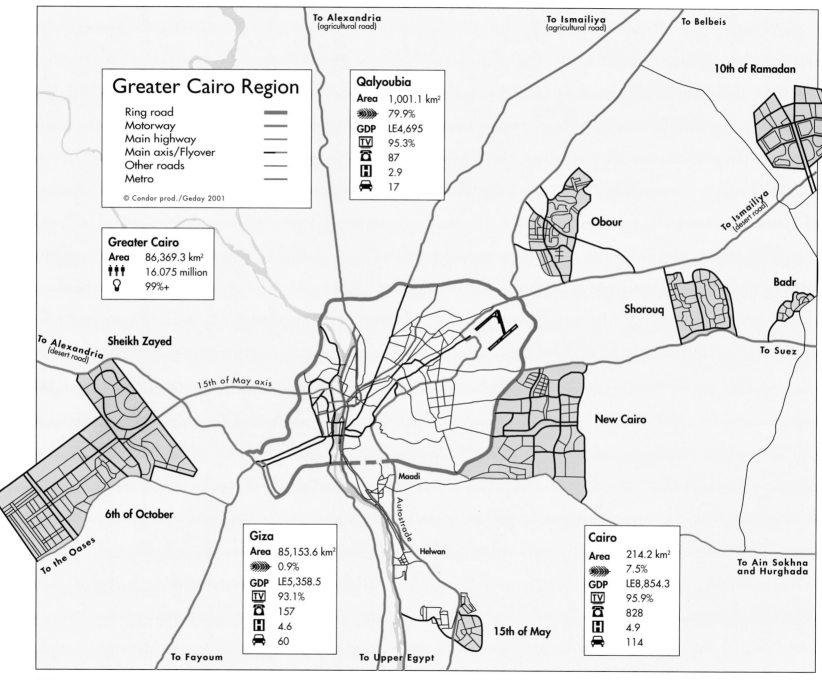

Greater Cairo Region

Ring road
Motorway
Main highway
Main axis/Flyover
Other roads
Metro

© Condor prod./Geday 2001

To Alexandria
(agricultural road)

To Ismailiya
(agricultural road)

To Belbeis

10th of Ramadan

Qalyoubia
Area   1,001.1 km²
          79.9%
GDP   LE4,695
TV   95.3%
          87
H   2.9
          17

To Ismailiya
(desert road)

Obour

Badr

Shorouq

To Suez

Greater Cairo
Area   86,369.3 km²
          16.075 million
          99%+

Sheikh Zayed

To Alexandria
(desert road)

15th of May axis

New Cairo

6th of October

To the Oases

Maadi

Autostrade

Helwan

Giza
Area   85,153.6 km²
          0.9%
GDP   LE5,358.5
TV   93.1%
          157
H   4.6
          60

15th of May

Cairo
Area   214.2 km²
          7.5%
GDP   LE8,854.3
TV   95.9%
          828
H   4.9
          114

To Ain Sokhna
and Hurghada

To Fayoum

To Upper Egypt

The people of Gezirat al-Dahab were relieved to see their environment preserved. Residents of Cairo's medieval quarters, and even more so scholars and aficionados of the old city, were not so sure what to make of a sudden burst of restoration activity on their turf. After decades of leaving the job to a handful of foreign institutes, or at best serially "restoring" the tested few monuments that are accessible by ministerial motorcade, the Ministry of Culture expanded the scope of its Islamic Monuments Sector last year. The result was a rash of hasty, heavy-on-the-cement jobs that certainly made many venerable buildings look newer, but that also alarmed experts so much that the ministry was obliged to call a conference to calm them down.

Drivers in Cairo, meanwhile, found some welcome changes. Belatedly recognizing that many streets were becoming impassable, the city government increased the number of one-way thoroughfares, most notably including Qasr al-Aini Street and the Garden City Corniche, and also started laying the groundwork for parking meters in the city center. Construction of new roads also continued apace. The controversial 2.65-km long tunnel under al-Azhar Street that cuts through the heart of the old city opened last October to a healthy roar of traffic. Fears that it would simply sluice more cars into the already swamped city center proved unfounded, but so, unfortunately, did hopes that the opening of the tunnel would allow for removal of the unsightly Azhar overpass along the same route. In 2002, work was completed on yet another extension to Cairo's coronary artery, the Sixth of October Bridge. This one links the bridge to another vital traffic vessel, the confusingly named 15th of May Bridge. And after a decade of earthmoving, Cairo's Ring Road finally began to look like a ring. When the last, long-delayed 3-km section through Basatin is finished, you will be able to cruise a grand 100 kilometer-long circle around the whole perimeter of the city.

Except that this is no longer Cairo's perimeter. The city bulges out of the ring like a swelling Stella belly. The big satellite suburbs that sprawl into the desert to the east and west, which together make up an area one and a half times the size of the old valley-bound Cairo, were mere sketchings in the sand a few years back. They have now taken solid shape. The speculative bubble of the late 90s, and subsequent crash,

led to a slowing-down of construction in places like Beverly Hills and New Cairo. It has hardly come to a stop, however.

Take Sixth of October City, for example. Despite market doldrums that have seen prices halved since 1998, it is looking more and more like a proper, lived-in suburb rather than a collection of factories and desolate wannabe institutions. Its grandiose Media Production City, the Ministry of Information's Universal Studios-cum-Cinecitta, now pulsates with what the ministry calls "production sector activity." Even the Arab

Key to Indicator Maps

Area	Total land area
†††	Population
†/km²	Population density (excluding desert in Alexandria, Delta, Upper Egypt, and Suez Canal zone)
⫸	Cultivated part of land area
GDP	Per capita gross domestic product
♀	Households with electricity (%)
TV	Households with TV (%)
☎	Phones per 1,000 households
H	Health units per 100,000
🚗	Vehicles per 1,000 people (cars, taxis, pick-up trucks

Source: CAPMAS 2001, UNDP/INP 1998

How Cairenes Get Around

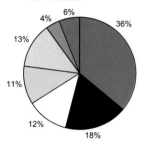

36%
6%
4%
13%
11%
12%
18%

■ Walking
■ Microbus
□ Bus
▨ Metro
▨ Car
▨ Taxi
■ Other public transport

Source: Célame Barge, 2000; SYSTRA, 1998

Cairenes use motorized transportation for about two-thirds of all daily trips around the city

world's most-watched show, MBC's *Who Wants to Be a Millionaire*, is being hosted there. Across the road, happy golfers swat at Dream City's spanking new links, while surgeons snip and tuck at the nearby Dar al-Fouad hospital, Egypt's latest and fanciest private medical institution. No wonder rush hour on Sixth of October City's main access road, the 26th of July Corridor that only opened in 1999, is now almost as packed as on the Corniche to Maadi, one of Cairo's oldest suburbs.

Which brings to mind one positive effect of prolonged economic depression. Traffic jams, thick enough already, would have been stickier yet if car sales hadn't plunged and redundancies obliged workers to stay home. Ramadan, normally a season of epic gridlock punctuated by bursts of manic driving frenzy, was notably empty in 2001 as shoppers shunned the markets in favor of watching TV.

Getting across the city was still difficult enough, however, to explain another phenomenon that grew more evident in 2001. Cairo is becoming a multi-nuclear organism. Districts like Giza, Mohandiseen, Maadi, Madinet Nasr, and Heliopolis have ceased to be mere dependencies of downtown Cairo. Their main shopping streets are just as busy as those of the city center, complete with the same chain stores and restaurants. Not surprisingly, the million or so people who inhabit each of these sub-cities feel less and less need to ever leave them.

Despite the clogged traffic, Cairo's pollution was generally reckoned to have improved over the previous year, believe it or not. Certainly, the most dreaded period in early November, when the burning of rice husks in the Delta blows in a thick pall of smoke, was much milder than the week-long Black Cloud experienced in 1999. The improvement may owe something to the ongoing campaign by Cairo's energetic governor, Abd al-Rahim Shehata, to remove polluting

industries, such as lead smelters, pottery furnaces, and tanneries, to outlying areas.

All cities change, yes, but there is something unique to the tensions of change in Cairo. Here, there is continuous competition between two kinds of city. One is a car-driving, middle-class metropolis that pretends to have well-planned, well-tended streets; in short, it tries to look and act like most modern cities. The other Cairo is the one that doesn't care about looks, it just tries to get by. This is the town that fills the cracks in the "formal" city, so that, for example, parked cars and street vendors fill up sidewalks that were designed for pedestrians. It is the town whose unfinished brick dwellings and unplanned alleyways clutter all the spaces between and around the districts with clean-cut buildings and streets.

The "informal" Cairo, of course, is the one where most people live, work, and play. When you talk about change in these areas, though, it is hard to be more specific than to say they grow ever-bigger in size, and ever more full of cars and mobile phones. The more evident change is in the balance of forces between formal and informal. Through much of the 1990s, it looked like the formal city was winning out. In 2001, though, even all the face

Moving in the City

Cairenes are incredibly more mobile than they were 30 years ago. In 1971, city dwellers made on average less than one trip a day (about 0.8). In 1998, they made almost twice as many trips per day (about 1.4). Increased urbanization and a larger city have also meant that when they do go out, they tend to go further. In 1998, almost half of all motorized trips (43%) were longer than 10 km, compared to only 13% in 1972. And although the use of mechanized means of transport increased 35% between 1972 and 1998, walking remains for many Cairenes the main mode of transport, accounting for 36% of all daily trips in 1998. CB

lifting could not disguise the continuing encroachment of what road planners call "side friction," in the guise of makeshift marketplaces, food stalls, and the like. The millennium may have changed, but the city some call the Big Mango is as messy as ever. *MR*

Bus Stop

A city built on public transport

To tell the story of how Cairo came to acquire its present day shape is, in many ways, to tell a story of transportation. In 1800, Cairo's radius was only 2.5 km, and the majority of its residents navigated the city on foot or in carriage. As a system of modern mass transit evolved in the early 20th century, it not only changed the way Cairenes moved around, it also fixed the contours of the burgeoning city.

The earliest mass transport network in Cairo was based on the tramway and the train, developed and run exclusively by private companies. The first tramway started operations in 1876. By 1917, 30 lines connected the central areas to the city's periphery, while two complementary networks operated inside the new quarters of Heliopolis and Helwan. New railway lines also linked the city center to more distant districts, like Helwan and Maadi in the south (est. 1877), and Qubba and Matariya in the northeast (est. 1888). These services put the outlying suburbs at a distance of only one hour from the city center. As the network extended from the Pyramids to Heliopolis, it determined the city's future growth pattern.

Starting in the 1950s, population growth, industrialization, and urbanization led to an influx of people to the center of Cairo. The state established its own system of public transport, while private means of getting around (cars and service taxis) developed. In 1960, the Cairo Tramway Society was nationalized and a public bus network was organized. Six years later, a riverboat bus service was introduced, serving both banks of the river from Rod al-Farag to Old Cairo.

Once in operation, the bus network proved more efficient than the old tramway. In 1963, buses moved about 510 million passengers, compared to less than 124 million on the tram. The tram's share in city transport continued to decrease, until in 1990 it was decided to discontinue service altogether. (The exception was the autonomous Heliopolis tram, which continues to run today, but carried only 0.7% of all transported passengers in 1998). Little by little, the bus became the principal mode of movement among Cairenes.

The 1970s, however, witnessed the beginning of changes that would eventually have a great impact on the way people moved around the city. For one thing, public transport faced a crisis, partly due to the state's lack of investment in the maintenance and upgrading of the sector. Buses ran infrequently, with waiting times of more than 25 minutes; the vehicles themselves were outdated (about 50% were more than 10 years old); and they carried two and half times the amount of passengers they were designed for. Between 1970 and 1985, the number of buses in service increased by less than 28% while the population almost doubled. Starting in 1980, the state started to reinvest in public transport. Minibuses were introduced in 1985, the first

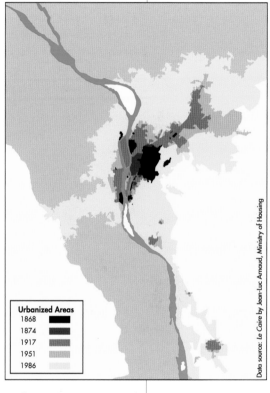

Urbanized Areas
- 1868
- 1874
- 1917
- 1951
- 1986

Data source: *Le Caire* by Jean-Luc Arnaud, Ministry of Housing

Cairo's growth in the last century mirrors expansions in the transport network

metro line opened in 1989, and bus service was improved throughout the decade.

As public transport struggled to cope with increasing demand, modes of private collective transport (taxis, private buses, school and administrative buses) stepped in to fill the gap. Between 1970 and 1998, the number of private buses increased 8.5 times and taxis about twelve-fold. But the most important development was undoubtedly the introduction of microbuses in 1980. These vehicles—minivans with a median capacity of 12 people—were and remain privately run, though the organization of the network is under the control of the public authorities who give licenses and fix the routes. Today, the microbus is the single most widely used motorized mode of transportation among Cairenes. In 1998, about 25,000 of them were operating in the Greater Cairo area, and they carried more than 1.2 million people every day, or about 30% of all motorized traffic (compared to 19% by bus).

The use of private cars also increased dramatically during the same period. In 1914, 656 cars were circulating in Cairo. Between 1970 and 1985, the number of cars on the road increased six-fold, reaching 500,000 in 1985; by 1998, the road network of Cairo had to absorb close to 760,000 cars a day. Important investments in infrastructure were made to adapt the urban fabric to this new mode of transport: flyovers,

Traffic Madness

At the beginning of 2001, there were 3.117 million vehicles registered in Egypt, including:
1. 1.389 million private cars
2. 303,918 taxis
3. 546,591 trucks
4. 53,483 buses
5. 498,891 motorcycles

In 2000, the latest year for which statistics are available, a total of 21,038,657 traffic tickets were doled out. That's almost one for every Egyptian over the legal driving age, or about seven per registered vehicle. The same year, on Egypt's roads there were:
1. 22,364 accidents
2. 4,844 deaths
3. 22,631 injuries

In general:
1. Losses (hospital care, lost working hours, damage to vehicles) incurred by road accidents are estimated at LE1 billion a year.
2. It takes an average of 45 minutes for ambulances to reach the accident scene.

According to the Traffic Authority, one of the most dangerous stretches of road in the country is in Beni Sueif, on the 120 km between al-Ayyat and Malatya. Beni Sueif also has the least kilometers of road of any governorate in the country.

In Cairo, it is estimated that less than 2,500 residential properties have underground parking facilities, about half of which are not used. According to a study carried out by the governorate, only 443 of Nasr City's 30,000 residential towers have parking garages. In Abdin, only 24 buildings do. The governorate estimates that close to 140,000 additional parking spaces are required this year to house cars in the central areas of the city.

Source: CAPMAS, Rose al-Youssef magazine, al-Akhbar newspaper, al-Ahram newspaper

new bridges, new main thoroughfares, and a Ring Road were built. The removal of the tram and the construction of an underground metro liberated precious space above ground for the flow of cars.

As Cairo's transport system evolved, it profoundly altered the shape of the city. The opening of tramlines between downtown and the suburbs sparked the first flight towards the periphery. Urban pockets sprang up around tram stations, rapidly merging into one another. The spatial enlargement of the city thus proceeded along fixed transit routes, spreading out from the center in finger-like extensions with a strong northeast-west pattern reflecting the Heliopolis-Pyramids route. In the 1970s, the diffusion of the car along with more flexible modes of transportation helped to fill the empty in-between spaces of the metropolitan area and conquer new space. Over the course of the last three decades, the built-up area of metropolitan Cairo has more than tripled, a physical expansion accompanied by the lengthening of the public transport network. The center, however, remains the hub. Almost 70% of buses operate in the inner city, and 30% serve the Pyramids-Heliopolis axis. As befits a dense urban fabric, collective transport in Cairo accounts for almost 50% of all daily trips, and walking for 36%.

As Cairo reaches further into the desert, however, a different pattern of urbanization has become visible, one that is no longer tied to public transport. Several

bus lines have been established in desert areas, but as these areas are less dense, they are less lucrative for the public sector. These new urban spaces depend above all on private transport: the car and the microbus. Since the early 1980s, more than 1,000 km of new roads have been constructed in the Greater Cairo area, nine-tenths of them in the desert. The recent extensions of the 26th of July axis and the Ring Road come within a policy of promoting the use of private cars. Yet, in 1998, less than one in five households owned a car, and they accounted for only 13% of all daily transit. In this context, microbuses, which adapt instantaneously to demand, represent the main mode of transportation in new urban areas like Sixth of October City.

Increasingly based on planning designed mainly for private cars, Cairo continues to expand, and as it does, it is leaving aside a great part of its population, held in enclaves captive to public transport. The future of the city as a sustainable environment will depend heavily on how these two competing visions of transportation facilities—public or private—are managed. *CB*

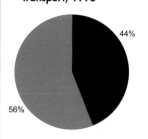

Cairenes' Use of Public Transport, 1998

44%

56%

 Private motorized transport

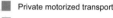 Public motorized transport

1971

19%

81%

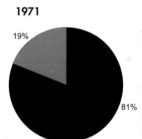

■ Private motorized transport

■ Public motorized transport

Source: Célame Barge, SYSTRA

The advent of the car and the microbus have reduced the usage of public transport

The Provinces
Once remote areas are rapidly developing

Second City

Alexandria began the first millennium of the Common Era as one of the greatest conurbations in the world. At the beginning of the third, Alex is still a big city with approximately four million inhabitants, a third of Egypt's shipping activity, and almost 40% of its manufacturing industries spread within and around the town.

For all that, Alex of late has become a shabby provincial place that can no longer manage to attract the once inevitable summer hordes from the capital. As life becomes more expensive, the poorer stay home and the wealthier head along the northwest coast to the ever-spreading holiday complexes. A city once dubbed "Bride of the Mediterranean" has become a bit of an old maid.

This, however, seems to be changing. Since his nomination to the post as governor, Mohammed Abd al-Salam Mahgoub has set in motion a massive campaign of urban beautification. Buildings in the downtown area as well as a long stretch of the Corniche have been repainted, public squares have been remodeled and replanted, bus stations have been relocated out of the city center, and every roundabout has become a mass of greenery, statuary, and bubbling fountains. While these changes are essentially cosmetic and often in dubious taste, they have done much to encourage some sort of optimism in the heart of the average Alexandrian.

The Corniche itself is receiving more than just a lick of paint. As a long thin city, trapped between the sea and Lake Maryout, Alexandria, with only two main longitudinal traffic axes, is well known for its gridlocks. The widening of the Corniche from four to twelve lanes is intended to ameliorate the situation. This four-stage project seems complete for the moment and has seen the once favored bathing beach of Stanley Bay transformed into Stanley Bridge. The downside is obvious: more traffic in the city center, less space for public beaches, and should one ever manage to cross the road and make it to the sea, the return journey will require waiting until the small hours of the morning.

A more positive note has been the recent disappearance of garbage from the streets. A $446-million deal with the French firm Onyx—the country's first experiment with comprehensive municipal trash collection—will hopefully assure Alexandria of a competent and rationalized waste collection, treatment, and disposal system for the next fifteen years. Already the streets are awash with new plastic rubbish bins and overalled workers. While there have been certain cavils over the cost and the fact that it is , in part, being passed on to the citizens through a supplement to electricity bills, for once the streets are noticeably clean.

In line with these initiatives in revamping the fading

Windows to the World

Gently sloping out to embrace the sea, its face tilted towards the horizon, the Bibliotheca Alexandrina looks eager to fulfill the daunting task that has been laid at its feet. "Egypt's window to the world and the world's window to Egypt" was how Suzanne Mubarak described it at the soft opening that took place in October last year, a grand meeting point for a dialogue of civilizations. If the battery of international luminaries that grace the Board of Trustees is any indication of the library's future, it seems prepared to achieve its global ambitions. The 27-member board includes Egyptian space scientist Farouq al-Baz, Palestinian stateswoman Hanan Ashrawi, Italian author Umberto Eco, Nigerian Nobel laureate Wole Soyinka, and Ecuadorean environmentalist Yolanda Kakabadse. The appointment of Ismail Serageldin to the post of director was the icing on the cake of the institution's international prestige. Former vice-president of the World Bank, the polyglot development specialist is a true citizen of the world, with just the right credentials needed to attract the necessary levels of international support.

But if the idea of resurrecting the ancient library makes good PR, it has also given the new Bibliotheca something of an identity complex. Drawing on the model of its ancient predecessor, some envision the new library primarily as a research institution, Egypt's loftiest ivory tower, capable of attracting scholars from across the globe and once again contributing to human scientific endeavor. Others see the library as a depository of universal knowledge, evolving into a truly public institution that embodies a more democratic conception of knowledge than that prevalent in Alexandria's Greco-Roman heyday. For the time being, the universal seems to be getting the upper hand. Officials have scrapped initial plans to close the library to the general public. Limits to use will remain—a small entrance fee will be imposed and it is still

unclear whether visitors will be allowed to check books out—but the public response in the month following the soft opening was promising. October witnessed about 6,000 people streaming in every day and at the mid-year school break, the place was packed with students. With a children's library, a science "exploratorium," and multilingual computer access, the library is striving to become a place of hands-on learning.

The universal received a further boost in April, when the US-based Internet Archive donated a copy of its entire archive to the library. The digital equivalent of about 100 million books, the archive holds the sum total of the web from 1996-2001. With the acquisition of what is essentially the history of the web—that most modern means of information dissemination and thus far the most democratic—the library took a great step into the 21st century, confirming its commitment to public access to information.

Ultimately, the library's agenda may be determined by practical considerations more than anything else. At this point, it still has a long way to go before it can rival the world's largest research libraries. By the grand opening on October 16, 2002, the library expects to have about 300,000 books on the shelves, in addition to several thousand manuscripts. The total operating budget of the Bibliotheca is only $20 million, and maintenance alone is expected to eat up about 30% of that, leaving the rest to cover salaries, acquisitions, and provide the kinds of services that distinguish the best research institutions. In contrast, Harvard University Library, the largest academic library in the US with a collection of over 14 million volumes, has an annual budget of over $80 million. Whatever shape the Bibliotheca eventually takes will be heavily dependent on what donors at home and abroad are willing to give. *MM*

The Bibliotheca is the second city's latest attempt to put itself back on the world map

city, a Heritage Management Unit has been set up within the governorate under the auspices of the National Center for the Documentation of Cultural and Natural Heritage. Funded jointly by the central government and the UNDP, this unit has already begun, in conjunction with NGOs, the identification and listing of buildings and zones requiring conservation and restoration. The effectiveness of these measures is yet to be seen. Reports still filter in of the wrecking ball illegally reshaping Alexandria's once stylish urban fabric, and archaeologists conducting salvage excavations have yet to enjoy the cooperation of construction companies.

But what has occasioned this flurry of activity? It could be that Alex had simply hit rock bottom and the only way was up. Alternatively it could be that the city now has a governor who is interested in working, unlike his predecessor who held the post for twelve long and inactive years. There is also the library factor. The brand spanking new, if yet unfilled,

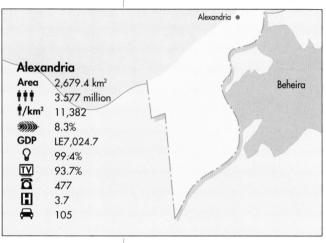

Alexandria

Area	2,679.4 km²
👥	3.577 million
👤/km²	11,382
📶	8.3%
GDP	LE7,024.7
💡	99.4%
📺	93.7%
☎	477
🅷	3.7
🚗	105

For key to indicator maps see page 41

Bibliotheca Alexandrina, envisaged to hold some four million volumes and serve as a new research pole for the Eastern Mediterranean, is scheduled to open officially on October 16, 2002, and is seen by many as a long-awaited kick start for the fading city. If Alexandria is to be put back on the world map as a center of culture and learning then the place had better not look like a dog's breakfast.

At a November conference organized by the new institution, "Alexandria in the 21st Century: Visions of Planning and Building," the governor outlined plans for other upcoming cultural ventures. These include the opening of a National (i.e. Pharaonic) Museum and a Mosaic Museum, while the former Mohammed Ali Theater is to be revamped and run by the Cairo Opera House. While the first should be easy enough to establish, the second may prove more problematic. Ancient Alexandria was an important and innovative center of mosaic production, and the city's Greco-Roman Museum holds a large collection. However, most of these are in a terrible state of repair and mosaic restoration is a very long and very costly procedure. Questions have also been asked as to why the town's biggest and oldest theater should be put in the hands of a Cairo-based organization dedicated to a rather elitist art form.

Alexandria's port, the very reason for the city's existence, is also heading for a clean up. Due to entrenched vested interests (notably in the customs), the port has become "a byword for corruption," in the words of the *Financial Times*. In any case, some $332 million has been earmarked for an upgrading, and the acronym BOT (Build, Operate, Transfer) is bouncing around the port's run-down wharves and crumbling passenger terminal. The idea is to get the private sector involved in a harbor through which passes some 60% of the country's imports before it is overshadowed by the construction of the East Port Said container terminal.

And it might just happen. The governor, it is

recognized by all, has been clever in involving the private sector in the regeneration of Alex and has effectively co-opted the erstwhile independent voices that once criticized his predecessor by turning them into unofficial advisors. With two business-oriented NGOs in action involving some of the real highfliers, newly digitized telephone exchanges, almost 50% of the country's petroleum industries, the recently discovered gas fields in the Mediterranean, and a pleasure boat marina projected for the eastern harbor, Alexandria may be on the way back. But there is something lacking: the city has still to rediscover its soul. As someone from the floor pointed out during the Bibliotheca conference, since the 1960s, the city has never been governed by Alexandrians and has never been properly represented in the central authorities. There is definitely something in that. And still the city has no daily newspaper. *CC*

Delta Dawn

The agricultural center is rapidly urbanizing

Cruising through the Delta these days, its is hard to reconcile the image conjured up by official statistics with the reality on the ground. While the 1996 census indicates that 72% of the Delta population lives in rural areas, disappearing farmland, bustling provincial centers, and sprawling villages tell another story. Even the word "village" itself is something of a misnomer—while the average population of an Egyptian village is about 7,000, it is often used to refer to towns of up to 20,000 people.

Since the late 1970s, when Egyptian laborers began migrating to the Gulf in record numbers, public investments to rural areas have been complemented by extensive private investments in modern housing and equipment, transportation, and shopping facilities for mass-produced consumer goods—all trappings previously identified with urban Egypt. The expansion of a transportation network throughout the Delta by privately owned cars, microbuses, and service taxis has reduced the distance between rural and urban environments, while major road-building projects like the northern coastal highway have made it easier and quicker to get from one place to the next.

Contact between village and town or city has intensified with the daily commuting of students and by the growing number of villagers who work in town.

Urban lifestyles have also spread to villages via the mass media and public education. Rural students are taught from standardized programs in school that are more or less identical for pupils whatever their social level or geographic origin. Radio and TV are found in most homes today, even among poor families. A high percentage of male villagers have worked abroad for extended periods, many in two or three different countries. They have thus been introduced to new styles of commodities and markets, housing, and cultural habits and have, in turn, passed some of this on to their own families. Indeed, in some villages, families affected by labor migration account for as much as two-thirds of the population. The extension of public services has reduced differences in access to health care, electricity, tapped water, and telecommunications.

These social changes are reflected in the physical transformation of the Delta landscape, with modern houses of

Delta	
Area	27,723.2 km²
👪	28.026 million
👤/km²	1,263
〰	58.9%
GDP	LE4,347.9
💡	99.9%
TV	90.4%
☎	153
H	3.2
🚗	20

burnt red brick and concrete rapidly replacing traditional mud-brick homes. The switch in housing styles is not merely aesthetic, but results from deeper social and changes. Mud-brick houses were constructed to fit the needs of a farming family, with an open-air inner courtyard for domestic activities and stables for livestock within the house. In the new houses, living areas are clearly set off from those assigned to livestock, which are being transferred to stables on the outskirts of the village or—more rarely—to the ground floor of the new house. Many new homes also include a space for a shop or workshop on the ground floor, an illustration of the new economic strategies of village residents and a sign of the expansion of a cash economy.

Even taking into account land reclamation projects, agricultural areas in the Delta are being rapidly decimated by new house building, the expansion of industrial areas, and road building. The shrinking supply of land has coincided with an increased demand, as remittances from abroad throughout the 1980s and 90s provided the capital for land purchase. As a result, land prices have skyrocketed over the last 15 years. In one village in Sharqiya, the price for a feddan of agricultural land (a feddan is approximately one acre) rose from LE10,000-18,000 in 1983 to LE84,000-108,000 in 1997 when the new tenancy law was implemented. The rural Delta has witnessed the rise of a new type of landless family: young

Cairo long ago ceased to be an attractive place to live for the young Delta generation, but commuting is on the rise

and educated, with jobs outside the agricultural sector. Other families have sold their inherited land to finance the building of a modern brick house or to cover debt, and many former tenant farmers became landless after the implementation of the new tenancy law.

Despite these transformations, farming is still an important part of the rural economy, and land ownership still holds high cultural value. But new economic realities, along with changing patterns in land ownership, have led to a boom in part-time, rather than full-time farming. Small- or micro-scale farmers with holdings of below one feddan comprise about 65% of all agricultural landowners in the Delta. There are a far smaller number of families who own more than ten feddans and who rent out their land or cultivate it with hired labor. Fragmentation of land holding is also high. Though the number of children per family has declined markedly among rural families in the Delta—from four-eight in the 1980s to only two-four today—the middle-aged villagers who are now inheriting from their parents and dividing the family holding have grown up in families with many children. Sons of medium-sized farmers of six feddans may become small-scale farmers of less than one feddan after the division. As the rise in crop prices and yields has not been high enough to balance out the decrease in holding size, many holdings are now unable to provide for a family even when combined with agricultural wage labor. At the same time, villagers with a job outside agriculture no longer tend to leave their share of the paternal holding for their farming brothers, but require the crop—as food and a source of cash income—to make ends meet.

Although the majority of farmers' sons and daughters now complete formal education at least to diploma levels and look for jobs outside agriculture, Cairo has long since ceased to be an attractive destination for the young generation of educated Delta villagers. With the extension of electricity, tapped water, and modern and comfortable housing, the rural setting competes favorably with a crammed flat in noisy and polluted Cairo. Looking for a solution to the lack of rural job opportunities, a growing number of villagers now commute daily over a considerable distance between work and home. Provincial centers like Tanta, Zaqaziq, and Benha attract the majority of these commuters, but young diploma-holders have also started taking jobs in the private-sector industries that have been set up in new desert cities like the Tenth of Ramadan and Sadat City. Often shuttled to and from home in company cars, the trip may take as much as three or four hours a day. In one village in Sharqiya, a large group of young men and women set out for the Tenth of Ramadan at 6 am, returning at 7 or 8 pm six days a week. With salaries ranging from LE120-150 per month (for diploma holders), most young factory workers prefer to set up a flat in the paternal house. There they remain close to their network of friends and family, while enjoying affordable housing, social security, and cheap food from a family holding or from the local markets. *KB*

Delta Shores

The Delta lakes are no longer wild

The area around the coastal lakes has always been a world apart from the rest of the Delta. The lakes' environment is wild, and access to it remote and difficult. Dotted with white sand dunes, the seashore has palm groves that wash into the sea. Where the Nile meets the sea, the sand of the beaches is black because of age-old silt deposits.

But the four Delta lakes—Manzala, Burullus, Edku, and Maryut—are sick. The backdrop for many smuggler thrillers in the 1950s, they are today only remnants of their former selves. The Bahr al-Baqar, a major drain, has contaminated the once bountiful waters of Manzala,

the largest of the four lakes. About three million m³ of wastewater flows into the lake every day, carrying heavy metals, toxins, and particulate matter. Even in the 1980s, over half the fish sampled in the four lakes showed traces of DDT. The extreme pollution of Lake Maryut, the primary dumping site of Alexandria's industrial run-off, has led to calls to drain what remains of it once and for all.

Land reclamation and road building have also taken a toll. The new coastal highway, part of a transnational endeavor, runs straight across the shoreline, cutting through the mouths of the lakes past hundreds of slender fishing fellucas. While it has cut the travel time between Alexandria and Port Said at least in half, it will inevitably alter even further the wild environment of the lakes as traffic in-

creases. Manzala has already shrunk many times over, from an area covering 400,000 feddans in the early 1930s to about 120,000 feddans today. But perhaps the greatest threat to the area is the erosion of its coasts and the resulting rising water table. Despite government efforts to halt the encroaching sea with a scheme to build break-waters at Rosetta, the coastline has receded in some places by as much as 100 meters. Sunken buildings are visible in the middle of the sea. This is a result of the disturbance of the natural cycle, as the silt of the Nile ceased to be deposited after the construction of the High Dam.

All this has not been good news for the communities of small-scale fishers that have depended on the lakes for their livelihood since time immemorial. The degradation of the lake environment has had a severe negative impact on the health of the fishers. A three-year field study conducted by the Land Center for Human Rights found that about 40% of fishers around Lake Edku suffer from kidney disease. Another study puts the average life span of Lake Manzala residents at around 40, compared to over 60 in the country as a whole.

Most disconcerting to the fishermen themselves, however, is the fallout they have suffered from another type of human encroachment on the lakes' environment: fish farms. Starting in the mid-1980s, the government began granting licenses for private fish farms on the perimeter of the lakes, in an effort to boost fish production and to encourage private investment in the sector. In terms of production, fish farms are booming. In 1993, the fish harvest from farms was only 35,000 tons; by 1999 it had risen to 215,000 tons, over 30% of Egypt's total fish harvest.

As more of the lakes' surface is cordoned off into private farms, small-scale fishers have had their access to the lake drastically restricted. At Lake Edku, more than 250 farms have been established. As a result, the 11,500 small fishers have seen the area available for their use steadily dwindle, from 20,000 feddans in 1985 to about 5,000 feddans today. Fishing villages along the northwestern shore of Lake Manzala have experienced a similar *de facto* privatization of what used to be collective fishing areas.

As man-made development has slowly reduced the diversity of the lakes' marine life, it threatens to do the same to its human denizens. Suffering the effects of both environmental and economic degradation, some fishers have already begun to migrate to other lakes in search of better opportunities, while others have given up fishing altogether. *MM*

The Canal Zone

The three canal cities part ways

If Egypt is the gift of the Nile, then the cities of Port Said, Ismailiya, and Suez are the gift of the Suez Canal. Prior to the digging of the canal, the whole area between the village of Suez and the Mediterranean Sea was one long sand bar. Port Said itself was only a 20-meter strip of sand separating Lake Manzala from the sea. As work proceeded on the canal, the rubble was used to fill in part of the lake, providing the foundation for the city and the harbor. All three cities grew up in the shadow of the canal and the British colonial presence, which remained in the zone until the 1956 war.

Evacuated during the years of war with Israel since they were on the front line, the Suez Canal cities were only re-inhabited after 1974. Though this shared past has infused the three cities with a distinctive flavor that sets them apart from the rest of Egypt, their destinies have parted ways over the past 30 years.

Port Said was declared a free zone in 1975 and became a bustling commercial center from which imported consumer goods flooded the country. Yet as customs duties came down and the quality of made-in-Egypt goods improved, the need to travel to Port Said to buy foreign goods diminished. The government's removal of

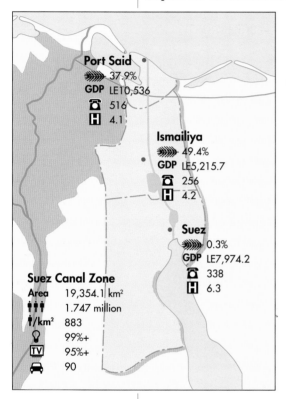

Ismailiya is statistiscally considered part of the Delta and is included on both indicator maps

the city's free zone status in early 2002 will probably spell its end as a retail center. Locals hope that the East Port Said megaproject will step in to fill the gap and compensate for the economic downturn that the city has suffered in recent years. Projected to stretch over an area of 220 km², the project includes plans for an industrial park, fisheries, a tourist zone, and a container port capable of handling 1.7 million containers annually. But the opening of the port has been postponed more than once—now it is scheduled to begin operations in 2004. Despite the setbacks, the developers hope to turn it into the region's prime hub port, where large container ships coming out of the canal can dock and reload their goods for distribution to Mediterranean markets. If it works, it is expected to eventually generate about LE1.5 billion in direct and indirect revenues. Less clear is the future of the industrial zone, which would act as the real stimulus for much-needed employment in the area. In mid-2001, the government put a lid on financing projects in the zone, claiming that the ground was not suitable for heavy industrial development.

Historically agriculture has been of little importance in Port Said; today, only about 5,500 feddans are cultivated. But that may change in the future as the Salam Canal comes to fruition. With about 10% of the canal in the Port Said governorate, 135,000 feddans of land have been slated for reclamation, and already several new farming plantations have been established.

Of the three canal cities, Ismailiya has remained the quietest. The headquarters of the long-defunct Companie Universelle du Canal de Suez is a sleepy town, famous for its mango orchards and vast gardens. It has a new university and its suburbs are sprawling to the northwest, but it has more in common with the Delta than its two sister cities on either end of the canal. About half of the land area is cultivated, and the provincial city itself has failed to attract many industries. To the south of the city, on the bitter lakes, lie the resorts of Fayed and Abu Sultan. To the north, two massive infrastructure projects were completed last year that may eventually bring more cross-continent travelers into the city's orbit. The old Cairo-Gaza railway line, once the line to the Levant and the Holy Land, is being resurrected to vie for the title of the New Orient Express. The centerpiece is the Ferdan Bridge, at 640 meters long, the world's longest rotating steel bridge. Further north at Qantara, a new suspension bridge over the Suez Canal was also inaugurated last year. Both bridges will relieve traffic at the overburdened Ahmed Hamdi tunnel and (officials hope) speed the flow of goods, industry, and people into the Sinai Peninsula.

Suez, meanwhile, has already shaken itself up. The city, which suffered heavily from a long siege by the Israelis in 1973 and was largely destroyed by bombardments, is undergoing massive reconstruction and expansion. Debris and mines from the years of war have been cleared. A multimillion-pound project is well underway to remove the railway tracks that run through the middle of the city and act as an obstacle to its southerly progression. Plans are in the works for an electrical tramway. Suez also has an impressive grand Corniche—created by landfill at the expense of the shallow waters—at the northernmost point of the Gulf of

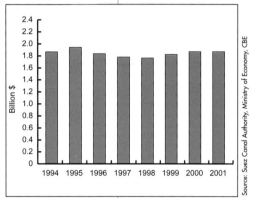

Source: Suez Canal Authority, Ministry of Economy, CBE

Despite a tough year, revenues from the canal in 2001 were slightly higher than the previous year

Suez, looking down the Red Sea.

And down the Red Sea seems increasingly to be where the economic future of the city lies, with the quarries along the Red Sea mountain range, the burgeoning oil industry, and the string of ports and industrial zones that start in Suez itself and stretch to Ain Sukhna, 40 km down the coast. The road to the older Attaqa port, until recently in a sorry state, has been upgraded to a two-lane highway to serve a new port—the first privately operated port in Egypt—and adjoining industrial zone at Ain Sukhna. Last year saw the completion of a new railway linking the Ain Sukhna port with Suez and the rest of the national railway network. The 25-km^2 port, still under construction, is intended to serve what will be a largely export-based industrial zone, catering to markets in Africa and Asia. In the industrial zone, a fertilizer and steel plant have already been established, and a bus factory is in the works, but the inauguration of the port has been delayed due to disputes between the government and the private operator. The project lies at the junction with the road to Cairo. Known as the Qatamiya road, it is narrow and dangerously crowded with trucks loaded with cement and marble from the nearby factories and quarries. There are plans to convert it in to a two-lane highway under a privately financed project.

The port and industrial zone cover dozens of square kilometers, right in the middle of a booming tourist destination—a sandy beach complete with a hot water spring that runs into the sea. Only 120 km from the capital, Ain Sukhna is an easily manageable day trip, the perfect beach for Cairenes. *MS & PAG*

Still a land of stunning beauty, the Said has its own way of blending the old with the new

Down South

The Said still suffers from neglect

In the standard geographical definition, Upper Egypt, or the Said, extends from Giza to Aswan, including the Fayyoum. Like most regional designations, this one glosses over many variations. The area, however, remains unified by a pervasive feeling among its inhabitants that they are marginalized, neglected, and forgotten, a feeling which is, to a great extent, justified. Upper Egypt still lags behind the rest of the country in key areas like infrastructure, health, and education. The latest figures from Egypt's Demographic and Health survey show that under-five child mortality rates in Upper Egypt are still twice that of urban governorates.

Given the overall condition of the Egyptian economy, this situation is not likely to improve in any significant way in the foreseeable future. It is a positive sign, however, that the region's need for attention is being increasingly acknowledged at the official level. In 2001, Aswan was the site of a high-profile conference, "Girls' Needs in Upper Egypt," presided over by Suzanne Mubarak and attended by the governors of Upper Egypt and a number of ministers and members of parliament. The city of Qena has also attracted considerable media attention, where the governor has initiated a major process of beautification that has been compared to Alexandria's recent facelift. The visible improvements include the cleaning of streets, the planting of trees, and the opening of new roads. The process is currently extending beyond the governorate capital to other towns in the Qena governorate. Elsewhere, infrastructure has seen a major push as a series of bridges have been built, or are under construction, at almost every major city. A desert highway on the west bank of the Nile now runs from Cairo all the way down to Assyout. When completed, it will reach Aswan.

Agriculture—and in particular sugarcane—still forms the backbone of the Upper Egyptian economy, but it is an increasing source of concern for the region's cultivators. The crop was hard hit by pests last year for the second year in a row, and it is expected to greatly affect productivity. The eight state-owned sugar mills that dot the valley from Hawamdiya in Giza to Kom Ombo in Aswan refused to receive cane from infected areas, accentuating the already problematic relationship with the cultivators, who complain of payment delays and disputes over the weighing of cane inside the mills. Competition from cheap imported sugar is also posing serious threats to local sugar production, while the growing need to rationalize water use may ultimately reduce the area planted with this water-demanding crop.

Although the state's fight against militant Islamists is practically over, Upper Egypt continues to suffer the consequences of a perceived lingering threat. The so-called security belt, referring to the ban on growing sugar cane in fields adjacent to main roads and the Nile bank, is still in place. Tourism is strictly regulated and supervised, and tourists are not allowed out of main cities except in police-guarded convoys. This not only deprives visitors from experiencing the richness of Upper Egyptian culture, but it deprives residents from a much-needed source of income as well. Villages like Garagos, Akhmim, and Nagada, famous for traditional crafts like pottery and weaving, have been especially hard hit by such policies. After the events of September 11, already strict security measures were tightened, even as the number of tourists visiting the Said fell drastically.

Government attempts to set up industrial cities that would provide much-needed employment for the region's youth have so far not been very effective, and the new cities in Upper Egypt are probably being used mainly to provide housing for the region's growing middle class. The only city that may have some industrial potential is New Beni Sueif—the closest of these cities to Cairo—with 38 factories up and running and 50 more under construction. According to government figures though, these factories only employ about 2,900 workers at present. Even as housing projects, achievements remain modest. According to official figures, over the last four years, 3,000 units were built in New Assyout, and less in the other new cities.

Yet, there is no denying that the face of rural Upper Egypt has changed drastically over the past two decades. Education has spread, agriculture is increasingly mechanized, transportation networks have expanded throughout the area, and the phenomenon of the part-time farmer is increasingly prominent. Perhaps the most visible aspect of change is seen in architectural preferences, as concrete red-brick, urban middle-class style structures replace the traditional mud-brick houses, a change linked to labor migration to oil-rich countries. But the visibility of this particular aspect of social change has led many observers to exaggerate the extent to which rural society, particularly in Upper Egypt, has actually changed. This is a society that seems unusually capable of accommodating many layers of history. The

The Fayyoum

Though the Fayyoum is commonly thought to be an oasis, it is not. Surrounded by the desert, it is linked to the Nile by the Bahr Youssef, which enters the depression at Lahoun. Yet, not unlike a far-flung oasis, the Fayyoum has lived its own history for thousands of years. It expanded under the pharaohs, when lands were reclaimed and irrigated at great cost under the reign of Sesotris II (1897-1878 BCE) and Amenemhat III (1842-1797 BCE). Centuries later, the Ptolemies turned the Fayyoum into a showcase for Greek civilization, establishing or enlarging towns and villages and introducing new cultures like the apricot and apple. Under Mamluk rule, the Fayyoum fell into decline, with the desert taking over reclaimed lands and Lake Qaroun shrinking to a fraction of its former size.

Quite the opposite of the desert oases, water in the Fayyoum flows by natural gravity, branching off the Bahr Youssef in multiple irrigation channels. The incline between Lahoun and Lake Qaroun, the lowest point of the depression, is 66 meters. As a result, Qaroun receives all the agricultural drainage in the Fayyoum. The waters are charged with pesticides and the residues of chemical fertilizers used indiscriminately by local farmers.

This lake was once full of crocodiles and other fauna, the former the living images of Sobek, the ancient god of the Fayyoum province. But as the lake has shrunk, salinity levels have been rising. Today, it is host to only a few varieties of fish: mullet, sole, gray shrimp, and *gambarod*, a small silver fish thin as an eel. When the fishing season opens in the summer, the lake is covered by boats coming from Shakshouk and other villages close to the shores, where locals live as both farmers and fishermen. Fishers say the factory near Shakshouk that extracts the lake's mineral salts is aggravating the pollution and impoverishing the lake.

A major scheme was implemented in the 1970s to relieve pressure on Lake Qaroun by diverting excess drainage water towards the Wadi Rayan depression, creating two new lakes in the middle of a pristine sea of sand that has since been turned into a protected area. More eco-friendly methods of pest control have been introduced to the depression—the use of predator insects, for example—but they are not yet widespread.

Only one hour away from Cairo, the Fayyoum today is still very much a part of Upper Egypt and one of the poorest regions in the country. However, over the last few years the shores of the three lakes have begun to attract throngs of weekend tourists, and holiday villas have sprung up along both tips of Lake Qaroun. But this northern-coast style of development does not seem to be working in the Fayyoum, and the resorts around Qaroun stand empty. Ezbat Tunis, on the other hand, the artists' colony near the eastern tip of the lake, is bustling. Part-time residents have adopted a more traditional eco-friendly mudbrick architecture that melts into the landscape, living in harmony with the adjacent village. Perhaps this type of development, which takes into account the Fayyoum's local identity while also benefiting the local economy, is a more appropriate model to follow. *PG*

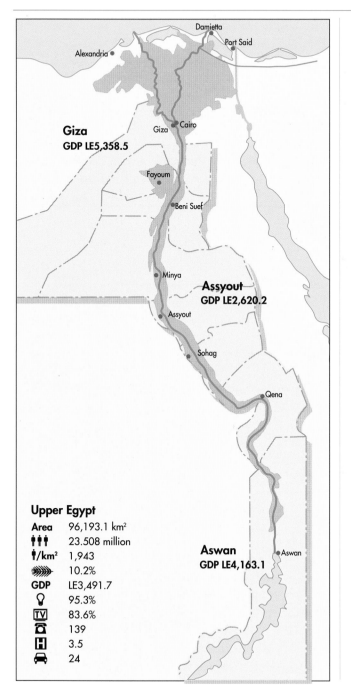

Giza
GDP LE5,358.5

Assyout
GDP LE2,620.2

Aswan
GDP LE4,163.1

Damietta
Port Said
Alexandria
Giza Cairo
Fayoum
Beni Suef
Minya
Assyout
Sohag
Qena
Aswan

Upper Egypt

Area	96,193.1 km²
👤👤👤	23.508 million
👤/km²	1,943
🌾	10.2%
GDP	LE3,491.7
💡	95.3%
📺	83.6%
☎	139
🏥	3.5
🚗	24

appearance of McDonalds, the Chinese *galabiya*, and a plastic culture is probably less interesting than the persistence of traditional (and even ancient) ways of preparing meals, of potters, blacksmiths and sieve-makers, of barter and ritual-related exchanges. In the southernmost governorates, mulukhiya and okra, the staple vegetables, are still cooked mainly in the clay *burma* pot. In certain parts of Aswan, cheaper blankets sold in department stores will coexist with, but not replace, the traditional *burdaya*, a blanket woven of sheep wool and made by Christian weavers in the area. Women still use eggs as currency to buy things for themselves, though this is more limited than it used to be. Though they always seem on the verge of extinction, many aspects of traditional culture are quite resilient.

As a form of social organization, tribalism, too, still plays an important role in the social, economic, and political life of Upper Egyptian society, especially in the three southernmost governorates of Aswan, Qena, and Sohag. Though often families that identify themselves as members in a tribe (*gabila*) have no obvious ancestral link, as an institution, the tribe performs vital social functions and is often an important determinant of marriage and residence patterns, as well as mediation and reconciliation. Apart from these "traditional" functions, tribes play a key role in electoral politics and more recently in the organization and running of NGOs and community development projects. For village-level development projects, like building a school or replacing water pipes, tribal representatives are in charge of allocating responsibilities and organizing villagers' contributions. These leaders use familiar and efficient ways of coordination and mobilization, and the results are often impressive. The changing form and function of tribalism is a notable example of the Said's peculiar way of connecting tradition and modernity, how the new never quite replaces the old but tends to coexist with it, often peacefully. *RS*

The Western Desert

Settling the desert is still a distant dream

Vast and sparsely inhabited, the Western or Libyan Desert covers 681,000 km², or two-thirds of Egyptian territory. One of the most arid regions in the world, rainfall is rare and water scarce. Three governorates, the New Valley, Giza, and Marsa Matrouh, administer this massive territory and its estimated 350,000 inhabitants.

Along the north coast the population is composed primarily of Bedouin, mainly from the Awlad Ali tribe, which migrated from the Libyan Desert a few hundred years ago. In the 1960s the government designed a sedentarization program (one of the most successful such state-sponsored projects in the Arab world) in which the Bedouin were given subsidized housing loans. Most built their houses in small clusters on their ancestral land on or near the coast, but many have now been pushed inland by the resorts that line the Mediterranean.

Elsewhere in the Western Desert the population is a mixture of indigenous oasis dwellers and settlers from the Nile Valley. Only in Siwa have the inhabitants retained their own distinct language and culture, thanks to the proximity of Berber-speaking tribes to the west and centuries of relative isolation from the Nile Valley.

In the five oasis depressions (Kharga, Dakhla, Farafra, Bahariya, and Siwa) water is easily accessible and for centuries artesian wells have sustained agriculture here (some 65% of the oases' population works in farming). The water is thought to have originated in equatorial rains in Africa hundreds or even thousands of years ago. It has gathered in vast underground cisterns and seeped slowly north to the Mediterranean, growing increasingly salty and brackish along the way.

Since the mid-20th century, the Egyptian government has looked to these wells and the seemingly empty desert as an outlet for its burgeoning population. Gamal Abd al-Nasser first created the New Valley governorate in the late 1950s, and Egyptian settlers were encouraged to leave the crowded "old" valley, reclaim desert land, and increase agricultural productivity. Although some small-scale projects were successful, many were not, and the massive transfer of population remains a dream, albeit one that is enshrined in policy.

No matter how alluring the idea of a brave new world in the desert is, the sustainability of using non-renewable artesian water for land reclamation is a matter of debate. According to some estimates, artesian water levels have been falling about a meter each year. Whether this is related to the Libyan government's Great Man-made River project, which taps artesian water from Kufra Oasis, is uncertain—opinion is split over whether or not Egypt's groundwater reservoir is linked to that of Libya. Nevertheless, water levels are falling in most of the oases, and some predict that if the current depletion levels continue, the water will run out in a little over a century.

Undeterred, the government is going ahead with its massive East Oweinat land reclamation project in the far southwest. Armed with reports that say water will last for 200 years, it aims to cultivate some 450,000 feddans here (a feddan is approximately equal to an acre). By the end of 2001, some 500 feddans of potatoes had been planted.

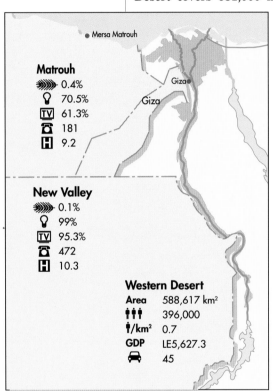

Mersa Matrouh

Matrouh
- 0.4%
- 70.5%
- TV 61.3%
- 181
- H 9.2

Giza

Giza

New Valley
- 0.1%
- 99%
- TV 95.3%
- 472
- H 10.3

Western Desert
Area	588,617 km²
👥	396,000
/km²	0.7
GDP	LE5,627.3
🚗	45

Desert Rush

Times are changing in Siwa. For centuries, its residents were suspicious of outsiders and had more in common with oasis dwellers to the west than the Egyptians from the east. With a thriving date trade, a strategic location on a caravan route, their own Berber language, and an efficient tribal legal system, they had little to do with their nominal overlords in Cairo until well into the 20th century. Since then, the Siwans have overcome their aversion to visitors. Over the past decade, a good road and the relaxation of military restrictions have opened the oasis to growing numbers of tourists, who return with glowing reports of Siwa's mineral springs, ancient remains, and unspoiled charm. Not slow to spot a trend, large developers and their friends at the Ministry of Tourism are now trying to get a piece of the action.

A blueprint for the future development of the oasis is currently under study by the prime minister's office but tourism, while an important component, is only one part of the plan. The government is also studying the possibilities for large-scale investment in industry and agriculture in the area. The oasis already has close to a million palm trees and is a major date producer. Soon it also may have millions of olive trees, which could help make Egypt an exporter of olive oil. Although the plans are still on the drawing board, Siwan residents report that the military, which maintains a large presence in the oasis, has already begun planting olive trees.

In order to turn into a major producer, however, Siwa's perennial water problems will have to be solved. While it may seem perverse given its surroundings, the oasis has a surplus of brackish water close to the surface, and lack of drainage is a major hindrance to expanding agriculture. A huge government-funded scheme currently underway uses dams and pumps in a high-cost, high-impact attempt to solve the problem. Critics say that

Siwa's 15,000 residents would be better served with low-impact, low-cost interventions at farm level. For now, the debate continues. Central to the success of all this planning is the building of an airport to make the remote oasis easily accessible. The plans are being blocked by critics, however, who say that making Siwa too easy to reach will destroy the special atmosphere that attracts tourists in the first place. Their fierce lobbying has kept Siwa off the list of upcoming airport projects for the time being. Large-scale development also seems at odds with Siwa's new status as a protected area. Though the reserve does not include the main town, limiting the impact of development may

prove difficult once the process is set in motion. However, sensitivity to delicate environments has never been the central government's strong point. (This is the place, after all, where a salmon pink, 10,000-seat sports stadium was built in the late 1990s.) While Siwans are being consulted about what form they think the future of their oasis should take, ominous signs of its direction are already there. In anticipation of the building frenzy that usually results from "development" in Egypt, land prices have skyrocketed beyond the means of most Siwans. In 2001 a local tourism giant reportedly bought a 40-feddan plot of land for LE2 million, more than four times the going rate. *SJ*

Siwans are gearing up for large-scale development

In late 1997, the state also began digging the New Valley Canal, which will take water from Toshka on Lake Nasser to the New Valley. The government claims this will provide some 2.8 million new jobs and add 49 million feddans to Egypt's cultivable area. The project is dogged by controversy, with most independent analysts fearing it may go the same way as Nasser's vision. As far as population transfer is concerned, the results so far are negligible. In 1996, the New Valley had 143,000 inhabitants; by 2001, the number had risen to a mere 156,000.

Water levels are falling in most of the oases—some predict the water will run out in a little over a century

Along the north coast, a very different approach is taken by the World Bank-financed Matrouh Resource Management Project, which is trying to development more efficient techniques for rain-fed agriculture. Working with the Bedouin and building on their traditional knowledge, it aims to manage dry areas in a sustainable, environmentally sensitive way that will also benefit the local population. New watershed management techniques have already increased the water supply by 45% in participating communities.

Apart from agriculture, the sands of the Western

Sand Trap

Driving west from Alexandria along Egypt's Mediterranean coast, it is easy to forget that this was the locale for one of the most vicious battles of World War II. The stark monuments and cemeteries of the thousands of allied and axis troops who lost their lives are almost hidden by the ubiquitous holiday villages that are gradually filling the coastline.

But lying in the sands from Alamein to Salloum is a menacing legacy that continues to maim and kill long after the Europeans protagonists have made peace. Some 17.5 million landmines, spread inland for up to 40 km, were left here by the warring parties. Their presence is a major hindrance to development plans in the area, causing a number of oil prospecting, farming, and energy projects to be put on hold. They are also a deadly hazard for thousands of Bedouin whose settlements lie close to the worst affected areas.

The scale of the clearing operation is staggering. Apart from the estimated $250 million it will cost, the few maps available are no longer accurate due to fifty years of shifting sands and rain. Moreover, although there is a highly trained mine-clearing unit in the Egyptian army, it is too small and ill-equipped to carry out such a huge effort.

Elsewhere in Egypt there are an estimated 5.5 million mines, most left over from wars with Israel. The government has pledged to remove them, but it says—not unreasonably considering who laid them in the first place—that it wants financial and technical assistance to remove those in the Western Desert.

So far the EU has contributed only about $1.6 million and Britain a paltry $500,000 towards the project. They say that they cannot commit more because Egypt has not signed the 1997 Ottawa Agreement banning anti-personnel mines and that it is continuing to lay mines along its southern and southwestern borders.

Egypt responds that the Ottawa Agreement prevents it from exercising its "legitimate right of self-defense," and maintains that the countries that battled on Egyptian land should help clean up the mess that they left irrespective of subsequent agreements.

With no end in sight to the diplomatic wrangling, the mines seem likely to remain for some time. *SJ*

Desert hide an impressive mineral wealth. Large natural gas reserves have been found here, particularly in the north. Three-quarters of Egypt's iron ore consumption (about three million tons per year) comes from Bahariya Oasis. Huge phosphate deposits—to the tune of seven billion tons, according to the government—have been found at Abu Tartour, between Kharga and Dakhla oases. A multi-billion dollar investment, which includes revamping the railway to the Red Sea port of Safaga, has been made for mining and processing. When fully functional it is supposed to produce the equivalent of 2.2 million tons of phosphate. However, like Toshka, the project has been controversial, with accusations of mismanagement and allegations of massive financial losses. Currently several years behind schedule, there have even been calls for it to be scrapped altogether.

Industry in the Western Desert is limited to a few small factories, a number of cottage-style craft projects in Dakhla and mineral water bottling in Siwa. Tourism has also made inroads, although the largest scale of development remains concentrated on the Mediterranean coast, where there are some 2,433 thousand beds and 752 under construction, primarily aimed at the domestic tourist market. There are also a number of villa and time-share developments that are not included in the Ministry of Tourism figures.

Although much of the land elsewhere in the Western Desert belongs to the Tourist Development Authority, it has yet to decide how it should be developed. In the meantime, small hotels are opening in the oasis settlements and the safari industry is flourishing. As the government announced plans for BOT (Build, Operate and Transfer) airports in Bahariya and Farafra in late 2001, to join those already in Dakhla and Kharga, this development may yet change in scale. *SJ*

The Eastern Desert

Tourism on the coast picks up speed

Arid and mountainous, the Eastern or Arabian Desert is to most people little more than a burgeoning number of coastal resorts and a few historic sites. Geologically divided into the northern Maaza Plateau, composed primarily of limestone, and the southern Ababda Plateau, its inhospitable wastes have historically been home to two tribes: the Ababda and the Bisharin, both of whom are descended from the African Beja people.

History has left a faint mark in this area of Egypt. Remains dating back to the Ptolemaic and Roman eras, with some evidence of Arab settlements, can still be seen. Most are either old mines, quarries, and villages, or parts of tracks, wells, and fortresses, several of which are interlinked. Their main purpose was to ensure the easy passage of goods from Red Sea ports to the Nile valley.

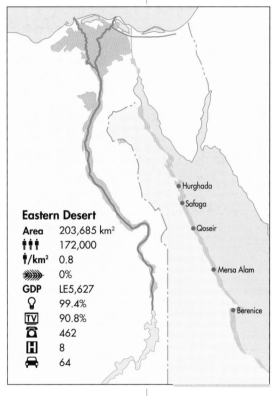

Eastern Desert	
Area	203,685 km²
👤👤👤	172,000
👤/km²	0.8
🌾	0%
GDP	LE5,627
💡	99.4%
📺	90.8%
☎	462
🏨	8
🚗	64

The Suez Canal changed that, although a modern port exists at Safaga for phosphate exports. Aside from the coastal road that runs from Ain Sukhna down to Halayeb on the Sudanese border, there are also good road links to the Nile Valley at Zaafarana (to Beni Suef), Safaga (to Qena), Quseir (to Qift, one of the main historical routes) and Marsa Alam (to Edfu). A new road linking Aswan with Shalateyn, some 135 km south of Marsa Alam, is currently under construction.

While industrial development is negligible in the Eastern Desert, its rocky, seemingly barren expanses are yielding new mining opportunities, much as they did for the pharaohs, who quarried the mountains for porphyry, granite, talc, gold, and emeralds. Indeed, one of the most high-profile mining finds in recent years was made by using a 3,000 year-old map of mining sites. The Pharaoh Company, a joint venture between Egyptian geologist

Sami al-Raghi and Austra-lian mining company Centamin, announced in October 2001 that it expected the rserves at the mine, in the Sukari area south of Marsa Alam, to amount to some 16 million ounces. If the lode fulfils its promise, it could yield some $1 billion a year and create thousands of jobs.

Other mining ventures in the area also look promising. In late 2001, Gippsland of Australia secured 50% ownership of a 48-million-ton tantalite deposit in an area known as Abu Dabbab, just north of Marsa Alam. Tantalum metal, which is derived from tantalite, is used in miniature high-efficiency electronic capacitors that are essential in cellular phones, computers, and other small electronic must-haves. The price of the rare metal jumped from about $40 per pound in the mid-1990s to $350 per pound in 2001. Until such gadgets become recyclable, the price is likely to jump higher still.

Less traditional but equally productive is the harnessing of the Red Sea's famous wind. The year 2001 saw the opening of a German/Danish-financed windfarm on the coast near Zaafarana. With winds reaching 9-10 meters per second (32.5 km per hour), the windfarm's fifty 41-meter tall turbines can generate 156,000 megawatt hours a year—the equivalent consumption of 300,000 modest Egyptian households. The electricity is fed into the national grid, and the New and Renewable Energy Authority has already signed a contract for another 50-turbine windfarm in the same area.

Tourism remains the largest single contributor to the Red Sea economy, however, and while the slump resulting from the World Trade Center attacks in the US led to a respite in the relentless expansion of tourist resorts down the coast, in the long term growth looks likely to continue. According to Ministry of Tourism figures, there are currently 172 hotels in the governorate, with 34,136 beds, and there are 114 more hotels, with a total of 74,794 beds, currently under construction. Proportionally, that is 34% of all hotels being built in Egypt.

The southward movement of construction was given a boost with the opening of Marsa Alam airport in November 2001. This was Egypt's first BOT (Build, Operate and Transfer) airport, and it was built by the Kuwaiti-based M.A. Kharafi Group, which has a 40-year concession for the site.

Kharafi is also the developer of Marsa Ghaleb, a 22-million square meter "mega-resort" adjacent to the airport, a spot that just two years ago was virgin territory. Currently there are about 2,000 hotel rooms in the airport's catchment area. By 2004, Kharafi estimates that this will have doubled and expects the airport to receive four flights each day, or 400,000 tourists annually.

The impact of such huge numbers of tourists on the corals and deserts that lie on either side of the resorts has yet to be quantified. Environmentalists charge that building so much so fast can only result in the destruction of this sensitive and highly perishable asset. Developers reply that because tourism is the most dynamic sector of the economy and employs thousands of people, it must be given precedence.

An attempt to address environmental concerns in a more concrete form is being made by the Tourist Development Authority in the far south near Ras Banas. Studies are underway to turn a 6,000 km² area into a special environmental zone where development will be strictly regulated. Whether this will give impetus for environmental preservation on a greater scale or serve as simply a safari destination for tourists at the many coastal resorts remains to be seen. *SJ*

The Sinai Peninsula

Tourism collides with nature

Pathway between Africa and Asia and route of marching armies for millennia, the Sinai Peninsula is a vast wilderness separated from mainland Egypt by the Suez Canal and by a very different outlook. Much of its 61,000 km² area is uninhabited, with desert in the north and granite mountains in the south, a division echoed in the administrative separation of the peninsula into North and South Sinai.

Occupied by Israel after the 1967 war, Sinai was returned to Egypt in 1982 and has since become the focus of ambitious plans for the large-scale transfer of population from the Nile Valley. The National Project for Sinai Development is a 23-year, LE75 billion blueprint for land reclamation and the development of infrastructure, mining, industry, and tourism that is to provide work and amenities to the 3.2 million people that are supposed to be living there by 2017. The current population is estimated at 340,000.

The jury is out on whether or not this huge population transfer is feasible—although most critics view the figures with skepticism—but 2001 saw the completion of some of the major infrastructure projects associated with the plan. At Qantara, the 9.5 km-long Mubarak Peace Bridge opened. Designed to encourage the building of more roads in Sinai, the huge four-lane structure sits 70 meters above the Suez Canal, allowing the largest of super-tankers to sail underneath. Transportation links with the mainland were also improved with the opening of the rotating Ferdan Bridge, 25 km north of Ismailiya. With a rail line and two traffic lanes it will swing into place twice daily to allow traffic to cross, and will revive the railway that used to link Egypt with Europe for the first half of the 20th century. Both will relieve traffic through the Ahmed Hamdi tunnel near Suez.

The Salam Canal, designed to transport Nile and recycled drainage water from mainland Egypt to Sinai, also neared completion by the end of 2001, a first step in the massive North Sinai Agricultural Development Program (NSADP), which aims to reclaim 400,000 feddans of desert along Sinai's Mediterranean coast.

Like many of the government's megaprojects, the NSADP is controversial. Apart from the huge cost (some LE2.75 billion), there are fears that Sinai's indigenous inhabitants, the Bedouin, will lose their livelihood. There are an estimated 100,000 Sinai Bedouin belonging to fourteen major tribes, many of which have affiliations with Bedouin in the Israeli Negev Desert,

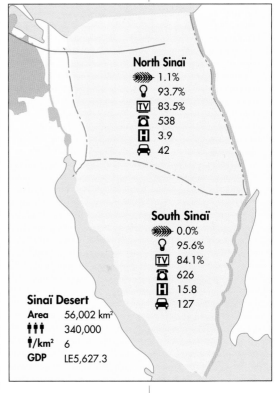

North Sinai
- 1.1%
- 93.7%
- TV 83.5%
- 538
- H 3.9
- 42

South Sinaï
- 0.0%
- 95.6%
- TV 84.1%
- 626
- H 15.8
- 127

Sinaï Desert
Area 56,002 km²
340,000
/km² 6
GDP LE5,627.3

With tourism development, South Sinai is much better off than the North

Egypt's Eastern Desert, Jordan, or Saudi Arabia. Four major tribes with as many as ten smaller tribes and clans live in north and central Sinai. Ten more live in the south.

With a strong traditional culture based on tribal law and nomadic farming, many have already been marginalized by the changes to their land over the past decade. Bedouin in the south have seen their traditional claims to coastal land ignored, and in some cases had their settlements bulldozed, as developers raced to build resorts for the booming tourism industry. Most have also been excluded from lucrative work in the sector by Egyptians from the Nile Valley who control the tourism companies.

In the north, where Bedouin are more populous, similar problems are feared. The NSADP ignores traditional land claims and relegates the Bedouin to the least productive lands, even though in the years since the Israeli withdrawal many have settled down and, using brackish groundwater, cultivated fruit trees and other crops on their ancestral lands. Under Egyptian law, making desert land productive can confer ownership (although the Bedouin would argue that this is their land anyway), and the North Sinai governorate has encouraged Bedouin small landholders to register their plots. However, the procedures are long and complicated and few have been able to get title. Those whose land is in areas allocated to the NSADP stand to lose everything.

Despite the state's grandiose plans to boost agriculture and industry, and notwithstanding the peninsula's mineral wealth (coal, petroleum, manganese, glass sand, gypsum, and kaolin are all found here and extracted for both domestic and export markets), for now tourism remains Sinai's main income generator. Almost all of this is concentrated on South Sinai's coasts, where the construction of hotels and resorts has been faster than any other part of the country. When Israel withdrew in 1982, the Sinai was a still a model of eco-friendly tourism, with only 312 hotel rooms in the entire peninsula. Now, according to the Ministry of Tourism, there are 23,846 hotel rooms in South Sinai alone, with another 49,904 under construction and thousands more planned.

While tourism is one of the quickest ways to generate employment and increase foreign currency, critics say the pace of development is too fast to be sustainable and risks destroying the very assets that attract tourists in the first place. From the world famous reefs at risk from too many divers and debris from construction, to the solid waste left on windblown dumping sites, there are many reasons to fear for the environment along the South Sinai coast.

However, efforts are being made to preserve Sinai's natural heritage. The country's first national park, Ras Mohammed at the peninsula's southern tip, has shown that environmental protection can coexist with tourism and development. The park, along with Nabaq, the only other protected area with an entrance fee, now brings in about LE3 million a year. More than 40% of South Sinai is now within national park or protectorate boundaries, where development is strictly controlled. Whether this will be sufficient to prevent the long-term damage that mass tourism leaves in its wake remains to be seen. *SJ*

Culture

Curtain Call

Setting the Scene

SURVEYING THE EGYPTIAN CULTURAL SCENE AT THE TURN OF THE THIRD MILLENIUM TURNS UP A MIXED BAG. THE LAST TWO years have seen more bums on seats in cinemas; theater has had its fine moments; and art has sprouted up everywhere. A dizzying parade of festivals and fairs in music, cinema, and art has raised the public profile of some art forms by trying to spread the fruits of cultural production across as wide a spectrum as possible, and a new generation in cinema, literature, and the arts have begun to take their place among the cultural establishment.

That is not to say that there are no clouds on the horizon. As cultural production in Egypt slowly but surely succumbs to globalization, many forms of culture appear to be at a crossroads. More frequent and different kinds of cross-cultural encounters have injected some fields with a burst of creativity, but the increased commercialization of culture and the erosion of clearly defined national cultural boundaries have made some uneasy. The state, still the major patron of the arts in Egypt, is also feeling the crunch. Unwilling to relinquish its role as the guardian of culture, it is caught between those clamoring for less censorship and state involvement, and others who see it flagging in its job as protector and provider.

All these tensions make for a vibrant, if uneven, cultural scene. Nowhere is this more apparent than in the art world, the sphere that has perhaps thrived the most over the past few years. New galleries have opened, providing more space to the burgeoning ranks of new artists, and the last year saw several strong retrospectives of established artists like

This page: Soad Hosni (center); opposite page: Moataz Nasr (top); David Hockney (center); Youssef Nabil (bottom)

painters Tahiya Halim, Vessela Farid, Hassan Soliman, Hamed Nada, and Gazbiya Serri. Spring 2001 kicked off with the second and, in retrospect, final Nitaq, a totally privately sponsored downtown arts festival. While there were logistic and organizational problems, art did manage to make it out of the galleries and into more public spaces, whether down-at-the-heels cafés or long-forgotten hotels. As it turned out, the Nitaq coincided with the opening of the state Biennale, where young artist Moataz Nasr took the grand prize for his installation, and the traveling London Nomad show, sponsored by the British Council. The latter brought the work of several big name international artists to the historic Zeinab Khatoun house in Islamic Cairo, and for a brief two weeks it seemed that art *was* everywhere. The Giza Pyramids were the site of an even more outlandish public display of art in 2002 when German conceptual artist H.A. Schult set up his traveling exhibition of "trash people"—1,000 human figures composed of trash. The exhibit was a coup for the Ministry of Culture and the city—so far Schult has set up his show in Paris, Moscow, and on the Great Wall of China—but the event occasioned a small ruckus in the local press, with some finding the opposition of modern detritus with the icons of ancient Egypt in poor taste.

Foreign cultural institutions have also done their part to promote fine arts, particularly the French, who have sponsored more than one extravaganza over the last two years. Cairo was the site of the May 2001 *Les Francais Aiment le Caire* (the French Love Cairo), a month-long festival that brought exhibits, lectures, and musical events to venues all over the city, including an unlikely concert in the Cairo metro. In 2002, it was Alexandria's turn to play host to a month of photography, literature, and seminars that featured French and Egyptian artists exploring the links between the two seaside cities of Alexandria and Marseille.

If the film world cannot lay claim to the same kind of diversity, at least it took a jump in the right direction in 2001, with 31 movies released across the country—the highest number in years. Highlights of the year included the commercial release of *al-Abwab al-Mughlaqa* (Closed Doors), which proved to audiences that Atef Hetata was one of the best new directors around, though, as usual, the critically acclaimed film bombed at the box office. *Asrar al-Banat* (Girls' Secrets) became one of the most talked-about movies of 2001. Director Magdi Ahmed Ali's frank look at teenage pregnancy filled cinemas and showed a new serious side to the youth movie phenomenon. It went on to pick up several awards on the international film circuit. Audiences and critics alike were also impressed with Dawoud Abd al-Sayed's *Muwaten, Mukhbir wa Harami* (Citizen, Detective, Thief), which swept the awards at the 2002 National Film Festival. Following the story of three disparate characters whose lives become intertwined by chance encounters, the film offered a cynical look at the sociopolitical changes of Egypt's last two decades. Veteran director Mohammed Khan also made a comeback with *Ayyam al-Sadat* (Days of Sadat), starring Ahmed Zaki. The movie provided much fodder for critical debate, not over the quality of the film per se, but over its historical take on the late president's life.

For the most part, however, audiences showed that they still were not ready for a return of serious cinema, and the lighter side of the youth movie continued to dominate, with Karim Abd al-Aziz, Mona Zaki, Ahmed al-Saqa, Ahmed Helmi, and Hanan Turk cementing their presence on the big screen. Even Adel Imam's summer 2002 celluloid comeback, *Amir al-Zalam* (Prince of Darkness), played a distant second-fiddle to *al-Limby*, starring

Mohammed Saad, best known for playing the sidekick of the same name in 2000's *al-Nazer* (The Headmaster). The two biggest comedians of the day parted ways, however, on their path to stardom. Alaa Wali al-Din and director Sherif Arafa flopped with *Ibn Ezz* (Rich Kid), putting a stop to the former's meteoric rise. The diminutive Mohammed Heneidi, meanwhile, continued to pull in the crowds, headlining the top-grossing film of 2001, *Gaana al-Bayan al-Tali* (We Have Received the Following Report). Amidst all the comedy fare, the film world—and Egypt at large—suffered a harsh blow with the death of screen idol Soad Hosni. For many, it symbolized the final passing of a golden era.

On the small screen, state television continued to battle it out with the satellite stations. If its news coverage did not quite match that of al-Jazeera, it came out a winner last Ramadan with *Ailat al-Hagg Mitwelli* (Hagg Metwalli's Family), which got everybody from Cairo to Beirut vocal on the issue of polygamy, momentarily distracting them from the global drama being staged elsewhere. The sudden proliferation of game shows also caught the attention of viewers, especially the Arabic version of *Who Wants to Be a Millionaire*. During Ramadan the show garnered the kind of following once associated with the musical variety *fawazir* programs.

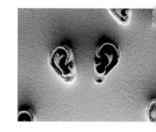

Best of 2001/2002

Critics' Tips

CINEMA
al-Abwab al-Mughlaqa
Muwatin, Mukhbir wa Harami
Ashiqat al-Cinema (documentary)
MUSIC
Arabic Music Festival
Reggae festival
ART
Nitaq 2001
Hamed Oweis
Vessela Farid
Sanaa Moussa
Intro photography exhibit
THEATER
Warsha Nights
Dance Theater Festival
King Lear
LITERATURE
Awraq al-Nargis (Somaya Ramadan)
Imarat Yaqoubian (Alaa al-Aswani)

Source: Egypt Almanac

Popular Favorites

CINEMA
Gaana al-Bayan al-Tali
Ayyam al-Sadat
al-Limby
Haramiya fi KG2
MUSIC
Amr Diab
Hakim
Mohammed Mounir
Shaaban Abd al-Rehim
ART
—
THEATER
Lamma Baba Yinam
People on the Third
King Lear
Children's theater
LITERATURE
Religious paperbacks
Computer tomes
Political books

Like cinema, the flagging theater scene showed some signs of life over the past two years. Surprisingly enough, it was the public sector that led the way, with the National Theater packing in the crowds two years in a row. Osama Anwar Okasha's play *al-Nas Illi fi al-Talet* (The People on The Third Floor), held up in censorship purgatory for several years, was finally unleashed upon an audience who evidently craved a return to more tangible threats than those posed by the economy. Featuring a star-studded cast, the play swept viewers up in a 1960s-style story of political repression and fragmented family ties. The follow up in the 2002 season, *King Lear*, proved even more successful with audiences, bringing in regular folks who long ago fled the theater along with the highbrow Shakespeare fans. Starring veteran actor Yehya al-Fakharani in the title role, the classic story of familial betrayal—performed largely in classical Arabic, no less—managed to strike a chord even as more dramatic events were being played out on the political stage next door. On the fun side, Fifi Abdou returned to the stage last year, though in a less than glamorous location. Despite the tatty venue, the grande dame pulled together a cast that featured many up and coming stars, such as Ahmed Zaher, Mohammed Nagati, Ahmed Rizq, and Maged al-Masri. The show proved to be a long running hit and even brought back to

This page: Made in Egypt, Four Women, Four Views, photo exhibition; opposite page: Mohsen Farouq at the Arabic Music Festival (top)

prominence *shaabi* singer Ahmed Adawiya, who influenced popular crooners like Shaaban Abd al-Rehim and Hakim.

Egyptian music produced one new certifiable star over the last year: Shaaban Abd al-Rehim. Riding on the wave of his hit *Bakrah Israil* (I Hate Israel), not even a rather embarrassing McDonald's campaign could move him out him out of the public eye. Two movies, one play, and one bug spray commercial later, his cassettes were still selling. Neither the first, nor the best of popular, or *shaabi* singers to make the crossover to the mainstream—Ahmed Adawiya did it in the 1970s, but with a better voice—Shaaban nonetheless injected the increasingly banal pop scene with some much needed street panache.

With the exception of Shaaban, though, Egyptian pop continued to get slicker. The introduction last year of Arabic MTV marked the coming of age of Arabpop. Unfortunately, the show underlined the dismal state of music video production in the Arab world, and the selection of the music did little to show off the best that modern Arabic pop has to offer. Sony Music also set up shop in Egypt, the first major international label to do so. While some in the industry hoped that the music giant would take Egyptian music global, so far the company has focused on bringing in quality international CDs to the local market. The only two acts it had signed to its label after almost a year in business were both Lebanese, perhaps an indication of where the real action is these days.

In other musical spheres, the Opera House is now operating smoothly under the directorship of ex-general Samir Farag. Programs actually managed to come out before the events, and the small hall came up for a revamping. But some embittered observers suggested renam-

ing it the Arabic Music House—not necessarily a bad thing—as opera took a back seat last year amid accusations of bias and neglect. The number of operas staged nose-dived, particularly the small, lighter operas that used to provide a nice counterpoint to the grand productions. Global events did not help matters, as soon after September 11, Aida at the Pyramids was cancelled, going belly up for the second year in a row after an entire year of planning. Even before that, the centennial Verdi celebrations were scaled down for lack of funds.

Arabizing the Airwaves

Cairo has long grown used to being the center of entertainment culture in the Arab world, exporting its films, music, and serial dramas for the eyes and ears of the rest of the Arab world. But Egyptians are not quite so accustomed to being on the receiving end of the cultural exchange. That started to change in 2001, however, when the game show Who *Wants to Be a Millionaire* hit Egyptian screens and George Qerdahi, the show's dapper, poetry-reciting Lebanese host, became a household name. Broadcast to 22 Arab countries, *Who Wants to Be a Millionaire* is a pan-Arab phenomenon, and the first non-Egyptian, Arabic program to gain a real foothold on local TV. Featuring contestants from across the Arab world and beyond, the show's questions reinforce a broader cultural identity, while bringing local audiences face to face with all the linguistic and cultural diversity the Arab world has to offer, whether it is in the form of a Syrian comedian, a Saudi journalist, or an Iraqi expatriate living in London. And then, there is the money. That combined with slick production and armchair erudition proved to be a wildly popular formula, and Qerdahi himself was catapulted into full-fledged stardom. The subject of gossipy columns in the local press and much female fawning, his status as cultural icon was cemented this year when he was appointed a goodwill ambassador for the UN Environment Program. If Qerdahi captivated audiences, not everyone was impressed. In July, Egypt's mufti, Nasr Farid Wassel, issued a *fatwa* against all game shows, announcing that they were tantamount to gambling, and thus forbidden in Islam.

Although Wassel's criticisms were largely dismissed by viewers—and contradicted by another *fatwa* issued by Sheikh al-Azhar Tantawi—more strident critiques were heard from certain press commentators, TV announcers, and even parliamentarians, who expressed dismay with the "Arabization" of their TV sets and insisted that Egypt has no need to import "foreign" programming or Lebanese hosts. Egyptian TV's own attempts to get on the game-show bandwagon proved abysmal failures, however, and its *Pyramid of Dreams*, hosted by the erstwhile Ezzat Abu Ouf, went off the air after a few short months.

There is a certain irony in the nationalist pique expressed by the show's detractors. *Who Wants to Be a Millionaire* is, of course, a foreign import, but the cultural protectionism is somewhat misplaced. Far from being a harbinger of an all-out Arabization of the Egyptian airwaves, the show is the most successful product yet of Western corporate media globalization. Started in Britain in 1998, *Who Wants to Be a Millionaire* has now spun off into over 30 versions—from Australia to Austria and India to Venezuela—each with the same format, tailored linguistically and culturally for its target audience.

Egypt's ego finally received a boost early this year when MBC, the Saudi-owned network that owns the program, moved production from London and Paris to Cairo, setting up shop in Media Production City. Lebanese host notwithstanding, the move proved that Egypt is still the entertainment mecca of the Arab world—enough to soothe the wounded national ego for the time being. *MM*

Despite the doom and gloom, a bright spot came in Spring 2002 when the opera orchestra, the Arabic Music Ensemble, and the Cairo Ballet teamed up for a ballet adaptation of Salah Jehin's puppet operetta *al-Leila al-Kebira* (The Feast Night). Though critics' gave the show mixed reviews, audiences piled in for the revival of one of the masterpieces of Egyptian theater. The hallowed grounds of the Opera House were even the site of four-day reggae festival in 2002. The event brought acts from France, the Ivory Coast, and Canada, but the biggest draw was undoubtedly Mohammed Mounir, who tried to rastify some of his own work for the occasion. With very few international music acts making their way to Egypt, the concert was a welcome respite from the standard fare, and it went much smoother than the much-vaunted Sting concert at the Pyramids the year before. Though not quite the fiasco that the millenium celebrations were, logistically the event was a disaster. Things turned even nastier when due to an issue of time-keeping—it never became clear quite who was to blame—local warm-up act Hakim was not allowed to perform.

Through it all, literature moseyed on, despite poor sales. Young writer Somaya Ramadan rose up the literary ladder with her novel *Awraq al-Nargis* (Leaves of Narcissus) netting the Naguib Mahfouz Prize for Literature, adding to publisher Dar Sharqiyat's reputation. The 90th birthday of the Nobel Laureate

himself occasioned a series of reprints of Mahfouz's most famous works, including the English translation of the once banned *Awlad Haritna* (Children of the Alley). Other translations, like that of Sonallah Ibrahim's *Zaat* and *al-Lagna* (The Committee), continued to bring Egyptian literature to a wider audience. One of the most talked about novels of last summer came from a relative unknown. First time novelist Alaa al-Aswani's *Imarat Yaqoubian* (The Yaqoubian Building), told a Mahfouzian tale of the life and times of downtown city-dwellers. If he did not reach the heights of that great novelist's descriptive powers and narrative finesse, his book was well received by readers looking a good piece of 1990s-style social realism.

For the most part, however, these literary goings-on were ignored by the majority of Egyptians. Popular literary festivals, like the annual book fair and this year's First International Book Forum, brought a little literature into the limelight, but the huge crowds turn out more in search of entertainment and cheap text books than literary stimulation. True to form, writers and intellectuals, too, proved themselves to be just as interested in politics as poetry. If the last year managed to pass without the eruption of the same kind of literary *kulturkampf* that marred 2000—when the publication of an obscure Syrian novel led to student riots, vicious media polemics, and shake-ups at the state publishing authority—the fallout from September 11 brought with it a different kind of culture war that Egyptian intellectuals and writers readily armed themselves for. Even the weekly literary rag *Akhbar al-Adab* (Literary News) seemed to forgo any pretence of living up to the second part of its name and dove head first into the so-called "clash of civilizations." *RW & MM*

Ballet Malgré Tout at the Cairo Opera House (above), retrospective of Nagui Yassa's photographs (right)

Performing Arts
Staving off stagnation

Box Office Blues

Though history tells us that the first cinema screening in Egypt took place on November 5, 1896, a truly Egyptian cinema was not born until 1923. That was the year that Mohammed Bayoumi returned from a stint studying cinema in Germany, took his place behind the camera, and became the first Egyptian to film an Egyptian movie: *Fi Bilad Tutankhamun* (In the Land of Tutankhamun). Over the next 12 years, Egyptian cinema produced about 45 long films, providing the fledgling industry with much-needed experience and laying the foundation for future development. Important milestones in this development include *Zeinab* (1930), the first film based on a novel by an Egyptian writer, Mohammed Hussein Heikal; *Awlad al-Dhawat* (Sons of the Chosen, 1932), the first Egyptian talkie; and *al-Warda al-Bayda* (The White Rose, 1933), the first musical featuring the soon-to-be erstwhile star Mohammed Abd al-Wahab.

Youssef Chahine and Latifa on the set of Sukout Hansawwar

During these early days, Egyptian cinema was enriched by the participation of a cadre of expatriate Arabs, most of whom came from the Levant. Ibrahim and Badr Lama, Asia, Mary Queenie, Naguib al-Rihani, Ahmed Galal, Fatima Rushdi, and Bahiga Hafez are only some of the most outstanding Levantine names that helped nurture along an infant cinema still trying to find its place in the sun.

A turning point came in 1936 with the release of *Widad*, the first long movie produced by Studio Misr, and the first film featuring the Star of the East, Umm Kulthoum. The

Egypt's Prize-Winning Films

National Film Festival 2001
Best Film: *Short wa Fanilla wa Cap*
Best Director: Khaled Youssef for *al-Asifa*
Best Actor: Ahmed al-Saqa in *Short wa Fanilla wa Cap*
Best Actress: Youssra in *al-Asifa*
Best Screenplay: Kawthar Heikal for *al-Ashiqan*

National Film Festival 2002
Best film: *Muwatin, Mukhbir wa Harami*
Best Director: Dawoud Abd al-Sayed for *Muwatin*
Best Actor: Salah Abdullah in *Muwatin*
Best Actress: Hind Sabri in *Muwatin*
Best Screenplay: Azza Shalabi for *Asrar al-Banat*

Alexandria Film Festival 2001
Best Film: *Deil al-Samaka*
Best Director: Samir Seif for *Deil al-Samaka*
Best Actor: Amr Waqed in *Deil al-Samaka*
Best Actress: Basma in *al-Naam wa al-Tawus*
Best Screenplay: Wahid Hamed for *Deil al-Samaka*

Cairo International Film Festival 2001
Silver Prize: Inas al-Degheidi for *Muzakarat Murahiqa*

movie ushered in the golden age of Egyptian cinema, which began to extend its reach all over the region. From that point until the end of the 1960s, Egyptian cinema dominated screens across the Arab world, spreading Egyptian culture, music, and even the Egyptian dialect from Iraq to Morocco.

But the Egyptian film industry today is not what it used to be. Once a rival to Hollywood and Bombay, it has fallen several notches since its golden age. In terms of worldwide feature film output, in 1999 it came in at number 27. Though the industry is still the largest in the Arab world (actually, the only industry per se) it no longer produces the quantity or quality of films that it once did. As a result, cinema admissions declined throughout most of the 1990s, from about 27 million in 1989 to 21.5 million in 1998. Taking a look back to 1970, when more than 65 million tickets were sold, one wonders where the downward spiral will end. The question of why audiences have fled the cinema is a matter of debate—critics cite everything from public-sector control over the industry to a decline in production standards to the rise of television to globalization. Whatever the causes, Egyptian cinema today is only a shadow of its former self.

Over the last couple of years, however, it looked like Egyptian cinema was finally witnessing an awakening of sorts. The number of films released last year reached 31, including the four films released during the Eid at the tail of the year. That's 12 more films than appeared in 1999, and almost the same as 2000.

The reasons for the relative upsurge are to be found in the release, five years ago, of the comedy *Ismailiya Rayeh Gayy* (Ismailiya Roundtrip). Featuring fresh new faces, catchy tunes, and young characters speaking the contemporary language of Egyptian youth, the movie was a box-office smash. Though artistically it was not a good film by any standards, it raked in a whopping LE20 million in revenues to become the largest grossing film in Egyptian history. Its unprecedented success—and that of other films that followed its lead—set a whole new slew of young actors on the path to stardom. Mohammed Heneidi (*Ismailiya Rayeh Gayy*), Ahmed al-Saqa (*Short wa Fanilla wa Cap*, or Shorts, T-shirt, and Cap), and Ala Wali al-Din (*al-Nazer*, or The Headmaster) became household names, bringing audiences—especially young ones—back to the movies. As their stars rose, those of the erstwhile favorites who had monopolized cinema for a quarter of a century began to wane: Nabila Ebeid, Nadia al-Gindi, and Adel Imam.

The success of films like *Ismailiya Rayeh Gayy* gave a shot in the arm to the industry as a whole. Its hopes raised by the new possibilities offered by eager

This page: Mona Zaki and Ahmed al-Saqqa in Africano; opposite page: Muwaten, Mukhbir wa Harami (top), Asrar al-Banat (center), Ashiqat al-Cinema (bottom), the first of a series of twelve documentaries on pioneering women

Top 10 Grossing Foreign Films of 2001

Film	Revenue LE
1. The Mummy Returns	2,072,036
2. Pearl Harbor	1,759,389
3. Hannibal	958,642
4. Evolution	945,049
5. Ms. Congeniality	929,678
6. Castaway	882,124
7. Jurassic Park III	855,343
8. Swordfish	846,459
9. What Women Want	816,359
10. Planet of the Apes	815,046

Source: Egyptian Film Society

audiences, Egyptian television began to bankroll an increasing number of films. The private sector got on board as well, and a number of production and distribution companies were established, the most important of which were Shuaa (The Arab Company for Media and Cultural Production) and the Arab Film Production Company (part of the Arab Company for Arts and Publishing, or Funoun).

Unfortunately, the high hopes seem be fizzling—indeed, 2001 may prove to be the year when the wave peaked. Most films produced by the public sector over the last couple of years, either by Egyptian Television itself or Media Production City, have met with unmitigated failure of a type rarely seen even in the darkest days of Egyptian cinema. It should not come as much of a surprise, however, as most of the offerings were things like *Jahim Taht al-Ard* (Hell Beneath the Earth), *Anbar wa al-Alwan* (Amber and Colors), *Yamin Talaq* (Divorce Vow), and *al-Ashiqan* (The Lovers)—all films of a former age, both in terms of subject matter and production standards, more suited to TV than the big screen. Indeed, this summer, Media Production City was reduced to releasing films that had clearly sat in the cans for a few years—*Ikhtifaa Gaafar al-Misri*

Top 10 Grossing Egyptian Films of 2001

Film	Revenue LE
1. Gana al-Bayan al-Tali	17,271,280
2. Ayyam al-Sadat	11,521,422
3. Africano	6,441,888
4. Saidi Rayeh Gayy	6,151,072
5. 55 Isaaf	5,666,251
6. Rihlat Hobb	5,287,526
7. Ibn Ezz	4,644,496
8. Ashab wala Bizness	4,452,072
9. Leh Khalitni Ahibbak	3,825,074
10. Ferqat Banat wa Bas	2,561,986

Source: Egyptian Film Society

(The Disappearance of Gaafar) was first screened at the Cairo International Film Festival four years ago. The only exception to the company's bad track record was *Ayyam al-Sadat* (Days of Sadat), easily the best film of summer 2001. Though it had a flawed screenplay, it was the most serious of the eight films released and made the best use of the language of cinema. It did well at the box office as well, pulling in almost LE11 million. Many of Media Production City's other films did not even manage to cover production and marketing costs.

Private-sector ventures have not met with great success either. Shuaa has stopped production completely, while Funoun—which produced about one-third of last year's movies—announced that it has temporarily halted all new Egyptian productions due to financial problems. Only a year ago the company was actively buying up the originals of classic Egyptian films and acquired the Renaissance Group cinema chain, with screens throughout the country. On the whole, this year film production is expected to decline to about one-third of what it was last year.

The question is why have these ventures failed, particularly given the optimism of the last few years? Though the general state of the Egyptian economy has not helped matters, the failure is largely due to misjudgments on the part of production companies. Simply put, cinema-goers were waiting for contemporary films that fit the age. Instead, with a few exceptions, they were met with generally low quality films that offered neither entertainment nor food for thought.

For its part, Shuaa, the producer of flicks like *Omar 2000* and *Ittfarag Ya Salam* (Take a Look at This), tended to underestimate its audience, producing politically-oriented films that smacked of naïve propaganda. *Ittfarag Ya Salam*, for example, offered a facile view of the social dimensions of the Arab-Israeli conflict. It appears that those in positions of

This page: al-Limby (top), Murabbaa Dayer (bottom); Ibn Ezz (inset); opposite page: al-Asifa

responsibility at the Libyan company have not the slightest idea about producing and marketing films. While Funoun's capital undoubtedly injected some much-needed financing into the sector, it was not savvy enough to turn its movies into money-making ventures. The genuinely good movies it helped to make, like *Asrar al-Banat* (Girls' Secrets), did not do well at the box office.

While a couple of big hits might have made up for the losses and kept the company in the black, its supposed crowd-pleasers failed financially as well. *Africano*, starring Ahmed al-Saqa and Mona Zaki, was hailed as the movie of summer 2001; though it did well relative to other films, its LE6.4 million in revenues did not even cover production costs. Again, it may be a problem of management. Funoun turned over directorship of the production and distribution sector of the company to a Jordanian businessman with little experience in making, distributing, and marketing films, a tricky business even for those with long experience in the field. Nor did the company's attempts to gain a monopoly over the market foster creativity.

Rules of the Game

When it comes to the Egyptian film industry, everyone is a critic. Scripts are bad, production standards are low, actors don't know how to act—these are all common complaints. But the major problems facing the industry are not artistic, but financial. Since the mid-1990s, rates commanded by top movie stars have skyrocketed, reaching unprecedented levels and making it difficult for local producers to invest in filmmaking. Whereas Adel Imam used to command the highest rate at LE1 million per film, he has been surpassed by Mohammed Heneidi, who gets upwards of LE5 million per film. With prices like these, a film that makes a few million pounds is still likely to come out in the red.

The way that film revenues are divvied up complicates the problem even more. Currently, the system is that the cinema house takes 50% of a film's revenues up front, while the distributor gets 20%. The remaining 30% is left to the producer, who must pay for advertising as well as production costs. Given this reality, it is difficult for producers to cover their costs. And with big-name stars being the main attraction for the public, they have little incentive to take risks or cast unknowns, which may further lessen their chances of making money. Creativity takes a back seat to profits, as producers stick to movies with well-worn themes and big names, sure to pack in the crowds.

Clearly, this system favors large production companies with major capital. While the Arab Film Production Company (Funoun) created a furor in 2000 when critics accused it of attempting to monopolize the market, it had a positive effect on the number of films being released, at least until the money ran out. The same holds true for Media Production City. While independent or young filmmakers face difficulties across the globe, the distribution system in Egypt is an added obstacle working against them. Last year, a group of young directors established a new production company, Simat, focused largely on digital production. Whether digital will catch on as a medium for full-length feature films is uncertain, but by substantially reducing costs, it may at least provide a means for up-and-coming filmsters to find their feet and actually get their ideas off the drawing board and onto the screen. *FT*

Given the current climate, there seems to be little hope for film production to exceed, or even come close to the number of films released last year. Though Media Production City has big plans this year, the recession is likely to throw a wrench in them. Indeed,

Hello Amrika

Critics of globalization in Egypt have only to point to cinema marquees to find an easy example of US cultural hegemony. While the summer film season and the two Eid holidays find local cinema houses awash with ads for made-in-Egypt movies, the rest of the year is a parade of dozens of American movie titles.

But the trend is not just in Egypt. All over the Arabic-speaking world, Hollywood has become the main supplier of movies. With less foreign films being shown throughout the region as whole—the number has fallen roughly by half from the mid-1970s—the US has crowded out all of its competitors, including Egypt. According to UNESCO figures, over the last 25 years, US films have pushed British films out of Syria, French and Italian films out of Morocco and Lebanon, and Egyptian films out of all the region's cinema houses. Only in Morocco, where Indian films still claimed a 21% market share in the mid-1990s, is there any serious competition to the US.

In Egypt, the number of US films coming into the country has not changed drastically over the last two decades, but they have become much more visible as they have cornered the foreign-film market and local production has declined. In 1975, a little less than half of the 200-plus non-Egyptian films shown were from the US; by 1994, over two-thirds were made in America, and of the 99 foreign films shown last year, the vast majority were from the US. But as far as audiences are concerned, Egyptian films win hands down: last year, homegrown movies made on average LE2.5 million each, while the average for imports was a piddling LE225,000. MM

all the indicators point to a drastic decline, with most industry sources predicting a maximum of ten films for 2002, even lower than the dark days of the mid-90s. Very few new cinemas are going up, and several have closed over the last year. The cost of filmmaking is still climbing, particularly after the devaluation of the Egyptian pound, and a pooling of government resources between the Ministries of Culture and Information—which might help offset the effects of the recession—is not even a remote possibility. Meanwhile, audiences are stuck with the same drab fare. The biggest grosser last summer was *al-Limby*, starring Mohammed Saad, who revived his goofy sidekick character from the 2000 hit *al-Nazer*.

Apart from current economic woes, there are other factors inhibiting the real return of Egyptian cinema. Little effort is being made to fight film piracy, widespread in both Egyptian and Arab markets. With films being sold on the video market before their official release, the industry has been deprived of important financial resources. A more long-standing problem is censorship in the cinema, which has put a damper on creative efforts in general. Barring another unexpected hit movie that would again revive the hopes of both audiences and the industry, Egyptian cinema is likely to go into even deeper hibernation, remaining, in the words of Oscar Wilde, an industry with a brilliant future behind it. *MD*

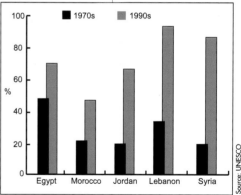

US Share of the Foreign Film Market

Source: UNESCO

US films are much more visible in cinema houses all over the region.

Upstaged

Independent theater offers hope

Like the rest of Egypt's culture industry, theater owes much of its existence to the state, and the public sector still sponsors the majority of plays put on across the country. The state theater legacy goes back to the 1960s, just as the first real generation of Egyptian playwrights appeared. The state-operated Theater Authority was formed, creating a number of theaters, each of which had a permanent troupe whose actors were paid like any civil servant, a system that has slowly gone by the way-side. As a result, public-sector the-ater has long been thought of as "real" theater, while the money-making glit-ter productions are left to the private sector. These days, however, both are suffering from atrophy.

Above: Nour al-Sherif in Jerusalem Shall Not Fall; opposite page: al-Halej at the Experimental Theater Festival (top); Ramadan fest at the Garage (inset)

The jewel in the crown of public-sector theater is the National. As its name suggests, it is the oldest and most traditional theater in the country. The National has always borne the mantle of "serious" theater, and until very recently, its repertoire was largely limited to the classics. Modern plays and even comedies did find their way to its stage, but only as long as they exhibited the proper *gravitas*. Though things have changed slightly, a perusal of the last two seasons shows that the theater has not strayed too far from its roots. The big hit last year was *al-Nas Illi fi al-Talet* (The People on the Third Floor). Written by screenwriter Osama Anwar Okasha, the offering was first and foremost a play with a message. It told the story of a middle-class Egyptian family, examining the tense web of relationships that bind them together, with each actor embodying some prototypical member of contemporary Egyptian society. Featuring a star-studded cast led by Samiha Ayoub, it proved an enormous success. (In only two months, it raked in more than half of the entire public sector's net revenues for the first six months of 2001.) Months after opening, the play was still selling sold-out shows, leading National manager Hoda Wasfi to extend its run into 2002. Okasha's play was followed up by a new production of *King Lear*, starring veteran actor Yehya al-Fakharani, another money-maker that found acclaim among audiences and critics alike.

The state also runs several specialized theaters. The Talia was originally the theater of the avant-garde, staging plays by the likes of Peter Weiss, Palestinian playwright Mouin Bessissou, Samuel Becket, and Eugene Ionesco as soon they hit theaters in Europe. Even in the 1970s, Samir al-Asfouri's witty productions came very close to creating a new form combining folkloric elements with contemporary theater. With time, however, the Talia has lost its progressive spirit. One of the best productions of last season was *Hikayat Ezbat Mahrous* (The Story of Mahrous Village), by storyteller Said al-Faramawi. Hardly cutting edge, the play carried viewers off to an Egyptian village, taking them on a sentimental historic journey.

Other state theaters continue to crank out productions, but they suffer from either inconsistent programming or general lackluster performances. The Modern Theater is set aside for contemporary plays by relatively new writers and directors. Instead of showcasing new talent, however, it only highlights the terrible state of Egyptian contemporary theater. Of the many plays that have come and gone over the last few years, none have left a lasting mark. The Youth Theater remains a troupe, but without an actual building to call its own, making it difficult for audiences to consistently follow their output. Meanwhile, the Comedy Theater had trouble last year even presenting a full program. One of their biggest hit was a holdover from last season, *Rusasa fi al-Qalb* (A Bullet to the Heart), by Tawfiq al-Hakim, an operetta with Ali al-Haggar and Angham.

One of the more successful public-sector experiments has been the Hanager Theater, which opened its doors in 1992 as a space to provide greater opportunities to the new generation. Although the quality of productions varies greatly, there have been signs of innovation,

particularly in the use of technology, dance, and approach, and several important new artists, like Karim al-Tonsi, have used the space to stage their productions. One of the more interesting productions in 2001 was *Doditello*, written and directed by Sameh Mahran, an attempt to deconstruct the relationship of Diana and Dodi within a cross-cultural context.

Children's theater is important as well, if only for its ability to draw audiences. In the 2000-2001 season, sales of tickets to productions by Egypt's two children's theater troupes, the Puppet Theater and the National Children's Theater, comprised about 60% of all ticket sales in the entire public sector. Both of these troupes put on matinee performances for schools, but the

Underground in Alex

Along Port Said Street in the Cleopatra Quarter of Alexandria sits a Jesuit retreat famous for its library and cinema club, run by Father Fayez. In 2000, it was decided to turn the garage next to the center into a multipurpose cultural space. Using moveable partitions, architect Tareq Abu al-Futouh designed a malleable performance space that could easily be arranged to suit the needs of an art exhibition one day, and a musical performance or theater event the next. Thus did the Garage come into being. Opening its doors in October, it played host to artists and the public with a week-long festival entitled "My Right to the City," featuring theater, dance, round-table discussions, and art installations. Luckily for Alexandrians, the Garage was not a flash in the pan. In a city that has only a precious few culture venues—and virtually no space for theater—the Garage has been a breath of fresh air blowing over the dormant theater scene in Egypt's second city, hosting dozens of musical, dance, and theater performances since its inception.

But the Garage is aspiring to be more than a performance space. It also runs a theater appreciation club, hosts visiting theater troupes, and last summer held a series of summer theater workshops open to both amateurs and professionals. Working in conjunction with Alexandria's Alternative Theater Group and the Young Arab Theater Fund, the Garage hopes to widen the city's cultural vistas by bringing in foreign artists and theater troupes as well, both from other parts of the Arab world and elsewhere. Beyond the obvious importance of providing Alexandria with a new venue, the Garage has proven that private collective endeavors are perhaps a real alternative to the vagaries of the public sector. So far the experiment has been highly successful. Performances have brought in healthy crowds, while the center's other activities have drawn students, amateur theater enthusiasts, and the city's intellectuals into its orbit. Who knows—perhaps the Alexandria Garage will provide the impetus for the creation of other garages in other places. Already in Minya, the Jesuit Theater is undergoing renovations, with plans to open soon. *MeB*

Opera Aida (top), the First Independent Theater Festival (bottom), Ballet de Prague (inset)

productions tend to resemble rote homework assignments more than anything else, with little attempt towards innovation or renewal. The Puppet Theater is still resting on the laurels of its most famous production, *al-Leila al-Kebira* (The Feast Night), written by Salah Jahin and first staged in the 1960s. More interesting children's theater has popped up in the private sector of late, with *Holahota Barakota* running for the third straight year in 2001.

Like the public sector, commercial theater has an illustrious history, going back to pre-revolutionary Egypt when playhouses were scattered in Rod al-Farag. The mainstays of today's private theaters are variety-show entertainment and big-name comedy stars along the lines of *Lamma Baba Yinam* (When Papa Goes to Sleep), a meleé of dancing, singing, and comedy hijinks performed by the likes of Youssra, Hisham Selim, and Alaa Wali al-Din, all actors largely known for their work in cinema. The Haram Theater, owned by Adel Imam, has been presenting his star-vehicle, *The Bodyguard*, for more than three years now. Financially, the private-sector strategy works. While state theater loses money, commercial theaters rake it in, packing in well-off audiences who come for a night of pure entertainment.

Private and public sector theaters differ greatly in their level of seriousness, approach, and their ability to attract audiences. In general, however, both tend to present moral, didactic theater, and each borrows some characteristics of the other to get along. Thus, the public sector includes a little lightness in its performances to try to distance itself from its notorious seriousness, while the private sector tries to be "relevant" or impart a moral message, no matter how entertainingly done. But neither differs substantially in the final product. Direction tends to be limited to moving the actors, and both show

characters who are more or less two-dimensional. Stage sets follows two modes, either completely realistic or completely symbolic. Shows in both almost always contain some singing or dancing, for entertainment in the private sector and perhaps as a Brechtian attempt to convey the message in the public sector.

In the midst of all this dreariness, the several independent theater troupes that have appeared over the last ten years are a real bright spot. Limited resources and a lack of places to show, however, are real obstacles to their growth. The Warsha, one of the oldest of these troupes, typically takes years to stage a new production. Director Ahmed al-Attar found one inventive solution to the lack of a space in 2001 when he staged *On the Road to Nowhere* entirely on a bus—a sensible marriage of practicality and experimentation. In Alexandria, the opening of the Garage has given that city's Alternative Theater Group a more regular venue for rehearsals and performances. Despite the difficult straits, new troupes continue to appear, reviving some hope in the future of independent theater. In March of this year, several troupes even managed to come together to organize a small independent theater festival. Featuring mostly re-runs of already staged productions, the festival at least served to remind the public of their existence.

While professional theater is centered almost exclusively in Cairo, amateur theater continues to thrive under the auspices of the Popular Culture Authority, with productions staged in cultural houses all over Egypt. These regional theaters flourished in the 1960s and 1970s, achieving a great deal of media and local attention. More recently however, they have been stricken by bureaucracy and conservatism, with the level of female cast members dropping noticeably. While some stage original productions, and even occasionally a real gem, they are only able to attract a wider audience during the Popular Culture festival, staged once a year in Cairo, or—if they are lucky—during the International Festival for Experimental Theater (IFET). Even so, there are many unsung heroes in the provinces, who kill themselves to keep theater alive if only for a few nights a year.

Despite state subsidization, theater enjoys precious few festivals compared to other performing arts. Of the three that exist, the IFET, running since 1989, is the largest. The festival's record is mixed. While critics complain about nonexistent organization and a noticeable lack of selection criteria, the festival continues to attract audiences and bring a breath of fresh air to an increasingly moribund theater scene. *MeB*

High Notes

The sentimental holds sway

Someone looking for amusement in the first few years of the last century would have had much to choose from: melodrama, vaudeville, and operettas, not to mention the eclecticism offered by a variety of music halls featuring singers, magicians, ventriloquists, acrobats, and comedy troupes. English, Egyptian, French, Syrian, and even Japanese artists marched across the stages of the Alcazar, the Printania, l'Arabe, the Belvédère, the Ambassadeurs and the Abbas. There were also open-air concerts, those potpourris of musical performance given free by Egyptian and English brass bands in the kiosks of the new Ezbekiya Gardens. In all festivities, music shared the top bill on advertisements with silent films.

The characteristic music of the traditional Egyptian orchestra, known then simply as oriental music, or *al-takht al-sharqi*, also found a place in this effervescent milieu, particularly in the cafés of Faggala and Bab al-Hadid and in the numerous cabarets found around Ezbekiya. A somewhat seedy reputation surrounded these orchestras and singers, or *awalim*, but it was in this environment that popular Egyptian song, the *taqtuqa*, evolved, though the stars of the day, for the most part women, are today largely forgotten.

Though record companies were making their debut at about the same time—the first official discs date to 1903-1904—their clientele did not frequent such places, except perhaps furtively. These companies were much more eager to find an audience in the gilt salons of the aristocracy. It was there that the music of the *takht*, the music of the *nahda*, or renaissance, was born and realized its true grandeur, in the pageantry of the khedival court in the last twenty years of the 19th century. The official court singer appointed by Khedive Ismail, the Tanta-born Abdu al-

Hamouli, abandoned his *gallabiya* for a frock coat and tarboush in the Istanbul style. He was sent to the Sublime Porte, and in turn Cairo received some of the great figures of Turkish music. This exchange breathed new life into what had recently been a learned, anemic musical tradition. Salama Higazi had the audacity to bring the *takht* into the theater hall, adapting the formula to the first melodrama sung in Arabic. The few years before his death in 1917 marked the last hours of glory of the musical tradition inherited from the *nahda*.

At the end of the Great War, the revolution of 1919 was ringing the death knell of this courtly music and its

Assala (top), Amr Diab (bottom)

Going Global

With the rise of a lucrative new clip culture beamed from the growing number of Arab satellite stations, Egyptian pop is getting slicker and more commercialized by the day. For the most part, though, the same constellation of stars have occupied the top billing spots for the last couple of years. Amr Diab, the foremost purveyor of Western-style pop and Egypt's chubby answer to Ricky Martin, is without a doubt the king of Egyptian pop. He hit it big again last year with his *Ana Aktar Wahed bi-Yihibbak* (I'm the One that Loves You Most). Never one to miss a trend, Diab outfitted this release with a techno-rap duet performed with expatriate Egyptian rapper SandMan. The song was accompanied by a glitzy video shot at a London disco by Sherif Sabri, one of the best—and most expensive—video directors around.

Hakim, whose loud anthemic brand of traditional *shaabi* music is the antithesis of Diab, was also a top seller yet again. The 2001 *Tammini Aleik* (Let Me Know You're Okay), like his album from the year before, benefited from plenty of publicity via television ads for MobiNil. He followed it up in 2002 with another hit single, *al-Salam Aleiku*, promoted by a well-produced video that was a radical departure from the kind of stuff normally seen on the screen. Forgoing the beach scenes and crowds of dancing women that provide the fodder for many an Egyptian video, the clip featured Hakim posing as a variety of working-class heroes, a daring move in a satellite market largely aimed at the upper-middle class. Mohammed Mounir also had two releases over the last year and a half, both of which cemented his status as the foremost popularizer of authentic, traditional sounds. The first, *Qalbi Masakin Shaabiya* (My Heart is a Ghetto), followed in the footsteps of his previous release with chicly produced, but still recognizable Nubian sounds, while the second, *al-Ard, al-Salam* (Earth, Peace) dove

into a different heritage, with the adaptation of Sufi rhythms and feel-good spiritual lyrics to stylized pop. No other contemporary Arab male vocalist has managed to make the same inroads with Egyptian audiences, though Iraqi heartthrob Kazem al-Saher probably has greater appeal across the Arab world than either Mounir or Hakim. When it comes to female pop vocalists, though, the top sellers are mostly foreign: Assala from Syria, Diana Haddad, and Nawal al-Zoghbi from Lebanon, and the Moroccan Samira Said. The most successful in the new age of the video clip have been Assala and Nawal al-Zoghbi. The latter followed up her hugely successful *Layali* with more of the same in *Tuul Omri* (All My Life) in 2001. Judging by the advance publicity for her new release—and her heavy presence in Pepsi ads during last summer's World Cup—it was sure to be a hit.

But it is Assala who best illustrates the changes that Arabpop has undergone over the last few years. Originally a dumpy singer of lengthy love poems, over her last three releases—the latest was last year's *Moshtaqa* (Missing You)—she has become made-for-video good-looking, and now sings extremely well-produced, if formulaic pop songs. Still noted for the same strong voice that got her started, the transformation has considerably widened her audience.

For the most part, you still need to have a great voice in Arabic music to become truly famous, but as Assala illustrates, in the world of Arab pop, more and more marketing counts. These days, with a rash of mutually beneficial advertising deals raising the stakes—whether it's Hakim adapting his songs to mobile phone jingles, or Amr Diab and Nawal al-Zoghbi peddling Pepsi—a pop star's cachet can be better assessed by just tuning in to TV commercials. *AH*

Voice of the People?

Sponsor of hate? Destroyer of good taste? Popular folk hero? These are only a few of the epithets used to describe *shaabi* pop idol, Shaaban Abd al-Rehim. Catapulted into fame with I Hate Israel—an anthem for the times if ever there was one—by year's end "Shaabola" (as his admirers call him) had proved himself to be more than just a flash in the pan—even though his songs still cannot be heard on the radio or TV.

As the high priests of culture like to point out, Shaaban cannot read, write, or carry a tune. He is, in short, the antithesis of everything the musical establishment stands for. The point was made comically clear when, in an interview on state television early in the year, the interviewer asked him what he thought of classical Arabic music. After the question was repeated more than once, Shaaban readily admitted that he didn't quite understand the meaning of the word "classical."

It is moments like these (and there have been plenty) that have gotten the cultural establishment all in a frenzy, and they have attacked him as a scourge on society, not to mention a no-talent lout. The vitriol reached a crescendo last Ramadan, when several critics complained that Shaaban had appeared on TV talk shows way too much, at the expense of "worthier" cultural figures who might actually have something to say.

But as critics bemoan his lack of taste and talent, they show that they have missed the point entirely. *I Hate Israel* proved to be such a success precisely because it is not the run-of-the-mill political anthem that cloaks raw sentiments in a mantle of high-flying prose, classical melody, and melodrama. Instead, the song personalizes the conflict in the way that most Egyptians today feel it—plus it throws in a heavy dose of street-wise humor and a danceable beat. That Shaaban is not the author of the lyrics has not affected his popularity in the least.

The jury is still out on whether Shaaban fell into his fame by accident, or is an ultra-savvy self-promoter who understands how to move markets. Perhaps both. In mid-year, his voice was used by McDonald's in a commercial jingle to promote its new McFelafel sandwich. He seemed to lose a little credibility for agreeing to do the ad in the first place, but he was just as quickly redeemed when McDonald's dropped the ad, after only three weeks of air play, allegedly due to pressure from US Jewish lobby groups who did not appreciate the fast-food chain's choice of spokesman. Shaaban turned the whole mess in his favor when he later said that he had no idea he was singing for McDonald's in the first place—a plausible claim from a man unable to read a contract.

While his popularity seemed to wane with his next release, *Amrika Ya Amrika*, the Nero of Egyptian high culture had the last laugh at the end of the year. Those who waited for him to crash and burn in his film debut, *Muwatin, Mukhbir, wa Harami*, had to be disappointed when the film proved a success, not only with the *shaab* but with high-brow film critics. Shaaban may not have proved that he can act—most everyone agreed that he was just playing himself—but he did manage to hold his own even in high culture settings.

Though his forays into cinema brought him fully into the mainstream last year, Shaaban has had a following among certain classes, like microbus drivers, at least since the late 1980s. Classicists take it all as one more sign of the degradation of Egyptian culture, but his crossover might be better read as the appearance of a new kind of truly contemporary musical voice, mirroring the rise of the youth comedy in film and even that of hip-hop culture in the US. Though Shaaban's roots may go back to traditional *shaabi* music, his feet are planted firmly in the modern Egyptian street. *MM*

Critics who bemoan Shaaban's lack of taste and talent have missed the point entirely

elitist aesthetic. It was in these years of intensity and greater social liberty that the *taqtuqa* knew its golden age. Musical couplets ranged from obscene ditties to social critique, their easy refrains being taken up by innumerable operettas, which remained quite popular until the cinema started to sing as well. But very quickly, over the next twenty years, the *taqtuqa* started to make its way into the past as well. A new type of elitist sensibility was in evidence, not only musical, despite the mythic figure and incontestable popularity of Sayed Darwish, who incarnates a certain moment both in national history and Egyptian song. In his day, he forsook the turban and the caftan for European attire and turned his back on the tradition of the *takht*. To be Egyptian is to be modern, he said.

The record market was growing, but the Hamoulien repertoire—too old, too marked by its Ottoman origins—no longer made money, nor did the vulgar accents of the *taqtuqa*, which grated on the ears of the new bourgeoisie. They wanted something new, yet tasteful. Taking the best the last half-century had produced, the new generation drew on outside influences as well, particularly from Europe. Mohammed al-Qasabji and Mohammed Abd al-Wahab developed the sentimental romance, while Zakariya Ahmed dressed the *taqtuqa* in more florid melodies (and more decent lyrics as well). Poets like Ahmed Rami, Bairam al-Tunsi, and Ahmed Shawqi were also part of the adventure. All instructed in the subtleties of classical poetry, but all devoted to the cause of a conquering modernism, together they helped to forge the modern Egyptian song. Umm Kulthoum and Abd al-Wahab became the irreplaceable icons of this latest incarnation—the Star of the East and the Composer for All Seasons.

When the first congress for Arabic music opened in Cairo in 1932, not only was the khedival school definitively consigned to the domain of the ancient, but the suspicious past of the pre-war song was completely effaced. Ignoring the preoccupations of the eminent European musicologists invited for the occasion, the event consecrated the total triumph of the New Egyptian and his newly born national music.

What followed is familiar. With the long compositions of Riyad al-Sunbati, Umm Kulthoum took Egyptian song to the summit of refinement, rediscovering the spirit of the khedival school. The mannerism of Abd al-Wahab is no less remote from the courtly song, but his continuous incorporation of instrumental collage opened the song to the contemporary spirit of the age. They exemplify the originality and great variety of the Egyptian song, but the cultural establishment's adoption of the form, as well as that of younger musicians like Abd al-Halim Hafez, has given it the status of classical music, in the Western sense of the word.

Though the last 20 years of Egyptian music has seen the relative explosion of artistic range, musical production today is dominated by two major currents: the sentimental pop song and popular, or *shaabi*, music. The first corresponds to a wide variety of pop music, from dance hits to ballads, heard on Egyptian radio waves and sung by stars like Amr Diab, Mustafa Qamar, Ihab Tawfiq, and Hani Shaker. *Shaabi* music, banned from the airwaves, is best known these days through its rising star, the highly publicized Shaaban Abd al-Rehim.

Destined for a large audience in the Arab world, Egyptian pop takes few risks in originality, neither in its lyrics nor music. Composers mix basic oriental rhythm to light melodies drawn from diverse sources: simplified Eastern melodic modes, Spanish or Latin-based, pentatonic, Nubian traditions, and others. The marketing of Egyptian music is principally directed to the Gulf and the Levant, quite the opposite of North African singers like Cheb Mami and Cheb Khaled, who export to Europe.

Parallel to this industry of Arabic showbiz, diffused through the media and accompanied by the

all-important video clip, popular music has developed within its own network. Banned from the airwaves as illegitimate by the guardians of normative culture, it finds its audience through the huge market of cheap audio cassettes, and is heard in non-institutional public spaces like microbuses, kiosks, and street parties of different sorts. Just because the music finds no official support, however, does not mean that its practitioners lack publicity. The media coverage they get does not promote their music, but comes in the context of polemics on cultural production. Focused on the social legitimacy of popular music, these polemics reflect the tensions of a strongly hierarchical urban society.

Contemporary popular constitutes the commercialization of wedding music, with its stars making their first appearances at street parties, weddings, and *moulids*. That was the case with Ahmed Adawiya, the emblem of *shaabi* music since the late 1960s who is currently in the process of making a comeback. Possessing *saltana*, the ability to change modes in the song, these singers have learned their musical techniques through apprenticeships, based on orality and repetition under the instruction of an experienced elder. A product of the local social tissue, popular musicians rarely know music from an academic point of view and few have studied it formally. As the system of apprenticeship has slowly run out of steam, however, the melodic and harmonic quality of popular music has declined. But the principle importance of the music lies elsewhere: in the lyrics that touch on the preoccupations of working-class, urban

Egyptians. Describing the difficulties of everyday life, they skillfully give voice to contemporary political resentments. In this regard, they are related to the likes of Bairam al-Tonsi, Ahmed Fouad Negm, and Salah Jehin, with one major caveat: these great Egyptian poets have been followed by much more modest wordsters who come from the working class, rather than an intellectual, progressive milieu, as was the case until the 1980s.

From the technical point of view, the increasing use of electronic equipment has little by little transformed the composition of *shaabi* orchestras, and has thus had an impact on their repertoire. In Egypt, as in other countries of the South, a new aesthetic of "aural saturation" has taken hold, accompanied by a distortion of sound produced by the use of reverb that prolongs certain notes. Both in *moulids* and in wedding celebrations, a new relationship has been established between aesthetics and the possibilities represented by these new techniques.

Aside from *shaabi* music and sentimental pop, the music of the great composers and divas of the 20th century continues to be regularly diffused over the radio and television, but the major influences of today lie elsewhere. Amidst the great voices of the past and the field of diverse, but limited musical experimentation—seen in oriental jazz, rediscoveries of the Delta and the Saidi traditions, and electronic music—sentimental pop and *shaabi* music continue to hold sway. *JFB & NP*

This page: oud master Nassir Shamma (top), Samira Said (bottom); opposite page: Mohammed Mounir (top), jazzman Yehya Khalil (middle)

Literature & Art
Talent abounds but audiences remain thin

On the Margins

The observer of the Egyptian literary scene at the turn of the millennium can only be bewildered by its latest evolution. While the heated political debates and the seemingly everlasting custodianship of the state apparatus over the literary field suggest that things are getting worse, the picture is not so bleak if one takes a look at the actual literary output of recent years.

Egyptian writers have to fight against the odds on several fronts, but the battle that absorbs them the most is the political one. Like other fellow intellectuals, they have been closely tied to the state throughout Egypt's modern history. To a large extent, the state and intellectuals—including writers—have grown together under the regime born of the 1952 revolution. The Ministries of Culture and Information have remarkably resisted the general trend of the state apparatus towards budget cuts and downsizing and remain, as in the Nasserist era, the almost unavoidable umbrella under which every writer or artist must work.

Never as much as in the 1990s have the state and state-controlled institutions published so many literary works, organized so many literary conferences, and funded so many sabbatical grants for writers. New merit prizes in literature, arts, and the social sciences are created in such quantities that the committees who grant them are often unable to find enough worthy candidates to take them. While many writers consider this a gift that cannot be refused, or a right to which they are entitled, others, especially within the young vanguard, do try to exist outside the umbrella.

One of the most puzzling paradoxes of Egyptian culture is the contrast between the very high symbolic value it attaches to the printed word (best seen in the heated polemics about book censorship, while censorship of other media, though much harsher and more systematic, is scarcely discussed) and the continuing marginality of the book in the market of symbolic goods. With roughly half of Egypt's population still illiterate, the problem for today's writers is that even the literate half reads very few books. When they do read, they tend to turn to things that are "useful" either in this world (school books) or in the other (religious books). While Sheikh Shaarawi's *tafsir* of the Quran sells hundreds of thousands of copies, the best-selling novels of the most prestigious living writers hardly sell a few thousand. Only vague figures are available because of the opacity and lack of regulation that prevail in the publishing sector, both private and public. Even Maktabat Misr, Naguib Mahfouz's publisher, has stopped mentioning the number and date of reprints of the author's works since he won the Nobel

What People Read

Egyptian publishers say that the wave of religious reading that washed over the country during the last decade is on the wane, with educational books—particularly computer tomes—now almost as popular. Leaving aside schoolbooks and children's books, though, today's best sellers remain political books. While there are no official statistics on Egypt's reading practices, an *Egypt Almanac* survey of the two leading non-state publishers, Dar al Shorouq and Madbouli, revealed the following:

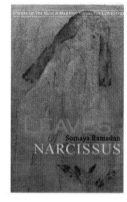

Top 10 at Madbouli:

1. *Bin Laden: Taliban al-Afghan al-Arab wa al-Umamiya al-Usuliya* (Bin Laden: The Arab Taliban of Afghanistan and the Fundamentalist Community)
Nabil Sharaf al-Din, 2001
2. *al-Quran wa al-Seif* (The Quran and the Sword)
Rifaat Sayed Ahmed, 2001
3. *al-Awlama wa Ahamm al-Tahawwulat al-Mujtamaiya fi al-Watan al-Arabi*
(Globalization and Social Change in the Arab World)
Ed. Abd al-Baset Abd al-Moati, 1999
4. *al-Hiroghlyfiya Tufassir al-Quran*
(Heiroglyphics and Quranic Exegesis)
Saad al-Adl, 2001
5. *al-Sajina* (The Prisoner), Malika Oufqeir, 2000
6. *Aam min al-Azamat* (A Year of Crises)
Mohammed Hassanein Heikal, 2001
7. *Dawaa li Kull Daa* (A Cure for Every Disease)
Amin al-Hudari, 1999
8. *Tanabuat Nostradamus*
(The Predictions of Nostradamus), 1999
9. *al-Muslimun wa al-Masihiyun taht al-Hisar al-Yehudi*
(Muslims and Christians under Jewish Siege)
Ahmed Hassan Sobhi, 2002
10. *Khitabat al-Rais Gamal Abd al-Nasser wa Muqabalatuhu al-Sahafiya*
(The Speeches and Interviews of President Gamal Abd al-Nasser, 2002

Survey: Egypt Almanac

Top 10 at Dar al Shorouq:

1. *Mushaf al-Tajwid* (The Reciter's Quran), 2001
2. *Silsilat al-Nahla Zeina*
(Zeina Bee series, for children), 1982
3. *Aam min al-Azamat* (A Year of Crises)
Mohammed Hassanein Heikal, 2001
4. *Silsilat Sindbad lil-Jeib*
(The Pocket Sindbad Series, for children), 1982
5. *Taliban Jund Allah fi al-Maarakat al-Ghalat*
(Taliban: Soldiers for God in the Wrong Battle)
Fahmi al-Howeidi, 2001
6. *Silsilat Ihki li Hikaya*
(Tell Me a Story Series, for children), 1998
7. *al-Ijaz al-Ilmi fi al-Quran*
(Scientific Inimitability in the Quran)
Zaghloul al-Naggar, 2001
8. *Hikayat Kalila wa Dimna*
(Stories from Kalila wa Dimna, for children), 1998
9. *Silsilat Qisas al-Quran* (Stories from the Quran)
Ahmed Bahgat, 2001
10. *Min New York ila Kabul*
(From New York to Kabul)
Mohammed Hassanein Heikal, 2002

This page: Dar Sharqiyat, premier literary publisher (top left); next page: Alaa al-Aswani's summer hit Imarat Yaqoubian

New Book Titles

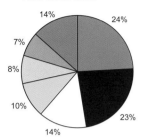

- 14%
- 24%
- 7%
- 8%
- 10%
- 23%
- 14%

■ Sciences
■ Literature
□ Religion
▨ Philology
░ Social Sciences
▨ Geography and History
■ Other

Total Number of Copies Printed

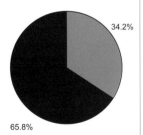

34.2%

65.8%

■ Textbooks
■ All other books

Source: UNESCO Statistical Yearbook, 1999

Of the more than 92 million books printed in Egypt in 1995, about two-thirds were textbooks

Prize in 1988. As for Maktabat al-Usra (The Family Library), the yearly operation of the state-owned GEBO patronized by Suzanne Mubarak (the publisher of millions of cheap, subsidized books aimed at "the masses" since 1993), there is, to date, no serious appraisal or investigation of its actual impact on the reading practices of its target audience.

In spite of these odds, more and more literature is published in Egypt every year: in the field of creative writing (fiction, poetry, drama), a low estimate would be an average of 500 new titles each year in the 1990s, compared to 100-150 in the 1960s. A good half of them are self-published, in one way or another, while the majority of the other half is published by state-owned or state-controlled publishers. In other words, not a single creative writer can make a living out of his book sales. Nevertheless, dozens of writers *do* make a living out of writing, by publishing their short stories, poems, or serialized novels or by contributing regular columns in the local and the Arabic press, writing songs and scripts for radio and TV, and selling their stories to filmmakers. While the book remains for the elite, these media allow writers to reach a much larger audience, but this sometimes has a price that the "purest" writers refuse to pay. The TV adaptation of Gamal al-Ghitani's *al-Zayni Barakat*, for example, stripped the work of any political critique, turning it into a flat historical series.

Caught between the hammer of the state and the anvil of society, many writers try to find alternative markets abroad. Since the 1970s especially, Egyptian writers have often turned to Beirut and other Arab capitals to publish or republish their works, as a mean to avoid local constraints but also to reach a broader Arab readership. Conversely, many Arab writers resort to Cairo publishers for the same reasons. A more significant change, especially visible since Mahfouz's Nobel, is the growth of the translation market. To date, Mahfouz remains the only Egyptian writer who can boast a wide readership in

the Euro-American market. But dozens of other titles by Egyptian writers are now available in translation. Al-Ghitani's classic *al-Zayni Barakat* has been translated into more than ten languages, all but one of Sonallah Ibrahim's novels are available in French, and most of their peers or the Generation of the 1960s can boast one or several translations. Another sign of improvement in this respect is the very swift access of the young vanguard of the 1990s to translation: the first novels of Miral al-Tahawi and May Telmissani were translated into more than one language within two or three years of their publication, and Somayya Ramadan's *Awraq al-Nargis* (Leaves of Narcissus) is on its way. The fact that these three young writers are women is a significant change in itself, as the Generation of the 60s is almost exclusively male.

Paradoxically, the impact of these translations, quite limited abroad, is much greater within the Egyptian literary field. Because of the prevailing nationalist mood, as well as the continuing misrepresentations of Arab and Islamic culture that dominate the Euro-American market, accusations of writing for export have become a common way to stigmatize rivals. As a whole, however, national literary production is increasingly adjusting to world literary trends, the most obvious of which is the triumph of the novel. True, poets like Abd al-Rahman al-Abnoudi or Ahmed Abd al-Moati Hegazi can still draw thousands to their readings at the yearly Cairo book fair—much more than a poetry reading any

European or American capital— but the evolution of poetic writing since the 1970s makes it difficult for their younger peers to attain the same status. In today's Egypt, as in Europe or the US, the consumption of poetic production is increasingly limited to textbooks and classrooms and the

song industry. Another declining genre is the short story: once thriving, when almost every newspaper and magazine had its regular short story section, it is increasingly identified with young writers and amateurs, who will turn to the novel as soon as they can afford it. This evolution is partly due to reasons internal to the literary field itself, but it also points to the influence of a translation market that concentrates almost exclusively on the novel.

In its content also, Egyptian literary input tends to follow international literary trends, although one can speculate whether this is a result of the influence of foreign models, or of similar internal dynamics at work in different areas. For instance, the current opposition between the Generation of the 1960s, once a revolutionary avant-garde and now in a position of domination over the field, and the Generation of the 1990s, today's avant-garde, seems analogous to similar oppositions in Latin American and certain European literatures. The individualistic, self-centered, provocative tone often adopted by the young Egyptian avant-garde has its parallels in many world literatures today, just as the innovations of its fathers in the 1960s were similar to the modernist tendencies at work in many world literatures from the 1950s onward.

In spite of all the odds, Egyptian literary input has not stopped growing and renewing itself, perhaps more successfully than other sectors of the cultural and intellectual field—the social and exact sciences, cinema, and theater—and in similar ways to those seen in the plastic arts. Not surprisingly, the sectors of intellectual creation that need less material investment and institutional support are the ones that better resist the on-going degradation in the material and symbolic conditions of intellectual work in Egypt. *RJ*

On Show
Quality vs. quantity

Over the last few years, the art scene in Cairo has exploded. Ten years ago, a few serious private galleries existed downtown and in Zamalek, but except in arty circles, they maintained a generally low profile. The focal point of contemporary art was the Center of Arts in Zamalek, the fortress of the state galleries, which hosted all the major shows and salons. Now there seems to be an art gallery wherever you turn—including a handful in the outposts of Heliopolis and Maadi. More non-traditional art spaces have also opened up, as Cairo's hippest restaurants and bars have begun hosting their own exhibitions or at least making a concerted effort to showcase contemporary Egyptian art in their businesses. Al-Ahram Beverages even got on the bandwagon last summer

when it unveiled its new Vine-Arts advertising campaign. Using works of contemporary artists to adorn the lables of its Gianaclis wine, the company hopes to promote young talent while selling a few extra bottles of wine in the process. Whether all this activity has improved the quality of art along with the quantity is still open for debate. Is a member of the public more likely to find a strong exhibition now than a decade ago?

This page: Vessela Farid (top), Hala El Koussy (bottom), Maha George (left inset), Hamed Nada (right inset); opposite page: Hassan Khan and Sherief El Azma (top), Anna Boghiguian (middle), Fathi Afifi (bottom), Dina al-Gharib, Maher Ali, Hoda Lutfi (bottom inset)

It probably depends on how determined he or she is and where they live. In the past, the Center of Arts always promised viewers some sort of visual entertainment. With the old villa split up into different galleries, a number of artists would exhibit at once, and there would generally be a big name or two as well as some new talent. While controversy invariably attended the selection of artists, Ahmed Fouad Selim, longtime head of the center, had the cream of the crop at his disposal. Now there is so much space to exhibit that gallerists have to fight to get the best work. With the opening of the Gezira Arts Center and to a lesser extent the rather misshapen Palace of Arts, the public galleries have even started competing with themselves.

Despite the increased importance of private galleries, artists know that the traditional path to fame and fortune is through the government institutions. The state sector controls the vast majority of scholarships abroad, representations at international biennales, and a bevy of local grants. It is therefore essential for most artists to exhibit in the national shows and, if they are still youngish, the Youth Salon. Even artists who have a strong profile in the private arts scene tend to keep one foot planted firmly in the state sector. Shady al-Nashouqati, Moataz Nasr, and Wael Shawqi—all bright young stars showcased in private galleries—have participated in (and often won) the Youth Salon or other state-sponsored shows.

It is an interesting balancing art for these artists. They like the higher profile that comes with being involved in the innovative private art scene, which gave

many of the 20- and 30-somethings their real starts, as well as the sales, but they soon realize the limitations of being a purely private-sector artist. This is changing as private galleries and foreign cultural organizations have begun contacting reputable foreign galleries directly, setting up cross-cultural exchanges outside of the normal state channels. Yet, even so, the state can intervene and stop both artists and art from traveling. To the private sector, this represents state interference to maintain its monopoly, while the state defends it as protecting the reputation of Egyptian contemporary art.

On a domestic level, the balancing act tends to produce repetition. The same pieces can appear in a private show, a national show, and group show all in one year. Popular artists, like Anna Boghiguian, Omar al-Fayyoumi, and Hoda Lutfi, can have show after show, sometimes running simultaneously. While more accomplished artists can carry this off, the majority cannot, and it has become far too easy to have too much of a good thing—never mind a bad thing. Even young artists are expected to stage two shows a year. The results are often exhibitions that feature little more than works in progress. This sort of approach will inevitably damage the art market that developed throughout the 1990s.

The increase in gallery space has also spawned fiercer competition among private galleries, who are ruled more by market forces than the heavily subsidized state sector. As a result, prices on art were inflated throughout the last decade, in some cases jumping from Egyptian pounds to US dollars, and it has reached the point where young artists who are still developing are charging as much for their works as major artists, both dead and alive. On the other hand, competition has forced gallerists to go out in search of more talent, allowing artists from outside Cairo—often left outside the loop altogether—to access the art scene more effectively. While there is no doubt that Cairo is still the center, Artists like Sanaa

Moussa and Amr Heiba, along with other artists from the so-called provinces are receiving more coverage.

While painting and sculpture have remained the dominant forms of Egyptian plastic arts, over the last decade local artists have begun to experiment more with other forms. Photography, previously neglected as an art form, has taken more of the limelight of late with talented young photographers like Lara Baladi, Heba Farid, and Susan Hefuna attracting attention. There are even plans to convert the planetarium on the Opera House grounds into a photography museum. Installations, too, are becoming a popular form. Using everything from grass to pitch and plastic bags to cotton wool, younger artists have been busy transforming galleries into mysterious and majestic spaces. There have been some disasters, particularly in the salons and national shows, but on the whole the experimentation has injected a positive shot of creativity into the arts, and some of the best new works are being created in this field.

Whereas downtown tends to be the playground of the young, in Zamalek, private galleries like the Safarkhana, the Zamalek Gallery, and the Khan al-Maghrabi are making a concerted effort to raise the profile of major league Egyptian artists, like Abd al-Hadi al-Gazzar, Hamed Nada, Sayed Abd al-Rassoul, Kamal Khalifa, Vessela Farid, and the Wanli brothers. Offering strong retrospectives of late artists and new shows, particularly painters, these galleries are,

because of their prime locations, bringing in new people who might be going to a gallery for the first time.

This work by the Zamalek galleries is essential, as fine arts do not get the attention they deserve in the media. There are some television shows devoted to fine art, but most are hopeless and hosted by people who know very little about what they are looking at. Sadly enough, the majority of coverage falls on two ends of the spectrum: either it is so simplistic as to be useless, or it is alienatingly academic. While some interesting articles and valuable art criticism are also published locally, it tends to go over the head of an average reader and lacks the quality color images that would bring in the crowds. Fine arts enjoy no television advertising like that which the Opera House receives, and major art events can occur without people outside the arts even knowing about it. In general, advertising tends to be limited to other galleries.

Overall, there is no doubt that fine arts are better off than they were ten years ago. There is much more art available to see, and that in itself is a good thing. It is now time to see the artistic world develop further to best utilize the new potential offered by more artists, more space, and a fervor towards experimentation. While state and private sectors will probably never really work together—it is rare now that either group can manage that within itself—as long as the relationship remains one of healthy rivalry, Egyptian art and artists can benefit. *RW*

هدى لطفى   ماهر على   دينا الغريب

The Built Heritage
The challenge of urbanization

Architecture

Throughout the 1980s, Egyptian cities both old and new witnessed a process of mass urbanization. As architects and builders have attempted to keep pace with the

changing environment, several distinctive architectural trends have emerged. Whether or not these can be considered appropriate reflections of the local culture, its climatic conditions, or the socioeconomic context is a question that remains unanswered. Over the past ten years, Egyptian architectural practice has undergone radical changes. For one thing, the scope of architectural practice has expanded considerably. Whereas the line between architect and client used to be short and direct, the relationship today is mediated more and more often by a battery of corporate business structures. This is seen in the increasing demand for new non-traditional architectural services, such as architectural programming, cost analysis, construction management, client relations, real estate development, and architectural marketing. These activities require skills beyond the capacity of the traditional architect, thereby threatening mainstream approaches. Some areas have escaped this professionalization, including interiors, façades, and shops. Trends in façades and commercial architecture, for example, are more a result of the client's belief that a building with a distinctive visual appearance will attract attention. A flagrant example of this is the Wonderland Mall in Nasr City.

At the same time, there is greater overlap (and thus competition) between the work of architects and other professionals, particularly interior designers and landscape architects. Indeed, interior design has increasingly come to replace building design per se. A less complementary crossover of professionals working to build our environment is represented in contracting companies, construction managers, and investment agencies.

The last ten years have also witnessed the entrance of large-scale multinational firms to the Egyptian scene, participating in joint-venture projects, companies, or consultancies. Collaboration is now taking place between local architectural firms and international corporate firms such as Skidmore, Owings and Merrill, and Hellmuth, Obata and Kassabaum. Conrad International Cairo Hotel, First Residence at Giza, Arkadia Mall, and Soma Bay Resort south of Hurghada are examples of this type of collaboration. Whether this development represents a positive or negative trend in Egyptian architecture is a point of debate—what is certain is that it has changed the face of Egypt's major urban centers.

Throughout this period, three government agencies have continued to exercise a formative influence on the

Egyptian landscape: the Supreme Council of Antiquities, the Tourism Development Authority, and the General Organization for Physical Planning. Often in collaboration with international bodies such as the UNDP, UNESCO, and the Aga Khan Trust for Culture, these agencies define architectural problems and envision solutions, although they rarely take steps towards implementing urban development plans or historic preservation policies. Nevertheless, these collaborations are important as they help to define the government agenda, which affects what sort of projects are promoted and what sort of structures get built.

These changes in the industry have resulted in a plurality of schools of architectural thought and a concomitant plurality of building styles. Certain socioeconomic processes (such as economic liberalization) have also left an imprint on the architectural landscape. With the push to privatization that began in the early 1990s, new private companies and banks were established, and government agencies upgraded their facilities. Consequently, there has been a surge in the construction of office buildings, commercial buildings and shopping centers, factories, tourist facilities, and public buildings.

In the midst of all these changes, local architects have struggled to address the practical realities of urbanization while simultaneously searching for an architectural identity that is contemporary, yet fully Egyptian. The most prominent product of this struggle has been the recent turn towards historical revivalism, embodied in the architectural mix of one or more of Egypt's historical periods. While its practitioners insist that simulating history in contemporary buildings establishes a sense of belonging and emotional ties between society and the built environment, all too often it devolves into a process of blindly selecting or copying from the past.

Examples representing contemporary attitudes towards historical revivalism are seen in everything from government structures to private homes. Completed in 2001, the Supreme Constitutional Court of Egypt, designed by Ahmed Mito, places emphasis on employing features of ancient Egyptian architecture while producing a quasi-new form. In the Heliopolis headquarters of Oriental Weavers, Farouk al-Gohary incorporates arches, an inner courtyard, and stucco screened windows in an attempt to put forth a new image of so-called "Arab" architecture. Ashraf Salah Abu Seif takes the integration of local designs one step further by avoiding the use of any modern visual features in apartment blocks in Nasr City and Agouza. Instead, he uses segmental arches and wooden pergolas to harmonize the overall building shell, in an attempt to simulate and adapt a Mediterranean pseudo-Islamic architecture.

Parallel to this, there are movements towards a more culturally and environmentally responsive architecture. An example that illustrates the participatory approach is Hager al-Dabiah Village, designed and built by Ahmed Abdou and Samy Abdel Aziz in 1996 to accommodate flood victims in the governorate of Qena. The village (a total of 124 units) was built using local material and traditional construction techniques, and helped create local employment opportunities.

Regional modernism—perhaps best described as a truly contemporary, yet truly indigenous architecture—

Opposite page: the Nubian Museum was the recipient of the Aga Khan award for architecture in 2001; next page: Rami El Dahan and Soheir Farid's work at Quseir also has its practitioners. One of the most well known examples of this trend is the Serena Beach Resort in Quseir, completed in 1994. Architects Ramy El Dahan and Soheir Farid show a sensitive approach to tourism development, using the same local material as the resort's neighboring buildings. It has established some momentum for other projects in the region, but the danger lies in a superficial adoption of this approach. In Qasr al-Funoun—an art gallery on the Opera House grounds in Cairo inaugurated in 1998—Abdelhalim

Ibrahim uses the Egyptian heritage as a reservoir for inspiration that serves a modern design for a building with a new function. His main concern was to link the current art movement in Egypt with a local, traditionalist Arab-Islamic cultural heritage. The project is a thoughtful attempt towards the development of a contemporary Egyptian cultural identity.

Public participation in architectural rehabilitation projects is a new realm for architectural practice in Egypt. One example is seen in a project directed by Salah Zaky Said, who worked on increasing residents' sense of belonging and appreciation of heritage in a series of still-ongoing restoration projects of domestic architecture in Fatimid Cairo. Adaptive reuse and architectural recycling is also explored in the work of Atef Fahim, who remodeled an existing farm house in Sharqiya into an artist's house by utilizing local techniques.

All told, the last decade does not appear to have produced one solid Egyptian architectural trend, but rather a collection of attitudes. There are honest attempts to tame architectural practices and urban development processes, but while Egyptian architects sometimes manage to build successful individual buildings, the overall built environment is increasingly mismanaged. This strongly suggests an urgent need to re-conceptualize Egyptian architecture, moving beyond the perception of architecture as an art form to its conception as a sociocultural act, one that has a role as a vehicle for the embodiment of community aspirations. *AG & AS*

Conservation

Preserving Egypt's past is a Herculean task

Egypt's built heritage spans at least five millennia and encompasses a variety of monuments unparalleled in the world. The legacy of the pharaohs is well known to tourists. Less well known are the vast number of Islamic monuments that make the city of Cairo a World Heritage Site, the multitude of Coptic churches and monasteries throughout the country, and the plethora of sites scattered throughout the more remote regions of Egypt. The inheritance of 19th- and early 20th-century architecture concentrated in Alexandria and Cairo, is only just beginning to be appreciated, with private enterprise contributing to the repainting of buildings and the pedestrianizing of streets. One prominent early 20th-century landmark facing the Qasr al-Nil bridge in Cairo, a villa belonging to the Ministry of Foreign Affairs, is now being restored by the government, which may raise awareness of the value of this architectural style. Other interesting projects are the renovation of the Zoological Gardens in Giza and the Fish Garden in Zamalek, which are both 19th-century French-designed

landscape gardens created for royal patrons.

The task of protecting and presenting most of this heritage devolves upon the Supreme Council for Antiquities (SCA), a department of the Ministry of Culture. This organization is responsible for coordinating the efforts of both local contractors and foreign missions to preserve the physical traces of Egypt's past, which attract millions of visitors to the country every year. While this task is relatively straightforward when it comes to the protection of ruins, it is fraught with complexity in urban situations when buildings are already occupied, ownership is disputed, and different interest groups are active. The major problems of a rising water table, a lack of basic infrastructure, and a public that is ill equipped to comprehend the value of its historic surroundings further complicate the situation. The method of assessment of what is actually worth preserving remains unrefined and essentially random. A final obstacle is the lack of a conceptual framework that would allow for the re-use of derelict historic buildings and their reintegration into the commercial and cultural life of the city. Without this, preservation attempts have often been little more than exercises in façadism: a facelift is all very well, but is possibly irrelevant when the body itself has rotted away.

Pharaonic sites continue to attract well-deserved conservation efforts. In Luxor on the West Bank, preservation and presentation work (including a site museum) at the Mortuary Temple of Merenptah is now complete thanks to a collaboration between the Swiss Institute and the SCA. The long-closed upper terrace of the temple of Deir al-Bahari opened to the public in April 2002 after years of conservation and reconstruction by a joint Polish and Egyptian team. The latter are also working on adjacent areas of this temple including the temple of Tuthmosis III. Restoration by the German Institute and the SCA is also in progress at the little visited temple of Seti I. At the Valley of the Kings, new etched aluminum signs giving visitor information for each tomb have recently been installed under the sponsorship of the World Monuments Fund. A new flood-water protection project has been implemented here by USAID and the American Research Center in Egypt, designed to divert potentially catastrophic floods away from tomb entrances. USAID is also funding the conservation of one of the small temples in the Medinet Habu complex by Chicago House. Across the river at Karnak's open-air museum, salvaged blocks from Hatshepsut's Red Chapel have now been reassembled by the French Mission to give these fragments architectural form.

In the Kharga Oasis in the Western Desert, a project reminiscent of the Nubian campaign is under way. This is the dismantling of the Greco-Roman sandstone temple of Hibis and its rebuilding on an adjacent site, a project that has been criticized as being an extreme and unnecessary measure. By contrast, the nearby Coptic cemetery of Baghawat, a remarkable collection of mud-brick funerary domes and chapels, has been saved from further disintegration by the replacement of many timber lintels which had been stolen for firewood over the years. Such small-scale, low-budget interventions are often more effective and sympathetic than grandiose projects.

Restored woodwork at the Gayer-Anderson museum

From the Coptic period, the interior of a chapel with wall paintings at the Monastery of St. Paul in the Eastern Desert is being cleaned and conserved. In Cairo, attention is still focused on the site of the Roman fortress of Babylon, now often referred to as "Old Cairo," which contains some of the oldest Coptic churches in the city. Here, a major project for the stabilization and restoration of the Hanging Church over the southern gateway into the fortress has been completed, with plans for the renovation of the adjacent Coptic Museum (*see box*).

Some 47 government-sponsored conservation projects are now being carried out in historic Cairo as part of an ambitious program to restore 157 monuments within eight years. This reflects a new concern for the appearance of this part of the city that is backed by the highest levels of government. All building types are included, from religious foundations to caravanserais to private houses. The work is being executed by four large local contractors. They include many large-scale prestige restoration projects, of which the most prominent are the mosque of Ibn Tulun, the mosque of al-Muayyad Sheikh, the mosque of Sarghatmish, the complex of Qalawun, and the Fatimid gates of Bab al-Nasr and Bab al-Futuh together with the Ayyubid northern city wall. Controversy attends most of these projects as the degree of intervention has been criticized as extreme, involving drastic structural adjustments and even rebuilding, as

The Mehlevi Dervish lodge, restored by the Italian mission (above), underground cisterns in Alexandria (right)

well as heavy surface treatments that result in the loss of the historic character so intrinsic to the appeal of these monuments. In the summer of 2001, a petition drawing attention to the treatment of these buildings, signed by numerous luminaries in the field of Islamic art, was submitted to First Lady Suzanne Mubarak, and a UNESCO report on the situation was drafted. This highlighted the need for a debate on the ethics of restoration versus conservation, which had hitherto been lacking, as well as for a much greater degree of transparency in the process from inception to execution. As a response to these criticisms, an international symposium on the restoration of Islamic and Coptic monuments was held in February 2002 under the auspices of the SCA. The stated objective of the symposium was to present the Egyptian experience of the restoration of these monuments in light of international legislation and to formulate a comprehensive strategy for the preservation and management of heritage sites. Though participants were pleased to be given the opportunity to voice their concerns over existing strategies and practices, many left the conference wondering how much of an impact the conference would ultimately have on government policies and future plans for Fatimid Cairo.

Foreign investment in Islamic Cairo has been markedly reduced of late, with American projects accounting for the bulk of those underway. These are principally directed at the area around the Bab Zuweila on the southern edge of Fatimid Cairo. The 11th-century gateway itself, and the two 15th-century minarets constructed upon it, have been cleaned and conserved, and attention is now focussed on the restoration of the 6.5-meter gates themselves. Adjacent projects include the

From the Bottom Up

Although the area commonly known today as Coptic Cairo has a history that predates the Roman Period, the earliest visible remains are those of the fortress called Babylon that Diocletian founded beside the Nile in AD 300. Two towers and an imposing gateway testify that this was once one of the largest military constructions of the Roman world. These elements, together with the walls of the fortress and the structures within it, have long been overlaid with dwellings (for both the living and the dead) and religious buildings that include churches, monasteries, and a synagogue. At the center of the site today stands the Coptic Museum, which contains the bulk of Egypt's collection of Byzantine and Coptic artifacts. For the last twenty years the site has suffered from a high ground water level that has rendered unusable certain key areas, such as the crypt of the Church of Abu Sarga where the infant Jesus and his mother are believed to have taken refuge. The increased water table can mostly be attributed to the fact that many thousands more people now live in the vicinity, where wastewater is inadequately provided for.

Since the mid-1990s, large sums of money have been allocated to different aspects of the renovation of the area within the fortress and its environs. Concerned parties include representatives of the Coptic, Greek Orthodox, Greek Catholic, and Jewish faiths, the Ministries of Tourism, Housing, and Culture, and international donors such as USAID. As might be expected with such a diverse group of interests, a coordinated vision of how best to improve the site for those who live, work, and visit there is hard to achieve. The first intervention to be initiated was the restoration of the Hanging Church and the Southern Roman Gateway upon which the church is built. The amount of LE35 million has been dedicated to this project, which involves the de-watering of a localized area through continuous pumping, as well as renovations to the church itself and the adjacent Coptic Museum (whose old wing has been closed for a decade). Ancillary is the creation of an outdoor theater facing the Roman gate.

In 1998 USAID, through the American Research Center in Egypt, commissioned a master plan for the preservation and presentation of the site. This was followed by a LE47-million localized de-watering project involving several parties whose limited aim is to reduce the level of the ground water within four selected monuments (the Churches of Abu Sarga and Mari Girgis, the Synagogue, and the Roman tower) to where it stood in 1979. The system adopted involves the sinking of a network of three-meter diameter concrete ring shafts connected to horizontal perforated drains that collect seepage. The water is then channeled by gravity to a remote pumping station. The possible long-term consequences of the rapid de-watering of this area and how to satisfactorily maintain the system remain valid concerns, although an archaeological monitoring program is fortunately in place which suggests that the bulk of remains lie beneath the level of current interventions.

Simultaneous with these endeavors has been the cosmetic upgrade of the architecture and environment surrounding the site, and the renovation of non-religious buildings within the complex. Undertaken by the Tourism Development Authority, these upgrades are largely superficial and seem to be aimed at drawing in tourists to the area. For now, the work appears to have petered out, leaving behind for another day the incomplete concrete frame structures that are the latest accretions within the fortress area. Money there may be in plenty, but something more is needed to create a sustainable heritage site that fulfills the disparate desires of ministries—be they ecclesiastical or governmental—archaeologists, and shopkeepers. *NW*

It is hoped that the de-watering project will help preserve the Roman-era structures in Coptic Cairo

conservation of the 19th-century *sabil*, or public drinking fountain, of Muhammad Ali (Tusun Pasha) and the small 15th-century prayer-hall and *sabil* of Farag Ibn Barquq. The Italian mission is persevering with its long-term program of conservation at the Mamluk tomb complex of Hassan Sadaqa and the later Mehlevi Dervish lodge and dancing-hall built around this. A small site museum has been installed under the latter space. The British team renovating the Gayer-Anderson Museum has completed the restoration of the roof terrace at the museum with its

remarkable collection of *mashrabiya* (wood screens), as well as the *sabil*, one of the courtyards, and associated display spaces.

Projects at two major commercial structures dating from the Ottoman period, the Wikalat al-Bazaraa in Gamaliya and the Street of the Tentmakers (the last covered street market in Cairo), have also recently been completed. Such work raises the further question of how non-religious structures can be appropriately and comprehensively reintegrated into the life of the city so that they do not suffer from the redundancy that afflicts so many restored structures.

Major urban regeneration projects are also being implemented throughout Cairo. A road tunnel has been built which connects Ezbekiya with the Salah Salem highway that skirts the eastern edge of the city. This will permit the creation of a major pedestrian square in the spiritual heart of Cairo between the mosques of al-Azhar and al-Hussein, although what this space will look like and which buildings should be demolished to achieve the grand plan is still unclear. Ancillary to the creation of this road tunnel is the widening of a parallel relief artery running immediately to the north of the Fatimid city. This has already resulted in the destruction of a part of the Bab al-Nasr cemetery, and it is expected that further demolitions will follow before the new route is established. Such a project demonstrates the extreme difficulty of reconciling infrastructure development with historic preservation in cities as densely populated as Cairo. Attention is also directed to the main artery of the medieval city itself: al-Muizz Street. Pedestrianizing this street and upgrading the façades that line it may now be closer to implementation, but this may result in the removal of the people and activities that give life and character to this area, and the ultimate "Disneyfication" of the historic city. Other major undertakings are the creation of public parks beyond the Ayyubid wall on the eastern edge of the city, and along the line of the aqueduct that runs from the Nile to the Citadel. This latter project involves the demolition of all houses within a 300-meter zone along the over two-kilometer stretch of the aqueduct: perhaps not the most sensitive of approaches. As public parks have often been closed to the public, just who will be allowed to use these facilities when they are completed is a question that remains unanswered. The project of the Aga Khan Trust for Culture along the Ayyubid Wall is making a great effort to provide a model for community development in the Darb al-Ahmar area on the inside of the wall and to forge links between that community and the park. Until many more similar projects come to fruition, whereby restored monuments can be reintegrated within an ever-enlarging urban and social context, it is difficult to remain optimistic about the future of Cairo's past. *NW*

Archaeology
Discovery gives way to preservation

Although travelers, antiquaries, and tomb robbers have been digging in Egypt for centuries, scientific excavation only began in the late nineteenth century with the work of W. M. F. Petrie and his associates. Petrie's controlled archaeological surveys and excavations at the Giza pyramids, Abydos, Hawara, and other sites yielded treasures like the Fayyoum mummy portraits, and they set a precedent for later scientific archaeology in Egypt. Over the last century, the search for museum pieces or collectors' items has been largely replaced by efforts to answer questions about the history, culture, and traditions of the ancient Egyptians. Now, in addition to the work being carried out by Egypt's Supreme Council of Antiquities (SCA), there are over 150 foreign missions working in Egypt.

The Nile Valley is, as usual, yielding more information about ancient Egypt. Work at Abydos has pushed back the date for the origins of writing to 3200 BCE, making Egypt, rather than Mesopotamia, the birthplace of writing, while work at Adaima and Hierakonpolis has shed new light on the history of mummification. The locations of Early Dynastic and Old Kingdom cities at Elephantine with their temples and palaces have been discovered, as has a lost tomb of the Seventeenth Dynasty ruler, Nebkheperre Inyotef, at Thebes.

Egypt's deserts and oases are also proving to be fertile ground for archaeological inquiry. Kuper's pioneering work in the Western Desert has shown that from the Old Kingdom onward (c. 2700 BCE) the ancient Egyptians used remote desert routes for commerce and conquest. In the Nabta Playa and the desert between Kharga and Dakhla oases, the remains of prehistoric Egyptian settlements have been identified. These include sacred stone emplacements, campsites, and industrial areas that produced weapons and beads. Archaeologists are also addressing more questions about the nitty-gritty of daily life in ancient Egypt, such as how the immense numbers of people who worked on the pyramids were housed and fed. More experts are coming to study botanical and zoological remains in an effort to better understand the diet and agricultural practices of the ancient inhabitants of the Nile valley.

Nautical archaeology continues along the Mediterranean and Red Sea coasts, with spectacular finds from the Ptolemaic period being made in Alexandria's harbors. Nearby, shipwrecks and portions of ancient Alexandria are being located and mapped, and a survey is scheduled to start in 2002 that will plot wrecks and submerged town sites along the entire Mediterranean  coast. On the Red Sea coast, archaeologists have documented shipwrecks from the Greco-Roman and Islamic periods, and diving is proceeding near Quseir in the hopes of locating evidence from the ancient port.

In contrast to the Nile Valley, the Delta has long been ignored aside from a handful of projects, such as those in Tell al-Dabaa, Qantir, Tell Ibrahim Awad, Sais, and Tell Balamun. This is due to the population density, extensive agricultural exploitation of land, damp weather, and the high water table, which requires costly pumping systems for excavations. Frequently land registered as an antiquities site is built upon or cultivated, cutting off access to the antiquities below. As a result, the history of the northern part of the country is largely unknown, and scholars have an imprecise idea of how the two portions of the country functioned together over time. However, the SCA has recently issued a plea to archaeologists to work in this area, and several missions are now responding to the request.

The same reasons that make it hard to work in the Delta are also significant in other areas of Egypt. Illegally expanding agricultural systems in Upper Egypt have caused excavators to shift their focus to these areas, both to reclaim them as antiquities sites and to establish what is buried under the soil before it is lost forever. Two prime examples of this kind of rescue archaeology are taking place in the Sinai and Western Deserts in advance of the Salam Canal and the Toshka project. Road building and widening in Alexandria, Thebes, Luxor, and other cities also requires rescue archaeology. The installation of sewage systems in populated areas—such Nazlet al-Saman, where the work revealed portions of Khufu's Valley Temple at the foot of the Giza pyramids—also provides rare opportunities for archaeologists to quickly examine what is otherwise inaccessible. The GIS map of Egypt, a project funded by the Finnish government, plans to eventually locate all archaeological sites in the country so that issues of building or planting over antiquities land can

be resolved (*see box*). This will also make it easy to identify trouble spots where rescue archaeology is urgently needed.

Today, archaeologists not only have to excavate and publish their results, but they must conserve the sites in some way. Object conservation is relatively straightforward, but site conservation is complicated and expensive. In tombs the architecture must be stabilized, plaster reattached to walls, and paintings cleaned and stabilized as well. In some instances, as with the Czech mission at Abu Sir, new roofs must be provided for excavated tombs to protect them from the elements and to act as a safeguard against antiquities thieves.

Temples are restored sometimes using anastylosis, a method that re-stacks fallen blocks in their original form, occasionally adding blocks when the originals are too destroyed or fragile. This sort of work is being carried out at the Step Pyramid complex at Saqqara. The French have almost completed the conservation and reconstruction of Hatshepsut's Red Granite Chapel at Karnak, while Chicago House is working on restoring and re-erecting portions of the Eighteenth Dynasty temples at Medinet Habu. Some of the finer and more delicate objects (or carved blocks) found during excavations are put into a site museum. The best example of this is the Swiss Institute's work, carried out by Dr. H. Jaritz, at the temple of Merenptah in Thebes. At Tell al-Amarna a column of the Small Aten Temple has been reconstructed so that visitors get a feel for the vertical space, while the plan is marked out so that the horizontal areas are also clearly visible.

Mudbrick poses a special problem for conservation, and in some instances it is covered over with sand to protect it or capped with new mudbrick, separated from the old by a layer of potsherds. Much time, money, and effort are going into preserving the large-scale mudbrick monument of Shunet al-Zebib at Abydos, in the hope that it will provide a prototype for the conservation of

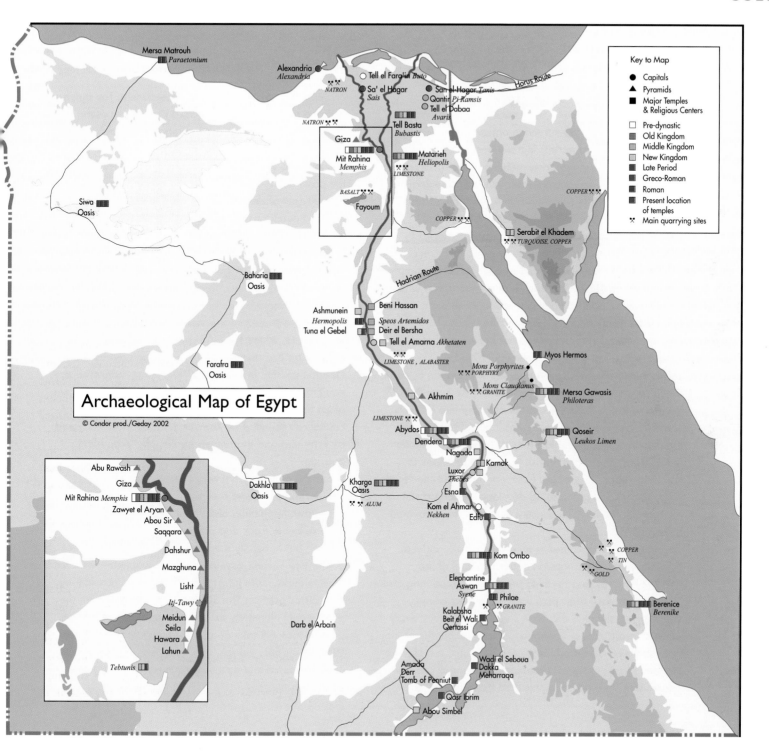

Archaeological Map of Egypt

© Condor prod./Geday 2002

Key to Map
- ● Capitals
- ▲ Pyramids
- ■ Major Temples & Religious Centers
- □ Pre-dynastic
- Old Kingdom
- Middle Kingdom
- New Kingdom
- Late Period
- Greco-Roman
- Roman
- Present location of temples
- ✕✕ Main quarrying sites

Mersa Matrouh
Paraetonium

Alexandria
Alexandria

Tell el Faraûn *Buto*

San el-Hagar *Tanis*
Qantir *Pi-Ramsis*
Tell el Dabaa
Avaris

Sa' el Hagar
Sais

Tell Basta
Bubastis

NATRON

NATRON

Giza ▲

Mit Rahina
Memphis

Matarieh
Heliopolis

LIMESTONE

BASALT

Fayoum

Siwa
Oasis

COPPER

COPPER

Serabit el Khadem
TURQUOISE, COPPER

Baharia
Oasis

Hadrian Route

Horus Route

Ashmunein
Hermopolis
Tuna el Gebel

Beni Hassan
Speos Artemidos
Deir el Bersha
Tell el Amarna *Akhetaten*

LIMESTONE , ALABASTER

Myos Hermos

Mons Porphyrites
PORPHYRY

Farafra
Oasis

Mons Claudianus
GRANITE

Akhmim ▲

LIMESTONE

Mersa Gawasis
Philoteras

Abydos
Dendera
Nagada
Karnak

Qoseir
Leukos Limen

Dakhla
Oasis

Kharga
Oasis

ALUM

Luxor
Thebes

Esna

Kom el Ahmar
Nekhen

Edfu

Darb el Arbain

COPPER
TIN
GOLD

Kom Ombo

Elephantine
Aswan
Syene

Philae

GRANITE

Berenice
Berenike

Kalabsha
Beit el Wali
Qertassi

Wadi el Seboua
Dakka
Meharraqa

Amada
Derr
Tomb of Penniut

Qasr Ibrim

Abou Simbel

Inset map

Abu Rawash ▲
Giza ▲
Mit Rahina *Memphis* ●
Zawyet el Aryan ▲
Abou Sir ▲
Saqqara ▲
Dahshur ▲
Mazghuna ▲
Lisht ▲
Itj-Tawy ●
Meidun ▲
Seila ▲
Hawara ▲
Lahun ▲
Tebtunis

Mapping the Past

Though it is difficult to quantify Egypt's vast historical heritage—by some counts, the country contains about one-third of the world's surviving antiquities—what is certain is that the country is literally packed with pieces of the past. Preserving it, documenting it, and analyzing all, though, is a monumental task. While archaeologists and conservationists complain about everything from a lack of sufficient funding to the mismanagement of antiquities sites, one of the major, unsung obstacles to preservation is that a comprehensive map of Egypt's antiquities sites, both registered and unregistered, simply does not exist. The lack of such a map means that when a government authority builds a road, hands out a permit to expand farmland, or implements an urban development scheme, it does so not knowing what it may be destroying just a meter under the ground.

This is where the Egyptian Antiquities Information System (EAIS) comes in. Funded by a grant from the Finnish government, the Supreme Council of Antiquities (SCA) is currently laying the basis for what it hopes will become the definitive archaeological map of Egypt. Set in motion in late 2000, the project chose three pilot locations to begin the mapping process: Northern Sinai and the North Coast, both undergoing rapid development, and a site in Sharqiya in the Delta, a densely populated area covered by farmland.

The mapping process itself is an arduous task—indeed, "map-making" is perhaps an understatement of the wealth of information the EAIS project is consolidating and creating. For each of its pilot sites, the project team is composing a detailed database containing virtually every scrap of geographical information known about the area, including a physical and historical description, a review of the land's legal status, a chronological record of previous excavations, and demographic data that will help to evaluate the site in terms of risk assessment. The database is linked to the actual map, which draws on existing archaeological and agricultural maps, cadastral surveys, satellite imagery, and aerial photos. Thus far, the project has involved little actual surveying; the real work lies in the painstaking comparison of the existing sources—some woefully out of date—that are used to delineate the precise boundaries of archaeological sites, many of which have already been covered by expanding villages. Once this information is compiled and digitized, the result is a many-layered grid that allows the user to see various archaeological sites in different formats and scales, including elaborately detailed views on a scale of 1/500. Much of the project's focus has thus far been in Sharqiya, near Qantir, where the EIAS group has benefited from the input of an archaeological survey carried out by the German mission in the mid-1990s. Using magnetometry equipment, German archaeologists mapped the remains of an ancient settlement thought to be Pi-Ramses, the capital city founded by Ramses II, today mostly covered by farmland and threatened by illegally expanding housing.

While the map may not help to save sites already encroached upon and built over, it can prevent the same thing from happening elsewhere. Not only will the SCA be able better track and preserve the sites under its control, but hopefully it will provide other government authorities—urban development, for example—with the keys to make more informed choices when considering projects or permits. The SCA plans to continue with the project until ultimately the entire country is mapped, a process that will take an extraordinary amount of time. When it is done, though, it is likely that Egypt will have "discovered" a few dozen more important antiquities' sites. *MM*

other mudbrick monuments.

The changing focus of archaeology from exploration and object discovery to rescue work and conservation has entailed a shift towards increasingly sophisticated archaeological tools. Computers are used for recording all sorts of finds, from bones and seeds to sculpted blocks, while elaborate computer programs are used to draw architectural plans. Archaeologists also use high quality scanning to make three-dimensional models of tombs in the hope that the precise replica that results from the process will be open to the public, while the fragile tomb will remain closed and thus preserved. Resistivity and magnetometry survey equipment can detect potentially useful areas for excavation without ever turning a stone. Satellite imaging and Global Positioning Systems (GPS) are used on surveys to locate and mark out-of-the-way sites. GPS is also used in conjunction with sonar scanning survey in nautical archaeology. The sonar scans the seabed, anomalies are marked by a GPS point, and divers are sent down to investigate the anomaly.

Next page: part of the EIAS mapping project. The colored dots represent possible archaeological sites

Despite the best efforts of the Egyptian government to wipe it out, illegal antiquities trading still hinders archaeological efforts, although it is less common than it was sixty years ago. Thieves steal objects from store-rooms or cut out reliefs and painted panels from tombs and temples to sell them to collectors abroad. The loss of the item itself is compounded by the damage done to the rest of the wall. It is not only remote sites that are prey to antiquities thieves: even well-guarded and central

Recently Unearthed

1. The Ramses-era tomb of Nemtymes at Saqqara, containing an unusual large rock-cut statue of a Hathor cow with the king standing under its muzzle. (Discovery by A. Zivie and the French Archaeological Mission of the Bubasteion)

2. The Sixth Dynasty tomb of a doctor, Kar, at Saqqara containing over 30 medical tools used in c. 2150 BCE. (Discovery by Zahi Hawass and SCA workers)

3. The tomb of Merire in the Saqqara necropolis, whose name in the tomb also appears as Merneith. He might be the same Merire who has a tomb at Tell al-Amarna. The find sheds new light on the political and religious upheavals of the Amarna period. (Discovery by a team from the Netherlands, headed by M. Raven, R. van Walsem, and G. T. Martin)

4. Tombs at Hierakonpolis, north of Edfu, revealed bodies that had false hair—evidence of the earliest wigs found in Egypt, and possibly the world (c. 3200-3100 BCE)—and parts of one of the world's earliest stone sculptures. A rare Pan Grave cemetery was also found, containing evidence of the originally nomadic Nubian people that functioned as police in ancient Egypt. (Discovery by R. Friedman and B. Adams)

5. The remains of a large bakery dating to the First Intermediate Period (c. 2000 BCE) found on Elephantine Island. The bakery was constructed using ten 3.2-meter wooden columns, eight of which are still preserved. These columns are one of, if not the earliest examples of octagonal wooden columns in the world. (Discovery by D. Raue of the German-Swiss Mission) *SI*

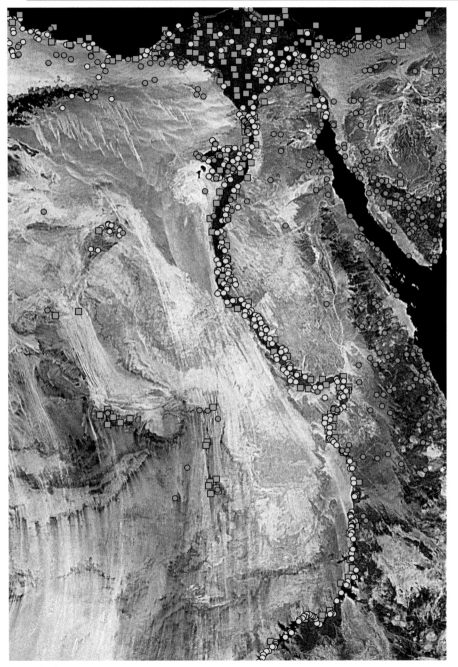

places such as the Valley of the Kings suffer from such vandalism, and on more than one occasion, antiquities guards have been shot while trying to defend a site from looting. In some instances, archaeologists have turned their attention to especially vulnerable sites to record them before they are destroyed by theft and vandalism. Over the last two years, however, a number of important objects stolen and transferred out of the country have been repatriated, including a large sculpted head of Amenhotep III and the base of Akhnaten's sarcophagus, which had long resided in the Munich Museum of Egyptian Art. Also this year, a respected US art dealer was convicted of knowingly trafficking in stolen artifacts and sentenced to 33 months in prison. Egyptian officials hope that high-profile cases like this one will help stem the international demand for stolen antiquities.

Although archaeological expeditions continue to yield new discoveries, both large and small, there are still mysteries to unearth and questions to answer. The location of the lost army of Cambyses in the desert sands (currently being searched for by an Egyptian team), the evolution of the pyramids, the organization of Egypt's bureaucracy, the origins of writing, the missing royal tombs in the Theban hills and Alexander the Great's tomb—these and other archaeological puzzles continue to inspire archaeologists to new research and excavation and undoubtedly will do so for years to come. *SI*

VILLA OF THE BIRDS

KOM EL DIKKA, ALEXANDRIA

Society

Roll Call

The Shape of the State

A VISITOR COMING TO EGYPT AFTER, SAY, A 15-YEAR HIATUS COULD BE FORGIVEN FOR THINKING THAT HIS PLANE HAD TOUCHED down in the wrong place. Economic liberalization and the explosion of a consumer culture, the invasion of technologies from the mobile phone to the internet, and massive improvements in basic infrastructure have transformed both the landscape and the social fabric. An evaluation of just how deep these changes are depends, of course, on how far under the surface you dig. Over the past few decades, no matter what kind of social or political forces held sway, the list of Egypt's mega-trends has read largely the same: an exploding population, a creaking educational system, a vast rural/urban infrastructure disparity and a constant and inevitable drift of the rural population into increasingly unlivable cities. Though social transformations are definitely underfoot, many of the disparities Egypt has been working to eradicate—between urban and rural populations, men and women, young and old—remain entrenched, while some, like the gap between rich and poor, seem to be growing.

Mark down January 2001 as the month when Egypt's population officially topped 66 million, according to government figures. That number is expected to reach 100 million by 2025. Concerted governmental efforts to stem the population tide through greater awareness and availability of birth control have borne some fruit, and the nationwide birth rate has declined. But the figures are badly skewed along class lines. The educated urban middle-and-upper classes have reacted to government pleas for population control. But it is a significantly harder sell among the urban and rural poor, where children represent a vital source of family income and a support mechanism for the parents in their old age. Many of these children still leave school early, thereby helping to perpetuate the cycle of poverty. Despite new laws prohibiting the employment of children under 14 and strictly regulating work conditions for children between 14 and 18, the practice remains widespread and the laws are largely unenforced. It is estimated that about 12% of children between the ages of 6-14 work, or about 1.5 million kids.

A brief breakdown of the population numbers reveals a fairly even male/female ratio: 51.2/48.8, and a serious balloon effect on the lower end of the age scale. Efforts focused on making life better for the female half have seen some progress. In tangible terms, recent studies have shown that the average marriage age is up, and the gender gap in education is slowly but surely closing. Women are also entering the workforce earlier and in greater numbers than they used to. But there are indications that the negative impact of structural adjustment has been felt most keenly among female workers, who are more likely to be laid off and less likely to make the transition from public- to private-sector jobs.

As for Egypt's younger generation, their future is still in the making. Almost a quarter of the Egyptian population is aged ten or under, a factor that could help fuel an economic resurgence—if only the education system and the labor market were prepared to handle the influx. The government is building schools at a frantic pace, and the number of children starting school has leveled off. Yet the nation's overburdened schools will still have to struggle to prepare this burgeoning new generation for a modern job market, and it is unclear just how healthy a job market will be waiting for them.

The International Labor Organization estimates that Egypt's unemployment rate is about 17%. That number does not take into account the ranks of the underemployed—those working low-paying menial jobs that are a far cry from their personal aspirations and the level of expertise they are trained for. To add to the difficulties, the public sector remains Egypt's single largest employer providing 42% of the nation's job opportunities according to one university study, and it is due to shrink steadily as the government continues its

Family Ties

Throughout the Arab world, long-standing marriage patterns are undergoing change in a process widespread enough to qualify as what sociologists call a "nuptiality transition." Marriage is occurring at later ages and the number of never-married women is growing.

In Egypt, rising unemployment and tighter economic conditions have also put a cramp in the marriage plans of many young adults, who simply cannot afford to get hitched. According to the latest figures from CAPMAS, only 513,000 marriages were registered in 2001, down from 579,000 the year before. At a rate of 7.9 marriages per 1,000 inhabitants, the number is the lowest since 1995. In contrast, divorce rates have remained steady, hovering between 1.1-1.2 since the late 1980s, despite the introduction of a new Personal Status Law in 2000 that makes it easier for women to get a divorce. AH & Egypt Almanac

privatization and structural economic reform efforts. The government's own estimates place the number of surplus public-sector workers at 185,000—some 18% of the total public sector workforce. A Ministry of Manpower spokesman said that independent audits of government companies by potential private investors have placed the portion of workers who are surplus to requirements at closer to 35%.

If reforms work the way their architects hope they will, the private sector will step in to pick up the slack, but the early indications do not look good. Sociologist Nader Fergany has estimated that of the 1.3 million jobs created between 1990 and 1995, the government provided about 60% of them, while the informal private sector absorbed the rest; meanwhile, the formal private

sector actually lost about 500,000 jobs.

Even as the gradual shift to a liberalized economy is promising large-scale unemployment and under-employment, the government's social safety net—represented in things like food subsidies, social insurance, and free health care—is showing a few holes. The end of the 20th century may have been a heady time for Egypt's richest, but things have not been quite so simple for the other 60 million Egyptians. A beleaguered white-collar middle class has struggled to hold on amid rising costs of living—officially up 16 fold since 1975—while the poorest Egyptians are falling farther and farther.

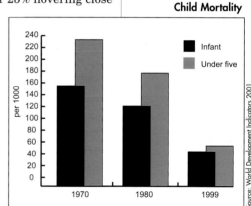

About 25% of Egyptians are estimated to be living below the poverty line, with another 25% hovering close by. According to the UNDP, the poorest 20% of Egyptians share 9.8% of the income, and the poorest 40% have 23% of the income. Fully 39% goes to the richest 20% of the country. That dynamic seems unlikely to abate any time soon. Numerous indices have shown an increase in both rural and urban poverty since structural reform began. One study by Cairo University economics professor Heba Nassar concluded that "the former lower middle expenditure category moved to a status of long-term or chronic poverty."

Though sociologists say that urban poverty is increasing at faster rates than rural poverty, a quick look at almost any economic, social, or health indicator reveals that rural areas, particularly in Upper Egypt, are still getting

Consumer Society

According to the latest CAPMAS study of Egyptian consumption patterns, Egypt's standard of living is on the rise, with families in both urban and rural areas spending more money on luxury items and less on basic necessities like food and drink. All told, Egyptian families spend about LE127.3 billion every year, broken down as follows (in LE billion):

Food and drink	56.1
Housing	18.7
Clothing	12.8
Transportation	7.2
Education	6
Private lessons	2.1
Sports, entertainment, and cultural activities	5.6
Health	5.3
Cigarettes	4
Furniture and household items	3.1
Cafes and hotels	2.6
Other	3.8

Source: CAPMAS, 2001

The 90s Generation

With increasing globalization, the rise of consumerism, and the communications revolution, Egypt's younger generation is being introduced to a brave new world. But how this is affecting their lives and attitudes is difficult to quantify. Despite the prevalence of "youth" in Egypt's public discourse, there is precious little talk about what Egyptian young people themselves want, what they think, and what they aspire to.

Though it is difficult to pin down a population of about 13 million teenagers, in 1997 the Population Council set out to do just that, initiating a nationwide survey of more than 9,000 adolescents between the ages of 10 and 19. The picture that emerges is as varied as one might expect given the range of ages, classes, and geographic locations surveyed. Nevertheless, the results of the survey do provide a rarely glimpsed look into the lives of the younger generation as they experience it. Like those anywhere, the life of Egyptian adolescents revolves largely around school, with work coming in a close second. Socialization patterns have undoubtedly been affected by increased urbanization, a loosening of social mores, and greater exposure to the rest of the world, but even so, Egyptian teens spend the greatest amount of time with their family and the familiar social network, and while some may be cruising the mall or bowling in their off hours, the vast majority are more likely to be watching TV or visiting friends or relatives. Ditto for consumer lifestyles. Today's youth may be bombarded from an early age by more consumer items than their parents ever dreamed of, but those who work—about a third of all adolescents—largely do so to help support their families, not to earn spending money for themselves.

The 90s generation is undoubtedly better educated than their parents or grandparents generation, but as the survey points out, education has affected girls' and boys' attitudes differently. The more girls move up the educational ladder, for example, the more likely they are to envision a future married life that is more egalitarian in terms of rights and duties. Not so for boys, who tend to cling to more traditional male-female roles. Perhaps the most striking aspect of the survey, however, is that the well-worn themes of teen rebellion and psychic angst are virtually absent from the picture. Considering the turmoil usually associated with these formative years, Egyptian adolescents come across as a surprisingly well-adjusted bunch: optimistic, with a positive view to life, family, and the future. The following is a sample of the survey results:

School

Adolescents enrolled in school: 69%
Urban enrollment: 81%
Enrollment in rural Upper Egypt: 61%
Those in school who like it: 47%
Group that likes school the most: rural students
Students who say they can express their view in class: 55%
Number one benefit of education cited by teens: increased social status
Least important reason for education: make more money
Number one reason for dropping out of school: bad grades
Girls in school who want to go to university: 70%
Fathers who want their girls to go to university: 71%

Work

Adolescents who work: 32%
Those who work 6+ hours/day: 42%
Working teens under the legal working age: 52%
Working teens who give all or part of their income to their family: 80%
Paid workers content with their jobs: two-thirds
Number one reason for dissatisfaction: big effort required
Average monthly earnings ages 10-19: LE122
Average monthly education costs per teen: LE28.89

Health and the Self

Adolescents with some degree of anemia: 47%
Girls who say they smoke: 0.3%
Boys aged 10-19 who smoke: 11%
Boys aged 16-19 who smoke: 28%
Boys' number one reason for starting: to imitate friends
Boys who say they sometimes differ from friends: 75%
Egyptian teens with a negative body image: 12%

Friends and Family

Teens who express opinions to their family: 75%
Those that say family respects their opinion: 80%
Talk to family about family problems: 75%
Talk to family about problems with friends: 53%

Free Time

Boys who play sports: 57%
Girls who do: 5%
Teens who watch TV in their spare time: 97%
Least favorite type of program: educational
Read a book in spare time: 15%
Ages 15-19 who read books in their spare time: 13%
Engage in religious activity: 49%
Least common leisure activity among adolescents: anything that costs money
Boys allowed to go out with friends: 67%
Girls allowed to go out with friends: 37%

The Birds and the Bees

Boys who say father talked to them about puberty: 7%
Fathers who said they did: 42%
Girls who do chores around the house: 80%
Boys who do: 11%
Boys ages 16-19 who said women should do the cleaning, washing, and cooking: 90%+
Girls ages 16-19 who said the same thing: 90%+
Number one quality sought in a mate by both boys and girls aged 16-19: politeness
Number two quality sought by girls in future husbands: good nature
Number two quality sought by boys in future wives: religiosity
Married adolescents: 12%
Never-married circumcised girls (ages 13-19): 86%
Circumcised girls who believe it's necessary: 42%
Boys ages 16-19 who say the husband should decide if his wife works: 63%
Girls ages 16-19 who say it should be shared decision: 58%
Girls ages 16-19 who say a wife needs her husband's permission for everything: 89%
Boys ages 16-19 who said the same thing: 91%
Boys ages 16-19 who say its okay for a woman to seek a divorce if her husband beats her: 77%
Girls ages 16-19 who said the same thing: 68%

The Future

Most popular role model: "I don't know"
Number two role model: father or male relative
Teens very satisfied with their life: 71%
Teens dissatisfied with their life: 2%
Well-off adolescents who see a brighter future: 87%
Poor adolescents who see a brighter future: 77%

Source: Population Council, *Transitions to Adulthood*, 1999

the short end of the stick. At last count, rural Upper Egypt had 25% of the total population, but 37% of the nation's poor. The incidence of what the UNDP calls "capability poverty"—a measure incorporating both health and educational indicators—is also twice as high in rural Upper Egypt than in urban areas. Infant mortality in Assyout, for example, is double the rate in Cairo.

Despite ongoing government efforts to spread Egypt's population over as wide an area as possible, the major cities continue to grow more and more densely packed. The most recent census figures show that Cairo governorate alone is home to 11.3% of the Egyptian population. The Greater Cairo sphere (consisting of Cairo, Giza and Qalyoubiya governorates) represents just under one-quarter of the population. The most recent government figures indicate that the rural-to-urban migration trend has decreased by a discernible margin in recent years, but further reduction is badly needed, government spokesmen say, and efforts to achieve this are in full swing. Large-scale development and land reclamation projects such as Toshka and North Sinai are necessary for demographic reasons as much as economic or agricultural ones.

Halfway through the 1990s it seemed that the

Population Growth

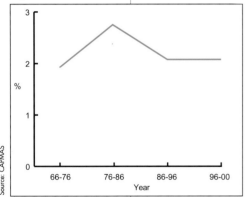

Growth has slowed markedly, but the population is still expected to hit 100 million by 2025

burgeoning Cairo desert development trend would finally begin siphoning people out of the central city and into the sprawling new suburbs. But recent economic woes have stalled the trend. As much of the investment was dumped in high-end housing, large-scale suburbanization remains a distant prospect.

One factor that may have helped slow the rural-to-urban migration flow is a gradual realization on the rural end that the streets of Cairo are not exactly paved with gold. With the cost of living and unemployment on the rise in Cairo, and the diffusion of transport and consumer products throughout the rest of the country, the costs of uprooting increasingly outweigh the benefits.

International assessments of Egypt's social and development trends have been mixed. The most recent Human Development Index report by the United Nations Development Program ranked Egypt at 105 out of 162 countries—up several notches from the last report. But the index, which measures a country's social progress in terms of life expectancy, income, educational enrollment, and adult literacy, still ranked Egypt low among its regional peers such as Libya (59), Lebanon (65), Jordan (88), Syria (97), and Algeria (100). The fact that Egypt ranked well-behind far weaker economies indicates, in the UNDP's view, a failure to effectively distribute the country's resources to social services in a meaningful way. *AK*

Stretching the Pound

The average annual income for an Egyptian family is LE12,000, or LE2,592 per person. About 30% of families make more than this every year, while 50% make between LE6,000-12,000, and 20% make less than LE6,000. The remaining 3% of families live on less than LE3,000 every year. On average, Egyptians save about 17% of their income every year.

Source: CAPMAS, 2001

Help Wanted

Chronic unemployment becomes a reality

While Prime Minister Atef Ebeid spent much of last year trying to convince the public that only about 1.5 million Egyptians were unemployed, a more accurate indicator of the state of unemployment in Egypt came in July 2001 when the Minister of Administrative Development, Zaki Abu Amer, issued a decree setting age requirements on the 170,000 public-sector jobs that had just come up for grabs. The announcement sparked protests in several governorates, some of which were only dispersed with tear gas. The reaction from generations of unemployed graduates—many of whom had already been waiting for a government appointment for ten years—was such that it forced Ebeid to rescind the decree only two days later.

The popular reaction was not really surprising—a February 2001 poll carried out by a researcher at the Ahram Center for Political and Strategic Studies found

The Young Working Life

A study of youth employment carried out by the Population Council found that employed young men and women (aged 15-24) work overwhelmingly in the private sector, which hosts 80% of young wage workers. Tracking changes in employment patterns from 1988 to 1998, the study found that agricultural employment for both men and women was way down, while work in construction, services, and transport showed the largest increases. Over the same ten-year period, working conditions declined across the board, with both men and women working longer hours—on average 50 hours a week—fewer enjoying benefits like social security coverage, and less having the security of permanent jobs and work contracts. The average monthly income of a private-sector female worker was LE115 per month.

that unemployment is overall Egyptians' number one concern, ahead of foreign policy, the general economy, and way ahead of issues like domestic politics and political reform.

While unemployment figures are notoriously spotty, most independent organizations put it at least at twice the official rate of 8%. What this number does not say is that unemployment in Egypt is largely a problem for youth. Young people between the ages of 15-24 constitute the largest segment of the unemployed, accounting for more than 60%. Although they tend to be more educated than their predecessors, this has not translated into more job opportunities or better wages. Unemployment rose throughout the last decade, even as wages declined. Indeed, CAPMAS figures show that by the mid-1990s real wages had dropped to levels lower than those in the early 1980s over almost all sectors of the economy.

As the government tries to move away from its Nasserist legacy of providing a job to every university and trade-school graduate, young women have been hit the hardest. A recent Population Council study found that unemployment levels among women aged 15-24 were an astounding 59% in 1998. It also showed that while both young men and women found some emerging opportunities in the private sector over the last decade—notably transportation for men and manufacturing for women—it has not been enough to compensate for steeper declines in agricultural and public-sector employment. With at least 500,000 new workers

Where Youth Work

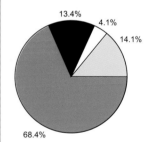

13.4%
4.1%
14.1%
68.4%

■ Private non-agricultural work
■ Private agricultural work
□ State-owned enterprises
  Government

Source: Population Council

entering the labor market every year, the chances of finding a job that will support a family—or even allow young people to marry—are getting slimmer as Egypt moves into the 21st century.

Looking for answers to the country's unemployment problem, some researchers lay the blame on structural adjustment, arguing that while public-sector companies were busy downsizing through the 1990s, new investments were focused in capital-intensive rather than labor-intensive enterprises. Thus, economic growth did not correspond to greater job opportunities. Others, like labor expert Samir Radwan, argue that it makes more sense to look at unemployment as a problem that has haunted modern Egypt for decades, but remained largely disguised until the last ten years. A more limited labor market and massive infrastructure investments meant that the state was able to provide most of the jobs throughout the 1960s, while in the 1970s and 1980s emigration to the oil-rich Gulf countries took care of excess labor. It is only in the 1990s that the problem of chronic unemployment has been unmasked. All sides of the debate, however, agree that the main obstacle to greater employment is that the skills taught in schools are increasingly at odds with the needs of the labor market. Thus, Egypt finds itself in the paradoxical position of still needing labor in certain technical fields, even as vocational schools are graduating students in record numbers.

So what is the state supposed to do? Despite some downsizing of public enterprises, it remains the largest non-agricultural employer, providing jobs for close to five million people. This in itself is disguised employment, a perpetuation of what is essentially a social welfare system, rather than a productive enterprise. But real job creation is expensive—about LE100,000 a job is an average estimate. In terms of social costs, it is easier in the short term for the state to keep expanding its employment rolls, even on a limited basis, rather than face public wrath. *MM*

The Great Migration
The impact of labor migration is still felt

As of January 1, 2001, there were officially 1.9 million Egyptians working abroad, most in Arab petroleum countries, and roughly half in Saudi Arabia. That's down from 2.1 million in 1996, and way down from the peak in the early 1980s when more than three million Egyptians left the country to work. All told, from about 1975 to 1985, it is estimated that about 10-15% of Egypt's labor force emigrated. Though the great migration is tapering off as the market abroad dries up, the impact of so many millions of souls—and dollars—crossing the border is still being felt in the economy and society at large.

Take the labor market, for example. Not only has the return of migrants had a direct impact on levels of unemployment, it has also contributed to a de-skilling of the labor force in certain key areas, like teaching. Many of the best qualified teachers left for work abroad at the same time that the number of students peaked after the establishment of new universities and schools all over the country. While the net return of migrants during the 1990s is likely to improve the situation in the future, the present cadre of teachers have themselves been taught by young, inexperienced teachers, and today's students are still suffering. A similar phenomenon occurred in the construction sector in the 1980s, when many skilled workers left for abroad just as the sector was experiencing a boom due to migrants' investments in housing.

The socioeconomic impact has been equally far-reaching. The dependence on remittances since the mid-1970s—within individual families as well as within the national economy—has made Egypt vulnerable to political and economic fluctuations in neighboring countries. But labor migration also stimulated an accumulation of private savings—just how much is a matter of some speculation. The flow of remittances promoted new consumption patterns in rural areas especially, where the economy had previously been subsistence oriented, and the import of mass-produced consumer goods escalated. The positive effects were felt in wider circles as well, as migrants' first-year savings were usually spent on gifts for the social network. Remittances thus created much new wealth, but at the same time it set in motion a new social dynamic, with the development of categories such as the "new" rich and the "new" poor. Non-migrant families got poorer as the cost of living rose.

Migrants' pattern of expenditure was influenced by their individual backgrounds and also by gradual changes in cultural status indicators. In the beginning, for example, the goal of most farmer migrants was to save for the purchase of land, though much money also went into the purchase of appliances and other durables. The subsequent strong demand for land gave rise to inflationary prices, and investment priorities gradually shifted into modern housing, spurring on a ten-year construction boom. Migrants from urban areas had more difficulties in finding areas for productive investments. Though privatization and the development of a stock market have increased the potential for investments in areas other than housing and consumption, unfortunately this opportunity did not mature until after savings from migration had already declined.

The effect of migration has not been limited to economic or social spheres, but has been felt more directly at the family level. In some villages, as many as two-thirds of families have participated in migration with the emigration of one or more male family members. Old patterns of authority within the family have been moderated, as both male migrants and their wives have absorbed new types of experience. Women have undertaken new burdens in the absence of their husbands, administering remittances, disciplining and bringing up children, supervising the renovation of the house or the building of a new one, and dealing with various government authorities. Generally speaking, the new roles have strengthened mutual respect among men and women, but they have rarely led to new divisions of labor within the family after the return of the migrant.

These days, however, the benefits of migration have been minimized, while many of the negative effects have become long-term. The surplus labor force once exported to oil-rich countries is expanding the rolls of the unemployed. Even as remittances decline, prices on agricultural land and new housing remain extremely high, as do marriage costs. New consumption patterns born in the days of plenty still exist, but it is getting increasingly difficult to finance them. *KB*

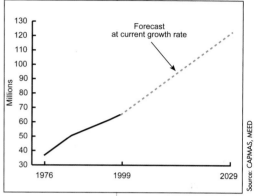

Population Forecast

Forecast at current growth rate

Millions

130
120
110
100
90
80
70
60
50
40
30

1976   1999   2029

Source: CAPMAS, MEED

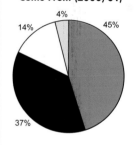

Where Remittances Come From (2000/01)

45%
4%
14%
37%

▮ Gulf States
▮ USA
☐ Europe
▮ Other

Source: Central Bank of Egypt

Of the estimated $2.8 billion that flowed into Egypt from abroad in 2001, almost half came from workers in the Gulf

Living
The state struggles to provide

Picture of Health

The architects of the long-term reform plans for Egypt's health system couldn't be blamed for throwing their hands up in frustration and wondering just where to start.

While the country faces far more high-profile difficulties in realms such as the economy and education, Egypt's health system continues to hold a daunting array of challenges and obstacles.

A partial list of the medical maladies:

A huge gap exists between public-sector health care and private hospitals—one that has fostered a growing public distrust of state-subsidized treatment. Public-sector hospitals are uniformly overcrowded, under-supplied and staffed by low-paid doctors who often save their energy for more profitable nighttime private clinic work. According to international audits, a full 60% of all Egyptian primary care visits now take place in private hospitals and clinics, indicating that only those who cannot afford anything else are willing to trust their healthcare to the state.

An equally large gap separates urban and rural health care options, with many doctors reluctant to leave large cities like Cairo and Alexandria to work in rural settings. As a result health figures for rural populations are often much worse than their urban brethren. While one in 12 Egyptian children die before the age of five, the ratio in rural Upper Egypt is one in seven.

Egypt's much maligned nursing corps is largely under-trained, disrespected, disgruntled, and regarded by the public as incompetent or corrupt. Nursing is not considered a respectable profession in Egypt; the media and cinema tend to portray nurses as either morally loose or as opportunistic sharks who extort money from patients in exchange for preferential treatment. The nurses complain that both doctors and patients treat them like an underclass. Any attempt to reform Egypt's health care system will be doomed to failure without a massive overhaul of the nurse's role in the scenario.

Blood-borne infectious diseases such as Hepatitis C continue to spread at levels that far exceed global standards. Up to 20% of the population has been infected by the Hep C virus, which is untreatable and often leads to chronic liver disease. A good portion of that number, it turns out, were infected during the massive campaign to wipe out bilharzia in the 1960s and 70s, when health workers embarked on mass innoculations in the countryside and failed to sterilize the needles used for injections. There is also an acknowledged hidden threat that Hep C today might be spread by doctors, nurses, and other health care workers infected with the disease.

The safety of Egypt's blood supply has been called into

Digesting Change

For years, the Egyptian diet has revolved largely around the ubiquitous loaf of *baladi* bread. According to CAPMAS, the average Egyptian consumes about 170.5 kg of wheat every year, and bread still provides the single largest source of caloric intake and protein. Throw in sugar, vegetable oil and *samna*, milk, and tea, and you've got the broad outlines of the Egyptian diet. According to a 1998 field study conducted by the national Nutrition Institute, about 50% of households around the country still consume these five staples every day.

But there are signs that changes are afoot. The shift to a more urban society, and from a centrally planned welfare state to a liberalized, consumer economy is slowly impacting what and how people eat. The Nutrition Institute study found that the number of meals eaten outside the home increased from 20% in 1981 to 46% in 1998. At the same time, the number of households baking their own bread declined from 56% to 18%. How Egyptian bodies are weathering these changes in eating patterns is still emerging, but the early indicators are not all positive.

On on hand, greater overall affluence and the proliferation of ready-made food options means that many Egyptians are eating more than they used to. Annual meat consumption, for example, has risen from 17 kg per capita to 21 kg over the last ten years. Sugar and oils are also more plentiful than they used to be; exercise, however, is not. As a result, a host of diet-related ailments like hypertension, cardiovascular disease, obesity, and diabetes are on the rise, especially among urban, better-off Egyptians. A Ministry of Health survey concluded that 20% of Cairenes in the high socioeconomic bracket suffer from diabetes; by 2025 it estimated that about 13.3% of the over-20 population—almost nine million people—will have the disease.

While affluence, and thus many ailments, are not evenly spread across all sectors of the population, the other end of the socioeconomic scale has its own, different set of nutritional problems. In the days before economic liberalization, Egypt consistently had one of the most well fed populations in the region in terms of caloric intake, largely due to extensive food subsidies, which accounted for 20% of state expenditures in 1981. By 1995, food subsidies only accounted for 5.5% of government expenditure, and there is evidence that the decrease is taking a nutritional toll. According to the Nutrition Institute, average per capita calorie consumption actually declined slightly from 1981 to 1998, while the World Bank has reported that the incidence of stunting among children—a malady directly related to inadequate nutrition and on the decline throughout the 1980s—increased in 1990s, despite an increase in overall wealth.

Not all diet-related health concerns are split along class lines, however. Iron deficiency still afflicts a large percentage of Egyptians of all ages and classes. The Population Council has found that a little less than half of all Egyptian adolescents have some degree of anemia. Nutritionists point the finger at the national institution of tea, which, when drunk with or shortly after meals, limits the ability of the body to absorb iron. *MM*

Doctors/1000 People

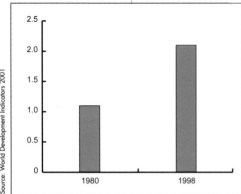

Source: World Development Indicators 2001

More doctors has not meant better public care

Beds/1000 People

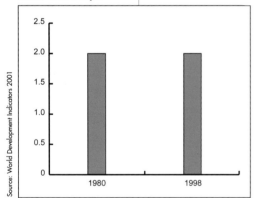

Source: World Development Indicators 2001

Hospital facilities have grown with the population

question several times, with private blood banks being blamed for depending on repeat "professional donors"—many of whom are IV drug users. The number of AIDS cases in Egypt is something of a mystery, and will likely remain so as long as there is no system for anonymous testing and no real treatment options for those who test positive. Egypt's AIDS rate is definitely far lower than that of sub-Saharan Africa, where whole generations have been cut down, but that is attributed more to Arab social conservatism than any kind of effective preventative, detection, or treatment procedures. Hoping to help fill the gap, the World Health Organization launched a new public-service campaign across the region late last year, while the Ministry of Health has maintained an AIDS hotline since 1996. Still, public awareness about the virus remains low.

Perhaps the greatest health challenge of all comes from Egypt's almost compulsively unhealthy population. Egyptians smoke a lot, eat a lot of fatty foods and do not exercise much—a Ministry of Health study concluded that Cairenes breathe some of the most polluted air on the planet. Illnesses tend to be handled by a visit to the pharmacist, who usually prescribes a semi-random handful of drugs. Patients mis-medicating or failing to complete antibiotic regimes has, according to researchers, already led to the development of several hard-to-kill super viral strains.

Strapped for resources in all fields, the state is financially ill-equipped to upgrade its services.

Throughout the 1990s, public spending on health averaged 1.8% of GDP on health expenditure—a low number even for many developing countries. Private spending came to 2% of GDP, meaning that more than half of the $48 per capita spent on health care counted as out-of-pocket expenses. The dream of universal health insurance, in place in principle since the 1960s, still has not come to fruition, and it is estimated that at least half of the population is uncovered.

The man charged with turning things around was, until recently, Ismail Sallam, Minister of Health and Population. Sallam came in for criticism from both health professionals, who pointed to a sometimes autocratic style, and the local press, who charged him with ignoring the needs of the poor. But Sallam did manage to get a sizeable chunk of foreign funding for a far-reaching reform package that included, among other things, efforts to set up a national health insurance system, establish professional quality control among doctors and nurses, and shift the focus of Egypt's health care from curative to preventative.

It is unclear if Sallam's successor, Mohammed Awad Tag al-Din, will continue along the same path. In any case, reform efforts are expected to take at least ten years before making a real difference, and the country's rapidly ticking population bomb makes speed a top priority. The national health infrastructure is already straining under the burden of more than 66 million citizens. Efforts to reduce the birthrate have been successful—population growth has slowed and family planning has increased dramatically. According to the latest Health and Demographic Survey, the rate of use of birth control among married women went from 24% in 1980 to 55% in 1997 to 56% in 2000. But the population is still expected to double by the year 2030.

Ironically, Egypt's economic reform efforts could, if successful, create an even bigger health reform challenge. For the last few years, population growth has, if anything, been artificially limited by economic hardship.

Young couples simply cannot afford to buy apartments, get married, and start having children. Once the economic picture brightens, all those delayed marriages could add up to another population boom—and with more than half the current population under age 20, there is already one on the horizon. *AK*

Problem Solving

Public education has gone private

At the beginning of the 1990s, educational specialists in Egypt could identify at least four flaws that crippled the educational system all the way from the primary level up to university: an insufficient numbers of schools, a curriculum that stressed rote learning over critical thinking, misallocated resources, and corruption. The state has made some progress over the past decade in tackling the first two issues; the last two, however, have so far shown themselves to be beyond the reach of reformers.

At the most basic level, progress has been made. Egypt's illiteracy rate fell between 1986 and 1999 from 55.5% to 45.4%. But the rate of population growth meant the actual number of illiterate Egyptians, in real terms, rose slightly. Moreover, the overall literacy rate hides certain gaps in the educational system, particularly those between men and women, rich and poor, and rural and urban residents. The poor still have literacy rates at about half that of the rich, and while literacy is on the rise in rural areas, it still lags behind urban governorates by about 30 percentage points. Recent research shows, however, that the gender gap is slowly closing, with female enrollment up over all levels of education. In urban areas, female enrollment in secondary school is slightly higher than that of males.

Bricks and mortar to build the future

Since the early 1990s, Minister of Education Hussein Kamel Baha al-Din has directed ministry resources towards the construction of new schools, particularly primary schools in poor districts. The number of primary schools rose to 15,566 in 1999 from 14,654 in 1993. In 2001, an extra 2,000 schools were slated to be built over the next two years. But

with a growing population and increasing enrollment rates, class size has remained about the same, falling overall from about 45 to 42 from 1993 to 1999. To relieve overcrowding and bring inadequate facilities up to par, the UNDP estimates that almost 20,000 new schools are still needed.

At the university level, the government has allowed the establishment of internationally accredited private universities. Their reputation is not good—they are viewed as places of last resort for rich kids who cannot get in anywhere else, and the state has attempted to close one down for not meeting standards—but they have been able to take some of the pressure off the state system. Indeed, the number of students enrolled in universities more than doubled to 1.2 million from 1992 to 1998.

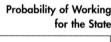

Probability of Working for the State

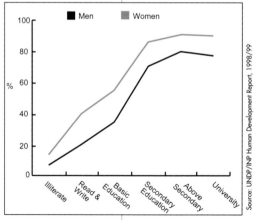

Source: UNDP/INP Human Development Report, 1998/99

The longer students stay in school, the more likely they are to end up working for the government

Illiteracy Rate (%)

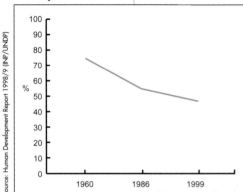

Overall literacy is up ...

Illiteracy Breakdown (%)

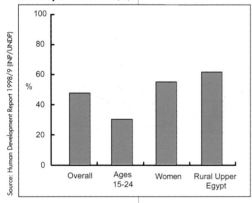

... but rates vary greatly among different segments of the population

The ministry has invested in up-to-date academic infrastructure as well, with increasing attention given to the need to bring schools into the computer age. By 1999, 11,500 state secondary schools had computers, and in 2001, the Ministry of Education unveiled the outline of a pilot "smart schools" project, aiming to introduce IT to classrooms in about 100 schools. The latter effort, however, is highly dependent on private-sector funding, and initially it will focus on private schools, thus benefiting upper-income students the most. In any case, getting students to use the equipment already in place—or allowing them, as the case may be—is another matter entirely. A Population Council study of 75 preparatory schools across Egypt found that although over half the schools have computers, only 18% of students actually used them.

Learning by rote

The school curriculum was the second area the ministry recognized as in dire need of reform. The Egyptian educational system, supposedly in order to combat favoritism, is largely focused on standardized, end-of-year tests, particularly the dreaded *thanawiya amma* secondary school exams that essentially determine a student's future career. Within the last few years, the ministry has introduced new textbooks intended to emphasize problem solving and critical thinking over mass memorization. But there is still an emphasis on quantity over quality. The number of Ministry of Education textbooks jumped from 59 to 106 between 1992 and 1998—and that is just at the primary level.

Moreover, new methods, where introduced, do not translate for students into success on the tests. Graders are ill-trained to handle imaginative test responses, and students would be ill-advised to do anything other than memorize the answers to questions they know will be on the test, even if those answers are themselves incorrect. Over the long haul, this system has tended to produce generations of graduates whose skills are severely mismatched to the needs of the modern labor market. Taught throughout all levels of schooling to play it safe, the system encourages students to seek the kind of security represented in the traditional government job. Indeed, the longer students remain in the educational system, the greater the chances they will end up working for the state, or as an employee rather than an employer.

Moonlighting for money

Sticking to its commitment to universal, free education, the state increased spending on education throughout the 1990s, from LE3.6 billion in 1991 to LE20.4 billion in 2001. Indeed, measured as a percentage of GDP, spending on education exceeds that of most developing countries and even many developed countries. Allocations, however, are heavily weighted to higher educational levels. While most of the students are concentrated in the primary and preparatory levels (79% in the 1990s), basic education received only 51% of government expenditure. Meanwhile, 31% of expenditure was allocated to the university level, although it accounted for only about 6% of total enrollment. As a result, the quality of basic education—the one level that boasts high levels of enrollment among all sectors of the population—is considerably worse than other developing countries. This ultimately has a tangible impact on income levels, one felt most severely among low-income students, who tend to drop out of the educational system earlier than other students. According to the UNDP, an Egyptian man who has completed primary education makes on average 8% more than one who has not; in other low-and middle-income countries the average wage increase for a similar educational jump is closer to 30%.

This is only one side of the government spending coin that tends to penalize poorer students. Although the majority of spending on education goes to pay wages, teachers' salaries remain absurdly low—a senior teacher at a public secondary school makes a few hundred pounds a month, barely enough to remain above the official poverty line. One reason for this is that some 38% of the Ministry of Education employees in 1998—or half a million people—were administrative staff, a legacy of the government's central planning pledge to employee all graduates. These administrators, who mostly kick their heels, absorb pay that could be going to improving teachers' salaries and to employing more teachers to lower class sizes. Given that student/teacher ratios are probably higher than the 40 or so reported, it is hardly surprising that only the most highly-motivated of educators might attempt to learn new methods and practice them in the classroom.

Creative teaching methods are also against the educators' own financial interests. Educators supplement their salaries through the infamous "private lessons" system. Teachers' may compromise on the quality of the teaching during classes to increase demand for private lessons and may limit the number of hours of formal classroom teaching to free up time for the more lucrative private lessons. They may even withhold answers to the questions they know will be on the test during ordinary office hours and give them out only during special after-school sessions to paying students.

Saving the state the necessity of raising teacher salaries, the proliferation of private lessons represents the ongoing, *de facto* privatization of the school system. About 70% of all students take private lessons, but the system clearly affects low-income families more than well-off ones. A working-class family with a child in secondary school might pay LE20 a session. Private lessons thus become one of many families' greatest household expenses, accounting for an average 65% of education-related expenses for an average middle income family.

Although the ministry has declared that it is at war with the so-called "private lessons mafia"—which in fact probably represents the vast majority of educators in the country—it appears to have done little to rectify a system that has turned into a burgeoning informal industry. According to CAPMAS, Egyptian families spend an estimated LE2 billion a year now on private lessons; independent estimates are even higher.

Cheating

The other problem is cheating. Peeking, cheat sheets, and answers passed around the test halls are among the most minor phenomena. Every year around exam time, stories of particularly creative or blatant examples of cheating make their way into the local press. In 2000, the state-owned newspaper *al-Ahram* published a copy of answers to the French examination held in a Delta village, claiming that it had been bought at a kiosk set up next to the testing center. One resident said that this kind of wholescale, open secret cheating had been going on in the village for years.

These cases are not exceptional, and some form of cheating is probably the norm at most schools in Egypt. Though technically illegal, there is little stigma attached. Invigilators tend to have sympathy for students caught up in a highly demanding testing system, in which one forgotten answer can easily disqualify a student from his or her chosen career. They will sometimes give hints during exams, refer one student to another, or otherwise make life easier for their wards. It happens all the way up from primary classes to medical school. Schools themselves will often overlook cheating because they risk being shut down if too many pupils fail. If an individual teacher wants to accuse a pupil, the burden of proof is on them—and if they fail to provide evidence they risk derailing their own career. Parents will often condone cheating, and sometimes encourage it—with tests being so hard, what else is one supposed to do?

The Egyptian educational system, then, is a major challenge. Designed with the best of intentions, to hold all students to a single empirical standard by way of objective testing, it has devolved into a system that favors rich over poor, memorization over critical thinking, and getting by over actual learning. *SN & MM*

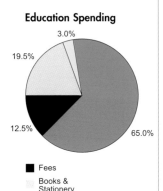

Education Spending

3.0%
19.5%
12.5%
65.0%

■ Fees
▨ Books & Stationery
▢ Transportation
▨ Private Lessons

Source: Egypt Human Development Report 1997/8 (INP, UNDP)

Expenses for a mid-income family with a child in secondary school

Mortgaged Hopes

Does Egypt have a housing crisis?

If you are one of millions of urban youth who want to start a family, the answer is yes. If you are one of the millions of families who live in a single room, the answer is yes. If you are one of the millions of families who continue to reside in tiny apartments even though the family is now three generations old and sleeping in shifts, the answer is yes.

But, if you are one of the lucky families who have amassed capital, who got in at the bottom of a housing scheme, who have cleverly speculated in land and property, or who have inherited rent-controlled accommodation, the answer is no. And if, like former parliamentarian Milad Hanna, you are an observer of the housing scene and know that there are millions of vacant units, you would say, no, there is not a housing crisis but a problem in the distribution of units.

New apartments on the market are plentiful, as a scan of any newspaper will tell you, but the prices are far beyond the means of the average middle-class family, let alone the mass of those with limited income. Couples commonly postpone marriage for years and years in attempts to save enough to enter the market. Due to the constrained offerings on the market (and the fact that there are no financing mechanisms which allow even bridging loans), there is little housing mobility. In fact, for most families the decision on where to live is a once-in-a-lifetime event, if that. Some consider housing to be the most serious problem facing the Egyptian household, especially for those who wish to start a family, and it is a source of frustration and social tension for all but the well-off.

Housing is a particularly important problem for the urban poor. In some areas, the number of families living in single rooms exceeds a third of the total, and substandard housing conditions are frequently the norm. In rural areas, housing is less of a problem, since there is room for a most families to expand their houses. With the increasing urbanization of the Egyptian village, however, even this option is becoming rare.

The housing sector in Egypt is characterized by a number of fundamental contradictions. The more visible of these are:

Mismatch of Supply and Demand: There is an increasing oversupply of up-market villas and apartments, many of which remain unoccupied, yet an almost complete absence of affordable units on the market (affordable by any definition).

Vacancies Galore: There are a very large number of vacant housing units, either those unsold or un-rented or simply held by owners in a vacant state for speculation or to house offspring when they marry. Similarly, there are extensive amounts of land parcels held vacant for the same purposes. CAPMAS has estimated that vacancies represent 18% of the urban housing stock.

Rent-controlled Units Off the Market: According to CAPMAS, in 1996 a full 48% of all occupied urban housing units were rented under inheritable fixed-rent contracts, based on a series of laws which date back to 1943. This means that these rents are usually a small fraction of market rates, that landlords cannot gain enough income even to maintain buildings, and that these units are held off the market for generations. (A number of dubious means have been devised to allow once-off transactions, but these frequently end in disputes.)

Informal Housing: Starting in the 1960s and accelerating during the oil-boom in the late 1970s and early 80s, huge areas on the fringes of cities have been settled illegally and spontaneously by families and small investors seeking housing solutions increasingly unavailable in the formal economy. Most of these settlements are built on agricultural land where builders buy the land from farmers and construct housing incrementally, without subdivision plans or approvals and without building licenses. Not only are these areas a planner's nightmare, but since they are totally unsanctioned, infrastructure services and public facilities arrive late, if at all, and properties are built and exchanged in a gray world of semi-legality. Were this phenomenon of urban informality a marginal one, it might be solvable if the state had the money. But today one is talking about a truly massive problem, and there are indications that the majority of urban Egyptians reside in these informal areas.

The Government Will Provide: The Egyptian government has maintained over the last 30 years a policy of directly supplying housing for those who cannot afford to find solutions in the private sector. The government currently builds roughly 40,000 units a year in public housing blocks, either in desert locations or sprinkled wherever state land can be found. The current Mubarak Housing scheme offers two-bedroom units in quite fancy blocks for sale to "youth," but in remote desert locations, for nominal down payments of LE2000 and monthly installments of LE72. While laudable from a social point of view, this attitude that "the state provides" requires massive subsidies (approaching 80% of the cost of the unit), involves considerable opportunity costs, and is becoming increas-

Some consider housing to be the most serious problem facing the Egyptian household

ingly unrealistic. It has also spawned a host of abuses to the system. It is remarkable that Egypt continues to maintain such a housing policy and continues to devote such enormous budget allocations in a world where housing solutions are increasingly seen as one of getting the market conditions right and enabling the private sector to operate efficiently.

Empty New Towns: The new-towns strategy has been a cornerstone of government development policy since Sadat announced it in 1976, and over the years city after city after city has been established with great fanfare, well into the desert on both sides of the Nile. Planned using modern, Western concepts of urban space, the new towns are seen as the appropriate direction for the modernization of Egyptian society and the solution to the overcrowding and chaos found in the Nile Valley. The state has devoted a considerable chunk of its development budget to building infrastructure and public housing in these towns, and has practically ignored housing problems in the Valley. Embarrassingly, few people want or can afford to live and work in these towns. A simple calculation reveals that by 1996, after 20 years of promotion, the total population in all new towns in Egypt represented less than the increase in population of Greater Cairo over a six-month period.

Egypt's Real Estate

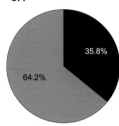

35.8%

64.2%

■ Informal

■ Formal

Source: Institute for Liberty and Democracy, ECES

Two-thirds of real estate by value—$241 billion—is unregistered, so can't be used as collateral, according to a study by Peruvian economist Hernando de Soto

Informalities

Most of what is known about housing in Egypt is anecdotal, and any statements about the subject need to be seriously qualified. The fact is that, currently, no focused look at the housing sector in Egypt exists. In the 1980s there were a number of housing sector investigations associated with projects sponsored by the World Bank, USAID, GTZ and others, most notably a USAID-financed survey of housing production and the informal sector in 1981. Since then, largely due to a drop in interest on the part of donors in the sector, little has been written. The Egyptian government, preoccupied with promoting new towns and desert settlements, has limited its attention to new urban development and the delivery of various forms of subsidized public housing.

There are a few efforts, however, that at least touch on private sector housing. One important investigation is the USAID-financed Egypt Property Formalization Study (1999-2000), which uncovered considerable information about tenure and informality in urban housing, including a quantification of the informality phenomenon. According to the study's findings, 92% of the urban population and 87% of the rural population lives in informal housing (whether built illegally or simply unregistered), the value of which is about $241 billion. The high incidence of informality was partially explained by the tortuous legal processes involved in acquiring or building "legal" housing. The study estimated that would take anywhere from 6-14 years of bureaucratic dealings for an average citizen to buy a piece of desert land and legally build a house on it.

The study was undertaken by the Institute for Liberty and Democracy of Lima, the brainchild of informality guru Hernando de Soto, under a contract with the Egyptian Center for Economic Studies. The intention was to come up with a national program to rapidly register and title extra-legal properties. The premise is that poor and moderate income families, for which housing represents the main form of equity, should be able to exchange and leverage this equity in formal financial systems, rather than having it remain unproductive "dead capital." It remains to be seen whether the Egyptian government has the political will to implement such a massive and complicated reform program. *DS*

Recent Trends

New suburbia: With very few exceptions, Egyptian cities have never had suburbs in the American or European sense. But starting in 1994, the minister in charge of urban development saw a way to rescue the most prestigious of his new towns—those surrounding Cairo—by the simple expedient of subdividing and selling vast tracts of desert which had been designated as buffer zones and green belts. Extremely high standards for subdivision and building were applied. Both individuals and real estate developers rushed to buy up land which, in the beginning at least, seemed a sure investment. Fancy villa developments, gated communities, golf cities, and amusement parks led the way. More and more land was carved up and sold, so that, on a map at least, the new settlements in the desert around Cairo now cover over one and a half times the total existing area of Greater Cairo. It is only during the past two years that what should have been obvious has become an unwelcome reality: there is a total oversupply of expensive, unaffordable units in remote and as yet unlivable neighborhoods coupled with a deflating land speculation bubble.

The real estate recession: Ever since the infitah in the 1970s every Egyptian family has come to believe one fact: property and land values always go up and investing in urban real estate is a sure bet. However, thanks to the recent suburban expansions, in the last two years this canon no longer holds, at least in Greater Cairo. So much liquid family capital has been absorbed by the new suburbs (and, it should be added, by seaside holiday home developments) that there is little demand for formal properties anywhere in the metropolis. As a result, prices are frozen or declining, with few buyers. This has hit developers in the new suburbs particularly hard, and many are defaulting on bank loans.

The new mortgage law: After considerable discussion and interest from various groups, the mortgage law (No. 148 of 2001) was passed by the Egyptian parliament and signed into law in June 2001. Great hopes are put on the impact that this law will have on housing markets. For the first time in Egypt, it will allow mortgage lenders to repossess units in the case of non-payment. However, there are different perceptions of the benefits of the law. On one hand, the very developers who are most hurt by the real estate recession see it as the silver bullet that will stimulate demand for their unsold up-market housing units. On the other hand, the government and politicians see it as a way to address the housing problem facing those of limited income by providing housing credit. Yet a third view, that of the World Bank and other donors, is that the law will allow the creation of mortgage institutions and eventually a secondary mortgage market which will strengthen Egypt's moribund financial sector and its capacity for securitization.

It is doubtful that this law (whose executive regulations, which spell out operational aspects, have not yet been issued) will satisfy all things for all people. If mortgages are offered on purely commercial terms, only those with steady incomes of LE2000 per month and up are likely to qualify. Moreover, only formally registered properties would be acceptable by banks. Thus, unless the government, itself under serious financial constraints, steps in with hefty subsidies on interest rates, the mortgage law will not address the fundamental issues underlying the housing crisis. *DS*

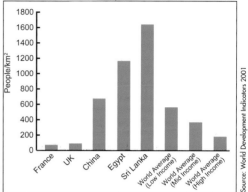

Rural Population Density

Source: World Development Indicators 2001

As rural areas urbanize, Egyptians in the countryside are also feeling the housing crunch

Civil Society
The state defends its prerogatives

The Civil Fabric

Among the 5,000 cooperatives, 25 professional syndicates, 23 trade unions, and about 20,000 non-governmental organizations (NGOs) that constitute what could be termed Egypt's civil society, NGOs represent the most significant group, both economically and politically. Historically, professional syndicates have played an important role in the political life of the country, but the government in 1993 granted itself greater powers to intervene in the internal elections of these organizations through the Unified Law of Syndicates. The law was used to control the mounting influence of Islamists, who had managed to dominate the boards of the most important syndicates, and it successfully marginalized the role of syndicates in most political activities. Despite the draconian nature of state control over civil society organizations in Egypt, reflected in tight administrative and legal constraints, today NGOs provide one of the most open spaces for political action and mobilization in the country. This often results in confrontations between state authorities

The majority of NGOs operate in charitable and service delivery activities

and more politically active NGOs. The majority of NGOs, however, are not politically active, operating in charitable and service delivery activities. As long as these organizations steer clear of challenging state policies, they are spared the harsher treatment of the state.

The legal framework for NGOs

The history of NGOs in Egypt is marked by the state's continuous attempts to control and co-opt the activities of this sector. A landmark in this history is Law 32 of 1964 which gave the state, represented mainly by the Ministry of Social Affairs (MOSA), full powers over all aspects of NGOs' work. Law 32 was finally superceded this year by Law 84/2002, but many observers believe the new law is even more repressive.

Though it is only a few months old, the new NGO law already has a somewhat checkered history, stretching back to 1999. In that year, the People's Assembly first approved a new associations law (Law 153). Although the drafting committee for the law included representatives of NGOs, they were unable to significantly influence its final form. Opposition to Law 153 came mainly from human rights organizations, believed to be the primary target of the stricter measures contained in the law. Article 11 of the law, which prohibited NGOs from carrying out any political activity, was a case in point. Most human rights NGOs engage in activities which could be labelled "political," for example, the defense of political prisoners. The new law also required the state's prior approval for the release of any foreign funding.

Law 153 was declared unconstitutional in 2000 by the Supreme Constitutional Court (SCC) on the grounds that it had not secured the approval of the Shura Council, and a new drafting committee, consisting only of government representatives, was formed to review the law. NGOs spent the year 2001 in nervous anticipation of the passage of the new law; as the SCC decision was based strictly on procedural, rather than substantive grounds, the new law promised to be no more liberal than its predecessor. These fears were confirmed late in the year when a draft of Law 84 was finally made public. Containing only minor changes, it left the most controversial parts of Law 153 in place. The final version of the law as ratified by President Mubarak on June 5, 2002, forbids NGOs from engaging in political activities, requires state approval for the release of all foreign donations, and gives the state the power to unilaterally dissolve NGOs that overstep these bounds.

Types of Egyptian NGOs

Law 32 divided all NGOs into two categories: welfare organizations and Community Development Associations (CDAs). This classification is simplistic and misleading, as it conceals the various—and sometimes conflicting—interests represented by groups lumped together under these vague categories. For example, the official CDA category puts advocacy groups together with Islamic NGOs, though the two have disparate agendas and worldviews. Alternatively, NGOs can be divided into five groups:

Islamic NGOs: Their wide popular base, access to resources, relative autonomy from the state, and ability to recruit large numbers of qualified volunteers make them some of the most active NGOs in the country. Their activities are largely focused on health and education.

Coptic NGOs: These include some of the largest, most professional, and most affluent NGOs working at the national level, for example, the Coptic Evangelical Organization for Social Services. Like their Islamic counterparts, they have a large popular base, access to

Double Jeopardy

The last two years have not been kind to Egypt's human rights and democracy advocacy groups. Already suffering from dwindling funding and occasional (if well-targeted) state harassment, the high-profile trial of AUC sociology professor Saad Eddin Ibrahim cast a long and enduring shadow over Egypt's civil society.

Ibrahim made international headlines in the summer of 2000 when he was arrested and later charged with illegally accepting foreign donations, forging voter registration cards, and besmirching Egypt's reputation abroad. The accusations centered on a voter awareness program conducted by his Ibn Khaldoun Center for Developmental Studies (ICDS) and funded by a grant from the European Commission. The subsequent trial dragged on for several months, but despite the parade character witnesses who stood up in Ibrahim's defense—many of whom have strong links to officialdom—he was convicted on May 21, 2001, and sentenced to seven years in prison. The verdict sent a sharp chill throughout many rights groups. Ibrahim, after all, is no rabble-rousing radical, but a well-known figure in both academic and official circles. Those with far less clout than he found themselves wondering if they could suffer the same fate.

Ibrahim was granted a retrial in 2002, but the state security court handed down the same verdict. Among the general public, Ibrahim's conviction cast further doubt on the already suspect notion of social research and its goals, and it reinforced a widely held view of foreign-funded activists and researchers as unpatriotic opportunists. The willingness of the state to avidly prosecute Ibrahim has been enough to make many organizations wary of foreign funding or controversial political activity. And without foreign funding, many human rights and democracy advocates will find it difficult to maintain an effective presence. *MM*

Showing Solidarity

Egyptians have plenty of domestic issues to be active about, but over the last year, none of these managed to galvanize public opinion quite like the Palestinian

intifada. Whether through direct protest, boycott, or charity work, Egyptians of all stripes came out in force to make their voices heard. Popular action took varied forms. While there were the usual student demonstrations and rallies at professional syndicates, other more indirect forms of solidarity were in evidence. In the capital, one couldn't help but notice a proliferation of all things Palestinian, from flags festooning taxis to the black-and-white checkered *kafiyas* that suddenly seemed to become *de riguer* winter gear. Popular associations with names like the Committee for the Boycott of Israeli Goods and the People's Committee in Support of the Palestinian Uprising, born in the early days of the intifada, gained greater public currency as they organized demonstrations and boycotts and collected donations for aid caravans to Palestinians in need. Egyptian superstars got on the bandwagon, organizing charity benefit concerts, while the Jawhara Company launched an alternative snack food for Egyptians wanting to show their solidarity. With a percentage of sales promised to go directly to the

Palestinian cause, those who indulged in Abu Ammar corn chips—the *nom de guerre* of Yasser Arafat—could rest assured that even as they sated their hunger, they were doing the right thing.

Things really heated up with the Israeli reinvasion of the West Bank in April this year. As television screens across the nation were ablaze with virtually nothing else, popular pro-Palestinian sentiment was running at an all-time high. The Ministry of Health and the Egyptian Red Crescent were literally flooded with blood donors. With no means to transport the blood to the West Bank, the Minister of Health was ultimately forced to ask Egyptians to refrain from donating more. The mood in the street reached a fever pitch as well, with large university protests from Zaqaziq to Minya. When in late April students at the American University in Cairo attempted to collect enough food and medicine to fill one truck headed for Rafah, they ended up collecting 30 truckloads of aid and about LE90,000 in cash aid for Palestinian refugees. The results of all this civil action were uneven. The impact on government policy, for example, was slight at best. Keenly aware of the potential explosiveness of public opinion, the state was more concerned with diffusing it than responding positively. If more students protested more loudly than they had in a decade, they were still largely confined to university campuses, unable to connect with the wider public. Particularly troublesome activists found themselves briefly detained. Even unauthorized charitable activities were subject to clampdowns. Ultimately, those actions that had the greatest tangible impact were not organized popular protests, but individual acts of solidarity, whether giving money or goods or choosing not to buy US or Israeli products. Effective broad-based political action, however, is still a thing of the future. *MM*

significant funds, and focus largely on issues of health and education. However, the majority of Coptic NGOs are small organizations working in local communities.

CDAs: In 1996, MOSA estimated that CDAs accounted for 25% of the total number of registered NGOs. Generally, CDAs are semi-governmental organizations, highly dependent on MOSA for funding, with their leadership drawn heavily from the state bureaucracy.

Advocacy groups: Consisting mainly of human rights, environmental, and the more active women's groups, these NGOs are the most outspoken of all Egyptian civil society organizations, and therefore, often involved in confrontations with the state.

Businessmen's associations: With membership constituting representatives of the private sector and leading state officials, and an objective of promoting the interests of their members, these associations qualify more as economic interest groups than NGOs. However, they operate within the same legal framework. The political nature of their activities, such as lobbying to acclerate privatization, are overlooked by the government.

Economic contribution

According to the latest official MOSA estimates, there were over 15,000 registered NGOs in 1996. A more recent study reports that there are nearly 20,000 NGOs. The dearth and inaccuracy of official data on NGOs is one of the main difficulties in understanding the real size of these organizations, and is believed by many activists and academics to be one of the main measures of state manipulation of the sector. Despite the lack of transparency, over the last decade it is clear that NGOs, especially religious NGOs, have made a substantial contribution to some service sectors, such as education and health, though estimates on their contributions vary widely. For example, the general census of 1992 showed that 14% of those who received health care at the national level did so through clinics run by NGOs.

An independent study showed that in 1994, 70-75% of health services offered to low-income communities were provided by religious NGOs and that the number of recipients of NGO health services increased to 14 million from 4.5 million in 1982. But yet another independent assessment estimated in 1997 that NGO health services reached no more than 3-5% of all those using health services in Egypt.

Economic and social contributions to the needy or to society at large are hindered by the poverty of most NGOs themselves. Although a few large organizations operate on multimillion-pound budgets, the majority of Egyptian NGOs are under-funded and work on very small-scale projects. In 1999, it was estimated that 33% of all NGOs have budgets of less than LE5,000.

Egyptian NGOs rely on various sources of finance: state support, membership fees, revenues from products and services, public donations, and foreign funding. Membership fees and revenues from services are the least consequential. Religious NGOs rely heavily on public donations, especially since those made to mosques and churches are not subject to MOSA supervision. State support in the form of MOSA grants, which range from LE100 to LE250,000, favors CDAs, most of which are regarded as an extension of MOSA. In 1996, it was estimated that MOSA farmed out 60,000 employees to NGOs, the majority of which were believed to be CDAs, to relieve them from the burden of paying staff salaries.

Foreign funding has been a major source of income for many NGOs since the mid-1980s. Most of this funding has come from USAID as part of its overall aid to Egypt although other donor agencies, such as the Netherlands Embassy, the Danish DANIDA, and Canada's CIDA, have also been major donors for local NGOs. Advocacy and human rights groups rely heavily on foreign donors, which has often rendered them vulnerable to both government harassment and public criticism. *MA*

The Association for the development and Enhancement of Women (ADEW) provides micro-loans and legal assistance

Sport
Football reigns supreme

The Score

An observer of the Egyptian sports scene might well ask what Egyptians did before the introduction of football in the early years of the 20th century.

Though the country has produced world champions in everything from swimming to bodybuilding to hockey, football is the undisputed king of Egyptian sport. Indeed, for many Egyptians, sport *is* football. It attracts the most public attention, the most money, and the most press coverage. And so it was that many in the country had a hard time remaining dry-eyed in July 2001 as the national team dramatically crashed out of the 2002 World Cup qualifiers for the third time in a row.

Those previous two failures, however, were not half as shameful as the elimination from last summer's football showpiece. In 1993, Egypt took Zimbabwe in Cairo, but misconduct by the Egyptian crowd at Cairo Stadium forced a replay on neutral ground in France, where pure bad luck came between Egypt and an open goal. In 1997, the Egyptian Football Association (EFA) brought in legendary coach Mahmoud al-Gohari to take the helm of the team just a few weeks before the crucial tie against Liberia, and time was clearly against him.

But in 2001, there were no such excuses. This time Egypt lost because of human error. In a group that

Highlights in Sports 2001/02

1. The national youth football team wins the bronze medal in the U-19 World Championship in Argentina, an unprecedented achievement (2001).
2. Ahli wins the African Champions League title for the third time in their history and for the first time since 1987 (2001).
3. Swimmer Abdel-Latif Abu Heif, conqueror of the English Channel in the 1950s, is named Swimmer of the Century by the US Swimming Higher Council (2001).
4. Ahli thrashes archrivals Zamalek 6-1 in the league championship (2002).
5. Ismaili captures the football league title for the third time in the club's history and the first time since 1990 (2002).
6. Heba Salah takes the gold medal in karate's World Youth Championship (2001).
7. The national handball team wins fourth place in the World Championship (2001).
8. Egypt amasses 36 medals in the Mediterranean Games held in Tunisia (2001).
9. Anwar al-Ammawi is selected Champion of the Century by the International Bodybuilding Federation (2001).
10. Ahli defeats Real Madrid 1-0 in a historic match at Cairo Stadium (2001). *AC*

contained Morocco (Africa's up-and-coming football power), Senegal, Algeria, and Namibia, there was no room for squandering scoring opportunities or conceding lousy goals. Still, the Egyptians allowed eight goals in their net, heading to Algeria in the last round of matches needing to win by a landslide on turf that has never allowed them a victory.

At the end of the qualifiers, Egypt came up third on 13 points, behind Morocco and Senegal. The latter snatched the group's lone ticket on goal difference, and world football's governing body FIFA turned down an Egyptian appeal for a rematch against Algeria due to a hostile and intimidating Algerian crowd.

Adding insult to injury, Senegal, the country that eliminated Egypt from the qualifiers, made an unexpectedly good showing at the World Cup finals. Though Egypt was not present in Japan or Korea, when South Korea won a controversial victory over Spain in the quarterfinals, it was Egypt, ironically, that took the blame. Egyptian referee, Gamal al-Ghandour, the country's only claim to fame in the championship, cancelled what were described by the Spanish media as "two valid goals" that could have booked Spain a place in the semifinals. Al-Ghandour, needless to say, slammed the accusations as "baseless" but his talked-about decisions in the match were enough to end his chances to officiate the final match.

Egypt's third successive failure to reach the World Cup was more painful to those who know its contributions to African football throughout the twentieth century. Egypt was among the founders of the Confederation of African Football (CAF) in 1957. It boasts a record four-time success in the African Cup of Nations, and it reached the World Cup finals twice, in 1934 and 1990. Egyptian teams also have the most successful record in CAF club competitions, with 14 continental titles. The country's powerhouses, Ahli and Zamalek, ranked first and second respectively in CAF's list of the best African clubs,

announced in March 2001, while the national team came in third on its list.

In contrast to the national team, Egypt's youth team shone in 2001, winning the bronze medal in the U-19 World Championship in Argentina, in an unprecedented achievement for Egyptian football, while Ahli closed the 2001 season by capturing the African Champions League title for the third time in their history. The victory was a record seventh continental title for the pride of Cairo. Ahli's success, however, was the first

for the Egyptians since the introduction of prize money in Africa' premier clubs competition in 1997. After their 4-1 aggregate win over South Africa's outfit, the Sundowns, Ahli walked out with $1 million. Ahli further confirmed their African supremacy by clinching the Super Cup for the first time in the club's history in 2002 after a humiliating 4-1 victory against the South African Kaizer Chiefs in Cairo.

On the domestic front, Ismaili won the precious league title for the third time in the club's history and for the first time since 1990, thus putting an end to the country's bifurcated soccer system that saw Ahli and Zamalek dominating the championship in the 1990s. Although Ahli came second, the team's supporters will long remember 2002 as the year their favorite team handed archrivals Zamalek a historic 6-1 defeat in May. The league title in 2001 went to Zamalek, thanks to the efforts of Ahli's former twin stars, Hossan and Ibrahim Hassan, who joined Zamalek in one of the most controversial deals in the history of Egyptian football.

Though Ahli has now lost the league title for two successive seasons, the balance of power in the country's premier soccer competition continues to swing in their favor. Since the championship was founded in 1948, Ahli has captured the title 29 times, Zamalek nine, Ismaili three, while Arab Contractors, Mahalla, Tersana, and Olympic have one title each.

After football, handball continued to rank as the

Pay for Play

For better or worse, pay TV seems to be the trend of the modern world. In their *Winners and Losers: the Business Strategy of Football*, Stefan Szymanski and Tim Kuypers explain that pay TV has moved from a loss-making, high-risk venture to a large, profitable, and still-growing business. In 1997, the British media giant BSkyB had a turnover of £1.2 billion, achieving a phenomenal £374 million in profits, a 26% increase on the previous year. In 2001, Egyptians also tried to grab a small slice of the ever-expanding pie.

Prior to the beginning of the 2001/2002 football league season, club powerhouse Ahli announced that it wanted more money from Egyptian Television for the rights to air the team's matches in the Egyptian football league. Rumors abounded that the club was studying an offer from a private Arab satellite channel interested in buying the TV rights of the Egyptian giants' matches. Although Ahli and Egyptian TV were able to reach a compromise at the end of the day—thus allaying the fears of millions of addicted TV fans—pay TV may soon become the norm. Sports pay TV was first introduced to Egypt in 1999 when private satellite network ART bought the exclusive TV rights of the Confederations Cup in Mexico in which both Egypt and Saudi Arabia were taking part. At the time, there were fewer public venues in Egypt with satellite subscriptions, and the resulting overcrowding inevitably led to quarrels. In several cases, the police were called in. Last year, the same network bought the exclusive rights of the Youth World Championship in Argentina and, again, Egypt took part in the event. This time around, however, audiences were much more agreeable, a response that observers chalk up to an increased understanding of the concept of pay TV and a growing number of satellite receivers. In 2002, millions of Egyptians almost missed the World Cup when private network ART bought the exclusive regional rights to air the tournament. Inititally ART demanded $40 million from Egyptian TV to license out the tournament, a price Egyptian TV refused to pay. Eventually a settlement was reached, but sports fans might not be so lucky the next time around.

The question now is if Egyptian entrepreneurs will be able to tap into the potentially lucrative local market, especially given the sacrosanct status of free televised sports. In 1998 Ehab Saleh, a businessman who owns a football marketing company, introduced a project to encode football matches: each family would pay LE150 for a simple UHF decoder, along with LE1 for a card to watch each match. Figuring that eight million families own televisions in Egypt, and that about half of them would pay to see sports, Saleh heard the unmistakable moo of the cash cow. He says today that he received verbal consent for his project from former Prime Minister Kamal al-Ganzouri, but that the project was later turned down. "The government evaluated the project on political grounds," he says. "They said football was like air and water for the Egyptian people. But don't we all pay for water nowadays?" *AC*

country's second most popular sport last year, a much-deserved status after the last decade's remarkable achievements. In 1993, the Egyptian youth team were world champions, while the senior national team ranked sixth in the 1995 and 1997 World Championships. The latter came seventh in the 1999 round before hitting top gear in 2001, when they came in fourth in the World Championship in France. The youth team was not as impressive as their seniors last year, failing to defend the third place they clinched in 1999 World Championship and coming in eighth.

In squash—a locally unpopular sport in which Egypt does well at the international level—the national team also failed to defend its world title in Australia in November 2001. It did gain respect, however, as the team managed to rank second despite the retirement of former world-seeded no. 2 player, Ahmed Barrada. Regardless of the international success, the game's popularity at home remains dependent on the organization of international events here, like the Ahram Championship that saw the rise of Barrada few years ago. But Egypt does boast a promising generation of players who are expected to rule the game in the coming few years.

Women's sports have gained more attention in Egypt throughout the last decade, especially with world-class champions like Egypt's golden fish, Rania Elwani, and Judo champion Heba Rashid. The retirement of Elwani after the 2000 Sydney Olympics and the decline in Rashid's performance have now left the way open for new female champions. One promising development is the introduction of women's boxing to Egypt. In July 2001, the country hosted the African championship of women's boxing for the first time. Fielding 12 competitors, the tournament showed how far Egypt has come since the Egyptian Association of Women's Boxing was founded four years ago. There are now 76 women registered in the association, between the ages of 15 and 29 and weighing from 45-91 kg. But the glory of 2001 was reserved for martial artist Heba Salah, 19, who won a gold medal at the world youth karate championships in Athens, an unprecedented achievement for Egyptian karate for either sex and in any age group. *AC*

On the Green

Egypt tries to draw golfers

The British introduced golfing in Egypt in the mid-19th century with an 18-hole course built inside the racetrack at the Gezira Club. Three "racetrack" courses were constructed at Merryland in Cairo, Alexandria Sporting, and Alexandria Smouha. After the turn of the century a club was established at Mena House near the Giza Pyramids, as well as a sand course in Maadi. The game was virtually reserved for the British, with only Egyptian caddies allowed to play occasionally.

After the 1952 revolution, golf became politically incorrect. The Gezira course was chopped up to make way for the youth club (Nadi al-Shebab) and the national club (Nadi al-Ahli). As the government nationalized the sporting clubs, the Merryland and Smouha courses disappeared. The Maadi club became an area of villas, which is to this day called "golf," leaving only Mena House at the pyramids and Alexandria Sporting relatively intact. All the courses fell into disuse as the number of golfers declined and money available for upkeep dried up.

With economic liberalization in the early 1990s came a renewed interest in golf. Modeling themselves after successful golf developments in the US, Europe, and parts of Asia, five courses began construction: Soleimaniya Golf Village on the Cairo-Alexandria desert road; Dreamland Golf and Tennis

Resort in Sixth of October City; Golf City on the Ismailiya desert road; and two courses along the road to Suez, Katameya Heights and Mirage City.

Katameya Heights, the vision of three golfing partners, Khaled and Tarek Abou Taleb and Mohammed Sabet, was the first of the modern clubs to open its doors in Egypt in 1996. Within a few months, most expatriate golfers and many Egyptians joined the club, which now has 5,000 members and about 1,000 golfers. It is by far the most active club in Egypt.

In the past three years Dreamland, Mirage, and Soleimania have opened around Cairo and are gradually building membership. The Pyramids Hilton hotel has opened at Dreamland. Soleimania is building a hotel and chalets and will open a night-lit course in August 2002. Mirage is attached to a JW Marriott hotel, scheduled to open December 1, 2002; it is adjacent to a theme water park next to the hotel. The latest course to open, al-Rabwa, is in a housing development along the Alexandria Desert Road. A nine-hole, part three executive course, it is designed for beginners and golfers looking to sharpen their short game. The Movenpick hotels are completing a clubhouse and expect to open Golf City in late 2002. All of these courses expect tourist golfers to keep their courses busy during the week.

As a national sport, golf is unlikely to become the obsession that it has reached in the US, Japan, and several European countries anytime soon. But it is definitely a sport attracting Egyptian players. Three years ago, Egypt had only 500 regular golfers. The number has more than quadrupled since then. Even in Alexandria, most of the tournaments are now won by golfers under 30 years old. Egypt saw its first televised tournament take place at Soleimania Golf Village in April 2002.

There are four resort courses: at Gouna, Soma Bay, Luxor, and Sharm al-Sheikh. But becoming a true golf destination, mainly for Europeans, will require more courses and aggressive marketing, both of which are happening. Except for the course at Luxor, which tourists visit for the cultural attractions, the other resort courses are mostly filled with tourist golfers during the October to April season. Additional courses are planned or being built in Sharm al-Sheikh, Taba Heights, Ain Sukhna, Marsa Alam, and west of Alexandria. Within a few years, Egypt should become a golf tourist destination. *TO*

Politics

The Art of Governance

- The Powers That Be
- Heads and Presidents
- Domestic Policy
- Local Government
- Crisis Management
- Egypt Abroad
- User-Friendly Government
- In the Arab League

The Game of Politics

- Under the Rotunda
- How a Law Gets Passed
- The Opposition
- Parliamentary Highlights

Other Power Bases

- The Fourth Estate
- On the Air
- Hollywood on the Nile?
- The Judiciary
- Egyptian Court System
- In the Courts

The Art of Governance

The Powers That Be

EGYPT HAS BEEN A REPUBLIC SINCE SOON AFTER THE ARMY OVERTHREW KING FAROUQ ON JULY 23, 1952, ENDING 150 YEARS of monarchy. The current constitution dates from 1971, when then-President Anwar Sadat instituted reforms to consolidate his power after the long rule of Gamal Abd al-Nasser. The constitution establishes an extremely strong executive branch and a weaker legislature, and enshrines a highly centralized administrative structure. It defines Egypt as a "socialist" state, but in practice the country has moved progressively away from the central planning of the Nasser era. A 1981 amendment to the constitution prescribes that Islamic Law (*shariaa*) should be the "principal source" of legislation, but outside of personal status issues, Egyptian law has remained an amalgam of Turkish, 19th-century European, and more modern legislation. Egypt's judiciary is substantially independent, although the Emergency Law that has been in force since 1981 allows some security offenses to be tried in parallel courts with limited rights of appeal.

Executive outcomes

Egyptian presidents serve six-year terms. They are not elected directly, but chosen by a two-thirds majority vote in the 454-member People's Assembly, which is then confirmed by popular referendum. The head of state has full discretion to appoint or remove the prime minister and his cabinet, as well as the governors of all 26 governorates, senior army and security chiefs, presidents of the 15 state universities, and a range of other key officials. Egypt's current cabinet has 34 ministers, who in theory report to the prime minister. By tradition, however, the key "sovereign" ministries, such as defense, interior, and foreign affairs, report directly to the presidency. Under the Emergency Law, the president has the authority to issue a broad range of administrative decrees. Egypt's parliament has also regularly delegated full discretion over military procurement to the presidency. In addition, Egypt's presidents have traditionally chaired the country's ruling party, currently the National Democratic Party (NDP).

Following the assassination of President Sadat on October 6, 1981, Mohammed Hosni Mubarak assumed office as president. He is now serving his fourth successive term, due to expire in 2005. Mubarak has usually pursued a supervisory style of rule, providing broad policy directives and allowing the four prime ministers who have served under him extensive leeway to implement them and manage day-to-day government. On occasions when government policy has proved to be unpopular, Mubarak has not hesitated to dismiss senior officials.

Mubarak's tenure has been characterized by cautious policies aimed at maintaining national and regional stability, at preserving the essentially secular character of the Egyptian state, and at opening the economy and encouraging private investment while trying to cushion the poor from the effects of reform. This conservatism has also been reflected in internal politics, where a battery of laws and administrative controls—many of them introduced to counter the religious extremism of the early 1990s—has kept the opposition weak and ineffective. Egypt's current president has kept a lower public profile than his predecessors, although the state's continuing dominance of the mass media still largely insulates him from criticism. While Mubarak has not inspired excessive public adulation, his aloofness from the fray of politics has preserved his popular stature, best embodied in his oft-repeated moniker, "the president of all Egyptians."

In the cabinet

In terms of constitutional authority, Prime Minister Atef Ebeid is the second most powerful man in the country. Ebeid became prime minister in October 1999. He had served in the cabinet since 1984, holding a number of economically related portfolios and gaining a reputation for understanding the complexity and rigidity of Egypt's administrative machinery.

Ebeid's appointment reflected a turn towards a more aggressive pursuit of economic reforms, coupled with stronger budgetary discipline. His predecessor, Kamal al-Ganzouri, had been criticized for sponsoring costly infrastructure projects that were subsequently blamed for the recession that hit in 2000. Ganzouri's ignominious departure, however, showed how tenuous the prime minister's position is. In the two years since his appointment, Ebeid's public profile has steadily waned, as complaints of ineffectiveness have become increasingly widespread. Ebeid's supporters, pointing to steady but slow progress, explain that the difficult nature of the job has hampered his efforts to speed reform. Critics, particularly in the business community, say that Ebeid has shied from grappling with

Heads and Presidents

President of the Republic
Mohammed Hosni Mubarak

Cabinet
Prime Minister Atef Ebeid
Deputy Prime Minister and Minister of Agriculture and Land Reclamation Youssef Wali
Minister of Awqaf (religious endowments)
Hamdi Zaqzouq
Minister of Civil Aviation** Ahmed Shafiq Zaki
Minister of Communications and Information Technology
Ahmed Nazif
Minister of Culture Farouq Hosni
Minister of Defense and Military Production
Field Marshal Mohammed Hussein Tantawi
Minister of Education Hussein Kamel Baha al-Din
Minister of Energy and Electricity* Hassan Ahmed Younes
Minister of Finance Medhat Hassanein
Minister of Foreign Affairs Ahmed Maher
Minister of Foreign Trade* Youssef Boutros Ghali
Minister of Health and Population**
Mohammed Awad Tag al-Din
Minister of Higher Education and Minister of State for Scientific Research Mufid Shehab
Minister of Housing, Utilities and Urban Communities
Mohammed Ibrahim Suleiman
Minister of Information Safwat al-Sherif
Minister of Insurance and Social Affairs Amina al-Gindi
Minister of the Interior Habib al-Adli
Minister of Justice Farouq Seif al-Nasr
Minister of Local Development Mostafa Abd al-Qader
Minister of Manpower and Emigration Ahmed al-Ammawi
Minister of Petroleum Sameh Fahmi
Minister of Planning* Osman Mohammed Osman
Minister of Public Enterprises Mokhtar Khattab
Minister of Public Works and Water Resources

Mahmoud Abd al-Halim Abu Zeid
Minister of State for Administrative Development
Mohammed Zaki Abu Amer
Minister of State for Environmental Affairs*
Mamdouh Riyad Tadros
Minister of State for Foreign Affairs*
Fayza Mohammed Abu al-Naga
Minister of State for Military Production Sayed Meshaal
Minister of State for People's Assembly and Shura Council Affairs Kamal al-Shazli
Minister of Supply and Internal Trade Hassan Khedr
Minister of Technological Development and Industry*
Ali Fahmi al-Saidi
Minister of Tourism Mamdouh al-Beltagui
Minister of Transport** Hamdi Abd al-Salam Shayeb
Minister of Youth Affairs Ali al-Din Hilal

HEADS OF MAIN PARTIES
National Democratic Party (NDP) President Mubarak
NDP secretary-general Safwat al-Sherif
New Wafd Party Noman Gomaa
Tagammu Party Khaled Mohi al-Din
Nasserist Arab Democratic Party Dia al-Din Dawoud

OTHER KEY FIGURES
Speaker of the People's Assembly Fathi Surour
Shura Council President Mustafa Kamal Helmi
Sheikh of al-Azhar Mohammed Sayed al-Tantawi
Patriarch of Coptic Church Pope Shenouda III
Armed Forces Chief of Staff Hamdi Weheiba
Public Prosecutor Maher Abd al-Wahed
Mufti of the Republic Mohammed Ahmed al-Tayeb

* Ministerial or portfolio changes in November 2001 (outgoing ministers: Ahmed al-Darsh, planning; Nadia Makram Ebeid, environment; Mostafa al-Rifai, technological development; Ali al-Saidi, electricity and energy; new ministry: Ministry of State for Foreign Affairs)
**Ministerial or portfolio changes in March 2002 (outgoing ministers: Ibrahim al-Demeiri, transport; Ismail Sallam, health and population; new ministry: civil aviation)
Source: Egypt Almanac

entrenched interests such as the six million-strong bureaucracy and state-owned industries.

Other than Ebeid, key figures in the cabinet include agriculture minister Youssef Wali, who is also deputy prime minister and secretary-general of the NDP, and parliamentary affairs minister Kamal al-Shazli, who functions as a sort of party whip. Both of them have served in the cabinet since the last decade. Despite murmurs early in 2001 that their position in the administration might have been undermined by the poor showing of the government's party in the 2000 parliamentary elections, neither has undergone a reversal of political fortune. Minister of Information Safwat al-Sherif, a former intelligence officer, has run the government's media machine for nearly two decades and shows no sign of losing his grip. Foreign Minister Ahmed Maher, the relative unknown who replaced Amr Moussa in May 2001, does not enjoy the same popularity as the former minister and has maintained a considerably lower profile. Perhaps more influential with the president on foreign policy matters is Osama al-Baz, the presidential adviser. Although not a minister, Mubarak's chief of staff, Zakariya Azmi, holds cabinet rank and plays a crucial role as the president's pointman in parliament, where he serves as an MP.

The remainder of the cabinet is mostly comprised of technocrats, such as Ahmed Nazif, the former university

professor who now heads the Ministry of Communications and Information Technology. Minister of Foreign Trade Youssef Boutros Ghali, the youngest cabinet minister and by many accounts the most economically savvy, is thought to be the architect of Egypt's economic reform program.

The legislature

Egypt's legislature is composed of two houses, the Shura (Consultative) Council and the People's Assembly or parliament. The first enjoys little power and, despite the inclusion of a few token members of the opposition, has little authority of its own. The People's Assembly began increasingly to exhibit a mind of its own in the wake of the November 2000 elections, even though it is still overwhelmingly dominated by the ruling party. Certain MPs—such as liberal Ayman Nour, leftist al-Badri Farghali, independent Kamal Ahmed, and even the government's own Zakariya Azmi—are known to grill ministers on incompetence and corruption in their portfolios. Assembly members are also reluctant to vote on government-sponsored legislation that can get them in trouble with their constituencies. Opposition from parliament held up the long-awaited new labor law for several years, while in 2001 pressure from the assembly led the government to introduce added provisions for low-income families in the controversial mortgage law. The assembly, however, is kept strictly in line by the iron fist of speaker Fathi Surour, who has been known to cut short debates when they enter into forbidden territory.

Political parties

The ruling National Democratic Party was created by President Sadat as part of a highly controlled experiment with democracy after decades of one-party rule. As the party of government, it has remained not much more than a collection of ambitious politicians with little ideological cohesion whose policy is dictated from above. Despite its stronghold on power, the party does seem to be suffering strains, particularly as new "clients" attempt to join what is in essence a vast patronage machine. A February 2000 shuffle of the general secretariat brought to power a handful of younger industrialists as well as Mubarak's younger son Gamal, who is considered to be close to business circles. The November 2000 parliamentary elections led to a further reshuffle, after more than half the candidates chosen by the NDP failed to win seats. The party only held its huge parliamentary majority by accepting a mass "conversion" of winning independent candidates into its ranks. Although these so-called renegade party members have yet to upset the parliamentary status quo in any substantial way, they represent an unknown element in the assembly whose voting patterns are not always predictable.

Egypt's opposition is notoriously weak and divided. The most important group by far is the banned Muslim Brotherhood, which in the late 1980s and early 1990s had built up a massive following in poor urban districts, on university campuses, and in the professional syndicates. By 1995, however, a campaign of arrests and military trials placed a good number of members in prison and encouraged the Brotherhood to lie low. They resurfaced as a force in the parliamentary elections in 2000, but Supreme Guide Mostafa Mashhour's subsequent calls to the government to grant the group official legal status have gone unheeded. Indeed, the government continued its crackdown on the movement, arresting a slew of members in 2001 and referring them to military tribunals.

Seven of the 16 legal parties that make up the secular opposition are no longer functioning, having been indefinitely suspended by administrative decree due to internal disputes or, in the case of the Islamist-oriented Labor Party, for running afoul of the government. Of the remaining active parties, the liberal Wafd, the leftist Tagammu, and the Nasserists have a small voice in parliament and some effect on public opinion via the party newspapers. The less-established parties have neither the financial resources, nor the membership cadres to influence politics in any meaningful way. *SN*

Domestic Policy

Security and stability

The world may have changed greatly in the past two decades, but the Egyptian government's domestic policy has not. Stability has been the chief watchword of President Mubarak's 20-year term in office. In practice, this means that key personnel have stayed in place, as have some opaque administrative systems dating from the Nasser years. Economic reforms have been pursued, but only gradually, with a view to cushioning the poor from shocks. Political change has been limited. The influence of the government's opponents has sometimes risen, sometimes fallen, but they have never been allowed to impede the wider prerogatives of the state.

Three main factors explain the government's instinct for caution. One is the personality of the president, a man who is careful by nature. Another is the hard lessons gained from the radical policy shifts of Mubarak's predecessors. In the 1950s and 60s President Gamal Abd al-Nasser pushed the country into centrally planned socialism and one-party rule. In the 1970s President Anwar Sadat abruptly reintroduced crony capitalism and political pluralism. In neither case was sufficient thought given to the long-term impact of such wrenching changes. Egypt emerged as a political and economic hybrid, an unwieldy mix of tendencies towards a more open and a more closed society.

A third reason for caution is the intractable nature of Egypt's most basic problems: poverty and over-population. Each problem has wide ramifications.

Maintaining subsidies on bread and essential medicines is an important pillar of government policy

Local Government

Investment Allocated to Governorates 2001/02

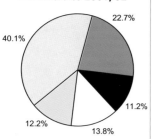

- 22.7%
- 40.1%
- 11.2%
- 12.2%
- 13.8%

■ Cairo
■ Alexandria
□ Delta
■ Upper Egypt
■ Suez Canal Zone

Source: State Information Service

Local Governorate Investment 2001/02

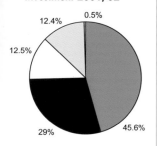

- 0.5%
- 12.4%
- 12.5%
- 29%
- 45.6%

■ Utilities
■ Transport
□ Services
■ Electricity
■ Industry

Source: State Information Service

Local government in Egypt is a poor cousin of the national legislature, which itself is the poor cousin of the executive in terms of the authority it exercises. While the 1971 constitution makes provisions for the creation of popular local councils, it defines their role vaguely: "Local People's Councils shall be gradually formed ... The law shall provide for the gradual transfer of authority to the local People's Councils." Theoretically, the councils are charged with providing infrastructure and social services to their district. They decide whether a certain street gets a light post, organize trash services, build schools and water disposal systems, and initiate other development projects. In reality, however, the distribution of power on the local level remains highly centralized. For each of the country's 26 governorates, 126 districts, and 4,695 municipalities, there is an elected popular council and a parallel executive council, whose members are appointed by the central government, largely drawn from the ranks of the civil service. A series of laws implemented since the councils were established have gradually eaten away at the authority of the elected bodies. Today, they function in a largely consultative role to the local executive councils, which have the real authority to determine what sorts of projects get implemented and how the local budget is spent. (However, since there is nothing in the law that prevents appointees to the executive councils from standing in elections for the popular councils, there is often overlap between the two.) In a relationship that mirrors that of the People's Assembly and the executive, local popular councils have little control over their purse strings, with about 90% of their funds allocated from the central government.

Of late, local councils have come under the gun for their poor performance. Last year, Zakariya Azmi, ruling party parliamentarian and confidant of President Hosni Muburak, declared before the People's Assembly that he wanted to revise an earlier declaration that local councils were "up to their knees in corruption." The councils, Azmi said, were in fact up to their necks in corruption. Azmi reopened his attack on local councils again early in 2002, claiming before the assembly that they had misappropriated public funds and failed to spend money allocated for infrastructure improvement, citing in particular improvements for the streets of Cairo to prevent flooding. According to a report produced by the Central Auditing Agency, some 25% of local council budgets never get spent, while a good portion of the money that they did spend went on such necessities as flowers, Eid greeting cards, and big ads in the state papers congratulating officials. Despite their limited authority, the elected popular councils are a good entry-level position for would-be powerbrokers in the ruling National Democratic Party, which has traditionally dominated the councils. Following the latest local elections on April 8, members of the NDP walked away with about 97% of the seats. Some complaints of foul play were heard following the elections, particularly since local elections were not supervised by the judiciary. The January decision to forgo judicial supervision had sparked some controversy, but the government argued that logistically it would be a nightmare. Given the limited number of judges, it would take about ten months to complete the election process.

The truth is that the NDP doesn't need strong-arm tactics to ensure its hegemony over local elections, as neither voters nor opposition parties seem to invest much time or interest in the process. A little more than half of the 46,000 seats won by NDP members were captured by default. All opposition parties combined fielded a little more than 1,000 candidates across the nation; in the end, they walked away with a mere 164 seats. *SN*

Poverty does not just mean that most Egyptians have extremely limited incomes, or that the state itself has limited resources. It also means that general levels of education and technical skill, of health, sanitation, and housing are low. It means that many of Egypt's best minds, impatient to gain rewards, have emigrated. Raising the level of the country's human development indicators would be a hard enough task, but population growth, and the pressure it places on schools, hospitals, the environment, infrastructure, housing, and employment, renders the job immensely difficult.

Much maligned and inefficient as it may be, the government has indeed set itself the task of raising all these standards. Its economic, social, and political policies all reflect this ambition. Even if its declared philosophy is to rely more on private participation, and even though many of the "social delivery" mechanisms created under socialism have been allowed to decay, the state remains committed to an actively development-oriented, rather than a regulatory and administrative role.

Stimulating the marketplace

In the early 1990s, encouraged by a write-off of a third of the country's foreign debt in reward for its role in the Gulf War, Egypt embarked on reforms designed to create a more dynamic, open market economy. The initial macroeconomic adjustments were broadly successful. By 1996 the balance of payments and the state budget deficit had stabilized at favorable levels. Economic growth was sustained at around 5%, a privatization program was launched, the stock market was revitalized, and foreign investment rose.

The course of reform has been less smooth and easy since then, with prolonged slumps in real estate and stock markets shaking business confidence. Still, the essential aims of economic policy have not changed. These include strengthening Egypt's physical infrastructure (transport, power, and communications networks)

with a continued high level of public investment, while inviting greater private participation—increasingly through the use of BOT mechanisms. They also include expanding the legal framework for a market economy. To this end, many commercial laws have been streamlined or overhauled, such as those governing company formation and capital markets. Long-awaited legislation to allow for the development of housing mortgages was finally approved in 2001. It is hoped that this will produce a range of positive effects, stimulating the housing market directly and financial markets indirectly as new forms of debt are securitized.

In pursuit of fiscal and monetary stability, the state sought for most of the last decade to limit inflation and to maintain the value of the Egyptian pound, largely by keeping local interest rates high. Contradictions began to emerge in this policy in late 1999. This was made evident by a rising trade deficit, a severe constriction in domestic liquidity, and mounting pressure on the pound. Following a 15% decline in the currency's value during 2000, a consensus began to emerge that the government needed to adopt a more flexible approach. A major step was taken towards this end with the imposition of a managed peg system in 2001, followed by several devaluations over the year. The blows Egypt's economy suffered in the wake of the World Trade Center attacks provoked more extreme responses, and a cabinet shuffle was effected with the

143

express aim of ameliorating the negative economic repercussions.

Providing for the poor

An important pillar of government policy is the effort to insulate the poor from the harsher effects of reform, both as an end in itself and as a means of defusing any potentially destabilizing backlash. Mubarak's repeated insistence that special attention should be paid to the

needs of the poor has, for instance, helped to slow parts of the privatization program, thus preserving jobs in a time of high unemployment. The state sugar, steel, and textile industries are woefully inefficient, but employ hundreds of thousands of people, often in relatively deprived regions. Not surprisingly, the government appears to have judged that the social cost of privatizing such industries remains too high.

While most consumer subsidies have been phased out,

Despite some minor cabinet shake-ups, government policies remained essentially unchanged over the past year

Crisis Management

In a year of global political and economic upheavals, the Egyptian government managed to survive the maelstrom largely intact. Though the cabinet underwent two minor facelifts over the last year—the first change in government since 1999—both were imminently pragmatic moves, aimed more at crisis management than major policy reform. The mandate of the new and improved cabinet that emerged after the first shuffle of late November was made clear by President Mubarak's inaugural address: catch the falling economy. To that end, the Ministry of Economy was abolished, leaving Youssef Boutros Ghali in charge of the Ministry of Foreign Trade and the primary task of raising exports. The Ministry of State for Foreign Affairs was brought out of the closet and brushed off after a ten-year hiatus, and the newly appointed minister, Fayza Abu al-Naga, was charged with cultivating and overseeing international economic cooperation agreements. At the same time, measures were taken to streamline the chain of command over certain key financial institutions in an effort to clearly define responsibilities and avoid unproductive policy tussles, like those seen between Boutros Ghali as economy minister and former governor of the Central Bank, Ismail Hassan. The Central Bank of Egypt was given full authority over monetary policy and made directly responsible to the prime minister, the insurance sector was brought under the domain of the Ministry of Planning, and

the National Investment Bank put under the authority of the Ministry of Finance.

The second shuffle took place in the aftermath of the Ayyat train disaster in late February, which saw the death of about 400 Egyptians and prompted the immediate resignation of transport minister Ibrahim al-Demeiri. Though some press commentators and parliamentarians were calling for the head of the prime minister himself, when the change came, it was largely limited to filling the vacant transport post and creating a new civil aviation ministry.

Despite the pragmatic nature of both shifts, there were a couple of unexpected victims. Nadia Makram Ebeid made a quiet exit from her post as environment minister in November, replaced by Mamdouh Riyad Tadros, formerly with the Ministry of Agriculture. When the head of the Egyptian Environmental Affairs Agency was also later replaced by an official from the agriculture ministry, some observers began to see Makram Ebeid's demise as part of an overall shift in priority towards agriculture at the expense of environmental protection. In the March shuffle, health minister Ismail Sallam got the boot. That move, too, seemed to have no immediate cause, but critics of the minister chalked it up to his inability to bring about real reform of the public health system and a tendency to ignore the population aspect of his portfolio. *MM*

the price of necessities such as bread, public transport, and essential medicines is still state supported or controlled. The state remains committed to providing low cost housing, most often in the form of stripped-down apartment complexes in new desert suburbs. The government also continues to provide most education and health care, although the low standard of its institutions has fostered a growth in parallel, private systems. A Social Development Fund, created specially to funnel investment into job creation schemes for the poor, continues to be generously financed from government resources as well as foreign aid, despite claims of inefficiency by critics, which became particularly strident in 2001.

Keeping the lid on

The priority placed on stability is most evident in the matrix of policies surrounding information and culture, party politics, and public security. These areas remain subject to controls that effectively limit dissent and that reinforce the government's "nationalist" vision of Egypt as a secular, Arab republic. However, the margin of civic freedom allowed to citizens is generally greater than in most countries in the region.

In the media, the state exerts its influence through an outright monopoly on broadcasting, and through indirect, but effective control of all but a fraction of the printed press. Government prerogatives are reflected not only in news coverage, but also in the content of, for example, television talk shows and even in popular serials that are designed to highlight issues that the ruling establishment deems pertinent. Those opposition papers that succeed in gaining licenses are not directly censored. However, ultra-tough licensing rules, high taxes on advertising, a harsh law on libel, and a tradition of avoiding certain taboo subjects serve to restrain their critical power. Despite occasional signs of opening, such as the recent establishment of private

satellite channels, the instinct for control continues to dominate information policy.

The same is true of policy regarding political activity. The government-appointed committee that vets applications to create parties rejects virtually all requests: since the National Democratic Party was formed in 1978, it has approved only one application. The remaining parties created in the intervening 23 years were established by court orders overturning rulings by the Political Parties Committee. With the exception of the government's NDP, all political parties operate under laws that effectively restrict their activity to publish newspapers, speak in parliament (if they win seats) and hold small, private meetings. An outright ban on parties based on religion has served to marginalize some political tendencies, notably both the radical and moderate wings of the Islamist movement.

A long-established system of massive, pervasive policing helps to keep Egypt relatively crime-free. However, this system is backed up by Emergency Laws, in force in one form or another for all but 8 of the past 63 years. Civil rights groups contend that these laws, along with more recent legislation that allows some civilians to be tried in military courts with no right of appeal, both encourage abuse and inhibit civic freedom. Laws that allow heavy state oversight of private and volunteer organizations are also often cited as being overly restrictive. *MR*

Egypt Abroad

Aiming for peace and economic prosperity

The president is the top decision-maker in all matters related to foreign policy and defense, and President Mubarak clearly belongs to the Egyptian school of thought that believes maintaining an active international role is necessary to help the Arab world's most populated country overcome some of its domestic problems. In practice, this means that Mubarak has led Egypt to play a key role in regional politics by cultivating ties on the Arab, African, and international levels. As in domestic policy, the pursuit of regional stability and economic development are the crux of the country's foreign policy goals. Egypt's strategic geographical and cultural position has put added weight behind Mubarak's efforts on both fronts.

After Anwar Sadat became the first Arab leader to sign a peace treaty with Israel in 1979, the majority of Arab governments boycotted Egypt, and Egypt's membership in both the Arab League and the Organization of Islamic Conference was frozen. Cairo had been a founding member of both organizations and the headquarters of the Arab League since its creation in 1945. While maintaining a strong commitment to a "special relationship" with the United States and peace with Israel, Mubarak sought to restore Egypt's ties with the Arab world after taking office in 1981. The policy culminated in Egypt regaining its full membership of the Arab League in 1989 and the return of its offices to Cairo.

Mubarak has since used his good ties with other Arab states to bring them closer to the Egyptian position, regarding peace with Israel as a "strategic option," and ending once and for all—at least on the official level—calls to end Israel's existence. From the Egyptian government's point of view, a comprehensive, just, and permanent deal with Israel is a pressing need for all countries in the region so that they can work on economic development and improve the living standards of their people. Despite a total lapse in peace efforts over the last year and increasingly frosty relations with the Jewish state, Mubarak has maintained this stance; even in the most charged moments in Egyptian-Israeli relations, he has consistently and expressly excluded the word "war" from his dictionary.

The inter-Arab honeymoon which followed Egypt's acceptance back into the Arab fold was short-lived. Iraqi President Saddam Hussein invaded Kuwait in August 1990, causing one of the deepest splits among Arab countries in recent history. Mubarak immediately sided with Washington in its efforts to build an alliance to end Kuwait's occupation. In making this decision, the president probably also had one eye on the domestic situation and the country's deteriorating economic conditions. Egypt was rewarded for its support by a massive debt write-off, and soon after embarked on an economic reform program after signing an agreement with the International Monetary Fund.

Since that time, Egyptian diplomatic efforts have increasingly turned towards the economic sphere, with the goal of developing a viable market economy domestically. Businessmen have become regular members of official Egyptian delegations abroad. Joint cooperation committees were established with scores of countries in Africa and Asia with the aim of boosting trade and investment. Egypt, after long years of negotiations, finally signed the trade partnership agreement with the European Union in June 2001. Cairo also sought to join African regional economic groupings in order to expand possibilities of joint investment, most notably COMESA, the Common Market for Eastern and Southern Africa. With the economic slowdown that hit in the wake of the attacks on the World Trade Center in the US, Mubarak took further steps to strengthen Egypt's economic ties abroad, reviving the Ministry of State for Foreign Affairs in November 2001 and charging the new minister, Fayza Abu al-Naga, with overseeing Egypt's foreign economic relations.

Mubarak sought to promote a similar economic approach towards the Arab world after the Iraqi invasion of Kuwait. Admitting that overcoming some disputes was nearly impossible in the short-run, he has repeatedly called for the establishment of an Arab Common Market, along the lines of the European Union. The argument is that if Arabs cannot agree on politics, they should at least do business. While sincere words of welcome

User-friendly Government

Want to know how much the Consumer Price Index went up last year? Time to renew your driver's license? Or maybe you want to apply for one of the 5,700 government jobs currently open in Qena? Thanks to the government's Information and Decision Support Center (IDSC), you can do it all online, at websites like economy.gov, idsc.gov, tawzeef.gov, alhokoma.gov, and a slew of other dotgovs. Established in 1985 to facilitate the flow of information among different parts of the Egyptian government and between the government and the public, the IDSC has been instrumental in setting up Egypt's digital information highway.

Alhokoma.gov is one of the latest additions to the country's fledgling e-government. A virtual mugamma, the site is considerably easier to navigate than that Kafkaesque bastion of bureaucracy that sits in Tahrir Square. It offers help and information for over 300 services—everything from renewing your passport to setting up an account at the post office to having your electricity meter checked. While users cannot yet complete the process online, the site lets visitors download the necessary forms and contains clear instructions on where to go, what to bring along, and how much it costs. Users can also choose to hear the instructions by clicking the phone icon next to the service.

Over the next few years, the IDSC hopes to expand the services offered by alhokoma and digitize other branches of government, ultimately creating a government portal where Egyptians at home and abroad can get information they need and actually do things like pay taxes and electricity bills online. But it isn't time to tear down the mugamma just yet—e-government is still in its very early stages in Egypt, and a myriad of obstacles need to be overcome before it is a viable enterprise. In addition to issues of technical capabilities, cost, and training, there is the challenge of adapting Egyptian bureaucratic structures to a user-friendly web format, with all the efficiency and transparency that entails. Already, some newly established government websites have managed to replicate the impenetrable bureaucracy that exists on the ground. Assembly.gov, for example, the site of the People's Assembly offers access in three different languages, but neither the French, English, nor Arabic pages offer the promised list of members, while capmas.gov, the site of the central statistics agency, is a virtual maze of hundreds of pages, navigable by a door at the bottom of every page that inevitably leads users on a wild goose chase. The biggest hurdle facing effective e-government, however, will be getting more Egyptians to use it. Though internet usage is growing fast, only about one million Egyptians at most are regular internet users. Even less own a computer. Nor will e-government be of much service to the 45% of the population that is still illiterate. Though the internet may provide the means to modernize state information systems, it will take a while for the benefit to trickle down to the general population. *MM*

The government is quickly modernizing its information systems, but it isn't time to tear down the mugamma yet

greeted the proposal, little has been accomplished on the ground. In terms of bilateral relations, however, there has been more progress. Despite political divisions, Iraq and Egypt have stepped up trade dramatically over the past few years, concluding a free trade agreement in January 2001. Egypt is now Iraq's biggest trade partner in the Arab world. A similar rapprochement with Iran is also visible, although formal diplomatic ties have not yet been restored.

The trend towards diversifying Egypt's ties with the outside world came at a time when key international players tended to believe a peaceful settlement for the

Ahmed Maher (left) and Amr Moussa (right)

In the Arab League

The Arab League has seen a breath of fresh air since Amr Moussa, Egypt's popular former foreign minister, became its secretary-general in May 2001. Analysts at the time surmised that the 65-year-old diplomat was being "kicked upstairs" to the toothless institution after ten years as the top diplomat in the largest Arab country. His replacement in the foreign ministry by the decidely more tactful Ahmed Maher gave credence to theories that Moussa had become too mouthy in front of the Americans over their pro-Israeli foreign policy. Moussa's stated aim when taking over as head of the 22-member league was to streamline its operations and make it an essential player in coordinating Arab positions quickly on the issues of the day. Thus far, he has certainly raised the public profile of the organization. One of his first acts was to appoint Palestinian politician Hanan Ashrawi as the League's Media Commissioner. An articulate woman and intelligent proponent of Palestinian rights respected in the West, Ashrawi's appointment was a shrewd move that signaled the league meant business.

As the Palestinian uprising against Israeli occupation raged on, the league was quick to issue press statements to the media. Moussa himself visited most Arab countries to ensure that support was maintained for Yasser Arafat's Palestinian Authority in the face of Israeli arguments to the international community that Arafat, and not its occupation, were the heart of the problem. Though Moussa's efforts have at times been thwarted by inter-Arab bickering—the March summit in Beirut that saw the walkout of the Palestinian delegation is the most obvious example—over the past year, the Arab League has started to wake up from its long slumber, and may eventually become a real forum for joint Arab action vis-à-vis Israel.

Perhaps most importantly, Moussa has made rare efforts to invigorate Arab groups abroad into more effective lobbying action on behalf of Arab issues, particularly the Palestinian issue. After spending the better of part last September in the US, in February he appointed the first of what are to be several Arab League liaison officers posted in Arab-American communities in the US. The first appointee, Nasser Beidoun, is based in Michigan, where it is hoped he can mobilize the sizeable Arab community there and help build a more productive relationship between the US and the Arab world. These sorts of grassroots efforts may ultimately do more than a dozen summits to make the league an effective tool for Arab diplomacy.

Moussa's plans to sort out the league's bureaucratic structures will take longer to tackle, though. The organization is way overstaffed, and Moussa himself has expressed the need to bring it down to a manageable size while raising the overall level of skill. His desire to triple the league's budget may also have to wait until Arab countries start to cough up their overdue annual dues, estimated at about $100 million. *AH*

50-year-old conflict between the Arabs and Israel could be near. Palestinians signed their Oslo peace deal with Israel in 1993, and Jordan followed one year later with a permanent peace treaty. Syria, despite refusing to take part in any form of normalization of relations with Israel until it withdrew from the Golan Heights, also kept open channels with Washington and engaged in on-and-off talks with Israel. Thus, several analysts argued that Egypt no longer had a regional role to play, since its main mission was to bring Arab countries to the negotiating table with Israel. Yet, this reasoning proved wrong, particularly in light of the dangerous escalation of violence in the occupied Palestinian territories throughout 2001 and the events following the attacks on the World Trade Center in the US.

The election of Ariel Sharon as Israel's prime minister in February 2001 coupled with the ongoing intifada ushered in a new stage in Egyptian-Israeli relations. Mubarak has repeatedly affirmed that Egypt was not negotiating on behalf of Palestinians. Yet, given the *de facto* retreat from the Oslo peace agreement by both sides of the conflict and the initial hands-off policy pursued by the new US administration, Egypt's diplomatic interventions proved essential to maintaining the possibility of renewed peace talks between Israel and Palestinians. While Egypt's basic stance towards Israel and the resolution of the conflict did not change, the Israeli government's brutal crackdown in the occupied territories, the re-invasion of the West Bank, and the universal hostility felt by the Arab street towards Sharon put unprecedented stress on Egyptian-Israeli relations. Unable to ignore Israel's excesses in the occupied territories, but still determined to keep the lines of communication with the Jewish state open, Egypt ultimately suspended all communication with Israel that was not immediately pertinent to the Palestinian situation. Though a flurry of diplomatic activity followed the announcement, by mid-year, Mubarak's attempts to broker a lasting cease-fire had come to naught.

Egypt's "special relationship" with the US managed to weather the escalating crisis next door, though it did start looking a little frayed around the edges. In the aftermath of September 11, the relationship actually received a boost, with Egypt stepping up to once again confirm its strategic importance in the region. As the US struggled to build a coalition against terror for its campaign in Afghanistan, Egypt proved an important ally, offering the use of its airspace, expedited transport through the Suez Canal, and—perhaps most importantly—moral support in selling its controversial war. In turn, the Bush administration officially announced its active re-engagement with the Palestinian-Israeli crisis and publicly acknowledged Egypt's positive role in the region. All of this official good will, however, did not completely mask the fissures in US-Egyptian relations. Unwavering US support for Sharon's policies, even throughout the April invasion of the West Bank, put to rest once and for all the myth of the US as an impartial mediator in the conflict, making it more difficult for the Egyptian government to justify its close ties with the US. The gap between the two allies became even starker when the US began calling for the ouster of Palestinian president Yasser Arafat in June, an idea Mubarak has consistently opposed. As the possibility loomed of a renewed US offensive against Iraq, Egypt was finding it increasingly difficult to square its own regional priorities with those of the Bush administration. *KD & MM*

The Game of Politics
The opposition tries to rise from its slumber

Under the Rotunda

The parliament elected in November 2000 took everyone by surprise with its extremely high turnover rate (75%), overwhelmingly youthful membership, and

the unusually intense and prolonged floor debates witnessed in its first session. The feisty performance of a handful of maverick and freshmen MPs captured the public imagination and gave vent to brewing popular frustrations over unemployment, the housing crisis, Israel's suppression of the Palestinian intifada, and government corruption.

High hopes for the 2001/02 session were soon dashed, however, when it got off to an uneventful start and remained decidedly low key for the duration of the term. The government passed all the key bills in the last month, deflated potentially embarrassing issues, and got away with minimal oversight by MPs. If the first session took a great step towards restoring parliament's historical role as a key arena of political debate and dissent, the assembly's mediocre performance during the second term illustrated the extent to which it still plays a subordinate role to the executive in Egypt's political system.

The 1971 constitution sets up a bicameral legislature consisting of the People's Assembly (Maglis al-Shaab) with 454 seats (444 elected by popular vote, 10 appointed by the president, members serve five-year terms) and the Shura Council (Maglis al-Shura) with 264 seats (176 elected by popular vote, 88 appointed by the president, members serve six-year terms). The Shura Council came into being in 1980 through a constitutional amendment by the president and functions largely in a consultative role. The constitution stipulates that certain types of legislation must pass through the council, but it does not have the power to initiate legislation on its own. Rather, its real power lies in its administration of several important government bodies, such as the Supreme Press Council and the Political Parties Committee. The People's Assembly is the real site of legislation and parliamentary oversight of executive performance. Since the return of multi-party politics in 1976, parliament's visibility in Egyptian politics has waxed and waned, its burgeoning rise in the 1980s eclipsed during the 1990s as legislative politics took a backseat to the government's battle against Islamist insurgents.

Parliament in Egypt has always played second fiddle to the much more powerful executive, earning the epithet of a rubber stamp legislature. It does not hold the power of the purse, requiring government approval before changing any items in the projected budget, and it does not have oversight of the defense budget. Legislation is overwhelmingly introduced by the executive and often swiftly railroaded through. The uninterrupted majority of the ruling party since 1976 means that parliament is

How a Law Gets Passed

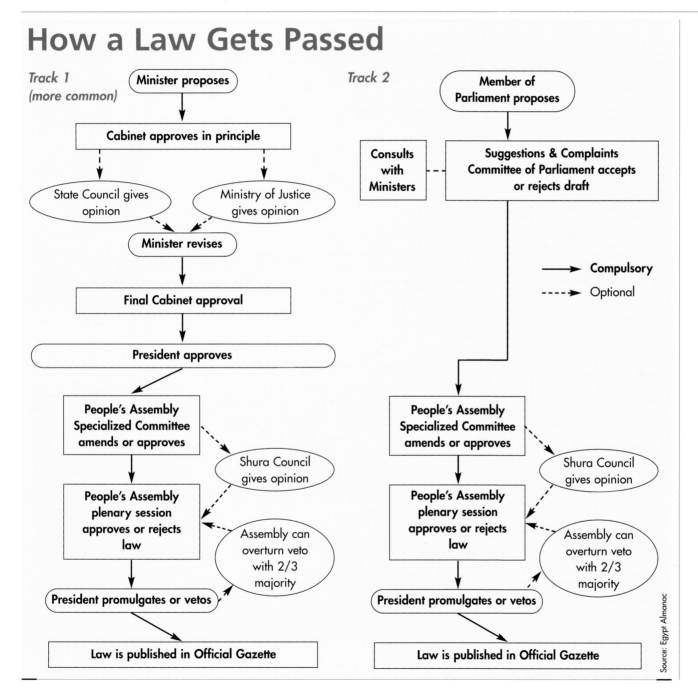

Track 1
(more common)

Minister proposes

Cabinet approves in principle

State Council gives opinion

Ministry of Justice gives opinion

Minister revises

Final Cabinet approval

President approves

People's Assembly Specialized Committee amends or approves

Shura Council gives opinion

People's Assembly plenary session approves or rejects law

Assembly can overturn veto with 2/3 majority

President promulgates or vetos

Law is published in Official Gazette

Track 2

Member of Parliament proposes

Consults with Ministers

Suggestions & Complaints Committee of Parliament accepts or rejects draft

People's Assembly Specialized Committee amends or approves

Shura Council gives opinion

People's Assembly plenary session approves or rejects law

Assembly can overturn veto with 2/3 majority

President promulgates or vetos

Law is published in Official Gazette

→ **Compulsory**

----→ Optional

All the laws passed over the last two years started in the cabinet

Source: Egypt Almanac

151

stacked with government supporters who forestall the opposition's ostensible power to block legislation.

By contrast, the 1971 constitution creates an extremely strong presidency. The president can both convene and dissolve parliament at any time. He can issue and block legislation and his decrees have the force of law. Articles 74 and 152 of the constitution empower the president to hold referenda by which parliament can be bypassed, as when the latter casts a vote of no-confidence in the sitting government. Article 134 enables the

executive to make further inroads into the legislature, allowing ministers to be MPs and granting nonmember ministers the right to sit in on plenary sessions and committee meetings. The president also has the power to appoint ten MPs, customarily used to raise the profile of underrepresented groups such as women and Copts.

A combination of factors conspired to make the People's Assembly elected in 2000 a vast improvement over its lackluster predecessor, which featured a 94% majority of the ruling NDP, the railroading of notorious legislation such as Press Law 95/1996, and the mechanical extension of the Emergency Law until 2003. The single most decisive cause of change was the highly significant ruling in July 2000 by the Supreme Constitutional Court (SCC) requiring judicial supervision of parliamentary elections for the first time in the nation's history, thus fulfilling a longtime opposition demand.

Relatively greater transparency and vigilance over the electoral process translated into a more representative parliament. Only 172 of the 444 seats in parliament were won by the NDP's official candidates. Although 216 nominal independents promptly joined the NDP's ranks (allowing it to claim an 85% majority), they were more beholden to their constituents than to the party and proved highly unpredictable in their voting behavior. On the opposition side, a batch of new faces along with experienced incumbents and a couple of old hands made for lively and more substantive floor debates. The return of seasoned MPs from the 1976 parliament such as Alexandrians Kamal Ahmed and Abu al-Ezz al-Hariri, the re-election of contentious mavericks such as al-Badri Farghali (Port Said) and Ayman Nour (Cairo), the first-time election of Nasserist activist Hamdin Sabahi (Baltim) and Wafdist scion Mounir Fakhri Abd al-Nour (Cairo), and the securing of 17 seats by Muslim Brother freshmen (larger than the share of opposition parties combined) made for some memorable moments.

During the first term, speaker Fathi Surour and Minister of State for Parliamentary Affairs Kamal al-Shazli were put to a severe test as MPs criticized government policy and budget priorities and delivered stinging interpellations of ministers. Shazli's role as enforcer of internal NDP discipline took a hit as NDP freshmen failed to consistently toe the party line and on more than one occasion wreaked havoc under the rotunda. In May 2001, 100 NDP freshmen staged a brief sit-in to protest the lifting of immunity from fellow NDP deputy and business tycoon Fawzi al-Sayed (East Cairo) for financial wrongdoing. It was only after the intercession of the majority leader and his assurance of an equitable resolution of the matter that the deputies called off their protest.

Key parliament posts also came in for intense competition. In the opening procedural session to elect the Speaker and his deputies, Ayman Nour received a startling 169 votes for deputy speaker, the majority from freshmen NDP deputies. NDP stalwart Amal Othman eventually won the post with 283 votes, but it was a loud wake-up call to NDP leaders that it would not be politics as usual. The battle for committee chairmanships was no less heated. Hamdin Sabahi almost made history by being the first opposition deputy to chair a committee (Media and Culture) when speaker Sorour quickly called a re-vote and prevailed upon NDP deputies to cast their votes for NDP fixture Fayda Kamel.

In terms of legislation, floor debates were more substantive and animated, and deputies' performance well above the usual mediocre average. By Speaker Surour's own count, 161 deputies spoke during the budget debate in May, the highest ever of any parliamentary budget debate since the ratification of the 1971 constitution. Several bills the government hoped to pass were held up to unprecedented scrutiny and sent back to committee. A bill establishing trade relations with Cameroon was sent back for re-translation when deputies pointed out serious flaws in the treaty's Arabic translation. A controversial bill debated in June on transplanting corneas from corpses extended well past 2 am and was eventually sent back to the Shura Council for reformulation.

Perhaps the most significant novelty of the 2001 session was the frequent coming together of ruling party and opposition MPs on key policy issues, such as their united stand against the controversial mortgage bill, their criticism of the government over soaring unemployment, and their uniform opposition to the implementation of the second and third stages of the General Sales Tax. In June, NDP and opposition MPs succeeded in suspending a ministerial decree evicting residents of the Dahab and Warraq Nile islands on the pretext of conserving the environment. If they did not always succeed in rolling back unpopular legislation (the mortgage and sales tax bills were later eventually

passed), deputies at least tried to live up to their watchdog function and embarrassed the government into conceding and addressing their criticisms. Press and TV coverage brought parliament into countless living rooms, engaging public opinion and popularizing the People's Assembly as entertaining political theater.

By contrast, the second term of parliament (December 2001–June 2002) was comparatively tamer than the first. The government adopted a successful strategy of containment, evidenced by its handling of the tragic Ayyat train disaster of February 19. The day after the accident, nearly a full house of opposition and government deputies made urgent statements, demanded fact-finding commissions, and some even called on the government to accept responsibility and resign. Surour and al-Shazli were able to delay a formal interrogation of responsible ministers until May 19, when the incident had receded from public memory.

The second term was also disappointing in terms of legislation. In time-honored fashion, the government saved the most contentious and important bills until the

The second session of the "parliament of hope" was much tamer than the first

Parliament in Action	2001	2002
Legislative Duties		
Laws passed	152	159
Treaties ratified	37	53
Presidential decrees approved	1	1
Hours spent in committee meetings	1,406	1,712
Committee reports discussed	661	667
Bills proposed by deputies	66	78
Of those, number that became law	0	0
Executive Oversight		
Formal questions	217	158
Requests for information	724	745
Urgent statements	515	492
Interpellations (interrogations of ministers)	9	9

Source: *al-Ahram* newspaper

last month, when the absentee rate among deputies is typically high. At breakneck speed, the government passed an export promotion law, a law establishing exclusive economic zones, a law regulating the affairs of non-governmental organizations (NGOs), and the controversial long-awaited labor law, which was passed in principle and awaits the 2002/03 session for article-

by-article deliberation and final approval.

While the assembly may not have appreciably enlarged its powers vis-à-vis the executive branch as evidenced by the 2002 session, the 2001 term definitively laid to rest its reputation as a politically marginal institution. Two episodes epitomize this mixed record. In May 2001, independent MP Kamal

The Opposition

The last two years have not been banner ones for Egypt's opposition political parties. Already enervated by the lack of popular and institutional support, the opposition lost two more parties when the government-affiliated Political Parties Committee froze the activities of the Misr Party and al-Wifaq al-Qawmi. The committee cited internal leadership struggles as the cause, but both parties claimed the government had incited the struggles as an excuse to shut them down. Two new parties, Egypt 2000 and the Democratic Generation, did make their entrance on the scene, but only after appealing the ruling of the Political Parties Committee. The committee compensated by rejecting the applications of nine more parties in 2001 alone.

More cracks appeared within the ranks of the opposition. Ibrahim Shukri, the 82-year-old leader of the frozen Labor Party, backed government candidate Ibrahim Nafie in the July 2001 elections at the Journalists' Syndicate over fellow party member Magdi Hussein, giving rise to rumors that he was making a deal with the government to revive his moribund party minus the Islamists. The liberal Wafd Party suffered a setback when party chair Noman Gomaa expelled three high-profile party members, all of them MPs, bringing the Wafd bloc in parliament down to four from seven seats. Expelled Wafdist Ayman Nour subsequently went shopping for a stake in a new party, making the rounds of the Greens, the Umma Party, the Nasserist Party, and the Misr Party. What was widely

perceived as Nour's opportunism is only the most exaggerated example of the general lack of a positive political vision among Egypt's opposition.

The Nasserist Party faced severe financial difficulties. Owing upwards of LE2 million in taxes, insurance payments, and printing costs, the party's weekly mouthpiece al-Arabi, was reduced to begging for alms on its front pages, while party members staged protests imploring the government itself to intervene and save the party from bankruptcy. As if that were not enough, four disaffected members briefly occupied the party's downtown headquarters last summer, threatening to blow it up if their demands for greater internal transparency were not met. Though riot police quickly diffused the situation, it served as a stark illustration of the internal strife that plagues more than one opposition party.

Throughout these routine fiascos, Egypt's opposition quietly grew one year older. The average age of the leaders of the three most established opposition parties—the Wafd, the leftist Tagammu, and the Arab Democratic Nasserist Party—is just shy of 75, three times older than well over half of the Egyptian population. Relics of a former age, their politics and oft-decried authoritarian styles of leadership are increasingly out of touch with the aspirations and needs of their would-be constituents. Egypt may have moved into the new millenium, but the opposition seems more suited to the Ice Age every year. *MM*

Voting in the 2000 Elections

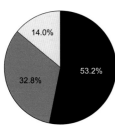

14.0%
53.2%
32.8%

■ Registered but didn't vote
■ Eligible but not registered
▨ Voted

Source: *al-Hayat* newspaper

In Egypt's last parliamentary elections, most voters shunned the polls

Ahmed became a household name when his interpellation of minister Youssef Boutros Ghali over alleged corruption at the Cairo and Alexandria Stock Exchange indirectly led to a probe by the public prosecutor. Ahmed's questioning prompted a series of investigations into additional high-profile cases of alleged corruption, leading to the trial and conviction of former public officials.

On June 3, 2002, over the dogged protests of independent and opposition MPs, the government rammed through Law 84/2002 regulating NGOs. The law gives the government the power to dissolve NGOs without court order (Article 42), bans them from engaging in political work (Article 11), and requires government approval of foreign funds before NGOs can access them. *MG*

Parliament after the 1995 Elections

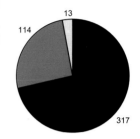

Parliament after the 2000 Elections

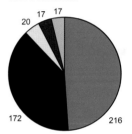

■ National Democratic Party
■ Independents who joined NDP
□ Remained Independents
■ Muslim Brotherhood
▨ Other opposition parties
(Appointed by the President 10)

Source: Egypt Almanac

Since the elections, the NDP has added three more seats to its total

Parliamentary Highlights

1. June 2002: During the discussion of the NGO bill, NDP whip Kamal al-Shazli explains the government's reasoning for prohibiting NGOs from pursuing political activities: "Parties are the proper venue for political work, syndicates for professional work, and NGOs for social work. If parties are there for politics, why should NGOs be involved in politics?"

2. February 2002: Deputies file 106 urgent statements, 25 requests for information, and 4 formal questions over the Ayyat train disaster. Independent Nasserist deputy Hamdin Sabahi calls on the cabinet to take responsibility and resign. Kamal al-Shazli answers, "Who are you to ask the government to resign?" Sabahi retorts, "And who are you to tell me I can't say that?"

3. January 2002: Independent MP Kamal Ahmed heckles Prime Minister Atef Ebeid during his delivery of the government's policy statement, saying "I don't respect the Egyptian government because it does not respect the rights of the Egyptian people." Told to calm down, he walks out in protest.

4. June 2001: Opposition and NDP deputies cause an uproar over a unilateral ministerial decree evicting residents of the Nile islands of Dahab and Warraq ostensibly to protect state property and the environment. The decree is suspended.

5. May 2001: Independent MP Kamal Ahmed delivers an interpellation of the economy minister over alleged cronyism at the Cairo and Alexandria Stock Exchange.

6. May 2001: NDP bigwig and presidential Chief-of-Staff Zakariya Azmi (Zeitoun) leads an attack against the government's long-awaited mortgage bill. Opposition and NDP deputies join in, lambasting the bill for ignoring low-income housing seekers.

7. May 2001: At a morning session, opposition and NDP deputies alike are up in arms against the implementation of the second and third stages of the General Sales Tax. At the evening session, NDP deputies are prevailed upon to vote for the tax, and opposition deputies walk out in protest.

8. April 2001: All 17 Muslim Brother deputies walk out in protest at the speaker's refusal to give them the floor to deliver an urgent statement about police harassment of Brother candidates for the Shura Council elections.

9. April 2001: As a sign of the enduring imbalance in executive-legislative relations, parliament votes 384-2 (with two abstentions) to extend for three years a 1974 law allowing the president to procure, produce, or export arms without referring his decisions to the People's Assembly.

10. January 2001: Brother MP Gamal Heshmat submits a request for information to the Ministry of Culture over the publication of three allegedly racy novels by the Cultural Palaces Authority. Forty-eight hours later, head of the authority, Ali Abu Shadi, is fired, and some NDP deputies applaud the original motion and government response. *MG*

Other Power Bases
The press and the judiciary liven up the scene

The Fourth Estate

There are three types of newspapers in Egypt: pro-government, opposition, and relatively independent. The pro-government papers (who prefer the label "nationalist press" arguing they represent the country's "national interests" which all Egyptians should agree on) came into being after the 1952 revolution. The Nasser regime first put the press under direct government censorship, then, in 1960, nationalized it. Egyptians grew accustomed to reading nothing but the government's line. The result was a high level of mistrust of what they read in the press.

Opposition papers were born under President Anwar al-Sadat. When he introduced the multi-party system in 1977, he also allowed opposition parties to publish newspapers. However, his tolerance was short-lived, and he soon became infuriated with the sharp criticism he faced in opposition papers. In September 1981, he ordered the arrests of his opponents, whether Islamists, leftists, or Nasserists, and the closure of all opposition newspapers. A month later he was assassinated.

President Mubarak has allowed a greater margin of freedom for the press, although several constraints remain. The form of ownership of the nationalist press is still ambiguous. According to laws tailored by Sadat, all newspapers in Egypt fall under the control of the Supreme Press Council, part of the upper house of parliament, the Shura Council. As in the People's Assembly, the ruling National Democratic Party holds the vast majority of its seats. The Supreme Press Council appoints editors-in-chief of the nationalist press, though it is the presidency that puts forward the names. It also has to approve any new publications by opposition parties. The People's Assembly approved a new, and ostensibly more liberal, press law in 1996, allowing individuals and companies to publish newspapers after depositing sums ranging from LE250,000 to LE1 million, depending on whether the publication was monthly, weekly, or daily. An amendment later introduced to the law that made it necessary to obtain cabinet approval for any new publication was declared unconstitutional by the Supreme Constitutional Court last year, thus eliminating at least one obstacle in the way of would-be press moguls. Still, the Supreme Press Council remains tight-fisted with the licenses it grants.

Other laws hinder publications in more subtle ways. If publications do not appear with a certain degree of regularity, they stand to lose their license. Small opposition papers are particularly vulnerable to this, as they have limited financial resources, and several have lost the right to publish.

The difficulties facing Egyptians who want to publish their own papers led many to register as offshore companies. They then seek a permit from the Ministry of Information to print the paper "offshore" in Egypt's Free Zones, and circulate it onshore in the rest of the country. Gaining such permission means that each issue has to be read first by the state censor. In the late 1990s, Cyprus was the favored choice for offshore registration, and the so-called "Cypriot press" received much negative attention from the nationalist press, who claimed that they were sensational and represented a threat to Egypt's national interest. Last year, however, the Cypriot government itself did away with the system, declaring that foreign publications were not conforming to that country's press law, which stipulates that Cypriot-licensed papers must be printed in Cyprus. Most of the 100-plus Egyptian publications licensed in Cyprus rushed to register as offshore companies in other countries.

Opposition papers, meanwhile, continue to complain that they cannot compete with the huge pro-government dailies. *Al-Arabi*, put out by the Arab Democratic Nasserist Party, was forced to go from a daily to a weekly in 1999 due to financial problems. It now owes the government-run al-Ahram printing house upwards of LE1 million in back printing costs. In any case, opposition papers have much lower rates of circulation than the government dailies. The largest daily opposition paper, put out by the Wafd Party and carrying the same name, does not release circulation figures. Yet it does not exceed 50,000 copies a day, down from about 250,000 in the mid-1980s. Some of the opposition papers circulate no more than a few thousand copies a week. The best-known opposition papers besides *al-Wafd* are *al-Ahali* (published by the leftist Tagammu Party), *al-Arabi*, and *Sawt al-Umma*, an upstart independent publication that hit the stands in late 2000. The independent business daily *al-Alam al-Yom* also has a following in its niche market, though it is known for its sensationalism.

Pressing Ahead

Al-Ahram, the venerable government mouthpiece, celebrated its 125th birthday last year. Founded by Lebanese brothers Selim and Bishara Takla, it is the country's oldest daily—indeed, the oldest daily in the Arab world. (Egypt also has the honor of being the site of the Arab world's first newspaper, *al-Waqaai al-Misriya*, established in 1828.) Though *al-Ahram's* age lends it an incontestable prestige, many other current publications have similarly illustrious histories. Prior to 1952, Dar al-Hilal, founded in 1890 by another Lebanese immigrant, Jurji Zeidan, boasted a variety of magazines and literary publications, such as the still-functioning *al-Musawwar* (est. 1924) and *al-Hilal* (est. 1892), and the now defunct *Image* and *Cineimage*. *Rose al-Youssef*, founded by former actress Fatma al-Youssef in 1925, was one of the most politically engaged magazines of the day. *Al-Akhbar*, first published in 1944 by Mostafa and Ali Amin, is a relative newcomer to the press scene.

Like the Arabic press, the foreign-language press has suffered somewhat with the onslaught of time, having been either nationalized or simply fallen into quiet oblivion. Three years ago, one of the last privately owned pre-revolutionary newspapers, the French *Journal d'Egypte*, closed down after the death of Litta Gallad, widow of founder Edgar Gallad. Of the many Greek, Armenian, and Italian dailies, only the Armenian *Arev*, established in 1915, still exists, along with once daily Greek *Neophos*, now printed bi-monthly. The once-flourishing pre-revolutionary French- and English-language press is represented only by the *Egyptian Gazette*, first issued in 1880, along with its sister publication *Le Progres Egyptien*, which came along a few years later in 1893. As for *al-Muqattam*, *al-Ahram's* main competitor in the pre-revolutionary days, it was simply closed down about 40 years ago. *PAG*

Al-Akhbar, al-Ahram, and *al-Gomhouriya* are Egypt's three largest nationalist newspapers. *Al-Akhbar* has the reputation of being the most popular, with a circulation of nearly one million copies a day. Its weekly edition, *Akhbar al-Yom*, is even more popular as it avoids lengthy articles by intellectuals and politicians and prefers short, newsy items. *Al-Ahram*, the country's oldest, has a daily circulation of 400,000 to 500,000 and is seen as the newspaper of the elite. While *al-Ahram* and *al-Akhbar* were among the publications nationalized in 1960, *al-Gomhouriya* was the product of the 1952 military regime. It is even more local in its nature than *al-Akhbar*, publishing dates of school exams and prices of vegetables and fruits. *Al-Gomhouriya's* back page, which carries the sports news, is particularly popular among soccer fans.

Dar al-Hilal, Dar al-Maaref, and Rose al-Youssef publication houses, also under government control, produce popular weekly magazines including *al-Mussawar, October, Rose al-Youssef*, and *Sabah al-Kheir*. Partly just to cope with the increasing number of staff in the nationalist press, the three largest dailies have opened more in-house publications. Al-Ahram as a publishing house now boasts more than a dozen publications including an English weekly (*al-Ahram Weekly*), the French *al-Ahram Hebdo*, a women's magazine (*Nisf al-Dunya*), one on sports (*al-Ahram al-Riyadi*), a children's magazine (*Alaa al-Din*), a glossy devoted to home décor (*al-Beit*), and a political Arabic weekly magazine (*al-Ahram al-Arabi*). Akhbar's publishing house, meantime, has issued tabloid papers such *Akhbar al-Adab* on literature, *Akhbar al-Negoum* on art and cinema, and *Akhbar al-Riyada* on sports.

Circulation figures in Egypt remain very low—about 40 copies a day are sold per 1000 people, or 2.6 million papers a day. Illiteracy of about 50% means TV is the medium with the most penetration, while many Egyptians can only afford one paper a day, and only a few would buy both a pro-government and an opposition paper on the same day. Newspaper headlines and editorials, however, get considerably more indirect circulation through TV news programs like *Rais al-Tahrir,* easily one of the most widely viewed shows on Egyptian television, in which host Hamdi Qandil gives a weekly rundown and commentary of the local press, both government and opposition.

While opposition and independent papers enjoy a certain degree of freedom, there remain unspoken "red lines" set by the government which should not be crossed. A cursory survey of the papers that have been shut down over the last few years clearly shows that the government does not hesitate to close publications that represent a threat to "national unity." In early 1998, the independent *al-Destour* was closed after it published a story about alleged death threats against three prominent Coptic businessmen, while *al-Shaab*, published by the Islamist Labor Party, was shut down in May 2000 after a hysterical campaign against the Ministry of Culture which led to riots. Last year, the sensationalist weekly *al-Naba* temporarily lost its license when it published a

Media Penetration per 1000 people

Newspaper Circulation:	39 (1997)
Households with radio:	81.9 (1999)
Households with TV:	89.3 (2000)

Source: World Development Indicators, World Bank; Human Development Report, INP, UNDP 1998/9; Health and Demographic Survey 2000

lurid exposé of a Coptic monk alleged to be involved in a sex scandal, and the paper's publisher, Mamdouh Mahran, was later sentenced to three years in prison. All of these cases stand as lessons to non-government publications. On a similar note, the government refuses to cancel articles in the law which allow the imprisonment of journalists convicted of libel, despite campaigns by the local Press Syndicate to have fines replace prison terms. Indeed, last year a little-known journalist spent a month in prison after being sued for libel by Ibrahim Nafie, the head of the Press Syndicate.

At a time when the opposition and independent press are struggling to gain licenses, Egypt has been witnessing a boom in the publication of glossy English-language magazines. The market for these publications is very limited. Some do not sell more than a few hundred copies an issue and several have had to close after their first number. Their owners seem to be more concerned with advertising revenue than readership. Besides the *Egyptian Gazette*, the venerable if slightly preposterous English daily newspaper issued by *al-Gomhouriya*, there are no other English dailies. *Al-Ahram Weekly,* the *Cairo Times* and the *Middle East Times* are the best-known English-language weeklies. *KD*

On the Air

Struggling to keep up with satellite networks

In a televised interview in 2001, the 80-year old Abd al-Qader Hatem, Egypt's post-1952 minister of information, said that he had not revealed the architectural plans of the giant television premise overlooking the Nile until the construction work was finally completed: the budget required would have been rejected as unjustifiable on the priority list of the socialist regime. Instead, he collected thousands of pounds from advance viewer subscriptions, building Maspero one floor at a time.

Today Maspero is a virtual empire, and Hatem's successor, Safwat al-Sherif, is regarded as one of the most powerful officials in Egypt. During the 20 years he has been in office, the country has witnessed major social, economic, and political changes. Al-Sherif's role has been to adapt to these changes and preserve Egypt's position as the premier broadcaster in the Arab world, while simultaneously holding on to the state media's watchdog role.

Radio broadcasting began in Egypt in 1923 with private, wireless stations run by amateurs. The sector soon came under government control, however, and in 1934, the State Radio Service started transmission to the Delta, Suez, and parts of Upper Egypt. After the 1952 revolution, the Free Officers recognized the importance of radio for their regime, using it to bypass the local illiteracy barrier and gain regional support. Late president Gamal Abd al-Nasser's fiery speeches and diva Umm Kulthoum's monthly concerts echoed throughout Arab streets in the 1950s and 60s, gluing millions in the region to their radios and helping to make Egypt the preeminent bearer of pan-Arab culture and sentiment in the region. Egyptian radio lost some of its credibility during the 1967 war with Israel when it broadcast totally misleading war coverage, leading many Arab listeners to turn to the Arabic services of the BBC and the Voice of America for a more objective reporting of events. Still, with its Foreign Language and Beamed Service transmitting in 34 languages, by the 1970s, Egypt was the sixth largest radio broadcaster in the world.

In 1971, the Egyptian Radio and Television Union (ERTU) was established under the Ministry of Information as the sole authority empowered to set up and own radio and television stations in the country, and it was given full control over all broadcast material. Though Anwar Sadat, and later, President Hosni Mubarak embarked on programs of social and economic

liberalization, radio and television remained firmly in the state's grip.

In its latest 1999-2000 General Media Plan, ERTU reiterated its well-worn strategy of "focusing on government achievements and shedding light on megaprojects." Its other objectives included "focusing on social development … and the effect of globalization," as well as "focusing on social problems that hinder development … like illiteracy and the environment." The former goal has been meticulously implemented in both radio and television, with long segments of news and serious programs dedicated to highlighting the government's arbitration role in regional conflicts and economic megaprojects like the Toshka project.

Although television now enjoys almost universal penetration, 70% of Egyptians still listen to the radio. Despite ERTU's efforts to use the media as a tool for development, their own studies indicate that educational, health awareness, and tourism programs hardly top the list of favorite radio programs among listeners. Much more popular among all cross-sections of Egyptian society is the FM song station that made its debut in 2000, featuring non-stop Arabic music from the 1940s to current pop hits. Other favorites include Quranic recitation, news, soap dramas, and sports.

A minor diversion in radio occurred in October 1998, when Mubarak visited al-Gouna beach resort and gave his approval for a radio venture run by an Italian expatriate couple. His blessing of the project, though never granted the proper government licensing, resulted in the establishment of the first private radio station in Egypt since 1934, but it did not signal the imminent privatization of the local airwaves. The community station transmits on a limited FM frequency, covering only Gouna, and its content is limited to Western music and the brief announcement of local events.

Like radio, Egyptian television also grew up under the control of the state. It began transmission on July 21, 1960, with Nasser giving the inaugural speech that kicked off the three-and-a-half-hours of daily programming on Channel One. The Egyptian film industry—then the third largest in the world after Hollywood and Bombay—was and remains a major provider of technical and artistic personnel for Egyptian television. Regionally, Egyptian movie stars became the heroes and heroines of millions of Arabs, making Egyptian dialect and culture the most popular around.

In the decades to come, Egyptian serial dramas inherited the iconic status of Egyptian films and became a major pillar of entertainment and culture for the rest of the region. Often dealing with nationalist themes or current social issues, the best are typically left for Ramadan, when Arabs feast equally on food and TV. Among the most memorable of these *musalsalat* are the

TV Facts

The Egyptian television industry boast nothing comparable to the US Nielson ratings, making it difficult to accurately assess the popularity—or lack thereof—of any one show on Egyptian TV. Recently, however, the Egyptian Radio and Television Union contracted a field study to evaluate the overall effectiveness of programming. Though the study did not ask viewers about individual programs, it does provide some insight into the habits of th TV viewing public:

Egyptians who watch 4 hours of TV daily: 24%
Those who watch 5 or more hours: 54%
Most popular viewing times: 7pm to 12am
Most popular channels: One and Two
Viewers tuning in to the Egyptian Satellite Channel: 3.1%
Viewers who regularly tune in to their local station: 70%
Most popular type of programs: Arabic films and serials
Second most popular: Religious programming
Viewers who watch commercials: 73%
Viewers who watch televised sports: 54%
Viewers who watch political and news programs: 47%

Source: ERTU, 2000

1991 *Raafat al-Haggan*, the dramatization of the true story of an Egyptian spy in Israel, and *Layali al-Helmiya* (Nights of Helmiya), which was broadcast for several years in a row and depicted a traditional neighborhood facing the repercussions of social and political changes. In 2001, the most talked-about serial was *Ailat al-Hagg Metwalli* (Hagg Metwalli's family), which featured seasoned actor Nour al-Sherif as a wealthy merchant who marries four wives. The show's treatment of polygamy provoked a heated debate in the press and on TV talk shows across the region. The *fawazir*—also once a staple of Ramadan TV—died a quiet death in 2001, to be replaced by the video clip, a slicker reincarnation of the musical variety show.

Like radio, television is used to promote pertinent social issues on the state's agenda. Perhaps Safwat al-Sherif's greatest success has been the media campaign waged against political Islam since the 1980s, which branded Islamists of all stripes as "terrorists" and "enemies of the nation." Despite the popularity of the veil among Egyptian women, only one Egyptian broadcaster, Kariman Hamza, has appeared with a veil on the screen—and that was on her regular religious program. Immediate coverage of local terrorist attacks is always followed by commentaries on their harmful social and economic impact, and TV dramas make good use of the "evil fundamentalist." Meanwhile, time is given to the state-supervised al-Azhar officials to preach and answer queries. Sheikh Metwalli al-Shaarawi, three years after his death, remains an important segment in religious programming on Fridays and in Ramadan.

A turning point for Egyptian television came with the outbreak of the Gulf War in 1990, when CNN offered free transmission to Egyptian TV, becoming the first foreign channel to be viewed locally. Egypt immediately started the Egyptian Space Network and established its first satellite channel on ArabSat. In 1994, Nile TV became the first satellite channel in the region to broadcast in English and Arabic.

In its race to join the satellite age, Egypt signed a contract with the French Matra Marconi Space to establish its first satellite, NileSat 101, in 1995. It was launched in 1998 at a cost of LE157 million, followed in 2000 by NileSat 102. The two have now taken over most of the regional and international TV satellite channels broadcasting in the region, totaling around 120 channels. Other space-age attempts have not been so successful. In 1998, ERTU launched eight thematic channels to be broadcast on Nile-Sat, running the gamut from news to sports to education. But instead of bringing in a greater audience, they suffered a deficit of more than LE750 million in a few years time and were later broadcast for free as part of the bouquet offered by the Dubai-based Showtime.

With more Egyptians tuning to Arab and foreign stations, Egyptian television has attempted to improve the quality of programming. In the news department, equipment was updated, and more reporters were dispatched to cover stories in Egypt and abroad, but there has been little change in the editorial context that endorses the government line. On the other hand, TV officials have been quick to respond to Egyptians' emotional response to the latest Palestinian intifada by dedicating ample airtime to coverage. A spate of new talk shows have made their appearance in the last couple of

Hollywood on the Nile?

After several years of hype, Egyptian Media Production City Co. (MPCC), the television production and entertainment zone in Sixth of October City, was officially inaugurated on June 17, 2002. Feted as a new Hollywood on the Nile that will bring in cash while breathing life back into the downtrodden film industry, the company garnered massive media attention and thousands of investors following its initial public offering in October 1999. Established on three million m² of desert next to the NileSat land station, MPCC includes three state-of-the-art studio complexes with 29 studios, 17 outdoor filming scenes with "typical" Egyptian sets, the amusement park Magicland, and a five-star hotel. The complex is also home to the newly established International Academy of Media, a 300-student TV and cinema academy that hopes to become a center for students from across the region. The first classes were to begin in September. The company lists paid-in capital of LE1.7 billion and a whopping LE2 billion in total assets. Even before the grand opening, MPCC had been working hard to attract customers to its complex. By the end of 2001, several private satellite channels had rented studios. For glitziness the coup of the year had to be Middle East Broadcasting Co.'s decision to move part of its production from London and Paris to Cairo, including its highly rated show, *Who Wants to Be a Millionaire*, which began production at MPCC in February. Other tenants included Orbit, the drama sector of the Egyptian Radio and Television Union (ERTU), ART, the Dubai-based TIBA satellite channel, Al-Jazeera, Tamima (the Egyptian shopping channel), and al-Mehwar and Dream TV, two Egyptian private satellite channels established in 2001. Terms of the leases were not disclosed.

Despite all this activity, lingering questions about the overall feasibility of the project remain. When the complex is fully operational, it will have the capacity to produce about 3,600 hours of TV programming and 100 films a year. According to chairman and CEO Abd al-Rahman Hafez, former president of ERTU, the company plans to raise film production from nine movies in 2001 to 40 this year. But if Media Production City is to really succeed, it will need need to improve the quality of its productions as well. Under the watchful eye of the Ministry of Information—its ERTU is the largest shareholder in the project with a 43% stake—can enough innovative programming make its way out of the studios to entice the necessary viewers and advertisers? Though the studios churned out a few serial dramas for Ramadan last year, the vast majority of the films bankrolled by the company thus far have proved flops. Questions of censorship have also reared their head. Fears that the state may exert editorial pressure on private satellite stations using MPCC's studios or broadcasting on NileSat next door were borne out by threats to close down the Qatari news channel al-Jazeera in October 2000 when it aired a particularly harsh critique of Egypt's stance vis-à-vis the Palestinian intifada.

Aside from issues of content, investors looking at the bottom line still have not been told how much money the project may earn. Since its inception, MPCC has been notoriously tight-fisted with the hard figures and information necessary to evaluate its financial health. Money has poured into the complex, but so far very little has come out. Construction and investments costs on studio complex A alone amounted to $315 million. Meanwhile the balance sheet for 2001 showed net earnings of only LE27.2 million, almost 50% less than the year before. With many of the studios only recently completed, it is still not clear when the real profits will be rolling in—or the quality broadcasting pouring out. *SP*

years, as Egyptian TV takes its cue from the popularity of such programs on Arab satellite stations, most notably the Qatar-based al-Jazeera network. Monday evening's *Rais al-Tahrir* (Editor-In-Chief) has proved a huge hit among Egyptians, who admire veteran broadcaster Hamdi Qandil's outspoken critique of local and foreign events. However, a red line is clearly drawn on top government officials and the military institution. Even Hamdi Qandil is not immune: a sizeable chunk of his program was censored in April, at the height of Israel's reinvasion of the West Bank.

In November 2001 (coinciding with the month of Ramadan), the first two private Egyptian satellite stations began transmission: al-Mehwar and Dream. Both were begun by well-known, politically connected businessmen—TV magnate Ahmed Bahgat began Dream, while ceramic king and parliamentarian Mohammed Abu al-Enein owns al-Mehwar, although ERTU has a 20% stake. With years of business experience, the two may be able to make good on their investment, but it is still too early to tell if the content will make any waves. Programming during Ramadan highlighted Jay Leno-styled talk shows, TV dramas, popular video clips, and moderate religious sermons by such rising stars as Amr Khaled. As the vast majority of Egyptians cannot afford even the reduced rates of satellite subscriptions, most stuck to local stations with their less glamorous entertainment.

As Egypt tries to maintain its lead in the Arab TV world, its main competition comes from Beirut and Dubai, with the former providing European-styled elegance and professionalism, and the latter offering meticulous hi-tech expertise. Egypt, however, is still outselling them with a well established artistic and entertainment culture that has deep roots in the entire region. *HF*

The Judiciary
Judges oversee creeping constitutionalism

On July 15, 2000, the Supreme Constitutional Court (SCC) issued what in retrospect may be viewed as one of the most significant legal decisions in Egypt's modern history. It ruled that the previous two parliamentary elections, in 1990 and 1995, were void because they did not honor the constitutional clause giving the judiciary authority over the voting. Faced with the ruling, the People's Assembly was forced to approve a new electoral law allowing judges access to all levels of the voting process, thus ushering in freer and cleaner elections. Following parliamentary elections in 2000, the ruling was extended to Shura Council elections last year.

The election issue is by no means the only case in which the judiciary has stood as a counterbalance to the government. Last year, the SCC overturned a clause in the penal code (article 48) that made discussing the commission of a possible crime a crime itself, regardless of whether the crime was actually carried out. It also declared unconstitutional a law requiring cabinet approval for the licensing of any new publication. Over the last ten years, the SCC has issued over a dozen rulings that have widened the margin of civil and individual liberties in Egypt, in

Egyptian Court System

State Council

Supreme Constitutional Court (SCC)

Cases referred by the executive or another court

Court of Cassation

High Court of Ethics

Military Judiciary

Under the Ministry of Defense, but the president can refer civilians

Legislative Division

Judicial Division

Legal Opinion Division

Referred for clarification on points of law only

Court of Ethics

High Administrative Court

Procedural appeal only

Administrative Courts

Where the state is a defendant

Disciplinary Courts

Where public officials and state employees are defendants for job-related charges

Court of Appeals

Courts of First Instance

State Security Courts

Emergency State Security Courts

No appeal

Criminal

Civil

With sections for commercial, civil, labor, and personal status cases

State Council: 655 member justices, established 1946
SCC: 15 justices, established 1979
Court of Cassation: 30 justices, established 1931
Court of Ethics: established 1980

Source: Egypt Almanac

In the Courts

Egypt's contemporary judicial system has its roots in the legal reforms of the 19th century, initiated by homegrown reformers who sought to modernize the Egyptian state and less altruistically motivated foreign powers. The outcome was Egypt's first modern civil court, established in 1875 in the form of the Mixed Courts, which stood in opposition to the *Ahli*, or Native Courts, instituted in 1883. As part of the Capitulations imposed on Egypt that granted foreigners privileged status, the Mixed Courts had the sole authority to adjudicate cases in which a foreigner was a party, while the latter had jurisdiction over criminal and civil cases involving Egyptian nationals. Personal status cases were heard in separate *shariaa* courts or the relevant sectarian *(milli)* courts for Copts and other Christian communities.

The dual court system survived until 1949, when the Mixed Courts were abolished and a new civil code was put in place. In 1956, separate *shariaa* courts were also done away with. Since then personal status cases have been heard in a special division of the civil court system, presided over by judges with training in Islamic law. Egyptian law as it stands today is an amalgamation of the various impulses that went into the earliest reforms, drawing heavily on Islamic Law and Napoleonic codes. In addition to the so-called "ordinary courts," over the past few decades several specialized judicial bodies have come into existence. The oldest of these is the State Council (*magles al-dawla*). Modeled on the French Conseil d'Etat, the State Council heads the administrative judiciary and a battery of other administrative tribunals and committees. It also has the authority to issue rulings on the legality of government decrees or proposed legislation, as in 1999 when it upheld a Ministry of Education decree banning the *niqab*, the full veil, on school campuses. The 1971 constitution made provisions

for the Supreme Constitutional Court and for state security courts, which officially have jurisdiction in cases involving threats to national security, such as espionage. President Sadat later established the Court of Ethics (*mahkamat al-qiyam*) as well, a nod to the office of the Socialist Prosecutor, who alone is authorized to bring cases before it. Its mandate is vague, allowing it to hear crimes related to threats to the public order and certain moral offenses. In recent years, it has been used to prosecute corruption cases and sequester funds related to drug-trafficking, but in general it has fallen by the wayside.

At the head of the ordinary courts stands the Supreme Judicial Council, composed of three members of the Court of Cassation (including the chief justice), the head of the Court of Appeals, the public prosecutor, and the assistant minister of justice. This body is responsible for the appointment and promotion of judges within the civil and criminal courts, chosen on a competitive basis from the ranks of the *niyaba*, or Public Prosecutor's Office, practicing lawyers, and law professors. Like the French system, there are no jury trials in the Egyptian system, but rather a panel of judges—or in lower courts, one judge—who issue verdicts and sentences.

Although attempts have been made to further modernize the Egyptian judiciary—recently a project was initiated to create an e-library of Egyptian jurisprudence—the court system is under severe strain due to high case loads, a lack of judicial infrastructure, and a labyrinthine court process that can mean endless delays in even the simplest of civil cases. A Ministry of Justice report estimated in 1996 that judges in lower courts hear at least 70 cases per day, allowing them about 4 minutes per case, and sometimes as many as 200. The same study also found that litigants in civil cases make on average 30-40 appearances before the first instance court before a case is resolved. *MM*

areas ranging from freedom of expression to workers' rights to the sanctity of private property.

Only recently has the judiciary been able to extend its authority to such crucial issues of state. Egypt's current constitution was enacted in 1971 by President Anwar Sadat, and the SCC was not established until 1979. Although the constitution is in principle extremely liberal, granting Egyptians rights comparable to those enjoyed by citizens of any country in the world, Sadat routinely violated both the letter and the spirit of the document. Only since the 1980s, and then haltingly at first, has the court really tried to enforce constitutional provisions. One prominent legal observer calls the constitution "a joke that turned serious," while legal scholar Nathan Brown argues that it is only because the SCC has not placed great emphasis on the intent of the authors of the constitution—i.e., Sadat—that the practice of judicial review has had relatively liberal results.

The judiciary is a patrician institution. Many judges are the sons of judges, and quite a few have family ties to the pre-Revolutionary elite. Judges are forbidden to get involved in partisan politics, a charge which they take very seriously. In 1968, for example, the judiciary took a unified stance against the regime by refusing to join the then-ruling party, the Arab Socialist Union. However, it is difficult for any institution to remain fully independent after 50 years of what has essentially been one-party, presidential rule.

While the judiciary has managed to expand its sphere of influence over the last decade, it is still relatively weak compared to other branches of government, particularly the executive. The constitution is vague concerning the jurisdiction of Egypt's major courts, a situation which has bred a certain degree of competition between the State Council, the Court of Cassation, and the SCC. Egypt's judiciary has no control over its budget. A two-tiered legal system whereby police academies grant officers law degrees after the completion of a shortened, two-year degree program has allowed serious encroachments into the legal profession, and by extension the judiciary. Moreover, as the implementation of court rulings depends largely on the executive, certain court rulings can be, and are, ignored at will. The case of the Islamist paper, *al-Shaab*, which has received over a dozen rulings authorizing its reappearance to no avail, is only the most striking example.

The most serious infringement on the independence of the judiciary is the Emergency Law, which has created a flourishing parallel court system susceptible to government influence. Whenever possible, in politically crucial cases, the state has bypassed the judiciary by establishing special courts. The regime of President Gamal Abd al-Nasser used revolutionary tribunals, President Sadat decreed into existence state security courts while President Mubarak has referred Islamists to military tribunals where presiding judges are military officers with only a bare minimum of legal training, appointed by the minister of defense. Last year alone, state security courts were used to try alleged spy Sherif al-Filali, sociologist and civil rights activist Saad Eddin Ibrahim, and 52 young men accused of debauchery. Verdicts in military courts cannot be appealed, while those in state security courts can only be contested on procedural grounds, not matters of substance.

Despite these limitations, the public and the opposition have more trust in the judiciary than they do in any other public institution. President Mubarak, too, appears to have accepted the trend towards creeping constitutionalism. Perhaps this is because the judicial system is a safety valve for opposition energies, or perhaps it is because the president genuinely wishes to preside over the transition to a more liberal political system, and is willing to let the authority of the judiciary grow. Either way, Egypt's judiciary has shown that it is increasingly a force to be reckoned with. *SN*

Economy

The Big Picture

Trade Challenges

The Big Picture

A Decade of Change

ALTHOUGH THE PAST DECADE MAY BE BUT A BRIEF EPISODE IN THE HISTORY OF EGYPT, THE ECONOMIC WHIRLWIND THAT HAS transpired since the onset of the 1990s is by all accounts monumental. The start of the country's steady transition into a new economic era can essentially be pinpointed to 1991, when Egypt chose to back the US-led coalition that pushed Iraqi forces out of Kuwait. For its pivotal role in winning the backing of key Arab states over misgivings on the Arab street, Egypt won a gradual debt write-off of $10 billion from the Paris Club of creditors. As a condition, Egypt agreed to follow an IMF-overseen economic reform program. It was an opportune time to shift gears. Beleaguered from aging Nasserist policies centered on state ownership and trade protectionism, the domestic economy was a mess, propped up by foreign aid, unproductive and forbidding to private enterprise. Abroad, the failure of central planning as an economic model was becoming ever more evident.

The reform program proposed by the IMF was the standard two-stage package of sorting out the macro-economy first, then tackling the "real" economy. On the first count, Egypt was so successful that in later years the IMF, embattled over failures in Asia, would sometimes hold the country up as an example of work well done. Inflation and government spending were reined in, and the exchange rate steadied as the Egyptian pound was pegged to the US dollar and the once rampant black market all but disappeared.

Egypt won its battles too. With the memory of sudden spells of economic pandemonium—particularly the 1977

GDP Growth Rate (%)

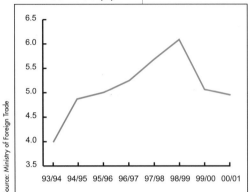

Source: Ministry of Foreign Trade

Breakdown of GDP (2000/01)

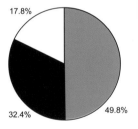

17.8%

32.4%   49.8%

■ Commodities
■ Production Services
□ Social Services
Source: Ministry of Planning

According to official figures, GDP growth dipped slightly to 4.9% in 2001, but outside observers peg growth at about 3%

bread riots under Anwar Sadat—looming large, policy makers refused IMF pressure to devalue the pound in 1994 and 1995 and always insisted reform would be homegrown. Shock tactics would simply not be considered.

By the mid-1990s, the powers that be felt the economic numbers were solid enough for reform to reach deeper. In January 1996, President Mubarak appointed Kamal al-Ganzouri as prime minister with a mandate to get cracking on privatization and to overhaul Egypt's socialist—or just plain ancient—commercial legislation.

After the rapid transfer of stakes from the government to 17 new industry-specific holding companies, about 30 state-owned companies were sold or liquidated. The stock market, awoken from a 40-year slumber by the 1992 capital markets law, was brought to life by a slew of IPOs. Private companies began to use the bourse to raise capital. By the late 1990s, Cairo had built a good case for its bid to become a financial services hub for the Arab world.

Laws that went to the very heart of Nasser's contract with the people were overhauled. Foreigners were to be allowed to own Egyptian real estate, landlords could raise the rents on new real estate contracts, and agricultural landlords were to be permitted to raise the rents of sitting tenants. Banks and insurance companies could be majority owned by private investors—not just Egyptian, but foreign.

In the meantime, and less successfully, the government went about courting foreign investors to set up in Egypt. As well as advertising Egypt's new investor-friendly credentials and tax exemptions, officials stressed the country's sizeable domestic market—at 66 million, the largest in the Arab world—and its "geographical

genius," astride the Suez Canal and linking Africa, Asia, and the sea routes from the south.

The pace and depth of reform was always heavily dependent on its social consequences. While profitable companies were sold, large loss-making companies remained propped up by the state since they employ many thousands of workers. The huge bureaucracy, employer of a staggering 4.6 million people, remained a deterrent to all but the most determined of entrepreneurs. Spending on subsidies stayed at about 14% of government non-capital expenditure throughout the 1990s. Utilities—telephones, electricity, and gas—continue to be provided cheap.

Come October 1998, the end of the IMF's conditional oversight drew near and, not surprisingly, Egypt decided to go it alone. The economy Egypt emerged with was a mixed bag. While the government can claim to have pulled out of some industrial activities—cement and mobile telephony are examples—it still owns much of the country's industry and controls the bulk of lending by dint of its enduring domination over the banking system through the four big state-owned commercial banks. In many cases, when the government says it has "privatized" a company because it divested more than 50% of the shares, it has retained control by remaining the single biggest shareholder. On the legal front, this also meant that the kind of arbitrary decision-making that governments can practice when they own the economy as well as regulate it continued to hinder investment through the late 1990s.

Though it may have been well intentioned, the shady public/private overlap has taken its toll on the economy. Imports still remain weak, as persisting public ownership has eliminated any incentive to modernize management practices, efficiency, and thus the international competitiveness of local goods. Furthermore, in many cases, the biggest movers and shakers in any given industry are either the ministers

Eurobonding

Egypt's maneuvers to join the club in the economic sense have not been limited to signing trade agreements. Last year marked the country's first foray into the sovereign bond market with a $1.5-billion issue of eurobonds on July 6. The move made Egypt one of 11 Arab countries to fish for funds on the international capital market. True to form, the government did not get around to making the big offering until after several years of consideration and foot-dragging. But this time around, the added caution was a good thing. The original plan was to launch the issue in 1997 when active neighbors like Lebanon, Oman, Bahrain, and Tunisia helped to push the MENA region's total bond issue value up to $1.2 billion. The outlook was positive until financial crisis stuck Asia later that year, and foreign investment was scared right out of the emerging markets.

But, as demonstrated by Russia's speedy rebound after defaulting on its Soviet-era bonds, the sovereign bond market does not require too long for forgiveness. By 1999, Qatar began rocking the boat with a $1-billion issue and a follow-up $1.4-billion issue in 2000.

In Egypt's case, deciding to join the club was based on more than just need. At launch time, the government could just have easily depended on internal sources or Arab soft loans to cover its needs. But tapping the sovereign bond market is an amazingly convenient way for emerging markets to build a wide and lasting interest in their market. Once listed on the regional index and assigned credit and currency ratings from international organizations like Fitch or Standard and Poor, the global investment community has a simple tool to assess a country's risk factor. If Egypt establishes a reputation for stability, the sovereign rating will also increase Egyptian companies' chances of getting foreign loans.

So in the usual fashion, the delay was a little long, but the thing was kicked off with a bang. In the months building up to the launch, most local commentators were anticipating a medium-term offer (5-7 year) not exceeding $500 million. Instead, the issue—primarily managed and distributed through Morgan Stanley and Merrill Lynch and Co.—was for three times that, broken into two different issues: a $500-million five-year maturity issue at an annual interest rate of 7.625% and a $1-billion 10-year maturity issue at an annual rate of 8.75%. The reception was overwhelmingly positive, garnering 100% subscription as soon as the bonds were launched.

This was a bit of a surprise, considering the biting pre-launch inquiries about whether it was advisable to borrow in dollars and what purpose the government expected the funds to serve. Although they have fiercely asserted that they will be used "for general budgetary purposes and for on-lending to certain economic authorities with foreign currency generating abilities," there is concern that the fresh stash of dollars will just be used to prop up the pound. Responsibility for the allocation of the proceeds has been solely assigned to Minister of Finance Medhat Hassanein.

Like most loans, there really is no way of knowing how it will be used, but the hope is always that the borrower will be in a better position when it comes time to pay it back than it was at the time of lending. *SV*

that head them or those lucky individuals who have the government's good favor.

While the power of Egyptian businessmen has invariably grown, they have rarely attempted to influence policy through lobby groups. Nor have they used the press much, except occasionally the business daily *al-Alam al-Yom*. Instead, they have chosen the inside track. Many of the biggest names in business are members of either the People's Assembly or the Shura Council. These businessmen—often unfairly reviled in what remains essentially a reactionary press—have created some eye-catching and highly successful enterprises.

The fact that even the biggest industrialists still operate from the inside, however, has highlighted a weakness in the system. Without the right connections or name, it is still hard to get a loan from the bank to start an enterprise. The court system, which should underpin all commercial transactions, is still slow and weak. While their parents' generation turned to the government for a job for life, the regime has long since stopped guaranteeing employment for young job-seekers. The half million or so graduates entering the job market each year must find employment elsewhere. Many, including Minister of Foreign Trade Youssef Boutros Ghali and the active Cairo office of the International Finance Corporation, see small and medium enterprises (SMEs) as the best way. The Social Development Fund (backed by multilateral institutions) was set up partly to lend funds to SMEs.

Nevertheless, unemployment—officially less than 10% but by independent estimates nearer 20%—remains a major problem and the gap between the haves and the have-nots has grown.

Tensions in this mixed system began to emerge at the turn of the millenium. The economy, though official figures disagree, seemed to slow from its impressive growth of 5% or so a year in the late 1990s. Locally, the reason given for this was a "liquidity crisis"—in fact a series of factors meeting head-on.

First, the late 1990s had seen an explosion of lending to the private sector, with outstanding loans rising 34% from April 1998 to the start of 2000. When the economy started to slow, payments became more difficult, especially among borrowers whose credentials were based on who, rather than what, they knew. Second, the government, having overspent on so-called megaprojects—grand-scale projects reminiscent of the days of central planning—stopped paying its bills, especially to contractors. A kind of crisis of trust spread through the economy as private companies in turn stopped payments to suppliers, and sometimes employees, and the whole economy slowed.

Third, two years of trying to maintain the Egyptian peg to the dollar following the foreign exchange shocks of the Luxor attack in November 1997, the emerging markets capital flight of the same year, and an oil price collapse, resulted in extremely tight monetary conditions and high interest rates. Fourth, a glut of up-market real estate soaked up much private and bank capital. Jazzy desert developments around Cairo intended for the rich came to a standstill.

Confidence in the economic management of the government was shaken. The economy's woes manifested themselves most clearly in the stock market. The benchmark Hermes Financial Index plummeted some 60% from mid-January to October 2000. The Telecom Egypt IPO, which would have been Egypt's biggest so far,

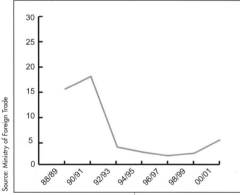

Rate of Inflation (%)

Source: Ministry of Foreign Trade

Projected

Inflation is tamed

Fiscal Deficit (% of GDP)

Source: Ministry of Foreign Trade

The deficit continued to creep up last year

was postponed indefinitely, largely because of the state of the bourse. But foreigners may in any case have shied away from buying in Egyptian currency since the exchange rate policy was far from clear. Companies reported falling earnings in most industries. Sales of cement and steel, bellwethers of the state of the construction industry, fell for the first time in years.

As 2000 came to a close, rising interest rates and dollar shortages had become so extreme that the government was finally forced to dip into the foreign exchange reserves to defend the peg. The drop to around US$14 billion by January 2001 from over US$19 billion in mid-1999 signaled that it was once again time to go back to the drawing board. But this time around, the necessary plan of attack was more obvious.

After allowing incremental depreciations to occur over the month without any official explanation, the government finally unveiled a new flexible exchange rate regime on January 29, whereby the pound was devalued to a rate of LE3.85 to the dollar. By making systematic adjustments in the central trading rate according to the forces of supply and demand, the new "banded peg" was to serve as an intermediate step towards an eventual floating rate.

Management was clumsy at first. A minor 1-piaster change in the rate in April and a 0.5% adjustment in the band in July made improvements in the dollar scarcity. But it was not until the surprise 8% devaluation to a central rate of LE4.15 to the dollar and an expansion in the band to 3% in early August that black market trading was stamped out.

In the meantime, other corrective measures were being executed at record speed. In April, the Central Bank shifted its discount rate not once, but twice, for the first time in three years, bringing it down to 11%, and then went on to ease up reserve and liquidity requirements. In June, Egypt made its first attempt at using the fixed income market to alleviate foreign debt, successfully raising $1.5 billion through two sovereign bond issues with five- and ten-year maturities (*see box*).

Various industries got cracking again, fueled by Egypt's emerging position in the world tourism market, the long-awaited ratification of the mortgage law, a new wave of acquisitions in the cement sector, a sudden drive to become the regional IT powerhouse, and the discovery of over 55 trillion ft^3 of

natural gas. On the trade front, the long-debated EU Association Agreement was finally signed, granting Egypt comfortable time margins and nearly EU2 billion in grants and loans to prepare for all out free trade with its leading regional trading partner.

Things were not perfect—interest rates remained sky-high, privatization efforts had come to a standstill, and the volume of exports still lagged far behind imports—but they were looking up. That is, until September.

As the world looked on in disbelief as hijacked planes began crashing into the World Trade Center and the Pentagon on September 11, few could even begin to think about what sort of economic impact such tragedy would have on the global market. But slowly it became evident: a crash in the American economy meant a crash in nearly every economy linked to it—Egypt included.

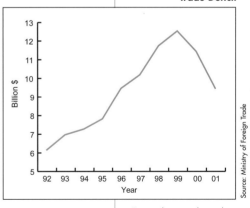

Trade Deficit

Source: Ministry of Foreign Trade

Egypt has reduced its trade deficit substantially over the past two years—but it's still not enough

Before you could even say crisis, the very foundations of the local economy—tourism, oil, and Suez Canal revenues—began to plummet, and government expenditure started to leap as the state clambered to hold down the fort. After a year of hard work equalizing foreign currency supply and demand, Egypt saw dollar sources dry up and desperate businessmen once again turn to the black market for foreign exchange.

By late November, the Egyptian stock exchange had bottomed out to new lows since its revival seven years prior. Foreign investors pulled out of the market, and stock prices were discounted beyond any forecast. A final devaluation for the year was executed on December 13, moving the rate down 8.4% to LE4.5 to the dollar (plus or minus 3%). The government set to securing grants and loans to keep the floundering tourism and travel industry afloat and make up for the steep drop in dollar proceeds.

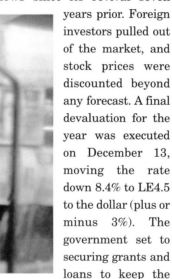

The year 2001 closed quietly, in sharp contrast to the millennial celebrations two years earlier that brought thousands of party-seeking tourists to the pyramids. The glum expectations for the New Year reflected a new sense of despair. As the drop in tourism hit its bleakest phase, Egypt's increasingly scarce dollar-denominated income led the government to estimate a mad hike in the current account deficit from $33 million in fiscal year 2000/01 to an astronomical $2 billion in 2001/02. This prompted new exchange rate speculation on the

black market and dollar hoarding, which in turn forced the national reserves to dip below the $14 billion mark for the first time since 1993. The stock market continued to lurch deeper into unknown depths, hitting an all-time low on January 28, 2002, when the benchmark Hermes Financial Index dropped to just 4762.31—a steep 71% decline from the heady days of 1997—stopping the privatization program dead in its tracks. The steady regression led the government to lower its estimate of GDP growth in 2001/02 to around 3%, a rosy figure in comparison to non-state projections of 0.6%-2.6%.

Such was the bleak state of affairs in early February, when the Egyptian government and the World Bank convened a Consultative Group meeting in Sharm al-Sheikh to lobby for help in covering the rapidly growing balance-of-payments deficit. By the close of the two-day meeting, Egypt walked away with pledges for a combined $10.3 billion in grants and favorable loans ($2.1 billion of which was supposedly marked for immediate disbursal) from the likes of the World Bank, the IMF, the African Development Bank, the Arab Monetary Fund, Japan, Denmark, and the Kuwaiti Fund for Arab Economic Development.

The success of the conference temporarily boosted morale, at least until it became clear that there were strings attached. As it turns out, the IMF's proposed $500 million in assistance came in the form of a compensatory financing facility (CFF), requiring Egypt to adopt a more flexible exchange rate policy, overhaul its banking sector, and make several other critical macroeconomic policy shifts. On second thought, the government turned out to be not so keen to succumb to these demands. Not only is it concerned about the inevitable hikes in inflation and the fiscal deficit such reforms would provoke, but it also seems put-off by the idea of accepting aid under the scolding finger of an organization largely seen as an instrument of the developed world and intimately associated with the economic demise of Argentina. However, should it officially decide to forgo the CFF, it is likely that the World Bank and the African Development Bank will veto the combined $1 billion they originally pledged.

The reluctance to change has many observers worried that the next several years will be tough ones for Egypt. But in some ways things have started to look up again. With tourism already recovering, and a stable flow of dollars from workers' remittances and Suez Canal revenues, the net current account deficit for the first half of fiscal year 2001/02 stood at only $379.20 million, giving hope that the original forecast of $2 billion is going to be way off the mark.

Egypt's biggest challenge now is to find a happy medium between what is good for the country short-term and what is best for it long-term. In order for real improvement to occur, the private sector needs to contribute more to the overall economy, which will require deep-seated reforms including a change in the peg to the dollar as well as a new push in privatization efforts. Though such moves will result in increasing inflation as well as significant job-losses in the short term, they will help the country to finally rid itself of the mess it inherited from its socialist days and reduce its dependence on foreign aid. With the global economy and political climate changing as rapidly as it is these days, it seems like there is no other choice. *BF & SV*

Shedding Pounds

Egypt's currency loses weight

Though many people might not have realized it, Cairo hosted a veritable economic dream team in late November 2000. Tucked into the grand ballroom of the Conrad International, an astounding collection of some of the world's foremost experts on exchange rate policy convened for two days to butt heads over the ongoing debate about what to do with the pound and discuss practical reform options for Egypt with local policymakers. Although pressure to do something about the pound's nine-year peg of approximately LE3.4/$1 had been brewing for years, there was no clear consensus on what exactly that something should be. What was clear, however, was that 2001 was going to have to be the year to start making calculated and well-defined changes.

The clock was ticking. While the peg originally steadied the economy in the early 1990s, by the turn of the century it faced increasing stress due to dispro-portionately fast credit expansion, slow structural reforms, dwindling global financing following the Asian crisis, sinking oil prices, and the steady strengthening of the greenback. By the end of 2000 there were only two reasonable choices: either throw away more of the highly treasured national reserves (which had already been cut down a hefty $5 billion since mid-1999) to artificially prop up the peg, or officially abandon the fixed peg.

It wasn't too hard to make the decision. The pound had already been allowed to depreciate by around 15% over the last quarter of 2000—a move that brought relief in some sense, but, without any clear statement of the new policy, also caused great anxiety. Nervous investors who could not anticipate what the next day might bring felt forced to take matters into their own hands by turning to the black market, which only made matters worse. By mid-January 2001, the unofficial rate diverged from the official rate by as much as 8%, and all eyes were on the government to set the record straight.

Sure enough, on January 29, Prime Minister Atef Ebeid announced Egypt's new forex brainchild: a crawling peg with a trading band, a sort of hybrid of the regimes discussed in November that was soon coined the "banded peg." In simpler terms, this meant that the pound's central rate to the dollar would be allowed to "crawl" per the forces of supply and demand. Added flexibility would then be granted by permitting banks

The pound took a beating last year, losing 31% of its value in 2001

and exchange houses to trade within a set percentage above or below that rate (i.e. a trading band). Thus, the initial central rate of LE3.85/$1 with a 1% bandwidth announced on January 29 translated into a legal trading band ranging from LE3.812 to LE3.899.

The implications of this decision were clear. Egypt was not deemed ready to adopt a full float, but moves were being made to gradually steer it in that direction. An ad-hoc committee headed by Ebeid himself was created to review the country's currency status on a weekly basis and shift the rate as necessary.

But it took time for the new regime to become effective. The initial 3% devaluation began the process of rerouting foreign currency exchange into formal institutions, but the rate still did not truly reflect market conditions. Black market trading continued to thrive despite minor adjustments in May (to 3.86 plus/minus 1%) and July (to 3.90 plus/minus 1.5%) and the threat of harsh penalties for anyone caught trading at unofficial rates. This failure to reflect the true value of the pound scared investors right out of the stock market. Now that it was clear that a new adjustment could be made at any time, it was considered safer to wait and see what would happen before sinking money in stocks.

The big step to stamp out the black market came in August. In a surprise move by the government, the pound was slashed by 8% to a new central rate of LE4.15/$1 and the width of the trading band was doubled to 3%, rendering the new maximum trading limit to as high as LE4.275 to the dollar. In many ways, the new central rate was more of a psychological milestone than an economic one. Everyone knew the pound was overvalued, but still, breaking the LE4 barrier was somewhat of a blow to the national ego.

Yet, in the weeks that followed, the new rate proved itself. The rates at banks crawled up toward the higher end of the band, but still, black market trading essentially dried up. Local banks were granting dollar requests and the government was commended for its dedication to continued adjustment and transparency in the regime.

Encouraged by the new liquidity in the market, investors stirred up a new storm of activity in the bourse. Share prices jumped across all sectors, although more cautiously for those companies that were carrying hefty dollar-denominated debts such as telecom giant MobiNil. By all accounts, it looked like Egypt was finally rectifying the valuation of the local currency and had found a viable means of keeping it on track. However, one catch to the plan was the assumption that the amount of dollars flowing into the country each year would stay the same, if not increase.

The wrench in the plan came in the form of the September 11 disaster. Egypt's four major sources of foreign currency are tourism, Suez Canal receipts, oil exports, and expatriate remittances—all of which were negatively impacted to varying degrees as the global market nose-dived into crisis. Taking the worst of it was Egypt's dollar-earning mainstay, the tourism market, which witnessed anywhere from a 30-50% dip in proceeds by November. Once again, banks grew strapped for cash, and requests for even a few hundred dollars remained unfulfilled.

All-out pandemonium broke out on November 19 when the government, in an effort to halt the outflow of dollars and cut the burgeoning trade deficit, announced that all ministries and government institutions were to cut imports by $1.5 billion. Banks would no longer be able to provide letters of credit to finance imports, except for the most basic needs. As the business community raised a loud and angry public outcry, investing halted on the stock market, and as expected, the black market raged once again—and this time the rates exceeded the next unthinkable limit: LE5/$1.

The decision was rescinded about a week later, although the controls on government spending remained. But something had to give to help remedy the spiraling losses that Egypt was facing as tourism worsened and global trade slumped. Not surprisingly, the pound was once again selected to carry the burden. The last devaluation of the year was executed on December 13, lessening the pound by another 8.4% to 4.50, plus/minus 3%. At a new upper limit of LE4.64/$1, the national currency stood an astounding 31.5% lower than it had at the start of the year. Unfortunately, the rate still lacked the full confidence of the investment community, already spooked by government waffling and the seemingly arbitrary nature of policy decision-making. The government was forced to fill the gap with the national reserves. All told, Egypt spent over $1 billion keeping the pound afloat from mid-2000 until the end of 2001.

Thus like 2000, 2001 ended with great uncertainty about the true value of the pound. Likewise, with increasingly sensational black market rates continuing to claim headlines in the daily press, the government has remained on the defensive for most of 2002.

Keen to keep up the image that everything was under control when Egypt's post-9/11 woes seemed insurmountable, the CBE effected what it termed a "minor depreciation, not a devaluation," on January 13 with a one-piaster shift in the central rate down to LE4.51 (the trading band remained steady). At the time, the country was fighting a gaggle of critics spread out from Beirut to New York that were saying the pound would be anywhere from LE5-7 to the dollar by the end of the year.

The one-piaster shuffle was supposed to be indicative of a new phase of the regime, in which the supposed "crawling" nature of the peg was going to be more obvious than it was over the year, when it crouched and leaped more than crawled. Minor everyday fluctuations, the CBE stated, would replace the sudden jumps that everyone found so jarring. But oddly, no further depreciations were announced after January.

Dollars continued to be scarce or plentiful depending on the week and what actions the government was taking, which meant that illicit trading was still taking place. Though the pound has officially held still, it is no indication that equilibrium in the forces of supply and demand has been achieved.

Given the heightened complexity of Egypt's economic challenges now in comparison to just a year and a half ago, the next obvious step is a diversification of the old currency approach. Whether that means expanding the peg to include a basket of currencies including the Euro and that of other major trade partners, or utilizing other instruments, such as the interest rate, is still unclear. Keeping the pound afloat will also largely depend on the revitalization of privatization efforts and keeping government spending under manageable levels—two accomplishments that the public and private sector alike are praying for in 2003. *SV*

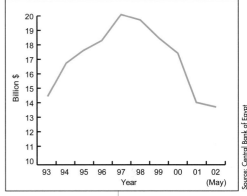

Foreign Reserves

Source: Central Bank of Egypt

Propping up the pound has cost about $5 billion since 1998

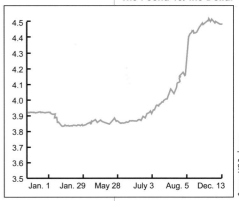

The Pound vs. the Dollar

Source: HC Brokerage

The pound gave way in 2001

For Sale

Privatization loses steam

If 2000 saw a significant slowdown in Egypt's privatization program, then 2001 witnessed outright stagnation. Despite the motley group of some 70 enterprises and assets put on the auction block at the start of the year, only 12 holdings were actually divested. The income from these sales, leases, and liquidations (there were no IPOs) totaled LE943 million, translating into just 6% of the total LE16.6 billion in privatization proceeds since 1994.

The regression was hardly a surprise. Activities had already begun to lose pace in 2000 when the liquidity crisis sapped the strength of both stock market investors and private companies to absorb assets, while prolonged devaluation fears kept foreign parties at bay. Coupled with the crippling slowdown in the economy as 2001 progressed, the country's chances of getting bids anywhere near what was hoped for became increasingly bleak. This led many companies, such as the Egypt Glass Co. and national department store chain Omar Effendi, to reject bids until the market climate improves.

But so far, it has not. During the first quarter of 2002, the only significant activity in the program was the sale of two companies back to their employee shareholders associations (ESAs), a method of privatization that has lost favor since 1998, but is considered better than no privatization at all. To save the year from being a total bust, the government agreed to relinquish its holdings in Helwan cement (a joint venture company) in September and Misr Hotels and Abu Zaabal Fertilizers in December at what many local commentators felt were bargain-basement prices.

But others argue that high hopes are precisely what is impeding progress at this stage in the plan. Even without an economic recession, privatization has gotten a whole lot harder in the last two years. By 2000 the best of the 314 enterprises originally earmarked for sale had been sold. The leftovers—now divided into ten holding companies—are mostly over-staffed, technologically outdated companies that owe their existence to the days when the government was their main patron and protector. The amount of money required just to bring them up to scratch is a considerable repellant to potential buyers, and should be factored into their valuations if they are ever to be sold.

And yet, this represents the very heart of the dilemma Egypt now finds itself in. If the country is truly dedicated to the goals of privatization, then emphasis should not only be placed on its short-term revenue-generating benefits, but also on the longer-term effects of stimulating economic development through growth in private enterprise and the capital market. Yet, at the same time, the lag before those longer-term economic gains materialize leaves ample space for acute short-term social tensions to surface. Many of the companies still left on the block, such as textile companies—said to employ as many as one million people, 30% of Egypt's industrial labor force—and Helwan steel, employer of some 23,000 workers, will not only require buyers to wipe out huge debts and upgrade new management and machinery, but also to

Most of the good stuff has already been sold

layoff employees on a scale that the government is unwilling to rush into. So far, Egypt's gradual "save the worst for last" approach has delayed shocks in the job market—but it cannot be put off much longer.

This may be a key reason for the shift of emphasis to utilities, banks, and insurance companies. However, while such sales would certainly raise much needed cash, they too present a host of complex issues. For several years, the government has been paving the way to sell state-owned banks and insurance companies, evaluating them and making the necessary legal changes. Progress has been slow. In 1998, the government found itself barraged by criticism in the People's Assembly when it passed legislation to allow for

Privatizations in 2001/02

Anchor Investors:
Egyptian Gypsum (Feb. 2001)
Arab Carpets (July 2001)
Alexandria Carpets (July 2001)
Abu Zaabal Fertilizer (Nov. 2001)

Sale to Employee Shareholder Associations:
Gharbiya Mills (July 2001)
Misr Import and Export (July 2001)
United Trade (Feb. 2002)
Arab Textiles (Feb. 2002)

Liquidations:
Egyptian Electrical Equipment (Jan. 2001)
Egyptian Co. for Metal Trade-Segal (Jan. 2001)

Production Asset Sales:
Alexandria Metal Production, Nozha (Jan. 2001)
Alexandria Metal Production, Minya (Jan. 2001)
Alexandria Confectionary, Nadler Factory (Jan. 2001)
Nasr Glass, Syringe Factory (Feb. 2002)

Leases:
Darfala Factory/Misr Aluminum (Feb. 2001)
Gypsum Factory-Sadat/GYMCO (Feb. 2001)

Source: Ministry of Public Enterprise

the privatization of banks and insurers. Many consider such institutions inalienable national assets that financed the construction of modern Egypt. Agreeing on a valuation for them is also fraught with difficulties. Banks and insurance companies were used under central planning to found government companies and to finance state-conceived projects. As a result, they now find themselves proud part owners of dozens of companies, some worthwhile, others worthless. More headway has been made in joint venture banks where, under the express order of the government, state banks have started to reduce their holdings to a maximum of 20%.

Selling utilities is just as tricky. For a start, Egyptian utilities are not companies at all, but arms of ministries. Hence they do not have a history of income statements and balance sheets and it has not been necessary to keep strict records of inventory. In many cases, they own the land that has been built on and it is often not clear what their debts are and to whom. Profits, losses, and debts within ministries were fungible, able to be shifted internally from one institution to another. Then there is the challenge of any utility privatization: how to regulate a monopoly so it does not exploit its customers.

The only utility sale has been the May 1998 sale of the Egyptian Company for Mobile Services, MobiNil, to Orascom Technologies, France Telecom, and Motorola. That sale was pretty straightforward. The company was without other holdings and not likely to attract

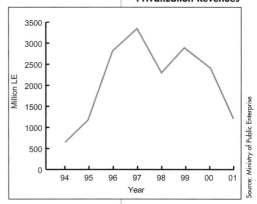

Privatization Revenues

Source: Ministry of Public Enterprise

Privatization seems to have past its heyday

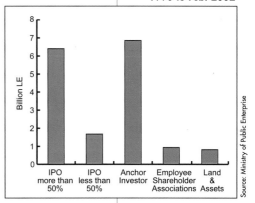

**PEO Asset Sales
1990 to Feb. 2002**

Source: Ministry of Public Enterprise

Sales to anchor investors have earned the most cash

criticism. In 2000, the government came close to its second majority sale. It delayed an IPO of 20% of Telecom Egypt at the last moment because of "unfavorable market conditions." The sale, due for October, was expected to raise some $1.2 billion and would have been Egypt's biggest. Now, three years since the plan was hatched, investors are still waiting. Elsewhere, plans for IPOs in the state-owned electricity distribution companies have been delayed, partly over debts owed them by other ministries. *SV & BF*

The old temples of commerce have proven a hard sell

Going, Going, and Still Going

They were once the pride of Egypt's retail sector. Massive, ornate temples to commerce, stores like Sednaoui and Cicurel dominated the trade in pre-revolutionary Egypt. It is difficult to remember that splendid past in light of their current tawdriness. Nationalized in the 1960s, Egypt's great department stores have slowly declined into gray bureaucratic mediocrity, selling undistinguished goods at inflated prices.

In 1996, the government announced that it would sell its department stores (Omar Effendi, Hannaux, Benzion, Ades, Rivoli, Sednaoui, Cicurel) to an anchor investor who would hopefully breathe some life into them. Despite being a little worn at the heels, they remain potentially lucrative investments. Omar Effendi alone (taking 50% of the public-sector department store market and over 10% of the retail market as a whole) has 82 outlets spread across the country and owns 108,000 m² of retail space. But department stores have proved a tough sell. From the beginning, analysts have agreed that the stores were overvalued. The chains are also plagued with bloated employment rolls, massive inventories of unsold (and often shoddy and unwanted) goods, cumbersome supply networks, and high receivables.

The government's attempts to make the stores more attractive to investors have not met with great success. After the first failed attempt to sell them in 1999, the state attempted to renovate the various Omar Effendi branches, pension off the work force (which dropped from 8,000 to 5,600 employees), and liquidate the unsold inventories. While tightening the companies' credit policies have resulted in a slight decrease in the receivables, the inventory of unsold goods has swelled. In 1996, Omar Effendi did LE661 million in sales, but that figure had dropped to LE463 million by 2000, with profit margins barely more than a few percentage points.

In the end, the biggest thing working against the department stores' sale may be the change in Egypt's consumer buying patterns, which have shifted away from department stores to either high-end boutiques or discount appliance stores. From 1996 to 1999, the retail market share of the large stores dropped from 47% to 27%. Potential investors—like Mohammed Farid Khamis of Oriental Weavers, who put in a bid for the stores in 1999—say they now prefer to start their own chains of specialty stores.

There may still be hope, however. The third round of bidding for Omar Effendi brought in three offers, from the Saudi Muhaydeb Group, a Spanish retail conglomerate, and the Saudi Industrial Investment Company, owned by Prince Abd al-Rahman Bin Saud. According to Khamis, the current offers for the company are around LE300 million, the same price offered by his consortium over a year ago. If successful, the sale could be the desperately needed shot in the arm for Egypt's privatization program-officials keep referring to it as a "milestone." As the Holding Company for Trade considers the offers, the tattered monuments to commerce remain, slowly moldering away as Egyptians have learned to look elsewhere for better products and better deals. *PS*

Trade Challenges
Narrowing the trade deficit is a priority

Making the Grade

Fitting the dramatic tone of last year, the Ministry of Foreign Trade raised a harrowing new battle cry: "exports: a matter of life or death." And really, the situation *is* dire. Although Egypt did make progress in hacking down its preposterous trade deficit over the year, import expenditure was still almost two and half times export revenues, resulting in a deficit of $9.4 billion for fiscal year 2000/01.

While Egypt's primary exports have remained the same for decades, mostly consisting of petroleum products, textiles, and steel, imports have increased and diversified over the last few years. Between 1992 and 1999, the trade deficit more than doubled, reaching $12.6 billion. The products flooding the market include just about everything from the most basic needs like wheat and other food products to luxury cars, designer sunglasses, and mobile phones. This can partly be blamed on the fact that Egypt's burgeoning population has simply outstripped its productive capabilities, in particular the capability of its land to provide enough food. Imports have also become more affordable since tariffs were slashed in compliance with various trade agreements. The foremost reason, however, is that the Egyptian people grew tired of shoddy goods churned out under central planning, and have thus chosen to buy foreign.

This is the bottom line of Egypt's current trade conundrum. While the government has placed new emphasis on making the so-called transition from "aid to trade" with its major allies, there is only so much that it can do. The Ministry of Foreign Trade has set up teams to tackle var-ious parts of the equation, such as the often controversial customs duty system, small- and medium-enterprise (SME) development, trade and investment legislation, capital markets, and free trade agreements, but policy cannot solve everything. Unless local products become more competitive in the global market, no one will be interested in buying them—either here or abroad.

As any of the ubiquitous hawkers on Cairo's crowded streets know, competitiveness is part price, part quality, and part targeting the right markets. In terms of price, the devaluation of the pound has helped make Egyptian goods more attractive, especially in the textile sector where countries like China and India have been pushing Egypt's once legendary hold on the cotton market into the history books. Quality will have to be enhanced through privatization, modernization, and old-fashioned ingenuity. Finding the right markets, however, has much to do with signing and honoring free trade agreements—a realm where the government got cracking in 2001.

In addition to its continued efforts to become fully WTO compliant by the 2010 deadline, Egypt made several big

Egypt's "geographic genius" makes it a trade hotspot, but not enough Egyptian products are catching the boat

moves to get trade borders opened up over the year. The biggest accomplishment of 2001 was the signing of the EU Association Agreement in June. After seven years of negotiations impeded by a change in parliament and fierce opposition from local producers afraid of being wiped out by European competitors, the deal was finally sealed. However, as Egyptian advocates steering the negotiations have said all along, there was no need for the ruckus—the terms of the deal are pretty good. The EU is Egypt's largest regional trade partner, claiming 28.4% of imports and 37.4% of exports in 2001. Upon full enactment of the agreement, which should occur within the next two years, Egyptian goods will immediately receive nearly unlimited access to European markets. The opportunities for agricultural and textile exports, in particular, are great.

The tariffs and other trade barriers Egypt places on European goods, on the other hand, will be scaled back in phases over an extended time frame. Products in which Egypt already has a competitive edge, such as raw materials and industrial capital goods, will be the first to shed tariffs, after three years. For those commodities that local manufacturers will need to work harder to improve, tariffs will remain in effect for much longer: semi-finished goods will wait 10 years, consumer goods and finished products 13, and automobiles 15. The government's stance on this is that if local producers cannot pull themselves together in that time, then they should probably not be producing at all.

In addition to the head start on market access, the EU has also agreed to provide EU615 million in grants and EU1.1 billion in loans to help bring Egyptian industry up to scratch.

Participation in the Common Market for Eastern and Southern Africa (COMESA)—a block comprising 21 member states with some 385 million people—has also brought a slow but steady stream of new trading opportunities. As one of the nine members that lowered tariffs to zero in late 2000, Egypt is now tapping previously untouched markets such as Kenya, Zimbabwe, and Mauritius. Some companies have benefited enormously from COMESA membership. Relying heavily on imported raw materials, Eastern Tobacco, Egypt's premier tobacco manufacturer, is now able to source one-third of its raw material needs duty free. What's more, under the terms of the agreement, they have also entered into attractive bartering deals with other COMESA country companies, whereby they partly pay for their imports with various Egyptian goods. The deal allows the company to combat foreign exchange losses, hang on to precious dollar supplies, and also helps create a market for Egyptian goods in neighboring countries.

Nonetheless, Egypt has yet to see a big payoff—the country's trade with COMESA members actually added up to a deficit of $127 million in the first nine months of 2001. But the gains from COMESA membership must be evaluated in terms of profits and politics. Membership is imperative, given that all countries within the Nile

Egypt's Top 10 Imports & Exports in fiscal year 2000/2001

(According to categories of the Harmonized Tariff System)

Imports	Million $
1. Crude petroleum	$2,276.8
2. Machines & electrical appliances	1,061.6
3. Petroleum products	892.1
4. Iron & steel products	552.6
5. Wheat	533.5
6. Plastic and plastic articles	503.6
7. Pharmaceutical products	469.4
8. Paper and cork	443.9
9. Maize	397.3
10. Chemicals	391.1

Exports	Million $
1. Petroleum products	$1,466.8
2. Crude petroleum	1,165.6
3. Iron & steel products	272.3
4. Ready-made clothes	232.8
5. Cotton	144.5
6. Cotton yarn	121.3
7. Cotton textiles	115.2
8. Raw aluminum	109.5
9. Semi-finished aluminum	82.8
10. Fertilizers	64.2

Source: Central Bank of Egypt

Basin are members. Furthermore, the association has allowed Egypt to establish a new leadership position with its non-Arab neighbors. Egypt played host to both the 2000 and 2001 summits, has taken an active role in laying the grounds for an eventual free trade zone, and

Tricks of the Trade

The opposition to Egypt's various free trade initiatives over the last few years has been large and loud—to be expected as the possibility looms of better made and cheaper products flooding the market. But while honoring commitments to free trade associations like the GATT or COMESA does demand adhering to many rules that level the global playing field, member countries are not left completely defenseless.

As with any game, the truly talented player is always the one who knows the rules inside and out and can therefore maneuver around them to his advantage. In this respect, Egypt is proving to be just as shrewd as many of its developed country counterparts.

As Gamal Bayoumi, former assistant minister of foreign affairs and one of Egypt's chief negotiators for the EU Association Agreement, stated in a recent interview with *Business Today Egypt*, "The beauty of the GATT is that there are a lot of hidden barriers to trade that you can implement in order to protect an industry without violating the regulations." So far the country has dreamed up all sorts of crafty measures to keep competitors at bay but still remain cleverly compliant. For example, although import bans on poultry have been eliminated, new rules stipulate that that every chicken must be stamped with the importer's name before the lot clears customs. Though as of January, importers now face new duties on ready-made garments, the law also stipulates that manufacturers must print washing instructions in four different languages on every article of clothing. The mere inconvenience, let alone expense, of such rules are amazingly effective. *SV*

initiated SME development projects for the benefit of COMESA countries.

In terms of trade with its Arab neighbors, Egypt has worked hard over the last decade to establish individual bilateral trade agreements with numerous Arab League members, including Libya (effective June 1991); Syria (December 1991); Jordan (December 1998); Morocco (April 1999); Lebanon (March 1999); and Tunisia (March 1999). The most recently sealed agreement was with Iraq. As of July 8, 2001, all tariffs between the two countries were eliminated, although trade is still tempered by the UN sanctions placed on Iraq.

While many Arab countries have forged similar one-on-one agreements with each other, the Arab world has yet to form a trade block similar to that of the EU or COMESA. For years, critics have stated that this is primarily due to the fact that most participating countries would have the same thing to offer—agricultural and textile goods, cement, and mineral products—so a regional trade block would not offer much opportunity for trade expansion. But the underlining political bonds implied by regional and bilateral trade agreements has led to renewed discussion of an Arab FTA in the last year, and even an Egypt-US agreement. Although there have still been no formal steps in this direction, it appeared that opposition—particularly from the American camp—lessened dramatically in the wake of September 11. It seems that Egypt's favored nation status has never been worth more. *SV*

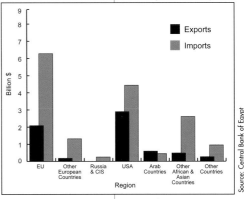

Imports vs. Exports

The EU is Egypt's largest trade partner

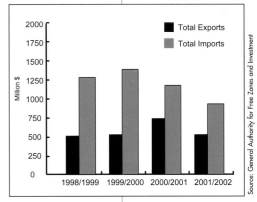

Free Zone Trade

Even exports in Egypt's free trade zones are half of imports

Microeconomy

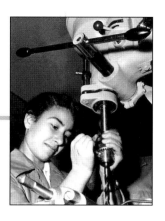

Finance

- **In the Money**
- **Insurance Eyes the 21st Century**
- **Holy Lending**
- **The Sale That Wasn't**
- **Trading Places**
- **Breaking the Speed Limit**
- **Alphabet Soup**

Industry

- **The Long View**
- **Empire Building**
- **Egypt's Mineral Wealth**
- **Buried Treasure**
- **Manufacturing**
- **Down in Damietta**
- **Chemical Reactions**
- **Food and Beverages**
- **Playing Monopoly**
- **Milking the Market**
- **Textiles**

Agriculture

- **On the Farm**
- **Borrowed Land**

Energy

- **Fueling Up**
- **Refined Partnerships**
- **Booting Up**

Services

- **Tourism**
- **The Real Importance of Tourism**
- **Advertising**
- **Retail**

Telecommunications

- **Wired**
- **Egyptian Dotcoms**
- **Soft Dreams**

Transport

- **In Transit**
- **Ailing EgyptAir**

The Small Picture

Finance

In the Money

Egypt's banking sector witnessed its share of groundbreaking developments and harsh disappointments in 2001. Positive highlights included the loosening of monetary and fiscal policies, a new mortgage law, the private sector's sudden push to give the Big Four a run for their money in retail banking, and the alliance of Egypt's two biggest investment banks, but low points such as post-devaluation pains, a botched acquisition, and the lack of any developments on the privatization front kept observers on a roller coaster all year long. The financial services sector (including trade, finance, and insurance activities) remains the single largest contributor to GDP, claiming 21.4% in 2000/01, compared to the 20.2% contribution of industry and mining, and 16.4% from agriculture. By the end of June 2001, the system's total lending stood at LE241.5 billion (67% of GDP), and total deposits were LE290.1 billion (81% of GDP).

State-owned banks

Despite Egypt's active decade of reform, the banking sector continues to be an area where state intervention runs deep. In addition to the rigid control of the Central Bank of Egypt (CBE) over banking operations, the government wields a sharply disproportionate dominance over the sector through its four massive public banks:

Bank of Alexandria, Banque du Caire, Banque Misr, and the National Bank of Egypt. The Big Four, as the group is commonly known, controls 55% of the banking sector's total assets, 52% of loans, and 60% of deposits. Three specialized banks focusing on real estate, agriculture, and industrial development further the government's grip on the sector. And, as if that were not enough, the state also holds sizeable stakes in many of the most successful private joint-venture banks in the country.

Answers to why the public banks have not been privatized, despite years of pleading from reformists and the IMF, are a bit of a catch-22. The reasons for holding on are also keeping the sector from reaching its fullest potential.

First of all, while financial development is essential to the evolution of the country, the tendency to focus on big businessmen, legislators, and bankers is skewed. Up until 1996, fully half of the population lived on less than LE3 a day, according to the UN Human Development Index. Thus for a good part of the Egyptian population, hiding one's life savings under the mattress is a far more likely option than opening a bank account, and the chances of getting a loan have pretty much been zero for decades.

The advent of experimental micro-financing programs and the explosion of retail banking targeted at Egypt's growing middle class have begun to change the tides, but there are still many people that are completely outside the system. Because the vast majority of Egypt's wealthy population is concentrated in major urban centers, private banks have little incentive to spread beyond Cairo and Alexandria. The public commercial and specialized banks, on the other hand, with a staggering 1,982 branches spread across the country (compared to the private sector's 499), are at least somewhat more accessible to the greater public.

Maintaining control of these massive organizations has also been a great way for the government to provide jobs—the financial sector alone claimed some two million employees in 2001. However, largely due to outdated operating systems and meager staff training, the Big Four have established a reputation for conservatism, inefficiency, and technological obsolescence. Furthermore, when employees are not trained to assess risk properly, the amount of non-performing loans (NPLs) can only be expected to increase. Although official figures state a sector NPL ratio of 12%, independent sources estimate a more realistic number of around 20% or more, particularly due to public banks. It was not until private banks began flooding the market with ATM, credit card, and specialized loan services that they began updating themselves—but old government employees can often be those most averse to change.

Finally, and perhaps most obviously, control over the bulk of Egypt's financial assets has permitted the state to lay a heavy hand on lending practices. Whether that translates into providing large and attractive loans to preferred customers, financing the rising fiscal deficit (which crept up to 5.4% of GDP in 2001), or funding its many costly megaprojects, it means that public banks have tacitly financed many ventures that private banks probably would have turned down.

As of June 2001, Egypt's industries claimed LE82.7 billion, or 34%, of total loans—LE18.5 billion of which (or 22%) went to public-sector companies. That's more

than two times the total lending to the agriculture sector (public and private) and more than 60% of total household lending. Privatization of the Big Four, either through the sale of existing capital or through a capital increase, will involve close scrutiny of their loan books, and the government may be reluctant to allow this until most state-owned companies—the banks' main clients—are themselves sold off.

Nonetheless, the government has tried to make steps in the right direction. A progressive law was passed in 1998 allowing private ownership of public banks, but it has yet to be acted on. Aside from governmental qualms, one of the largest obstacles is the disapproving public. Bank of Alexandria, the smallest of the four, was expected to be the first to be sold in 1999, but popular dissent indefinitely postponed the sale.

To get around to putting a large segment of employees out to pasture, the government has chosen a creative top-

Insurance Eyes the 21st Century

Minister of Foreign Trade Youssef Boutros Ghali once joked that it would be unfair to describe Egypt's insurance industry as fit only for the 18th century—it's "well into the 19th century." But that was nearly five years ago. A good deal has been done since then to pave the way for an industry overhaul.

Even so, few Egyptian industries remain so dominated by the state. There are 13 insurance companies in Egypt and one reinsurer. The three state-owned giants, Misr Insurance, al-Sharq Insurance and al-Ahli Insurance, account for around 90% of the market. Lack of competition and isolation from developments taking place elsewhere have meant that their products lag years behind. Uneducated by the industry, the Egyptian public is still largely unaware of the benefits of insurance. Premiums total just 1.5% of GDP, well short of the 4% to 5% mark that the government has targeted, and far less than the global average of 7.5%.

While in charge of the cabinet's economy portfolio, Boutros Ghali led the drive to change all that. In 1998, legislation was passed that lifted the 49% restriction on foreign ownership of insurance companies and scrapped the rule that managers must be Egyptian. That allowed foreign companies to set up and opened up the way for a sell-off of state-owned insurers.

Early in 1999, Merrill Lynch and Morgan Stanley Dean Witter were mandated to evaluate the big three state-owned insurance companies and Egypt Reinsurance with a view to privatization. Agreeing on how much the companies are worth, though, was an arduous process that was not completed until 2001 had almost run out. Under central planning, insurance companies, like banks, were used as vehicles for government investment and have ended up owning stakes in dozens of state-owned enterprises. The results of the evaluation still have not been made public.

A faster track to modernizing the industry may be through foreign companies setting up, bringing new skills and products and ratcheting up the competition. However, an unwieldy—and some say resistant to change—regulatory process run by the Egyptian Insurance Supervisory Authority means approving new participants and products is slow.

Indeed, since 1998 newcomers have been few and far between. A life-insurance joint venture between Commercial International Bank and Legal and General of the UK set up in 2000 while American International Group took control of Pharaonic Insurance Company. The WTO liberalization of services due to kick in at the start of 2005 is likely to speed up the trend towards more foreign participation. *BF*

down approach. The appointment of Ahmed Bardie—former head of Citibank's North African operations—as Chairman of Banque du Caire in 2000 marked the first privatization of management in one of the Big Four. Along with a team of four other private-turned-public bankers, he has met success in cleaning up the bank for state divestiture, although it is still not clear when that will be.

Central Bank of Egypt

Another way the government keeps a leash on banking is through the CBE's strict regulation of the sector. In addition to controlling the liquidity and reserve requirements, the exchange rate, and open market operations (including all treasury bond, T-bill, and REPO operations), the organization also closely monitors all 56 banks operating within the system. With new governor Mohammed Abu al-Uyoun at the helm and the placement of the CBE directly under the president's supervision (rather than the now-defunct Ministry of Economy), many hope that the CBE will ease its tight grip on banks in the coming years.

The track record from the last ten years shows interest in liberalization. Rigid interest rate ceilings on deposits and floors on loans were removed in 1991; an edict to reduce holdings in private banks to less than 20% was issued in 1997; and a decision was made to allow 100% foreign ownership of local banks' equity in 1998. But there is still much to do. If Egypt really wants to attract foreign participation, as these legislations imply, then complementary measures to improve the general market climate should be taken as well. Banks' major gripe over late 2000 and 2001 was the lack of liquidity and foreign currency pressures crippling their activities.

Accordingly, the CBE spent last year on the defensive, implementing small policy adjustments to try to keep the market liquid. This included cutting the discount rate by a total of 100 basis points to 11% in April, dropping the reserve requirement for Egyptian pound deposits with a maturity of three years or more, and allowing bonds issued by banks to count towards liquidity requirements (set at 20% of local currency deposits and 25% of foreign currency deposits). Increased open market operations, particularly in terms of REPOs, in which the CBE buys back treasury bills from banks, also helped to restore cold hard cash to the market, but the gap between supply and demand was just too large. In the end, the CBE still had to resort to pumping funds from the national reserves into the sector.

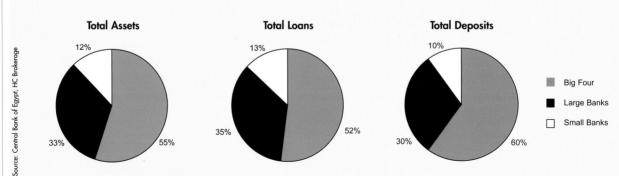

Banking Activity

Total Assets

12%
33%
55%

Total Loans

13%
35%
52%

Total Deposits

10%
30%
60%

Source: Central Bank of Egypt, HC Brokerage

- �(gray) Big Four
- ■ Large Banks
- □ Small Banks

With combined assets of over LE80 billion, the Big Four are big by any standard. They also account for the lion's share of loans and deposits

Many feel that it is high time the CBE starts utilizing the interest rate more aggressively to alleviate pressure and encourage investment, especially now that a post-September recession prevails. The cut in the discount rate to 11% was a start, but it will not make much of an impact since banks seldom actually offer loans at that rate. The average market lending rate, based on banks' varying cost of funds-plus-spread formulas, actually hovers around 14%.

Joint-venture banks

Over the last several years, foreign banks have discovered that the easiest way to get a foothold in the Egyptian market is to either increase their stakes in a joint venture or through acquisition. Given the language barrier and the massive expense of setting up shop from scratch, taking over an already established entity has many benefits, and can be managed if the interested party acts diligently when the state decides to release one of its holdings.

The Big Four own substantial stakes in Egypt's many joint-venture banks, such as Commercial International Bank (CIB) and Misr International Bank (MIBank). This persists despite the government's request in 1996 that they reduce their holdings to no more than 20%. To date, the National Bank of Egypt, which was involved in the creation of two of Egypt's most impressive joint-venture banks, CIB and National Société Générale Bank (NSGB), has been the most compliant. Most notably it has retained just 20% of CIB and allowed France's Société Générale to up its stake in NSGB to 51%, keeping only 18%.

Other successful share buy-outs include HSBC's stealthy move to scoop up an extra 50% of Egyptian British Bank to raise its holdings to 90% in 2000, and Barclays' boost in its share of Cairo Barclays International to 60%. In terms of acquisitions, only two have transpired so far. First, Arab Banking Corporation bought Egypt Arab African Bank in 1999, and just last May, Credit Agricole Indosuez captured HSBC's 75% stake in Credit International d'Egypte.

The acquisition of a bank that is held, at least in part, by the government remains a tricky ordeal. Not only are they usually loathe to resign the large profits granted by their stakes, but the size of their holdings are enough to make them key shareholders, and thus able to influence sale negotiations. A recent example was London-based Standard Chartered's attempts last year to buy Egyptian American Bank (EAB), in which American Express holds a 40.8% stake and Bank of Alexandria still retains a 33% interest (*see box*).

Private-sector banks

Despite, or perhaps because of, their small branch networks, Egypt's 24 private and joint-venture banks are the sector's most profitable. Outstanding among them are CIB, NSGB, MIB, and EAB. CIB is Egypt's biggest private-sector bank, with 4.8% of total market assets in 2000, and is also one of the most conservative banks in the group. Though it is a private entity, the head of the bank, like all others operating within the system, must be approved by the prime minister. NSGB is one of the country's most efficient banks, with a cost-to-income ratio of only 22.3%.

Up until very recently, such banks—particularly CIB—concentrated on lending to large corporate clients. MIBank has extended this to medium-sized enterprises, and NSGB has used its international ties through

Société Générale to serve multinationals working in Egypt. But because of the increased competition in the corporate banking market in the last two years, inviting more foreign banks into the fray, Egypt's existing private banks have been forced to look for new growth options.

They have discovered it in retail banking. Recognizing Egypt's vast middle class, who had previously found it near impossible to get credit, in late 1999 private banks began inundating the market with all sorts of new products, ranging from ATM, debit, and credit cards to personal loans of every variety, and even mobile and e-banking services. All of a sudden, private banks were giving the Big Four a run for their money in a sub-market the latter had dominated for decades. State banks reacted quickly to offer similar services of their own, and the market began to transform itself. Among the most aggressive banks in the sector are NSGB, which was the first to launch car loans in 1999; National Bank of Egypt, currently the largest credit card provider in Egypt; and Citibank, which attracted scores of customers in 2001 with its top-notch 24-hour customer services.

The short-term results are astounding: domestic credit card holders increased from around 200,000 in 2000 to an estimated one million in 2001. The number is expected to reach six million by 2005. There are also now around 820 ATMs across the country, 435 of which are linked by the 22-member 123

Holy Lending

An ever-expanding enclave of Egypt's banking network is the growing group of Islamic banks. Centered on the basic Quranic premises that usury is strictly forbidden, and that risk and reward should be shared collectively amongst a community of peers, these banks invite customers to deposit or invest at no pre-determined rate of profit and even borrow in special interest-free packages. Instead of interest, clients earn money on their pounds according to a profit-sharing ratio based on the bank's performance. The practice has gained such international support in recent years that private banks like Citibank, Deutsche Bank, and HSBC have created specialized Islamic banking branches, and Dow Jones launched several Islamic Market Indexes in 1999. Although once associated with scandals for conniving innocent people in the late 1980s—hundreds of thousands of Egyptians lost their life savings after investing in banking companies like al-Rayan, Sherif, al-Hoda Misr, and al-Saad—Egypt's Islamic investment institutions have cleaned up in recent years, establishing a sizeable stake in the local market. The country's most well known Islamic bank is Faisal Islamic Bank of Egypt, which was established in 1977 and relocated to a spectacular building in Doqqi in 2000, the entire exterior of which is adorned with Quranic calligraphy from earth to sky. Faisal Bank's assets of over LE9 billion in 2000 placed it near the top of the large and medium bank segment, although its earnings of LE32.2 million were considerably less than its peers. MIB, for example, with assets of LE11.3 billion, earned LE204.8 million that same year. But clients of Islamic banks do not seem to mind the reduced profits. They invest with a higher purpose in mind, content to know that their gains are not reaped from the losses of others. SV

network, which allows customers to use them interchangeably. And perhaps making the largest impact on everyday life, many regular citizens are using personal loans to finally get that car, or washing machine, or even the education they always dreamed of. Mobile phone and e-banking services, such as Citibank's CitiDirect service, have been slower to gain acceptance.

Banks have been making good business off this new wellspring, especially because the largely uninformed public is still willing to pay exorbitant service fees. Currently, customers whose cards are issued by state banks pay rates in the range of 15%-22%. Those with MasterCards issued by Citibank pay 33% interest. Time, competition, and the sudden drop in the economy at the end of 2001 should adjust this next year.

Despite the sudden expansion in retail banking, loans to the household sector only comprised a low 13% of total sector lending. Most analysts still see a vastly under-

The Sale That Wasn't

For a few months last year, it looked like something big was afoot in Egypt's banking world. In May 2001, the joint-venture Egyptian American Bank (EAB) announced that it was up for sale. The two major shareholders—American Express with a 40.8% stake and the Bank of Alexandria with a 33% stake—said they would be willing to unload their combined shares to an outside investor. Seen as one of Egypt's most lucrative banks, the offer presented a tantalizing opportunity for a private company seeking to gain a foothold in the Egyptian market.

When word got around that a prospective buyer had been found in Standard Chartered, the news electrified observers in the financial sector. Although public banks have shed part of their holdings in joint-venture banks over the past several years, their shares have largely gone to other major shareholders; this, on the other hand, would mark the first full acquisition of an Egyptian bank by an outside company. Moreover, if both parties could agree on a fair price, the deal could provide a benchmark for pricing other leading Egyptian banks, thus clearing the way for further privatization in the sector. The next few months of negotiations, however, proved unfruitful. After several bids were proposed and rejected

by the shareholders, Standard Chartered finally gave up and retreated to England. By late September, word was out that talks had resumed, but by then, global events had already started taking their toll. In the end, Standard Chartered was unwilling to pay the price EAB had in mind, and when the Middle East became too much of a gamble in itself, they pulled out. The ongoing saga of negotiations kept EAB's stock rallying on the exchange until December 18—up 80% from its March price—when it was finally announced that the deal was a no-go. As the back-and-forth of negotiations wore on, it highlighted the obstacles hampering the further liberalization of the banking sector. Many feel that the shareholders at EAB were expecting too much. While it is one of the better private-sector banks in the country, it did not perform as well as its peers over the last year, particularly in terms of its non-performing loan ratio. Its net profit also slipped as a result of the ongoing economic crunch, to LE72.5 million in 2000 from LE100 million in 1999. The very unfortunate epilogue to the tale is that on the night the deal fell through, EAB's managing director, James Vaughn, passed away unexpectedly. Since then, the bank has been taken off the market, although rumors of other interested buyers persist. Whether EAB will be able to price itself attractively enough to actually make the sell has yet to be seen. *MK*

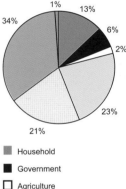

Bank Lending by Sector

1%
13%
34%
6%
2%
23%
21%

- ■ Household
- ■ Government
- □ Agriculture
- Services
- Trade
- Industry
- Foreign

Source: Central Bank of Egypt

Egyptian industries claim LE82 billion in loans, with one-fifth of that going to public-sector companies

Get a Cash Loan
In a blink of an eye

serviced market, providing extraordinary opportunities for growth. The next big step will be to harness the new mortgage law, which was finally passed last year. While it may be slow to take off, given the current recessionary climate, rich or poor, there are a lot of young Egyptian families in need of sufficient housing, and private banks look forward to helping them secure it.

Investment banks

Two investment banks, Commercial International Investment Co. (CIIC, created by CIB) and EFG-Hermes, have dominated corporate finance in Egypt over the last few years. Both have participated in major public and private sector offerings, most recently for Orascom Telecom in July 2000. Again though, competition in the industry has intensified. The government's privatization program slowed considerably in 2000 and 2001, reducing demand for the advisory services necessary to turn around inefficient enterprises. The economic slowdown and credit crunch have also reduced demand for new equity and debt.

Given the moratorium on initial public offerings in 2001, it is no surprise that investment bankers found themselves with a lot of time on their hands. Who could have asked for a better moment for some major internal restructuring? Come August, CIIC and EFG-Hermes did just that, initiating a strategic alliance. The terms of the deal entailed a share swap in which EFG-Hermes bought 100% of Flemings CIIC (an arm of CIIC formed in 1999 through a merger with Flemings Mansour) and 16% of CIIC, while CIIC took on a 34% stake in EFG-Hermes through a capital increase. As the biggest, most competitive investment banking houses in the country, some believe that the move granted the new superpower over half of the market in one fell swoop.

The consolidation has allowed CIIC/EFG-Hermes to streamline their operations—with EFG-Hermes and Flemings CIIC tackling investment banking and CIIC

becoming the investment holding company—in preparation of intense foreign rivalry once the market get active again. Already in 2001, Merrill Lynch and Morgan Stanley beat out the competition to handle the government's eurobond issue. Personal relationships are important in Egyptian banking, and multinationals have realized the importance of establishing links with local firms. ABN Amro bought Delta Securities in 2000, and Morgan Stanley has a 20% stake in HC Securities. Once privatization efforts rekindle and the stock market starts climbing again, it will be all out war amongst these big league players. *SV*

Trading Places

The bourse drops to new lows

Spending any time around the Cairo and Alexandria Stock Exchange (CASE) these days is likely to make you feel slightly nearsighted. Most investors are not looking too far ahead. They are out for short-term profits—by, say, tomorrow, at the latest—and tracking any given security back to 1995 ... well, that was just an eternity ago. True, the market has seen an astounding turnaround in the last nine years since it was pulled out of its 30-year socialist era slumber. But it is not as if Egypt had never seen its share of spirited trading before. The country's stock exchange has a long and bold history, dating back to 1865 when the Alexandria Cotton Bourse was first formulated in the cosmopolitan coffee shops of that city's elite European quarter.

At the time, Egyptian cotton was swaddling the globe, and the country's ambitious industrialists had made a habit of gathering informally to cut deals with European exporters. In those days—before terms like transparency and investor relations had been coined—local producers' main strategy to beat the fierce competition was to establish a strong reputation for reliability, make sure their crops met deadlines, and provide top quality goods. When the practice became bigger than the men themselves, they organized, forming the Alexandria General Produce Association (AGPA) to trade cotton, seeds, and cereals in the spot and future markets. In 1899, the AGPA formally established the Alexandria Cotton Bourse in Mohammed Ali Square.

Not wanting to be outdone by their northern neighbors, the businessmen of Cairo—already representing some 79 limited liability companies—began considering shifting their trading venue from café to exchange. In 1903 the Bourse and Banking Company of Egypt Ltd., headed by Maurice Cattaui, was established in the former building of the Ottoman Bank. Within four short years, the Cairo bourse had grown to such a size—228 listed companies with a combined capital of LE91 million—that it was necessary to relocate to a larger building in the heart of Cairo. Counting this exchange and its Alexandrian counterpart, Egypt was considered to have one of the top five stock markets in the world.

For the next 50 years, the bourse was a force to be reckoned with, rising on agricultural strength that seemed inexhaustible. The market survived a near fatal crash in the summer of 1907, stemming from overly zealous real estate and bank speculation, and even carried on through the US stock market crash of 1929. By the 1930s, the exchange had moved into its third building on Sherifein Street, where it still presides today. The Egyptian pound itself was trading at £1.025, giving root to the trading that would still make and break fortunes well into the 1950s. The catch, however, was that even though there was some degree of Egyptian involvement, the wealth being reaped from Egypt's soil was, for the most part, going straight into the coffers of Great Britain. By the time Egyptians were finally forging strong positions for themselves on the bourse, the whole political climate of the county was inches away from being turned on its head. In 1956, in a speech actually delivered from the parapet of the Alexandria bourse, Gamal Abd al-Nasser proclaimed to the world that he had nationalized the Suez Canal.

Before long, Abd al-Nasser's campaign to reclaim "Egypt for the Egyptians" placed the entire private sector under state control. Inevitably, the bourse closed its doors in 1961.

But though the bears and bulls were in hibernation for nearly 30 years, they have not found it too difficult to come out and play again. The bourse received the push it needed from the Economic Reform Law of 1992 and the subsequent Capital Market Law, which created the Capital Market Authority (CMA) in 1995. When the moves towards privatization came in the 1990s, the framework provided by this legislation enabled CASE to become a stand-out amongst emerging markets. Ironically, one of the biggest goals of CASE these days is to attract foreign participation.

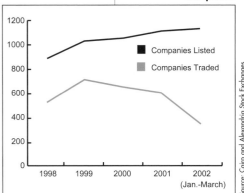

Traded vs. Listed Companies

- Companies Listed
- Companies Traded

Source: Cairo and Alexandria Stock Exchanges

As the market has stagnated the number of companies actually traded has nosedived

2001/02: that sinking feeling

If, as many believe, the stock market can be considered a mirror of the overall economy, then it would be fair to say that Egypt suffered from low self-esteem over 2001 and the first half of 2002. Last year started with the odds against it: when the IT bubble burst, domestic liquidity

Market Capitalization

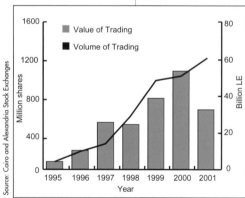

Source: Cairo and Alexandria Stock Exchanges

Market cap fell by LE8.5 billion in 2001

Trading Volume vs. Value

Source: Cairo and Alexandria Stock Exchanges

The value of stocks traded fell sharply in 2001

dropped. With the devaluation dilemma that started in late 2000, CASE took a steep slide that made it clear that hard work and some luck would be required to turn things around.

A brief period of optimism flashed by in January 2001 when a local subsidiary of Pepsi Co., Tasty Foods Egypt, acquired Chipsy, a local snack food company, at a price of LE420 million. But as the macro-economic obstacles multiplied, the bourse went into a steady decline. The period's few highlights—including the addition of Egypt to the Morgan Stanley EMF index in May 2001 and a spell of cement acquisitions four months later—pulled CASE up temporarily. But as a whole, the last year and a half was a bust. According to the Egypt's benchmark Hermes Financial Index (HFI), the market sank 29.8% over 2001 to end the year at 5272.5 and bottomed out to a new all-time low of 4762.31 by late January 2002, an unimaginable distance from the high of 16,448.5 in 1997. Despite periodic glimmers of hope for a turnaround following the international donors' meeting in February 2002, the CASE had only repaired slightly by the end of June 2002 to close at 5300.22.

A quick glance over the annual statistics for 2001 shows that market capitalization declined by LE8.5 billion from the previous year to LE111.3 billion, average daily turnover shrunk to almost half from LE195 million in 2000 to just LE101 million, and the percentage of listed companies that were actually traded dropped to 50% for the first time since 1995.

From the way 2002 has gone so far, it looks like it will be another record year, in a bad way. Daily trading volumes remained severely depressed into the first half of 2002, often with total market turnover of just around LE20 million. This is sorrowfully evident in the steep decline in average daily trading values for the market's most active stocks, such as MobiNil, which traded at an average daily turnover of LE7.56 million over 2001 but just LE2.6 million for the first half of 2002, as well as Suez Cement, which fell from an average daily turnover of LE7.27 million in 2001 to LE2.12 million in the first half of 2002.

The reasons for the fall are both tangible and intangible. Concrete factors like the deceleration of privatization efforts over 2001, particularly in terms of IPOs, concerns about the government's waning fiscal discipline, the liquidity crisis, and the deep recession following September 11 surely had an impact on the market. The bourse is also still underdeveloped, with more than half of market cap concentrated in the telecom, construction and building materials, and banking sectors. Yet, a great deal of CASE's volatility can only be explained by the elusive "psychological factors" at play.

For example, though Egypt has one of the most stable governments in the region, it is still highly susceptible to any vague perceptions of political or military risk in the area. This made for strange commentary over the last year and a half, when local analysts would ascribe a day's decline on the bourse to the Palestinian uprising or the US bombing campaigns in Afghanistan. No matter how far away or how removed from Egyptian affairs they are, whenever tensions arise in the region, foreign investors—who accounted for 16.5% of the buying and 15.4% of the selling in fiscal year 2000/01—liquidate their holdings and get out quick.

While out-of-country investors can be excused for overlooking fundamentals in favor of more random and sometimes unsubstantiated fears, local investors cannot. Most of the time, however, the thick stew of gossip making its rounds each day wins out over solid financial results.

This might be the biggest reason that CASE has remained relatively shallow despite the high speed of its technological advancements. The staple diet of rumors—which are often given room to fester on the pages of Egypt's daily business newspaper, *al-Alam al-Yom*—egg on the large number of local retail investors. These investors are not interested in market development. They are hungry for an edge that will enable them to buy low and sell high quickly. For that reason, many companies that fail to submit financials on time or keep investors posted on any developments, whether good or bad, still

manage to drum up large sums of cash on the bourse.

The most fitting example of this phenomenon can be found in Egyptian Media Production City (EMPC). Although it is notoriously lacking in transparency, EMPC was still the third most active stock in 2001, with an average trading value of LE5.35 million, due to persistent rumors of foreign acquisition interests, which have, as yet, failed to come true.

The rumor mill sometimes even picks up companies with good investor relations departments. Pfizer Pharmaceuticals, for instance, ended up on 2001's top 20 list due to whispers mid-year that it had received a license to

Breaking the Speed Limit

The bourse may not have moved from its Sharifein Street building since 1931, but it has hardly stayed the same. The implementation of a high-tech electronic trading floor, opened in March 2001, now has the bourse all decked out to compete with the big boys. The new Automated Trading System, designed by a Canadian company, EFA Software Services Ltd., has transformed the exchange's settlement system, the process of filing all the required documentation following the purchase or sale of securities. From a cumbersome procedure requiring vast numbers of paper slips in favor it has become one clean, mean machine that handles all trading, clearing, settlement, registry, and central deposit operations electronically. By law, the whole system is under the supervision of one organization—Misr Company for Clearance, Settlement, and Depository (MCSD)—which received the highest possible rating for a central-depository company (1.25) from JP Morgan in July 2001. Though implementation cost near LE6 million, CASE sees big returns for its investment: without the automated system, Egypt would not have been able to cut its settlement cycle down to a guaranteed T+3 (3 days after the transaction) for available funds and T+4 for physical

shares. This places the bourse on equal footing with European and American markets.

The MCSD is also betting on the fact that when foreign investors can count on quick, organized returns, they will be more inclined to invest—and even more so when settlement is guaranteed in dollars. With this audience in mind, the MCSD has developed a system with the Central Bank whereby foreign investors receive their selling receipts denominated in US dollars based on the official exchange rate on the day of transaction. A new mechanism also allows dollar earnings to be shifted abroad by as early as T+4.

To counter another big potential snag in trading—securities and cash defaults, which occur when brokers execute trades before their positions have settled—the MCSD has set up the Settlement Guarantee Fund (SGF) with CASE and the CMA. Under the system, if a trade is still held up five days after the transaction order, the SGF steps in to settle the cash position. The fund keeps the market fluid, but it is not designed to let transgressors off the hook. Brokers that default receive harsh warnings from the CMA and can be shut down if the problem persists. *SV*

Market Capitalization by Sector

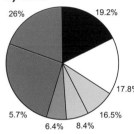

26% 19.2%

17.8%

5.7% 16.5%

6.4% 8.4%

■ Utilities

■ Building Materials and Construction

□ Financial Services

▨ Entertainment

▨ Food and Beverage

■ Mining and Gas

■ Other

Source: Cairo and Alexandria Stock Exchanges

The stock exchange has started to diversify, but more than half of market cap is still concentrated in the telecom, construction, and banking sectors

produce Viagra in Egypt. This kept the stock artificially inflated even after the company publicly stated, on more than one occasion, that although it had applied, it had not been granted the license. The gossip-mongers may have felt vindicated in June 2002 when the government announced out of the blue that Viagra would in fact be allowed to be manufactured in Egypt. Pfizer was not the only winning horse, since the government decided to award manufacturing licenses to seven or eight local firms, some of which still remain unidentified. As many speculators have learned the hard way, getting too carried away with visions of grandeur also tends to detract from positive developments when they actually happen. The bourse was reeling from February to April when word spread that Morgan Stanley Dean Witter was finally going to add Egypt and Morocco to its Emerging Market Free and All Country World indices, as they had proposed in July 2000. By the time the news was actually confirmed on April 10, 2001, some had gone so far as to speculate that inclusion would bring an inflow of anywhere from $3.6 to $5 billion from international fund managers who passively allocate their investments in line with the indices.

With imaginary millions flashing before their eyes,

Hermes Financial Index

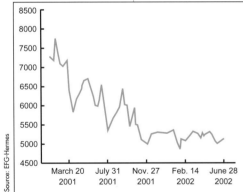

Source: EFG-Hermes

The exchange reached a new low in January 2002, dipping to 4,762.31

local investors went wild buying into blue chip stocks like Orascom Telecom and Commercial International Bank in hopes of pre-empting the foreign investors they expected to flood the market within the next few weeks. The HFI jumped 11.4% from 6092 on April 10 to 6786 on May 28 as frantic optimism kept driving the market up despite indications that Egypt's weight would only account for 0.28% of the index (as opposed to the originally forecasted 0.8%) and warnings by local Morgan Stanley affiliate, HC Securities, that potential inflows were likely to be more to the tune of $14 million. When the big day came, investors felt let down. The fireworks they had imagined hardly made a spark on the bourse. Not long after, Egypt's weight on the index was scaled down to just 0.23%. The HFI slid to 5969 by the end of June and kept on falling well into August. Precisely because of the

Second Chances

With equity valuations bottoming out over the year, institutional traders made a noticeable shift to the more conservative bond market in 2001. Following September 11, they swept in to pick up Egypt's sovereign issues, which were trading cheap. But despite Egypt's big launch into the sovereign bond market this year, the secondary market is still undeveloped in comparison to other emerging markets, particularly in terms of corporate bonds. Companies are often conservative and rely on bank debt for financing. Outstanding bonds, including government housing and treasury bonds, and 28 corporate bonds are worth LE19 billion. The main players in the market are banks, insurers and funds.

In an effort to encourage development of the fixed income market, CASE announced in late December that price change limits on bonds were to be removed as of January 2002, allowing closing prices to be set according to market forces. The new policy will apply to all bonds except convertible bonds, which will be subject to the 5% price limits currently applied. *SV*

devastating effect rumors can have on a market of this size, the CMA has been slow to remove the 5% ceiling on daily price increases or decreases. By last summer, however, the need to stimulate trading overrode caution, and it was announced that the ceiling would be gradually eliminated, starting with those stocks that normally experience the heaviest trading.

The bourse witnessed its first big insider trading scandal in 2000 when Arabian International Construction (AIC) executives were investigated for dumping shares just before the company announced that originally predicted profits of LE48 million had actually only come to LE7 million. As punishment, the CMA canceled several days worth of AIC transactions and forced the company to buy back 1.5 million shares. Given the cultural emphasis on personal business relationships and the expected favors that they entail, many felt that this was one instance of what is considered standard practice in the

Alphabet Soup

In the acronym-laden world of finance, sometimes it is easy to get confused—when the analyst said ABC, did he mean Arab Banking Corporation or al-Ahram Beverages Co.? Mention GDRs, however, and most local investors' eyes will perk up with immediate recognition. The term instantly conjures up images of large, rain-making companies and dollar inflows.

A GDR, or Global Depository Receipt, is a mechanism that allows companies listed on one exchange to simultaneously list on another (non-American) foreign exchange through an intermediary custodian bank. The way it works is straightforward: a broker submits local shares in an international depository bank, which then issues the certificate of receipt in another market to be traded freely. GDRs provide investors with dollar dividends and eliminate intermediary charges. The systems is a perfect marriage for companies that feel limited by their local investor pool, and foreign investors who would like to diversify their portfolios, but are hesitant to hassle with foreign bureaucracy and exchange rates. In fact, GDRs have proven to be such an attractive investment option that there are now nearly 2,000 trading around the world, and they are increasing at an annual rate of 40%.

Currently, nine lucky Egyptian companies have tapped European markets through the use of GDRs. The first was Commercial International Bank (CIB), which listed on the London Stock Exchange in 1996, followed shortly afterward by Suez Cement, al-Ahram Beverages (ABC) and PACHIN in 1997, MIBank and EFG-Hermes in 1998, al-Ezz Steel and Lakah Group in 1999, and finally, Orascom Telecom in 2000. All are listed on the London exchange, although Lakah Group is also additionally listed on the Luxembourg exchange. The group's choice of custodian bank is split between Bank of New York and London-based Banker's Trust.

Their success has been mixed. Those that have failed to cater to their foreign investors with the utmost commitment to transparency and detailed reporting, such as Lakah Group and al-Ezz Steel, have not fared well, as proven by their valuations, which are lower abroad than they are at home. Others, like ABC and CIB, have impressed fund managers with their forthcoming manner of conducting investor relations and have certainly prospered for it.

Looking at the turn of global stock exchanges over the last two years towards recession, it is now clear that the nine Egyptian companies chose the perfect moment to launch their issues. The current climate has not only put off IPOs, but GDR issues as well. Companies that failed to seize the moment in the late 1990s missed the boat, and it still is not clear when the next one is coming. *SV*

market. But citing the damaging effect such behavior has on Egypt's credibility in the eyes of the global market, the CMA has made efforts to show that it means business.

After the round of big cement acquisitions in September, when French firm Ciments Français gained a 25% stake in Suez Cement and the government relinquished it 50% interest in Helwan Portland Cement to ASEC, investors got the feeling that the Egyptian cement bonanza was just getting started. Prices soared across the sector as they bet on which company would be the next to catch a foreign operator's eye. But whenever mysterious rumors cropped up without much to back them up, CASE moved in to protect investors. On October 2, it was announced that trading on shares of South Valley Cement would be suspended until they published up-to-date financial results. The red flag was also thrown in the closing days of 2001 when suspicions arose that a privileged few had known about Standard Chartered's decision to pull out of the EAB acquisition before the news hit the wire. Investigations were initiated, but have still not reached any conclusions.

The menacing effects of these myopic and sometimes underhanded approaches to trading are unfortunate when considering, as Egypt's 100-odd institutional brokers are continuously pointing out, that with a low price-to-earnings ratio of 7.69 and high dividend yield of 16.62% as of December 2001, CASE is still one of the cheapest and most attractive emerging markets in the world.

The combination of steady devaluation and declining interest in securities following September 11 left most stocks severely discounted by the close of 2001. In such conditions, some might say that the bourse offered some attractive investments. But the tall order for macroeconomic reform, regional peace, renewed privatization efforts, and increased transparency in the market suggests that the following year or two are likely to be tough ones for the CASE. *SV*

Top 30 Companies by Market Capitalization as of March 31, 2002

Company	LE Billion
Egypt Telecom	17.11
MIDOR	3.51
MobiNil	3.09
Orascom Construction Industries	2.41
Suez Cement	2.32
Commercial International Bank	1.98
Golden Pyramids Plaza	1.85
Egyptian Media Production City	1.71
Assyout Cement	1.67
Abu Qir Fertilizer	1.50
Orascom Telecom	1.42
Egyptian Iron and Steel	1.40
Exxon Mobil Egypt	1.30
CIIC	1.20
Arab International Investment Co.	1.16
Delta Sugar	1.14
HSBC Bank Egypt	1.00
Eastern Tobacco	0.95
Alexandria National Iron and Steel	0.93
National Cement	0.92
Sugar & Integrated Industries	0.90
Helwan Portland Cement	0.85
Egyptian Cement Company	0.81
Al-Ahram Beverages	0.80
Dreamland Urban Development	0.79
Tora Cement	0.76
Glaxo Wellcome	0.76
Egyptian Kuwaiti Holding	0.74
Misr Exterior Bank	0.72
National Societe Generale Bank	0.71
Total	56.40
As a percentage of whole market	48%

Source: Cairo and Alexandria Stock Exchanges

Industry
Growth and competitiveness remain uneven

The Long View

With full-fledged WTO membership in 2005 looming closer and the COMESA and new EU Partnership agreements promising a whole new era of liberalized trade, Egyptian industrialists are busy these days gearing up for survival of the fittest. Manufacturers understand that unless they are busy modernizing, fine-tuning, and gearing their activities towards exporting, there is little hope that they will still be around by the end of the decade.

Though the current situation seems dire—President Mubarak's "export or die" proclamation sums it up succinctly—Egyptian industry has weathered many rocky years in the past and more than one economic revolution. Indeed, the challenges now facing Egyptian industry are just the latest of many to rear their head since Mohammed Ali first embarked on industrialization in the first half of the 19th century.

While Mohammed Ali made a concerted effort to create a manufacturing sector, laying the foundation for basic industries like sugar refining, milling, and textile production, as British rule tightened its grip over the country, the agenda changed. Given the choice between exploiting cotton for quick riches, or actually investing in more widespread industrialization for the good of the country, the British chose the first. As a result, Egypt became disproportionately dependent on this mighty agricultural crop (by 1914 cotton constituted 90 percent of Egypt's exports) and the rest of Egypt's manufacturing capabilities were sidelined.

Despite the prominence of cotton, a very limited manufacturing sector devoted primarily to processing raw materials and producing perishable or bulky goods gave birth to Egypt's first modern working class engaged in factory labor. By 1916 there were 30,000 to 35,000 workers employed in modern factories, and it was these humble origins that led to greater industry in the following decades after the cotton market withered.

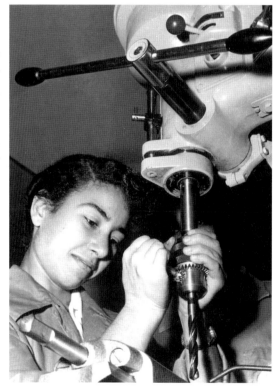

Expansion hastened during the Great Depression and World War II, feeding into the inter-war period when local manufacturers made their first real drive to combat imports. Under the aegis of Banque Misr, for example, a dozen different industrial enterprises were created, ranging from printing to tobacco manufacturing, cotton ginning to fisheries. Aiming to promote industrial development and self-sufficiency, these and other burgeoning local industries helped to raise exports and substantially reduce the dependency on imports for such commodities as cement, refined sugar, soap, and even lightbulbs. One of the most successful enterprises—and a point of national pride—

Industrial Growth in Emerging Markets

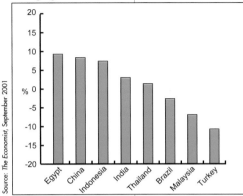

Source: The Economist, September 2001

Egypt compares well to other developing economies

Industrial Growth

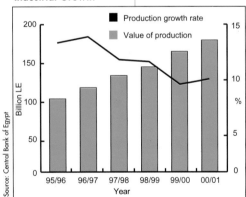

Source: Central Bank of Egypt

Production is on the rise, but actual growth is slowing

was the so-called piaster project, which built a tarboush-making factory with the proceeds of a one-piaster subscription fee paid by Egyptians. Before the factory was established, Egypt imported almost all its tarboushes—660,000 of them in 1928. By 1937, the number had declined to 34,000. With the input of both local and foreign capital, Egypt was rapidly industrializing. Industrial output ballooned by nearly 63 percent between 1946 and 1951.

The tide turned after the 1952 revolution, when the government drastically increased investment in industry and mining. This went hand in hand with the nationalization program: the state took hold of nearly all large-scale firms (with 500+ employees) in the chemicals, pharmaceuticals, engineering, electrical textile and sugar refining sectors. By the late 1960s, the public sector's output value accounted for about two-thirds of Egypt's total manufacturing output. Public investment in industry throughout the 1960s and 1970s rose to 85%-90% of total manufacturing investment.

But as national debt mounted and oil prices sank toward the end of the 1980s, the sector began facing increasing difficulties. By then, Egypt had emerged from its socialist era to make a new go at open market activity, but persisting governmental price regulation was damaging both production and distribution activities. In terms of production, public sector companies were given unfair advantages over private companies by being able to purchase inputs, such as energy, at subsidized prices. To even the scales, the government increased energy prices and lifted controls on agricultural prices.

Distribution was equally skewed due to the unrealistically low fixed prices for locally manufactured consumer products like beverages, soap, and even cars. In a nod to the policies that would characterize the next twenty years, the government decided to ease price controls in 1982 and permit gradual increases so long as they did not threaten social and political stability.

Egyptian industry has emerged from this decades-long roller-coaster ride as fit as can be expected, but it is still dogged by a lingering lethargy caused by years of governmental protection and subsidies. The industry and non-petroleum mining sector contributed 20.2% of GDP in fiscal year 2000/01 and employed a weighty 2.533 million citizens, or roughly 14% of the national workforce. The primary and secondary effects of privatization—namely, improved efficiency in production, increased product variety, and the steady widening of Egypt's consumer base—have enabled the country to maintain industrial growth of around 10% or more over the last eight years. This rate puts Egypt at the top among its emerging market peers.

But when scrutinized closely, it is clear that growth has been unbalanced among different industries, and global competitiveness differs drastically from one to the next. Those sectors that have been most sheltered, such as the textiles, pharmaceuticals, and milling industries, are finding it much more difficult to get in shape. Though they may be large in terms of value, years of preferential treatment as "strategic" sectors have left them overstaffed, mismanaged, and woefully in need of modernization. But others such as the cement, food and beverage, and furniture industries, which prospered from the wave of privatization in the 1990s or have just demonstrated enough ingenuity to thrive, are seen as defensive industries that will do well in an open market.

To help encourage growth and combat unemployment, the government has created a series of large industrial cities that offer cheap land and attractive tax breaks to companies that utilize them. Some of these cities have proven quite successful. The two largest, Tenth of Ramadan and Sixth of October, currently boast over 1,500 factories (with 700 more under construction) that provide almost 220,000 jobs. But these success stories tend to be concentrated around Cairo—the industrial cities of Upper Egypt have failed to bring in many investors and thus have not had the same economic impact in these communities. New Minya, for example, has only one factory that employs about 375 workers. *SV*

Empire Building

The housing bust hurts cement and steel

As the Pyramids demonstrate, the ancient Egyptians well understood the intrinsic connection between empire building and massive construction. Operating with a similar motivation, Egypt has targeted the construction sector as the key to economic stimulus over the last decade. Building the economy depends, in many ways, on physically building Egypt, whether in terms of improving infrastructure like roads, bridges, and airports; expanding and modernizing commercial space; or providing enough affordable housing for the rapidly multiplying population. Accordingly, construction activities have grown at an average annual rate of 20% and total spending on infrastructure has topped LE400 billion since the 1980s, according to the US Department of State.

For obvious reasons, the sector is rarely discussed in isolation. Investment in construction trickles down into the highly lucrative engineering, machinery, building materials, and housing and real estate markets. Their extreme interconnectedness was advantageous in the mid-1990s when intense growth in the demand for one fed the others. This culminated in the period from 1997 to 1999 when spending on glitzy new residential communities in and around Cairo as well as massive hotels and tourist villages in Cairo, Sinai, and the now-trendy Northern Coast shot up to unprecedented levels.

But dwindling resources stemming from the liquidity crisis in 2000 and misdirected development left the market with a surplus of half-finished resorts and expensive up-scale homes but not enough lower-income level digs. This means that the last two years have been tough for the whole group. According to the Business Barometer, a twice yearly survey of 165 of Egypt's biggest manufacturing firms and 35 construction companies, 71% of the surveyed construction firms reported stagnant or declining activity in the first half of 2001. By the end of the second half of the year, that number increased to 83%. The top two constraints cited by participants were lack of capital and low market demand.

How such firms have weathered the bust depends on their nature. There are currently 42 state-owned construction companies and about 2,000 private construction firms, most of which are small. Nearly every major company is exposed in some way to government debt. Over two years ago, the government vowed to pay back some LE25 billion in debts, much of it owed to local contractors. So far, about LE3.5 billion

203

has been paid. Since the government is still the main client, the key players in the sector are the state-controlled giants who are not in a position to demand swift payment, and who may do work cheaper, if less well. The behemoth Arab Contractors, together with smaller state firms like Mokhtar Ibrahim, enjoy an estimated 40% of the market.

The yellow livery of Arab Contractors is ubiquitous. Its crowning achievements last year include the completion of two state-of-the-art underground tunnels from al-

Azhar to Saleh Salem in October as well as the inauguration of the 70-meter high Mubarak Peace Bridge over the Suez Canal that same month. Arab Contractors is also currently wrapping up the tenth and final stage of the May 15th flyover from Mohandessin to Nasr City. While public firms continue to dominate state infrastructure projects, there is little evidence that these workhorses can compete for luxury projects, or of the privatization that might make them leaner. Non-state companies, not so government-dependent, are better positioned to compete during these belt-tightening times. The biggest contender among them is Orascom Construction Industries (OCI), a conglomerate made up of 20 companies, which is involved in just about everything. In addition to wrapping up the other big bridge project—the $66 million Ferdan swinging rail bridge—in October, OCI kept busy over the year working in consortia with various international firms on upscale retail and residence projects, like the Royal Méridien Tower, the Nile City complex in Boulaq, and the Heliopolis Citystars project. It also continued working on the new port at Ain Sukhna. OCI has expanded its activities to include local and regional cement enterprises, primarily in Algeria and Palestine, to offset the local slowdown. Its local cement concern, Egyptian Cement Company, exported approximately 30,000 tons of cement in 2001 and secured contracts to send another 500,000 tons to various African countries in the first half of 2002.

The darker side of last year was in the Egyptian housing sector. Despite much fanfare, the new desert cities—which currently total ten completed and 44 planned developments, according to the Ministry of Housing and New Communities—have yet to prove successful.

Private companies have been most stung by this reality. After increasingly moving into housing in the 1990s in pursuit of big returns from the luxury market, they suffered in 2000 as sales slowed to a trickle and bottomed out in 2001's larger economic struggles. Of the estimated million Egyptians that enter the housing market each year, only about 12.5% of these home-seekers are destined for high income and luxury housing, while 25% look at middle-income housing and the remaining 62.5% head for the low-income housing market. The bulk of Egyptians simply cannot afford the type of homes being built, or the transportation required to live even a half hour outside of Cairo.

Unofficially, demand for lower-income housing is also being met by hand-to-mouth construction, the haphazardly thrown up edifices that characterize the informal industry and whose figures do not show up on the balance books. But this is risky business. Indeed, much building is illegal, carried out without permits by returnee workers spending their precious savings after a stint in the Gulf.

In an attempt to tackle this problem, the government finally ratified Egypt's first mortgage law in late 2001.

Operative as of September 26, the new law gives priority to the low-income segment of the economy (defined as those individuals earning a maximum of LE6,000 a year or families earning a maximum of LE9,000 a year) and stipulates that the government will subsidize 50% of the total cost of land and infrastructure for projects planned in lower-income housing areas. Although it may take a few years to get worked out, the passing of the law has made many hopeful that the coming years will bring a turnaround in this section of the industry.

Cement

Though the Egyptian cement industry has received much attention from foreign investors only over the last few years, cement has been a key industry for over eighty years—and for good reason. The wealth of raw materials found locally such as limestone, clay, gypsum, and manpower, for that matter, make it a natural choice. In 1928, one year before Egypt's first local factory, Tora Cement, went into production, Egypt imported 250,924 tons of cement. The following year, Tora Cement went online with an operating capacity of 160,000 tons of cement a year. Just one year later, Helwan Cement entered the scene. By 1939, the two factories were fulfilling 90% of local demand with a combined production of 320,000 tons per year. Alexandria Portland Cement was established next in 1948 and National

Cement followed in 1956 under the Nasserist regime, when cement was directed toward massive projects like the High Dam in Aswan and the west bank of Cairo sprouted up Mohandessin and Doqqi. These four companies managed to carry Egypt all the way through the nationalization era, but by the 1970s they could no longer keep up with mounting demand. Fueled by returns on migrant labor and a push to new infrastructure investments, the 1980s and 90s boomed as cement factories started popping up all over the country in places like Minya, Assyout, Suez, and Sinai.

With the slowdown in construction over the last two years, however, the Egyptian cement sector has suffered, and it looks as though the damage is not done yet. The surge in local demand in the mid-1990s inspired the nine local companies to rapidly increase their production capacities so that they would be able to produce 56% more by 2002 (from 1999 levels). In addition, four new companies were formed to compete for market share by 2002. In the meantime, declining market demand and increased capacities have almost wiped out the need for imports. By

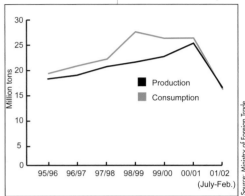

Cement Production vs. Consumption

Source: Ministry of Foreign Trade

The housing slowdown put a dent in cement consumption

Major Cement Industry Acquisitions since 1996

Buyer	Target	Year	Share acquired (%)	Market Share 2001 (%)
Holcim	ECC	1996	36	17.1
Cemex	Asyut Cement	1999	96	13.5
Lafarge	Beni Sueif	1999	95	4.8
Blue Circle	Alexandria Cement	2000	76	2.7
Cimpor	Ameriyah Cement	2000	91	7.5
Suez	Tora Cement	2000	65	13.0
ASEC	Helwan Cement	2001	100	11.0
Ciments Français	Suez Cement	2001	25	13.9

Source: HC Brokerage

the time the new companies get rolling, Egypt will have a heavy oversupply on its hands that will lower utilization rates and wreak havoc on prices until serious steps are taken to increase exports or redress supply/demand imbalances, as expected in 2006.

Despite the general acknowledgement that the sector is just beginning an ugly slump, it is still extremely attractive in the long term. The global cement market has seen a frenzy of consolidation in recent years, and Egypt has certainly not been left out. Continuing the wave of privatizations and acquisitions that began in 1996, 2001 brought more of the world's biggest building materials companies into the fray. Last year, the two major targets were Helwan Cement and national giant, Suez Cement.

The Helwan deal got a false start at the beginning of the year after the government announced on December 19, 2000, that its 47.9% stake in the company would be put on the block. Helwan's shares rallied well into February 2001 on the stock exchange, when many thought the buyer would be local Suez Cement. But as time moved on and rumors grew cold, investors lost hope. Devaluation of the pound took its toll on the market, further complicating the valuation for the sale, and so it was not until August 16, 2001, that the Ministry of Public Enterprise announced again that Helwan was on the block. Within a week, Ciments Français announced its intention to bid for a 25% stake in Helwan at LE51 per share. This was followed shortly after by an offer from the Arab Swiss Engineering Company (ASEC) for up to 100% of the company at a price of LE51.10 per share plus a LE4 per share dividend, raising the full bid to LE55.10/share. The sudden bidding war was reported to catch the interest of two other global giants, the Irish Building Group, CRH, and the Portuguese firm Secil, but they did not submit competing bids by the deadline. On September 9, the Ministerial Committee for Privatization announced ASEC as the winning bidder.

Some felt that Helwan was sold far too cheaply; indeed, according to HC Brokerage, it was the cheapest cement acquisition yet to take place in the market in terms of production value. But then again, the market is not as attractive as it was just two yeas ago, and Helwan will require large investment to bring its production up to global environmental standards. Furthermore, although ASEC is a joint venture, Egyptian companies have a majority stake. While the government is anxious to privatize, there is a limit to how much of the national assets it (and Egyptians in general) is comfortable selling off to foreign investors.

In comparison to the Helwan acquisition, the deal involving Suez Cement was much tamer. But the timing of Suez's decision to assign an 18.7% stake (10.1 million shares at LE51 per share) to Ciments Français—which effectively granted Ciments Français a 25% total share in the company—on September 17, 2001, meant that it was lumped together in the cement storm. According to HC, these two major transactions pushed the percentage of foreign holdings in the local market up to a stout 44%.

Despite the arrival of private-sector producers, the government still sets cement prices through the grandly named High Council for Cement, a body made up of cement companies' chairmen and representatives. Although it has contributed to cutting down the volume of imports in the market over the last two years, the concept of the government dictating the prices charged by private companies is somewhat jarring and the producers are expected to demand more flexibility as time goes on.

Steel

Like many Egyptian industries, the steel industry is dominated by one giant, in this case the Alexandria National Iron and Steel Company (ANSDK). But unlike some other state giants, this one has experienced a shake-up over the last couple of years. In 2000, Ezz Steel Rebars—headed by Ahmed Ezz, one of Egypt's biggest businessmen—gradually acquired a 30% stake in the firm. Ezz was subsequently appointed as Alexandria Steel's chairman and managing director, granting him control of about 70% of the Egyptian steel market. The two companies have started to consolidate operations under his management, and unify their brands under the label Ezz-Dekheila (EZDK).

Ezz has two main facilities, in Sadat City and Tenth of Ramadan City, while ANSDK's operations are in Alexandria. EZDK Steel Europe was incorporated in Duisburg, Germany, in July 2000 as EZDK's European marketing arm with the aim of enhancing exports.

The changes in management had many observers hoping that Ezz's private-sector know-how would increase efficiency and production, but the market—again largely dependent on construction—slowed. Reinforced bars, known as rebars, account for around 80% of steel sales in Egypt, and since they are used in construction, are vulnerable to any slowdown in building. Egypt's steel sales (both imports and exports) dropped from a total of around 4.17 million tons in 1999 to just 3.26 million in 2000. Over the first six months of 2001, volume stood at 1.62 million tons compared to 1.603 million in the first half of 2000, indicating that the slowdown has now prevailed for two years. This is quite a shock after growth of 18% over the previous five years.

Competition for Ezz's domination in the near future appears slight—EZDK has an estimated 67% of the market. The Kouta Steel Group and Suez Steel are the next largest private local players. There has been talk for years about selling off state-owned Helwan Steel, an employer of some 23,000 workers. Inefficiency, outmoded equipment, and overstaffing mean the company has failed to compete as private-sector competition has grown. Given the number of lay-offs necessary to make privatization viable most do not see it happening any time soon.

A much smaller segment of the market is claimed by flat steel, which is used to manufacture goods such as cars, ships, consumer durables, and piping. However, because local production currently does not come anywhere close to meeting demand, the market is much more advantageous for producers. Unlike rebar producers, devaluation has actually helped them, since the cost of imported flat steel rose. But Ezz, too, is looking forward to stirring up this sub-market soon as well with the opening of a $700-million flat steel plant in Ain Sokhna. Though the plant is still going through test runs, it will ultimately have a capacity to produce 1.2 million tons per year, geared largely to export.

Aluminum

No progress has been made towards attracting international investors to state-controlled Egypt Aluminum—Egypt's only primary aluminum producer—since an initial public offering of 10% took place in 1997. The rest of the company is owned by public-sector institutions. The government seems wary of the social upheaval a sale might cause the company's 10,000 employees in Nagaa Hamadi, 100 km north of Luxor.

However Egypt Aluminum is recognized as one of the gems of the state-owned industry, with exports totaling LE513.4 million in 1999/00, representing 53% of its production. Discussions have apparently taken place on selling a state of the art rolling mill, but there has been little progress as the government is demanding very high prices. *SV & PS-S*

Egypt's Mineral Wealth

Mineral	Description	Location	Reserves
Albitite	White rock used in ceramics, refractories, and some medical industries	South Sinai (Wadi al-Tor, Wadi al-Samra, Wadi Ghorab)	Estimated 239 million tons Possible: 1.5 billion tons
Bentonite	Super absorbant clay used in drilling operations for oil or underground water	Uyoun Mousa, Ras Sedr (southwest Sinai)	At least 450 million tons
Black Sands	Rich sands deposited from Nile silt with high content of industrial materials	Arish, Delta coast near Rashid and Damietta	848 million tons with 4.1 million tons in valuable industrial materials
Building Materials	Various rocks, minerals, and sands used in building	Found throughout the country	Annual production: Limestone: 25 million m³; Sandstone: 0.8 million m³; Dolomite: 1.5 million tons; Gravel: 12 million m³
Carbonaceous Shale	Mineral deposits burned to generate power, as in cement industry kilns	Abu Zeneima in the Sinai	140 million tons
Feldspar	Mineral mixed with quartz for use in the glass and ceramic industries	Gabal Eish and Shamam (both near Hurghada)	9.3 million tons
Gold	Precious metal	Eastern Desert	At least 2 million ounces
Gypsum	Absorbant mineral used to make Plaster of Paris and cement	Eastern Desert, Western Desert, and Sinai	At least 275.9 million tons
Kaolin	Clay used in ceramic, white cement, textiles, medicinal industries, and some special types of plastic	Abu Zeneima, al-Tih Plateau (Sinai)	At least 100 million tons
Ilmenite	Mineral used to produce titanium white paint and titanium metal	Eastern Desert and Abu Galaga	Estimated 18 million tons
Niobium & Tantalum	Metals used for high-tech alloys in the optical, electrical, and IT industries	Abu Dabbab and Umm Nagat (Eastern Desert)	156 million tons
Ornamental Stones	High gloss stones used to decorate living spaces	Throughout the country	Marble: 150,000 m³ Granite: 30,000 m³
Phosphate	Mineral used to produce fertilizers	Abu Tartour, Eastern Desert	969 million tons
Sodium Chloride	Rock salt used by the food and chemical industries	Red Sea Coast	Annual production: 2 million tons
Tin	Multi-purpose metal	Wadi Dib, Igla, Muelha and other places in the Eastern Desert	280,000 tons
White Sand	High silica sand used for making glass	Throughout the Sinai and Eastern Desert	Annual production: 400,000 tons

Source: Egyptian Geological Survey and Mining Authority

Buried Treasure

In addition to wealth of gypsum, kaolin, and limestone deposits that feed Egypt's large cement industry, the country has stores of other minerals and precious metals hidden under its sand and buried in the rocky expanses of desert. Valuable materials currently being mined in Egypt include tin, gold, marble, granite, phosphate, and black and white sands.

Despite all this natural wealth, the mining industry remains underdeveloped. But this may change in the coming years. Through joint contracts with the Egyptian Geological Survey and Mining Authority (EGSMA)—the state agency that oversees all exploration and mining activities in the country—some multinationals have sunk millions of dollars into Egypt in the last five years in search of buried treasures.

The most high profile discovery—or re-discovery—in recent years has been gold. In 1998, the EGSMA and Centamin NL, an Australian mining company, discovered an impressive reserve of about 1.6 million ounces of gold in the Eastern Desert after three years of exploration. Egyptian-born Australian Sami al-Raghi, who owns 40% of Centamin and was the instigator of the firm's interests in the Eastern Desert, says that he was inspired by a framed reproduction of the oldest mining map in the world, which he saw hanging in the EGSMA offices. The map depicted the extensive Fawakhir gold mines under the reign of King Seti I, who ruled from 1350-1205 BC.

Al-Raghi has big plans for Egypt. In addition to proven reserves, exploratory drilling suggests that Centamin's 1,400-km^2 Sukari concession may contain as much as 16 million ounces of gold. Once the mining locations are fully operational, Centamin anticipates production of about 610,000 ounces per year at an estimated cost of $100-$160 per ounce. Such a yield and operational expense ratio will grant Egypt one of the top ten gold mines in the world, and also one of the cheapest. Despite the steep drop in world gold prices over the last two decades—in 1980, the price per ounce on the New York Commodities Exchange topped $825, but it's now hovering around $320 per ounce—Centamin plans on making revenues of up to $1 billion per year from the mining concession in return for its $17 million investment.

In addition to Centamin, the US-based Cresset International has also set up shop in the Eastern Desert. Exploration in their Umm Tundub mine has shown possible gold reserves of about 23 million ounces.

The year 2001 revealed that Egypt's mother earth is home to both ancient riches and space-age fortunes. The latter comes in the form of tantalum—an extremely expensive high-tech metal (currently selling for around $150,000 per ton) used to make the electronic capacitors needed for popular modern appliances like cellular phones, PDAs, computers, and video game systems. In an announcement in October, Gippsland, another Australian mining firm, announced that it had signed a $40-million deal with the Egyptian government to mine a 48-million-ton tantalum deposit in Abu Dabbab, located in the Eastern Desert.

Gippsland made use of previous studies conducted by EGSMA, the Geological Research Institute of Moscow, and Geominera Italiana to home in on the Abu Dabbab site. As it turns out, 50-70% of the mining wastes will be composed of feldspar, a material used in the production of high-grade ceramics that sells for around $70 per ton. With such discoveries, it may not be long before the mining industry witnesses an expansion. *SV*

Manufacturing

Local manufacturers strive to compete

Cars

Since 1993, when the government liberalized the commercial import of passenger cars, opening the industry up to outside competition, foreign companies have poured in. Egypt now boasts 11 car assembly plants and roughly 350 car-part manufacturers. Consumers

have real choice these days, a far cry from pre-1993 when state-owned Nasco had a monopoly and the options were uninspiring cars made in technological alliances with foreign car companies such as Fiat and Turkey's Dogan.

Yet while the market has grown to around 70,000 automobiles a year from 20,000 in 1992, it is still tiny. A study distributed by FORSA—a business matchmaking organization created by AmCham Egypt and the US Chamber of Commerce last year—found that Egypt's annual production of around 50,000 passenger cars and another 20,000 trucks and buses does not compare well to the four million registered vehicles already on the road.

The adverse economic conditions of the last two years have obviously hindered new car sales. FORSA reports that the number of newly licensed vehicles was almost 50% lower in the first two months of 2001 than in the same period in 2000, primarily due to the massive decline in commercial rather than private vehicles. As a result, most assemblers and parts factories are operating far below capacity, with some averaging just 30%. The inefficiency of this system renders it anti-competitive: cars made abroad under proper economies of scale cost 20% to 30% less to make.

Recognizing the enticing prospect of simply buying foreign, the government has chosen to protect the nascent industry with whopping import tariffs. These range from 40% for cars with engines smaller than 1,000 cm^3 to 135% for those with engines larger than 1,600 cm^3. A loophole in the scheme is that foreign cars assembled locally with a minimum of 45% local content enjoy a considerable cut in duties. This has successfully convinced multinationals to set up their own plants in Egypt. Currently, GM, Fiat, Chrysler, Suzuki, and Mercedes Benz all have considerable operations here.

The 45% local-parts requirement along with the prevalence of older cars in the market leads most analysts to believe that the future of Egypt's automotive parts industry looks far brighter than that of car assemblers. The US embassy estimated in 1998 that the feeder sector accounted for about $600 million in sales to original equipment manufacturers and another $400 million in replacement parts. But even this sub-segment is going to need to shape up. Right now, Egyptian car parts producers make only low-tech, highly labor-intensive parts such as seats, radiators, batteries, air conditioning, radio-cassette decks, wiring harnesses, and exhaust systems. Modernizing their factories will help attract more multinationals and will also raise the companies' export potential.

Many firms have already begun exporting to Europe, hoping to cash in on the eventual reduction of tariffs under the EU-Med Association Agreement. These are primarily foreign companies with local operations, but Egyptian feeder companies are planning to give the multinationals a run for their money by earning ISO

9000 ratings as well as more stringent American "quality standard" QS 9000 ratings. This can only help to improve the overall industry.

The big question is what will happen come 2005 when under the World Trade Organization tariffs will be set at a maximum 30%. Some say it could be the end of the line for the local industry. Others say the government will protect the local assemblers by piling on non-tariff trade barriers and raising sales tax on imported cars. One thing is for sure, Egypt's automotive industry is working hard to prepare itself.

Household appliances

Understanding the boom in Egypt's household appliance industries over the last thirty years depends a lot on one's perception of the term "luxury." Air conditioners, refrigerators, televisions, and washing machines might have been among the basic accoutrements of domestic life in Europe and America since the 1950s, but in countries like Egypt such conveniences did not start finding a wide consumer base until a couple of decades later—and many households are still without them. The advent of cheap, locally made household appliances has radically transformed life in Egypt. Such products have improved lives through increased hygiene and savings provided by refrigeration, granted more spare time from automatic washing machines, and

Imports of Durable Consumer Goods				
(Million $)	98/99	99/00	00/01	01/02 July-March
Durable Consumer Goods of which:	582.2	603.0	681.4	526.3
Cars	130.3	170.6	156.7	98.3
Refrigerators, Freezers	76.2	73.4	71.1	46.5
TVs & Parts	20.4	50.1	42.5	29.9
Source: Central Bank of Egypt				

supplied vital access to information through televisions. World Bank Development Indicators show that Egypt's television density per 1,000 people increased from 118 in 1995 to 189 in 2000.

The local giant in the sector is without a doubt the Olympic Group, which has made millions by supplying the masses with affordable appliances produced locally under license from some of the world's leading manufacturers like Zanussi and the Electrolux Group. Their product line includes refrigerators, manual and fully automatic washing machines, water heaters, and metallic office furniture—all markets in which it has carved out a near monopoly.

The fastest growing domestic appliance industry, however, is air-conditioning. The market is still highly fragmented, but Miraco dominates. In 1979, the company launched its first factory with a production capacity of 1,400 units per year. In 1992, Miraco entered a joint-venture agreement with Carrier Corporation and quickly became the largest heating, ventilation, and air-conditioning company in the African continent. Today, Miraco-Carrier claims a 54% market share in Egypt and produces roughly 100,000 units per year. Among its most recent crowning achievements was the award of a multimillion dollar contract in 1999 to keep Alexandria's

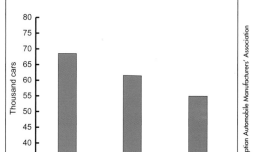

Cars Sales

Thousand cars

Source: Egyptian Automobile Manufacturers' Association

With money tighter, fewer people are buying new cars

new Bibliotheca Alexandrina comfortably cool all year.

In the realm of televisions, International Electronics, another major firm controlled by the Bahgat family, dominates the market. It makes Philips and Grundig televisions under license, as well as its own Goldi and Goldstar brands, which have become quite popular.

Again, considering the low average income of most Egyptians, it is a wonder that so many can afford such appliances. In order to maintain sales margins, most retailers have devised installment programs whereby customers can place a sizeable down payment up front and then pay the rest over an agreed upon timeframe ranging anywhere from six months to two years. In order to make sure they get paid, many shops have created their own customer evaluation teams that require detailed personal information from their prospective clients such as their jobs, salaries, bank statements, and electricity bills.

Down in Damietta

Known in the beginning of last century as a center for silk, cottons, and fish production, these days Damietta is synonymous with carved wood furniture. An offshoot of the boat building industry that flourished here in days gone by, today Damietta's furniture industry is home to some 37,000 registered manufacturers. Although there are no official numbers on Damietta's share of the domestic sector, local industry sources estimate that up to 90% of all Egyptian wooden furniture is manufactured here.

Egypt exports furniture to about 70 countries in Europe, North America, and the Middle East, and with furniture exports on the rise throughout the 1990s, Damietta has become something of an Egyptian success story, an example a local small-scale industry that is managing to adapt to the competitive global market. Indeed, President Mubarak himself has held up Damietta as a model to be followed in Egypt's drive to develop local industry and exports. But to hear some local craftsmen speak, the success has not been evenly spread.

Exports of Wooden Bedroom Furniture

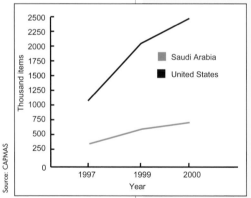

Exports of wooden furniture rose from $6.4 million in 1997 to $9.5 million in 1999

Traditionally, Damietta's industry has been based on a chain of small workshops, each employing about five or six workers specializing in some aspect of the manufacturing process, from carving to inlaying, finishing to upholstery. Based on custom orders, the system gives buyers more input into the final product, but it is not conducive to large scale manufacturing or export. The 1980s, however, saw the development of nearby New Damietta, which houses large, mostly export-oriented furniture factories. Many of these have set up showrooms on the roads leading into the old city, allowing customers to peruse ready-made goods. Offering more convenience to the consumer and more secure wages to local workers, the factories of new Damietta have taken a big bite out of the domestic market, once the almost exclusive province of small manufacturers.

As small furniture makers struggle to stay afloat in the midst of a changing industry, the last year has not been kind to them. The devaluation of the pound has meant a steep increase in the price of lumber, and the higher prices have affected business. The implementation of the general sales tax in 2001 also put a dent in domestic sales by tacking on another 10% to the retail price. Indeed, small manufacturers claim that many workshops shut down because they believed the tax would do them in. *ScB*

But one can hardly blame them. In the last two years the market has slowed down significantly as economic recession has squashed the real estate market and cut back customers' expendable incomes. Tourism development briefly offset the losses suffered from the slowdown in the residential real estate market, but the tourism crisis that followed September 11 eliminated that as well. Salesmen are being forced to devise ways to attract customers, but still keep their necks above water in case of defaults.

Similar to the automobile industry, Egyptian household appliance producers are also finding it more difficult to compete with imports. As products become more sophisticated, local production is falling and imports from countries with better economies of scale are on the rise.

Always trying to stay ahead of the market, the Olympic Group undertook a major restructuring of its washing machine and refrigerator production lines in 2001. The two-phase project included relocation to modernized factories in Tenth of Ramadan City. Upon completion, the new facility will be able to turn out 250,000 washing machines and 500,000 refrigerators each year, as well as develop new models of refrigerators and deep freezers. With a population of 66 million people, the domestic appliance market may suffer a bit for a few years, but as soon as the economy turns around demand is sure to shoot through the roof again.

Furniture

Despite Egypt's utter lack of any lumber resources to speak of, it is home to a thriving and wildly creative furniture-making industry. Generations of family apprenticeship have left the country with a strong industry comprising over half a million employees. Unlike other consumer durable sub-sectors, Egypt's furniture industry is dominated by the private sector, and most companies are small to medium-sized. Production of wooden furniture is concentrated in the towns of Damietta and New Damietta, where thousands of craftsmen still practice the fine arts of hand woodcarving, inlaying, and high-grade reproduction (*see box*). While styles remain heavily influenced by colonial British and French aesthetics, heavy on the gold leaf and brocade, many have also done well producing modernist custom-fitted furnishings for large buyers like hotels and office buildings.

Though furniture exports do not comprise a significant part of Egypt's total exports, the number has been steadily rising over the last few years. According to CAPMAS, total domestic furniture production was estimated at $100 million in 1996-97, with exports of $10 million. By 1999, exports were up to $15.4 million, with the greatest demand coming from the United States, Europe, and the Arab Gulf. Home furnishing exports to the United States, the largest importer, totaled $7.6 million in 2000, but dipped to $6.1 million in 2001 after a rough second half of the year. Total exports over January and February of 2002 had fallen by a third from the previous two years to just $844,000.

The small group of imported furniture outlets in Egypt has also suffered with the recession. While a good portion of furniture imports are parts (rather than finished goods) used in local production, there are some international retailers doing business in Egypt. But challenges abound from all fronts. In addition to stiff import tariffs of around 40% plus 10% sales tax, many name-brand retailers like Ethan Allen, which opened two showrooms in Mohandessin and Heliopolis in 2001, have to watch out that their catalogs are not scooped up by customers and brought to Damietta for cheaper replications. For the moment, they appear to be suffering most from the slow market. *SV, SK, & MK*

Despite low average expendable income, most households have a TV

Chemical Reactions

The drug industry gears up for WTO

Pharmaceuticals

Egypt's pharmaceutical industry is the largest in the Middle East and North Africa. According to a sector report put out in February 2001 by the American Chamber of Commerce's Business Studies and Analysis Center, Egypt claims 30% of the regional market with products worth more than $1 billion a year. Almost all of this is consumed domestically with just 6% exported. Nonetheless, per capita consumption remains low due to low average income.

Companies can be divided into three groups: multinational, state-owned, and local privately owned firms. Like wheat and tobacco, the government considers drugs of strategic importance, meaning that rapid price fluctuations have the potential to provoke major social distress and, consequently, violent public response. For this reason, it retains a tight grip on pricing policies, subsidizes essential drugs, and does not want to let go of state-owned companies. Although it has sold stakes of up to 40% in some through the stock exchange, most local companies still have some degree of state ownership.

Devaluation has negatively affected local drug companies. Though consumers hardly felt the squeeze, pharmaceutical firms were hit hard by the fall of the pound. Pricing in the industry is strictly regulated by the government's cost-plus formula, which sets prices with a pre-determined profit margin for local producers. But because companies must import between 80%-85% of their active ingredients, manufacturing is now 40% more expensive than it was two years ago. Without a governmental move to increase the retail prices of the products themselves, producers will continue to shoulder all losses. Health care professionals are also suffering from rising expenses since many drugs that they need for surgery and other complex procedures are too sophisticated to be produced in Egypt.

The question of whether to keep vital drugs available to the greater public, who often cannot afford the medical services to begin with, or grant the drug companies the profits needed to keep them growing, is a pressing one. While the government has been trying to make compromises that would keep both sides of the fence happy, it is getting tougher by the minute.

One of the key reasons that producers are able to provide cheap drugs is because they are not spending millions on research and development each year. According to a report produced by the Ahram Center for Political and Strategic Studies, R&D spending in public-sector drug companies is, in the best of cases, about 2.9% of sales revenues, while the world average is a little more than 17%. Local drug manufacturers capture 82% of the domestic market. More than half the output of these companies is generic, essentially copied. Currently, this type of co-opting is legal in Egypt. However, under the forthcoming Trade Related Aspects of Intellectual Property Rights (TRIPS) agreement, patented pharmaceutical products will be protected by copyright for 20 years.

Multinationals have lobbied the government to implement the accord before the grace period allowed to emerging markets ends December 31, 2004. They say early implementation would allow Egypt to get a head start on the rest of the region and could attract companies to set up here, making the nation a regional pharmaceutical hub. Local producers, however, are dead set against implementation of the accord any earlier than is necessary, saying they need the time to adjust—but "adjusting" is a relative term.

Right now, most companies are busying themselves with introducing as many new generic products as possible before January 1, 2005. The TRIPS law will not be retroactive, so any products that are on the market before it takes hold will remain in the public domain, and will be priced accordingly.

The government, meanwhile, has taken several steps to lessen the impact of TRIPS—forming a French-African company to export drugs to Africa and laying out a special clause in the agreement that allows them to breach the law in cases of public health emergencies—but much depends on the stance multinationals take.

Several multinationals, including Hoechst Marion Russell, Glaxo-Wellcome, Novartis, and Bristol Myers-Squibb, already have operations in Egypt—Pfizer set up here in 1961. Will they choose to import copyrighted medicines to Egypt, scaling back their operations, or will they use Egypt as a base for exporting to Africa? The signs seem promising. Glaxo-Wellcome increased its stake in Amoun Pharmaceuticals to 100% in March 2000, while Pfizer announced seven months later that it would spend LE140 million on a new plant designed to export to Africa and Arab countries.

Egypt's largest private-sector drug company, EIPICO, is also Egypt's largest exporter, accounting for a quarter of Egypt's drug sales abroad. It is comparatively well protected from the effects of TRIPS, making 185 products. Nevertheless, it is spending heavily on research and development, opening labs for biotechnology and raw material research.

Cosmetics and Paramedical Products

The modern cosmetic industry owes much to ancient Egyptian beauty rituals. Historians have found proof that all Egyptians—including men, women and children of all classes—wore eye makeup. French Egyptologists and chemists discovered in 1999 that Egypt's ancestors also understood the deeper connection between health and beauty. Remnants found in 4,000 year-old make-up containers had traces of chemical compounds that were used by the Greeks and Romans in later millennia to treat eye diseases like conjunctivitis and trachoma.

Today, Egypt's beauty industry—and that in the rest of the world—still draws on this ancient wisdom. The cosmetic and paramedical (including soaps, shampoos, and moisturizers) sectors are increasingly dependent on modern medical and chemical sciences to meet the growing demand for products like anti-aging moisturizers, anti-perspirant deodorants, sunblock, whitening toothpaste, and hypo-allergenic makeup.

One of the largest Egyptian cosmetic firms is the

Drug	Unit	US	Egypt*	Egypt**
Aspirin (US: Tylenol, EG: Rivo)	1 tablet	$0.20	$0.17	$0.54
Cipro (antibiotic)	500 mg tablet	$4.20	$0.89	$2.86
Afrin Nasal spray	20 ml bottle	$5.79	$0.83	$2.68
Prozac	20 mg capsule	$2.97	$0.93	$3.00
Antihistamine (US: Chlor Trimetron, EG: Allergex)	20 mg capsule	$0.25	$0.01	$0.04
Amoxicillin (antibiotic)	500 mg capsule	$0.47	$0.10	$0.36

An Informal Retail Price Comparison of Popular Drugs

*Based on an exchange rate of $1/LE4.5 **Based on purchasing price parity of $1/LE1.4 (World Bank)

Source: Egypt Almanac

privately owned Luna Group, which specializes in local and licensed cosmetic lines; hair, nail and skin products; flavors and fragrances; food and chemicals; as well as industrial paints, inks, and packaging. With factories in Cairo and Sixth of October City and branches in the Alexandria free zone, Romania, and Russia, Luna has a workforce of over 600 employees.

While the cosmetics industry is growing in Egypt, the local market is still trying to escape what local manufacturers have called the "foreign complex," which influences consumers to buy imports or locally-made foreign products over Egyptian goods. The preference is clearly seen in a comparison of local manufacturers, like Luna, and the two mammoth multinationals competing for the market: Proctor and Gamble and Unilever. Proctor and Gamble set up shop in Egypt in 1986 with the launch of just two products, Camay soap and Crest toothpaste. Today, the Egyptian office markets ten brands of detergents, soaps, shampoos, toilet soaps, and sanitary products with the help of nearly 1,000 employees. The company manufactures from a 100,000 m² complex in Sixth of October City, and has increased investment in Egypt from just LE10 million in 1986 to LE750 million in 2001.

Egyptian corporate spending on research and development is a fraction of the global average

Unilever Egypt is part of a regional operation covering 48 African and 30 Middle Eastern companies. The company's MENA network managed to increase overall sales by 2% and profits by 13% over 2001 despite substantial threats to margins from devaluation in Egypt, South Africa, and Turkey.

Fertilizers

Like many things in Egypt, the fertilizer market—though it may have many similarities to those in other parts of the world—operates according to its own traditions and dictates. Whereas the global market these days is busy manufacturing compound fertilizers using a cocktail of phosphates, nitrates and potassium, Egypt's local companies are strictly divided into phosphate-based fertilizer producers and nitrate-based producers (ignoring potassium all together). Though this may seem old fashioned, the fact is that they know their market. All hybrid fertilizers introduced to the market have failed, so local producers have simply stuck to the tried-and-true products. Phosphate fertilizers dominate the market, which is convenient since Egypt's natural phosphate reserves currently total a colossal 969 million tons. The three major crops that require such fertilizers are Egypt's three biggest—rice, cotton, and wheat. According to the State Information Service, 1.44 million tons of phosphate fertilizers were produced in 2001, a number that is likely to increase over 2002 since it was a good crop year.

Non-state Egyptian Financial and Industrial Company (EFIC) has about 53% of the phosphate-based fertilizers, and its only rival, Abu Zaabal, has the remainder. EFIC is better run and more profitable, and is looking to tap into the export market with a new compound fertilizer plant in Sadat City planned to open in 2003.

But it is likely that Abu Zaabal will build up its market share in the next coming years, given that it was finally privatized in late 2001. Under the terms of the agreement approved by the Holding Company for Chemical Industries on October 28, 2001, a consortium of Egyptian investors including Sherif al-Gabali of Misr Fertilizers, Adel Salam al-Gabali, Mohammed Farid Khamis of Oriental Weavers, and five fertilizer traders will lease the company for three years at a cost of LE51 million plus an additional payment of LE83 million for inventory. After the three-year leasing period, the consortium will fully acquire the company at a price of LE149 million. Though the company is sure to improve under tighter management, it is unlikely that the building competition will force one of these two big companies out of the market. According to one local sector analyst, the market can probably absorb them both.

Abu Qir Fertilizers has about 54% of the nitrogen-based market and three state-controlled rivals. The SIS pegged nitrous fertilizer production at around 9 million tons in 2001.

Paints

Paints and Chemicals Industries, known as Pachin, Egypt's biggest paint maker with about 30% of the market, has had a torrid few years. The company has failed to maintain market share in an increasingly competitive field. Over-capacity in Egypt is estimated at about 30% to 40%. The Holding Company for Chemical Industries has not allowed Pachin to buy out rivals or invest huge cash balances elsewhere, since it wants to wait until a corporate buyer is found for the controlling 38.25% stake it still holds on behalf of the government. Devaluation put a dent in profits over 2001, given the company's dependence on imports for nearly 90% of raw materials. As a way of crawling out of the hole, Pachin hinted all year that it was looking to expand its operations by entering the printing ink market—a sub-sector so far completely dominated by imports—but nothing came of it. Many believe, however, that 2002 may bring better luck for the company and the sector as whole. *SV, SK & MK*

Food and Beverages
The market expands with the population

Egypt's food and beverage industry is enormous—quite simply because the country has a lot of mouths to feed. Food by far accounts for the largest segment of household spending, summing up LE56.1 billion annually, according to CAMPAS, compared to LE12.8 billion on clothes, LE6 billion on education, LE2.1 billion on private lessons, and LE4 billion on tobacco. Even in belt-tightening times like the last two years, the market has continued to expand and diversify at a rate slightly above 10% per year. Today, total production for the food industry stands at around $4.6 billion per year.

Bread—called *eish* in Egyptian Arabic, meaning "life"—is the nation's staple food and is viewed by the government as a strategic industry. Egyptians consume on average three loaves a day, costing the government LE2.9 billion in subsidies. Over the last few years, consumption of flour has grown at 2.5% annually, slightly above the population growth rate. Egypt produces three types of flour: dark, or 82% extraction (so called because that is the proportion of the grain extracted for use); white, or 72% extraction; and whole grain. The government controls the production of dark flour by providing state-controlled mills with wheat and paying a fixed rate for the work. Dark flour is used to make the subsidized *baladi* bread and forms the basis of most Egyptians' diet.

There are no pricing restrictions on white flour—used in pasta, cakes, and French-type bread—making it ostensibly more profitable. Consumption of white flour is growing at 9%-10% a year as economic reform raises the incomes and expectations of the richer segments of society. In the late 1990s, state mills started boosting white flour output since it is where they have room to make money. Private mills, eyeing fat margins and a growing market, sprouted up left, right, and

center. The result has been enormous oversupply. Some private mills that took out loans to build white flour mills find themselves watching as interest payments consume their profits.

Aside from the milling industry, the market boasts several giants like Bisco Misr, al-Ahram Beverage Company, Americana Food Group, Kaha Preserved Foods, Faragalla, Delta Sugar, Chipsy, and Eastern Tobacco, some of which are over a hundred years old and have survived the transition from private ownership to public to private again. In fact, some argue that one reason for the sector's success is the avid privatizations

The World Health Organization estimates that 5% of family income is spent on tobacco

Playing Monopoly

Al-Ahram Beverages, parent to Stella beer and now the popular upstart Sakkara as well, showed its strengths and weaknesses in 2001. Its successful buyout of its only beer and wine competitor, Gouna Beverages, for $66 million was the most talked about deal of the year and demonstrated its ability as a player in the fledgling Egypt mergers-and-acquisitions market. But a sales slump that began when it hiked prices on key beer and wine brands only a few weeks after the buyout, compounded with the crash in tourism, showed that even a monopoly has to nurture its clients. Expecting reduced profits for 2001, at year end ABC was reducing staff through voluntary buyouts and consolidating beer and wine production facilities. Financial results for the year, released in March, showed the company was right: net profit fell by 18%, from LE112.0 million in 2000 to LE92.2 million in 2001. Known for its flagship beer Stella, ABC has been diversifying since the company was privatized in 1997, branching out into the non-alcoholic beverage market with its flavored soft drink Fayrouz and the non-alcoholic beer Birell. And it's a good thing, too. Although vast improvements in quality control and aggressive

advertising helped to spur beer and wine sales, HC securities predicts that the local beer market will reach the saturation point by 2004. ABC already saw beer and wine sales decline in the wake of the tourist drop that hit Egypt after September 11. As the bulk of its wine sales—85%—and 19% of its beer sales go to tourists, both lines were seriously affected. In addition, the company said both markets were already shrinking.

To compensate for the expected market downsize, ABC is concentrating on expanding its non-alcoholic beverage segment. As of September 30, 2001, Fayrouz and Birell were available in nearly half the retail outlets in Egypt, and in August last year, the company signed a distribution agreement with Saudi Dairy and Food Stuff Co. covering Saudi Arabia, Kuwait, Bahrain, and Qatar—a significant boost to its export business and its presence in the Gulf. According to the company, its non-alcoholic beverage segment is growing fast, with Birell and Fayrouz summing up a 26% increase in sales over 2001, and unlike beer and wine, it is not exposed to fluctuations in tourism. *SP*

that have taken place within it: out of the 185 privatized companies logged by the Ministry of Public Enterprise since 1990, 51 involve giant agricultural and processed foods companies.

Added to this are hundreds of small-scale operations competing for the hungry market. Despite their large quantity and diversity of products, their efforts are not enough. With a population that is growing at nearly one million people per year, there is simply no possible way to produce enough food to feed everyone. Despite years of active campaigns to promote self-sufficiency, Egypt is among the top food importers in the world. The designation persists despite complex customs clearance procedures and prohibitive tariffs that can reach up to 80% for some types of food and up to 3,000% for some types of alcohol. According to CAPMAS, Egypt imported around $1 billion in agricultural products from the United States in 2000, in addition to another $697 million from the EU. While basic commodities like wheat account for the bulk of these imports, the US Department of Agriculture estimates that imported processed and packaged foods comprised around $523 million of Egypt's total agricultural imports that same year.

At the same time, however, an increasing number of local companies are doing very successful business exporting all over the world. According to a study published by FORSA in July 2001, Egypt's processed food exports (excluding staples like rice and sugar) leaped from $45.2 million in 1994 to an impressive $82.5 million by 2000. This is because while Egypt does import a very wide variety of food products, it has a surplus

of fruits and vegetables that feed into an extremely competitive frozen, canned, and preserved food market. From that $82.5 million total, $36.9 million was from dehy-drated vegetables, $17.1 million was from frozen vegetables and fruits, $3.6 million was from fruit and vegetable juices and concentrates, and $2.2 million was from jams and preserves. One enterprising company has even started exporting frozen molokhiya to Japan. Successes like these validate the Ministry of Foreign Trade's argument that Egypt can build a strong exporting economy if it utilizes its competitive advantages and targets markets carefully. Accordingly, its focus on this sector has increased in recent years.

Food industries are also a major selling point in the government's other big campaign to improve the trade balance—the "buy Egyptian" campaign. While it may seem that the burden of this scheme is being placed on consumers, the state is pushing local companies to work harder to

provide goods that satisfy the increasingly sophisticated tastes of the domestic market, which is exactly what is happening in the food sector. Particular goods that have seen major improvement over the last two years include baked goods, cheeses, alcoholic and carbonated beverages, dairy products, and bottled mineral water.

Aside from improving taste and variety, Egyptian companies are also trying to make food more practical for modern families. Due to the increasing number of women taking to the workplace, eating habits are now turning more towards convenience. This is manifested in the increasing variety of pre-cooked and packaged

Egyptians consume about three loaves of bread a day

foods, fast food outlets, frozen meats and vegetables and the phasing out of small grocers specializing in one food type (such as eggs, fruits and vegetables, meat, poultry, or baked goods) in favor of supermarkets and hypermarts. One sharp difference from wealthier countries, however, is that such "convenience" foods (often fast or junk food) are primarily consumed by Egypt's rich, not the poor. Upper income bracket moms are more likely to pay for the convenience of frozen pre-cooked meals, and their kids more likely to pay for expensive snacks like Doritos, Hostess Cupcakes, and Snicker bars. Furthermore, because the working day is still rarely punctuated by a lunch break in local corporate culture, the hungry white-collar class tends

Milking the Market

After a hiatus of 30 years, fresh pasteurized milk returned to Egypt in July 2001 with the launching of Labanita by the Mansour Group. Packaged in pristine white plastic bottles with Guernsey-cow-like blue patches, Labanita found immediate popular success with its TV ad campaign featuring the friendly milk cows Sawsan and Soad.

Though Egypt had fresh pasteurized milk in glass bottles for home delivery in the 1960s, the quality of the products went into decline with the nationalization of the Misr Dairy Company, and the once popular milkman fell by the wayside as cities grew increasingly crowded. In more recent times, the only liquid milk available on the market was the Ultra Heated Treatment (UHT) milk sold in Swedish tetrapacks or, more commonly, "loose milk," sold in markets, street carts, and other informal outlets. When the Mansour Group bought its Alexandria Seclam factory from the government in 1999, it began conducting market research to determine what consumers wanted in a new dairy product. The answer? The pasteurized milk of 30 years ago, perceived as healthier than UHT milk and more hygienic than loose milk.

The introduction of fresh milk on the market, however, faced several obstacles. For one thing, the Egyptian milk industry is dominated by informal producers—according to the Egyptian Dairy Association, in 1998 the informal sector produced almost eight times more milk than the formal industry—and many retailers are still unequipped to distribute a product with such a short shelf life. UHT milk does not require refrigeration, making it ideal for storage on the tightly packed shelves of small grocers. The company ultimately solved the problem by supplying retailers with branded Labanita refrigerators, effectively limiting distribution to supermarkets and medium-sized grocers with enough space to accommodate an additional refrigerator.

Deciding to target "C-plus" consumers—middle-class households with refrigerators, televisions, and disposable income—a major $2 million plus advertising campaign in newspapers, television, and radio created by J. Walter Thompson accompanied the introduction and deserves some of the credit for the milk's early consumer cachet. The ads feature two chatty cows discussing the merits of fresh pasteurized milk and the new yogurt, made from a mixture of cow's milk and buffalo milk "to make it more delicious."

By the end of the year, the newly renovated Seclam factory was at full production and unable to keep up with demand. Although the company is reluctant to release production figures, at least one measure of the milk's success is the competition it has spawned. Juhayna, a leader in the UHT market, introduced its own brand of fresh milk, Taza, soon after Labanita hit the market, while last fall Domty introduced UHT milk packaged in bottles that looked suspiciously like those used by Labanita, cow spots and all. *SP*

to depend on fast food delivery services. According to a study published by FORSA in August 2001, food franchises are currently making around $150 million a year in Egypt, 80% of which are US-based chains.

This explains why inflation in food, beverage, and tobacco products is currently the highest in the market: as devaluation has hit the economy, this import-heavy sector is paying the price. While the national inflation rate has hovered at around 2.2% for the last year and a half, food and beverages have risen from an average of 1.3% over the second half of 2001 to a rate of 3.5% since the start of 2002.

To many, the increasing prices are particularly alarming in tobacco products. More than half of the Egyptian male population smokes, either cigarettes or the ever-present *shisha*, or water pipe, and according to the World Health Organization, about 5% of family income is spent in one form or another on smoking. The market is monopolized by Eastern Tobacco Company, which claims about an 85% share (the main competition comes in the form of smuggled cigarettes). Currently the company sells about 55 billion cigarettes

and 17.3 million kg of molasses tobacco to the nicotine-craving Egyptian market every year. The giant boasts a range of products from their own brand stuff—primarily the ubiquitous Cleopatra regular—to L&M, Marlboro, and other smokes made under license. Still 66% owned by the state, it has been able to shore up prices until recently. But the company imports 100% of its tobacco leaf requirements, and with their inventories running out, devaluation is striking a mighty blow. Over the last year and a half, the price of a pack of Marlboro went up by 38%.

The food and beverage sector tends to be one of Egypt's most visibly politicized industries. In the early 1990s any product perceived to be foreign, particularly American, was generally considered to be of high quality and desirable by consumers, no matter the price. Yet since September 11 and the escalation of the Palestinian uprising against Israel, things have changed. Many food products and consumer chains have been boycotted and sometimes even vandalized over the last year and a half if perceived to represent an unwanted US presence and/or economic support for Israel. Many products that once espoused a certain "American-ness" either changed their image or launched defensive campaigns to defend their "Egyptian-ness" to the market. Another more direct approach is that of al-Jawhara food group, which launched its own line of Abu Ammar (a.k.a. Yasser Arafat) corn chips in May of 2002. Although the company may actually be helping the Palestinian cause (they claim to donate 50 piasters for every 25 bags sold to medical care in the Palestinian territories), the emergence of such a product just goes to show that local companies have realized that the old saying that "a way to a man's heart is through his stomach," may in fact be the other way around. *SV & SK*

Textiles

Trapped in the cotton club

If there were a black sheep in the Egyptian industrial family, then it would certainly be the textile sector. Once the pride of Egyptian industry, it is now suffering astronomical losses due to a combination of sorrowful mismanagement, addled pricing and trade policies, and stiff international competition. This is a shame, considering the sector's enormous potential. Regardless of its business shortcomings, Egypt still grows some of the finest cotton in the world, and it has captured an average of 57% of the country's total agricultural exports since 1996.

To understand where things have gone wrong, one must first grasp the number of players involved. Foremost are the government and semi-official agencies whose efforts to protect the national spinning and weaving industries by hedging against highly volatile world cotton prices have resulted in a mess of counteractive and essentially anti-competitive laws and policies. The government players include four different ministries, along with the Principal Bank for Development and Agricultural Credit, the Alexandria Cotton Exporters Association (Alcotexa), the Cotton Prices Stabilization Fund, the Cotton Supervisory Committee, the Textile Consolidation Fund, the Cotton and International Trade Holding Company, and the Holding Company for Spinning and Weaving. This hulking group sets the policies followed by Egypt's cotton farmers, textile traders, cotton mills, and the 31 public and 2,356 private spinning and weaving enterprises. Altogether, the industrial side of the sector (that is, everything excluding the farmers) employs over one million people—a hefty 35% of the industrial workforce.

According to a study by Omnia Helmy published by ECES in late 2001, the government started with honorable intentions. Cotton prices oscillate wildly from year to year. In order to protect farmers, the state established a system in 1997 that sets price guarantees on the cotton crop at the start of each growing season. If prices end up higher than the set price, then the sector makes a profit. If prices are lower, then the government uses a deficiency payment system to make up the difference.

The problem with this system is threefold: first, Egyptian cotton prices are isolated from world prices; second, set prices do not offer any incentive for farmers to improve efficiency; and third, the policy does not take the potential earnings from competing crop rotations into consideration. More often than not, deficiency payments are required at the end of the season, and the government finds it difficult to cover them. To make matters worse, price guarantees are not set consistently. They were never announced for the 1998/99 growing season, when farmers stomached an average 25% decline in prices. This has given farmers little incentive to continue growing cotton—and it shows from the 41.3% decline in area planted with cotton since 1996/97.

Similar problems exist in the pricing policy for exported lint cotton. The quasi-governmental Alcotexa is encouraged to overprice cotton by exaggerating lint prices and underestimating local processing and marketing expenses, which results in lower exports and encourages local private firms to seek cheaper imported cotton. The catch is that the backlog of unsold cotton is hoarded and then sold at a discount by the government as a "buyer of last resort" to traders.

Cotton sales are executed through pre-determined sales rings organized by the Principal Bank for Development and Agricultural Credit, with the majority of the slots held for public-sector companies. As a member of a ring, traders are obligated to buy all cotton delivered, regardless of its quality, at the pre-set prices. Because they are forced to buy expensive local cotton that they can ill afford, Egypt's public spinning and weaving firms are currently running themselves into the ground. This means that the government is, once again, shouldering the losses. According to the Carana Corporation, the 36 state-owned companies at the end of 1998 had accrued some LE5.8 billion in bank debts. Just ten of the textile companies affiliated with the Ministry of Public Enterprises account for 75% of its losses.

The companies do not know how to market, suffer from poor management, and face stiff competition from imports—Far Eastern products, even with customs duties, are just too cheap. In addition, the factories are in grave need of upgrading. According to a recent report in the business daily *al-Alam al-Yom*, useable production capacities in the sector as a whole are around 25%; 35% are in need of partial overhauls and replacement, and 40% need to be entirely replaced and renewed. Privatization would alleviate a great deal of these problems, but the state is reluctant to make swift moves since that would require total restructuring, which would inevitably lead to huge and unpopular lay-offs. Besides, a private firm would probably find it easier to simply start from scratch than fix an overstaffed and obsolete operation.

Faced with this vicious circle, the government is now desperately trying to find a way out of the hole. They have no other option—the sector is a mess at home, and exports are sliding. According to a study published by the Spinning and Weaving Industries Fund last September, spinning exports for the year had declined by 9.5%, while mixed blend export fell by 59.9% and textiles by 33.3%.

To increase the prospects for privatization, the government created a company for the development of the textile industry in October 1999, which is responsible for diagnosing the problems of troubled companies, drawing up business plans, contracting specialized companies to manage and implement solutions, and overseeing the long-term health of the sector. The company is now working on restructuring Misr Helwan Spinning and Weaving, al-Nasr al-Mahalla and al-Nasr Shorbagi. It also sold the Arab  Company for Carpets (including two Damanhour area textile plants and a dyeing plant in Alexandria) to the Ministry of Religious Endowments for LE50.1 million last July. The 56,000 mosques controlled by the ministry consume carpets worth LE43 million every year.

Another practical scheme is the initiation of early retirement programs. This was first tested out in August on Misr Spinning and Weaving where 1,600 employees were offered a combined severance package of LE35 million.

Perhaps the most interesting effort made over the year, however, was the public and (mostly) private initiative to bring the sector into the information age through the creation of an interactive website (www.egytex.com). The site was launched in April 2001 by Sahara Group, a local textile trading company, and the Ministry of Communications and Information Technology. The creators hope to attract foreign and local interest in the Egyptian industry through a host of features, including a database of over 2,500 local factories and related companies, regularly updated sector news, an interactive calendar, chatting facilities, and message boards for job listings and classified ads—all currently available in both Arabic and English. While the creators aimed at facilitating communication between the various subgroups in the sector, it is still questionable how successful it will be—many industry members are still not very e-savvy. To combat that problem, the ministry plans to hold educational seminars to teach people to use the site and harness its full potential.

The most striking irony of Egypt's textile sector is that it is also home to the extremely successful Oriental Weavers Group. The company is not just a standout in the sector, but is widely acknowledged as one of the country's greatest exporting success stories.

Private textile companies, free of government controls, generally fare much better than their public counterparts. Given that 10 cents per garment can mean the difference between winning and losing a contract, devaluations enacted since 2000 have been to their benefit. But even without the benefits of devaluation, Oriental Weavers would have continued to blow the competition away.

The company, founded in 1980 by Mohammed Farid Khamis, produces all types of floor coverings from inexpensive wall-to-wall carpets to super-luxe silk rugs. Unlike many other local competitors, Farid first researched the market carefully and then built his company accordingly. The Weavers Group currently comprises 13 subsidiaries and affiliates that specialize in every step of the rug-making process from the production of chemicals and synthetic fibers to spinning, dyeing and weaving, and, finally, distribution. A special focus on the continuous technical and artistic training of its 3,000 employees has enabled the Weavers to win numerous international design awards and hence build up massive demand in over 80 countries around the world, which are fed by strategically placed international distribution outlets. Today, exports account for 56% of Oriental Weavers' sales while its local outlets dominate 80% of the local market. Over the five-year period from 1997 to 2001, revenues soared from LE337.4 million to LE689.7 million, while net profits have jumped from LE69.7 million to LE133.2 million. Organization, efficiency, and creativity are the hallmarks of the company, and more than anything, show what the public sector firms could be if they got their act together. *SV*

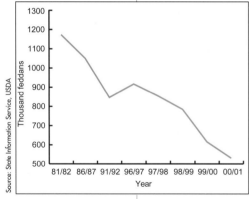

Area Planted in Cotton

Source: State Information Service, USDA

Thousand feddans

Year

Inconsistent pricing policies have led many farmers to give up on cotton

Agriculture
The drive to self-sufficiency propels growth

On the Farm

Egypt may owe its existence to the Nile, but it can no longer survive on Nile waters alone. Egypt was a net exporter of agricultural commodities as recently as the early 1970s—now it is one of the biggest food importers in the world. Food usually accounts for between 10% and 15% of Egypt's imports, though that can rise if international wheat prices are high.

Agriculture has made huge advances over the last 30 years. The government has backed off controlling what farmers grow, research has raised crop yields, and land has been gradually reclaimed. But these advances are not enough to keep up with population growth, which has seen the number of Egyptians double since the early 1970s. To compound the problem, crowding has often meant building on valuable arable land. Egypt can no longer truly be called a rural society—many so-called "villages" are the size of large towns and the Nile Valley is one of the most densely populated places on the planet.

At the same time the nation's economy has become more sophisticated. Other industries, which can be set up in custom-made desert cities and demand less water, have grown in importance. Yet, agriculture remains central to the Egyptian economy. Today it accounts for 16% of GDP and officially employs 28% of the country's workforce—compared to 30% of GDP and about 52% of the labor force in 1970. Agriculture-related industries such as fertilizers, pesticides and seeds, and the processing and marketing of commodities account for another 20% of GDP and many more jobs. The textile industry is also an important spin-off of agriculture.

According to the Ministry of Agriculture, agricultural production rose on average 3.1% annually over the last 20 years from LE5.7 billion in 1981 to LE74.02 billion in 2001. Cotton is the main summer crop, taking up about one-fifth of the country's arable land. Next most important are cereal crops (wheat, rice and corn), followed by sugar, potatoes, onions, and citrus fruits.

The most valuable agricultural export by far is cotton, a spot it has occupied since Mohammed Ali introduced large-scale cotton cultivation in 1820, radically changing age-old agricultural patterns in only a few years. In 1821, Egypt exported about 950 qintars of cotton (a qintar is about 45 kg); by 1824, cotton exports had risen to almost 230,000 qintars, replacing wheat as Egypt's principal export commodity. Though cotton no longer occupies the pride of place it once did, it is still Egypt's no. 2 export, albeit far behind petroleum. Cotton, cotton yarn, clothes, and cotton textiles earned Egypt $613.8 million in fiscal year 2000/01, up from $496.2 million the previous year. The next largest export crop is rice, earning $78.5 million, up from $41.9 million the previous year. Potatoes and citrus

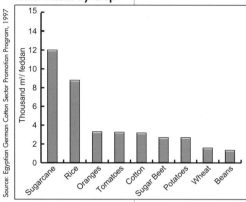

Water Needs by Crop

Source: Egyptian German Cotton Sector Promotion Program, 1997

Thousand m³/ feddan

Sugarcane, the main crop in the south, devours water

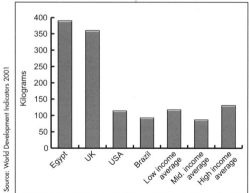

Fertilizer Use/Hectare

Source: World Development Indicators 2001

Kilograms

Average Egyptian crop yields are exceptionally high, but so is fertilizer use

fruits are also export crops. Egypt's biggest agricultural imports are wheat and corn, which together cost $930.7 million in the last fiscal year, up from $835.5 million the year before.

Egypt has invested huge amounts of money and energy in enlarging its cultivable land. Cultivated land stands at some 8.3 million feddans (a feddan is roughly an acre). That's up from 6.2 million feddans in 1981. Plans for the future are, if anything, even more dramatic. The government hopes to raise its usable surface area to 25% of the total from the current 4% within 20 years. The viability of some projects, costly and water-intensive, has raised eyebrows.

To understand what farmers grow today requires a brief look at Egypt's recent agricultural history. Up to the mid-1980s the government's central planning mentality, the need to provide cheap food for burgeoning urban populations, and national pride over self-sufficiency led to enormous distortions and misallocation of resources. The government provided the key inputs, said what could be grown where, fixed farm-gate prices, and controlled distribution, marketing, and loans. Farmers turned away from growing basic commodities such as cotton, rice, and sugar and towards less regulated crops, mostly animal fodder, which were more profitable.

In the mid-1980s, however, the government started removing many of the controls. Subsidies for fertilizers, seeds, and pesticides have been largely abolished. Marketing by non-state companies is now permitted.

However, distortions remain. The government still encourages the planting of some crops by guaranteeing prices to farmers beforehand. The best example is cotton (*see textiles*), though renewed efforts to encourage farmers to plant the lucrative crop have so far failed. Another example is wheat. It varies from year to year, but Egypt—once the bread basket of the Roman empire—is often the world's biggest wheat importer, buying some 6.5 million tons a year. The government has encouraged local growing of wheat, making a drive towards self-sufficiency a matter of national pride.

The country's main state wheat buying authority, the General Authority for Supply Commodities (GASC) imports some 4 to 4.5 million tons a year for use in Egypt's subsidized bread program, making it a major mover of the world's commodity markets. That's about half of Egypt's total consumption. The other half is bought from local farmers. However, the government often pays local wheat growers more than the going international price—for this year's crop it paid on average about 20% more, but only a couple of years ago it paid almost 90% more for locally grown wheat. Such subsidies have on occasion tempted producers to buy imports from private buyers and then sell them on to the government.

On the other hand, the high prices have worked. Wheat production rose to 7 million tons in 2001 from 2.1 million tons in 1982. But some suggest that Egypt's exceptionally rich arable land—the average wheat yield of 126 ft³ per feddan and rice yields of 3.8 tons per feddan are bettered by only a handful of countries worldwide—and year-round sun would be better used for technologically more tricky but much more lucrative crops. A hectare's worth of horticultural produce exported to neighboring Europe would earn enough to buy far more than a hectare's worth of wheat from prairie-blessed countries such as France, Australia, and the US. Nor do Egypt's land-holding patterns lend themselves to crops that are usually grown extensively. An estimated

3.5 million farmers cultivate holdings averaging 2 feddans. Given the size of the holdings and the wealth of labor available, Egyptian agriculture remains extremely labor intensive. There are, for example, just 11 tractors per 1,000 agricultural workers compared to 1,133 in Denmark and 167 in the Czech Republic. A law that went into effect in 1997 allowed raising agricultural rents and eviction of the tenant farmers for the first time in 40 years. At the time there were an estimated 1.3 million agricultural leases, which accounted for more than a million feddans. In theory, the law could promote the massing of small plots together and encourage economies of scale, which could change agricultural patterns.

For many years, export barriers have been another significant disincentive to choosing more adventurous crops. Marketing is still underdeveloped, while sloppy packaging can mean the loss of produce during transportation. But change should come around once the EU Partnership agreement, finally ratified in June 2001, comes into full swing. The agriculture issue was a huge bone of contention over the drawn-out years of negotiations. The Egyptians felt that the EU was unwilling to tread on the toes of its own powerful farming lobbies and would not allow Egypt enough access, but in the end, both parties settled on terms they can live with. Agricultural exports will be included in those goods that will lose their tariffs over the next three years.

Egypt's other major crops include rice, sugar, and vegetables. Being extremely profitable, farmers have flocked to rice in recent years. Production climbed to 6 million tons in 2001 from 2.3 million tons in 1982 and it now accounts for 10% of planted area. However, rice devours precious water, so the government restricts where it can be grown. For example, it is allowed in Kafr al-Sheikh in the Delta, but not in the Fayyoum, an oasis. In theory, farmers who break the rules get fined.

Sugar production suffered in the mid-1990s when the government ordered many cane fields to be cleared to remove cover for Islamist militants. Sugarcane is the largest source of Egypt's sugar supply, representing 72% (1 million tons) of total production in 2001. This number is expected to rise by 2.7% in 2002 due to successful efforts to combat rust scaling plant disease that plagued farms in the Qena region in 2001. The other 28% of 2001's output was sourced from sugar beet crops, which yielded 400,000 tons of sugar and are expected to produce 410,000 tons in 2002. But the combined total would still leave a 585,000-ton gap between sugar production and consumption—estimated at 2.04 million tons. Imports were curtailed after the government hiked tariffs in October 1999 to ease chronic oversupply that was causing mounting losses for traders and producers. In November 2000, facing a supply shortage and rising prices, the government brought the tariffs back down.

Production of vegetables, mainly potatoes, tomatoes, onions and *fuul*, or fava beans, more than doubled to 18.9 million tons in 2001 up from 8.9 million tons in 1981. Production of dates and fruit—mainly oranges, lemons, mangos, and watermelons—rose to 9.1 million tons in 2001 from 2.4 million tons in 1982.

The Egyptian livestock herd is estimated at 6.2 million animals, of which 3 million are cows and 3.2 million are buffaloes. Most local livestock are used for dairy purposes, with meat being of secondary importance. Increased fears about BSE-tainted meat have led to a steep decline in European imports, with Australia stepping in to fill the gap. According to the latest figures, Australia provided over 90% of live cattle imports in 1999, up from 51% the year before. *MK*

Crop Production

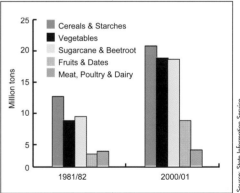

Crop production has almost doubled over the last 20 years

Borrowed Land

Egypt may no longer be the traditional agricultural society it once was, but according to the last census, about 28% of the labor force still makes a living cultivating the land. From the Delta to Upper Egypt, though, farming has changed drastically over the last ten years as a result of the gradual liberalization of Egyptian agriculture. Fluctuating markets, the withdrawal of government subsidies, and price rises across the board have hurt small-scale farmers—the vast majority of Egyptian farmers. Nowhere is the social and economic impact clearer than in the reversal of fortunes among tenant farmers.

The decade-long liberalization of agriculture has gone to the very heart of the Nasserist socialist reforms of the 1950s. By introducing rent ceilings, providing security in holding, and offering favorable conditions for the purchase of rented land, the early land reforms tremendously improved the lot of tenant farmers all over Egypt. Many tenants ended up buying their land, particular in the 1980s when returns from labor migration provided the necessary capital. Although tenancy was not eradicated, with the heavy inflation of the 1980s, the purchasing value of rent payments declined substantially, and the economic differences between tenants and those farmers who owned their land almost disappeared.

The new tenancy law that was passed in 1992 as part of structural adjustment policies led to a radical change in the patterns of land tenure, abolishing tenants' privileges and returning full control over the land to its owner. From 1992-1997, the interim phase of the law's implementation, rent ceilings were raised over 300%, from seven times to 22 times the land tax. Although there is as yet no countrywide data detailing the impact of the law, it is estimated that when it went into full force in 1997, it affected about one million families. Many left the land they had farmed for generations, either because they could no longer afford the raised rents or because they were expelled from their tenancies. Those who remained paid the new market rent, which has soared to about ten times the rent before the law. This has led to increased poverty and indebtedness among tenants, many of whom have been forced to sell their cattle to cover debts or to leave the land. In some areas, the law has also given rise to a new class of farmer. Large-scale commercial tenants have taken over leases, cultivating high market vegetables like cauliflower, cabbage, and tomatoes using cheap labor, in many cases children from poor landless families.

At the same time, the cost of agricultural inputs has shot up with deregulation—the price of fertilizer, for example, increased drastically from 1987 to 1993, in some cases by as much as six-fold—while prices on important cash crops such as cotton and rice have fluctuated. This has intensified the problems of the tenants whose rent payments are now determined by market forces. Isolated studies of different areas suggest that the effect has been disastrous for many tenants. In one village in Sharqiya, cotton yields fell from 7-8 qintars per feddan in 1997 to only 3-4 qintars in 1998, the first year after the full implementation of the new tenancy law, and prices per qintar similarly dropped about 50%. Rents for tenants had been fixed at LE2,000 per feddan, based on the yields and prices of 1997. The decline thus translated into negative or nearly negative revenues. Though this generated a slight decrease in rent prices for 1999, many tenant farmers were already ruined. *KB*

Energy
Egypt hits it big with natural gas

Fueling Up

Though oil and gas have been a mainstay of the Egyptian economy for the past 20 years, it was not until very recently that Egypt joined its rich Arab Gulf neighbors as a designated world-class petroleum source. Discovery of a colossal proven reserve of 55 trillion cubic meters (tcm) of natural gas in 2000 (and probable reserves of 120 tcm), as well as a spell of sizeable new offshore oil sites has placed the country among the top twenty energy producing countries in the world. This is great news, considering that petroleum exports are one of the country's major sources of foreign currency revenues.

The petroleum sector currently contributes 7.7% of GDP, but given that the new national darling—natural gas—is expected to see production double between 1999 and 2002, that number should rise in the very near future. Already, Minister of Petroleum Sameh Fahmi was very pleased to announce that receipts from the sale of crude oil and natural gas hit LE1.1 billion in fiscal year 2001, nearly 30% above target.

As can be expected, the findings have sparked renewed interest in the sector from both the government and the foreign community. Due to the anticipated production of 1,020 million cubic feet (mcf) of natural gas per day in the West Delta region, the government is building a new port in Edku that should draw in $2 billion from exports. Once a second factory for liquefying natural gas is completed in the area, that number is expected to double to $4 billion. Now everyone seems to be rushing in to get their share— and not only the usual European, Arab, and American firms, but even newcomers like Russia, South Africa, and Malaysia as well. The Egyptian British Chamber of Commerce announced that they expect $1 billion in new British investments in the Egyptian gas sector through 2004, and the French ambassador to Egypt was quoted in the local press in May stating that France estimates a minimum of EU9 billion in proceeds from their bilateral gas agreement within the coming 20 years.

Oil woes

The gas discoveries could not have come at a better time. Though it would be all too easy for the government to sit back and wait for the dollars to roll in from gas revenues, there's one ugly blight on the dreamscape that has been raising concerns: the petroleum trade balance. The balance slipped into the red for the first time in decades in 1999, and has continued to worsen at an alarming rate ever since. This is because, despite the increase in exports, local demand has grown along with it and production has steadily declined as the existing wells have reached maturity. At first, the deficit started out small, summing a manageable $167.6 million in fiscal year 1999/00, but it widened abruptly to $583.7 million by the following year, and it

appears that 2002 will be even worse. According to the US Department of Energy, Egypt's production averaged about 639,000 barrels per day (bpd) of crude oil during the first ten months of 2001, signaling a steep decline from the average of 710,000 bpd in 2000 and a far cry from the all-time peak in 1996 at 922,000 bpd.

The deterioration is primarily due to the rapid decline in output from Gulf of Suez basin, which supplies 70% of Egypt's total oil supply. The main oil producer in this region is Gupco (Gulf of Suez Petroleum Company), a joint venture between BP and the Egyptian General Petroleum Corp (EGPC) that has been operating since the 1960s. In order to combat the decline of its fields, Gupco is now investing large amounts of money in developing advanced techniques to draw oil from the earth and launching new explorations. Egypt's second largest producer, Petrobel, which operates near the Gulf of Suez basin, is undertaking similar programs to slow down the decline in output, but new anti-aging technologies can only go so far.

What the country is really hoping for is the discovery of new areas to mine, which it has already begun to find—offshore. In February 1999, Shell won the bid for a new deepwater concession in a large area off Egypt's Mediterranean coast. Shortly afterward, BP Amoco, Elf Aquitaine Shell, and Italy's ENI-Agip followed with other explorations in the area. More recently in October 2001, American firm Ocean Energy discovered a new site 70 km north of Hurghada with reserves estimated at 60 million barrels. That same month, Canada's Cabre Exploration reported a new find in the Gulf of Suez off the West Ish al-Mallah block with reserves estimated at 30 million barrels. These two discoveries are some of the largest finds in the Gulf of Suez in years. President Mubarak inaugurated a new site in the area on January 15, 2002, that is now operating at a rate of 8,000 bpd.

Egypt has made great efforts to compensate for its local shortcomings by improving its facilities to transport oil passing through from the Persian Gulf, whether through the Suez Canal or the new Sumed pipeline. In an attempt to win back the oil tanker traffic it lost over the last decade, Egypt has recently deepened the Suez Canal to 58 feet. However, these efforts have not been enough to attract their main targets. The new depth accommodates the majority of the world's bulk carriers, but not the very large crude carriers (VLCCs) and ultra large crude carriers (ULCCs), which require a depth of at least 68 feet. VLCCs and ULCCs are now forced to take the much longer (and more expensive) route around South Africa's Cape of Good Hope. The government plans to further deepen the canal to facilitate these supertankers, but the renovations will probably not be completed until 2010. A better option for now is the Sumed pipeline, a 200-mile line connecting Ain Sukhna on the Gulf of Suez to Sidi Krir on the Mediterranean. The Sumed's original capacity of 1.6 million bpd was pushed up to 3.1 million bpd by adding new pumping stations, but actual transfer averaged about 2.2 million bpd in 2000. Even when operating below full capacity, this is significantly greater than the Suez Canal's total petroleum transfer of 820,000 bpd in 2000. The Sumed is owned by the Arab Petroleum Pipeline Company, a joint venture in which Egypt holds a 50% stake, along with Saudi Arabia (15%), Kuwait (15%), the UAE (15%), and Qatar (5%).

Another obvious measure to increase the national oil output is to expand its refineries. Currently, nine refineries produce around 726,250 bpd of crude each year. The government is seeking to improve the existing plants by updating their technical facilities and diversifying their products. Rather than simply focusing on crude oil, they are increasing the production of lighter products, petrochemicals, and higher-octane gasoline. The Ministry of Petroleum has also earmarked $2.5 billion to erect five more refineries.

Last year brought added attention to Egypt's refining activities when Midor, the $1.5 billion Middle East Oil Refinery formed jointly by Egypt and Israel in 1997, stopped being a symbol of peace and economic partnership with Israel, and turned into tangible evidence of the two countries' further distancing from each other (*see box*). Though Israel's Merhav and Masaka Groups divested their 23% stake in the project in May 2001, recent rumors suggest that a 39% holding may be picked up by another neighboring country—Libya, which still remains on the US's sanctioned country list. The acquisition would come in line with Egypt's plans to increase energy cooperation in North Africa. Early in 2000, Libya and Egypt had sketched out

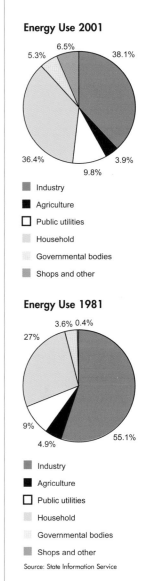

Energy Use 2001

- 6.5%
- 38.1%
- 5.3%
- 3.9%
- 9.8%
- 36.4%

■ Industry
■ Agriculture
□ Public utilities
  Household
  Governmental bodies
■ Shops and other

Energy Use 1981

- 3.6%
- 0.4%
- 27%
- 55.1%
- 9%
- 4.9%

■ Industry
■ Agriculture
□ Public utilities
  Household
  Governmental bodies
■ Shops and other

Source: State Information Service

Refined Partnerships

Egypt upped the ante in the oil and gas refining business in 2001 with the opening of the $1.3-billion state-of-the-art Midor refinery outside Alexandria in April. But Middle East politics threw its shadow over the project even before the refinery began operations when Egyptian officials announced the government wanted new investors to buy the ownership stake of Israeli partner Merhav Group. On May 30, 2001, the National Bank of Egypt (NBE), already a minor shareholder in the plant, bought the 20% Israeli share. Egypt's Ministry of Petroleum continued to try for the rest of the year to find a Gulf investor to take over the NBE investment, but no deal solidified.

When Merhav teamed up with Egyptian businessman Hussein K. Salem and the Egyptian General Petroleum Corp. seven years ago to build the 100,000 barrel per day refinery, the partnership was hailed as the biggest joint Arab-Israeli investment ever and a symbol of neighborly reconciliation. After months of intifada and bitterness, however, the refinery found its planned supplies of crude oil were blocked by unhappy Arab neighbors, and it became clear to Egypt that Israel's Merhav would have to go.

The original plan for the refinery was to process a mix of light and heavy crudes from the Gulf and Iran and export the petroleum products to Israel and other Mediterranean markets. Now, instead of serving international markets as originally planned, the government has integrated Midor

into its domestic refinery system. Midor's first major tender for crude oil was issued on May 14, 2001. The volume sought for the July-October period was 12 million barrels, or 100,000 barrels per day, to be delivered to Sidi Krir after being shipped from Ain Sukhna through the Sumed pipeline. Arab crudes specifying a destination could not be sent due to Israeli ownership. Ultimately a mix of non-destination specific Oman and Dubai crude was bought. By the time of the second tender later in the year, Israeli ownership was out and the supply problem solved.

The move to oust Israel's Merhav Group was a harsh blow to economic cooperation in the Middle East, but it did not leave Israeli investors entirely bereft. By selling its 20% investment in the Midor refinery to the state-run NBE for $158 million, Merhav Group profited nicely on its original $60-$70 million investment. Merhav official Nimrod Novik says the sale was purely a business decision, but others in the industry said the sale was never what Merhav intended. The plan had been to help Egypt build the refinery, then team up with Hussein Salem to sell Egyptian natural gas to Israel via the so-called Peace Pipeline. The episode threw into doubt the extent of future Israeli-Egyptian cooperation in natural gas, but Merhav remains a partner with Salem in the Eastern Mediterranean Gas Pipeline Co., and contract negotiations are continuing in Israel to finalize a long-term agreement by which Egypt would supply gas to Israel. *SP* plans to build twin pipelines spanning a 620-km stretch between Alexandria and Tobruk to import crude oil from Libya and export natural gas from Egypt. This was followed up with the creation of the Arab Company for Oil and Gas Lines, a Libyan-Egyptian joint venture, in August 2001, which will build and operate the lines.

A natural high

According to the Ministry of Petroleum, total investment in the natural gas sector is expected to reach $2.3 billion in the next four years. The throng of new activities in the sector has rapidly increased production from 2.3 bcf/day at the end of 1999 to an estimated 3 bcf/day by the end of 2002—and this is just the beginning. The 16 new discoveries since 2000 alone are expected to add an additional 11.69 bcf/day to the current production rate.

As a result of the accelerated activities in the field, the Egyptian government formed a new state-owned entity, the Egyptian Natural Gas Holding Company (EGAS), in early 2002 to manage the natural gas sector. Currently, the largest operator in the field is the International Egyptian Oil Company (IEOC), a subsidiary of Italy's ENI-Agip group, which has concessions in the Gulf of Suez, the Nile Delta, and the Western Desert regions. Yet, as in the oil sub-sector, most of the newest and most exciting new finds are offshore. The most active companies in offshore gas activities are Edison, BG, BP Amoco, Shell, and ExxonMobil, though their operations have not yet been initiated.

The dilemma of just what to do with this newly discovered bounty has fueled major expansions of Egypt's distribution network, both at home and abroad. Domestically, demand has grown as the country's thermal power plants, which account for about 79% of Egypt's total electricity generating capacity, have switched from oil to gas. From 2000 to 2001 alone, local demand jumped 20% from 417 mcf/day to 501 mcf/day, an astounding 136% increase from the slim 212 mcf/day demand in 1990. To feed local consumers, several private distributing franchises were set up in late 1998. Notably, a team comprised of BG, Orascom Construction Industries, and Edison is currently developing distribution infrastructure in Upper Egypt as far south as Assyout, where piped natural gas had previously been unavailable. After the completion of the $220 million initial phase, the group may extend the natural gas grid south to Aswan.

But even with this growing local demand, there is still a sizeable surplus that is growing bigger with each new discovery. As a result, the government is heavily advocating the establishment of new export agreements, which will certainly help to improve the faltering trade balance.

The means to this end has been the creation of several large multi-national pipelines. Since, as with oil, Egypt's current focus is to develop stronger gas trade relations with its Arab Middle East neighbors (with the pointed exclusion of Israel), the most ambitious of these efforts is the $700-million project currently underway to construct a regional natural gas pipeline connecting Egypt, Jordan, Syria, and Lebanon by 2006. The project has been broken into three major phases, the first involving the construction of a 278-km line running from Arish in the northern Sinai peninsula across the desert and then 18 km under the Gulf of Aqaba to Jordan's port of Aqaba

Booting up

With the further devaluation of Egypt's currency on December 12, 2001, energy from the new Sidi Krir power plant got a little more expensive. In fact, since InterGen and Edison were awarded the contract to build the third and fourth stages of the Sidi Krir plant, 30 km west of Alexandria, its electricity has increased 36% in price for the Egyptian government. Suddenly the 2.6 cents/kilowatt hour (kWh) does not look so good. For that matter, neither does the 2.37 cents/kWh price tag of the power coming from the two Electricité du France (EdF) plants in East Port Said and Suez. When the EdF bid was accepted in 1999, this price was considered outrageously low, but not any more.

For the past ten years, developing countries have been turning to Build, Own, Operate, Transfer (BOOT or BOT, without the 'own') projects to develop their infrastructure. The idea is that several companies bid on a contract to finance and build a project. They run it for a specified period of time, making a return on their investment before turning it back over to the government.

This approach has been used extensively in Asia and elsewhere and was hailed as a cost-effective way to get the private sector to invest in infrastructure, leaving the government to spend its money on health and education projects. Moreover, it encouraged private sector efficiency while ultimately leaving the sector under the control of the government.

With the passing of Law 100 in 1996 allowing for private sector power suppliers, the government of Egypt paved the way for BOT projects here. In 1998, the Sidi Krir contract was signed, followed a year later by the EdF plants. The Egyptian Electricity Authority plans to add another 11,000 megawatts to its generating capacity by 2012, about half of which is to be supplied through BOT plants. According to the government, $21 billion was invested in BOT projects in 1999-2000.

The next scheduled BOT power plants were to be north Cairo and Nubariya, in the Delta, but by late 2001 the government was looking to finance these through development funds. Paying hard currency for power (or water, or whatever services the project supplies) presents problems when the local currency is prone to fluctuations. Although future agreements may stipulate that partial payment be made in local currency, companies whose expenses are largely in foreign currency may not welcome such a move. Moreover, BOTs may face problems finding adequate funds, especially if foreign companies start borrowing from the hard currency-starved Egyptian banks. Most deals now require the contractors to find their funds from abroad.

While enthusiasm for power plants has lagged, BOTs remain all the rage in the air transport sector. Hurghada, Marsa Allam, and Sharm al-Sheikh are just a few of the new airport or airport expansion projects now being done under the BOT system. Ports have also come in for the BOT treatment, most notably the massive East Port Said container terminal as well as a port in Ain Sukhna. Canada's SNC Lavalin has won the bid for a number of water projects in 2001 in the Suez area as well. What has not taken off, however, are proposed plans for toll roads, which have less of a guaranteed income than power plants or ports.

Though not seen as the panacea for development that they once were, BOTs are still considered a useful and expedient way of getting private sector financing and expertise in to build necessary projects at a minimal cost to the government. Barring a currency crash or some other event that makes the cost prohibitive, they will in all likelihood continue to be a tool in Egypt's infrastructure development. *PS*

Sources of Electricity (1980)

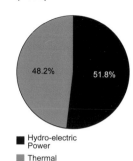

Hydro-electric Power
Thermal

(1998)

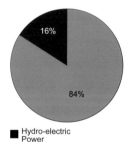

Hydro-electric Power
Thermal

Source: World Development Indicators 2000 (World Bank)

The Aswan Dam no longer provides the bulk of Egypt's power

Sources of Carbon Emissions

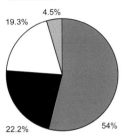

- ■ Industrial
- ■ Residential
- □ Transportational
- ▨ Commercial

Source: US Energy Information Administration

by the first half of 2003. The sub-sea leg was devised specifically to avoid Israel, which was included in Egypt's regional expansion plans until mid-2001 when political relations took a sharp turn for the worse following the renewed Palestinian uprising against Israeli occupation. The second phase, which is planned to be completed by 2004, will extend the lines to Syria and Lebanon, and then, finally, the third phase will connect Syria to Cyprus via an underwater pipeline that is estimated to cost $250 million. The third phase may also include expansion to Turkey, although it is not yet confirmed. Both the Cyprus and Turkey branches will then open up opportunities to export to Europe. So far, the first phase has proceeded well, thanks to the $50 million in financing provided by the Arab Fund for Economic and Social Development as well as the $101 million loan awarded in March 2002 by the Kuwaiti Fund for Arab Economic Development.

Jordan and Egypt have already set the foundation for their Arish-Aqaba pipeline with a 30-year agreement signed in June 2001 whereby Egypt will provide Jordan with 38.85 bcf/year starting in 2003, to be increased to

Egypt's Annual Energy Count

	Oil (barrels)	Natural Gas (cubic feet)	Coal (metric tons)	Electricity (megawatt hours)
Reserves	2.9 billion	55 trillion	22 million	--
Production	713,000/day	614 million/day	400,000	75.6 million
Consumption	585,000/day	501 million/day	2.3 million	64.5 million
Refining/ Generation Capacity	726,250/day	--	--	13.3 gigawatts

Source: HC Brokerage

70.63 bcf/year by 2008. Also looking ahead, the four participating Arab parties agreed in June 2002 to establish an Arab Natural Gas Authority to oversee and regulate the natural gas pipeline and to establish a company headquartered in Syria to transfer, distribute,

and market natural gas by the end of 2002.

Export arrangements to Europe, on the other hand, have mostly involved liquefied natural gas (LNG) projects. The two most likely to see solid progress in the near future include Spanish utility firm Union Fenosa's LNG plant in Damietta, which should be completed by mid-2004, and BG/Edison's project to build a LNG plant in Edku. Both sites have been designed to operate at a capacity of 141bcf/year. Union Fenosa intends to use most of its LNG products in its power plants in Spain and sell the remainder to consumers in Spain and the rest of Europe.

Electric slide

Egypt's electricity sector has not been as prosperous as its other energy-sector counterparts in recent years. Though electricity demand is growing, the rate has decelerated as economic growth has waned, critical privatization of the sector has been postponed, and expansion plans have come into question. At present, Egypt is generating around 75,600 megawatt hours (mwh) per year, of which about 85% is being utilized. Generating capacity sits at some 13.3 gigawatts (gw), the majority of which (79%) comes from thermal plants using natural gas, while the rest is supplied by hydropower primarily from the Aswan High Dam.

The sector is characterized by a tangle of state regulation and operation, a classic monopoly situation that raises the hackles of most liberal economists. Currently, electricity is provided by seven regional state-owned power production and distribution companies that are overseen by the Egyptian Electricity Holding Company (EEHC). The state's role as both the operator and regulator of all generation, transmission, and distribution activities in the sector has been the source of great criticism in recent years, and calls for privatization in the sector have been strongly voiced. Without any competition, the general population has had no choice but to put up with the power outages, surges, and even theft (by illegally connecting one's lines to the neighbor's, for example) that are all still fairly regular today. Despite their recognition of the problems at hand, the government has been slow to move on liberalization.

The EEHC itself is an example of the government's half-hearted attempts to appease this demand. The EEHC was formerly the Egyptian Electricity Authority (EEA) until it was turned into a "private" holding company in July 2000. The catch is that all shares of the company are still held by the government. Nonetheless, the new structure enables the company to raise money on the capital markets (should the government decide to release some of its holdings) and the state has professed an intention to begin privatization by first separating one or two distribution companies from the fold, though no specific timeline for such a move has been established yet.

The cause for the heel-dragging is believed to be the EEHC's massive debts. Taking over a company in deep arrears to operate in a highly regulated sector, where the government retains the right to set both distribution rates and prices, will not sound particularly attractive to potential investors. To be fair, though, the state is also concerned about fair coverage across the country: if electricity distribution were completely in private hands, it is unlikely that service would be provided to many of the poorest sections of the population. Clearly, serious internal re-organization and planning will be required before private investment is likely.

Despite the domestic impasse, Egypt is working hard to multiply its generating capacity so that it can become a major power supplier in the region. Already, a multimillion dollar link with Jordan was completed in October 1998 and Libya was connected in December 1999. Syria, Turkey, and Iraq should be connected to the national power grid by the end of 2002. Once completed, the regional network will fit into the larger Mediterranean Power Pool project intended to connect the Middle East, North Africa and Europe by 2015.

But where is this added electricity coming from? In a lofty plan to push its generating capacity up from its current level of 13.3 gw to 22.6 gw by 2010, Egypt has almost exclusively pursued privately funded Build, Own, Operate, and Transfer (BOOT) projects. That is, they have invited foreign companies to build the infra-structure needed in Egypt with their own money, make some profits for a while, and then hand the whole thing over to the government after a set amount of time. The two big power-plant BOOT projects currently taking place are the Sidi Krir project on the Gulf of Suez headed by InterGen and the Port Said project run by Electricité de France (*see box*). Both have come under question in recent months since President Mubarak announced in mid-November 2001 that the government had had a change of heart regarding the benefits of such schemes. According to President Mubarak, the new goal is to limit the expansion of BOOT projects in Egypt, as they are expected to eventually become a burden on the economy. As a means to keep profits from BOOTs in the country, President Mubarak suggests a number of restrictions, including mandatory reinvestment of 50% of profits realized from these projects in Egypt. *SV*

Services
Growth continues despite a recession

Tourism

If there was one sector that officially bore the brunt of September 11's harsh economic aftermath, it was tourism. When fear of flying suddenly gripped even the most seasoned travelers and world sentiment towards Arab and Muslim countries indiscriminately took a turn for the worse, the industry went overnight from being Egypt's cash cow to its sacrificial lamb. Minister of Tourism Mamdouh al-Beltagui stated in March that the lucrative flow of tourist traffic took an unheard of 54.4% fall in November 2001 in comparison to 2000 figures. Changes like that reaffirm what many local economists have been saying for years: that tourism is a dangerous sector to depend on so heavily for dollar revenues. As Egypt's hospitality industry has grown exponentially over the last four years, it has become one of the anchors of the economy, accounting for 36.9% of Egypt's total current account receipts in fiscal year 2000/01 with foreign currency revenues summing $4.3 billion. But, as September

11 and several other crises have proven, basing the nation's budget on expected growth in the sector, or even static performance, is risky for the government when it is so vulnerable to factors that are beyond its control.

Still, the Egyptian tourism industry is nothing if not resilient. The bounce back up to a more tolerable -11.8% slide on tourist numbers by February 2002 is reminiscent of the sector's rebounds following other major catastrophes in years past. Egypt was buffeted by shocks throughout the 1990s—the Gulf War, attacks on Nile cruise boats and buses by Muslim militants, the bloody Luxor massacre, and a faltering Middle East peace process—often making it difficult for industry players to remain upbeat.

But such is the heritage bequeathed Egyptians by their ancient ancestors that tourists just can't stay away. Countries that do not boast the Pyramids, the Sphinx, Abu Simbel, and Karnak would not be able to always bounce back like Egypt has. The government, realizing that tourism is becoming an increasingly important driver of economic growth, a major employer, and the nation's top foreign currency earner, has helped by advertising hard abroad and making security a priority to the point of strangulation.

Up until September, the policy had worked well enough. But this year, it was time for the government to pull some new tricks out of its bag, which it did—and uncharacteristically fast, too. First of all, it set about trying to capture the millions of pounds spent abroad each year by traveling Egyptians—it is estimated that about LE6 billion is spent annually on the *umra*, the lesser pilgrimage to Mecca, alone. The government pushed a strong campaign to travel domestically, supported by cheap flights and severely discounted hotel rates. In the face of foreigners' fears about Egypt's national security, Egypt then launched an aggressive campaign targeting all its key markets to affirm that Egypt is not only a fun and beautiful place to visit, but also one with a long-standing commitment to ensuring tourists' security and safety. This was followed up with state-sponsorship of over 1,000 travel agents and travel writers to prove it. To make it that much easier to enter the country for its most-favored tourists, the government also decided to drop the visa requirement for Gulf Cooperational Council citizens, who flood the country each summer, and agreed to do away with the passport requirement for Italian and German nationals altogether, deciding that personal identity cards were good enough. European travelers were given further incentive by the government's EU33 million fund to help maintain a steady flow of chartered planes into the coastal cities. And to spark interest from the American camp, several millions of dollars worth of some of Egypt's finest antiquities were packed up and sent off to the Metropolitan Museum of Art in New York for a huge traveling exhibit that was kicked off amidst great fanfare by Egypt's eminent Egyptologist and head of the Supreme Council of Antiquities Zahi Hawass.

The effort just goes to show that Egypt has no interest in being a good loser. The prize is just too much to give up. Over the span of 20 years, the sector grew from a gross total of $300 million in revenues from one million tourists to a record $4.5 billion in 2000 from about 5.4 million visitors. The government wants to see revenues hit $10 billion a year in five years and the number of tourists rise to 9.5 million.

It sees the number of hotel rooms doubling to 187,000 in the same period.

In addition to adding sizeable revenues to the current account each year, tourism is also of critical importance to the economy for its role in creating jobs and feeding many other related industries like transportation, construction, furniture, food and beverages, and recreation, to name a few. In times of prosperity, such linkages go unnoticed and unappreciated; but this year's fallout made many firms wisen up to the importance of maintaining a stable group of tourist consumers. Of course, the typical Khan al-Khalili merchants hawking papyrus, statuettes, and alabaster were hurting. Egypt Air also saw a harrowing fall in revenues. But even firms like al-Ahram Beverages cited the drop in tourists as a critical reason for their weak performance in the second half of 2001. The key to maintaining that lifeline is the continued diversification of Egypt's tourism package.

Nile Valley holidays—the traditional safari shorts and Pyramids type—may have been what kept the tourists coming, but the growth is elsewhere: religious holidays, health holidays, desert treks, golf holidays, and most importantly sun, sea, sand, and diving holidays in the Red Sea. Key are the mainland Red Sea resorts and Sinai which boast the northernmost and some of the best

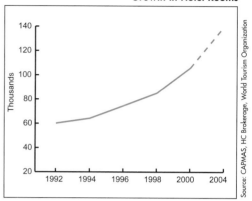

Growth in Hotel Rooms

Source: CAPMAS, HC Brokerage, World Tourism Organization

Despite regional instability, hotels keep rising out of the earth

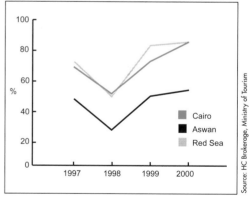

Occupancy Trends

- Cairo
- Aswan
- Red Sea

Source: HC Brokerage, Ministry of Tourism

Beach tourism is winning out over the traditional antiquities tour

237

diving in the world, and certainly the closest to the huge European markets. By Ministry of Tourism figures, in 1982 there were only three hotels on the Red Sea mainland, with 327 rooms. South Sinai had only 312 rooms. By 1996, there were 10,826 rooms on the Red Sea and 6,089 in South Sinai. Over the past four years the figures have exploded. There are now 30,150 rooms on the Red Sea mainland coast, with some 87,301 under construction, and by 2012, according to official projections, there will be some 115,000 rooms between Hurghada and Marsa Allam 300 km to the south. Coastal holidays, available year round a mere three hours or so from the nearest European markets such as Italy, already account for up to 40% of visitors to Egypt.

To encourage development, the government offers a 10-year tax exemption for tourism and hotel investment projects in new tourist areas, as well as land at cheap prices. Eyeing quick profits, the industry is growing so fast that many worry haphazard building will ruin the landscape, cheap and quick building methods hurt the environment, and the sheer weight of numbers crush coastal infrastructure. Scarred stretches of coastline near Hurghada are held up as examples of what to avoid.

By law, developers are not allowed to use more than 16% of the total area of tourist development sites for construction. They must maintain a buffer zone of 10 to 15 km between each tourist development center. But in reality a little cash changing hands can see these rules

waived. It's a fine balance. While the country badly needs the foreign currency, too much, too fast could destroy the very resources visitors come for.

One company that claims to have taken a different approach is Orascom Projects and Touristic

The Real Importance of Tourism

By official figures, hotels and restaurants, the nearest item corresponding to tourism, account for just 2% of Egypt's GDP. But according to a study entitled *The Real Impact of Tourism in Egypt* published by the Egyptian Center for Economic Studies, when all tourism's spin-offs are totted up, the industry is probably worth more than 10% of GDP.

The industry directly employs some one million people in hotels, restaurants, entertainment, cultural services, and transportation. Yet according to the study, tourists spend some 60% to 70% of their money outside of their hotels and designated restaurants. They buy souvenirs which need to be manufactured, transported, and sold; they eat food outside of their itinerary which needs growing, preparing, and serving; and they ride on horses and camels and in carts. They need their sheets and clothes cleaned, and hotels, swimming pools, and airports must be built and maintained.

These are indirect spin-offs, but the study takes it one step further. What about the money Egyptians spend from their tourism-related earnings and the people that employs? Tourism is linked to so many activities that its impact is much greater than other key Egyptian industries. According to the study, every $1 million spent by foreign tourists generates no fewer than 329 jobs. That compares to just 13 jobs in oil extraction, 183 jobs in construction and 192 jobs in the clothes industry for $1 million worth of output or exports. All told, the survey estimates that 12.6% of Egypt's workforce—about 4.1 million people—are kept gainfully active in one way or another by tourism. *BF*

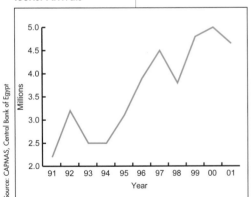

Tourism Receipts

Source: Central Bank of Egypt, World Tourism Organization

Receipts dipped last year from an all-time high of $4.35 billion

Tourist Arrivals

Source: CAPMAS, Central Bank of Egypt

Tourist arrivals are highly sensitive to perceived local or regional threats

Development, which built a fully-owned tourist town off the beaten track at Gouna on the Red Sea, even providing its own infrastructure. The site was such a success that Saudi investors bought into it in June 2002 and Bahrain announced plans to copy it on their home turf. But Orascom might have overstepped its bounds with its latest application of the Gouna formula at Taba Heights, near Egypt's border with Israel. Usually a huge attraction for Israeli tourists in Egypt, the area has been a ghost town for much of the year.

In the meantime, facing heavy bills to keep up with infrastructure needs, the government has started to turn to private financing through build-own-operate-transfer projects (BOOT), most notably for new airports.

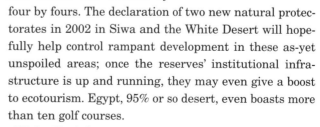

Airports are important since tourists with a week to spend increasingly fly straight in to coastal towns for package holidays, rather than taking in Egypt's coast as part of a wider tour of the country.

The government awarded the 40-year contract to build and run an airport at Marsa Allam—in pretty much virgin territory—to the Kuwaiti Khorafi Group. It opened in November 2001, unlocking the southern tract of Egypt's Red Sea coast. As part of the contract, Khorafi was allocated land to sell or lease to developers, and hotels have already sprung up. Elsewhere, the government awarded a $170-million contract to expand the Sharm al-Sheikh airport, while a BOOT airport in Alamein is well underway. Other areas slated for airport development include Bahariya and Farafra oases, Assyout, and Sohag.

Meantime, Nile cruises, which essentially stopped in the wake of the Luxor attack in November 1997, are back on track. Put on the tourist map by Thomas Cook in the 19th century and immortalized by Agatha Christie's *Death on the Nile* in the 20th, cruising the artifact-rich 200-mile stretch between Luxor and Aswan was Egypt's number one tourist attraction before Islamic militant insurgency of the early 1990s. There are now 229 Nile cruise boats with a capacity of 12,300 rooms, according to the Ministry of Tourism. The government plans to expand docking facilities at Aswan, Komombo, Edfu, Esna, and Luxor.

In an effort to lift religious tourism, Egypt has restored churches along the biblical route the Holy Family is supposed to have taken in Egypt to escape King Herod. That drive was given a publicity shot in the arm in February 2001, when Pope Jean Paul II fulfilled his lifelong ambition to make the pilgrimage to the 2,285-meter high Mount Sinai deep in Sinai's desert.

Desert tourism, for the more adventurous, is also taking off, both in the Sinai and the Western Desert. More and more are flocking to the oases, islands of tranquillity, which are also straining under the weight of new hotels and scarred by four by fours. The declaration of two new natural protectorates in 2002 in Siwa and the White Desert will hopefully help control rampant development in these as-yet unspoiled areas; once the reserves' institutional infrastructure is up and running, they may even give a boost to ecotourism. Egypt, 95% or so desert, even boasts more than ten golf courses.

With all of these attractions, it comes as no surprise that tourists are trickling back into the country. But is

Egypt hanging on to the revenues? Not yet. Due to the massive discounts required to win its prized visitors back, the industry is still suffering. As of late as March 2002, many of the big hotels were complaining that while bookings were only around 10% below 2001's levels, revenues were down by half. The reduced spending is felt by other feeder industries too. While American and Western European travelers tend to spend a lot on vacations, the more thrifty tourists now visiting the country in increasing numbers, like Russians, Eastern Europeans, and Chinese, tend to forgo add-ons like expensive souvenirs and guided tours. But still, it is too early to tell how the year will pan out. The summer months are expected to bring more carloads of Gulf Arabs than ever before, along with their extravagant spending habits. The mix of nationalities flooding the country at any given moment almost seems like an attraction in itself. *MK & SV*

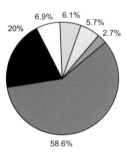

Where Tourists Come From

- 58.6% Western Europe
- 20% Middle East
- 6.9% Eastern Europe
- 6.1% The Americas
- 5.7% East Asia & the Pacific
- 2.7% Africa

Source: CAPMAS

Advertising

Spending is on the rise

Though 2001 and 2002 might have been pound-pinching times for consumers, it was certainly not the case for the local advertising industry. Unlike the rest of the world, where agency growth has cooled in reaction to the global economic malaise, advertising in the Middle East is on a sharp upswing. This has a lot to do with the increasing number of multinational firms that are now operating in the region, either individually or jointly with local companies. According to a special report produced by *Ad Age* magazine in June 2002, the Middle East showed an impressive 22.2% growth in agency performance over 2001 to a total of $454.3 million in gross income. The rise stands in sharp contrast to the 2.7% slide worldwide. The increasing maturity of the

jingle-crafting art has been obvious in Egypt, where campaigns are becoming more targeted, memorable, and thus more effective.

Take last year's Ramadan face-off, for example: akin to the US advertising extravaganza during the Superbowl, Ramadan is the season when almost the entire Egyptian population buckles down every evening to watch several hours of television. Programs include everything from provocative melodramas and talk shows, to silly game shows and comedy series, informative history and social awareness programs, and even nightly cartoons for the kiddies. Knowing that they have a captive audience spanning almost the entire demographic universe,

Egypt's Top 20 Ad Spenders in all Media 2001	Million $
1. Click Vodafone	11.250
2. MobiNil	10.838
3. Toshiba	5.917
4. Family Planning	5.818
5. EgyptAir	4.514
6. Goldi	3.982
7. Ariel	3.982
8. Daewoo	3.772
9. Coca Cola	3.536
10. Pepsi	3.525
11. National Bank of Egypt International	3.442
12. National Bank of Egypt	3.436
13. Fiat	2.880
14. Persil	2.606
15. Telecom Egypt	2.596
16. Power	2,538
17. Egyptian Arab L.	2.413
18. Banque Misr	2.103
19. Chevrolet	2.015
20. Union	1.939

Source: Pan Arab Research Center

advertisers compete to outdo each other as if their very lives depended on it. Last year's star campaigns included the return of Labanita's two cute and gabby cows, Sawsan and Soad, McDonald's spots to plug the new children's hospital it is funding in Mohandessin, Amr Diab and Nawal al-Zoghbi's sexy sing-offs for Pepsi, sports from the new City Stars complex showing posh 30-somethings living in style, and, of course, the two heavyweights, MobiNil and Click Vodafone, who duked it out using different but equally effective angles of superstars vs. superservice. While MobiNil pressed on with ads featuring the likes of Amr Diab, local *shaabi* singer Hakim, and *Who Wants to Be a Millionaire* host George Qerdahi, Click Vodafone spent the season building its image in connection to its new affiliation with the biggest mobile service provider in the world, Vodafone.

The diversity of the companies competing for ad space and their different approaches gives evidence of the growing sophistication of the market, both in terms of the ad agencies and the consumers. A couple of decades ago, ad production was controlled by a handful of select agencies. There was no competition and ads were churned out factory-line style—cheap and fast. The businesses had money to spend, but the lack of competition together with untrained, undemanding audiences allowed agencies to compromise on quality. So when multinational ad agencies saw local companies hemorrhaging money into the black hole of the market, they heard opportunity knock loudly. As more multinationals stepped into the Egyptian arena, the competition became fierce, pushing agencies to spend more, use up-to-date technology, and continue to develop artistically.

There are now more than 170 companies claiming to offer advertising services in Egypt. While the likes of Fortune Promoseven, Ama Leo Burrnett, and Saatchi and Saatchi are doing some mean business in the market, that's not to say that Egyptian companies are not getting their share too. Tarek Nour's TN Communications has been a mainstay in the market for over 20 years, and continues to hold many of the biggest accounts in town. The firm made headlines in December 2001 when they dumped MobiNil and joined forces with Click Vodafone, claiming that MobiNil had breached contract by subcontracting Echo Media for some projects. Other sources state that the fault was with Nour himself, who had reportedly inflamed MobiNil by approaching Click Vodafone on the media buying front. The ugly affair ended in the exchange of full-page newspaper ads, with one telecom operator announcing their disassociation with Tarek Nour and the other then following up with an announcement of their new professional association with him. As these accounts are the two largest in Egypt, the dispute demonstrates the growing importance placed on ad management.

Consumers, for their part, have been schooled in recent years by the explosion of Arab satellite TV networks and print publications flooding the market. The sensory overload of new images, jingles, promotions, spokespeople, and logos coming from a variety of markets have led Egyptian audiences to expect a higher standard of advertising and push companies to work harder to win them over. As a result, more effort is being spent than ever before to tailor the pitch for different types of consumers, whether the value-conscious, socially-minded, or the just plain wanna-be-cool set. And as indicated by the growing use of film and pop stars in Egyptian advertising campaigns, more money is being spent than ever before.

End-of-year figures published by the Pan Arab Research

Total Ad Spending

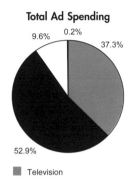

- 37.3%
- 0.2%
- 9.6%
- 52.9%

- ■ Television
- ■ Newspaper
- □ Magazine
- ▨ Radio & other

Source: Pan Arab Research Center

Who Spends on Ads?

- 7%
- 7%
- 5%
- 5%
- 9%
- 13%
- 54%

- ■ Services
- ■ Food, beverage & tobacco
- □ Household appliances
- ▨ Clothes & jewelry
- ▨ Cars & accessories
- ▨ Toiletries & personal care
- ■ Other

Source: Pan Arab Research Center

Center (PARC) show that companies spent more than $170 million on television advertising and $242 million on newspaper ads over 2001. Total advertising spending for the year grew to more than $457 million, indicating an impressive 12% increase from the previous year's figure of $407.4 million.

But are they hitting the mark? According to leading industry figures, there remains the major problem of defining target groups. How do you classify? Wealthy does not necessarily imply educated nor vice-versa. The most successful ads in terms of viewership are those targeted at Madame Housewife as she is the most easily definable. Not surprisingly, PARC studies show that food and house care products were among the highest spending sectors for the year.

Despite the improving face of advertising, to truly mature the industry needs a more sophisticated understanding of how and where to reach people. Enter public relations and market research. The basic purpose of public relations as understood in the West is to communicate and reinforce a corporate image to the public, normally via the media. In the US and Europe, the average PR budget is now 2%-3% of the marketing budget. In Egypt, PR is just starting to develop from being an extra within the advertising team to acquiring its own independent role. Market research—collecting and analyzing data to help define advertisers' target groups—is also showing signs of life.

But it may be a while before Egypt witnesses flourishing PR and market research industries. Marketing here is based around immediate, tangible results, and PR departments are often an afterthought, if they exist at all. For one thing, local business people may not like the notion of paying for an idea. They would rather pay for a tangible service with immediate results. Secondly, in

Egypt most business is built around personal relationships and trust, and many firms are family businesses at the core. Executives may be reluctant to put their trust in outside firms. Another obstacle is transparency, the notion that being open with the customer is a selling point, not a weakness.

Eyeing the growth possibilities in this fledgling market, JPA (Jack Pearce Associates) in 2000 became the first specialized foreign PR company to set up in Cairo. Start-up regional agency, Trans-Arabian Creative Communications Services (TRACCS) was next to set up in Cairo in 2001. And upping the competition one big notch, Fortune Promoseven's PR leg announced in June 2002 that it will be rebranded as Promoseven Weber Shandwick, reflecting its full integration into Weber Shandwick's (the world's biggest PR network) global operations.

These developments suggest that there is beginning to be a greater understanding of what the industry can offer. The preconception many Egyptian companies had (and still have, to some extent) of the market research industry is rooted in its origins as a data collector, while overlooking the very important task of helping to shape a corporate image for their clients. However, given the many companies with business dealings in Egypt that suffered immeasurable losses after 9/11 due to anti-Israeli and anti-US boycott campaigns, many are realizing the importance of reaching out to the population. *JZ & SV*

Retail

Commerce comes of age

With all the emphasis being placed on budding "new economy" sectors like natural gas, frozen processed foods, and mobile telephone and internet services, it is easy to forget that Egypt's links to its mercantile past still shape business and commerce in many ways. More than any of the other medieval-turned-modern cities in the Middle East, Cairo demonstrates that evolution has not necessarily meant tearing down and rebuilding things from scratch, but rather building on top of, around, and next to the existing labyrinth of the old city structures.

This is particularly true of Egypt's bustling and wildly diverse world of retail. Strolling downtown or around Khan al-Khalili, one gets the sense that the distinctive honeycomb structure of old Arab urban centers— whereby the city is divided into a network of concentrated cells, one for each product or trade—is still very much alive and well. For household appliances and electronics, head to Abd al-Aziz Street; for musical instruments, Mohammed Ali Street is your best bet; for wholesale produce, al-Obour; for fabric and sewing notions, Wikalat al-Balah or Muski. In such places, deals are often still made over a glass of tea with some banter about family and soccer before you get down to business. Prices are rarely set, but determined more by your ability to bargain. At times it seems like shops are built into almost every nook and cranny, often just big enough to house one or two employees and a single shabby display case. In addition, there are the thousands of tiny mom-and-pop groceries and makeshift kiosks sprinkled throughout crowded neighborhoods. The 1996 census showed that these small businesses comprise the bulk of all retail in Egypt, with the number of employees in Cairo's business establishments averaging 2.3. The wide spectrum makes it nearly impossible to gather reliable data on the sector, and very few comprehensive studies exist. At present, there are believed to be roughly three million wholesale and retail merchants in the country, but who really knows for sure? Many activities go unreported in fear of tax collectors.

But change is afoot. Modern shopping malls, hypermarkets, and all-purpose retail, tourism, residence, and entertainment centers are slowly taking hold and threatening to run the old-style merchants out of business. According to Retail International, Egypt is one of the leading countries in the region in terms of its total area of modern retail space, meaning Western shopping-mall type spaces. The combined total of completed space in Cairo and Alexandria currently stands at 450,000 m², with another 500,000 m² under construction. Once completed, Cairo will have the second highest amount of such shopping space in the region and Alexandria will be seventh out of the top fifteen cities. Already, Cairo has many large malls in Downtown and Heliopolis, but these are just the tip of the iceberg. The plans for the future are big.

Right now, the biggest developments are concentrated in two areas: the Corniche in Boulaq on the northwestern skirt of downtown (quickly gentrifying its working-class residents out of the area), and the area close to the

airport in Heliopolis. Already, the Corniche is home to the World Trade Center and the Arkadia Mall. The WTC, which serves as a corporate, retail, entertainment, and residential complex, opened in the early 1990s with a business tower, a mall, and two residential towers run by Hilton International and then expanded in 1996 with the addition of the WTC annex, which holds more retail space as well as a movie theatre, a food court, and a bowling alley. It is currently one of the most prestigious office complexes in town, housing multinational organizations like the World Bank, the IMF, and the UNDP as well as embassies, investment banks, and local NGOs. The mall, however, has proven to be far less successful due to its poor layout, with many strange narrow corridors that seem like dead-ends. As a result, many retailers have closed up and moved out over the last two years to the point that the WTC operators are now considering converting the entire annex into office space.

The increasing competition on the block has been the biggest factor for the change. Arkadia mall did not enter into the scene until January 2001, but the slick, airy mall has had little trouble filling up its spaces. In fact, many of the shops that vacated the WTC relocated down the block at Arkadia. It, too, has corporate and residential towers as well as a skating rink and food court, and, more importantly, underground parking.

But Arkadia does not have long to bask in its preferred venue status. In January 2003, the new Nile City complex being built just a few hundred yards away by Orascom Construction Industries (OCI) will open its doors. The $500 million project has taken some twenty years to come through due to the complications involved in buying out the hundreds of tiny land plots owned by residents and workshops in the area. If it lives up to the hype, it looks like the WTC will also have to struggle to hang on to its corporate clients as well. Already, by April 2001, 60% of the two 34-story towers had already been reserved.

In Heliopolis, the-Dubai based Majid al-Futtaim Group (MAF Group) has begun implementing its large-scale plans for Egypt. MAF has gained a reputation in recent years for introducing the hypermarket concept to the Middle East. Due to the overwhelming success of its Deira City Center in Dubai, which now attracts an estimated 50,000 visitors a day to its huge conglomeration of big name international retailers, the group is rolling out an entire web of "City Centers" throughout the region in collaboration with the French supermarket chain Carrefour. Its first local launch was the relatively smaller Heliopolis City Center complex in early 2002, but the group began construction for a larger 22,500 m^2 complex outside of Cairo in November 2001. MAF started operations in Egypt with an initial investment of $45 million, and plans to invest a total of $500 million over ten years as it builds anywhere from 13-15 hypermarkets across the country.

Never one to be outdone, OCI is involved in the fantastically promoted City Stars project just down the block from MAF's City Center in Heliopolis. This one will put all others to shame. The LE1.2 billion complex, which reached the halfway point for construction in September 2001, will be the largest private-sector urban development project ever in Egypt when it is completed in 2003. The site is so enormous that it almost rivals a pharaoh's sense of scale: with three upscale hotels, a mall, a convention center, office buildings, a parking lot for 5,200 cars, and even its own modern pyramid in the center, the complex will cover a staggering 115,000 m^2, and include 70,000 m^2 of office space. The pièce de résistance, however, will be the hypermarket-style shopping mall, which will make Cairo the site of the biggest shopping outlet in the Middle East (much to the chagrin of its Arab Gulf neighbors). The secondary

economic impact of this one multiplex in terms of employment creation is astounding. Already, OCI has some 7,500 on-site employees involved in the construction, and once the place gets going, several thousand other employees will be required to run it. Such developments will also be a substantial source of tax money for the government.

This complete re-conception of retail spaces has had the beneficial result of attracting franchises and international brand principals to Egypt and the rest of the region. At first, fast food ruled the local franchise industry through the strong and omnipotent arm of the Americana Group. Operating in Egypt for nearly 40 years (though it is headquartered in Kuwait), Americana now owns the exclusive franchise licenses to operate American chains like Hardee's, Kentucky Fried Chicken, Pizza Hut, Subway, Baskin Robbins, and TGI Friday's as well their own local chains, Grand Café, Chicken Tikka, Samadi, and Fish Market. Though it is not run by Americana, McDonald's also has extensive operations in Egypt. According to a study published by FORSA in August 2001, franchise activities started out with a small family of seven fast food chains in 1993. Today, there are over 30 chains doing business worth $150 million per year, and the number of non-food chains is on the rise. Although OCI has not publicly stated which stores its City Stars hypermarket will contain, it is rumored that international retailers such as the Gap, Ikea, and even some high-end names will all reside in

the megacomplex. Other examples include car rental outlets like Budget and Hertz as well as Gold's Gym and Berlitz Language Schools.

The growth in the sector has as much to do with the increasing consumer demand for high-quality goods in modern, organized space as it does with Egypt's membership in the

World Trade Organization and its concerted efforts in recent years to crack down on counterfeiting, rampant clothes smuggling, and intellectual property rights violations. Retail International estimates that international retailers' recognition of the growing importance of the regional market should bring some $500 billion into the Middle East over the next ten years.

Egyptian consumers' increasing sophistication is also making a major impact on the country's burgeoning supermarket business. More and more, today's shoppers want a wide variety of products in a clean and spacious store, and they want to get in and out of it in as little time as possible. This has resulted in a rapid transformation from the old schedule of grocers, butchers, fruit and vegetable sellers, and bakers to the one-stop supermarket. Currently, the biggest chain in operation is the locally-owned Metro Supermarket group. Their sudden rise over the last year was largely a result of the failure of England's mega-chain, Sainsbury's, in Egypt. Sainsbury's created a storm when it swept into Cairo in 2000, wooing customers with its enormous variety at wholesale prices. Though it managed to put several smaller local chains out of business in a few short months, it could not sustain its success due to problems with importing products and a nasty smear campaign that labeled it as a supporter of Israel. With losses reported at around

$150 million, Sainsbury's closed up shop in 2001 leaving a huge vacuum in its wake. Metro was quick to flood the market with well-placed stores in all of the busiest sections of town and has been the leading supermarket chain in Egypt ever since. Currently, it operates 15 outlets in Cairo and Alexandria, with annual sales of around $90 million. It plans to open four more stores over 2002.

There are only six other real competitors in the market, but that too is about to change. Carrefour/MAF Group's City Center complexes will certainly include supermarkets and other foreign multinational chains have already started building their positions in the market. These include the South African chain, Shoprite, which has already opened three outlets with plans to open eight more within a year, as well as Germany's Metro chain (not related to the local Metro supermarkets), which has committed $100 million to begin operating its Metro Cash-and-Carry stores in Egypt by the end of 2002.

Though there are only 148 supermarkets in the country, most market analysts believe that they will put the majority of the existing 65,000 medium-sized mom-and-pop groceries out of business within the next five years. The smaller stores and kiosks are expected to be more resilient, given that they primarily function as small stops to pick up cigarettes, drinks, and candy— but even they are facing some competition from the new convenience marts popping up at local gas stations. This is particularly true of the new On the Run chain introduced by Mobil Exxon in 2001. The strong positive reaction to the three pilot stores in Cairo has encouraged the company to open up another 25-30 over the next year. Though average sales differ depending on the location of the station and the size of the store, sales from medium outlets are estimated at around $14,000 per month while the large outlets earn some $58,000 per month.

With all this radical growth in the retail sector, there is now one big question looming on the horizon: will Egypt be able to absorb it all? Without a doubt, many investors have been hypnotized by the massive market size. Egypt's population of 66 million people makes it the greatest consumer block in the region. But at the same time, many of the projects currently under construction are banking on the expectation that what worked well in the Gulf will work in Egypt. That might be a stretch, considering that Egypt's GDP is not even one quarter of Kuwait's, for example. With the pound continuing to slide against the dollar, local purchasing power is becoming weaker by the minute, and there have been bad reactionary symptoms. The Sainsbury's experience might raise the red flag for some. Even the first big international chain to set up in Egypt, Benneton, gave up and pulled out in 2001. Still, Cairo and Alexandria do boast numerous upper-income consumers that have up until now depended on travels abroad to do their shopping. The large number of projects targeting these areas might alter this pattern. The hundreds of thousands of tourists that visit these two cities each year also present a large potential market. It is most likely that the two systems, both old and new, will end up co-existing à la Dickens' *Tale of Two Cities*. The Egyptian population is in transition, and such developments will further cement the divide between the rich and the poor. *SV*

Retail Space in the Middle East

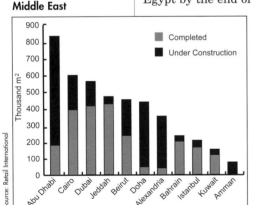

Source: Retail International

Cairo is trying to catch up to the Gulf as a shopping center

Telecommunications
On the way to becoming an IT hub

Wired

In the early 1980s, it was easier to get in a car and brave the infamous Cairo traffic to deliver a message than to use the telephone. Scarce dial tones meant hours of queuing for a line, whether twiddling your thumbs at home or waiting your turn at an exchange. And if you were lucky enough to make a connection, you faced a minefield of crossed lines, hung lines, squeaking lines, and engaged signals. The country had grown to such a size people-wise that it was nearly impossible to build lines as quickly as the population was expanding. The waiting list for new phone lines was several million long, and it often took not months, but years for requests to be honored. Furthermore, the budding IT revolution was quickly rendering all the existing systems obsolete.

This was the moment that the government established the Arab Republic of Egypt National Telecommunications Organization (ARENTO)—which would eventually become Telecom Egypt in 1996—to pick up the torch. ARENTO set out on an ambitious program that placed network expansion and the installation of new electronic digital exchanges as its top priorities. By the mid-1990s, telecommunication service had been introduced to remote areas that had never before been connected to the national web and provisions had been made for an emergency telephone service using solar energy. This massive investment—backed by USAID, which has coughed up over $700 million since 1980—raised teledensity (the number of lines per 100 people) to 9.5 by 2001 from 1.2 in 1981. That's below the world average of 13, but above the regional average of 6.5.

In addition to fixing up the domestic systems, ARENTO also made great efforts to improve the lucrative international network and introduce new value-added services. In hopes of increasing the country's alternatives to satellite communications, ARENTO implemented the Transoceanic Fiber Optic Cable (SEA-ME-WE 2) linking Southeast Asia, the Middle East, and Western Europe. The capacity of the Cairo International Exchange was increased to 3,680  international circuits (versus just 160 in 1980) and in 1990, a second international gateway in Alexandria with a capacity of 1,000 circuits was put in service, bringing the total number of Egypt's international circuits to 4,680.

Before long, the rapid transformation of the sector began to catalyze Egypt's corporate communications potential, and soon the business sector was lobbying for improved mobile, facsimile, and data network systems. The push spawned Egypt's huge mobile telecommunications industry, now one of the most active sectors in the country. By the mid-1990s, mobile telephone service coverage had been extended to all cities and roads in the

Delta region as well as the Suez Canal Zone, and capacity for mobile sets in Cairo alone jumped from under 500 in 1981 to 56,000 in 1991.

Egypt's e-volution

The reason for all the excitement in recent years, however, is the policy shift away from simply providing telecommunication services toward the provision of diversified state-of-the-art internet and information technology services. The dawning of Egypt's e-volution was heralded by the separation of telecommunictions from the Ministry of Transport and Communication in October 1999 to create the new Ministry of Communications and Information Technology (MCIT). Under the direction of former Cairo University professor of computer engineering Ahmed Nazif, MCIT immediately embarked upon an aggressive five-year strategy to make Egypt's CIT network strong enough to become the regional IT hub, and perhaps even eventually compete with IT exporting countries like India, Israel, and Korea.

The plan revolves around four major goals: establishing a solid telecommunications backbone for Egypt; building a large workforce of highly skilled IT professionals; increasing local demand for the internet and other value-added services; and fostering new IT corporate communities through the creation of attractive "Smart Villages." To make it happen,

Egypt's telephone network has grown by leaps and bounds over the last decade

investment in the sector jumped from a slim LE23.95 million in 1999/00 to LE537.75 million in 2001/02, almost 90% of which targets human resource and information base development.

So far, the plan has proven to be amazingly successful. As Nazif himself is fond of highlighting these days, while Egypt's overall economic growth settled at around 4.5% in 2001, the CIT sector charged ahead at a rate of 17%.

The government's plan is built on the concept of well-planned teamwork. The creation of the MCIT was followed up in July 2000 with the appointment of a new board of directors for Telecom Egypt (TE, still the national landline monopoly), as it supposedly made ready for an initial public offering (IPO) planned for later in the year. More than half the new board came from the private sector. Aqil Beshir was appointed chairman from Mohammed Nosseir's Alkan Group—one of the first non-state companies in Egypt to invest in telecommunications and IT—where he had run the group's software development affiliate. It was a far cry from the lifetime public servants the government had usually opted for.

Telecom Egypt's new management has played a huge role in the drive to forge a solid backbone for the country, already making great strides in network development in the two short years since the plan got rolling. In 2000, TE directed $620 million of its own funds and another $300 million from USAID towards expanding and updating Egypt's entire switching and transmission facilities from outdated analog voice switching to digital switches and modernizing the local network with fiber optic cables and digital microwave links. The digital switches enable the company to provide advanced services such as call waiting, call forwarding, caller ID, and hotlines that were previously unavailable in Egypt. Since June 1999, TE has installed an additional 2.2 million lines (translating into an astonishing 92,000 new lines per month) and brought the percentage of lines using digital switching up to

Egyptian Dotcoms

Egypt's nascent dotcom scene did not wait for the US internet bubble to pop before wising up to the perils of IT investments. As the US high-tech slowdown began, several colossal failures had made it clear that a radical rethinking of how to invest in the internet was needed. As recently as a year and a half ago, enthusiastic dotcoms proliferated in the Egyptian market, with startups racing to set up portals that would have first-comers advantage in an exponentially growing market. Most notable among them was a company called Nomad International, which launched in September 2000 the first part of its portal, minhina.com. The upstart, staffed with over 50 editorial staff (more than many print publications), produced quality original content. Income generation, however, was almost an afterthought. By January 2001, Nomad had laid off most of its staff and lived only a few more months as a sports portal before completely closing down.

The entry of global software giant Microsoft into the Arab world portal race in September 2001 with the creation of MSN Arabia, a site that customizes the MSN brand's well-known portal for the Arab world, led some to wonder whether there is room for any other competition. MSN Arabia, a partnership between Microsoft and Egyptian ISP LinkdotNet (as well as a Dubai company) brought 2.4 million Arab-world users of Microsoft's popular Hotmail online email service to the portal. Industry insiders say that pan-Arab portals will face an uphill struggle against the newcomer, but that national or city-based portals may well find a niche in which to survive.

LinkdotNet's enthusiastic young CEO, Khaled Bishara, made another bold move to assert his dominance over the local dotcom scene in May 2002 when it bought nine websites to add to its online services section: arabfinance.com (business), careermideast.com (recruitment), e-dar.com (real estate), el3ab.com (gaming), masrawy.com (yahoo!-like portal), mazika.com (music), nilemart.com (shopping) and otlob.com (food, flowers, pharmaceuticals and video ordering). The purchase, made through a share-swap deal that increased LinkdotNet's market capitalization to LE365 million, drew a gasp from industry pundits: while it certainly helped the company assert its dominance over the local online services market, was it too ambitious a move?

Although they are popular, most if not all of these sites were loss-making. LinkdotNet's purchase prolonged their life, at least for a while, but it is not clear how the company intends to transform them into profitable websites—perhaps the synergetic advantages of having these sites operating under one umbrella (presumably MSN Arabia) will pay off. In the meantime, it can rely on the deep pockets of its parent company, IT and telephony giant Orascom Telecom, to keep it going.

Since the NASDAQ crash, the Egyptian dotcom scene has matured greatly, moving from a pioneering spirit that had little regard for the bottom line to a more careful and business-driven approach. Funds for startups are rarer as financial institutions such as EFG-Hermes and CIIC, which once provided the bulk of funding for Egyptian startups, have adopted stricter standards. Since they announced their merger in the summer of 2001, the two brokerage houses have created a distinct entity, Ideavelopers, to deal with IT investments separately from their main business. Another major financial institution to have taken a more practical approach to online business is Citibank, which in partnership with Egyptian IT giant Raya Holdings created CiraNet, Egypt's first true business-to-business (B2B) marketplace. To date, although it has not made any money yet, CiraNet (whose first marketplace, Ciranet Pharma, deals with pharmaceutical products) is the dotcom with the most potential in the country. *IE*

around 98%. The total number of fixed lines now reaches 8.4 million, and it is expected to hit 12 million by 2005. These efforts hacked the waiting list for new lines down from 1.7 million in December 1999 to just 700,000 by 2001. Anticipating further demand, TE signed a $175-million deal with Swedish equipment manufacturer LM Ericsson in February 2002 to help them further expand and modernize its fixed-telephone network over the next five years.

Though the government started with firm intentions for the 20% IPO of TE in 2001, it was indefinitely called off due to the subsequent decline in the markets here and abroad and the sharp deceleration of the government's privatization program. The "adverse market conditions" delaying the sale have been a grave disappointment for the government, which could certainly have used the estimated $1.2 billion infusion from the offering—Egypt's biggest yet. But in retrospect, the setback was useful since it gave TE time to devise a clearer strategy on how it intends to proceed into the millennium. Realizing that the key to survival is to merge fixed line services with mobile services, the company is now focusing more on how it will roll out and operate Egypt's third mobile network, which it plans to launch in the first quarter of 2003. According to Aqil Bashir, TE will not consider an IPO until it finds a strategic investor to pick up a 20-34% stake in the company and play an active role in its mobile operations. While a torrent of announcements have been issued from MCIT since January regarding developments in the selection process (TE is purported to be seriously evaluating five bids from international firms), no company has been named yet. The delay also afforded MCIT time to finish drafting its new Telecommunications Act, which proposes guidelines on how to ensure proper regulation of telecom services, the licensing of fixed-line and wireless services, the promotion of fair competition and consumer protection, and ensuring fair pricing and coverage in the market. This landmark legislature, which was approved by the cabinet in September 2001—it still needs parliamentary approval—is sure to make a huge impact on the future of Telecom Egypt and other telecom services providers.

While TE is the sole provider of fixed lines in the country, mobile services are open to private enterprises with licensing from the Telecommunications Regulatory Authority, established in 1998. Currently only two providers exist in the market, and with the future of TE undecided, they have not wasted their window of opportunity. The Egyptian Co. for Mobile Services, commonly known as MobiNil and backed by Orascom Telecom and France Telecom, is the leader of the two. It

Egypt's Telecoms and IT Profile (as of January 2002)

Number of	Total	Per 100 people
Phone lines	8.8 million	13.2
Mobile phone subscribers	3.4 million	5.1
Pay phones	36,000	0.05
Internet users	1 million	1.5
ISPs	64	--
IT companies	625	--
Workers in IT sector	21,850	--
Software exports	$50 million	--

Source: MCIT

picked up its millionth subscriber in September 2000 and within the year and a half since, it has now more than doubled that to 2.1 million subscribers. Though it began operating six months after MobiNil, rival Click Vodafone (formerly Misrfone but now backed by UK giant Vodafone and Egypt's Alkan Group) has nearly caught up with around 1,800,000 subscribers—not bad in market that consisted of only 7,400 lines in 1996. The watershed industry has already siphoned off billions of pounds from the market—revenue from GSM lines hit $1.3 billion in 2001—and executives at the two companies say they expect penetration rates in Egypt of upwards of 10% (15% in one optimistic estimation) in the next six or seven years, which means that there are still millions of customers and even more profits to come. A study published in March 2002 by the Arab Advisors Group estimates that the liberalizations enforced by the proposed telecom law, which will allow GSM operators to install their own switches, will mean that GSM lines in Egypt will actually outnumber fixed lines by 2005. They forecast that revenues from these lines will hit $3.17 billion by 2006. It's no wonder that Telecom Egypt is scurrying to enter this market as soon as possible.

The existing exclusionary agreement for licenses keeps the market limited to just MobiNil and Click Vodafone until November 2002, which some analysts say has kept the prices higher than average in the region. Competition between the two has heated up as illustrated by advertising wars: Click Vodafone and MobiNil are the top two spenders on advertising in the entire Egyptian market, shelling out $11.25 million and $10.84 million, respectively, in 2001.

The companies have also been keen to show they are providing their customers with the latest options, so that Wireless Application Protocal (WAP) services are now offered by both—though the handsets capable of using them remain rare. Both MobiNil and Click currently boast partnership agreements with local banks to provide customer account information services, and MobiNil even announced in May 2001 that it will provide customers with an ability to get up-to-the-minute information on EgyptAir flights and lost luggage tracking. Indeed, the mobile companies have put considerable pressure on Telecom Egypt by offering their customers service and quality that the public sector cannot always match.

Not that it has been entirely rosy for the mobile market. Rapid attempts at expansion have occasionally caused breakdowns in service as companies' reach sometimes exceeded their grasp. The massive increase in mobile lines, coupled with the excellent new public payphones (now reaching some 32,000, 50% of which are operated by Menatel) as well as increased internet usage caused a system overload in the summer of 1999 that brought the phone system in some neighborhoods back to the level of the 1970s. Fingers were pointed both at Telecom Egypt for not anticipating the growth and expanding its infrastructure fast enough and at MobiNil for being overly ambitious, but in any event it appeared to be a case of periodic growing pains. No one was immune. Click had similar problems when its network took a day-long break in September 2000. Both networks claim they now have at least six months more capacity than subscribers. The various glitches have shown just how interconnected the three companies are, with one's mistakes bringing down the other two.

Teledensity

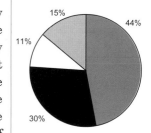

Teledensity has increased five fold since 1983

IT Market Structure

44%
15%
11%
30%

■ Hardware Industry
■ IT Services
□ Data Communications
▨ Packaged Software

Source: BSAC ICT, International Data Corporation, 2001

The Egyptian IT market is expected to hit $1.32 billion by 2004

IT intentions

Even with all this activity in the telecom market, phone services are now just one small part of Egypt's big CIT picture. The push to become a strong internet services and software exporting country is manifested in the hundreds of different projects and initiatives all simultaneously moving forward at breakneck speed. According to an April report by the American Chamber of Commerce's Business Studies and Analysis Center, Egypt is now home to an $849-million IT market, including the hardware, software, services, and data communications sub-markets. If things go as planned, the market will be worth some $1.32 billion by 2004.

The government believes that the key to making this dream possible is threefold. First, it must build a massive work force of highly trained professionals; second, it needs to convince leading multinational firms to set up office in Egypt; and third, it needs to radically increase the number of internet users in the country. As can be expected, efforts to accomplish these goals often overlap.

Building Human Resources: Much to the credit of Minister Nazif, MCIT has successfully enticed a host of giant IT firms to begin operating training and certification programs in Egypt. Participating firms include the likes of IBM, Microsoft, Cisco, and Lucent Technologies. Currently, some 5,500 students are enrolled in these programs, which run anywhere from three weeks to six months in duration.

Measures have also been taken to upgrade the computer science programs already offered by universities and create special colleges dedicated entirely to the field. One of these is the Information Technology Institute (ITI), which was established by the Information and Decision Support Center (IDSC) in

In Touch

1854: Telegraphic communication systems—the first in Africa—link Cairo and Alexandria.

1881: The first telephones are introduced when the US Edison Bell Company sets up a cable connecting Cairo to Alexandria.

1930: Egypt's network of automatic exchanges and underground cables make it a hub for international traffic spanning from China to Bombay, Yemen, Jordan, London, and the rest of Europe.

1932: Radio stations connect Egypt to over 90% of the telephone users in the world.

1963: The first telex exchange is established.

1972: The first submarine cable laid, connecting Egypt and Italy.

1979: The first international exchange is built with an initial capacity of 160 circuits.

1981: There are 1.2 telephone lines per every 100 Egyptians.

1985: First digital local exchange established, and the first fibre optic cables installed.

1992: First ISP in Egypt established.

1998: MobiNil and Click given the licenses for GSM service in Egypt.

1999: Egypt has about 300,000 internet users.

2001: There are 9.5 telephone lines per every 100 Egyptians; about 1 million Egyptians are internet users.

2002: The government introduces free internet usage.

1993 in partnership with the University of Nottingham, the University of Rennes, ENST and GDTA of France, and the National Sugar Company and Mentor Graphics of Egypt. So far, the institute has met great success, graduating 1,633 students by July 2001 in specialties ranging from software and multi-media development to network design and e-commerce.

Other training venues include the IDSC's National Education Technology Program and the E-Business Institute, as well as the courses provided by Gamal Mubarak's Future Generation Foundation and the Raya Academy. Most recently, MCIT signed a $113-million pact with Alcatel in June 2002 to expand its local training activities into a regional training organization in line with its worldwide Alcatel University organization. The new site will work alongside the ITI to train around 4,000 new graduates (more than half being non-Egyptian) over a five-year period. In addition, Alcatel will develop its Cairo-based International Service Center focused on advanced telecom software applications staffed by local experts and promote research and development into third generation cellular services. The skills are expected to generate over US$132 million in export-led activity over the next five years.

Smart Villages: Egypt is also creating tailor-made IT corporate communities. The concept hinges on the premise that if you gather all the leading companies in one compact (and beautiful) space, the synergies from close proximity will result in a nurturing environment that pushes research and development as far as it can go—a theory Korea has already proven can result in outstanding financial gains.

According to MCIT, the policy is that these "Smart Villages," as they have been termed, should be located near vital residential and service centers and include state-of-the-art facilities such as high-speed communication links, fiber-optic cables, and satellite connections for company offices, as well as business-oriented hotels, convention centers, and even restaurants. Moreover, as Nazif added at the September 2000 Euromoney Conference, they should be small enough be duplicated in different parts of the country. The government is offering attractive incentives to promote the concept, such as the provision of government-subsidized land, ten-year tax holidays, and reduced tariffs for participating companies.

Currently, villages are being built in Giza, Sixth of October City, Mansoura, and Assyout, and advertisements offering space on them are already cropping up in local business magazines. Already, IBM and KPMG have signed up to move into the slick new Pyramids Heights complex in Sixth of October City. Other state-owned residents will include MCIT, the Telecommunications Regulatory Authority, as well as new state-funded IT incubators.

To put some numbers on what they expect to gain from all this, the government has stated that it hopes the Smart Villages will kick-start local software production up to $2 billion by 2003 and raise IT exports to $25 billion annually by 2017. They also expect the new complexes to help alleviate unemployment by creating an estimated 300,000 new job opportunities.

Promoting Internet Use: With all these opportunities, one would think that just about everyone in Egypt knew their way around the internet, but this could not be

further from the case. The monetary resources necessary to own a computer (or even temporarily use one in an internet café) are non-existent for a large percentage of the Egyptian population. Current estimates peg Egyptian internet users at around one million—one of the highest rates in the region, but still not even 2% of the population. Moreover, use is split along gender lines, with the vast majority of regular users being men. Although that may be changing as the internet gains more general currency, according to UNESCO, in 1998, only 5% of internet users across the Arab world were women.

In addition to the financial obstacles, there are other reasons for the low numbers. Many blame it on the minimal Arabic-content sites currently in existence. Others point fingers at the lack of trust in web security and e-commerce. Some argue that there is still little awareness of the value-added provided by the internet, as

Soft Dreams

If 2001 was anything for Egypt's burgeoning IT industry, it was the year of software exports. Amidst a generalized economic depression and a government urging to "export or die," plans were laid out to turn Egypt into an exporter of IT know-how to rival India, Ireland, or Israel. The charismatic Minister of Telecommunications and Information Technology, Ahmed Nazif, spent the year championing the cause of software exports and praising companies such as IT Worx that have specialized in offshore software development for clients in North America and Europe. Nazif said that he hopes that the offshore software development industry, today worth around $50 million, will double every year until it reaches $500 million. The minister thinks software exports can become Egypt's biggest foreign currency earner, ahead of the country's traditional breadwinners: tourism, oil, and Suez Canal revenues. Although observers agree that he is a tad too ambitious, many are impressed by the IT sector's sustained growth despite a three-year economic malaise.

Egypt's IT graduates are also recognized to be of good caliber, while the country's location in relation to North America helps make it a good base for graveyard-shift maintenance of websites and other systems. For the past three years, international corporations from Alcatel to IBM have invested in the country as a regional base and started training programs across the country. The government has also encouraged software exports by granting IT companies special permission to set up IT free zones anywhere they want.

Egypt also has an existing lead in developing and exporting software applications for the Arabic-speaking world. Companies such as Sakhr Software, a developer of Arabic-language software since the early 1980s, have a long-standing reputation in translating standard software packages and are also developing technologies to use the Arabic script online—a key aspect of spreading internet usage in the Arab world. With Dubai as the only regional competitor and Cairo's place as an Arab cultural center, Egyptian IT firms have an opportunity to provide 23 Arabic-speaking countries with native-language software.

Nevertheless, dark clouds lurk on the horizon. Offshore developers complain that they cannot compete without top-of-the-line infrastructure that can ensure no time lag with their clients. They are also facing human resources problems, as Egyptian graduates are increasingly being recruited to work in North America, Europe, and the Arabian Gulf. While this brain drain may in some years turn into a brain gain as migrant IT workers return to Egypt, in the short-term it is making it more difficult for Egyptian firms to recruit top-notch staff. *IE*

opposed to other IT services like mobile phone lines and pagers. Up until very recently, others stated that the cost and inconvenience of registering accounts with Internet Service Providers (ISPs) was a leading deterrent.

All of these issues are matters that the government hopes private companies will help to resolve, whether by increasing the volume of on-line content and services that appeal to Arab consumer, producing affordable, locally-made hardware, or demonstrating the gains in store for internet-savvy individuals.

In one of its biggest moves yet, MCIT and Telecom Egypt set out to cut out the middleman expense of ISPs with the launch of free internet services in January 2002. Under the new model, the existing 64 ISPs in the market agreed to do away with their membership, monthly bill, and pre-paid card systems in return for a special eight-digit number that anyone with a computer and a modem can dial up to access the web for the cost of a regular call. The revolutionary program is one of the government's most aggressive ploys to increase internet use in the country. The way it works is this: in order to participate, an ISP must purchase a 07-prefix number from Telecom Egypt and then lease access ports

from its data carriers. When an internet user connects using the ISP's number, the state phone company charges that person for the cost of the local call, ceding 70% of the revenue to the ISP that provides the internet service. While this may seem unusually generous for the government, many ISPs say that the leasing rates are high and profit margins are very low. Furthermore, they must lease enough lines from any particular exchange to accommodate all their dial-in consumers. If a user dials an ISP through an exchange that does not have sufficient ports, then the ISP loses all revenues from the call.

While the government argues that the plan should introduce a greater degree of competition in the market (which, in the end, will benefit the consumer) and encourage mergers in the fragmented industry, many ISPs have argued that it is simply an ingenious way for Telecom Egypt to increase its profits. Because no outside regulatory authority is monitoring the traffic flow, there is no way to ascertain if the ISPs are getting their due. What is certain, however, is that many of the smaller ISPs who did not invest as much in advertising and leasing lines have already folded. This might be a necessary evil if the program does in fact increase internet use as is expected. Only time will tell. In the meantime, great hopes continue to be pinned on the future of Egypt's IT industry. *SV & PS*

Transport
Taking advantage of "geographical genius"

In Transit

The last two decades have seen a major effort to improve Egypt's transportation networks. By the mid-1990s, however, it became clear that the government could not keep pace with the needs of the transport sector, and, in keeping with the new ethos of the day, the private sector was invited back into what had been the unique domain of the state since the 1960s. While the state reports that it invested LE46.3 billion between 1997 and 2001 on transportation and communications, the Ministry of Transportation said in March 2001 that transportation projects over the next 30 years would require another $150 billion—money the government cannot provide all on its own.

Starting around 1997, private sector participation in nearly all areas of transportation infrastructure has been seen, usually through BOOT-style projects (buy, own, operate, transfer), in which the government turns over the building and operation of a facility, along with the revenues it earns, to a private firm for a specified period of time. While the trains, airplanes, and canals themselves remain state property, some services and stations are now being built by the private sector, and often by international companies.

Railroads

June 2001 marked the 150th anniversary of railroads in Egypt, as well as an important turning point in the recent history of rail in Egypt. Once again the government is investing in its iron roads to improve existing networks and extend them into new areas of the country.

While railroads once held pride of place in Egypt, the past half century saw a greater emphasis on using them to move as many people as cheaply as possible. While low fares and plenty of discounts meant heavy usage (2.3 million passengers per day), it did not translate into profit—or even breaking even. Prime Minister Atef Ebeid revealed earlier this year that over the last 30 years, the Egyptian National Railways (ENR) had racked up LE17 billion in debts. In 2001 alone, it ran a deficit of almost LE1.3 billion. About 70% of its revenues were spent paying the wages of its 80,000 employees.

It might not be so bad—after all, plenty of European railways operate firmly in the red—if it were not for the periodic horrific accident caused by underpaid employees, bad maintenance, and out-of-date equipment. This was made poignantly clear in mid-February when Egypt experienced the worst rail disaster in the country's history. The death of about 400 Egyptians in Ayyat led to the dismissal of both transport minister Ibrahim al-Demeiri and ENR chair Maher Mostafa, but whether the tragedy will spark a much-needed shake-up in general operations has yet to be seen. Shortly after the accident, the Spanish government loaned Egypt $300 million, earmarked for improving maintenance, service, and employee training, and the ENR implemented a passenger insurance policy.

Aside from these upgrades, a host of BOOT projects have been proposed to build new lines and put in new signaling equipment, and the possibility of contracting maintenance duties out to the private sector has been raised even more seriously since the Ayyat accident. High-profile projects, most of which are still in the bidding or planning stages, include a rapid rail line from Sidi Gaber to Borg al-Arab, an electric train service from Ain Shams to Tenth of Ramadan City, and a LE10-billion "supertrain" from Alexandria to Aswan. Railway station services at Cairo, Alexandria, Maragha, and Abu Qurqas (the latter two in Upper Egypt) are soon to be contracted out via BOOT as well.

Meanwhile, the government has been building new lines, including a railway extending from Ismailiya, across the Suez at the Ferdan bridge (one of the world's highest flat land rail bridges), all the way to Rafah. Other lines under construction include one out to Salloum on the Libyan border and one from Qena to Safaga on the Red Sea, an extension of a line that already runs to Kharga and Baris oases. Over the past twenty years 1,540 km of new lines have been laid (out of a total of 9,400 km).

Suez Canal

After railroads, the Suez Canal is modern Egypt's oldest and certainly highest profile infrastructure project. One of the world's two great maritime shortcuts, the digging, losing, and reacquiring of the canal by Egypt provides plenty of fodder for history and national legend—in addition to bringing in a hefty supply of foreign exchange.

For the past decade, however, revenues from the canal have gone soft, showing a steady decline throughout the 1990s and reaching a depressing low point in 1997. Bigger ships, cheaper oil prices, and changing patterns of global trade made the Red-Med shortcut less of a necessity for shipping companies.

The last two years, however, witnessed a reversal. While there are still less ships than there used to be, the ones coming through are growing larger and carrying more cargo, resulting in more fees. The year 2000 saw the highest revenues in years with $1.9 billion in receipts, an increase of 10% on 1998. The first ten months of 2001 looked even better, but come November, the fallout of September 11 began to make an impact. The attack on the US ushered in a global recession, leading to less shipping trade, while lower oil prices and increased insurance premiums on ships passing through the area made it cheaper to go around the Horn. Returns

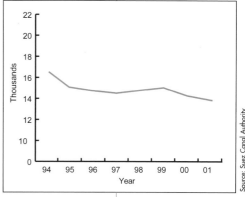

Number of Ships Transiting the Canal

Source: Suez Canal Authority

Less ships are using the Suez Canal ...

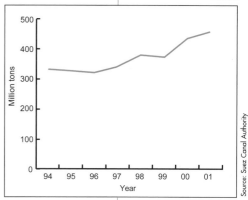

Tonnage in the Suez Canal

Source: Suez Canal Authority

... but they are carrying heavier loads

About the Suez Canal

About 7% of all sea-transported trade passes through the Suez Canal. Most of it (39%) is shipped to or from the Far East; 35% is shipped to or from the Red Sea and Arabian Gulf ports; and 20% is shipped to or from India and Southeast Asia.

Total canal length: 193 km
From Port Said to Ismailiya: 78.5 km
From Ismailiya to Port Tawfiq: 83.65 km
Width at water level: 300-365 m
Navigable width: 180-205 m
Maximum permissible draught for ships: 17.68 m (58 ft)
Canal depth: 21 m

Source: Rafimar

from November showed an 8.8% drop in traffic on the year before, and revenues declined 6% to $150 million for the month. In the first three months of 2002, the canal was still depressed, with revenues down 9.5% from the same period in 2001. This is even after international insurers agreed to remove Egypt from its list of war zones in January, slashing insurance premiums by 50%.

Despite the recent setback, the Suez Canal remains relevant to global shipping. Companies have cited improved canal services, especially since the 1998 privatization of the canal shipping agencies that speed the boats through the crossing procedures. Once the current malaise blows over, the ships will undoubtedly return, including the very large and lucrative ones. Current expansion efforts begun in 2000 and scheduled to end in 2010 will increase the breadth and depth of the canal to accomdate very large crude carriers and ultra large crude carriers with drafts of up to 72 feet. (Currently the canal can only accommodate ships with a 58-foot draft.) Oil, however, is no longer the lifeblood of the canal—bigger ships and pipelines have taken care of that. Now 80% of the canal's traffic consists of container ships carrying finished products rather than raw materials between the busy ports of the Mediterranean and East Asia. Once consumer appetites return, these goods should start flowing through the world's most famous shortcut again.

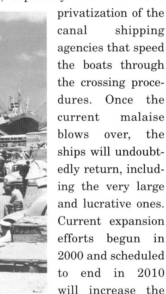

Sea ports

Egypt has spent the last few years aiming to regain its status in antiquity (and early last century) as a major maritime entrepot. Currently, the country's ports have a total capacity of 58.8 million tons, but with major port expansion underway on both the Mediterranean and Red Seas, the government hopes to see that number top 100 by 2017.

Alexandria's port, long in decline, is currently slated for major renovations as part of the comprehensive effort to restore Egypt's second city. Chalking up over 4,000 vessels and 32 million tons of cargo in 2001, it is still the country's single largest port in terms of overall traffic, but it has been eclipsed in certain areas—most notably the container trade—by newer, better outfitted ports in recent years.

Down the coast to the east, Damietta's star is rising, with plans to turn it into a major center for the export of natural gas. The Damietta for Liquid Gas Export project, a much-hyped $1.6 billion Spanish-Egyptian joint venture, includes the building of a liquefied natural gas (LNG) plant and export facilities at the port. As of July, the project was running a little ahead of schedule, with 14% already completed. If all goes as planned, by 2004, about five million tons a year of LNG will be shipped out of Damietta—a major boon to the port and the country's foreign reserves. Damietta is also undergoing renovations intended to double its container capacity. Though it sees much less overall traffic than Alexandria, Damietta is Egypt's second busiest port, and it has been the biggest magnet for transshipment since the early 1990s. In 2001, it moved 600,000 containers, about 85% of those transit shipments. With transshipment growing in importance all over the area, Damietta is poised to become an important regional hub, hoping to take a larger chunk of the 25 million or so containers that are expected to pass through central and eastern

Mediterranean ports by 2010.

But the most high-profile development in seaports in recent years has been around the Suez Canal. The East Port Said port and industrial complex, a BOOT project initiated in 1999, is also envisioned as a major hub in the east Mediterranean. When completed, it will be able to handle the largest container ships and some 1.5 million containers a year. With about 50% of Mediterranean container traffic passing through the Suez Canal, the port's location is a major draw, and project managers estimate operating revenues of LE515 million, with indirect revenues of LE1.5 billion. Phase one for the new "Rotterdam of the East" is currently being completed at a cost of LE750 million, but the project has been delayed more than once. Originally scheduled to open this year, the opening date has been pushed back to 2004.

On the other end of the canal sits the North Sukhna port, another BOOT project that is already partly operational. While East Port Said will handle the European trade from the north, Sukhna is focused towards the trade from Africa and Asia coming from the south. Though both these projects have been farmed out to private contractors and managers, the government has invested substantial amounts of money—in Sukhna, upwards of LE1 billion—to prepare the site for the ports. Like East Port Said, Sukhna has an adjacent industrial complex, and is meant to serve as an outlet for industrial exports. Thus far, it has done a better job of attracting clients than its northern sister—some steel, fertilizer, and petroleum industries have set up shop—but like Port Said, the Sukhna project has been plagued with delays. Last year it was set back due to a dispute between the customs authority and the port's management over whether the port area was really a free trade zone. Currently, trade is minimal, and container traffic negligible, but if the industrial zone proves viable, it does hold out promise for the future.

With all this activity, Egypt's maritime sector will undoubtedly increase in importance in coming years, but there are still some stiff hurdles to overcome. Egyptian ports have traditionally been poorly managed, which makes them slow and therefore expensive. A report by USAID and the Ministry of Economy found that in the mid-1990s terminal handling charges in Alexandria, for example, were almost double those of northern European ports, despite the stark differences in labor costs. It also noted that cargo handling practices were some of the worst in the world. The industry has seen some improvement since 1998, when maritime services were opened up to private investment, and recent technical upgrades have also improved efficiency, cutting down the time that ships spend in port. It is hoped that under private management both Sukhna and East Port Said will flourish— similar arrangements have given a boost to other ports in the region, like Beirut—but analysts say that customs procedures and port bureaucracy still require streamlining if Egypt hopes to compete with other well-established ports in the area.

Airports

In November, the country's first all-private airport opened in Marsa Allam to somewhat muted fanfare. The opening was delayed due to the September events, raising the question of whether the project was inaugurating a new era of BOOT airports to cope with increased tourism flows, or just establishing a lonely

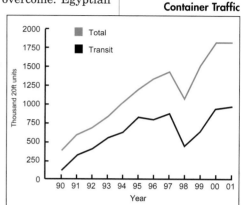

Container Traffic

Source: Rahmar

Trade took a sharp dip after the Southeast Asian crisis

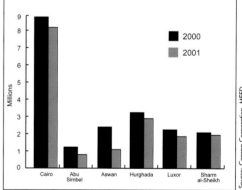

Passengers at Egyptian Airports

Source: Carana Corporation, MEED

Passenger loads fell across the board in 2001

outpost on the southern shores of the Red Sea.

Aside from the temporary decrease in 1998 following the Luxor tragedy, Egypt's tourism arrivals have been growing steadily, up 30% over previous years in both 1999 and 2000. It was clear to everyone, at that time, that Egypt's airports, especially those in high interest areas like Hurghada, Luxor, and Sharm al-Sheikh, not to mention the ghastly nightmare of the Cairo terminal, were simply not up to the increased numbers.

Following global trends, it was decided that BOOT was the answer. Law 3/1997 authorizing private sector participation in airports was passed, and tenders were put out for renovating airports, building new terminals, and even entire new airports. Marsa Allam is the first, built by the Kuwaiti Kharafi Group at an initial investment of $50 million, but agreements have already been signed for new airports in Bahariya and Farafra oases, as well as Alamein.

Meanwhile, airport expansions are moving forward at full speed, with a new tent-terminal completed

Ailing EgyptAir

Even the most seasoned observer of Egyptian domestic politics couldn't help but be a little surprised when EgyptAir's long-time chairman, Fahim Rayan, was given the axe on June 17, 2002. Though Rayan had faced plenty of criticism over the years for his management of the national carrier, more than 20 years at the helm seemed to have inured him against any sudden mood swings by higher ups.

But changes are afoot in Egyptian aviation, and particularly at EgyptAir. The announcement of Rayan's retirement came only two weeks after the airline was broken up into six independent companies, each responsible for some aspect of the carrier's operations. All were placed under the brand new EgyptAir Holding Company. Officials at the Ministry of Civil Aviation said the breakup was an attempt to improve performance and efficiency, but many observers took the move as a sign of impending privatization. The airline had already paid off its $38.5 million in foreign debts in April. Now, with Rayan (a major foe of liberalization) out of the way, the time seemed right for further shake-ups.

Though ministry officials have repeatedly denied such speculation, saying there are no plans to privatize the national carrier, they have spoken of the need to bring a little private-sector ethos to the management of the company. How deep reform can go with no private-sector involvement is still unclear, but there are signs that the government is committed to some liberalization. In April this year, the carrier lost its monopoly on some domestic air routes when the cabinet allowed private companies to edge in, a move applauded by resort managers whose customer base had long been held captive by EgyptAir's pricing and schedules.

Whether or not the government ultimately brings in the private sector, perhaps through some sort of management scheme, something must be done to restore confidence in the ailing airline. Still suffering from the unresolved crash of flight 990 in 1999, the airline suffered another hit with a May crash in Tunisia that left 14 dead. As is the case in the global industry, the airline is also still feeling the fallout of September 11. The first four months of 2002 saw revenue per passenger per kilometers flown (RPK) down 10% on 2001, with freight movement down 16%. Though so far the government has been reluctant to slim down the company's bloated workforce, analysts say it's one of the surest ways to improve efficiency and boost revenues. With 18,000 employees in 2000, EgyptAir was the world's 24th largest airline in terms of staff, though it came nowhere near that spot in terms of revenues or passengers moved. *MM*

in September for the Hurghada airport, increasing capacity five-fold. Construction on the new Sharm al-Sheikh expansion was set to begin in January, while renovations for Luxor and Aswan are under way. There are also plans for an airport in Sixth of October City and Borg al-Arab near Alexandria.

How these projects will fair in light of the slowdown in tourism arrivals remains to be seen. November saw a 20% drop in arrivals and a 13% drop in the number of flights on the year before. Still, airports are in need of the increased investment, if only due to years of government neglect. Most government spending on air transport over the past few decades has gone to EgyptAir rather than the airports themselves.

Cairo Airport, held under a separate company directly under the Ministry of Civil Aviation, is currently undergoing renovations on terminals 1 and 2. Officials say they are considering bids from international companies to build a LE3 billion third terminal and even operate its services. Like the national carrier, however, there will be no substantial privatization of a public sector giant like the Cairo Airport. The privatization of airport management or retail services is another matter, however. This

About EgyptAir

In 2001, EgyptAir moved:

2,980,559 international passengers

1,408,604 domestic passengers

75,231 tons of freight cargo

The airline has:

35 aircraft

24,000 employees

Source: MEED, IATA World Air Transport Statistics

possibility has been raised with increasing frequency since the creation of the civil aviation ministry in March, when newly appointed minister Ahmed Shafiq expressed his determination to bring Egyptian airports more in line with international standards. Those pushing for greater private sector participation in aviation argue that Egypt could get a substantial boost just by corporatizing non-aviation services at airports, like retail outlets, advertising, and parking. Globally, airports make 40% of their money through retail sales, but Egypt falls woefully short of this. According to the Carana Corporation, passengers at Egyptian airports spend on average $4 a visit, compared to $12-$16 at other Middle Eastern airports.

Increasing the variety and efficiency of airport services could provide a windfall, but whether the sudden rush of BOOT projects in the air travel sector will last is highly dependent on tourism-related developments. There is little incentive for investors to build new airports in places like Assyout, where tourists still cannot move freely, or even the desert oases. The high-traffic airports for monuments and beach tourism are safe investments as soon as tourism picks up again. *PS*

The back of the book

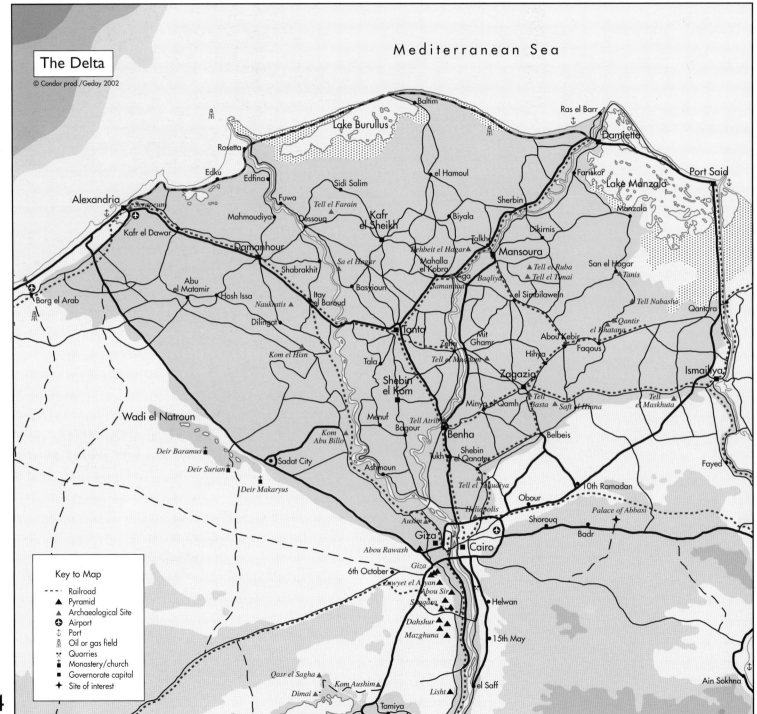

The Delta

© Condor prod./Geday 2002

Mediterranean Sea

Baltim
Ras el Barr
Lake Burullus
Rosetta
Damietta
Edku
Port Said
Edfina
Fariskor
Lake Manzala
Alexandria
Fuwa
Sidi Salim
el Hamoul
Sherbin
Manzala
Serapeum
Mahmoudiya
Dessouq
Tell el Farain
Kafr
el Sheikh
Biyala
Dikirnis
Kafr el Dawar
Talkha
Damanhour
Behbeit el Hagar
Mansoura
San el Hagar
Shabrakhit
Sa el Hagur
Mahalla
el Kobra
Tell el Ruba
Tanis
Abu
el Matamir
Naukratis
Itay
el Baroud
Basyioun
Aga
Samannud
Baqliya
Tell el Timai
el Simbilawein
Tell Nabasha
Hosh Issa
Dilingat
Qantir
el Khatana
Qantara
Borg el Arab
Kom el Hisn
Tanta
Zefta
Mit
Ghamr
Abou Kebir
Faqous
Tell el Maghlum
Hihya
Tala
Shebin
el Kom
Zagazig
Ismailiya
Wadi el Natroun
Menuf
Tell Atrib
Bagour
Benha
Minya el Qamh
Tell
Basta
Saft el Hinna
Tell
el Maskhuta
Deir Baramus
Kom
Abu Billo
Belbeis
Deir Surian
Sadat City
Ashmoun
Shebin
el Qanater
Fayed
Deir Makaryus
Tukh
Tell el Yahudiya
10th Ramadan
Palace of Abbasi
Obour
Shorouq
Badr
Heliopolis
Ausim
Abou Rawash
Giza
Cairo
6th October
Giza
Helwan
Zawyet el Aryan
Abou Sir
Saqqara
15th May
Dahshur
Mazghuna
Qasr el Sagha
Kom Aushim
Ain Sokhna
Dimai
Lisht
el Saff
Tamiya

Key to Map

- – – – Railroad
- ▲ Pyramid
- ▲ Archaeological Site
- ✈ Airport
- ⚓ Port
- Oil or gas field
- Quarries
- ✝ Monastery/church
- ■ Governorate capital
- ✦ Site of interest

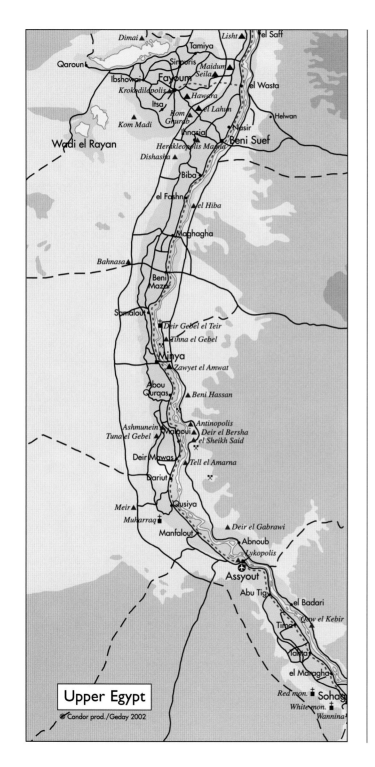

Upper Egypt

© Condor prod./Geday 2002

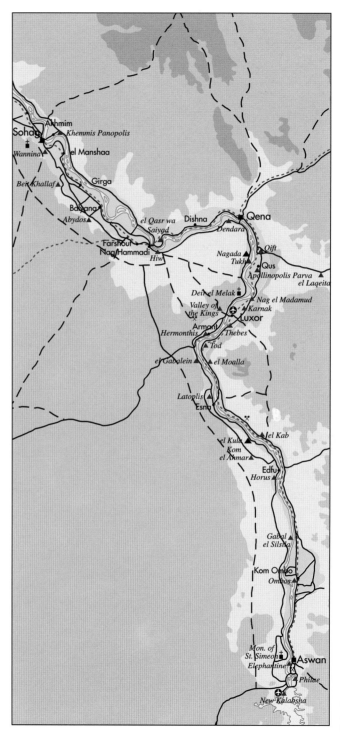

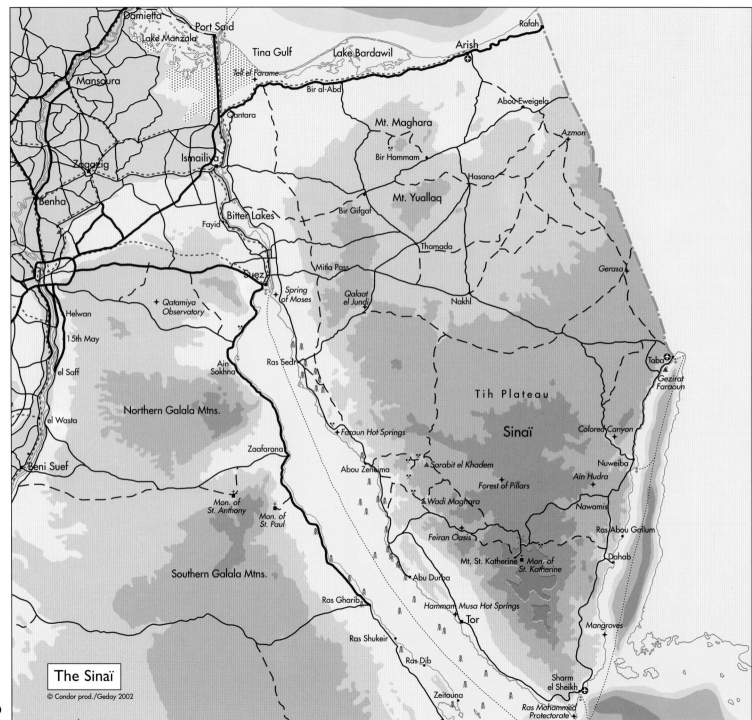

The Sinaï

© Condor prod./Geday 2002

266

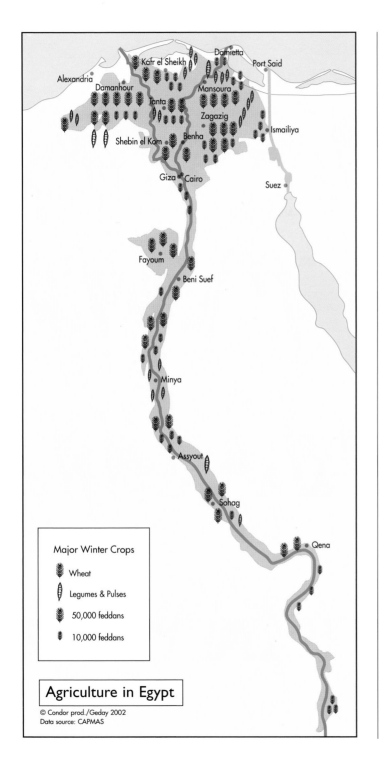

Major Winter Crops

Wheat

Legumes & Pulses

50,000 feddans

10,000 feddans

Agriculture in Egypt

© Condor prod./Geday 2002
Data source: CAPMAS

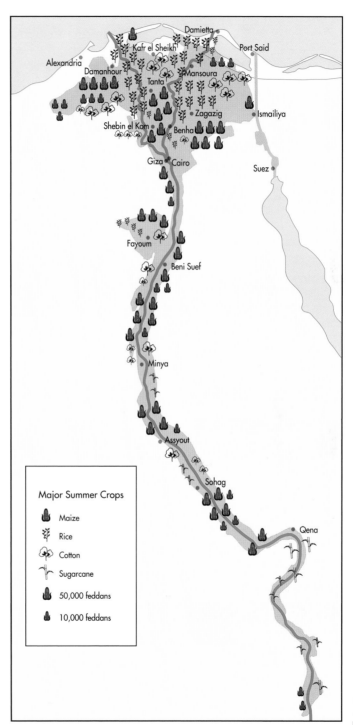

Major Summer Crops

Maize

Rice

Cotton

Sugarcane

50,000 feddans

10,000 feddans

267

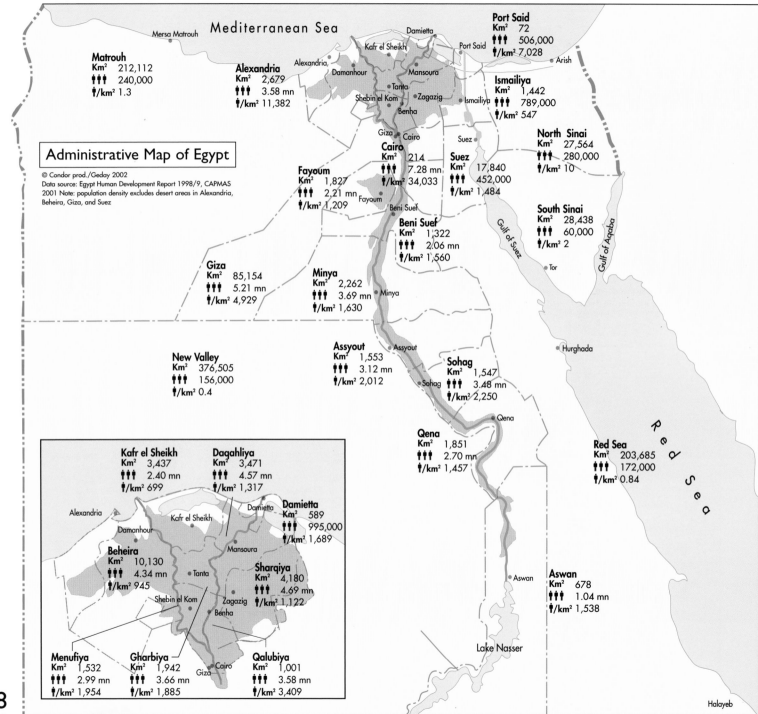

Mediterranean Sea

Port Said
Km² 72
♦♦♦ 506,000
♦/km² 7,028

Matrouh
Km² 212,112
♦♦♦ 240,000
♦/km² 1.3

Alexandria
Km² 2,679
♦♦♦ 3.58 mn
♦/km² 11,382

Ismailiya
Km² 1,442
♦♦♦ 789,000
♦/km² 547

North Sinai
Km² 27,564
♦♦♦ 280,000
♦/km² 10

Administrative Map of Egypt

© Condor prod./Geday 2002
Data source: Egypt Human Development Report 1998/9, CAPMAS
2001 Note: population density excludes desert areas in Alexandria,
Beheira, Giza, and Suez

Cairo
Km² 214
♦♦♦ 7.28 mn
♦/km² 34,033

Fayoum
Km² 1,827
♦♦♦ 2.21 mn
♦/km² 1,209

Suez
Km² 17,840
♦♦♦ 452,000
♦/km² 1,484

South Sinai
Km² 28,438
♦♦♦ 60,000
♦/km² 2

Beni Suef
Km² 1,322
♦♦♦ 2.06 mn
♦/km² 1,560

Giza
Km² 85,154
♦♦♦ 5.21 mn
♦/km² 4,929

Minya
Km² 2,262
♦♦♦ 3.69 mn
♦/km² 1,630

New Valley
Km² 376,505
♦♦♦ 156,000
♦/km² 0.4

Assyout
Km² 1,553
♦♦♦ 3.12 mn
♦/km² 2,012

Sohag
Km² 1,547
♦♦♦ 3.48 mn
♦/km² 2,250

Qena
Km² 1,851
♦♦♦ 2.70 mn
♦/km² 1,457

Red Sea
Km² 203,685
♦♦♦ 172,000
♦/km² 0.84

Kafr el Sheikh
Km² 3,437
♦♦♦ 2.40 mn
♦/km² 699

Dagahliya
Km² 3,471
♦♦♦ 4.57 mn
♦/km² 1,317

Damietta
Km² 589
♦♦♦ 995,000
♦/km² 1,689

Beheira
Km² 10,130
♦♦♦ 4.34 mn
♦/km² 945

Sharqiya
Km² 4,180
♦♦♦ 4.69 mn
♦/km² 1,122

Menufiya
Km² 1,532
♦♦♦ 2.99 mn
♦/km² 1,954

Gharbiya
Km² 1,942
♦♦♦ 3.66 mn
♦/km² 1,885

Qalubiya
Km² 1,001
♦♦♦ 3.58 mn
♦/km² 3,409

Aswan
Km² 678
♦♦♦ 1.04 mn
♦/km² 1,538

Lake Nasser

Red Sea

Halayeb

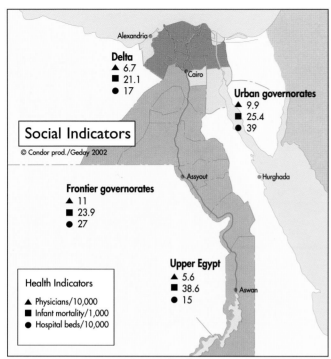

Delta
▲ 6.7
■ 21.1
● 17

Urban governorates
▲ 9.9
■ 25.4
● 39

Social Indicators

© Condor prod./Geday 2002

Frontier governorates
▲ 11
■ 23.9
● 27

Upper Egypt
▲ 5.6
■ 38.6
● 15

Health Indicators

▲ Physicians/10,000
■ Infant mortality/1,000
● Hospital beds/10,000

Data source: Egypt Human Development Report 1998/9 (INP/UNDP)

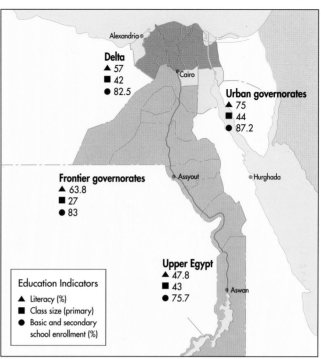

Delta
▲ 57
■ 42
● 82.5

Urban governorates
▲ 75
■ 44
● 87.2

Frontier governorates
▲ 63.8
■ 27
● 83

Upper Egypt
▲ 47.8
■ 43
● 75.7

Education Indicators

▲ Literacy (%)
■ Class size (primary)
● Basic and secondary school enrollment (%)

Data source: Egypt Human Development Report 1998/9 (INP/UNDP)

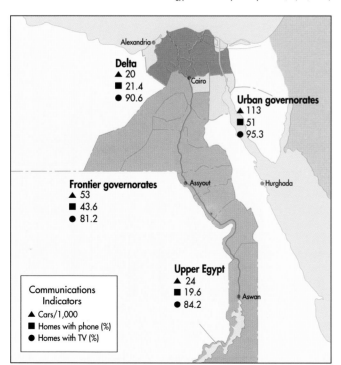

Delta
▲ 20
■ 21.4
● 90.6

Urban governorates
▲ 113
■ 51
● 95.3

Frontier governorates
▲ 53
■ 43.6
● 81.2

Upper Egypt
▲ 24
■ 19.6
● 84.2

Communications Indicators

▲ Cars/1,000
■ Homes with phone (%)
● Homes with TV (%)

Data source: CAPMAS 2001, Health and Demographic Survey 2000

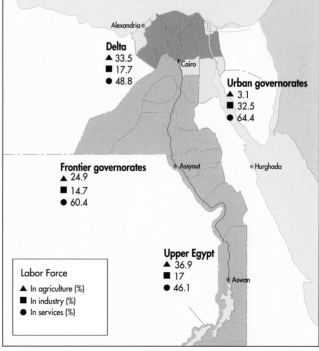

Delta
▲ 33.5
■ 17.7
● 48.8

Urban governorates
▲ 3.1
■ 32.5
● 64.4

Frontier governorates
▲ 24.9
■ 14.7
● 60.4

Upper Egypt
▲ 36.9
■ 17
● 46.1

Labor Force

▲ In agriculture (%)
■ In industry (%)
● In services (%)

269

Data source: Egypt Human Development Report 1998/9 (INP/UNDP)

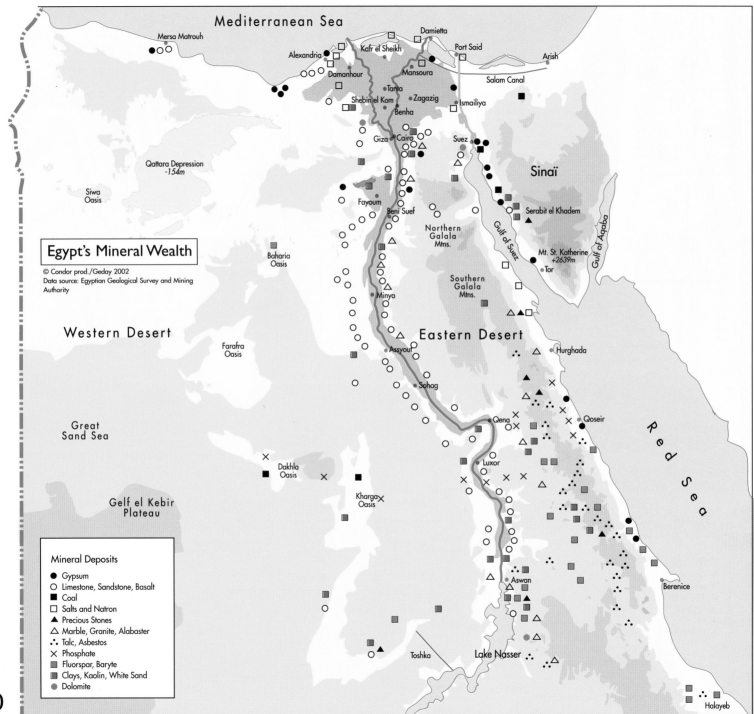

Mediterranean Sea

Mersa Matrouh

Damietta
Alexandria
Kafr el Sheikh
Port Said
Arish
Damanhour
Mansoura
Salam Canal
Tanta
Shebin el Kom
Zagazig
Benha
Ismailiya
Qattara Depression
-154m

Siwa
Oasis

Giza · Cairo
Suez

Sinaï

Egypt's Mineral Wealth

© Condor prod./Geday 2002
Data source: Egyptian Geological Survey and Mining
Authority

Fayoum
Beni Suef
Northern
Galala
Mtns.
Serabit el Khadem

Baharia
Oasis
Mt. St. Katherine
+2639m

Tor

Southern
Galala
Mtns.

Western Desert
Farafra
Oasis
Minya

Great
Sand Sea
Assyout
Eastern Desert
Hurghada

Sohag
Qoseir

Dakhla
Oasis
Qena
Red Sea

Gelf el Kebir
Plateau
Kharga
Oasis
Luxor

Aswan
Berenice

Mineral Deposits

● Gypsum
○ Limestone, Sandstone, Basalt
■ Coal
□ Salts and Natron
▲ Precious Stones
△ Marble, Granite, Alabaster
∴ Talc, Asbestos
✕ Phosphate
▪ Fluorspar, Baryte
▪ Clays, Kaolin, White Sand
● Dolomite

Toshka
Lake Nasser

Halayeb

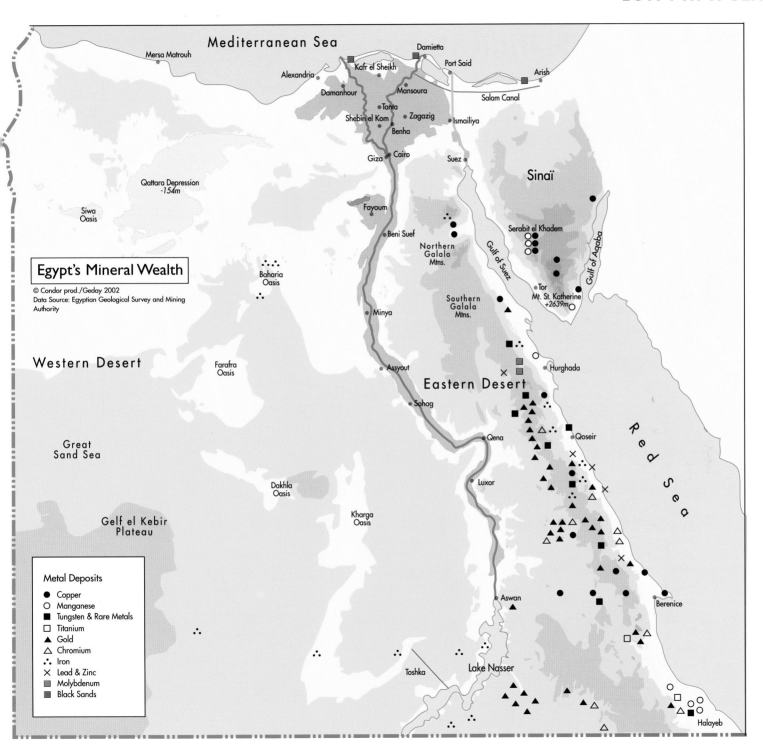

Mediterranean Sea

Mersa Matrouh

Damietta

Alexandria · Kafr el Sheikh · Port Said · Arish

Damanhour · Mansoura

Tanta · Zagazig · Salam Canal

Shebin el Kom · Benha · Ismailiya

Giza · Cairo · Suez

Qattara Depression -154m

Sinaï

Siwa Oasis

Fayoum

Beni Suef

Egypt's Mineral Wealth

© Condor prod./Geday 2002
Data Source: Egyptian Geological Survey and Mining Authority

Baharia Oasis

Northern Galala Mtns.

Serabit el Khadem

Minya · Southern Galala Mtns. · Tor

Mt. St. Katherine +2639m

Gulf of Suez

Gulf of Aqaba

Western Desert

Farafra Oasis

Assyout

Eastern Desert

Hurghada

Sohag

Great Sand Sea

Qena · Qoseir

Dakhla Oasis

Luxor

Red Sea

Kharga Oasis

Gelf el Kebir Plateau

Aswan · Berenice

Metal Deposits

- ● Copper
- ○ Manganese
- ■ Tungsten & Rare Metals
- □ Titanium
- ▲ Gold
- △ Chromium
- ∴ Iron
- ✕ Lead & Zinc
- ▨ Molybdenum
- ▦ Black Sands

Toshka · **Lake Nasser**

Halayeb

Economic Indicators

GDP Growth

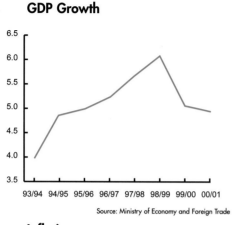

Officially, GDP growth remained strong in the late 1990s though analysts put the 2000/01 rate at more like 3%

Source: Ministry of Economy and Foreign Trade

Breakdown of GDP

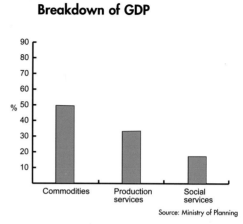

The economy has diversified, but work in basic commodities still accounts for about half of GDP

Source: Ministry of Planning

Inflation

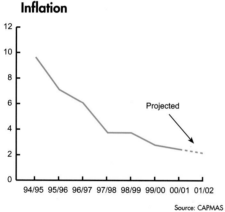

Inflation was brought under control during the 1990s

Source: CAPMAS

Foreign Reserves

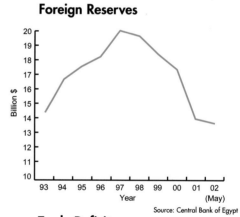

Since 1998 Egypt has spent some $5 billion propping up the pound

Source: Central Bank of Egypt

Fiscal Deficit as % of GDP

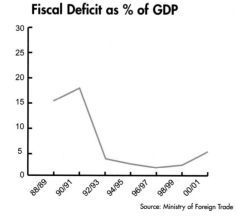

The budget deficit started to crawl up again in 1998

Source: Ministry of Foreign Trade

Trade Deficit

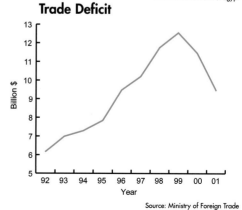

The trade deficit contracts in 2001 but is still gaping

Source: Ministry of Foreign Trade

Economic Indicators

Industrial Production

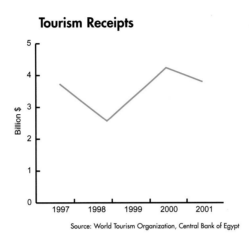

Industrial output is steadily rising, but the rate of growth is on the decline

Tourism Receipts

Source: World Tourism Organization, Central Bank of Egypt

Tourism is Egypt's biggest foreign currency earner but it is extremely sensitive to regional and global events

Suez Canal Revenues

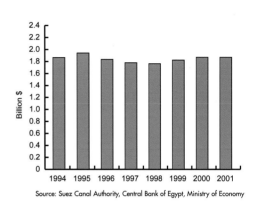

Source: Suez Canal Authority, Central Bank of Egypt, Ministry of Economy

The Suez Canal does not see the traffic it once did, but revenues have remained steady

Trade Patterns

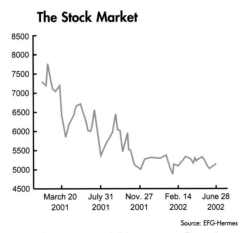

Source: Central Bank of Egypt

Egypt trades most with the EU but imports much more than it exports

The Stock Market

Source: EFG-Hermes

Egypt's economic doldrums are reflected in the benchmark Hermes Financial Index, which fell to new lows in 2001

Bourse Make-up

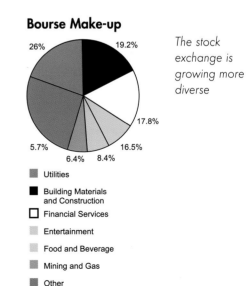

The stock exchange is growing more diverse

- Utilities
- Building Materials and Construction
- Financial Services
- Entertainment
- Food and Beverage
- Mining and Gas
- Other

Source: Cairo & Alexandria Stock Exchanges

Agricultural Indicators

Crop Production

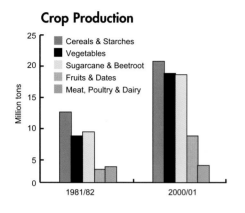

Legend:
- Cereals & Starches
- Vegetables
- Sugarcane & Beetroot
- Fruits & Dates
- Meat, Poultry & Dairy

Million tons

1981/82   2000/01

Source: State Information Service

Crop productivity has grown markedly over the past 20 years

Cereal Yield per Hectare

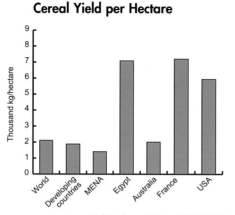

Thousand kg/hectare

World, Developing countries, MENA, Egypt, Australia, France, USA

Source: World Development Indicators 2002 (World Bank)

Egypt boasts some of the highest wheat yields per hectare planted in the world ...

Food Sufficiency

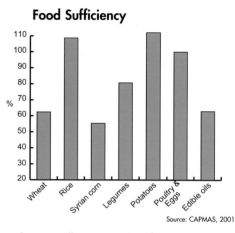

%

Wheat, Rice, Syrian corn, Legumes, Potatoes, Poultry & Eggs, Edible oils

Source: CAPMAS, 2001

... but it is still not enough to feed the growing population

Social Indicators

Population Growth Rate

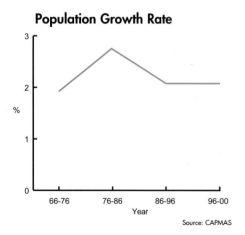

%

66-76   76-86   86-96   96-00
Year

Source: CAPMAS

The population growth rate has slowed to around 2%

Population Forecast

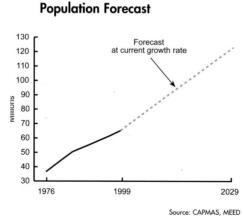

Forecast at current growth rate

Millions

1976   1999   2029

Source: CAPMAS, MEED

Even at the current slower growth rate, Egypt's population will double between 1996 and 2029

Population Breakdown

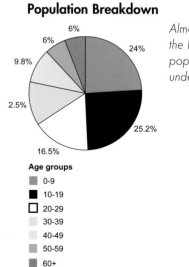

6%
6%
9.8%
2.5%
16.5%
25.2%
24%

Almost half of the Egyptian population is under 20

Age groups
- 0-9
- 10-19
- 20-29
- 30-39
- 40-49
- 50-59
- 60+

Source: Health and Demographic Survey 2000

Social indicators

Household Ownership

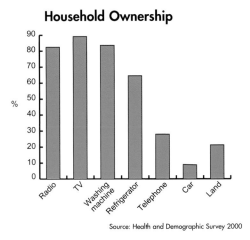

Source: Health and Demographic Survey 2000

The vast majority of Egyptian households own a TV, but other durable goods are less widespread

Consumer Profile

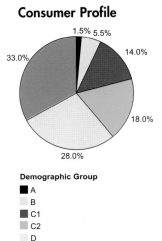

33.0% 1.5% 5.5% 14.0% 18.0% 28.0%

Demographic Group
- A
- B
- C1
- C2
- D
- E

Source: Sainsbury's Egypt

Spending power has grown with liberalization. Some 14 million people come under A, B, or C1 spending brackets

Household Spending

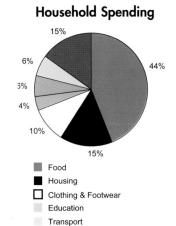

15% 6% 3% 4% 10% 15% 44%

- Food
- Housing
- Clothing & Footwear
- Education
- Transport
- Healthcare
- Other

Source: CAPMAS, 2001

Food accounts for almost half of average household expenses. Housing is the second biggest drain

Fertility Rate

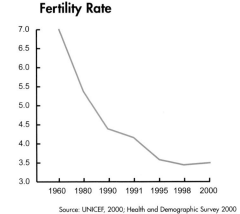

Source: UNICEF, 2000; Health and Demographic Survey 2000

Contraceptive use in Egypt more than doubled from 1980-2000, from 24% to 56%

Doctors per 1000 People

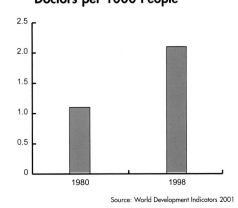

Source: World Development Indicators 2001

The number of doctors has increased, but there's a huge gulf between private and state-provided medical care

Spending on Health

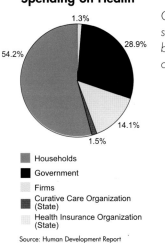

54.2% 1.3% 28.9% 14.1% 1.5%

- Households
- Government
- Firms
- Curative Care Organization (State)
- Health Insurance Organization (State)

Source: Human Development Report 1997/8 (INP, UNDP)

Citizens shoulder the bulk of health costs

275

Social Indicators

Illiteracy Rate

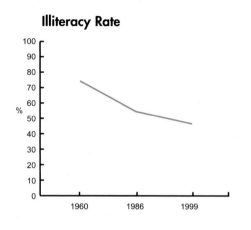

Source: Human Development Report 1998/9 (INP, UNDP)

Overall literacy is up ...

Breakdown of Illiteracy

Source: Human Development Report 1997/8 (INP, UNDP)

... but rates vary greatly among different segments of the population

Spending on Education

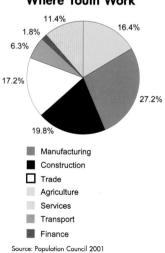

3.0%
19.5%
12.5%
65.0%

- ■ Fees
- Books & Stationery
- Transportation
- Private Lessons

Source: Human Development Report 1997/8 (INP, UNDP)

Almost two-thirds of education costs are spent on private lessons

Unemployment by Educational Status

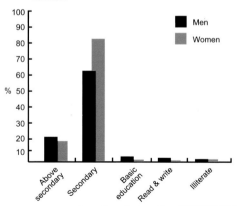

■ Men
■ Women

Source: Human Development Report 1998/9 (INP/UNDP)

Official figures put unemployment at about 7.5%, with the vast majority of the unemployed being educated

Students Enrolled in Universites

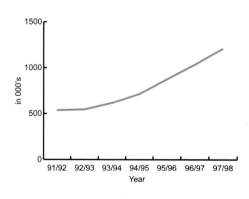

Source: CAPMAS

The number of university students more than doubled between 1992 and 1998

Where Youth Work

11.4%
1.8%
6.3%
17.2%
19.8%
16.4%
27.2%

- Manufacturing
- ■ Construction
- □ Trade
- Agriculture
- Services
- Transport
- Finance

Source: Population Council 2001

Almost 70% of young people aged 15-24 work in the private sector. Of those, over a quarter work in manufacturing

Fingertip Facts

Geography

Surface Area:

Total: 1,001,450 km²

Land: 995,450 km²

Water: 6,000 km²

Inhabited: 52,500 km²

Built-up: 19,740 km²

Cultivated: 31,000 km²

Land boundaries:

Total: 2,689 km

Border countries: Gaza Strip 11 km, Israel 255 km, Libya 1,150 km, Sudan 1,273 km

Coastline: 2,450 km

Maritime claims:

Contiguous zone: 24 nautical miles

Continental shelf: 200 m depth or to depth of exploitation

Exclusive economic zone: 200 nautical miles

Territorial sea: 12 nautical miles

Terrain:

Vast desert plateau interrupted by Nile Valley and Delta

Elevation extremes:

Lowest point: Qattara Depression -154 m

Highest point: Mount St. Katherine 2,639 m

Climate:

	Max Temp	Min Temp	Humidity (%)	Rain per month (mm)
(mean daily temperatures in January)				
Cairo:	18.8	8.9	59	5.2
Alexandria:	18.3	9.1	70	51.8
Aswan:	22.7	8.5	39	Less than 0.1
(mean daily temperatures in August)				
Cairo:	34.2	22.0	59	0.0
Alexandria:	30.4	23.6	71	0.2
Aswan:	40.8	25.6	20	0.8

Capital City:

Cairo

Major Cities:

Alexandria, Aswan, Assyout, Ismailiya, Port Said, Tanta, Mansoura

Society

Population: 66.5 million

Labor force: 19.5 million

Population growth rate: 2.1%

Fertility rate: 3.5%

Life expectancy (men): 67 years

Life expectancy (women): 69 years

Infant mortality rate: 41/1000

Under 5 mortality rate: 52/1000

Literacy: 54.6%

Students enrolled in university (2000/01): 1.7 million

Infrastructure

IT	Total	Per 100 people
Phone lines (capacity):	8.8 million	13.2
Mobile phone subscribers:	3.4 million	5.1
Pay phones:	36,048	0.05
Internet service providers:	64	--
Internet users:	1 million	1.5
Personal computers:	800,000	1.2

Physical

Length of rail lines: 9,400 km

Electrification of signals (1999): 1,560 km

Length of metro: 63 km

Length of roads: 44,000 km

Seaport quays (1999): 141

Port capacity (million tons): 58.8

Civil Airports: 20

Irrigation canals: 34,200 km

Politics

Head of state: President Mohammed Hosni Mubarak

Ruling party: National Democratic Party

Opposition parties: 16

Macroeconomy

Official exchange rate (June 30, 2002): LE4.51 to $1 (± 3%)

Foreign reserves (May 31, 2002): $13.73 billion

Real GDP 2000/01 (fiscal year ends June 30): LE316 billion

Real GDP Growth Rate 2000/01: 4.9% (official)

Unemployment: 7.4% (official)

Inflation 2000/01: 2.4%

Budget deficit 2000/01: 5.4% of GDP

Trade deficit 2000/01: $9.354 billion

Total Exports 2000/01: $7.078 billion

Total Imports 2000/01: $16.432 billion

Current account deficit 2000/01: $33 million

Balance of payments deficit 2000/01: $852.8 million

Total public domestic debt

(government and state industry, 2000/01): LE193.81 billion

External debt 2000/01: $26.56 billion

Total banking credit 2000/01: LE243.6 billion (of which LE13.6 billion to government, LE230 billion to private sector)

Total liquidity 2000/01: LE284.9 billion

Dollarization 2000/01: 21% of total liquidity

Interest rate on 6-month T-bills: 7.631% (July 2002)

Interest rate on 3-month T-bills: 7.199% (July 2002)

Cairo Interbank Offered Rate (Caibor):
10.439% (July 25, 2002)

Real Economy

Sectors' share of GDP:

Government services 7.8%; social & personal services 7.6%; agriculture 16.4%; industry & mining 20.2%; petroleum 5.4%; electricity 1.8%; construction 6%; transportation 9%; trade, finance & insurance 21.4%; hotels & restaurants 2%; housing & real estate 1.9%; social insurance 0.1%; utilities 0.4%

Income from Suez Canal (2001): $1.9 billion

(Jan.-June 2002): $891.1 million)

Tourist arrivals (2001): 4.6 million

(Jan.-June 2002: 2.2 million)

Total tourist nights (2001): 29.8 million

(Jan-June 2002: 14.6 million)

Electricity generated 2000/01: 77 billion kw/h

Cement production (2000/01): 25.2 million tons

(first half 2001/2002: 13.1 million tons)

Bankruptcies (2001): 196

Companies listed on stock exchange (2001): 1,110

Number of companies traded on stock exchange (2001): 643

Volume of trading (2001): 1.26 billion shares

Value of trading (2001): LE31.8 billion

Turnover ratio (2001): 21.97%

Market capitalization (March 2002): LE112.3 billion

Weights and Measures

Length

1 diraa baladi (local cubit): 58 cm (used for textiles)

1 qasaba (rod): 3.55 m (used for surveying)

1 qadam: 1 ft or 0.3048 m (used in leather industry)

1 busa: 1 in (used for nails, screws, and raw metal)

1 linya: 1/8 in (used for nails, screws, drill bits)

1 qirat barsum: 1/6 habbit shair, or 0.087 cm

1 habbit shair: 1/144 diraa mimari, or 0.521 cm

1 usbaa (fingerbreadth): 1/24 diraa mimari, or 3.125 cm

1 qabda (handsbreadth): 1/6 diraa mimari, or 12.5 cm

1 diraa mimari or naggari (architects' cubit): 75 cm

1 baa (fathom): 4 diraa mimari or 3 m

Area

1 sahtut: 1/24 sahm, or 0.304 m²

1 sahm: 1/24 qirat, or 7.293 m²

1 daneq: 1/6 qirat, or 29.172 m²

1 habba: 1/3 qirat, or 58.345 m²

1 qirat: 1/24 feddan, or 175.035 m²

1 feddan: 4,200.833 m², or 1.038 acres

1 diraa mimari²: 0.5625 m²

1 qasaba²: 12.6025 m²

Dry Measure

1 qirat: 1/32 qadah, or 0.064 lt

1 kharuba: 1/16 qadah, or 0.129 lt

1 tumna: 1/8 qadah, or 0.258 lt

1 rubaa: 1/4 qadah, or 0.516 lt

1 qadah: 2.062 lt

1 melwa: 2 qadahs, or 4.125 lt

1 rub: 4 qadahs, or 8.25 lt

1 keila: 8 qadahs, or 16.5 lt

1 weiba: 16 qadahs, or 33 lt

1 ardabb: 6 weibas, or 96 qadahs, or 198 lt

1 shikara: 20 kg (cement and plaster)

Volume

1 safiha: 20 liters, or 4.4 gallons (gasoline and kerosene)

Standard Weight

1 dirham: 3.12 g

1 wiqiya: 12 dirhams, or 37.44 g (often used to mean one ounce, but it is 1.321 ounces; used for silver, hashish, and opium)

1 ratl: 144 dirhams, or 449.28 g

1 wiqqa (oka): 400 dirhams, or 1.248 kg

1 qintar: 100 ratls, or 44.928 kg

Precious metals and stones

1 qamha: 1/4 qirat, or 0.04875 g

1 qirat: 1 carat, or 0.195 g

1 dirham: 3.12 g

1 magar: 18 qirats, or 3.51 g (also used to refer to 18-carat gold)

1 mitqal: 24 qirats, or 4.68 g

Agricultural produce (approximate)

1 ardabb wheat: 150 kg

1 ardabb barley: 120 kg

1 ardabb maize: 140 kg

1 ardabb beans: 155 kg

1 ardabb whole lentils: 160 kg

1 ardabb split lentils: 148 kg

1 ardabb cotton-seed: 270 ratls, or 121.3 kg

Cotton

1 qintar unginned cotton: 315 ratls, or 141.5 kg

1 qintar ginned cotton: 100 ratls, or 44.928 kg

Money

1 milleme: 1/10 qirsh (piaster)

1 taarifa: 5 millemes

1 qirsh sagh: 10 millemes, 1/100 Egyptian pound ("sagh" is used to refer to 10 qirsh sagh or less, while "qirsh" is used for amounts of 11 qirsh or more)

1 shillin: 5 qirsh (used colloquially to refer to 5 pounds)

1 bariza: 10 qirsh (used colloquially to refer to 10 pounds)

1 riyal: 20 qirsh (used colloquially to refer to 20 pounds)

1 guinea: 100 qirsh, or one Egyptian pound

alf guinea: 1000 pounds (colloquially referred to as "bako")

milyun guinea: 1 million pounds (colloquially referred to as "arnab")

milyar guinea: 1 billion pounds

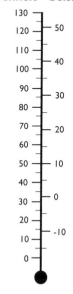

Farenheit   Celsius

*Boiling point:
212° F=100° C
Freezing point:
32° F=0° C*

A Century in Numbers

Indicator	Pre-1952	1952-1979	1980-Present
Demography			
Population of Egypt	1897: 9.734 million	1957: 23.21 million	1986: 48.254 million
	1927: 14.218 million	1966: 30.076 million	1996: 59.272 million
	1947: 18.967 million	1976: 36.626 million	2001: 66.552 million
Population growth rate	1897-1907: 1.16%	1947-1957: 1.22%	1976-1986: 2.75%
	1937-1947: 1.19%	1960-1966: 2.52%	1986-1996: 2.1%
Population density in inhabited areas	1927: 450 per km^2		1998: 1,743 per km^2
Urban population	1947: 36.2%	1960: 43.9%	1986: 62.5%
		1976: 53.5%	1996: 66.8%
Number of towns with a population of more than 10,000	1947: 40		1996: 600
Population living in Cairo	1897: 5.9%		1986: 19.3%
	1907: 5.5%		1996: 17%
	1947: 11%		
Social Indicators			
Male literacy	1897: 4.8%	1960: 41.7%	1996: 71%
	1947: 33.9%		
Female literacy	1897: 0.7%	1960: 12.5%	1980: 25.5%
	1947: 11.8%		1998: 45.7%
Spending on education as % of total government spending	1936/7: 11%	1954/5: 12.6%	2000/1: 17.4%
Number of pupils in basic education per 1,000 people	1925: 15	1958: 102	1996: 189
	1951: 66	1974: 151	
Number of students in secondary education per 1,000 people	1937: 1.2	1957: 4.7	1996: 14
		1974: 9.8	
Number of hospital beds per 10,000 people	1923: 3.2		1981: 20.2
	1944: 11.7		2001: 20.4
Economy and Industry			
Local exchange rate (official)	1939: LE1=£1.025, or LE1=$5	1950: LE1=£1.025	1980: LE1=$1.43
		1975: LE1=$2.56	1990: LE1=$0.50

Exports as a percentage of imports	1920: 83.5% 1936: 105% 1949: 92.3%	1953: 77% 1975: 35.7%	1981: 44.5% 2000: 43.1%
Biggest export product in terms of value	1900: cotton 1937: cotton 1949: cotton	1953: cotton 1973: cotton 1978: crude oil	1994: crude oil 2000: petroleum products
Biggest import product in terms of value	1900: cotton goods 1937: cotton goods 1949: wheat	1953: wheat 1973: wheat 1978: vehicles	1994: machinery 2000: crude oil
Biggest trading partner	1900: Britain 1937: Britain	1958: Soviet Union 1973: Soviet Union 1978: USA	2000: EU
Number of tourists		1952: 206,000 1959: 417,801 1978: 1.004 million	1981: 1.4 million 1995: 3.133 million 2001: 4.648 million
Number of hotel rooms in the country		1959: 6,653 1975: 21,568	1981: 31,166 2000: 113,611

Agriculture

Workforce in agriculture		1970: 52%	1981: 39% 2001: 28%
Percentage of landowners holding less than 1 feddan of land	1923: 65.8% 1944: 70.3%		1995: 69.3%
Percentage of land held by owners of less than 1 feddan	1923: 9.5% 1944: 12.6%		1995: 18.5%
Percentage of landowners holding over 100 feddans of land	1923: 0.3% 1944: 0.2%		1995: 0.001%
Percentage of land held by owners of more than 100 feddans	1923: 31.3% 1944: 28.7%		1995: 8.1%
Average plot size among landowners	1940s: 6 feddans	1950s: 3.8 feddans	1982: 2.7 feddans 1990: 2.7 feddans
Area planted in cotton	1935: 1.716 mn feddans 1949: 1.628 mn feddans	1970-74 average: 1.551 mn feddans	1993: 884,000 feddans 199: 789,000 feddans

Sources: UNDP, CAPMAS, Economist Intelligence Unit, in addition to a series of annual government publications and almanacs dating from the turn of the 20th century through 1964.

Chronology

Year/Dynasty	Political History	Culture and Technology
Prehistoric	c. 250,000 BCE: Earliest human traces in Egypt c. 25,000: Following climate change, settlements centered in Delta, Upper Egypt and Nubia, and Western Desert oases. Neolithic period sees the introduction of cereal agriculture.	Rock drawings and carvings, stone implements.
Pre-dynastic c. 4500-2920 BCE	Local cultures appear in Upper and Lower Egypt. Towards the end of the period, they have evolved into two competing federations, with the capital of Upper Egypt in Kom Ahmar and Lower Egypt in Tell al-Farain.	Narmer Palette, showing unification of North and South. Religious centers in Heliopolis and Karnak.
Early Dynastic 2920-2575 BCE Dynasties 1-3	Memphis is established as the capital of a united Egypt. Cultural uniformity from Aswan to the Delta. Hieroglyphs and canons of Egyptian art make their first appearance.	Mastaba tombs constructed and temples established in major cult centers like Abydos, Heliopolis, and Saïs.
Old Kingdom 2575-2134 BCE Dynasties 4-6	Capital in Memphis. Period of great bureaucratic centralization. King regarded as absolute ruler, more god than man. Last king of the 6th Dynasty, Pepi II, rules more than 90 years.	Pyramid age: Djoser (3rd Dynasty) constructs step pyramid at Saqqara. Three great pyramids of Giza built in 4th Dynasty. Pyramid texts appear in late 5th and 6th Dynasty pyramids.
First Intermediate Period 2134-2040 BCE Dynasties 7-11	Local rulers gain power and the influence of the royal house declines. Theban princes of the 11th Dynasty reassert control over the country.	Tombs of local nobles grow in size. Nobleman Ankhtify of Moalla leaves a tomb biography recounting his battles with rivals in Middle Egypt. Development of classical Middle Egyptian, providing one of the bases of the literary flourishing of the Middle Kingdom.
Middle Kingdom 2040-1640 BCE Dynasties 11-13	The start of incursions into Asia and Nubia for trade. New capital at Itj-Tawi, on the outskirts of Memphis. Thebes grows in stature as an important religious center.	11th and 12th Dynasty pyramids at Dahshur and Lisht.

Second Intermediate Period 1640-1550 BCE Dynasties 14-17	Near Eastern kings—the so-called Hyksos—rule as far south as Abydos. The Nubian kingdom of Kush penetrates north. Theban rulers of the 17th and early 18th Dynasties regain the land and cross Sinai to destroy the last of the Hyksos.	Mycenean wall paintings of bull leapers found in the Hyksos capital, Avaris, in the Delta. Similar paintings from this period found in Knossos in Crete and northern Syria indicative of a high level of cultural exchange.
New Kingdom 1550-1070 BCE Dynasties 18-20	18th and 19th Dynasty kings build empire in Syria-Palestine and Nubia. Akhenaten (18th Dynasty) imposes "monotheistic" religion directed to the sun-disc, Aten. Capital moved to Amarna. His legacy is erased shortly afterwards. Ramses II (19th Dynasty) battles against the Hittite empire at Kadesh. Capital moved to Pi-Ramses in the Delta during the 19th Dynasty. Population of the Delta exceeds that of the Nile Valley for the first time.	Valley of the Kings initiated. Temple to Amun, Karnak, expands to its current size in the 18th Dynasty. Hatshepsut's mortuary complex at Deir al-Bahari (18th Dynasty). Akhenaton (18th Dynasty) builds a new capital and temple to the sun-god Aten at Amarna. Tutankhamun burial in the Valley of the Kings. Ramses II (19th Dynasty) builds temple at Abu Simbel. Ramses III (20th Dynasty) builds Ramesseum on the Theban West Bank.
Third Intermediate Period 1070-712 BCE Dynasties 21-24	Libyan, Egyptian, and priestly rulers from Thebes divide the country amongst themselves. Medinet Habu becomes a fortified town inhabited by remnants of Theban community.	Royal mummies moved from Valley of the Kings to Deir al-Bahari for safekeeping.
Late Period 712-332 BCE Dynasties 25-30	Nubian rulers, from Napata, revive a strict form of Amun worship. The last native Egyptian dynasties rule from Saïs in the western Delta between periods of occupation by Nubian and Persian invaders. A Greek trading colony, Naukratis, is founded in the Delta in the 7th century BCE.	The stele of the Nubian king Piye recounts his conquests of Libyan and Egyptian princedoms. Archaizing style in art.
Ptolemaic Period 332-30 BCE	332 BCE: Alexander invades and visits the oracle at Amun. 30 BCE: Cleopatra's death brings an end to the Ptolemies. Final period of independent sovereignty before	Foundation of Alexandria (331 BCE) and the building of the lighthouse (Pharos, c. 279 BCE) and great library. Temples constructed at Edfu, Dendera, and Philae.

the country becomes part of the Roman Empire.

Euclid (c. 300 BCE) lays down the foundations of geometry.
A priestly decree engraved in stone is issued c. 200 BCE: the Rosetta Stone.

Romano-Byzantine Period
30 BCE-641

Egypt becomes the main wheat supplier to the Roman Empire and Egyptian religious cults spread throughout the empire.
c. 54: Christianity established in Egypt with the arrival of St. Mark.
270: St. Anthony retires to the desert, establishing monasticism.
284: Beginning of the Coptic calendar, marking persecutions under Diocletian.
395: Roman Empire divided; Egypt falls under the authority of Byzantine emperors.
451: Council of Chalcedon ushers in the establishment of an independent Egyptian church.
553: Justinian evicts the last Egyptian priests from the temples at Philae and Siwa.
End of period marked by attacks by Persian Empire.
639: Arab army under Amr Ibn al-Aas enters Egypt.

c. 100: Romans build fortress at Babylon.
c. 140: Claudius Ptolemy draws his map of the world.
300: Pompey's Pillar.
c. 350: St. Anthony's Monastery.
c. 450: Coptic basilica at Dendera, one of the oldest surviving Coptic structures.
Fayyoum portraits.

Early Islamic Period
641-868

641: Fortress at Babylon falls to the army of Amr Ibn al-Aas. Coptic population of Egypt estimated at 12 million.
705: Arabic becomes official language of administration.
832: The Abbasid caliph Mamoun arrives in Egypt to put down Coptic Bashmouric revolt; tries to gain entry to the Giza Pyramids.

641: Mosque of Amr Ibn al-Aas raised and Fustat established as the capital.
715: Nilometer built on Roda Island.
820: Imam al-Shafii, founder of one of the four schools of Islamic Law, dies in Fustat.
861: Nilometer built at Roda.

Tulunids
868-905

Ahmed Ibn Tulun comes as governor for Abbasid caliph and establishes his own dynasty.

879: Mosque of Ibn Tulun completed, built in the center of the new city of al-Qatai, now destroyed.

Ikhshidids 935-969	Mohammed Ibn Tughj appointed by the Abbasid caliph as governor of Egypt Repels invasion attempts by the Fatimids and spawns short-lived dynasty.	
Fatimids 969-1171	969: Fatimid general Jawhar enters Fustat and lays the foundation of the city of Cairo. 996-1021: Rule of al-Hakim, marked by persecution of Christians and bizarre state decrees; presumed murdered. 1074: Following a period of chaos, drought, and famine, Badr al-Gamali, governor of Acre, enters Egypt and forms a mini-dynasty of emirs that rule the Fatimid caliphs. 1168: Crusaders launch an attack on Egypt, and Salah al-Din assumes the wazirate of the Fatimid caliphate; the great Fustat fire.	972: al-Azhar Mosque completed. 1013: The mosque of al-Hakim completed. 1087-1092: Bab al-Futuh added to city as Badr al-Gamali reinforces and expands Cairo's walls.
Ayyubids 1171-1250	1171: Salah al-Din has the Friday sermon announced in the name of the Abbasid caliph, officially ending the Fatimid dynasty; the last Fatimid caliph, Adid, dies soon after. 1187: Muslim army led by Salah al-Din captures Jerusalem. 1218: al-Kamil becomes the first sultan to take up residence in the Citadel. 1249: The last of the Crusaders led by King Louis IX capture Damietta and Mansoura; king later taken captive. 1249: Shagarat al-Dorr rules after her husband, al-Saleh Ayyub, dies; she is briefly proclaimed sultan before marrying Aybak, a Kipçak Turkish mamluk, thus bringing the Mamluk dynasty to power.	Institution of the madrasa (legal religious school) introduced in Egypt. 1176-1182: Citadel built and the city's walls enlarged and fortified. 1180: Tomb and madrasa of Imam al-Shafii established. 1249: Shagarat al-Dorr builds a tomb for her late husband adjacent to his madrasa, establishing an architectural precedent for later Mamluk rulers.
Bahri Mamluks 1250-1382	1260: Mamluk army led by al-Zahir Baybars defeats the Mongols at Ain Jalut. 1261: Baghdad destroyed, Baybars proclaims a	1305: Madrasa and tomb of al-Nasir Mohammed Ibn Qalawun completed. 1307: Earthquake brings down the remains of

new Abbasid caliph with his seat in Egypt.

1294-1340: Rule of al-Nasir Mohammed Ibn Qalawun; Cairo expands into Boulaq. His rule also sees the beginning of a wave of mob riots against Copts.

1347: The first of dozens of plague epidemics hit Egypt.

the Alexandria lighthouse.

1347: Blue Mosque built.

1360: Mosque of Sultan Hassan completed.

1382: Khan al-Khalili market built.

Burgi Mamluks
1382-1517

1382: Barquq, a Circassian Turk, seizes the crown of the last Bahri Mamluk sultan, initiating a new dynasty.

1426: Cyprus conquered and brought under Mamluk control.

1491: Qait Bey concludes a temporary peace with the Ottomans after several skirmishes.

1498: Vasco de Gama sails to India, breaking the Mamluk spice monopoly.

1516: Sultan al-Ghuri dies of a stroke fighting the Ottoman army at Marj Dabiq.

1517: On the last day of the hijri year, the The Ottoman sultan Selim enters Cairo, executing the last Mamluk sultan, Tuman Bey II.

1396: Madrasa and tomb of Sultan Barquq completed.

1406: Ibn Khaldoun—historian, jurist, and politician—dies in Cairo.

1420: Muayyad Sheikh mosque and tomb built.

1442: Death of al-Maqrizi, Mamluk historian.

1474: Qait Bey's madrasa and tomb completed.

1505: Wikalat al-Ghuri completed.

Ottoman Rule
1517-1805

A series of Ottoman governors, and later Mamluk beys, wrestle for control of the country.

1798: French invasion; the British land at Abu Qir and destroy the French fleet in the bay.

1524: Death of Ibn Iyas, Mamluk historian.

1571: Mosque of Sinan Pasha goes up.

1799: Discovery of the Rosetta Stone.

Mohammed Ali Pasha
1805-September 1848

1811: Mohammed Ali has Mamluk beys assassinated after a banquet at the Citadel.

1820: Conquest of Nubia and Sudan begun.

c. 1820: Development of long-staple cotton plant in Egypt.

1841: Sudan put officially under Egyptian control.

1809-22: Publication of *Description de l'Egypte*.

1819: Mahmoudiya Canal dug.

1822: Amiriya press established.

1825: Death of al-Gabarti, historian.

1827: School of Medicine.

1830: Mosque of Mohammed Ali begun.

Ibrahim Pasha
September 1848-
November 1848

After pursuing military campaigns from Saudi Arabia to Greece, Ibrahim succeeds his father, but dies of pneumonia a few months later.

Abbas Pasha I
1848-1854

1851: Abbas attempts to forestall the implementation of a new Ottoman legal code.

1849: Shepheard's Hotel opens.
1851: Monesterly Palace built.

Said Pasha
1854-1863

1857: First Egyptian ministries established; Egyptians admitted to army officer corps.
1860: Said Pasha wins Egypt's first international loan.

1854: First telegraph line laid, between Cairo and Alexandria.
1855: First railway opens, between Cairo and Alexandria.
1859: Work begins on the Suez Canal.
1861: City of Ismailiya established.

Khedive Ismail
1863-1879

1870: Ismail begins to make forays further south into Equatorial Africa.
1874: Ismail takes up residence in Abdin Palace, quitting the Citadel that has housed Egypt's rulers since 1218.
1875: Bankrupt, Ismail is forced to sell Egypt's stake in the Suez Canal to the British.

1863: First Egyptian Museum opens in Boulaq; work on Abdin Palace begins.
1866: First Egyptian postal stamp issued.
1869: Suez Canal opens, along with the Opera House; founding of the National Library.
1872: First Qasr al-Nil bridge opens.
1873: Mosque of Hussein initiated.
1873: Death of Rifaa al-Tahtawi, educator, reformer, and father of Egyptian journalism.
1875: Mixed Courts established.

Khedive Mohammed Tawfiq
1879-1892

1882: Orabi uprising and his defeat at Tell al-Kebir; British occupation begins.
1885: Anglo-Egyptian campaign into Sudan to put down Mahdist revolt.
1890: Alexandria given the sole right to form a municipal government.

1881: First phone line laid, between Cairo and Alexandria.
1889: Edfina Barrage built.
1891: Zifta Barrage up; zoological Gardens established.

Khedive Abbas Helmi II
1892-1914

1906: Dinshaway incident.
1908: Death of Mostafa Kamel, nationalist leader.
1914: Egypt officially becomes a British protectorate; British depose Abbas while he is away receiving medical treatment in Istanbul.

1893: Death of Ali Pasha Mubarak, historian, politician, reformer.
1896: Cairo's first tramway up and running, between Ataba and Abbasiya.
1902: Inauguration of the new Egyptian Museum; Aswan Dam goes up.

1906: Baron Empain's Heliopolis is born.
1908: Cairo University (then the Egyptian University) and School of Fine Arts established.
1911: al-Rifai Mosque built.

Sultan Hussein Kamel
1914-1917

1917: Sultan deposed by the British for his pro-German sympathies.

King Fouad
1917-1936

1918: A nationalist delegation (*wafd*) to Versaille gives birth to Egypt's premier political party.
1919: Popular uprising against the British; nationalist leader Saad Zaghloul temporarily exiled to Malta.
1921: Caliphate abolished.
1922: Egypt receives limited independence.
1923: First constitution promulgated.
1924: First parliamentary elections held.
1927: Saad Zaghloul dies.

1920: Talaat Harb establishes Banque Misr.
1922: Discovery of Tutankhamun's tomb.
1923: Hoda Shaarawi casts off her face veil and later founds the Egyptian Feminist Union.
1924: Federation of Industries founded.
1928: Mahmoud Mukhtar completes "Nahdat Misr"; the statue is placed in Ramses Sq.
1932: Ahmed Shawqi, "prince of poets," dies.
1934: State Radio Service established.
1935: Talaat Harb establishes Studio Misr.

King Farouq
1936-1952

1936: Anglo-Egyptian Treaty signed, formally, if symbolically, ending the British occupation.
1942: British tanks surround Abdin Palace and force the king to accept a Wafd government.
1942: Battle of al-Alamein.
1948: Foundation of Israel; Egypt goes to war.
January 1952: Great Cairo Fire, Black Saturday.

1945: Gnostic texts discovered at Nagaa Hamadi.
1949: Hassan al-Banna, Muslim Brotherhood founder, assassinated.
1949: Mixed Courts abolished.
1950: Minister of Education Taha Hussein institutes free secondary education.

King Fouad II (Ahmed Fouad)
July 1952-June 1953
(Under control of regency council)

1952: Free Officers Revolution; Mohammed Naguib becomes Prime Minister.
January 1953: All political parties suspended.

President Mohammed Naguib
June 1953- November 1954

June 1953: The monarchy is abolished and Egypt is formally declared a republic.
July 1953: Royal properties nationalized.
March 1954: Naguib announces impending

elections; loses the post of prime minister one
month later to Gamal Abd al-Nasser.
October 1954: Lavon affair; an attempted
assassination is made against Nasser.

President Gamal Abd al-Nasser
1954-1970

November 1954: Mohammed Naguib is put
under house arrest.
1954: Anglo-Egyptian evacuation agreement
signed.
June 1956: Last British soldier leaves Egypt;
Nasser officially elected president.
July 1956: Suez Canal nationalized.
October 1956: Israel attacks Egypt.
1958-1961: Union with Syria (UAR).
1959: New Valley Land Reclamation Scheme
begun.
1967: Six-Day War.

1956: Religious courts abolished.
1960: Work on High Dam begins; TV comes to
Egypt; Cairo Tower goes up; the press is
nationalized.
1962: Maspero TV building opened.

President Anwar al-Sadat
1970-1981

1971: Corrective revolution.
1971: New constitution promulgated.
1972: Sadat expels Soviet technicians in Egypt.
1973: Egyptian forces cross the Canal Zone.
1974: Economic *infitah* begins.
1977: Bread riots.
1977: Sadat goes to Jerusalem.
1979: Peace treaty signed with Israel.
1981: Sadat assassinated.

1971: High Dam completed; Opera House
burns.
1973: Death of Taha Hussein.
1975: Death of Umm Kulthoum.
1977: Death of Abd al-Halim Hafez.

President Mohammed Hosni Mubarak
1981-present

1986: Central Security riots.
1990: Gulf War.
1991: Agreement signed with IMF; structural
adjustment begins.
1997: New land reform law goes into effect,
reversing Nasserist reforms.

1988: Naguib Mahfouz awarded Nobel Prize in
literature.
1989: First line of metro operative.
1996: Toshka project inaugurated.
1998: NileSat 1 launched; death of Sheikh
Shaarawi.
1999: Ahmed Zuweil awarded Nobel Prize in
chemistry; final phase of Sixth of October
Bridge completed.
2001: Azhar Tunnel opens.

Calendars

Nawat

Originally used by the Arabs to denote a whole system of time-keeping and weather forecast based on stellar constellations, the nawat today refer to seasonal wind storms that blow along the Mediterranean Coast. Dates may vary by a day or two.

Ras al-Sana (New Year's storm): January 2-6
West winds and rain, force 6-8

al-Fayda al-Kebira ("the great downpour"): January 9-13
Southwest winds and rain, force 6-8

al-Ghutas (storm of the Epiphany): January 18-22
Southwest winds and rain, force 6-8

al-Karam ("the generous"): January 27-February 1
Northwest winds and heavy rain, force 6-8

Tail of al-Karam: February 3-9
Northwest winds, force 6-8

al-Shams al-Sughayara ("the lesser sun"): February 14-15
Northwest winds, force 6-8

al-Salloum: March 4-6
Northwest winds and rain, force 6-8

al-Husoum ("the inauspicious"): March 8-9
Northeast or northwest winds and partly rainy, force 6-8

Tail of al-Husoum: March 14-15
Northwest and partly rainy, force 6-8

al-Shams al-Kebira ("the great sun"): March 22-24
West winds and partly rainy, force 6-8

al-Awwa ("the howler"): March 29-31
Northwest winds and partly rainy, force 6-9

Tail of al-Awwa: April 2-3
Northwest winds, force 6-7

al-Muknisa ("the broom"): November 20-23
Northwest winds and heavy rain, force 6-8

Tail of al-Muknisa: November 26-27
Northwest winds, force 5-6

al-Qasem ("the decisive"): December 4-7
Southwest winds, force 6-8

Tail of al-Qasem: December 10-11
Northwest winds, force 6-7

al-Fayda al-Sughayara ("the lesser downpour"):
December 13-14, northwest winds, force 6-7

Tail of al-Fayda al-Sughayara: December 21-22
Southwest winds, force 6-7

Eid al-Milad ("Christmas storm"): December 29-30
Northwest winds, force 6-8

Coptic Calendar

The Coptic calendar has 12 months of 30 days each, plus an intercalary month of five days. In leap years, al-Nasi has six days instead of five, and the first six months of the year start one day later. The next leap year is 2003/2004. Each month has a proverb associated with it that illustrates the calendar's links to traditional Egyptian agricultural practices.

Tut (September 11-October 10): Irrigate the fields, Tut, or get gone (*Tut, irwi wala fuut*).

Baba (October 11-November 9): Sow in Baba and harvest enough for the plunder (*zaraa Baba yighlib al-nahhaba*).

Hatour (November 10-December 9): Wheat turns golden in Hatour (*Hatour abu al-dahab al-mantur*).

Kiyak (December 10-January 8): Kiyak's dawn grows into dusk, so have breakfast before it becomes lunch (*Kiyak sabahak masak yikhalli fatourak huwwa ashak*).

Tuba (January 9-February 7): The cold of Tuba turns the maiden gray (*Tuba tisayyar al-sabiya karkouba*).

Amshir (February 8-March 9): When Amshir flies by, rise, plants, arise! (*yifout Amshir wa sir ya zaraa sir.*)

Baramhat (March 10-April 8, the first seven days of the month are called "husum," thought to be an inauspicious time for planting): Baramhat go to the fields and reap (*Baramhat rouh al-gheit wa hat*).

Baramuda (April 9-May 8): Baramuda pound the barley until there isn't a stalk standing (*Baramuda duqq al-shiir bi al-amouda wala yibqa fi al-gheit wala ouda*).

Bashans (May 9-June 7): Bashans sweeps the cupboards clean (*Bashans bi-yiknis al-beit*).

Bauna (June 8-July 7): Mix neither bricks nor mortar in Bauna (*fi Bauna la yindirib toub wala titimil mouna*).

Abib (July 8-August 6): Under Abib's spell, grapes and raisins swell (*Abib tabbakh al-inab wa al-zabib*); eating molokhiya in Abib will bring the doctor with due speed (*min yakoul al-molokhiya fi Abib yigib li batnu tabib*).

Misra (August 7-September 5):Misra's heat sours the bread (*israt Misra tiaffin al-kisra*).

al-Nasi (September 6-September 10)

Islamic Calendar

The Islamic calendar is based on a lunar year, about 11 days shorter than the solar year. However, the names of some of the months, with their references to seasons, suggest that the ancient Arabs used an intercalary period to ensure that certain months— and thus certain festivals like the annual pilgrimage—fell at approximately the same time every year. The year starts with Moharram.

Ragab (the holy month): September 9-October 7, 2002; August 29-September 27, 2003

Shaaban (the month of division): October 8-November 5, 2002; September 28-October 26, 2003

Ramadan (the month of heat): November 6-December 5, 2002; October 27-November 24, 2003

Shawwal (the month of hunting): December 6, 2002-January 3, 2003; November 25-December 24, 2003

Dhu al-Qaeda (the month of rest): January 4-February 2, 2003; December 25, 2003-January 22, 2004

Dhu al-Higga (the month of pilgrimage): February 3-March 3, 2003

Moharram (the sacred month): March 4-April 2, 2003

Safar (the void month): April 3-May 2, 2003

Rabi al-Awwal (the first spring): May 3-June 1, 2003

Rabi al-Thani (the second spring): June 2-June 30, 2003

Gumada al-Awwal (the first month of dryness): July 1-July 30, 2003

Gumada al-Thaniya (the second month of dryness): July 31-August 28, 2003

Syrian Calendar

Widely used throughout the Levant, the Syrian calendar today corresponds to the Gregorian calendar. The names of the months are derived from the Jewish calendar, which begins with October.

Kanoun al-Thani: January
Shubat: February
Azar: March
Nisan: April
Ayyar: May
Huzayran: June
Tammouz: July
Ab: August
Aylul: September
Tashrin al-Awwal: October
Tashrin al-Thani: November
Kanoun al-Awwal: December

Calendar of Events

September

1-11: 14th Cairo International Festival for Experimental Theater

2: 11th Annual Sharqiya Arabian Horse Show

9: Sharqiya National Day marks Farmer's Day, commemorating the Orabi uprising against the Khedive and the British colonialist authorities

11: Nawrouz and Coptic New Year (year 1719)

18-23: The 18th Alexandria International Film Festival

21: Autumn equinox

24: Beheira National Day

26: Daylight Savings Time begins at midnight—set your clock one hour back (last Thursday of the month)

27-October 3: Ismailiya International Festival for

Documentary and Short Films
28: Feast of the Cross
28: Anniversary of Gamal Abd al-Nasser's death

October

1: Moulid of Sayeda Zeinab (last Tuesday in Ragab), Cairo, with festivities beginning two weeks in advance
3: New Valley National Day, marking the beginning of land reclamation efforts in 1959
5: Israa wa al-Miraag (Ragab 27), commemorating the Prophet's night journey to Jerusalem and the heavens
6: Armed Forces Day, Sadat's death
7: Gharbiya National Day, celebrating the Egyptian victory over French forces at Tanta
9-20: the 26th Cairo International Film Festival
10-13: Opera Aida at the Pyramids
12: Moulid of al-Shafii (Shaaban 5), Cairo
12-24: Abu Simbel Festival marking the sun's position perpendicular to the temple
15: Fall arrives as traffic police switch to their winter black uniforms
16: Ismailiya National Day, marking local resistance against British occupation; grand opening of the Alexandria Library
21: Moulid of Abu al-Haggag (Shaaban 14), Luxor
22: Leilat al-Baraa (Shaaban 15), a day of fasting and prayers in which the year's sins are said to be forgiven
22-25: Siyaha Festival in Siwa (starts with the full moon)
23: National Liberation Day
24: Suez National Day, marking civilian engagement with Israeli troops
The moulid of al-Sayed al-Badawi in Tanta begins after the cotton harvest and is followed directly by the moulid of Abu al-Einein al-Dessouqi in Gharbiya

1-3: Intex International, ready-made garment expo, Cairo Fairgrounds
9-12: Hace Exhibition, hotel supplies and catering equipment, Cairo International Conference Center (CICC)

11-14: Progas, 5th Arab and African expo for the oil and gas industry, Cairo Fairgrounds
13-15: Annual conference of the International Public Relations Association (IPRA), JW Marriott, Mirage City Golf Resort Hotel
17-20: Arabian Stone Expo 2002, 4th international exhibition for marble, granite, and stone-processing equipment, Cairo Fairgrounds
19-22: Electrix 2002, Middle East power and energy expo, CICC
25-28: Painting and Coating 2002, 2nd pan-Arab and African expo for paints, Cairo Fairgrounds
25-November 3: Wahawee Exhibition, fair for Ramadan consumer items, CICC
27-30: Ancient Oil, New Energy, an international petroleum conference and exhibition, CICC
29-30: MEED 1st Mediterranean Petrochemicals Conference, CICC

November

1: National Fair for Plastic Arts (held every two years)
4: Egyptian Valentine's day. Also Luxor National Day, chosen to commemorate the discovery of King Tutanhkamen's tomb in 1922
6: Ramadan begins
10-16: Moulid commemorating the consecration of the Church of Saint George in Deir Mari Girgis at Ruzyqat near Luxor
25: Advent (Christmas fast) begins
11th Annual Arabic Music Festival (usually early in the month)
International Fishing Competition and Festival, Sharm al-Sheikh

2-5: Supermarket expo, international exhibition for food and beverages, CICC
14-17: Journalism XXI Century, forum for advertising, publishing, and journalism industries, Cairo Fairgrounds

December

2: Leilat al-Qadr, marking the day the Quran was first revealed (Ramadan 27)

6: Eid al-Fitr (Shawwal 1); the first Friday of the month also marks the opening of bird hunting season (until March 28, last Friday of the month)

7-12: (Shawwal 2-7); Six White Days of fasting and prayer

21: Winter solstice

23: Victory Day and Port Said National Day, marking the repulsion of British, French, and Israeli troops

15-19: Plastex 8, Arab and African exhibition for plastics and petrochemicals, Cairo Fairgrounds

15-21: Motor Show Formula 2002, international motor show, Cairo Fairgrounds

18-21: 7th national expo for interior design and lighting, CICC

22-26: Christmas fair, toys and gifts, Cairo Fairgrounds

January 2003

1: New Year's Day and Egyptian Post Day

7: Coptic Christmas

9: Aswan National Day, marking the anniversary of the construction of the High Dam

16: Proclamation of the 1971 Constitution of the Arab Republic of Egypt

19: Feast of the Epiphany

22: Red Sea National Day

25: Police Day

The two-week Cairo International Book Fair usually starts in January with the mid-year school break.

12-15: Cairo Telecomp, 6th international fair for telecommunications, IT, networking, and satellite and broadcast technology, CICC

February

3: Anniversary of Umm Kulthoum's death

4-11: Moulid of Sayed al-Shazili (Dhu al-Higga 2-9), near Mahamid, Eastern Desert

12: Eid al-Adha (Dhu al-Higga 10)

13-16: Textile Week, expo at the Cairo Fairgrounds

March

3: Lent begins and Qena celebrates its National Day, marking local victory over French expeditionary forces

4: Islamic New Year, year 1424 (Moharram 1)

8: Minya National Day and International Women's Day

13: Ashoura (Moharram 10), a day of atonement commemorating the death of Hussein at Karbala. Also said to be the day that Noah left the ark

15: Beni Sueif National Day

19: Fayyoum National Day, marking local opposition to British occupation in the 1919 revolution. Also South Sinai National Day, commemorating the day Egypt's flag was raised over Taba in 1989

21: Mother's Day and the vernal equinox

31: Giza National Day, commemorating local battle with British occupation troops

Commercial fishing in Lake Nasser is closed during March and April

6-8: Photo Egypt 2003, international image expo, CICC

15-21: Beauty Egypt 2003, international fair for cosmetics, fashion, and pharmaceuticals, in front of the pyramids

18-21: Mother's Day Festival, CICC

April

1: April Fool's Day. Also the annual commemoration of the death of singer Abd al-Halim Hafez

7: Feast of the Annunciation

10: Sohag National Day

15: Traffic police switch to their summer white uniforms

18: Assyout National Day

20: Palm Sunday

23: The Greek Orthodox feast of St. George (the Panegyris)

24: Holy Thursday; daylight savings time ends at midnight (last Thursday of the month)—set your clock forward one hour

25: Sinai Liberation Day, commemorating the return of the peninsula to Egypt; also Good Friday

27: Coptic Easter
28: Sham al-Nessim
Commercial fishing in Lake Nasser is closed during April

24-27: Red Sea Hotel and Restaurant Expo, the Pharaoh Resort in Hurghada

May

1: Labor Day
7: Daqahliya National Day
8: Damietta National Day
12-20: Moulid of St. Damiana at the Convent of St. Damiana, near Bilqas, Delta
14: Moulid al-Nabi, the Prophet's birthday (Rabi al-Awwal 12)
30-June 5: Moulid at the Monastery of St. George in Fayyoum, in celebration of the Feast of the Ascension
Commercial fishing in the Mediterranean Sea is closed during May and June
Moulid of Fatma al-Nabawiya usually occurs on the 3rd or 4th Monday of Rabi al-Awwal (May 19 or 26)

5-7: Mefsec 2003, fire and security exhibition at the CICC

June

5: Feast of the Ascension
5-15: Large moulid at Gabal al-Teir in anticipation of Pentecost
15: Pentecost
16: The Apostle's Fast begins (until July 12)
18: Evacuation Day, celebrating the exit of British colonial troops from Egypt in 1956
21: Summer solstice
21-28: Moulid at al-Muharraq Monastery, commemorating the establishment of the first church of the Virgin at Philippi
24: Moulid of Hussein (last Tuesday in Rabi al-Thani), Cairo, Festivities begin up to two weeks in advance
Both the Modern Dance Theater Festival and the Cairo Oriental Dance Festival are usually held in June every year

July

6: Cairo Day, marking the founding of al-Qahira by the Fatimid general Jawhar in 969
12: Feast of the Apostles
23: Revolution Day, 51st anniversary of the Free Officers revolution
31: Moulid of Aba Anub of Samanud, near to Tanta

3-6: IT Wireless Fair, international IT fair, Cairo Fairgrounds
20-August 20: The annual Shopping and Tourism Festival

August

14: Dormition fast begins
19: Transfiguration
22: Feast of the Assumption, with Coptic moulids all over Egypt in the two weeks preceding the feast. Major moulids and pilgrimage sites: Durunka Monastery near Assyout (7-22), Musturud near Matariya (7-22), the Monastery of the Holy Virgin in Fayyoum (15-22), Deir al-Garnus north of Bahnasa (21-22), and the Church of the Holy Virgin at Gabal al-Teir (7-22).
24: Matrouh National Day
15th Annual Youth Salon (usually opens at the end of the month)

September

9: Sharqiya National Day marks Farmer's Day, commemorating the Orabi uprising against the Khedive and the British colonial authorities
12: Nawrouz and Coptic New Year (year 1720 is a leap year)
21: Autumn equinox
23: Moulid of Sayeda Zeinab (last Tuesday in Ragab), Cairo, with festivities beginning two weeks in advance
24: Beheira National Day; al-Israa wa al-Miraag (Ragab 27), commemorating the Prophet's night journey to Jerusalem and the heavens
25: Daylight Savings Time begins at midnight—set your clock one hour back (last Thursday of the month)

28: Feast of the Cross

28: Anniversary of Gamal Abd al-Nasser's death

15th Cairo International Festival for Experimental Theater (usually opens at the first of the month)

1-4: IAAPW 2003, international paper, printing, and packaging fair, CICC

4-7: Leather, footwear and clothing expo, Cairo Fairgrounds

23-26: Sahara 2003, exhibit for agriculture products and equipment, CICC

October

2: Moulid of al-Shafii (Shaaban 5), Cairo

3: New Valley National Day, marking the beginning of land reclamation efforts in 1959

6: Armed Forces Day, Sadat's death

7: Gharbiya National Day, celebrating Egyptian victory over French forces at Tanta

11: Moulid of Abu al-Haggag (Shaaban 14), Luxor

12: Leilat al-Baraa (Shaaban 15), a day of fasting and prayers in which the year's sins are said to be forgiven

12-15: Siyaha Festival in Siwa (starts with the full moon)

12-24: Abu Simbel Festival marking the sun's position perpendicular to the temple

15: Traffic police switch to their winter black uniforms

16: Ismailiya National Day, marking local resistance against British occupation

23: National Liberation Day

24: Suez National Day, marking civilian engagement with Israeli troops

27: Ramadan begins

Moulid of al-Sayed al-Badawi, Tanta, begins after the cotton harvest and is followed directly by the moulid of Abu al-Einein al-Dessouqi, Gharbiya

Opera Aida at the Pyramids

3-6: World of Children Exhibition, Cairo Fairgrounds

November

4: Luxor National Day, chosen to commemorate the discovery of King Tutankhamen's tomb in 1922. Also Egyptian Valentine's day

10-16: Moulid commemorating the consecration of the Church of Saint George in Deir Mari Girgis at Ruzyqat near Luxor

22: Leilat al-Qadr, marking the day the Quran was first revealed (Ramadan 27)

25: Advent (Christmas fast) begins

25: Eid al-Fitr (Shawwal 1)

26-December 1: Six White Days (Shawwal 2-7), marked by fasting and prayer

12th Annual Arabic Music Festival (usually early in the month)

International Fishing Competition and Festival, Sharm al-Sheikh

December

5: The first Friday of the month marks the opening of bird hunting season (until March 28, last Friday of the month)

21: Winter solstice

25: Western Christmas

23: Port Said National Day, marking the repulsion of British, French, and Israeli troops

6-9: Automechanical Africa 2003, Cairo Fairgrounds

14-17: Electricx 2003, electrical equipment exhibition, CICC

22-26: Christmas Fair, Cairo Fairgrounds

Note: Trade fairs compiled with the help of Fianni & Partners.
Excepting national holidays, dates do change, venues get moved, and events are cancelled at the last minute. It is best to confirm the exact dates of trade fairs and cultural events in advance. The dates given for Islamic holidays are based on the lunar calendar, and thus may vary by a day or two. Moulids, both Muslim and Christian, are also fluid, and may involve festivities that stretch over several days, both before and after the main feast day.

Countdown to 2003

January 2001

The year kicks off with the strict enforcement of the **new traffic law**. More than 3,000 people in Cairo are ticketed on January 1 for not wearing their seatbelts.

A minor culture war erupts on January 2 when Muslim Brother MP Gamal Heshmat submits a formal request for clarification to Minister of Culture Farouq Hosni over three novels published by the ministry that allegedly fly in the face of public morality. One week later, Hosni bans the three books and fires the head of the General Authority of Culture Palaces, Ali Abu Shadi, for allowing their publication.

On January 3, a group of Egyptian businessmen, doctors, and artists land in Baghdad on a humanitarian aid mission.

On January 4, it is announced that Egypt has received a $200-million loan from the World Bank to finance development, social security, and technology programs. France Telecom buys 21.5% of Motorola's 35.5% stake in MobiNil for LE66 per share, increasing its stake in the company to 71.25%.

On January 6, Tagammu MP al-Badri Farghali asks Prime Minister Atef Ebeid to demand an official inquiry into the deaths of Egyptian prisoners of war held by Israel in the 1956 and 1967 wars.

Egypt's Copts celebrate **Christmas** on January 7, as Pope Shenouda leads the traditional mass at St. Mark's Cathedral in Abbasiya.

On January 8, an administrative court issues a ruling declaring the results of November 2000's parliamentary elections invalid in seven districts.

The Egyptian pound is trading at LE3.76-3.77 on the dollar at local banks on January 10, and LE3.96-3.97 at exchange bureaus.

On January 11, the British Blue Circle Cement, owner of Alexandria Cement, announces that it has accepted Lafarge Cement's offer of $4.6 billion to buy Blue Circle. The deal makes Lafarge the world's largest cement producer and increases its share of the Egyptian market to 15%. The Central Bank releases $250 million to meet foreign currency needs. Demand had gone up after Prime Minister Atef Ebeid said that the bank's reserves were "not going to be touched." The exchange rate rises as well, reaching LE4.06 on the dollar.

On January 14, Egypt meets Libya on the soccer field for the first time in 23 years, and the Pharaohs win 4-0.

A high state security court sentences Mohammed Bahgat and Mohammed al-Shimi to 15 and 10 years in prison on January 15 for their part in the Aswan Steel scandal. Both are convicted of forging documents to obtain bank loans for an iron-ore mining project. The government detains 16 Bahais in Sohag, later charging them with debauchery.

On January 16, Minister of Culture Farouq Hosni's former secretary Mohammed Foda is sentenced to five years in prison for accepting bribes.

On January 17, the People's Assembly ratifies an Egyptian-Qatari investment agreement, and the following day Egypt and Iraq sign a **free trade accord**.

Famed criminal attorney Farid al-Dib announces on January 18 that his clients, the Sadat family, are raising a libel suit against the Nasserist paper *al-Arabi* for $1.3 million. The paper had called former President Anwar al-Sadat "the greatest traitor" of the 20th century in its special millennial issue. The Sadat family drops its suit a month later after the paper publishes a retraction.

On January 19, the two-day conference of the Euro-Mediterranean Chambers of Commerce is postponed after the Egyptian chamber refuses to invite Israel to the Cairo meeting.

On January 20, the High Administrative Court dissolves the board of directors of the Azhar Scholars Front, a long-time thorn in the side of the official Azhar establishment. The 17th annual Cairo International Children's Book Fair opens, featuring 686 publishers from 47 countries with 2.8 million books on display.

On **January 22**, five exchange bureaus are closed for violating foreign exchange rules. The move comes as part of the government's efforts to crack down on incipient black market trading in dollars.

On **January 24**, President Mubarak inaugurates the 33rd annual **Cairo International Book Fair**, with more than 85 countries and 2,700 publishers participating. The threat of some intellectuals to boycott the fair comes to naught.

Egypt celebrates Police Day on **January 25**, while Israeli public television announces that Israel has accepted Egypt's bid to supply it with 1.7 billion m³ annually of natural gas for ten years.

On **January 26**, EgyptAir announces that it will settle the claims of families of the victims of **flight 990**, which crashed under mysterious circumstances off the US coast in 1999. The airline maintains its position of denying responsibility for the crash. Egypt commemorates the Palestinian Aqsa intifada with the release of three new postal stamps, one featuring a picture of Mohammed al-Durra.

Little-known writer Salah al-Din Mohsen is sentenced to three years in jail on **January 27** for publishing novels accused of belittling religion.

On **January 28**, Egypt, Lebanon, Syria, and Jordan sign a deal estimated at $1 billion for the sale and transport of **natural gas**.

On **January 29**, the Central Bank announces a long-awaited currency devaluation, setting the **pound** at **3.85 to the dolla**r and implementing a new managed peg system.

February 2001

On **February 4**, the webmaster for the Central Bank says the bank's website has been vandalized by hackers, who allegedly left a message in Portuguese. Part of the message read: "Ha-ha, and you still say Brazilians are stupid."

On **February 7**, a criminal court in Shebin al-Kom convicts four prison officials in the case of a prisoner who was tortured to death. The verdict comes one day after prisoner rights group HRCAP issues its annual report on the state of Egyptian prisons.

Culture minister Farouq Hosni upsets Minister of Education Hussein Kamel Baha al-Din on **February 10** when he suggests before the parliamentary culture committee that **sexual education** classes be introduced in schools.

On **February 12**, Africa Online, one of **Africa's largest ISPs**, acquires the local ISP MenaNet Communications in a deal totaling $8.7 million, hoping to extend its reach in North Africa.

US Ambassador to Egypt Daniel Kurtzer announces on **February 14** that the US has officially lifted its travel warning for US citizens visiting Upper Egypt. The warning had expired in late January.

On **February 11**, archaeologists in the Saqqara necropolis announce that they have uncovered the **tomb of Merire**, a high priest under Akhenaten. The finding sheds new light on the political and religious upheavals of the Amarna period (when Akhenaten introduced monotheism as the state religion), showing how professional priests adapted to the changing climes. Chipsy Food Industries sells 28 million shares to Chipsy International in a deal worth $144 million. The sale gives the latter 70% of the local potato chip market.

On **February 18**, head of the Supreme Council of Antiquities Gaballa Ali Gaballa announces that archaeologists have uncovered **6,000-year-old rock drawings** of the Goddess Hathor on Mount Nabta, located in the southern Western Desert only a few kilometers from the earliest known human settlements in Egypt. Islamist writer Mohammed Abbas is cleared of charges of incitement, brought for an article he wrote against Syrian novelist Haydar Haydar's work *A Banquet for Seaweed*. The article provoked massive student riots in 2000.

On **February 20**, the highway connecting **Abu Simbel** with Aswan reopens after a three-year closure.

The government kicks off its international privatization tour in London on **February 22**, showcasing 13 companies slated for sale by 2003, including Omar Effendi, Haneaux, Shepheard's Hotel, Amoun Hotel, and some subsidiaries of the Holding Company for Chemical Industries.

The second round of voting in the **Law Syndicate elections** ends on February 24 with the election of Nasserist lawyer Sameh Ashour as syndicate head. The election ends the five-year government-enforced sequestration of the syndicate.

The D8 summit is held in Cairo on February 25, with the leaders of eight developing countries coming together to discuss economic and technological cooperation. The Supreme Council of Antiquities withdraws permission given to a Japanese university to extract DNA samples from King Tut's mummy. Head of the SCA Gaballa Ali Gaballa cites security concerns as the cause.

Al-Ahram Beverages announces on February 27 that it has acquired its sole competitor, Gouna Beverages, in a **buyout** worth LE225 million. The move puts ABC in a position of total dominance over the local beer market.

On February 28, Kuwaiti princess in residence, the notorious Hind al-Fassi, is sentenced in absentia to three years in prison for her involvement in a jewel theft. She remains at large in the Ramses Hilton hotel.

March 2001

The completion of restoration work on the 13th-century wall paintings at St. Anthony's Monastery is officially marked on March 1.

On March 3, President Mubarak releases 800 prisoners in his annual Eid pardon.

Egyptians celebrate the first day of **Eid al-Adha** on March 5.

On March 6, four Syrians are caught at Cairo Airport attempting to smuggle in 15,000 Viagra tablets. *Al-Ahram* estimates that the black-market trade in the anti-impotence drug is about LE7 billion every year, although Ministry of Health estimates are much lower.

Mufti Nasr Farid Wassel travels to Afghanistan on March 10 in an attempt to persuade the Taliban to halt their destruction of the **Bamiyan Buddhas**, the tallest Buddha statues in the world.

Wafd president Noman Gomaa creates a stir on March 11 when he expels Ayman Nour and Farid Hassanein from the party following a scuffle at the party's Doqqi headquarters. Both Nour and Hassanein are parliamentarians.

March 13 sees the opening ceremony of the 11th Cairo International Film Festival for Children.

On March 14, the presidents of Syria, Egypt, and Jordan inaugurate the $300-million **electricity grid** linking the three nations. Turkey, Lebanon, and Iraq will connect to the network in the coming years. The project enables any of the participating countries to use the common electricity grid in case of an emergency in their own system.

The Cairo downtown arts festival, **al-Nitaq**, kicks off its second year on March 15.

On March 17, the **new trading floor** of the Cairo bourse is opened to much fanfare after three years of renovations and upgrades costing almost $7 million. Officials hope the state-of-the-art trading floor will lead to more transparency in transactions and boost the flagging stock market. Elections proceed for the **Magles al-Milli**, the Coptic Community Council. Eight defendants are convicted in the case of the radioactive cylinder found in the village of Mit Halfa in June. The "lost" object was found by a local family and caused the death of two people.

On March 19, in a retrial of the so-called "loan deputies" case, a state security court releases the defendants on bail after having spent a year and a half in prison. In January, the Court of Cassation had allowed a retrial of the case, which saw the conviction in July 2000 of 31 businessmen, bankers, and MPs on charges of fraudulently obtaining bank loans totaling $450 million.

On March 20, the US Commission on International Religious Freedom kicks off its regional tour with a visit to Egypt, sparking controversy and a boycott among the majority of Egypt's intellectuals and civil society groups. A week later, Presidential Advisor Osama al-Baz says that Egypt will no longer receive such commissions, adding that religious freedom in Egypt is an internal affair. An administrative court issues its eighth ruling authorizing the banned Islamist *al-Shaab* to reappear. At Cairo

Airport, police arrest Mohammed Mursi Omar, son of Medhat Mursi Omar, who is thought to be a close associate of Saudi terrorist Osama Bin Laden.

On **March 21**, Mother's Day, 11 **Roman-era mummies** are found in Bahariya Oasis, adding to the cache of more than 300 found there since 1999. The number of the mummies unearthed in the area and the riches found in the tombs indicate that Bahariya was a large, prosperous settlement during the Roman era.

On **March 22**, an Alexandria court orders a French school to pay $160,000 in damages to the family of 12-year old Azza Mohammed Zaki, expelled for wearing a head scarf, and states that the school must open its doors to Zaki.

The Supreme Council of Antiquities institutes a **new horse-riding policy** at the Giza Plateau on **March 24**, charging entrance fees and prohibiting night rides into the desert.

On **March 27**, leaders from across the Arab world convene for a summit in Amman amid growing pressure to support the Palestinian intifada.

The **March 29** issue of *Construction News* awards its prestigious International Performance of the Year Award to the project team that built the **Alexandria Library**. The award committee commends the multi-cultural, collaborative approach taken by the library contractors.

On **March 30**, Islamist pundit Fahmi Howeidi publishes an article in *al-Wafd*

accusing journalists of taking bribes in exchange for favorable coverage. The accusation sparks a heated press debate.

On **March 31**, **khamasin** winds cause a road accident in Fayyoum that leaves six dead. The former vice-chairman of the General Authority for Supply Commodities, Sami Shaqanqiri, loses a libel case against Minister of Supply and Internal Trade Hassan Khidr. Khidr had publicly accused Shaqanqiri of purchasing wheat unfit for consumption.

April 2001

Egyptians commemorate the death of crooner Abd al-Halim Hafez on **April 1**, as radio and TV blast out the former idol's songs and films. Sheikh of al-Azhar Mohammed Sayed al-Tantawi issues a fatwa against surrogate mothers, calling it a violation of the bonds of matrimony.

On **April 2**, President Mubarak arrives for his annual **visit to Washington**, becoming the first Arab leader to meet the new US president, George Bush. Back in Egypt, students at Ain Shams University stage a **protest against Israel**. The next day, students at Cairo University follow suit, burning Israeli flags

On **April 3**, the European Investment Bank announces that it will give Egypt an **EU36-million loan** to boost business and technology. A week later, the bank gives Egypt LE300,000 for a study on the reduction of rice-straw burning, said to cause the seasonal black cloud of pollution that hovers over

Cairo every fall.

On **April 5**, Minister of Information Technology and Communications Ahmed Nazif signs an agreement with software giant Microsoft to eliminate **software piracy** and beef up Egypt's governmental networks.

The government releases its budget for 2001/02 on **April 8**, to be put before the parliament later in the week. The budget raises total expenditure LE14 billion to LE126 billion, including LE15 billion for infrastructure development. The government says it wants to reduce the deficit to 3.4% of GDP in the coming year.

After much speculation in the local press, UK supermarket chain **Sainsbury's** announces on **April 9** that it will pull out of Egypt, selling its 80% stake to a minority partner and losing about £100-124 million. Analysts blame the supermarket's failure on too rapid expansion and complex import procedures. Since moving into the local market in 2000, the chain has also been subject to an on-and-off boycott based on rumors that it is Jewish- or Israeli-owned. The store has 111 outlets in the country and employs some 5,000 Egyptians.

On **April 11**, Pope Shenouda criticizes the lack of Arab support for the Palestinian intifada in an interview with the weekly *Musawwar*.

On **April 12**, lawyer Nabih al-Wahsh sues to have writer Nawal al-Saadawi divorced from her husband on the grounds that she is an apostate, based on remarks she made to the local *al-Midan* the month before. Among other things, al-Saadawi called the pilgrimage to Mecca a leftover of pagan ritual. A personal status court later rejects the suit.

On April 14, environment minister Nadia Makram Ebeid announces that her office will no longer hire smokers.

Egyptians sniff the breeze on April 16 with the arrival of **Sham al-Nessim**.

On April 17, a merger is announced between EVC, owner of 20 cinemas and the rights to distribute MGM, Universal, and Dreamworks pictures in Egypt, and the Arab Company for Arts and Publishing (Funoun), a LE500-million company and currently Egypt's largest film producer. The deal is worth LE70 million and will increase Funoun's hold on the film market.

Sara Shahin is chosen as the new **Miss Egypt** on April 18.

Pope Shenouda begins a US tour on April 19. A parliamentary confrontation on April 21 leads to a walkout by the Muslim Brother bloc. Speaker Fathi Surour refused to give them the floor to deliver an urgent statement about police harassment of Brother candidates standing in the Shura elections. Dar al-Kutub inaugurates its website on April 23.

On April 25, thousands flock to the Pyramids for a concert with **Sting**, Hakim, Cheb Mami, and Alyssa. The night ends in fiasco following major logistical problems and a walkout by Hakim, who arrives late and is unable to perform his set.

May 2001

May 2 kicks off a month-long **Francophilic festival** of arts and culture in Cairo, with *Les Francais aiment le Caire*. Organized by the city of Paris and the Cairo governorate, the festival features exhibitions, concerts, lectures, and conferences all over town, celebrating one thousand years of Umm al-Dunya.

On May 3, head of the Journalists' Syndicate and *al-Ahram* editor-in-chief Ibrahim Nafie says he is withdrawing his libel suit against fellow journalist Mohammed Abu Liwaya, already serving a one-month prison term following his conviction.

The Supreme Constitutional Court strikes again on May 6 when it declares unconstitutional a decree requiring cabinet approval for the licensing of any independent local publication. Egypt gets one step closer to the World Cup 2002 when it **beats Senegal 1-0**.

On May 7, CAPMAS announces that the population of Egypt reached **66.6 million** at the end of 2000, a 2.1% increase over the previous year.

On May 8, Presidential Advisor Osama al-Baz denies Israeli allegations that Egypt is smuggling arms to Palestinians.

On May 12, **khamasin** winds rage, causing the closure of Cairo Airport and two ports in Alexandria.

On May 13, the Nile Pharmaceutical Company announces that it will start distributing two generic drugs to treat AIDS and leukemia. The drugs will be 40% less than their rival name-brand products.

On May 14, Mufti Nasr Farid Wassel issues a **fatwa against beauty pageants**. The Middle East Oil Refinery (MIDOR) receives its first major tender, for 12 million barrels of crude. The first privately owned operation in Egypt, it started full production in April despite growing disquiet over Israeli participation. A new trading system goes into effect on the Egyptian bourse. The Automated Trading System will streamline clearing and settlement procedures by handling them electronically. The LE6-million system will enable the exchange to speed up its current settlement cycle, bringing it in line with European and American exchanges.

About 100 people gather outside the Arab League building on May 15 to protest on the 53rd anniversary of the founding of Israel. Ahmed Maher is sworn in as Egypt's **new foreign minister**. The next day, former foreign minister Amr Moussa takes up his post as the new head of the Arab League. One of his first acts is to appoint Palestinian politician Hanan Ashrawi as the League's Media Commissioner. The first of the three-stage Shura Council elections begin.

President Mubarak tells journalists on May 20 that the situation in the Middle East may have reached "a point of no return" after Israel launches F-16 attacks on Palestinians towns.

On May 21, the four-month trial of civil society activist and sociologist **Saad Eddin Ibrahim** draws to a close with the conviction of Ibrahim and his 27 co-defendants. Ibrahim, founder and head of the Ibn Khaldoun Center for Developmental Studies, is sentenced to seven years in prison for tarnishing Egypt's reputation abroad and alleged financial misdeeds. The verdict sparks an outcry from local and international human rights' organizations.

Representatives of the 20 member-countries of COMESA meet in Cairo on May 22 for their sixth summit, while the head of EgyptAir, Mohammed Fahim Rayan, meets with a group from Boeing to further discuss the October 1999 crash of flight 990.

On May 23, the Egyptian Historical Society inaugurates its new headquarters in Nasr City. The society, founded in 1945, has been homeless since it was forced to vacate its old offices downtown several years ago. The new building is funded by Emirati Sultan Ibn Mohammed al-Qasimi.

On May 24, the Writers' Syndicate votes to expel renowned playwright Ali Salem for his support of normalization of ties with Israel.

On May 28, drinking water contaminated with sewage causes over one hundred villagers near Zaqaziq to fall ill. The press publishes a prime ministerial decree announcing the state's eminent domain over the houses and farmland on **Dahab and Warraq Islands**, the home of about 60,000 informal residents. Amid rumors that the land will be turned over to developers, protest from parliament, island residents, and the larger public leads to the temporary suspension of the decree. The Central Bank raises the exchange rate to LE3.86 on the dollar, and an early **summer heat wave** hits its peak, as temperatures in Cairo register a high of 43 degrees.

On May 29, the officially disbanded Azhar Scholar's Front issues a statement condemning a book by Khaled Abd al-Karim, the so-called "red sheikh," as heretical.

On May 30, Egypt signs an agreement with Jordan to build a **natural gas pipeline** from Arish through the Gulf of Aqaba. The proposed pipeline will ultimately carry 12 million m^3 of gas per day from Egypt to Jordan, Syria, and Lebanon. A Luxor judge is sentenced to five years in prison for accepting a bribe. The Israeli investment firm Merhav announces that it has sold its 18% stake in **MIDOR**, Egypt's first privately operated oil refinery.

On May 31, Egypt is included on Morgan Stanley's Index of Emerging Markets, and McDonald's Egypt introduces the **McFalafel** sandwich, sold for LE1.50. Local phenomenon Shaaban Abd al-Rehim sings the TV jingle, which is later canned, allegedly following protests from US Jewish groups, who object to Abd al-Rehim's hit song *I Hate Israel*.

June 2001

On June 1, *Science* magazine reveals the discovery of an amphibious dinosaur in Bahariya in 1999, the **second largest dinosaur** known to have walked the earth. The article estimates that the animal, weighing about 65 tons, lived about 150 million years ago. Egyptians celebrate **moulid al-nabi**, the Prophet Mohammed's birthday. As part of the government's anti-smoking campaign, Cairo governor Abd al-Rehim Shehata issues a decree banning youth under the age of 18 from the city's coffee shops.

On June 6, NDP parliamentarian Fawzi al-Sayed is charged with misappropriations of LE28 million. The so-called "whale of Nasr City," who owns about 40 apartment buildings in Nasr City, allegedly forged construction licenses in order to avoid paying contracting fees owed to the state. He is later convicted and sentenced to three years in prison.

On June 7 a team of French explorers diving in Alexandria's waters present their latest finds, including a large black granite stele, a black basalt royal statue, and several pink granite statues.

Microsoft and LinkdotNet sign an

agreement on June 11 to create a regional megaportal, **MSN Arabia**, run from Cairo. Modeled after Microsoft's other regional portals, the site will include the popular Hotmail email program in Arabic, as well as general content for Arab users.

An earthquake briefly shakes Cairo on June 12, measuring 4.9 on the Richter scale.

On June 13, alleged spy Sherif al-Filali is acquitted before a state security court after a six-month trial. Filali had been accused of providing sensitive military information to Israel.

The final results of the **Shura Council elections** are announced, with the NDP taking 74 of the available 88 seats. Interior Minister Habib al-Adli says that voter turnout was somewhere between 10-20%. EgyptAir challenges the preliminary finding of the NTSB regarding the 1999 crash of flight 990. The NTSB argues that co-pilot Gamil al-Batuti downed the plane on purpose.

On June 15, Alexandria kicks off its 12-day cultural walk, a multi-faceted cultural offering featuring music, dance, theater, film, art, and poetry readings.

On June 17, 3,000 Coptic protestors clash with police at **St. Mark's Cathedral** after local rag *al-Nabaa* publishes the story of a monk's alleged sexual escapades with married women, complete with pictures. The fallout from the scandal continues in coming months. In July, an administrative court revokes the publishing license of *al-*

Nabaa and its sister publication *Akher Khabar*, while in September, *al-Nabaa* **publisher Mamdouh Mahran** is sentenced to three years in prison for inciting hatred of Copts, undermining public order, and publishing offensive material. Mahran claims that he had simply published excerpts from a video tape that had been circulating informally in Assyout. The People's Assembly passes the Real Estate Financing Law—the so-called **"mortgage law"**—after more than three years on the table. The bill had been criticized by some deputies for ignoring low-income families, but others hope that it will give a shot in the arm to the depressed housing market.

The country grieves on June 23 after 1960s screen sweetheart **Soad Hosni** falls to her death from the sixth floor of a London apartment. The same day, a fire in a ceramic tile factory in Ushim, 100 km south of Cairo, leaves 19 dead. Culture minister Farouq Hosni announces the annual state awards in literature, the arts, and the sciences.

Speaking before the opening session of the Shura Council, Mubarak says on June 24 that judicial rulings against certain MPs need to be respected and implemented. In Assyout, 15,000 people gather for a moulid at the Muharraq Monastery, the site of the alleged sexual scandal published by *al-Nabaa*.

On June 26, and after much foot-dragging, Egypt finally ratifies its **partnership agreement** with the EU.

On June 28 the 3,500-year-old tomb of Pharaoh Nub-Kheper-Re is discovered with the help of papyrus documents.

July 2001

On July 1, the second and third levels of the **general sales tax** go into effect, with consumers complaining of rising prices and merchants worrying about a decline in sales. The tax, which ranges from 10-40%, will be levied on retailers and wholesalers of certain goods who sell more than LE150,000 worth of merchandise every year. Elections at the Journalists' Syndicate see government editor Ibrahim Nafie selected once more to head the syndicate.

On July 2, Mufti Nasr Farid Wassel issues a fatwa against TV game shows, saying they are akin to gambling, which is forbidden in Islam. Less than a month later, Sheikh of al-Azhar Mohammed Sayed al-Tantawi answers with his own fatwa, declaring such shows to be lawful. The 7th annual Cairo Festival for Radio and Television opens.

On July 3, the official exchange rate goes up to **LE3.90 on the dollar**.

Cairo celebrates the birth of the city on July 6 during Cairo Day, a holiday instituted two years ago to mark the founding of al-Qahira by the Fatimid general Jawhar in 969.

On July 11, the Cyprus government announces that it will revoke the licenses of all offshore publications that do not adhere to its press law, a move that affects dozens of independent Egyptian publications licensed on the Mediterranean island. Egypt and Italy sign an agreement that will funnel $147 million of Egyptian debt into development projects.

On July 15, **protests break out** in nine governorates after the government issues new minimum age requirements for public employment. Prime Minister Atef Ebeid later rescinds the order in the face of public outcry. British Petroleum announces that about 15 billion m^3 of gas has been discovered off the Mediterranean Coast in its North Alexandria concession, raising Egypt's already sizeable reserves. The trial of Sayed Ragab al-Sawirki begins. The millionaire retail owner stands accused of keeping more than the legal limit of four wives at one time. In Germany, Egypt rowing duo Akram Abd al-Shafei and al-Bakri Yehya walk away with the bronze medal in the World Rowing Championship.

On July 16, President Mubarak inaugurates the new Supreme Constitutional Court building on the Nile Corniche in Cairo, and police arrest 25 Muslim Brothers, charging them with trying to overthrow the government.

Thousands flock to Hussein Square on July 17 in celebration of the **moulid of Hussein**, the Prophet's grandson. President Mubarak implements a governorate shuffle, naming several high-ranking officers to top civilian posts.

On July 21, head of the Supreme Council of Antiquities Gaballa Ali Gaballa announces that several smuggled antiquities are being returned from Britain, including the head of 19th Dynasty Queen Merit. The antiquities arrive a few days later. Egypt's hopes for a trip to the **World Cup** 2002 are dashed when the Pharaohs tie with Algeria and Senegal beats Namibia.

On July 24, Egypt increases its police force at the border town of Rafah as Israeli security prevents hundreds of Palestinians from entering the Gaza Strip.

On July 27, Foreign Minister Ahmed Maher denies a report on the Qatari Jazeera network that Egypt is considering political and economic sanctions against Israel.

On July 30, the Court of Cassation overturns the verdict in the so-called **Kosheh trial**, named for the Upper Egyptian village that in early 2000 saw sectarian clashes that left 22 people dead. In the first trial, 92 of 96 defendants were acquitted and released amidst cries of protest among Egypt's Coptic community.

Outgoing Israeli ambassador to Egypt Zvi Mazel directs an attack on the Egyptian press at a press conference on July 31 prior to his departure.

August 2001

In mid-month, the Auberge des Pyramids, established in 1943, is razed to the ground, marking the destruction of another venerable landmark of Cairo's *ancien regime*. A favorite hangout of King Farouq, in its heyday the nightclub played host to the best in foreign and local entertainment, drawing an eclectic, if elite crowd. Damaged by the Cairo fire in 1952 and later during the bread riots of 1977, the Auberge finally closed its doors in 1986 following the Central Security forces riots.

On August 3, 2,000 people rally outside al-Azhar and Hussein mosques after Friday prayers in support of the Palestinian intifada.

On August 4, Egypt's Ahli team trounces **Real Madrid** before a disbelieving audience. The same day, Wafd MP Seif Mahmoud leaves the party and the Wafd's parliamentary bloc shrinks to four.

On August 5, the Central Bank **devalues the pound** by 6.5%, raising it to LE4.15 on the dollar and widening the legal trading band to plus or minus 3%. *Al-Ahram* celebrates its 125th anniversary. Egypt announces that the World Bank is providing a $400-million grant to upgrade education and infrastructure. The so-called Arkadia murder trial draws to a close, as the court sentences Omar al-Hawari to life imprisonment for the April murder of Mahmoud Rawhi. The murder, which took place at an upscale nightclub in the Arkadia Mall, had attracted much press attention due to the upper-class background of those involved—the 37-year-old Rawhi was the head of Hertz rental cars in Egypt, while al-Hawari, 29, was a successful businessman.

The Central Bank on August 7 injects $59 million into the banking sector in an attempt to meet the **rising demand for dollars.** It says it will release further reserves in coming days, though no exact figure is given. The average exchange rate at local banks is LE4.20 on the dollar.

Princess Hind al-Fassi makes headlines again on August 12 when she is acquitted on charges of spending the salaries of 50 of her employees. The Telecom Regulatory Authority meets to determine the licensing fee to be paid by Egypt Telecom to operate the country's third GSM network. The fee is set at LE1.975 billion. MobiNil and Click each paid $516 million, or LE1.755 billion, to obtain their licenses.

Following Israel's occupation of Orient House, the Egyptian Doctors' Syndicate holds a symbolic strike in solidarity with Palestinians on August 13. In the occupied territories, Israeli soldiers beat up an Egyptian TV news crew. The incident is broadcast on the local news.

On August 14, the Central Bank says that it has released $150 million into the banking sector over the last week to fill the need for foreign currency. The bank says it used its internal resources and did not touch foreign exchange reserves.

A court sentences tour guide Ibrahim Moussa to 15 years in prison on August 16 for kidnapping four German tourists in Luxor earlier in the year.

Moussa held the tourists hostage for three days before releasing them, claiming he wanted to go to Germany to see his kids, taken there against his will by his German wife. President Mubarak later commutes his sentence.

The **new US ambassador** to Egypt, David Welch, arrives in Cairo on August 17, replacing Daniel Kurtzer, who was posted as the US ambassador to Israel. Welch has already served in US missions in Jordan, Syria, and Saudi Arabia.

On August 19, the Political Parties Committee freezes the marginal Wifaq al-Qawmi party following internal disputes among the leadership.

The week-long Seventh Cairo International Song Festival opens on August 20.

On August 21, Azhar's Center for Islamic Research okays the first feature cartoon on the Prophet Mohammed's life. The film is to appear in both Arabic and English. The Ahram Beverage Company signs a lucrative deal with Saudi Dairy and Foodstuff Company (SADAFCO) to distribute its non-alcoholic Fayrouz and Birell. Minister of Tourism Mamdouh al-Beltagui announces that **three million tourists** have already visited Egypt during the first seven months of the year, a record.

On August 22, more than 100 families living in the Bab al-Nasr cemetery are given notice to evacuate their homes, which will be razed to make way for a road linking Port Said

Street with Salah Salem.

The international ratings agency Fitch says on August 23 that it has cut Egypt's long-term currency rating in light of overruns on investment and a higher budget deficit.

On August 26, Israeli forces start building a sandbag wall on the Egyptian border, following several stray bullet incidents since the start of the intifada.

On August 28, 25 private banks raise the price of the dollar to LE4.27, the maximum limit allowed by the Central Bank, in an attempt to close the gap between the official and black market exchange rates. Two days later, Minister of Economy and Foreign Trade Youssef Boutros Ghali says that the devaluation of the pound has not raised inflation rates, but it has increased Egypt's exports by 22%.

September 2001

September 1 sees the opening of the 10th Annual Sharqiya Arabian Horse Show and the 13th Cairo International Experimental Theater Festival.

Sinai White Cement Company begins production on September 4. Churning out 410,000 tons of clinker annually, it is the world's largest producer of white cement.

On September 5, the 17th **Alexandria Film Festival** kicks off. A retrial is ordered in the case of Sherif al-Filali, acquitted on charges of spying for Israel in June. An administrative court in Alexandria strikes down a decree from

Minister of Culture Farouq Hosni that would have registered the tomb of Jewish rabbi Abu Hasira, located in Damanhour, as a religious landmark. The ruling opens the door on a ban of the annual Jewish pilgrimage to the site.

On September 8, a Japanese archaeological team uncovers a 2,500-year-old tomb in Saqqara, believed to date to the 26th dynasty.

Hundreds of Egyptians **stage a protest** in Tahrir Square on September 10 in solidarity with the Palestinian intifada.

On September 11, stunned Egyptians watch live CNN coverage of the **World Trade Center** attacks on local TV. President Mubarak sends his condolences to the US.

On September 14, EgyptAir bans metal knives and forks aboard its flights to "preserve the safety of passengers." Mubarak calls for a UN conference on terrorism.

On September 15, Foreign Minister Ahmed Maher accuses Israel of exploiting the terror attacks in the US to block the peace process. About 17 million kids across Egypt head back to school.

On September 18, EgyptAir resumes its flights to New York with increased security, and the Cairo Opera House cancels the **Aida performance** at the Pyramids.

On September 19, Egyptian authorities demolish dozens of Palestinian refugee homes in Rafah in an effort to uncover smuggling tunnels.

In an interview with *Le Figaro*, President Mubarak warns the US on September 21 against making any hasty decisions in the wake of the terror attacks. In Cairo, July 26th becomes a one-way street, part of the traffic realignments the city has been implementing throughout the year in an attempt to ease traffic jams near the center.

On September 22, villagers near Mit Halfa clash with police when a 16-year-old girl is hit by car on the Cairo-Alexandria road, a year after a similar incident near Mit Nama.

President Mubarak begins a European tour to discuss terrorism on September 23, as EgyptAir indefinitely cancels flights to Yemen and Pakistan.

On September 24, the Muslim Brotherhood issue a statement supporting President Mubarak's call for a conference on international terrorism.

French and US troops begin arriving in Egypt for Bright Star, the world's biggest war games on September 25, with Egypt hosting 70,000 troops from ten countries. The head of the Insurance Supervisory Authority, Kheiri Selim, announces that Egyptian insurance companies will pay $4.1 million as compensation to the US following the attacks on the World Trade Center. Following negotiations with international insurers, Egypt's burden is reduced to $670,000.

September 28 marks the one-year anniversary of the second **Palestinian intifada** and the 22nd anniversary of Gamal Abd al-Nasser's death. Italian Premier Silvio Berlusconi tells journalists that Western civilization is superior to Islam, only three days after meeting with President Mubarak in Rome. The remarks spark a storm of protest in the Egyptian press, while Berlusconi claims his statement was misinterpreted.

On September 30, Egypt takes fourth place in the World Youth Volleyball Championships.

October 2001

Iranian Foreign Minister Kamal Kharazi visits Cairo on October 1 in the ongoing thaw in relations between the two countries. The **Alexandria Library** gathers more than 1,000 people for its soft opening.

On October 2, 14 people are detained in a Cairo suburb for proselytizing a false version of Islam. Foreign Minister Ahmed Maher welcomes Bush's endorsement of a Palestinian state.

On October 3, 4,000 students at Cairo University protest in support of the Palestinian intifada. Minister of Information Safwat al-Sherif announces that **hotel occupancy** has fallen 40-50% since September 11. Head of the Popular Committee in Support of the Palestinian Intifada, Farid Zahran, is released on LE5,000 bail following his arrest for disseminating information "harmful to national security and the public welfare." Zahran was arrested after organizing a pro-Palestinian protest in Tahrir Square one day before the attacks on the World Trade Center.

October 6 celebrations mark 20 years of President Mubarak's rule. More than 2,000 prisoners are released on the occasion. The US begins its **bombing campaign in Afghanistan** and security is tightened at the US embassy in Cairo.

October 8 sees more student protests across the country. The Egyptian government recognizes the right of the US to retaliate for the September 11 terror attacks, but expresses concern for Afghan civilians. The first of the three-stage elections to the General Federation of Trade Unions begins.

The telephone information service (140) opens its website, 140online.com, on October 9, and the **Mubarak Peace Bridge** over the Suez Canal is opened after more than three years of construction.

On October 10, Egyptian TV runs old footage of terrorist attacks in Cairo without removing the "transmitted live" mark, causing confusion and a minor panic among the city's inhabitants. The **Cairo International Film Festival** opens on October 11, with noticeably less fanfare than in past years, as several honored guests cancel their appearances. At festival's end, actor Hussein Fahmi announces that he will be stepping down as the festival director, a post he has occupied since 1998.

Following Friday prayers at al-Azhar mosque on October 12, 5,000 worshippers protest the US and British bombing in Afghanistan. The Nobel committee awards this year's peace prize to Kofi Annan and the UN.

EgyptAir announces on October 13 that the company will lay off 90% of its part-time work force, about 900 employees, as part of its cost-cutting measures in the wake of September 11. The trial of former minister of finance Mohi al-Din Gharib begins. He and five customs officials are charged with embezzling LE29 million in customs receipts. President Mubarak refers 83 men to a military court on charges of plotting terrorist attacks and trying to destabilize the nation.

Al-Wafd reports the death of Amina Hasabo in Daqahliya, at the ripe old age of 137, on October 14. President Mubarak appears on Israeli TV warning of future terror attacks if current Israeli policies continue. Aboud al-Zumor, convicted in the plot to assassinate former president Anwar al-Sadat, completes his 20-year prison sentence. He is not released.

On October 15, Egypt says it will lift a 30% tariff on Kenyan tea after 10 million kg have stacked up in Port Said.

On October 16, 170 men accused of membership in al-Gamaa al-Islamiya are referred to a military court. **Israel's new ambassador**, Gideon Ben Ami, arrives in Cairo. An anthrax scare in an American Express branch in Giza proves to be a false alarm. The government announces that it will pay about LE900 million of its arrears to local contracting companies within the week.

Israeli tourism minister Rehavam Zeevi is assassinated on October 17 by members of the Popular Front for the Liberation of Palestine. Zeevi is the first Israeli cabinet minister ever assassinated by Palestinians. EgyptAir reports a 30% decline in passenger loads since September 11, and it expects a 45% decline by the end of the month.

On October 19, EgyptAir announces that it will reduce the price of domestic flights for foreign travelers by 40% starting in November.

London police arrest Egyptian Yasser al-Serri on October 23 and later charge him with complicity in the murder of Afghan opposition commander Ahmed Shah Masoud on September 9. Director of the Islamic Observation Center, al-Serri faces a death sentence in Egypt for his alleged involvement in the plot to assassinate former Prime Minister Atef Sidqi in 1994. **An anthrax scare** leads to the evacuation of a building at the US embassy in Cairo.

After a five-year hiatus, the 5th Ismailiya International Film Festival for Documentaries and Short Features opens on October 27. Eight men are referred to a state security court for insulting Islam.

The 2.5-km **tunnel under al-Azhar** is officially opened on October 28. Four US warships pass through the Suez Canal on their way to join forces in Afghanistan. The Political Parties Committee freezes the Arab Socialist Misr Party, citing internal disputes as the reason. In light of the adverse affects of September 11 on the tourism sector, the ministers of tourism and economy say that they have agreed to reschedule debt payments owed to local banks by companies operating in the sector.

Mahmoud Abu al-Uyoun is made governor of the Central Bank on October 30, replacing Ismail Hassan, whose term was not renewed. Centamin Egypt holds a press conference to announce Egypt's coming **gold rush.** After spending $17 million on exploration over the past seven years, officials say the company's first gold mine—Sukari, in the Eastern Desert—is set to come on line within six months. It will initially produce about 610,000 ounces a year, but the company believes that their 14,000-km^2 concession could eventually yield more.

November 2001

The month opens with a government warning of an economic slowdown following a drop in tourism and shipping revenues since September 11. The 10th Annual Arabic Music Festival begins.

A Condor charter flight from Munich lands in **Marsa Alam International Airport** on November 5 with 252 passengers, inaugurating the country's first privately run airport.

Swiss authorities start an investigation into the Taqwa Bank on November 6, questioning the Egyptian owner, a supporter of the Muslim Brothers alleged to have ties to Bin Laden. Three days later, several Egyptians have their assets in the bank frozen, among them Seif al-Islam Hassan al-Banna and popular sheikhs Youssef Qaradawi and Zaghloul al-Naggar. A new batch of 21 Muslim Brothers are arrested and remanded to a military court a few days later. They are charged with seeking "to incite public opinion by exploiting the ongoing US military campaign against Afghanistan." The **Nubian Museum** is given the Aga Khan award for architecture. Minister of Planning Ahmed al-Darsh announces that the African Development Bank will give Egypt $500 million to help the country face the negative repercussions of the September 11 attack on the US.

On November 7, the corruption trial of former Giza governor **Maher al-Gindi** begins. Charged with accepting LE1 million in bribes in return for the sale of state land at bargain prices, he faces a life sentence.

Pope Shenouda marks his 30th year as patriarch on November 9.

On November 11, an extraordinary Arab Women's summit is held in Cairo. Prime Minister Atef Ebeid talks of changes to come in the cabinet over the next few days. The Ministry of Economy's monthly report, released today, shows that foreign direct investment from January to September declined to LE814 million from LE1,906 million in the same period last year. The capital of newly incorporated companies also fell over the same period, from LE2.616 billion to LE1.137 billion.

The controversial **Queen Boat trial** comes to an end on November 14. The case started in May, when police raided a tourist boat docked outside the Marriott Hotel, detaining scores of young men and charging them with debauchery and other illegal activities. Of the 52 defendants in the trial, 23 are acquitted, and 29 receive sentences ranging from one to five years in prison. The case attracts international attention from gay rights groups, while at home the defendants are vilified in the local press.

On November 16, Egyptians fast for the **first day of Ramadan** as Egyptian TV starts cranking out the yearly soap operas.

As the 2001/02 parliament convenes for its first session on November 17, speaker Fathi Surour announces that according to the body's internal statutes, no interpellations will be debated unless they are accompanied by corroborating evidence. The next day, the assembly votes to strip the membership of MPs **Rami Lakah** and Misbah Mutawaa due to their dual citizenship. A military trial begins of 94 men accused of forming an underground terrorist group, al-Waad, which allegedly planned to assassinate public figures. The men were originally charged in May with illegally collecting money for Palestine and Chechnya.

On November 19, Egyptian banks begin monitoring transactions in accordance with a UN Security Council decision aimed at cutting off financial support to terrorist networks.

On November 20, the Central Bank announces that it will introduce temporary measures to **limit certain imports** in an effort to increase foreign currency and jumpstart the economy. The measures are quickly reversed, but not before inflicting a blow to investor confidence. The **dollar is up to about LE4.90** on the black market. USAID announces that it will give Egypt LE400 million to meet budget deficits following the slump in tourism. An Emirati doctor becomes the first to win one million Saudi riyals on the popular TV game show, Who Wants to Be a Millionaire.

On November 21, Edison and British Gas announce a new **natural gas discovery** 120 km north of Alexandria. A long-awaited **cabinet change** brings in four new faces and rearranges ministerial portfolios. The new cabinet is charged with improving the ailing economy.

On November 22, the vice squad arrests Shohdi Naguib, son of controversial poet Naguib Surour, for allegedly posting some of his late father's more obscene poetry on the

internet. Naguib denied being the author of the website. The poem has been posted on the website for the last three years. President Mubarak urges Egyptians against repeat pilgrimages to Saudi Arabia in an effort to limit spending abroad.

On November 23, Zamalek beats Ahli on the football field during their biannual match.

President Mubarak warns on November 25 that exports "are **a matter of life and death"** for the Egyptian economy. Two journalists at the weekly al-Mowagaha are sentenced to two years in prison for publishing potentially offensive articles and photos.

On November 26, the Arab League organizes a two-day conference entitled "Civilizations: Dialogue not Confrontation." More than 100 intellectuals from all over the Arab world come to Cairo to attend. The press announces that CEO of **Arab Contractors**, Ismail Osman, will be stepping down from his post, amidst rumors that he was forced out of Egypt's biggest contracting firm, founded by his father.

Foreign Minister Ahmed Maher warns the US on November 27 that extending its war to Iraq would pose serious domestic problems for US allies in the region.

The Egyptian-US Mutual Legal Assistance Treaty goes into effect on November 29. The treaty is aimed at combating terrorism, drug trafficking,

and money laundering. The US State Department confirms the sale of more than 50 Harpoon anti-ship missiles to Egypt, despite protests from the pro-Israel bloc in the US Congress. Foreign Minister Ahmed Maher expresses concern over Egyptians detained in the US following the September 11 attacks.

December 2001

A court rules on December 4 that an AUC student can wear the niqab, overturning the university's ban on the full-face veil. AUC says it will appeal the decision. President Mubarak announces a shuffle in the NDP general secretariat. Following the changes, the secretariat includes eight cabinet ministers, four women, four Copts, and four youth members between the ages of 35-45. The business daily al-Alam al-Yom reports that the black market dollar rate has fallen slightly to LE4.33 on the dollar, down from LE4.38. The dollar sell rate at banks is averaging LE4.27.

Four Egyptians who had been detained by US authorities following the September 11 attacks return home to Cairo on December 5. The Capital Markets Authority announces that it has stopped trading shares in Arabian International Construction (AIC) after the company had rejected repeated requests by the CMA to submit its financial results. The firm was accused of insider trading in June 2000.

Nobel laureate **Naguib Mahfouz** celebrates his 90th birthday on

December 11. The annual Mahfouz literary prize is awarded to writer Somaya Ramadan for her novel *Awraq al-Nargis*.

On December 12, the Central Bank announces the third and **final devaluation of the year,** with the pound up to 4.50 on the dollar (plus or minus 3%). At its upper limit of LE4.64, the pound is worth 31.5% less than it was in January.

The Pentagon releases the much-hyped **Bin Laden tape** on December 13. The Egyptian press remains skeptical about its authenticity. An Abdin court sentences MP Ragab Helal Hemeida to six months in prison for writing a bad check. This is the 15th time the deputy has faced similar charges. Prime Minister Atef Ebeid says that the Central Bank will supply local banks with $2 billion to meet the rising demand for foreign currency, $500 million of which will be injected immediately from the Central Bank's reserves. The remaining $1.5 billion will come from international funds and will be disbursed at around $250 million per month until June 2002.

On December 14, 52 Egyptian pilgrims returning from Mecca die in a bus accident in Aqaba, Jordan.

In a December 15 interview with *al-Gomhouriya*, President Mubarak supports the new US policy of referring civilians to military trials, arguing that September 11 has forced a reassessment of the limits of individual freedom.

Egyptians celebrate the first day of **Eid al-Fitr** on December 16.

Egypt is shaken by the second minor **earthquake** of the year on December 17, registering 4.4 on the Richter scale.

On December 18, two students are convicted for soliciting gay sex on the internet after being caught by a police sting. The Cairo and Alexandria Stock Exchanges issue a surprise statement that the UK-based Standard Chartered is no longer interested in acquiring a stake of the Egyptian American Bank. The announcement comes after long months of negotiations that had seen EAB's stock price rise 80% in anticipation of the landmark sale. CASE later launches an investigation into charges of insider trading after irregularities in EAB share trading are noticed in the days leading up to the announcment.

On December 19, the Court of Cassation postpones the appeal hearing for sociologist **Saad Eddin Ibrahim**, convicted and sentenced in May of tarnishing Egypt's reputation abroad.

Arab foreign ministers meet in Cairo on December 20 to discuss the Palestinian situation.

The **Ahli club** wins the African Champions League title on December 21 for the first time since 1987.

The Cairo Opera House heads south on December 23, sponsoring a one-day cultural celebration in Minya that features jazz, opera selections, and a flute concert. The People's Assembly

passes a law outlawing flogging in prisons, legalizing a Ministry of Interior decree issued in 2000. President Mubarak inaugurates a newly refurbished **Abu Simbel**, marking the end of an LE8-million project to upgrade security and infrastructure at the complex.

The military trial of 22 Muslim Brothers starts on December 24. The Arab Monetary Fund will give Egypt a loan of $150 million to help it meet a deficit in the balance of payments, reports *al-Akhbar*.

Actress Wafaa Mekki is sentenced to 10 years in prison on December 26 for torturing her two maids.

British Prime Minister Tony Blair arrives in Egypt for a vacation and visits the Pyramids on December 27.

The **Umm Kulthoum** Museum is inaugurated on December 28 in Monesterly Palace.

Three judges are convicted of taking bribes from a businessman on December 29.

Head of the Supreme Council of Antiquities Gaballa Ali Gaballa announces on December 30 that archaeologists have discovered a funeral chapel dedicated to Ramses II in an ancient military base on the North Coast.

On December 31, the Ministry of Tourism says that about 40,000 tourists have flocked to Egypt to celebrate the coming of the new year. Hotels in Luxor and Aswan are booked to full capacity.

January 2002

The year opens on January 1 with the government effectively revoking the free zone status of **Port Said** when it imposes stiff tariffs on ready-made imported garments. Riots in the city the next day lead the government to revoke the tariffs, but later in the month the People's Assembly approves a law to formally end the city's free zone status over five years. A free zone since 1976, the decision is a blow to the port town, whose economy is largely based on the trade of imported clothes.

On January 3, the Egyptian Foreign Ministry says that of the more than 110 Egyptian citizens detained in the US after September 11, only 20 have been released. Archaeologists announce that three Greco-Roman sites have been discovered in North Sinai near the border town of Rafah. They believe the sites may have served as military outposts.

On January 4, authorities catch a customs agent and an engineer with the **Atomic Energy Authority** trying to smuggle an undisclosed quantity of uranium and thorium into the country.

On January 6, the People's Assembly votes to forgo judicial supervision of municipal elections, scheduled for April, sparking protests from opposition deputies who believe it will open the door to widespread election rigging. A sudden cold snap hits Cairo as two high-profile Israeli peaceniks come to the capital. Yossi Sarid, head of the leftist Meretz Party, and former justice minister Yossi Beilin meet with the president to discuss opportunities for peace in the region.

January 7 marks the celebration of Coptic Christmas, and Pope Shenouda gives his customary sermon after mass at St. Mark's Cathedral in Abbasiya.

On January 9, Minister of Culture Farouq Hosni holds a press conference to announce the design competition for the new **$350-million Egyptian museum** near the Giza Plateau. Once completed, the museum will hold 150,000 items and be the largest antiquities museum in the world. The winner of the competition, to be chosen in May 2003, will have his or her design executed and will receive a cash prize.

A huge downpour on January 10 leaves Cairo's streets flooded as the deluge overpowers the city's insufficient drainage system. Rough weather is reported all over Egypt, and 39 fishermen die off the Red Sea coast when their boat capsizes due to high waves. The 18th Cairo International Children's Book Fair opens at the fairgrounds at Nasr City. The Central Bank releases $100 million to local banks to relieve pressure on the pound, reportedly trading on the **black market** for LE5.05 to the dollar.

On January 14, the CBE devalues the pound by one piaster, setting the **new exchange rate** at LE4.51 to the dollar, plus or minus 3%. After more than a year in the making, **free internet** finally comes to Egypt with the opening of the 6th annual Cairo Telecomp fair. Users no longer need a subscription with a local internet service provider to access the web, and they can now log on for the price of a local phone call. About one million people currently use the net in Egypt, but it is hoped that the plan will boost the numbers considerably.

On January 15, Nasr City MP Fawzi al-Sayed is sentenced to three years in prison for forging documents to receive construction licenses valued at about LE28.2 million. Known as "the whale of Nasr City," al-Sayed is subsequently stripped of his parliamentary membership and his seat is opened to new elections.

On January 17, President Mubarak inaugurates the 34th Cairo International **Book Fair** with his annual meeting with Egyptian intellectuals. The fair, featuring almost 3,000 publishers from more than 90 countries, will run for two weeks.

Former US president Bill Clinton comes to town on January 18 to give a speech to Gamal Mubarak's Future Generation Fund.

On January 20, Police Day marks its 50th anniversary. The French-Cypriot Cyprien Katsaris, one of the world's leading concert pianists, gives a recital at Cairo's Monasterly Palace. The Ministry of Public Enterprise announces that all of the remaining 135 state-owned companies up for privatization will be put on the block this year.

On January 21, Egypt starts to cash in on its natural gas reserves when it signs a contract to sell 4.8 billion m³ of liquefied **natural gas** (LNG) every year to France. The deal involves plans for a $900-million liquefication plant on the Mediterranean Coast at Edku, to be completed by 2005.

On January 22, the 52-year-old Ragab al-Sawirki is sentenced to seven years in prison for exceeding the legal limit of four wives, and of marrying 29 minors. The millionaire owner of the chain of Tawhid and Nour shops denies that he ever married more than four women at once, but he does say that he had married a total of 19 times. A minor earthquake shakes Cairo.

January 23 witnesses a crackdown on **black market currency trading** as the government closes more than a dozen foreign exchange bureaus in Cairo, the Delta, and Alexandria and arrests ten people. The pound has reportedly reached LE5.80 on the dollar on the black market, compared to the legal maximum trading rate of LE4.65.

On January 25, Germany finally hands over the long-contested base of **Akhnaten's sarcophagus**. Discovered in 1907, the base was spirited out of the country a few years later and had resided in the Munich Museum of Egyptian Art until its return to native soil.

On January 27, police say they have arrested eight members of the banned Muslim Brotherhood. Currently, 22 members of the illegal organization are undergoing a military trial.

February 2002

On February 2, Egypt participates in the Winter Olympics, held in Utah, for the first time when it sends eight bridge players to participate in the first, experimental round of bridge at the games. Of the International Bridge Federation's 90 member countries, only 10 were selected to participate in the games.

On February 3, the state-owned Eastern Tobacco says it will increase production during 2002 from 179 million to 200 million cigarettes a day. Company head Mohammed Sadeq Ragab says that the price on local brands will not be raised, even though devaluation has considerably increased the price of imported raw tobacco.

President Mubarak on February 4 lays the cornerstone for the new Egyptian antiquities museum. Egypt crashes out of the **African Cup** when it loses to Cameroon 0-1 in the quarter-finals.

The Consultative Group donors' meeting in Sharm al-Sheikh closes on February 6. By the end of the session, Egypt has secured **loan commitments of $10.3 billion** over the next three years. About $2.1 billion of that is to be disbursed in 2002. Prime Minister Atef Ebeid tells the group in his inaugural speech that Egypt lost 387,000 jobs after September 11, or about 2% of total employment.

On February 7, sociologist Saad Eddin Ibrahim is released from prison after the Court of Cassation overturns his seven-year sentence and orders a retrial. Ibrahim and 27 co-defendants had been convicted in May 2001 of fraud and tarnishing Egypt's reputation abroad in what was broadly seen by rights groups and the international community in a politically motivated case. Ahmed Omar Hashem, the president of Azhar University, says the university will waive all fees for the some 200 Palestinian students enrolled in 2002.

February 9 sees clashes between Copts and Muslims in a village in Minya. Fights break out when Muslim villagers protest the ringing of bells during the inauguration of a new church. The flare-up leaves 11 injured and several homes damaged. Police detain 50 people.

The sale of the state-owned Abu Zaabal Fertilizer for LE201 million is finalized on February 11. The deal is one of the few privatization ventures to go through over the last year.

On February 12, a downpour in the capital brings traffic to a halt, while a benefit auction of late actress Soad Hosni's possessions is held to raise money for the children's cancer hospital currently going up, the first facility of its kind in the Middle East. The auction brings in over LE700,000.

On February 13, the Saudi Fund for Development agrees to give Egypt a

$26.6 million loan to upgrade and build 55 schools across Egypt.

Another political party makes its way onto the stage on February 14, when the Political Parties Court overturns a rejection by the Political Parties Committee. The new party, the Democratic Generation, was founded by disgruntled members of the Islamist Labor Party, frozen in 2000. A group of Egyptian young people head to Media Production City for an international video conference with US Secretary of State Colin Powell. The proceedings are part of an MTV special, aired the next day, called *Be Heard: an MTV Global Discussion with Colin Powell*. The Cairo audience grills Powell on US foreign policy in Iraq and Palestine.

On February 16, an international symposium is held on the **conservation and restoration of Islamic Cairo**. Organized by the Ministry of Culture and UNESCO, the conference is held after several local and foreign specialists send a petition to First Lady Suzanne Mubarak expressing concern over restoration practices in Fatimid Cairo.

On February 17, Ericsson signs a deal with Telecom Egypt to establish a EU200-million regional telecommunications center over the next five years. As part of the terms of the deal, Ericsson agrees to reinvest a percentage of its proceeds in the Egyptian market.

On February 19, the State Council issues a ruling reiterating the protected status of Wadi Digla and calling on the Cairo governorate to enforce its status. One of 21 nature reserves in the country, the area has been the site of illegal garbage dumping and urban encroachment. The court appoints an expert to determine the damage inflicted on the wadi and forces the governorate to pay for the clean up.

Disaster strikes Egypt on February 20 when a train heading to Upper Egypt catches on fire at **al-Ayyat** in Beni Sueif, causing the deaths of about 360 people. The result of negligence and substandard safety precautions, the accident throws the spotlight on the poor state of the national railway system and leads to the resignation of Minister of Transportation Ibrahim al-Demeiri. The accident comes as travelers are heading home to celebrate Eid al-Adha.

On February 28, a high state security court sentences former minister of finance Mohi al-Din Gharib to eight years in prison for personally profiting from his post. The judge charges Gharib to pay back the LE16 million he made from customs kickbacks and fines him an additional LE16 million. Nine other defendants in the case receive sentences ranging from 3 to 11 years.

March 2002

On March 3, Amr Moussa, secretary general of the Arab League, feels the dollar crunch when, set to head off to Libya on official league business, he is held up after being unable to pay a $152 plane refueling fee. Moussa and the Libyan official with him at the Cairo airport offer to pay the fee in Egyptian pounds or euros, but officials at the state-run petroleum company insist on dollars.

President Mubarak meets with US president, George Bush, in Washington on March 5, the first meeting between the two men since September 11. Meanwhile, thousands of Alexandria students hold **pro-Palestinian protests** as the situation in the Occupied Territories degenerates.

On March 7, Cairo governor Abd al-Rehim Sheha signs a deal with an Egyptian subsidiary of the Sony Corporation to install and run **parking meters** in downtown Cairo. Under the terms of the agreement, the private company will install and run the system for five years before turning it over to the city.

Coming on the heels of the Ayyat tragedy, another train accident occurs on March 8 when a train derails in the Delta, injuring 13 people. Egyptian foreign minister Ahmed Maher calls on the US to release 70 Egyptians detained after September 11.

On March 9, Foreign Minister Ahmed Maher announces that passport requirements have been lifted for Italians and Germans visiting Egypt. In an effort to boost tourism, these two countries' nationals will be allowed to enter the country with only a personal identity card.

Mufti of the republic, Nasser Farid Wassel, is replaced on March 10 by Ahmed Mohammed al-Tayyeb. Wassel had served as the mufti for five years; no reason is given for the switch.

More **government shuffling** occurs on March 11, when a new transport minister is named to replace Ibrahim al-Demeiri, who resigned in the wake of the Ayyat train disaster in late February. New transport minister Hamdi al-Shayeb is joined by Ahmed Shafiq, in charge of the newly created Ministry of Civil Aviation. Health minister Ismail Sallam is also replaced by Mohammed Awad Tag al-Din.

US Vice-President Dick Cheney meets with President Mubarak on March 13 as part of his Middle Eastern tour to garner support for a US offensive against Iraq. Details of the meeting are not released, but Mubarak comments later that Iraqi president Saddam Hussein will most likely accept a new batch of UN inspectors.

On March 17, Telecom Egypt announces **new phone rates**, effective April. Under the new tariffs, charges on local calls will be assessed in one-minute increments, rather than six-minute blocs. The change makes shorter phone calls cheaper and longer ones more expensive. The number of free minutes is also reduced, down from 1,600 per year to 500 per year. A family court refuses

to grant a Coptic woman a divorce using *khulaa*, a provision set out in the 2000 **personal status law** whereby a woman can receive a divorce automatically by giving up all financial claims on her husband. Though family courts in Egypt are part of the civil court system, the judge rules that *khulaa* is an Islamic principle and is not recognized by the Coptic Church. Minister of Tourism Mamdouh al-Beltagui says that tourist arrivals for February are down only 11.8% from the same period last year, promising a speedy **recovery in the tourism sector**.

On March 18, Foreign Minister Ahmed Maher says that Arab countries will put their support behind the Saudi peace initiative in the upcoming Arab summit in Beirut, scheduled for the end of March. It is still unclear if Palestinian president Yasser Arafat will be able to attend the summit.

On March 19, Galal Ghorab, head of the Holding Company for Pharmaceuticals, announces that local pharmaceutical companies will start **producing insulin** within three years. Investment costs for the project are estimated at LE50 million.

On March 20, Public Prosecutor Maher Abd al-Wahed charges 11 people with negligence and building violations in connection with two building collapses in Damietta and Mansoura that left 36 people dead. These two collapses are only the latest in a spate of tragedies that have

highlighted the widespread violation of Egypt's housing and zoning laws. Zahi Hawass, the flamboyant director of the Giza Plateau, is appointed director of the **Supreme Council of Antiquities**, replacing Gaballa Ali Gaballa, who had quietly resigned from the position the previous month.

Two more journalists fall prey to Egypt's harsh libel laws on March 21. Adel Hammouda and Essam Fahmi, editor and publisher of the weekly *Sawt al-Umma* are sentenced to six months in prison and fined LE500 after being convicted of slandering businessman Naguib Sawiris. Hammouda had accused the tycoon of gaining his license to run the first mobile phone company in Egypt through illegal procedures. The US National Transportation and Safety Board releases its long-awaited report on the crash of **EgyptAir flight 990** in 1999. The report blames the accident on the actions of co-pilot Gamil al-Batouti, but does not give a reason for his behavior. The board has long held that al-Batouti deliberately crashed the plane, a theory that most Egyptians reject. The Egyptian Civil Aviation Authority says it will file an appeal of the ruling.

On March 23, twice-tried and once-acquitted alleged spy Sherif al-Filali is found guilty of espionage by a state security emergency court. He is sentenced to 15 years in prison and fined LE1,000 for passing on sensitive state secrets to Israeli intelligence.

Another gold mining company sets up in Egypt on March 25 when the US-based Cresset International teams up with the Egyptian Geological Survey and Mining Authority to create the Hamash Egypt Gold Mines. The company believes that its Umm Tundub concession in the Eastern Desert contains **23 million ounces of gold**.

On March 26, President Mubarak suddenly announces that he will not attend the **Arab summit** in Beirut, scheduled to begin the next day. Though he says he supports the Saudi peace plan, he will stay in Cairo in a show of solidarity with Yasser Arafat, who is unable to attend. Mubarak is one of many Arab leaders who do not show up in Beirut.

On March 28, the authorities announce that a large granite head has been discovered in Tell Basta by Egyptian and German archaeologists. The archaeological team believes that the head, which measures 11 ft high, represents Queen Nefertari, the favorite wife of Ramses II.

On March 30, a family court agrees to give Christian actress Hala Sidqi a **divorce** based on *khulaa*, a principle in Islamic law that allows a woman an automatic divorce if she gives up financial claims on her husbands. This is the first time *khulaa* has been granted in a Christian divorce case. Sidqi, however, had left the Coptic Church, which does not recognize *khulaa*, for another Christian denomination.

Prime Minister Atef Ebeid on March 31 announces the preliminary 2002/03 state budget. Set at LE141.4 billion, it provides LE34.8 billion for state salaries, LE56 billion for health, education, and social services, and LE18.9 billion for infrastructure improvements.

April 2002

As the Israeli reinvasion of the West Bank continues, urban centers all over Egypt witness **demonstrations** on April 1. Egyptians turn out at universities, mosques, and professional associations in solidarity with Palestinians. Sheikh of al-Azhar Mohammed Sayed al-Tantawi denounces suicide attacks on civilians, but declares that those who die in attacks on soldiers are martyrs. Hamdi Qandil's popular weekly news program *Rais al-Tahrir* is heavily censored, with only 10 minutes airing of the usually hour-long show.

On April 3, Egypt announces that it will cut all contacts with the Israeli government except those that are directly linked to the issue of Palestine.

On April 6, a special Arab League session is convened in Cairo in support of Palestine. Though the session draws only about half of all Arab foreign ministers, it closes with a statement condemning Israeli actions and calling on the US to take a more balanced approach to the conflict.

Egyptians head to the polls to vote in **local council elections** on April 8. The ruling National Democratic Party captures about 97% of the 46,000 seats up for grabs across the nation.

The families of Israeli embassy personnel leave the country on April 9 for an unspecified vacation period in Israel. Student protests at Alexandria University turn nasty when students leave the campus to march towards the US cultural center. **Riot police** shoot and kill student Mohammed Ali al-Saqqa, and about 200 students are wounded and 68 more arrested in the mêlée. The detainees are released five days later.

On April 11, 2,000 people rally at St. Mark's Cathedral in Abbasiya in support of Palestine. The rally is attended by Pope Shenouda, Sheikh of al-Azhar Tantawi, and, via telephone, Palestinian president Yasser Arafat.

On April 14, President Mubarak cancels the long-awaited grand opening of the **Alexandria Library**, scheduled for April 23. The opening is later rescheduled for October 16.

On April 16, 23-year-old Milad Mohammed Hemeida is shot and killed by Israeli soldiers while crossing the Egyptian-Israeli border at Rafah. Hemeida said he was strapped with explosives, but is later found to be carrying nothing. He is only the latest in a string of young Egyptians who have tried to cross the border and join the Palestinian resistance. Egypt announces that it will bring a halt to its extensive **agricultural cooperation with Israel**, including joint research projects and training exchanges. Fares at the

Cairo metro go up by 5-10 piasters.

On April 20, the Alexandria Library holds a press conference announcing that the US-based Internet Archive has donated a copy of its entire archive to the library. The digital equivalent of about 100 million books, the archive holds the sum total of the world wide web from 1996-2001.

Police arrest seven people in Mansoura and Zaqaziq on April 22 for illegally collecting funds for the Palestinians. They are later released.

On April 24, students at AUC load up 500 tons of donated food, medicine, and clothing into 30 trucks destined for Rafah and ultimately Palestinian refugee camps. Like many **charity convoys**, however, this one has problems crossing the border.

Families of Israeli diplomats in Cairo return to Egypt on April 25.

On April 27, the trial of 11 state employees held responsible for the February Ayyat train disaster opens in Cairo. The defendants are charged with negligence, the falsification of documents, and committing errors that caused the death of 361 people. The defendants are all relatively low-ranking civil servants who claim that they are scapegoats for a fundamentally flawed railway system.

On April 28, a high state security court sentences Mohammed Hassan al-Sayed to ten years in prison for belonging to an illegal organization. He is suspected of ties to Osama Bin Laden.

On April 29, Suzanne Mubarak, head of the Egyptian Red Crescent, leads a public protest march at the Egyptian border with several hundred Red Crescent volunteers. The march is part of a convoy bringing **food and medical supplies** to Palestinians in need.

May 2002

On May 2, Egypt's Police Club hockey team lands at Cairo airport after winning the African hockey club championship. The club dethroned 12-time champions and fellow national club Sharqiya to win the title. German conceptual artist H.A. Schult sets up his traveling exhibition of 1,000 trash figures at the Giza Pyramids. The exhibit has shown in Paris, Moscow, and the Great Wall of China. The Red Crescent organizes a benefit concert at the Cairo Opera House with the proceeds going to Palestinian relief efforts. Participants include Latifa, Assala, Angham, Ali al-Haggar, and Hani Shaker.

On May 4, Egyptian border police arrest two more men attempting to cross from Rafah into Gaza. Since mid-April ten Egyptians have been arrested at the border. The Ministry of Interior cancels the **Limby celebrations** in Port Said, traditionally held on Easter day. A popular festival that involves burning effigies of notorious figures of the day, the event has been held since 1917. The ministry announces that anyone burning anything will be detained and fined.

On May 5, head of the Supreme Council of Antiquities Zahi Hawass announces that archaeologists have discovered the base of **another pyramid** ten miles north of the great pyramid. Estimated to be 4,500 years old, the pyramid is thought to have been built for the wife of the son of Cheops, builder of the great pyramid.

May 6 marks Sham al-Nessim, the national spring holiday devoted to picnics, salted fish, onions, and lettuce.

On May 7, an EgyptAir flight en route from Cairo to Tunis crashes outside of Tunis, leaving 14 dead, including seven Egyptians. Bad weather conditions are blamed for the crash, but the national carrier is put on the spot for its performance. Head of the Supreme Council of Antiquities Zahi Hawass announces that Belgian archaeologists have discovered a **30,000-year-old skeleton** in Upper Egypt, one of the oldest ever found in North Africa. Pottery shards found next to the skeleton are estimated to be 35,000 years old.

On May 10, two students from the American University in Cairo are arrested in Bethlehem. The year-abroad students are two of ten international volunteers present in the standoff at the Church of the Nativity. After lying in prison for two weeks, Israeli officials deport them to the US on May 28.

On May 12, President Mubarak holds a small summit meeting with Prince Abdullah of Saudi Arabia and President

Bashar al-Assad of Syria. The three leaders issue a statement rejecting the use of all violence in dealings with Israel.

May 15 marks the 54th anniversary of the *nakba*, or disaster of the creation of the state of Israel. Both Cairo and Alexandria witness protest demonstrations on the occasion.

On May 16, the Ahli football club stomps Zamalek in an unprecedented 6-1 victory. The match between the arch-rivals takes place a week after the death of legendary footballer and head of the Ahli club Saleh Selim.

On May 20, the People's Assembly passes an **anti-money laundering law**, more than three years in the making. The law calls for the establishment of a task force at the Central Bank of Egypt to monitor suspicious financial transfers. Egypt had come under fire from the Financial Action Task Force in 2001 for its insufficient efforts to combat money laundering.

Local internet giant LinkdotNet, partly owned by Orascom Telecom, acquires eight websites on May 21 in a deal worth LE365 million. The acquisition includes local ISP internet Egypt in addition to other service-oriented websites, such as the local online delivery service otlob.com. Shorouq Airlines pilot Nerine Salem wins a suit against the air carrier after it had fired her for donning the veil. Salem had started wearing the veil last year under her pilot's cap until she was forbidden from flying for "altering her uniform." The court orders the airline to pay Salem her monthly salary, but it does not reinstate her on the job.

On May 22, international ratings agency Standard and Poor lowers Egypt's sovereign credit rating. Most local analysts are unsurprised by the move. The World Bank says that it will join the African Development Bank in giving Egypt a $1-billion 17-year loan, to be disbursed in October.

In his capacity as military governor, President Mubarak on May 23 rescinds the jail terms for 21 men convicted in the controversial **Queen Boat case** and orders the prosecutor to review the case. Two of those convicted, however, are granted no reprieve. Sherif Farahat and Mahmoud Ahmed Allam were convicted not only for debauchery, but for contempt of religion as well. Their sentences stand. A retrial is later set to begin in September.

Egyptians celebrate moulid al-nabi, the Prophet Mohammed's birthday, on May 24.

On May 25, a court reverses the July order that banned the weekly *al-Nabaa* after it published a lurid expose of a sexual scandal involving a Coptic monk. The weekly will be allowed to reappear, but minus its former publisher, Mamdouh Mahran, who is still serving a three-year sentence for allowing the publication of the story. The local press reports that Minister of Health Mohammed Awad Tag al-Din has agreed to allow the local production of the anti-impotence drug Viagra. Thirteen local companies apply to the ministry for licenses to produce the drug.

On May 27, the weekly *al-Midan* publishes a picture of the late president Anwar al-Sadat, naked from the chest up and riddled with bullet holes. The photo causes a stir, with some calling for the closure of the paper. The paper's publisher fires editor-in-chief Said Abd al-Khaleq, and Sadat's nephew later sues the Egyptian intelligence service for releasing the photo to the paper.

On May 29, the People's Assembly passes the long-awaited law on **intellectual property rights**. The law fulfills Egypt's commitments under the World Trade Organization's TRIPS accord, to be fully implemented in 2005, but critics fear it will have negative ramifications for local manufacturers and particularly for the price of pharmaceuticals.

The **World Cup** kicks off on May 31, with the opening game between last round's champion team, France, and Senegal, the team that beat Egypt for a spot in the football extravaganza. For the next month, televisions across the country are ablaze with non-stop soccer in coffee shops, homes, offices, and other places of business.

June 2002

Ismaili takes the championship in the Egyptian football league for the third time ever on June 2 after securing a 3-

2 victory over Misri.

On June 3, the Ministry of Communications and Information Technology announces an $18-million e-government initiative that will ultimately allow Egyptians to pay utility bills, traffic fines, and more online. The five-year project is to be launched in July.

On June 4, the illustrious Arabic Music Institute reopens after undergoing a LE6-million facelift. The institute contains a small museum to composer **Mohammed Abd al-Wahab**, who sang at the institute's original opening night in 1929 before King Fouad.

On June 5, President Mubarak ratifies a new law regulating **non-governmental associations** before heading off to the US. Subject to hot debate in parliament, the law is widely criticized by civil society activists for increasing the government's stranglehold on civil society. The law prohibits NGOs from engaging in political activity, gives the government the right to unilaterally dissolve NGOs, and requires government permission for the release of any foreign funds to be used by NGOs. The president also issues a decree establishing the **EgyptAir** Holding Company and breaking up the national carrier into six independent companies, each specialized in some aspect of the airline's operations. The move leads to speculation that the carrier will be up for privatization soon, but officials deny the rumors. Former

governor of Giza Maher al-Gindi is sentenced to seven years in prison and fined LE2,000 for accepting kickbacks during his term in office in return for sweetheart land deals.

On June 10, the unemployed 52-year-old Magdi Anwar Mohammed Tawfiq is sentenced to ten years in prison after being convicted of espionage. The public prosecutor had charged him with spying for Israel after he allegedly faxed a letter to the Israeli consulate in Alexandria offering his services to Israeli intelligence, but his lawyer claims that Tawfiq is mentally unstable.

On June 11, a US court sentences Frederick Schultz, gallery owner and former president of the American Association of Ancient Art Dealers, to 33 months in prison and fines him $55,000 for **trafficking in stolen Egyptian artifacts**. Schultz's conviction and sentencing is welcomed by Egyptian antiquities officials, who hope that high-profile cases like this one will help discourage the illegal antiquities trade and keep ancient Egyptian art in Egypt. Just days before it adjourns for the year, the People's Assembly approves in principle the controversial **unified labor law**. Critics of the law have long claimed that it curtails workers' rights even further and gives the government greater control over trade unions. The article-by-article debate over the law is postponed to the next session. The stock market sees heavy turnover as the Egyptian Kuwaiti

Holding consortium buys a 90% stake of the state-owned Egyptian Glass Company for LE271 million. The sale is one of the few advances made on the privatization front for several months.

On June 12, Minister of Finance Medhat Hassanein tells the press that the government has paid LE31.1 billion in arrears, including LE22.2 billion to local contractors, fully covering the period through June 2001.

Just two weeks after the national carrier was restructured, on June 17, it is announced that long-standing head of EgyptAir Fahim Rayan will be replaced by former air force general Abd al-Fattah Kato

On June 18, head of the Supreme Council for Antiquities Zahi Hawass says that a sarcophagus has been discovered near the Giza pyramids that may be the oldest ever found intact. Found in a tomb for the pyramid builders, the **limestone sarcophagus** dates back to the Fourth Dynasty. Hawass has hopes that the sarcophagus contains an equally ancient mummy, but says he will wait until September 16 to open it live on a National Geographic television program.

On June 24, Egypt turns down an invitation to attend the G8 summit in Canada due to regional tensions. This is the first time that the economic group has invited non-G8 member countries to attend a summit. US president George Bush gives a policy statement on the Middle East, calling for the ouster of Palestinian president Yasser Arafat. While rejecting that principle, President Mubarak receives the speech optimistically, though local observers are disappointed with the pro-Israeli stance taken by Bush.

On June 27, **elections** are held in Alexandria for two parliamentary seats left open since the fall 2000 elections. In November of that year, two Muslim Brother candidates—including the much-publicized female Brother candidate Jihan al-Halafawi—won the elections, but the results were cancelled by court order. This time around, the ruling National Democratic Party takes both seats by wide margins, amidst widespread accusations that hundreds of pro-Brother voters were turned away at the polls. On voting day, about 200 Muslim Brother supporters are arrested.

On June 28, the US releases $202 million in aid to Egypt, largely in recognition of its efforts to fight money laundering. At a meeting in Budapest, the UNESCO World Heritage Committee adds **St. Katherine's Monastery** to its list of protected sites. The heritage site includes the monastery and about 600 km^2 around it, already part of a national protected area.

On June 30, the business daily *al-Alam al-Yom* reports that the Egyptian pound has appreciated slightly in the black market over the last few days, falling to LE4.95 on the dollar, only about 30

piasters higher than the maximum official trading ceiling.

July 2002

July 1 marks the beginning of the International Flying Circus Festival at the national circus in Cairo. The event brings international performers to the big top in Agouza.

On July 2, the first **Arab Human Development Report** is released. Authored by a group of independent Arab researchers headed by Egyptian sociologist Nader Fergani, the report concludes that the slow pace of development in the Arab world is largely due to the absence of political freedom, the state of women, and a poor knowledge base.

On July 4, the Middle East News Agency reports that Pope Shenouda has excommunicated 13 clerics for heresy and contesting the leadership of the Coptic Church. The announcement marks a break with traditional church policy, which in the past has sought to hide conflicts within the church. An Egyptian national, Hisham Mohammed Ali Hedayat, kills two Israelis and injures five more at the El Al counter in Los Angeles. He is shot and killed by airport security.

On July 6, Shohdi Surour, son of the late revolutionary poet Naguib Surour, is sentenced to one year in prison for posting excerpts of his father's poetry on the web. Naguib Surour's politically and sexually explicit poetry has

circulated on cassette recordings since the 1970s, but the collection posted on the internet does not exist in print. Shohdi Surour appeals the ruling, arguing that it cannot be proven that it was he who posted the poetry.

On July 7, Mohammed al-Wakil, director of the news section at Egyptian television, is arrested in a sting operation as he receives LE10,000 in return for a promise to feature a particular guest on the popular *Good Morning Egypt*. Prosecutors say that he will go to trial, but no date is set. The first artifacts from the collection of convicted smuggler Frederick Schultz arrive in Cairo.

The Cairo headquarters of the **Nasserist party** witness a brief ruckus on July 9 when four young party members storm the headquarters and threaten to blow it up in protest over the party's internal elections. Two small homemade bombs are thrown on the street before riot police take the men into custody.

On July 11, the Capital Markets Authority attempts to breathe some life into the stock exchange by announcing that it will remove the **5% trading band** on certain stocks at the bourse and that it will allow margin trading.

Security forces say on July 13 they have arrested 28 members of the Muslim Brotherhood for planning a demonstration at the Azhar mosque, banned under the Emergency Law.

On July 15, the daily *al-Akhbar* reports

that 83% of students who took the yearly *thanawiya al-amma* exams this year passed. Several companies sign on to be part of the government's new **Smart Village** complex, including ISP giant LinkdotNet, Raya Holdings, Alcatel, and the Cairo and Alexandria Stock Exchanges. The complex, touted as Egypt's silicon valley, will hold hi-tech offices, a conference center, recreation and shopping facilities, and a hotel. The companies are scheduled to set up shop in the Smart Village in early 2003, but construction will continue on the area until 2006. As a prelude to the celebrations coming up for the 50th anniversary of the revolution, Prime Minister Atef Ebeid unveils a statue of war hero Abd al-Meneim Riyad in Cairo's Tahrir Square. The general participated in the wars of 1948, 1956, and 1967 before being killed in the 1973 War of Attrition.

On July 19, citywide blackouts strike the capital in the midst of a **heat wave** that sees temperatures reach a scorching 45 degrees Celsius. Thousands of passengers in the metro are trapped underground, and some try to make their way out of the tunnels.

On July 21, police say they have arrested 34 more members of the banned Muslim Brotherhood group while attending a clandestine meeting in a home about 70 km north of Cairo. The suspects are charged with being part of an illegal organization and are detained 15 days pending investigation.

The 1st International Book Forum opens in Cairo on July 22. The cultural extravaganza features music, seminars, theater, and poetry recitals held in honor of the **July 23 revolution**. About 50 publishing houses are represented at the fair. Abd al-Shakour Shaalan, an executive director with the IMF, gives Egypt a thumbs up for its recent **economic performance** at a press conference. Before a somewhat incredulous audience, he praises the government's recent attempts at economic reform and commends the flexible exchange rate policy. Observers believed that a $500-million loan Egypt reportedly requested from the organization was being held up due to the slow pace of reform, but Shaalan says that Egypt had asked for no loan.

Fireworks, concerts, and other festivities mark the 50th anniversary of the July 23 revolution, which saw the Free Officers coup and the rise to power of Gamal Abd al-Nasser.

On July 27, an administrative court ruling reinstates playwright Ali Salem in Writers' Syndicate. Salem had been expelled from the syndicate in May 2001 for his pro-normalization stance vis-à-vis Israel. The head of the syndicate says that he will appeal the ruling.

On July 28, Sudanese vice-president Ali Osman Taha pays a visit to Cairo to meet with President Mubarak about the interim peace accord recently signed between north and south Sudan, engaged in a bloody 20-year civil war.

The agreement was brokered by the US-sponsored IGAD initiative with no input from Egypt. It calls for two, temporary separate confederations in Sudan and may open up the way for a divided Sudan, something long-opposed by Egypt.

On July 29, international observers and local civil rights activists are stunned when sociologist **Saad Eddin Ibrahim** is convicted once more and sentenced to seven years in prison. The head of the Ibn Khaldoun Center for Social and Developmental Studies, Ibrahim plans to appeal.

The state-owned tobacco giant Eastern Tobacco raises prices on many of its cigarette brands, including some types of the local favorite Cleopatra.

After twice postponing its ruling, a military court on July 30 sentences 16 members of the Muslim Brotherhood to prison terms ranging from three to five years. Five of the 22 defendants are acquitted on charges of joining an illegal organization to overthrow the government. Many of the defendants are university professors, arrested in the wake of the US bombing campaign in Afghanistan.

Who's Who

Business

Abd al-Aziz, Mahmoud. The former chairman of CIB and the National Bank is now the deputy governor at the CBE.

Abd al-Wadood, Mostafa. The young financier is the co-founder and managing director of Sigma Capital, a leading investment bank.

Abu al-Enein, Mohammed. The Ceramica Cleopatra magnate also dabbles in politics as an MP for the ruling party.

Abu al-Fotouh, Hossam. Mr. BMW and chairman of Daewoo Egypt.

Adib, Emad al-Din. Chairman of the board and driving force behind *al-Alam al-Yom*, the only business daily in Egypt. Also a high-profile presenter for satellite TV channel Orbit's *Ala al-Hawa* (On the Air).

Alfi, Moataz al-. Represents the Kuwaiti-owned Americana foods group in Egypt, with franchises for everything from KFC to TGI Fridays. Also an important player in the Future Generations Foundation, Gamal Mubarak's initiative to improve the job skills of Egyptian grads.

Ayub, Mahmood. World Bank rep in Egypt, Yemen, and Djibouti.

Bahgat, Ahmed. Egypt's leading maker of TV sets under international brands like Grundig and own labels such as Goldi. Last year moved into content as well, starting one the first private satellite stations in Egypt, Dream TV. Also into medical equipment and real estate projects like Dreamland in Sixth of October City.

Barakat, Hazem. Scion of the Barakat family, major shareholders in Miraco-Carrier air conditioners.

Baradie, Ahmed. Headed Citibank's North African operations before taking over the helm of Banque du Caire in order to oversee the bank's restructuring program. Recently appointed to the US-Egypt Presidents' Council.

Beleidi, Mostafa al-. Cosmetics tycoon who acted as agent for big French names, but skipped the country owing Egyptian banks about LE150 million.

Bennett, Adam. IMF representative in Egypt.

Beshir, Aqil. Before being appointed chairman and CEO of Telecom Egypt he worked in the software development arm of Alkan Group, one of the first non-state companies in Egypt to invest in telecoms and IT.

Bishara, Khaled. Young founder of Link Egypt, Egypt's number one ISP. Last year signed a deal with Microsoft to create a new portal, MSN Arabia.

Bishara, Louis. Chairman of Bishara Textile and Garment Manufacturing.

Choucri, Hussein. Cool-headed ex-Wall Street operator runs HC Securities, one of Cairo's most respected private finance houses. Expanded to Turkey last year.

Cordano, Francesco. Managing director of Fiat Egypt and president of the Egyptian-Italian Chamber of Commerce.

Danish, Adel. The IT entrepreneur is the CEO of Masriya Information Systems and a member of the US-Egypt Presidents' Council.

Dessouqi, Mohammed Said. Chairman of state-controlled Suez Cement, by far Egypt's biggest cement producer after its year 2000 purchase of Tora Cement.

Diab, Kamel. Has turned PICO into one of the biggest names in Egyptian agriculture. Also has interests in petroleum.

Ezz, Ahmed. The king of Egyptian steel. Parlayed the family scrap-metal business into Egypt's biggest private steel producer, then merged with state-owned ANSDK to form a regional steel giant. Also runs Jawhara Ceramics company, sits in parliament and on the US-Egypt Presidents' Council, and is a big wheel in the North Gulf of Suez Free Zone.

Ezz al-Arab, Hisham. Acting managing director of Egypt's top private bank, Commercial International Bank, brought a wealth of international banking experience with him when he took over at CIB early in 1999 having worked for Deutsche

Bank, JP Morgan, and Merrill Lynch.

Fabian, Igor. Managing Director of Edison Egypt, a major player in the sector and partner with British Gas in the new LNG plant, the largest petrochemical project in Egypt. Also owner of Intergen, along with Shell and Bechtel.

Fahmy, Hisham. Formerly of Egyptian Center for Economic Studies, now executive director of the American Chamber of Commerce.

Farag Amer, Mohammed. Faragallah processed and packed foods supremo, runs operations from Borg al-Arab industrial city near Cairo. Also serves as an MP.

Faramawi, Ali. A big name in IT circles, he heads Microsoft Egypt's regional operations. Also sits on the US-Egypt Presidents' Council.

Ferguson, Curtis. Egypt's biggest coke dealer—cola that is. As GM of Coca-Cola Egypt, he keeps the nation's thirst quenched.

Fiani, Josse Dora. Created Egypt's business bible, the Kompass directory.

Frystacki, Henryk. MD of Siemens Ltd, the Egypt-based arm of Siemens which has operations in many fields and has built almost half of Egypt's thermal power plants.

Fysh, Stuart. Country manager for British Gas, a major investor in both gas production and distribution.

Gabr, Shafiq. Talking head in international business forums. Owns Artoc Trading, imports Skoda cars, and runs a series of publications. His aggressive style has earned him plenty of critics.

Galal, Ahmed. Economist and former World Bank brain, now executive head of the independent think tank, the Egyptian Center for Economic Studies.

Ghabbour, Raouf. Egypt's bus supremo as head of ITAMCO, plus assembles Hyundai cars. Also a member of the US-Egypt Presidents' Council.

Gobran, Maged. Chairman and MD of Glaxo Wellcome Egypt, the country's biggest pharmaceutical producer.

Granryd, Mats. President of Ericsson Egypt.

Guemei, Omar. The head of the Arab Swiss Engineering Co. (ASEC) has his hands all over cement, from engineering to production. Added Helwan Cement to ASEC's holding early in

the year.

Guweili, Ahmed. Former minister of trade and supply, now head of Saudi billionaire Prince Walid Bin Talal's Kingdom Agricultural Development Co., a huge investor in Toshka.

Hamza, Samir. The Hamza half of Baker & McKenzie (Helmy & Hamza) law firm.

Handousa, Heba. Prominent economist and driving force behind the Economic Research Forum, a think tank that covers the Arab world, Turkey, and Iran.

Hassan, Hazem Zaki. Chairman of KPMG Hazem Hassan. Has a Central Bank board seat.

Hefnawy, Ali el-. As chairman and CEO of Smart Village Development Co., he hopes to turn Egypt into the Silicon Valley of the East.

Heikal, Ahmed. With brother Hassan, one of the driving forces behind EFG-Hermes, Egypt's top home-grown investment bank. Son of Egypt's most famous journalist and one-time confidant of Nasser, Mohammed Hassanein Heikal. Now involved with the Arab Company for Arts (Funoun).

Heikal, Hassan. Younger brother of Ahmed and son of Mohammed Hassanein is head of investment banking at EFG-Hermes.

Helmi, Atef. GM of Oracle Egypt.

Helmi, Baha al-Din. Chairman of Banque Misr, Egypt's second biggest state-owned bank.

Helmy, Taher. Co-runs top law firm Helmy and Hamza, the Cairo branch of Baker and Mackenzie. Also chairs Egyptian Center for Economic Studies and the 2000-appointed Telecom Egypt board.

Helw, Ahmed al-. Left EFG-Hermes to found own brokerage, which quickly became a market leader before being bought out by Flemings Mansour. Left after Flemings published controversial research document on Egyptian economy. Talented young financier, now setting up consultancy to advise "new economy" companies.

Kabil, Tarek. A formerly expatriate Egyptian who has returned home to run Pepsi Egypt, the country's no. 2 beverage company.

Kamel, Ibrahim. High-profile businessman with interests in aromatics, Russian aircraft, airports, real estate, North Coast resorts, and more.

Kamhawi, Nabil. Chairman of Arthur Anderson Egypt.

Khalil, Medhat. CEO and driving force behind the founding of Raya Holding Company, a computer services company with interests in information systems, software development, and e-business. Also a member of the US-Egypt Presidents' Council.

Khamis, Mohammed Farid. Carpet king of Egypt. His Oriental Weavers is the world's no. 3 coverer of floors.

Khayat, Dina. Savvy fund manager for Lazard Frères.

Lakah, Rami. Builder of turnkey hospitals, importer of medical equipment, and creator of controversy. Egypt's first Catholic MP was stripped of membership in the parliament last year for his dual nationality, and his stock went through the floor when he defaulted on eurobonds in July.

Lehata, Ossama. Chairman of Mena Tours, one of Egypt's largest travel agencies, and general agent for British Airways.

Lutz, Hans-Georg Managing director of Mercedes-Benz Egypt.

Maghrabi, Akef. Head of Maghrabi Optics and financer of a new eye hospital in Fustat.

Malas, Iyad. An IT mover and shaker, the man behind Arabia.com.

Mallawani, Yasser al-. Chairman of Flemings CIIC. Like many senior bankers in Egypt schooled at the Commercial International Bank. Also sits on the Amcham board.

Mansour, Mohammed. Along with Youssef and Yasin, forms one of the biggest family conglomerates in Egypt: GM cars, Caterpillar equipment, Fleming Mansour investment bank, McDonalds, Metro supermarkets, and more. Mohammed is the current president of Amcham and sits on the US-Egypt Presidents' Council.

McArthur, Dan, Chairman of General Motors Egypt.

Mekawy, Hisham. President and GM of BP Amoco Egypt. Given Egypt's burgeoning gas reserves, his role of focusing on gas exploration, development, and marketing both domestic and foreign is growing in importance.

Metwalli, Mohammed. Winning tenders for Toshka turned his Arabian International Construction into a big league player, but an insider trading scandal and refusal to turn over financial statements to the CMA got AIC in hot water at the bourse.

Moallem, Ibrahim al-. Founder of Dar al-Shorouq, the biggest private publisher in Egypt. Heads the Arab Publishing Association and also sits on the board at the Ahli Club.

Mohanna, Omar. Chairman of Accor Hotels, the number one foreign manager of hotels in Egypt.

Moharem, Gamal. Former chief representative for the Bank of New York is now the president of Misr Commercial Bank.

Mohieldin, Mahmoud. The Cairo University prof is an advisor to Youssef Boutros Ghali and also a member of the CBE board.

Mostafa, Talaat. Major developer from Alexandria, with interests in San Stefano, the Garden City Four Seasons, Beverly Hills housing development, and several tourist proects. Now semi-retired, he has passed the chair of his company on to his son Hisham.

Nasrallah, Khalil. With his brother Ramzy, runs Wadi Foods, producing gourmet olives and olive oil, and other organic food.

Nasser, Farouq. As chairman of International Development Consultants, he has brokered some of the big cement sales.

Nesci, Vincenzo. Runs Alcatel's operations in Egypt and the Middle East.

Nosseir, Mohammed. Big tycoon. His Alkan group does everything from telecoms to developing Cairo's new financial center.

Nour, Tareq. The guy who brought jingles to TV and made Americana Advertising Egypt's top biller. Now trades under his own name. Made headlines last year when he dropped MobiNil and switched to Vodafone.

Osman, Ismail. Nephew of Arab Contractors founder Osman Ahmed Osman, he ran the family holdings until he was kicked upstairs last year and made a consultant to the Ministry of Housing, supposedly after making noises about government debts to construction companies.

Oswald, George. Heads the Jeep and Chrysler half of DaimlerChrysler. Chairman of operations in Egypt.

Raafat, Sherif. Former popular and outspoken chairman of the Egyptian stock exchange, rejoined Concord International Investments after his action-packed 18-month stint.

Rachid, Rachid Mohammed. Unilever and Fine Foods supremo. Claims to be the biggest producer of quick turnover goods (from Lipton Tea to Dove soap and Axe and Impulse deodorants) in Egypt.

Rae, Paul. Chairman of Exxon Mobil Egypt.

Ragab, Abd al-Fattah. Chairman of Ford Egypt and son of Mohammed, head of the Alexandria Businessmen's Association.

Ragab, Mohammed Sadeq. Chairman of Eastern Tobacco, the giant state-owned cigarette monopoly and producers of the ubiquitous Cleopatra smokes.

Rifaie, Faika el-. A former sub-governor at the CBE, now she's a prominent analyst and talking head.

Rizq, Hani. Confectionery king, Milkyland supremo, and president of International Foods, which makes the products of US sweet company Hostess.

Saad, Farid. Egyptian Finance Co. whose front line project is Soma Bay, Egypt's second integrated mega-resort after Gouna.

Saad, Sami. Assembles Mercedes-Benz in Egypt and has interests in concrete and infrastructure construction.

Saba, Aladdin. Wall Street whiz helped kick-start Egypt's financial industry by co-founding Hermes. Now in the process of setting up his own investment company.

Sabbour, Hussein. Among other projects, his company, Sabbour Associates, built the Cairo metro and Arkadia Mall, now run by his son Omar. Also chairman of the Shooting Club.

Sallam, Saad. Head of family-controlled Olympic Group for Financial Investments, Egypt's number one maker of washing machines and water heaters. Systematically bought out rival makers of domestic appliances, including Ideal, to leave Olympic with a near monopoly in the local market.

Sawiris, Naguib. Runs the telecoms and IT arm of the Sawiris empire, with pay-phones, internet and, of course, cellular phones among the interests. Now carving out a mobile phone empire in Africa and parts of the Middle East.

Sawiris, Nassef. Heads Orascom Construction Industries, which groups the family's building interests together, with companies ranging from cement to gas. Expanding regionally.

Sawiris, Onsi. Head of the Sawiris family, indisputedly Egypt's most successful business clan. Founded the family fortune with the construction company he started in Upper Egypt. His three sons are listed above and below.

Sawiris, Samih. Mr. Tourism. Behind Gouna, the highly successful, totally-owned tourist town north of Hurghada.

Schmidt, Hans Juergen. Chairman of Bayer Egypt.

Seoudi, Abd al-Meneim. Chairman of Suzuki Egypt, plus head of the Federation of Egyptian Industries.

Shaalan, Abd al-Shakour. Bigwig in the IMF meets regularly with the powers that be over matters at the heart of Egypt's economic performance.

Shawqi, Ahmed. Big name accountant and former president of Amcham. Executive Vice President of Shawqi and Co.

Shawqi, Mohammed. Agent for Mitsubishi Elevators, an ever-expanding market.

Shedid, Khaled. Managing director of the Swiss-based Schindler elevator company (not to be confused with the state-owned elevator company of the same name).

Sherif, Hisham al-. Egypt's IT supremo. Set up the Cabinet Information Decision Support Center.

Sheta, Mohammed Abd al-Mohsen. Heads the diverse IGI Group which made its name trading oil and chemicals, but whose activities now range from cosmetics to petroleum, industrial services, and food processing.

Shobokshi, Fahd. Saudi businessman with big real estate investments in Egypt.

Stevenson, Shanon. Vice-president and GM of Proctor and Gamble Egypt and East Africa.

Sultan, Fouad. A former minister of tourism turned venture capitalist and fund manager with his Ahli for Development. Chairman of the Board at the Heliopolis Sporting Club.

Sultan, Osman. CEO of MobiNil, Egypt's biggest mobile phone operator and one of the biggest companies on the Egyptian exchange by market capitalization.

Tahri, Nevine El-. Leading lady in the Cairo bourse, a stage usually dominated by men. Dutch banking giant ABN Amro bought a controlling stake in her brokerage, Delta, in 1999.

Talal, Prince Walid Bin. Saudi financier and one of the world's wealthiest men. Interests in Egypt include a huge swathe of the southern land reclamation project, Toshka, and hotels.

Tawfiq, Amr. General manager of IBM Egypt. and a key player in e-business solutions.

Tawfiq, Hani. A big name in financial circles, runs Egycap Investment.

Tawil, Said Ahmed al-. Chairman of Setcore, with interests ranging from oil and gas to construction, food processing, and steel structures.

Tawil, Ahmed al-. Of Triangle Trading and Engineering fame, big IT and systems players.

Taymour, Mohammed. Chairman of EFG-Hermes and doyen of the financial services industry. Merged his Egyptian Financial Group with Hermes to form Egypt's leading investment bank.

Thomason, Thomas E. Runs Intergen's operations in Egypt. The company's headline project is the nation's first privately financed electricity plant at Sidi Krir near Alexandria.

Vaughan, Andrew. Chairman of Shell Egypt.

Viney, Ian. Head of Commercial International Life Insurance,

Wahba, Mahmoud. US-Egyptian businessman and cotton trader. Won huge damages for government meddling with cotton prices.

Younis, Mohammed. The brains behind Concord Investments, Egypt's biggest fund manager.

Zahran, Mahmoud. Managing director of the household manufacturer and Tefal agent in Egypt. Also has many development projects.

Zaklama, Loula. Queen and pioneer of market research in Egypt. Runs Rada Research and Public Relations Co.

Zayat, Ahmed el-. Pulled off the deal of the century by leveraging a takeover of state beermaker Ahram Beverages. ABC is now one of Egypt's most profitable businesses, expanding into the Gulf with its non-alcoholic Fayrouz and Birell. Also sits on the Egypt-US Presidents' Council.

Zayat, Elhamy. Chairman and CEO of Emeco Travel and general tourism talking head.

Zorba, Galal. Chairman of Nile Clothing Co., which produces clothes under license for Van Heusen and Pierre Cardin. Sits on the US-Egypt Presidents' Council and also chairs Expolink, the Egyptian exporters association.

Politics

Abd al-Nour, Mounir Fakhri. Rising star in the Wafd party who won a seat for a north Cairo district despite heavy government fire—and he's a Copt, to boot. Scion of the Vitrac jelly and juice family empire.

Abd al-Razeq, Mohammed. As state wheat buyer, or vice-chairman of the General Authority for Supply Commodities, he is a major mover of futures markets.

Abu al-Fotouh, Abd al-Meneim. Top ranking Muslim Brotherhood physician imprisoned between 1995-2000. He engineered the Brother's electoral alliance with other parties in the 1984 and 1987 parliamentary elections and oversaw the group's pragmatic turn to centrist politics.

Abu al-Magd, Kamal. Former minister of information is now a talking head for the middle-of-the-road brand of Islamism. Also the international dialogue chief at the Arab League.

Adli, Habib al-. Interior minister appointed in the wake of the Luxor massacre of November 1997. He has kept a lid on Islamist insurgency since then.

Ahmed, Kamal. Longtime independent Nasserist and MP from Alexandria who became a household name in May 2001 when he directed a blistering attack on alleged corruption at the bourse.

Azmi, Zakariya. MP for the Zeitoun district in Cairo. As Mubarak's chief-of-staff he is the president's pointman in parliament, where he plays the role of the "critical wing" of the NDP to signal the president's displeasure at the party hacks.

Badrawi, Hossam. Scion of a powerful political family and an MP who holds the Qasr al-Nil seat in the heart of Cairo. He heads the parliament's education committee and also owns one of Egypt's most prestigious private hospitals.

Baha al-Din, Hussein Kamel. Consummate politician and former pediatrician of the Nasser children has been a controversial education minister, drawing criticism for banning the *higab* in school a few years back and taken to task for rapidly declining school standards.

Bassyouni, Amin. Head of NileSat, Egypt's ambitious project aimed at staying ahead in the media game. Former head of the Egyptian Radio and Television Union.

Bayoumi, Gamal. As assistant minister for foreign affairs he was Egypt's pointman in the difficult negotiations with the EU over the partnership agreement, signed in March 2001.

Baz, Osama al-. The presidential spokesman is among Mubarak's key advisers, particularly in the foreign arena. Often deals with Israel and the foreign press.

Beltagui, Mamdouh. As tourism minister oversees one of the key engines of Egypt's economic growth.

Beshir, Aqil. Before being appointed chairman and CEO of Telecom Egypt he worked in the software development arm of Alkan Group, one of the first non-state companies in Egypt to invest in telecoms and IT.

Boutros Ghali, Boutros. Former secretary-general of United Nations and deputy foreign minister under Sadat. Part of the delegation that negotiated peace with Israel.

Boutros Ghali, Youssef. Francophone, Anglophone minister of foreign trade. A former IMF economist who won his PhD at MIT, he is thought to be the architect of Egypt's economic reform program. A Coptic Christian born into an illustrious family. Nephew of Boutros.

Dawoud, Dia al-Din. Head of the Nasserist party and former minister of social affairs. Has overseen the defection of the party's young cadres due to his reportedly heavy-handed leadership style.

Ebeid, Atef. Prime minister and former minister of public enterprises who headed Egypt's missions to the World Bank and IMF. Considered to have a greater understanding of investors' needs than Kamal al-Ganzouri, whom he replaced as PM in October 1999.

Eryan, Essam al-. One of the prime representatives of the new guard of the Muslim Brotherhood. Former secretary-general of the Doctors' Syndicate and MP from 1987-1990. Arrested and imprisoned from 1995-2000.

Farghali, al-Badri. Colorful and outspoken gadfly MP of the leftist Tagammu Party famed for his tirades against alleged government corruption and irregularities. Represents Port Said.

Gindi, Amina al-. Social affairs minister, a portfolio traditionally reserved for women since the Nasser regime. One of two women in the cabinet.

Gomaa, Noman. Elected new head of the Wafd Party following the death of Fouad Serageddin in August 2000. Seems to be following in the footsteps of Serageddin by ruling the party as his own personal fiefdom after unilaterally expelling two Wafd MPs from the party in March 2001.

Hafez, Abd al-Rahman. Head of Media Production City, the state-owned TV and film production complex.

Hamed, Hassan. Appointed as head of the Egyptian Radio and Television Union in April last year.

Hassan, Farkhonda. Geology prof, Shura Council member, and NDP bigwig. Head of the National Women's Council.

Hassan al-Banna, Ahmed Seif al-Islam. Lawyer son of Brotherhood founder Hassan al-Banna and former MP, he is the secretary-general of the bar association.

Hassanein, Medhat. Finance minister and former financial consultant and AUC professor. Understands the needs of the business and the investment community having sat on numerous boards of directors.

Helmi, Mostafa Kamal. Long-serving president of the Shura Council.

Hemeida, Ragab Helal. Sole liberal party MP and self-styled politico who loves the limelight.

Heshmat, Gamal. Unknown second-tier Muslim Brother and freshman MP who made a splash in January 2001 with a motion protesting the publication of three allegedly racy novels by a government printing agency.

Hodeibi, Mamoun al-. Official spokesman of the Muslim Brotherhood, former judge and MP. Son of Hassan al-Hodeibi, the supreme guide who built the rapprochement with the military regime in 1952 before the group's official banning in 1954. Hodeibi Junior inherited cautious moderation from his father and a desire to build bridges with the government.

Hosni, Farouq. Artist and long-time culture minister, he is a convenient punching bag for critics, who charge him with everything from appeasing Islamists to ignoring hungry artists to mismanaging the nation's monumental heritage.

Hussein, Magdi. Editor of the frozen *al-Shaab* newspaper. Imprisoned twice for libeling prominent government figures, he now sits on the board at the Journalists' Syndicate.

Ibrahim, Abd al-Hamid. Chairman of the Capital Markets Authority, responsible for fair play on the bourse.

Madi, Abu al-Ela. Politically skillful engineer and former Muslim Brother who broke away in 1996 to form the Wasat (Center) Party, which included a prominent Copt as a founding member. Turned down twice by the Political Parties Committee. He was tried (and acquitted) before a military tribunal.

Makram Ebeid, Mona. Former Wafd MP, women's rights activist, and conservationist. Member of a well-known Coptic family.

Makram Ebeid, Nadia. Former high-profile environment minister replaced by Mamdouh Riyad Tadros in last November's cabinet shuffle. She was famous for her sometimes overly ambitious campaigns, like banning smoking in government offices.

Mashhour, Mostafa. Supreme guide of the Muslim Brotherhood. An old-guard Muslim Brother who was a member of the group's secret military wing in the 1940s. Imprisoned by Nasser and released by Sadat. After the 2000 elections and the Brothers' surprise bag of 17 seats he publicly called on the government to give the group official legal status.

Mohi al-Din, Khaled. One of the original Free Officers who led the 1952 military coup. Was a proponent of bringing back multi-party politics. When Sadat did allow political pluralism in 1976, Mohi al-Din set up the leftist Tagammu Party which he still heads. Oldest sitting member of parliament.

Morr, Awad al-. Former chief justice of the Supreme

Constitutional Court given credit for raising the profile of the institution. Runs a private law practice that attracts prominent clients and has participated in drafting a new press code.

Moussa, Amr. Egypt's most popular politician and former foreign minister now heads the Arab League. Best known for his uncompromising statements regarding the Middle East peace process.

Mubarak, Gamal. Banker son of the president is now a senior figure in the ruling National Democratic Party.

Nazif, Ahmed. The dapper former university professor was handed the IT and telecommunications ministerial duties in October 1999. The industry has been singled out by the president himself as one to back.

Nour, Ayman. One of the youngest members of parliament, and also one of the most controversial. A former Wafdist, he was kicked out of the party in 2001 after a run-in with party leader Noman Gomaa and still has not found a new party.

Osman, Amal. Former social affairs minister and current deputy speaker of parliament. Osman is an NDP pillar and a no-nonsense lawyer who has taken a leading role in drafting some notorious legislation, such as the maligned NGO law 153/1999, passed in a new guise as Law 84 in 2002.

Osman, Mohammed. Of the Osman construction family fame. He was appointed minister of planning in last year's cabinet shuffle.

Osman, Nabil. Head of the State Information Service.

Sabahi, Hamdin. Prominent independent Nasserist MP who also serves on the board of the Journalists' Syndicate. Almost became the first opposition MP to head a parliamentary committee when speaker Surour called for a re-vote.

Sabet, Madkour. State censor. Responsible for checking all films and music.

Said, Refaat al-. Secretary-general of the leftist Tagammu party, sometime historian, and former member of Nasser's secret vanguard organization. The *de facto* head of the party in place of the ailing Mohi al-Din.

Shazli, Kamal al-. Parliamentary affairs minister and NDP bigwig who acts as a kind of party whip for the majority in parliament. His job got harder with the election of 213 independents who later officially joined the NDP but proved highly unpredictable in their voting behavior. Reportedly writing his memoirs.

Sherif, Safwat al-. The minister of information has been in the job for two decades and shows no sign of losing his grip. Also serves as the NDP's secretary general.

Shukri, Ibrahim. One of the most durable fixtures of the political scene: a student activist in the 1940s, a founder of the nationalist Young Egypt party before the 1952 revolution, and agriculture minister under Sadat, who allowed him to set up the Socialist Labor Party. Still president of the party, he has been less in the limelight since it was frozen in 2000.

Suleiman, Omar. State security chief and one of the most powerful men in Egypt. His name is frequently thrown around as a possible Mubarak choice for veep.

Surour, Fathi. Longest standing speaker of the People's Assembly and MP for Sayeda Zeinab. The wily former law professor maintains a delicate balancing act in parliament, keeping a lid on contentious debates and making sure dissent remains in the confines of the chamber.

Takla, Laila. Former MP with an interest in environmental affairs.

Tantawi, Mohammed Hussein. Has kept a very low profile as minister of defense.

Tantawi, Sheikh Mohammed al-Sayed. Appointed Sheikh of al-Azhar by President Mubarak in 1996. Praised by some as a moderate, reviled by others. Succeeded hard-liner Gad al-Haqq Ali Gad al-Haqq.

Tayeb, Mohammed Ahmed al-. The former awqaf employee from Upper Egypt was appointed head mufti early this year.

Torgoman, Sameh al-. Chairman of Cairo and Alexandria Stock Exchanges. The Stanford-educated lawyer and one-time former deputy district attorney has risen through the ranks of the government legal profession to his current post, but he faced heat from parliament last year over alleged corruption at the bourse.

Wali, Youssef. Deputy prime minister as well as minister of agriculture, Wali is rarely outspoken but is a powerful insider.

Welch, David. He replaced Daniel Kutzer last year as the US ambassador to Egypt.

Zayat, Montasser al-. A leading Islamist lawyer. A *de facto* spokesman of the Gamaa Islamiya in the 1990s after it launched an insurgency to topple the government. Regarded as the mastermind of the group's 1997 truce with the government.

Public Service

Government

Ahli Insurance Chairman, Mohammed Abu al-Yazid

al-Ahram newspaper Editor-in-Chief, Ibrahim Nafie

Ain Shams University President, Hassan Ahmed Ghallab

Air Defense Forces Commander, Sami Hafez Anan

Airforce Commander, Magdi Gamal Shaarawi

al-Akhbar newspaper Editor-in-Chief, Galal Deweidar

Alexandria University President, Essam Ahmed Salem

(Antiquities) Supreme Council of Antiquities Secretary-General, Zahi Hawass

Arab League Secretary-General, Amr Moussa

Armed Forces Chief-of-Staff, Hamdi Weheiba

Aswan High Dam Chairman, Taher Mohammed Zidan

al-Azhar, Sheikh of Mohammed Sayed al-Tantawi

al-Azhar University President, Ahmed Omar Hashem

Bank of Alexandria Chairman, Mahmoud Abd al-Latif

Banque du Caire Chairman, Ahmed Mounir al-Bardie

Banque Misr Chairman, Baha al-Din Helmi

Cairo University President, Naguib al-Helali

Capital Markets Authority Chairman, Abd al-Hamid Ibrahim

Censor Madkour Sabet

Central Agency for Public Mobilization and Statistics (CAPMAS) President, Ihab Mostafa Elwi

Central Bank of Egypt Governor, Mahmoud Abu al-Uyoun

Court of Cassation Chief Justice, Zakariya Shalash

Customs Authority Chairman, Mohammed Ibrahim Bushisha

Eastern Tobacco Chairman, Mohammed Sadeq Ragab

EgyptAir Chairman, Abd al-Fattah Kato

Egyptian Environmental Affairs Agency (EEAA)
CEO, Ayman Abu Hadid

Egyptian Insurance Supervisory Authority
Chairman, Kheiry Selim

European Union Ambassador, Raouf Saad

General Authority for Investment and Free Zones
Chairman, Mohammed al-Ghamrawi

General Egyptian Book Organization (GEBO)
Chairman, Samir Sarhan

al-Gomhouriya **newspaper** Editor-in-Chief, Samir Ragab

Information and Decision Support Center (IDSC)
Chairman, Raafat Radwan

Media Production City Chairman, Abd al-Rahman Hafez

Misr Insurance Chairman, Mohammed Mohammed al-Teir

Mufti of the Republic Mohammed Ahmed al-Tayeb

National Archives President, Mohammed Saber Arab

National Bank of Egypt Chairman, Diaa Fahmi

National Council of Women President, Farkhonda Hassan

National Library (Dar al-Kutub) Director, Salah Fadl

Navy Commander, Tamer Abd al-Alim Ismail

(Petroleum) Egyptian General Petroleum Corporation
Chairman, Ibrahim Saleh

Pharaonic Insurance Chairman, Peter Hammer

Public Prosecutor Maher Abd al-Wahed

al-Sharq Insurance Chairman, Anwar Zekri

Shura Council President, Mostafa Kamel Helmi

Social Fund for Development Chairman, Hani Seif

(Stock Exchange) Cairo and Alexandria Stock Exchanges Chairman, Sameh al-Turgoman

Suez Canal Authority Chairman, Ahmed Ali Fadel

Supreme Constitutional Court Chief Justice, Fathi Naguib

Supreme Council of Culture
Secretary-General, Gaber Asfour

Tax Authority Chairman, Talaat Hamam

Telecom Egypt Chairman and CEO, Aqil Beshir

(Tourism) Egyptian Tourist Authority
Chairman, Adel Abd al-Aziz

Tourist Development Authority
Acting Chairman, Fateh al-Negoumi

(TV) Egyptian Radio and Television Union (ERTU)
Chairman, Hassan Hamed

United States Ambassador, Nabil Fahmi

United Nations Ambassador, Ahmed Abu al-Gheit

(Wheat) General Authority for Supply Commodities
Vice-Chairman or State Wheat Buyer, Mohammed Abdel Razeq

Heads of Holding Companies

Building and Construction Ahmed Ahmed al-Sayed

Chemical Industries Mohammed Adel al-Mouzi

Cotton and Foreign Trade Nabil al-Marsafawi

Engineering Industries Ibrahim al-Sebaai

Food Industries Adel Ibrahim al-Shahawi

Housing, Tourism and Cinema Mostafa Eid Mostafa

Maritime Transport Atef Hassan Marouni

Metallurgical Industries Mohammed Adel al-Danaf

Pharmaceutical Mohammed Galal Ghorab

Spinning and Weaving Mohsen Gilani

Sporting Clubs

Ahli Club Hassan Hamdi (acting president)

Gezira Club Ramzi Rushdi

Heliopolis Club Fouad Sultan

Shooting Club Hussein Sabbour

Zamalek Club Kamal Darwish

Academic and Research Centers and Societies

Ahram Center for Political and Strategic Studies
Director, Abd al-Meneim Said

American Research Center in Egypt (ARCE)
Director, Robert Springborg

American University in Cairo (AUC) Acting President, Thomas A. Bartlett

Bibliotheca Alexandrina Director, Ismail Serageldin

Centre d'Etudes et de Documentation Economique,

Juridique et Sociale (CEDEJ) Director, Ghislaine Alleaume

Economic Research Forum (ERF) Managing Director, Heba Handoussa

Egyptian Center for Economic Studies (ECES) Executive Director, Ahmed Galal

Ford Foundation Representative in Egypt, Emma Playfair

Fulbright Commission Director, Ann Radwan

IFAO (French archaeological mission) Director, Bernard Mathieu

Mishkat Economic Research Center Director, Nader Fergani

Pro Helvetia Center (Swiss) Acting Director, Mayson Mahfouz

Religious Organizations

Coptic Evangelical Church Pastor Safwat al-Bayadi

Coptic Orthodox Church Pope Shenouda III

Business Organizations

American Chamber of Commerce President, Mohammed Mansour

Club D'Affaires Franco-Egyptien (CAFE) Director, Atef Mokhtar

British Egyptian Businessmen's Association (BEBA) Chairman, Mohammed Nosseir

Federation of Egyptian Industries President, Abd al-Meneim Seoudi

German-Arab Chamber of Industry and Commerce President, Udo Scherf

Italian Chamber of Commerce President, Francesco Cordano

Japanese External Trade Organization (JETRO) Managing Director, Koi Ta Bashi

Political Party Heads

Arab Socialist Misr (Egypt) Party* Gamal al-Din Rabie (disputed)

Democratic Generation** Nagi al-Shehabi

Democratic People's Party* Anwar Afifi (disputed)

Egypt 2000** Fawzi Khalil

Green Party Abd al-Meneim al-Aasar

Labor Party* Ibrahim Shukri

Liberal Party* Disputed after death of Mostafa Kamel Murad in 1998

Misr al-Fatah Party (Young Egyptians Party)* Ahmed Ezz al-Din

Nasserist Arab Democratic Party Dia al-Din Dawoud

National Democratic Party (NDP) President, President Mubarak

NDP Secretary-General, Safwat al-Sherif

New Wafd Party Noman Gomaa

Social Justice Party* Mohammed Abd al-Aal

Socialist Liberal Party Ibrahim Tork

Tagammu Party Khaled Mohi al-Din

Takaful Party Osama Shaltout

Umma Party Ahmed al-Sabahi

al-Wifaq al Qawmi (National Conciliation Party)* Ahmed Shoheib

* Indefinitely frozen by adminstrative decree
** New in 2001-2002

Governors

Alexandria Abd al-Salam Mahgoub

Aswan Samir Mahmoud Youssef

Assyout Ahmed Hammam Mohammed

Beheira Ahmed Abd al-Meneim al-Leithi

Beni Sueif Said Mohammed al-Naggar

Cairo Abd al-Rehim Shehata

Damietta Abd al-Azim Wazir Abdullah

Daqahliya Ahmed Said Sawwan

Fayyoum Saad Nasser

Gharbiya Fathi al-Sayed Ibrahim

Giza Mahmoud Abu al-Leil

Ismailiya Fouad Saad al-Din Mohammed

Kafr al-Sheikh Ali Abd al-Shakour

Matrouh Mohammed al-Shahhat

Menoufiya Ahmed Metwalli Shahin
Minya Hassan Mohammed Ahmed Hemeida
New Valley Ahmed Medhat Abd al-Rahman
North Sinai Ahmed Abd al-Hamid Mohammed
Port Said Mostafa Kamel al-Sayed
Qalyoubiya Adli Hussein
Qena Adel Ali Labib
Red Sea Saad Hassan Abu Reda
Sohag Mamdouh Kedwani
South Sinai Mostafa Mohammed Afifi
Sharqiya Hamed Shatla
Suez Mohammed Seif al-Din Ahmed

Culture

Abbas, Hisham. Mr. Nice Guy of the pop music scene. Latest release: *Guwa fi Qalbi.*

Abd al-Aziz, Karim. Young heartthrob of the silver screen.

Abd al-Aziz, Lubna. Former classic film star turned critic and jury member at the Cairo Film Festival.

Abd al-Aziz, Mahmoud. Hunky, soulful star of classic 80s films like *Kit Kat, al-Aar,* and *al-Saher.*

Abd al-Aziz, Nesma. Resident drummer at the Cairo Opera House.

Abd al-Aziz, Yasmin. Most familiar face of the college-age generation who plays giggly yet precocious Egyptian everygirl roles.

Abd al-Baqi, Ashraf. Comedy actor who got off to a good start in 90s, but is still trying to make it as a leading star.

Abd al-Fadil, Mahmoud. Economics professor at Cairo University and top economic analyst of a leftward persuasion.

Abd al-Hamid, Ferdous. With her unassuming all-Egyptian looks, she specializes in playing strong, independent women. A staple of the *musalsalat* scene.

Abd al-Hayy, Abd al-Badie. Pioneering self-taught sculptor hails from a village in Upper Egypt. Now entering his ninth decade.

Abd al-Megid, Wahid. Incisive liberal analyst at the Ahram Center and former editor of the *Arab Strategic Report.*

Abd al-Nasser, Gamal. Creates colorful, painterly sculptures out of shoes, chairs, and other detritus.

Abd al-Quddous, Mohammad. Muslim Brother journalist and son of the late pulp fiction doyen Ihsan Abd al-Quddous. Writes weekly column in *al-Wafd* and elsewhere.

Abd al-Rahman, Ibrahim. Owner of Zamalek's Picasso gallery and renowned art collector.

Abd al-Razeq, Hussein. Longtime leftie and Tagammu party bigwig. Writes column in weekly *al-Ahali.*

Abd al-Rehim, Shaaban. Former *makwagi* (ironing man) turned *shaabi* idol turned film star. The bane of the cultural establishment, but his *I Hate Israel* made him a popular hero.

Abd al-Sayed, Dawoud. Director of serious, mainstream movies like *Kit Kat, Ard al-Ahlam,* and last year's *Muwatin, Mukhbir wa Harami.*

Abdou, Fifi. From *baladi* origins became the hottest belly dancer of the 80s. Her wealth is the stuff of legends. Returned to the stage last year with *Iddalai Ya Dosa.*

Abla, Mohammed. The Alexandria-born painter has been a popular staple of the arts scene for more than 20 years, with several European exhibitions under his belt.

Abnoudi, Abd al-Rahman al-. Voice of the Said. The colloquial verse of this poetic phenomenon from the South draws thousands at readings.

Abnoudi, Atiyat al-. Egypt's foremost documentary filmmaker is also an activist for women's rights.

Abu al-Naga, Khaled. Former Nile TV announcer turned film star. He played the citizen in last year's critically acclaimed *Muwatin, Mukhbir wa Harami.*

Abu Heif, Abd al-Latif. The man who crossed the English Channel in the 1950s was named the century's best swimmer last year by the US Higher Swimming Council.

Abu Seif, Onsi. Top set designer in the film industry.

Abu Shadi, Ali. Ex-censor who got censored: he took the rap this year when the Ministry of Culture decided to clean up its publishing act.

Adam, Ahmed. Comedy star of *Wala fi al-Niyya Filippiniya,*

Shahatin wa Nubala, and the musical *Huda Karama*.

Adawiya, Ahmed. The original *shaabi* singer of the 1970s started a comeback last year on the stage with Fifi Abdou.

Adl, Medhat and Sami. Producer brothers behind hit flicks like *Ismailiya Rayeh Gayy*.

Afifi, Fathi. Self-taught painter whose favorite themes are the workers' world and the factory.

Ahmed, Mohsen. Contender for title of Egypt's star cinematographer.

Ahmed, Samira. The actress lit up the screen in the 1950s and 60s. Now appears in the occasional TV soap drama.

Albert, Antoine. Long-standing top photographer at *al-Ahram*.

Ali, Magdi Ahmed. Director of critically-acclaimed *Ya Dunya Ya Gharami* who made a comeback last year with the controversial *Asrar al-Banat*.

Alim, Mahmoud Amin al-. Literary critic, commentator, and general talking head.

Allam, Tareq. TV presenter with great teeth who has turned a Ramadan pop quiz show into a social welfare agency.

Allouba, Nevine. Prize-winning soprano at the Cairo Opera, with a German PhD under her belt.

Allouba, Samia. Former student of choreographer Walid Ouni is now a dance instructor.

Amer, Ghada. The Egyptian expatriate artist has garnered both controversy and praise for her hand-stitched and painted erotic scenes.

Amin, Galal. Tweedy, provocative AUC professor and author of the best-selling *Whatever Happened to the Egyptians?*

Amin, Hussein. Galal's brother is ex-ambassador to Algeria and a leading liberal. Best-known book: *Dalil al-Muslim al-Hazin*.

Amin, Mervat. Top-billing starlet of the 70s, and still going strong.

Amin, Nora. Prominent playwright and director in the independent theater scene.

Ammawi, Anwar al-. Bodybuilding legend was named the champion of the century by the International Bodybuilding Federation last year.

Angarano, Stefania. Pioneer of the downtown arts scene, runs the Mashrabia Gallery.

Angham. Serious vocalist with a powerful voice keeps a foot in the pop scene with video clips.

Anoushka. Pop music singer who also hit the stage in last year's *Awlad al-Ghadab wa al-Hubb*.

Arafa, Sherif. Big-time director of Adel Imam vehicles and other blockbusters, including this summer's action flick *Mafia*.

Armand. Old school artist and photographer who still keeps his downtown studio. Also the son of Armand, another famed Egyptian photographer.

Asfour, Gaber. Intellectual heavyweight who heads the Higher Council for Culture.

Ashour, Radwa. Leading Arabic literature professor at Cairo University. Best-known book: *Gharnata*.

Aslan, Ibrahim. Tousled novelist since the 60s. Best known work: *al-Malak al-Hazin*, adapted to the screen as *Kit Kat*.

Aswani, Alaa al-. Dentist by profession, he wowed the literary crowd with his first novel *Imarat Yaqoubian*.

Attar, Ahmed al-. Independent theater director who got rave reviews for his *Life is Beautiful or Waiting for My Uncle from America*.

Avedissian, Chant. All-round artist who gyrates between whimsy, irony and, lately, Armenia.

Awa, Mohammed Selim al-. Islamist moderate thinker and prominent lawyer who participated in authoring the fatwa last year that ruled that American Muslim soldiers can join the Afghanistan war effort.

Awad, Mohammed. Architect bent on saving Alexandria from itself.

Badawi, El-Said. Directs the Teaching Arabic as a Foreign Language department at AUC, and the man behind *the* dictionary of Egyptian colloquial Arabic.

Badr, Sawsan. Versatile actress of the silver and small screen, and theater to boot. She picked up the Egyptian Film Society's best actress award in 2000 for her role in *al-Abwab al-Mughlaqa*.

Bahgat, Ahmed. See his conservative column on page 2 of *al-Ahram*. Best known book: *Qisas al-Anbiya*. Not to be confused with Ahmed Bahgat, the tycoon.

Bahgouri, George. Prodigal Saidi cartoonist and Paris resident, his creations show up every week in *al-Ahram Weekly*.

Bakr, Salwa. Eminent novelist. Best-known works: *Maqam Atiya, The Golden Chariot Doesn't Rise to Heaven, Bashmouri*.

Bakri, Asma al-. Director of *al-Shahatin wa al-Nubala*, among other artsy features.

Baladi, Lara. Francophone expatriate photographer with Lebanese roots who made a splash internationally after the Cartier Foundation for Contemporary Art commissioned one of her works.

Banna, Gamal al-. Trade unionist brother of Muslim Brothers' founder Hassan al-Banna. Extremely prolific author of books on trade and professional union issues and Islam and politics.

Barada, Ahmed. Squash star ranked no. 3 in the world. Survived mysterious stabbing in 1998 but retired last year.

Baroudi, Shams al-. Sexy 60s screen star who now sports a *niqab*.

Batroui, Menha el-. Long-time theater critic now writes for *al-Ahram Hebdo*.

Baz, Farouq al-. Ex-NASA brain is star science advisor to the president and founder of the Remote Sensing outfit at Boston University.

Bedeir, Sobhi. Director of the Opera Company at the Opera House.

Bikar, Hussein. Founder of the kids magazine *Sindbad*, and illustrious illustrator, painter, and art critic.

Bilal, Ahmed. Star of the Egyptian handball team.

Bisatie, Mohammed al-. Prominent writer of the Generation of the 60s and the former editor of the Ministry of Culture's Literary Voices series.

Bishai, Adel. AUC economics don and member of the Shura Council

Bishara, Kheiri. Director who started with artsy, neorealist stuff like *Yom Helw, Yom Murr* but switched to tosh like *Kaburiya*.

Bishri, Tareq al-. Top legal mind and ex-vice president of the State Council is an Islamist public intellectual.

Boghiguian, Anna. Brilliant, eccentric painter.

Boraie, Sherif. His Zeitouna Press brought aesthetics back to Egyptian publishing.

Chahine, Youssef. Egypt's best known filmmaker, at least in foreign climes. Won't give up after 40 years in the director's chair. Major films: *Bab al-Hadid, al-Ard, Iskandariya Leeh?*, and, most recently, *Sukout Hansawwar*.

Cossery, Albert. Franco-Egyptian writer who writes in French and whose stories have provided the basis for films like *al-Shahatin wa al-Nubala*.

Dagher, Abdo. Silver-toothed maestro of the Arabic violin.

Dahan, Ramy El-. This talented disciple of mudbrick guru Hassan Fathi has ended up doing architecture for the rich at Gouna and elsewhere.

Darwish, Mostafa. Doyen of Egyptian film critics and former chief censor.

Dawestashi, Esmat al-. Brash painter and eminent art critic.

Degheidi, Inas al-. The oft-hyped (and oft-panned) director won the Silver Pyramid at last year's Cairo Film Fest for her *Muzakirat Murahiqa*.

Dewey, Marwan al-. Leading art photographer spends most of his time on some Aegean island.

Diab, Amr. Slick crooner from Port Said known for the east-west mix in megahits like *Awaduni, Nur al-Ain,* and *Walla Ala Balo*.

Dina. Hottest, sassiest dancer of the moment, with an MA in philosophy.

Ebeid, Nabila. Doe-eyed starlet now fading. Last film: *al-Akher*.

Eissa, Ibrahim. Outspoken no-holds-barred young journalist. Former editor of the now defunct *al-Dustour*, he now hosts his own show on Dream TV.

Eissa, Salah. Editor of *al-Qahira* weekly, history buff, and a lonely non-dogmatic voice.

Eleili, Ezzat al-. One of his generation's best but lesser-known actors, he was the young radical peasant in *al-Ard* and is a staple supporting actor in Ramadan soaps.

Elias, Nadim. Sahara printing house owner in the Free Zone and the premier dictionary publisher, with brother Ramez and late sister Eva. Also father of Sami, an up-and-coming young video and photo artist.

Elwani, Rania. Egypt's "golden fish." The top swimmer announced her retirement in 2000 at age 22, taking the veil.

Elwi, Leila. Fave pin-up actress in the 80s and early 90s whose weight struggles have become fodder for gossip mags.

Enani, Salah. His whimsical, Egyptian Rubenesque figures are favorite poster and bookcover material.

Etrebi, Soheir al-. Graduated from heading Channel 1 to a top job in state TV.

Ezz al-Din, Hamada. Natty presenter of *Good Morning Egypt* has a sideline in decor.

Fahmi, Azza. Ain gallery owner and designer who made Bedouin jewelry chic.

Fahmi, Hussein. The blue-eyed movie star resigned last year as head of the Cairo Film Festival.

Fahmi, Mostafa. Hussein's lesser-known, dark-haired brother, stuck close to reality by playing rich playboys in 1980s B-movies. Lately doing commercials for gated communities with golf clubs.

Fahmi, Shahira. Cairo's top taste-maker, from Mix and Match clothes to neo-rustic décor at Gouna's Dar al-Omda.

Fakharani, Yehia al-. The roly-poly actor with a mirthful laugh is one of the best character actors around. Hit the stage this year playing the title role in *King Lear*.

Farag, Alfred. Prolific playwright since the 1960s.

Farag, Samir. A former general turned director of the Cairo Opera House.

Farahat, Amr. Leader of the religious music ensemble at the Opera House.

Farid, Vessela. Painter who came to Cairo from Bulgaria in 1938 and stayed. Her portraits of women delve into the unseen. Wife of late artist Morris Farid.

Farouq, Dalia. The American-trained soprano is an up-and-coming voice at the Cairo Opera.

Fathi, Nagla. Former sex symbol of the 1960s and 70s still occasionally pops up on the silver screen. Also married to TV's most popular man, Hamdi Qandil.

Fawzi, Mufid. TV's bulldog interviewer with a unique fashion sense. Tackles hot issues but knows where to stop.

Fawzi, Osama. Young director of arty flicks like *Gannat al-Shayatin*.

Fayyoumi, Omar al-. Artist from the downtown crowd, best known for iconic look-alikes of the Fayyoum portraits.

Fishawi, Farouq al-. Specialized in streetwise bad-boy roles until drug problems put a crimp in his acting style. Starred in last year's theater hit *al-Nas Illi fi al-Talet*.

Fouad, Karam. The doyen of traditional Nubian music.

Fouad, Mohammed. Crooner who hit it big with a role in *Ismailiya Rayeh Gayy*. Latest success: last year's *Rihlat Hubb*.

Fouad, Nagwa. Star dancer of the 1950s and 60s occasionally pops up on TV these days.

Francis, Karim. Suave owner of Espace gallery and a big man in the downtown arts scene.

Gamal al-Din, Karim. Owner of the Elixir Sound Studio, plus the recently acquired Studio Misr.

Gamil, Sanaa. Grande dame of the Cairo stage and screen. She's worked with everyone from the late Salah Abu Seif to Omar Sherif to Soad Hosni.

Gebali, Hussein al-. Head of the Artists' Syndicate and renowned painter.

Geretli, Hassan al-. Dynamo of independent theater leads the Warsha troupe.

Ghadban, Mary. Eminent film critic at Dar al-Hilal, and one of the founders of the Cairo Film Fest.

Ghanem, Samir. First made it big in the 60s with the cool comedy trio Tulati Adwa al-Masrah with Deif Ahmed and George Seidhom, now he stars in over-the-top commercial theater productions like *Do Re Mi Fasouliya*.

Ghitani, Gamal al-. Feisty novelist and editor of weekly *Akhbar al-Adab*. Best known of his 40 books: *al-Zayni Barakat*.

Ghobashi, Salah. Head of the Abd al-Halim Nawwara Group for Arabic Music at Opera House.

Gibril, Mohammed. Top grossing Quran reciter of the 1990s.

Gindi, Nadia al-. Fading damsel-in-distress of the screen and the self-described "darling of the masses."

Girgis, Sobhi. The still-working sculptor first gained renown decades ago for his iconoclastic metalworks.

Gohar, Mohammed. The founder and CEO of Cairo Video Sat has his hands in numerous productions for satellite TV.

Gohari, Mahmoud al-. The legendary coach took Egypt's squad to the 1990 World Cup and won the African Cup of Nations in 1998.

Golo. Brings Gallic panache and elfin wit to Egyptian cartoons.

Habib, Rafiq. Intellectual scion of a prominent Protestant family who joined up with the neo-Islamist Wasat group.

Haddad, Diana. Lebanese pop diva with a big market in Egypt.

Haggar, Ali al-. The Voice. One of the few post-1980s singers to stick to serious ballads.

Hakim. The *shaabi* singer has struck gold with mobile phone jingles, but caused a stir in 2001 when he showed up late for a gig at the Pyramids with British rocker Sting.

Halim, Tahiya. One of Egypt's most renowned old-school painters.

Hamama, Faten. Egypt's leading lady of the cinema started on screen at age 7 back in 1934, topped the marquees in the 50s and 60s, and now keeps a low public profile.

Hamed, Wahid. Screenwriter extraordinaire best known for his sometimes controversial, always melodramatic TV soap operas, like 2000's *Awan al Ward*, which featured mixed Christian-Muslim marriages.

Hammouda, Adel. Self-styled muckraker edits Egypt's independent weekly, *Sawt al-Umma*.

Hanafi, Hassan. Maverick philospher and darling of the intellectual set.

Hanna, Milad. Housing activist, professional Copt, Church critic, and all-round politico since the Sadat years. Author of the touchy-feely *Seven Pillars of Egyptian Identity*.

Hashem, Mohammed. Owner of the chic new publishing house, Merit.

Hassan, Hossam and Ibrahim. The celebrated soccer twins turned heads in 2000 by dumping Ahli for Zamalek.

Hefni, Ratiba al-. Dean of the Arabic Music Institute and director of the Arabic Music Festival.

Hegazi, Ahmed Abd al-Moati. The 60s-generation poet and critic is is now the primary defender of classical style Arabic poetry against the free verse of the 90s generation.

Heggy, Tarek. The former head of Shell Egypt is a management guru, petroleum expert, and socioeconomic thinker prominent on the international lecture circuit.

Heiba, Amr. Alexandrian painter who creates memorable canvas versions of his native city.

Heikal, Awny. Eminent sculptor of the 1960s generation still going strong.

Heikal, Mohammed Hassanein. For many years Egypt's top journalist and confidant of Nasser who has since turned eminence grise of political punditry. Best known book: *Autumn of Fury*.

Helmi, Mona. Poet and social commentator and daughter of Nawal al-Saadawi.

Hemeida, Mahmoud. Accessibly handsome and serious actor has appeared in everything from Chahine's *al-Masir* to *Afarit al-Asfalt*.

Heneidi, Mohammed. The short, cuddly comedian was the top box office draw in 2001.

Henein, Adam. One of Egypt's foremost artists and director of the Aswan Sculpture Symposium.

Hilal, Ahmed. Owner of IPH, leading printshop in the free zone.

Howeidi, Fahmi. His weekly column in *al-Ahram* is virtual holy writ to Islamists, but well-known among the wider intellectual set.

Hussein, Mostafa. The king of Egyptian cartoons has created a kingdom of familiar characters. With writer and partner Ahmed Ragab, makes the daily *al-Akhbar* a must-read.

Hussein, Taha. Respected graphic artist.

Ibrahim, Abdelhalim. Architect and purveyor of regional modernism. Designed the Qasr al-Funoun and the prize-winning children's park in Sayeda Zeinab.

Ibrahim, Saad Eddin. The AUC sociology bigwig and democracy advocate was sentenced to seven years in jail in 2001 and 2002 for making Egypt look bad abroad.

Ibrahim, Sonallah. Wry, soft-spoken novelist. Best-known works: *al-Lagna, Zat, Tilka al-Raiha*.

Imam, Adel. Premier comic of the 70s and 80s. The impish star debuted on stage in 1972 with *Madrasat al-Mushaghebin*, but his 2002 celluloid comeback, *Amir al-Zalam*, was a flop.

Ismail, Amr. Founder of al-Rahil, a band that offers fusion oriental music.

Ismail, Fatma. Head of the Arts Museum sector in the Ministry of Culture and a big name in the public-sector arts scene.

Johnson-Davis, Denys. White-haired scholar is the doyen of translators from Arabic.

Kamel, Abd al-Meneim. Head of the Egyptian ballet and ex-first dancer. Married to first ballerina, Erminia Kamel.

Kamel, Abla. Her anti-glamorous persona has made her a favorite among audiences. She's acted in everything from artsy films to popular TV melodramas to detergent commercials to last summer's blockbuster comedy *al-Limby*.

Kami, Hassan. The long-time opera tenor first joined the company when it was formed in 1964. Also produces Opera Aida.

Kassem, Hisham. Publishes *Cairo Times* and heads the Egyptian Organization for Human Rights.

Kazazian, Georges. Multi-talented musician fuses east and west. Best known album: *Sabil*.

Kazem, Safinaz. Quick-witted leftist of the 70s turned Islamist in the 80s. A theater critic by profession.

Khaled, Amr. Society preacher of the moment who draws thousands to his sermons in Sixth of October City. Also popular on the satellite networks.

Khalil, Yehia. Drummer whose beat helped revive jazz in Egypt.

Khan, Hassan. Young theater and video artist who keeps up with the cutting-edge regional art scene.

Khan, Mohammed. Bluff director of 80s with hits like *Ahlam Hind wa Camelia* and *Zawgat Ragul Mohem*. Chimed in last year with the long-awaited *Ayyam al-Sadat*.

Kharrat, Edwar al-. Alexandrian writer of eliptical, evocative novels like *The Girls of Alexandria*.

Khatib, Magda al-. One of the remnants of the glory days of Egyptian film appeared in last year's *Sukout Hansawwar*.

Khatib, Mahmoud al-. Egypt's football legend of the 1970s now sits on the board at the Ahli Club and does commercials for Coca-Cola.

Khawaga, Alaa al-. Shady big money behind Funoun, once Egypt's biggest—but now broke—film production group.

Kheirat, Omar. Composer, pianist. King of the Egyptian film score, and therefore Arabic muzak.

Khouri, Marianne and Gaby. Duo who head Youssef Chahine's film production outfit, Misr International Films.

Labbad, Mohi al-Din al-. Celebrated illustrator, graphic artist, and book designer who helped found the children's publishing house Dar al-Fata al-Arabi.

Latifa. Tunisian bombshell who pioneered the Arab video clip and tried her hand at acting last year in Youssef Chahine's *Sukout Hansawwar*.

Leithi, Gamal and Mamdouh al-. Brother duo have built a virtual empire in broadcasting, with their hands in production, distribution, state TV, and screenwriting.

Linz, Mark. Head of AUC Press.

Lotfi, Nadia. The 1960s film star is retired now, but still active in the Actors' Syndicate.

Lozy, Mahmoud al-. Director and AUC theater professor.

Lucy. Top belly dancer who successfully crossed over into film. Specializes in playing streetwise vixens with hearts of gold.

Lutfi al-Sayed, Afaf. Prolific historian of modern Egypt teaches in L.A.

Lutfi, Hoda. AUC history prof and hip collage artist.

Madbouli, Abd al-Meniem. Godfather of the male comedy role. Though aged considerably he appears in the occasional cameo. Played the forgetful grandpa in last year's *al-Ashiqan*.

Madbouli, Hagg Mohammed. Venerable owner of venerable downtown bookshop and publishing outfit.

Madkour, Nazli. The self-taught artist is a respected abstract painter with several international exhibitions under her belt.

Mahfouz, Naguib. Biggest name in modern Arabic liteature. Prolific novelist and Nobel laureate. Best known work: the Cairo trilogy.

Mahmoud, Mostafa. Long-running presenter of TV's *Science and Faith* masterminded Cairo's biggest charity hospital, and so has both a Mohandessin mosque and square named after him.

Makhyoun, Abd al-Aziz. Serious, choosy actor who also takes positions on public issues. Appeared last year on the stage in *al-Nas Illi fi al-Talet.*

Mansour, Anis. Loose-cannon editor of *October* magazine and back page columnist in *al-Ahram.* Likes Sadat so much he is said to have ghosted his bio, *In Search of Identity.*

Mansour, Karima. Renowned London-educated choreographer and modern dancer.

Maqar, Violette. Opera singer and illustrious voice coach.

Marai, Salah. Set designer and alter-ego of the late Shadi Abd al-Salam.

Marsafi, Tareq. Owner of Arabesque Gallery.

Marzouq, Ramses. One of the film industry's most respected cinematographers has worked on more than 40 films.

Masri, Suzanne al-. Innovative jeweller and part owner of the trendiest boutique of the moment, Khatoun.

Mazhar, Shehab. Renowned architect and landscape artist. Also the son of the late actor Ahmed Mazhar.

Mehrez, Samia. Literary critic and AUC prof.

Mehrez, Shahira. Master purveyor of the ethnic Egyptian style: architecture prof, boutique owner, and director of the Center of Traditional Embroidery in Arish.

Messiri, Abd al-Wahab al-. Incisive intellectual, sometime Islamist, and author of an encyclopedia of Judaism.

Mestikawy, Hazem al-. Cutting-edge modern sculptor and critic recently appointed as the director of the Egyptian Museum of Modern Art.

Mito, Ahmed. Young architect who wowed Cairo with the Pharaonesque Supreme Constitutional Court building.

Mohandes, Fouad al-. The aging king of classic comedy is still seen regularly on TV in the reruns of his dozens of films.

Mohi al-Din, Manal. No. 1 harpist in Egypt and the winner of several international prizes.

Mohi al-Din, Sherif. The viola player and former conductor at the Opera House now heads the culture and art division at the Alexandria Library.

Montasser, Salah. Heavyweight op-ed columnist for *al-Ahram.*

Morsi, Gihan. A long-time staple at the Cairo Opera, she is more often behind the scenes these days in the role of director.

Morsi, Mahmoud. Seventy-something actor made his mark on the screen in the 60s before turning to TV in the 80s. Last year he popped up on the Ramadan serial *Banat Afkari.*

Mostafa, Iman. Aida diva and prize-winning soprano.

Mounir, Mohammed. Nubian pop idol who has been going strong since the late 1970s. Latest release: the Sufi-inspired *Earth, Peace.*

Mukhtar, Karima. Buxom, fussy, kindly Egyptian everymom of the screen. These days she's active in population control campaigns.

Nabil, Gohar. Current star of the Egyptian handball team.

Nabil, Youssef. Young glam photographer whose pics grace both gallery walls and glossy celeb mags.

Nafaa, Hassan. Political science don at Cairo University.

Nagui, Mostafa. Conductor and former head of the Opera House.

Naoum, Nabil. Short story writer who resides mostly in Paris.

Naqqash, Amina. Farida's more retiring yet no less intellectual sister. Writes column in weekly *al-Ahali,* married to Salah Eissa.

Naqqash, Farida. Secular leftist women's rights advocate and literary critic. Edits the literary monthly *al-Adab wa al-Naqd,* often the token female at all-male intellectual forums.

Nashaat, Sandra. The young director has already made several commercial hits like *Leh Khalitni Ahibbak* and *Haramiya fi KG2.*

Nasr, Ibrahim. The man behind the wig of entertainment's most obnoxious comedienne, Zakiya Zakariya.

Nasr, Moataz. One of Egypt's brightest young artists, last year he won first prize for his installation at the Cairo Biennale.

Nasrallah, Sylvia. With Michel Pastor, runs the fashionable Nagada Gallery.

Nasrallah, Yousri. Survived Youssef Chahine to become an accomplished director of flicks like *al-Madina, Saruqat Sayfiya,* and *Mercedes.*

Nawar, Ahmed. Painter and head of the Fine Arts Sector at the Ministry of Culture.

Negm, Ahmed Fouad. Bad boy colloquial poet wrote satirical songs performed by blind Sheikh Imam in 70s and was tried by Sadat in a military court.

Nelly. Rambunctious blond on stage and screen who hosted Ramadan's *fawazir* for many years.

Noushouqati, Shadi al-. Young painter from Damietta whose star rose after taking the grand prize at the Youth Salon in 1996.

Okasha, Osama Anwar. The Nasserist screenwriter and self-appointed historian of the times is the author of TV's longest-playing serial, *Layali al-Helmiya* and of last year's stage hit, *al-Nas Illi fi al-Talet.*

Ouf, Ezzat Abu. Former pop musician turned ubiquitous actor who hosted Egypt's short-lived game show, *Haram al-Ahlam.*

Ouni, Walid. Diminutive Lebanese choreographer who learned his steps with Maurice Bejart.

Porret, Evelyne. Swiss expatriate potter and pioneer at the Tunis artists' colony, where she runs a pottery school for kids.

Qaid, Youssef al-. Prolific novelist, short-story writer, and commentator. His classic *War in the Land of Egypt* (1975) was banned.

Qamar, Mostafa. Singer of the 1990s new pop wave who headed into movies with *al-Batal* and *Ashab wala Bizness.*

Qandil, Hamdi. His sassy, ironic Monday night political talk show, *Rais al-Tahrir*, has made him a celebrity.

Qaradawi, Sheikh Youssef. Bushy-bearded cleric preaches a relatively sophisticated, tolerant breed of political Islam from the safety of Qatar.

Raafat, Samir. Popular historian of belle-epoque Cairo. His website keeps the nation's memory alive.

Ragab, Ahmed. Snappy, fearless wordsmith is the brains behind Mostafa Hussein's cartoons in *al-Akhbar.*

Ramadan, Somaya. The young writer nabbed the Naguib Mahfouz Medal for Literature last year with *Awraq al-Nargis.*

Ramli, Lenin al-. Top drawing playwright teamed with Muhammad Sobhi in the 80s, now goes alone. Hit the bullseye with plays like *Bi al-Arabi al-Fasih*, making theater-goers wonder if they should laugh or cry.

Ramzi, Ahmed. Screen hearthrob of the 1940s and 1950s who specialized in playing the bad boy. Now retired, but occasionally shows up in cameo roles.

Ramzi, Hani. The beefy young comedian started on the stage and is now a familiar face on the big screen in commercial flicks like last year's *Gawaz bi Qarar Gomhouri.*

Rateb, Gamil. Francophone theatrical actor debuted in a cameo on *Lawrence of Arabia* and has done everything since then from the 1970s B-movie to the TV melodrama. Lately has become TV's milk industry spokesman.

Reda, Mahmoud. Top folk dancer whose eponymous dance troupe (now nationalized) has won international acclaim.

Rizq, Amina. The aging thespian is still going strong after five decades of acting.

Rizq, Mohammed. Director of the Gezira Arts Center.

Rizq, Yunan Labib. Ain Shams history prof has been spinning *al-Ahram*'s archives into a full scale chronicle of modern Egypt.

Rizqallah, Adli. Preeminent artist famed for his watercolors since the 1960s.

Rizqallah, Youssef Sherif. Film critic and head of Nile TV.

Rostom, Hind. Egypt's answer to Marilyn Monroe, since retired. Her classic 1950s films are favorite TV re-run material.

Roussillon, Christine. Arts impressaria, critic, and former downtown gallerist. Now into textile design.

Saad, Mohammed. Formerly known to cinema audiences for his goofy sidekick roles, his summer 2002 hit, *al-Limby*, may turn out to be the top-grossing Egyptian film of all time.

Saad Eddine, Mursi. Quaint *al-Ahram Weekly* columnist, former head of the State Information Service, and brother of late composer Baligh Hamdi.

Saadawi, Nawal al-. The fearless feminist and seeker of controversy is one of Egypt's most translated authors.

Sabban, Rafiq al-. Eminent film critic, screenwriter, and frequent jury member at regional film fests.

Sabri, Samir. Screen comedian and now Egypt's premier kitsch emcee.

Sabri, Sherif. Top video clip director and head of the eponymous advertising agency, one of the most expensive in Egypt.

Sadeq, Rehab al-. The young artist from Matrouh has garnered acclaim for both her paintings and textile installations.

Saher, Kazem al-. Iraqi singer is a top Arab heartthrob and a sometime Egypt resident.

Said, Rushdie. Celebrated scholar and former head of the Geological Survey.

Saidi, Ahmed al-. Opera conductor.

Salah, Heba. The 19-year-old girl wonder became the world youth karate champion last year.

Salama, Fathi. Part-time Paris resident whose Sharqiyat ensemble blends jazz and oriental music,

Salama, Hani. A Youssef Chahine protégé who is now a regular on the big screen. He appeared in last year's *Ashab wala Bizness* and *al-Sellem wa al-Teaaban*.

Salama, Salama Ahmed. His daily column in *al-Ahram* is a voice of reason. Also edits the monthly *al-Kutub Weghat Nazar*, Egypt's *New York Review of Books*.

Salmawi, Mohammed. Playwright, man of letters and editor-in-chief of *al-Ahram Hebdo*.

Saqqa, Ahmed al-. Actor who rose with the youth comedy film. Appeared in last year's *Africano* and this summer's big budget action thriller *Mafia*.

Sarhan, Hala. Egypt's satellite Oprah with an American Ph.D in dance.

Sarhan, Samir. Chairman of the General Egyptian Book Organization who presides over the Cairo Book Fair.

Sayed, Mostafa Kamel al-. Political science guru at Cairo University.

Selim, Hisham. Actor and son of the late football legend Saleh Selim. Shot to stardom as a teenager in movies like *Awdat al-Ibn al-Dall*. Now acts as TV's Chipsy spokesman.

Scanlon, Georges. The archaeologist and Islamic arts prof taught a generation at AUC.

Schleiffer, Abdulla. Founded and heads AUC's Adham Center for Television Journalism.

Sehab, Selim. Founder and conductor of the National Arabic Music Ensemble since 1989. Also conducts the Children's Choir at the Opera House.

Seleiha, Nehad. Eminent theater critic writes for *al-Ahram Weekly*.

Selim, Ahmed Fouad. Long-time head of the state-run Akhnaton Galleries and fixture of the public-sector arts scene.

Seweilam, Ashraf. Bass at the Cairo Opera and AUC music prof.

Shaaban, Youssef. Aging mustachioed leading man who shone briefly in the 1960s. Head of the Actors' Syndicate.

Shadia. Now retired and in a *higab*, she had a long and varied 40-year career as a vocalist and actress. Most memorable roles: Fouada in *Shay min al-Khof* and Zuhra in Mahfouz's *Miramar*.

Shafei, Shirwet. Owner of the discreet, classy Safarkhana gallery, which she runs with daughter Mona Said.

Shafiq, Amina. Veteran scribbler for *al-Ahram*, and once a big wheel in the Journalists' Syndicate. Also a member of the National Women's Council.

Shafiq, Gamil. His familiar ink drawings regularly light up the pages of *al-Ahram Weekly*.

Shaker, Hossam. Qanun player extraordinaire and co-founder of the east-west jazz ensemble Rahala.

Shamma, Nasir. Iraqi master of the oud has been gracing Cairo's Opera House since 1998.

Sharaf al-Din, Doria. Erudite PhD presenter of TVs venerable *Nadi al-Cinema*. Former chief censor.

Sharaf, Assem. Painter of whimsical, waxy Chagall-ish stuff.

Sharara, Mohsen. Premier minimalist modern artist.

Shawqi, Wael. Young maverick artist took the grand prize at the Cairo Biennale in 1999.

Shehata, Yasmine. Editor of *Enigma*, Egypt's answer to *Cosmopolitan*.

Sherif, Nour al-. Versatile movie lead since the 1970s. Specializes in playing bewildered, decent men out of step with their unforgiving circumstances. Made a controversial splash last Ramadan with *Ailat al-Hagg Metwalli*.

Sherif, Omar. Screen idol of Egypt in the 50s and Hollywood in the 60s. Back home and still charming since the 80s.

Shiha, Hala. Up-and-coming young actress. Latest film: *al- Limby.*

Shobashi, Sherif al-. The writer and state culture bigwig was appointed director of the Cairo International Film Festival this year.

Sid Ahmed, Mohammed. Veteran political analyst and commentator.

Sirry, Gazbia. Leading painter since the 1950s known for her independence and formidable talent.

Siwi, Adel al-. Ex-doctor turned painter of contemporary art. Husband of Mashrabia gallerist Stefania Angarano.

Sobhi, Mohammed. Master comedian of the stage. His project on the Desert Road, Qaryat Sonbol, brings kids off Cairo streets to have some fun and fresh air.

Soliman, Hassan. Egypt's foremost painter of still-lifes, a master of light and shadow.

Soliman, Hosni. Head of the small publishing outfit Dar Sharqiyat, which launched the hottest novelists of 1990s.

Soueif, Ahdaf. Zamalek born-and-bred novelist writes in English. Best-known book: *In the Eye of the Sun.*

Tahawi, Miral al-. Brilliant young novelist. Best-known work: *al-Khibaa.*

Taher, Bahaa. One of the most widely read contemporary novelists in the Arab world. Best known works: *Khalti Safiya wa al-Deir, Ana al-Malak Jitu, al-Hobb fi al-Manfa.*

Taher, Salah. Pioneering and prolific nonogenarian painter.

Tarawi, Mohammed al-. Illustrator for *Rose al-Youssef* and premier watercolorist.

Tawfiq, Mohsena. Accomplished stage actress has worked with everyone from Chahine to Okasha, lending an engaged and lyrical quality to all her roles.

Telmissani, May. One of the most prominent writers of the Generation of the 90s, with two novels, several short story collections, and two screenplays under her belt.

Telmissani, Tareq al-. As Egypt's top cinematographer, his shots are featured in dozens of movies, videos, and commercials.

Telpian, Vahan. Armenian sculptor who makes modern obelisks out of concrete and cement.

Tohami, Sheikh Yasin al-. Top-billing *munshid*, or sufi singer.

Tonsi, Karim al-. The former first dancer and instructor of the Modern Dance Theatre Troupe now has his own troupe.

Touni, Helmi al-. Cartoonist, illustrator, childrens' book writer, and painter of Cairo nostalgia.

Turk, Hanan. The bubbly thirty-something actress is one of the most visible in the crop of new young actresses. Starred in last year's Eid flick *Gawaz bi Qarar Gomhouri.*

Vartan. Cairo's top jeweller.

Veillon, Margo. The renowned Cairo-born, Swiss artist has been evoking Egypt's people and landscapes for eight decades.

Wahba, Wagih. Painter and head of the Cairo Atelier.

Wakil, Abd al-Wahed al-. Architect with a passion for the Islamic who contributed to expanding holy sanctuaries of Mecca, Medina.

Wakil, Reda al-. Lead baritone at the Cairo Opera and winner of several international competitions.

Wali al-Din, Alaa. Blubbery comedian has made size an asset in flicks like *Abboud ala al-Hudoud, al-Nazer,* but started to fade with last year's *Ibn Ezz.*

Warda. Willowy, Algerian-born queen of the pop scene since the 1970s.

Wasfi, Hoda. Formidable head of the Hanager and National Theater.

Weeks, Kent. Archeologist who reopened a derelict tomb in the Valley of the Kings and found it was the grandest of them all. Best known book: *The Lost Tomb.*

Wells, William. Gallery impresario who kick-started Cairo's downtown arts scene with his ever-expanding Townhouse Gallery.

Yacoub, Sir Magdy. One of Egypt's most sucessful exports, his skill as a London heart surgeon earned him a knighthood.

Yamin, Charles. Creative director at TMI-GWI advertising agency, a living legend in the field.

Yasin, Mahmoud. Melodrama hero of the 1960s and 70s still appears in the occasional Ramadan historical soap.

Yasin, Sayed. Leftist political commentator who used to head the Ahram Center for Strategic Studies.

Yassa, Ramzi. Egypt's top pianist and international concertist.

Youssef, Khaled. Chahine protégé director whose film, *al-Asifa*, took the Silver Pyramid at the Cairo International Film Festival in 2000.

Yousra. Golden-haired leading lady in films since the 80s, her latest forays into pop music have fizzled.

Zaki, Ahmed. Top paid actor since the 80s. Last year made a splash playing the late president in *Ayyam al-Sadat*.

Zaki, Mona. Most popular young actress around. Not related to Ahmed, although she played the young Jihan Sadat in this year's *Ayyam al-Sadat*.

Zaki, Suheir. Renowned dancer of the 1970s and 1980s on screen and on stage.

Zeidan, Raouf. Star tenor of the Cairo Opera.

Zewail, Ahmed. Caltech scientist whose discovery of the femto-second nabbed Egypt's second Nobel.

Zoghbi, Nawal al-. Lebanese pop star who is a top grosser in Egypt. Most visible in her role as the Pepsi songstress.

Obituaries

Abaza, Sarwat. Scion of a prominent Delta family, Abaza was a prolific writer, producing upwards of 30 novels, two plays, ten books on literary criticism, and a regular column in the state-owned *al-Ahram*. Of his many novels adapted to the large and small screens, the 1969 *Shay min al-Khof* (A Touch of Fear) is perhaps the best remembered among audiences for its timeless portrayal of a village terrorized by a local strongman. Abaza received the state merit award in literature and was a long-standing member of the Shura Council. He died on March 17, 2002, at the age of 75.

Alami, Yehya al-. Passing away on January 19, 2002, the 61-year-old director left behind a prodigious number of films and television serials spanning his 40-year career. Though not all are memorable, al-Alami left his mark on Egyptian television with hits like *Raafat al-Haggan*, a Ramadan serial about the true

adventures of an Egyptian spy in Israel, and the popular, if short-lived, dramatic series *Huwwa wa Hiyya* (He and She), starring Soad Hosni and Ahmed Zaki.

Badawi, Abd al-Rahman. After spending the last 20 years of his life in exile in Paris, the celebrated philosopher only returned to Egypt at the age of 85 to die. Notorious for his arrogance and an almost pathological hatred of the country of his birth, Badawi was a controversial figure at home. He was a staunch critic of the politics and culture of the contemporary Middle East, and his polemics extended to some of Egypt's most sanctified figures, including Taha Hussein and Saad Zaghloul. Nevertheless, his philosophical work—which includes original treatises and copious translations and commentary—is a monument to scholarship. He died on July 25, 2002.

Bashir, Tahsin. The 77-year-old former diplomat passed away in London on June 12, 2002, while undergoing treatment for heart problems. Known for his candor, wit, and sometimes controversial politics, Bashir held a variety of official posts in his long career, serving as a spokesman to both Gamal Abd al-Nasser and Anwar al-Sadat, Egypt's representative to the Arab League, and later its ambassador to Canada. Though he retired in 1985, he remained involved in public life, dispensing thought-provoking analysis and memorable soundbites to both the local and foreign media.

Brown, Frank. Australian by birth, the 85-year-old music lover was an unrepentant peripatetic, roving Europe, the Middle East, and India before settling down in Egypt over ten years ago. Adopting the *nom de plume* of David Blake, he became the music critic for the young *Ahram Weekly*, and remained a constant on the culture pages there until his death on February 15, 2002.

Elias, Eva. Egypt premier dictionnary publisher, Eva spent ten years of her life updating Elias Modern English-Arabic Dictionary and a few more translating and editing the Illustrated Junior Dictionary. She was a fervent promoter of translation both into and from the arabic with many titles to her credit both as an editor or as a translator. Eva was also a short story writer and a theater director mainly with AUC theater company. She passed away on august 3rd 2002 in Montreal at the age of 47 after having fought cancer for five years

Fouad, Moharram. The 71-one-year old singer passed away on June 27, 2002, as a result of kidney and heart failure. A graduate of the Arabic Music Institute, Fouad left behind some 900 songs to his name. Like many popular singers of his generation, he enjoyed a fruitful career on the big screen, starring in 13 films, including the classic *Hassan wa Naima*, where he played opposite a young Soad Hosni in her screen debut.

Francis, Youssef. A true Renaissance man, Francis was an accomplished painter, a sensitive writer, and a fine director. Starting his career as an illustrator with *Rose al-Youssef* in the late 1950s, he later moved into writing (both books and screenplays) before taking up cinema in the 1970s. Among his most well known films was his adaptation of Tawfiq al-Hakim's *Asfour min al-Sharq* (Bird from the East), for which he wrote the screenplay in addition to directing. He died of a heart attack on April 15, 2001, at the age of 67, only a month after the opening of his latest art exhibition and a year after his most recent film *Habibati Man Takun* (Who Is My Lover) won first prize at the Cairo Radio and Television Festival.

Haroun, Shehata. One of the last remaining members of Egypt's tiny Jewish community passed away on March 16, 2001, at the age of 82. Like many of his Egyptian co-religionists, Haroun was an unreformed old-school leftist, one of the founding members of Egypt's communist party in the 1940s. A lawyer by profession, he was a regular contributor to the press and an active member of the leftist Tagammu Party until declining health forced him to retire from public life. A staunch anti-Zionist until his death, Haroun nevertheless refused to give up the religion of his birth, as did a number of Jews who stayed in Egypt after 1956. His essentially humanist version of socialism made room for all of his myriad identities: religious, national, and political. He was buried at the Jewish cemetery in Basatin.

Hosni, Soad. The Cinderella of the silver screen died on June 23, 2001, at age 58, after falling from a sixth-floor London apartment in what appeared to be a suicide. Half-sister of the younger Nagat, Hosni entered showbiz at a tender age, singing on the children's radio show *Baba Sharo*. At age 17, she was catapulted into full-fledged stardom with her film debut, *Hassan wa Naima*, playing opposite teen idol and pop star Moharram Fouad. A talented actress and singer, Hosni went on to star in more than 80 films, acquiring the status of an Egyptian icon. Married several times, Hosni's tumultuous personal life was the source of much speculation and gossip. Suffering recurring bouts of depression, she spent the last few years of her life in London in self-imposed exile.

Hussein, Adel. A born activist, Hussein made the long, and often tortuous, journey from Marxism to Nasserism to Islamism, his own political development mirroring in many ways that of the entire nation. Imprisoned as a communist under Nasser, he later clashed with Sadat over his espousal of Nasserist ideology. In 1984, he joined the Labor Party and was instrumental in forging its alliance with the Muslim Brothers and transforming the party into a platform for political Islam. As secretary-general and effective head of the party, Hussein led the 2000 campaign against an obscure Syrian novel that led to student riots and ultimately the party's closure. He died on March 15, 2001, at the age of 69.

Ibrahim, Laila. Having suffered from a debilitating disease for several years, Ibrahim passed away on July 14, 2002, at the age of 85. The daughter of celebrated doctor Ali Ibrahim Pasha and the mother of Alexandria Library director Ismail Serageldin, Laila Ibrahim kept a comparatively low public profile. But she was renowned in certain circles for her commitment to and extensive knowledge of Cairo's medieval architectural heritage, actively contributing to its documentation, study, and preservation. Though she had no formal training in art history, Ibrahim used her erudition to raise public awareness of the city's treasures through lectures, teaching, and advocacy, authoring a small corpus of scholarly publications as well.

Jordan, Renate. With her inevitable cigarette and almost theatrical appearance, Jordan cut a striking figure on the downtown Cairo arts circuit. Relocating from her native Germany a decade ago, she set up the Cairo Berlin gallery, one of the earliest private galleries to open its doors to the burgeoning art scene. Despite the gallery's modest size, it competed with the rest by offering an eclectic mix of exhibits by well-established and younger, more obscure artists, along with the occasional show by European artists. Jordan passed away at the age of 57 on October 29, 2001.

Kamel, Mohammed Ibrahim. Although he enjoyed a 45-year career in state politics, serving as Egypt's ambassador to several American, European, and African countries, Kamel is largely remembered for his brief stint as Sadat's foreign minister in 1977-78. He initially participated in the Camp David negotiations, but later resigned in protest and made his criticism of the peace treaty public in his 1983 *al-Salam al-Daiaa fi Camp David* (Lost Peace at Camp David). Kamel was a founding member of the Egyptian Organization for Human Rights and served as the association's president from its establishment in 1985 until 1993. He died on November 21, 2001, at the age of 74.

Kashef, Radwan al-. The 50-year-old Sohag-born director died in his sleep on June 5, 2002, a few weeks after his latest film, *al-Saher* (The Magician) was released in theaters. Part of the generation of realist directors that came of age in the 1980s, al-Kashef won critical acclaim with his 1992 *Leh Ya Banafsag* (Violets Are Blue) and his 1997 *Araq al-Balah* (Date Wine). Before his death, he was working on a screen adaptation of *Layali Okhra* (Other Nights), a novel by Mohammed al-Bisatie.

Lauer, Jean-Philippe. After joining the Egyptian Antiquities Department in 1926, the eminent French archaeologist was chosen to lead excavations at the Saqqara Plateau in 1932. And that is where he remained until his death on May 16, 2001, at the age of 99, having devoted his life to an exploration of the ancient site. Lauer made important contributions to Egyptology and was largely responsible for the reconstruction of Djoser's famed step pyramid, the focus of much of his academic work.

Mazhar, Ahmed. The "knight of Egyptian cinema" started his career as military man, joining the military academy in 1937, where he rubbed elbows with both Gamal Abd al-Nasser and Anwar al-Sadat. An equestrian champion and cavalry officer, he eventually attained the rank of colonel before turning his

attention to the silver screen. His big break in cinema came in 1957 with the quintessential tale of life in pre-revolutionary Egypt, *Rudda Qalbi* (Return My Heart). He went on to star in 91 films, including several classics like *Doa al-Karawan* (The Dove's Keening), but he is perhaps best remembered for his role as medieval military hero Saladdin in Youssef Chahine's 1963 *al-Nasser Salah al-Din*. Mazhar passed away on May 8, 2002, at the age of 85.

Mortada, Saad. The former diplomat died in his home in Virginia on September 25, 2001, at the age of 78. Egypt's first ambassador to Israel after the signing of the Camp David Accords in 1979, Mortada held several senior diplomatic posts in his long career, serving as an ambassador to Morocco, Senegal, and the United Arab Emirates. He retired in 1982 and later resettled in the US.

Osman, Bahgat. The celebrated caricaturist, known more familiarly by his signature byline of "Bahgat," entertained generations of Egyptian readers with his wit and his instantly recognizable cartoon creations. Starting his career in the late 1950s with *Rose al-Youssef*, Osman was a regular contributor to several publications, including *Sabah al-Kheir*, *al-Musawwar*, and *al-Ahali*. He passed away at the age of 70 on June 3, 2001.

Qutt, Abd al-Qader al-. The *sheikh al-nuqad*, the master critic, passed away on June 16, 2002, at the ripe old age of 85. The Delta-born scholar devoted his life to Arabic literature and poetry, leaving behind several seminal works on contemporary and classical poetry, along with a batch of translations of English and American literature. The editor of a slew of literary journals, he received several awards in honor of his academic achievements, including the prestigious King Faisal Award for Literature and the state merit award.

Rahmi, Mahmoud. The renowned puppeteer who introduced television audiences to Hamada and Amm Shafiq, and more recently Boogi and Tamtam, died on July 25, 2001, at the age of 62. An Alexandria native, Rahmi channeled his formal arts training into creating a world somewhere between the real and the imaginary that captivated children and adults alike. Though his wildly popular Hamada was ultimately taken off the air—the three-dimensional character was deemed unsuitable for child audiences—Boogi and Tamtam continued to be a staple of Ramadan viewing from their introduction in 1982 up until the artist's death.

Sabet, Adel. The great raconteur, historian, and famously generous host passed away on January 19, 2001, after being struck by a hit-and-run driver. Born into the royal household in 1919—he was a second cousin of King Fouad—Sabet initially survived the transition into Nasser's Egypt, becoming the editor and publisher of *The Egyptian Economic and Political Review*. His later fall from grace, however, led him briefly to prison and then into a ten-year exile. More recently, Sabet gained renown for his biography of King Farouq, *A King Betrayed*, which went through five editions in Egypt.

Salem, Atef. Already in poor health, the 75-year-old film director suffered a stroke and passed away on July 30, 2002. Salem started his career in the 1940s, working from the bottom up. Initially helping out with sets, makeup, lighting, or any other odd jobs behind the scenes, he rose in the industry ranks to become an assistant director to such early giants as Ahmed Badrakhan and Henri Barakat. Following his first film in 1954, *al-Hirman* (Deprivation), he went on to direct more than 50 movies over the next 30 years, producing a body of work that reads like a catalogue of classic Egyptian film—*Gaaluni Mugriman* (They Made Me a Criminal), *Yom min Omri* (A Day of My Life), *Ihna al-Talamdha* (We're the Students), *Umm al-Arousa* (Mother of the Bride), *Qaher al-Zalam* (Vanquisher of Darkness), and *Ayyamna al-Helwa* (The Good Old Days) are only some of the most well remembered.

Selim, Saleh. Egypt's most beloved sports figure passed away on May 6, 2002, after a long battle with liver cancer. A seemingly permanent fixture of the Ahli Club, Selim joined the team in 1948 at the age of 17, and, with the exception of a short stint in Europe, played there until his retirement in 1967. A brief foray into the cinema cemented his status as an icon on the Egyptian cultural scene—*al-Shamou al-Sawda* (The Black Candles), in which Saleh played a blind man opposite Nagat al-Saghira, is something of a cult classic. For the last 22 years he served as the head of the Ahli Club. He is survived by two sons, Hisham and Khaled, both familiar to movie-going audiences.

Shihata, Ibrahim. One of Egypt's most celebrated legal minds passed away on May 28, 2001, at the age of 64. Starting his career with the State Council, Shehata taught international law for several years in Egypt before becoming a consultant and legal advisor to such institutions as the Kuwaiti Fund for Arab Economic Development and OPEC. A specialist in international finance law, Shehata served as the general counsel at the World Bank from 1983-1998, where he was instrumental in establishing and running several of the bank's development and investment programs.

Tawfiq, Tumadir. Anyone who has dialed 15 has probably heard Tawfiq's voice clearly ringing out the time of day. But she achieved much more in her 80 years than simply becoming the voice of the speaking clock. A media pioneer, Tawfiq chalked up several firsts to her name: the first female news anchor on Egyptian radio, the first woman to join the ranks of Egyptian television, the first female television director, and the first female director of Egyptian television. In addition to occupying several senior posts at both radio and TV, Tawfiq gained the respect of Egyptian viewers with her seriousness of purpose, seen on several successful television programs, including *Waghan li-Wagh* (Face to Face) and *Maa al-Nuqad* (With the Critics). She passed away on June 8, 2001.

Van Leo. Levon Boyadijian spent the last few years of his long life enjoying a well-deserved comeback to the public eye as one of Egypt's premier studio photographers. Known for his iconic photos of cultural figures like Doria Shafiq, Taha Hussein, child star Sherihan, and Farid al-Atrash, Van Leo himself was an icon of fading Cairene cosmopolitanism. Before his death, the Armenia-born artist donated most of what was left of his voluminous archive—he burned part of his collection in the late 1980s in fear of rising fundamentalism—to the American University in Cairo. He passed away in his downtown apartment on March 18, 2002, at the age of 80.

Contacts

Emergency/Help

Ambulance: 123/230
Cairo Airport: 291-4255/66/77
Terminal 1: 244-1460
Terminal 2: 245-9332
Clock: 15
Electricity service complaints: 121
Fire brigade: 180
Operator service:
International: 574-5620
National: 10
Police: 122
Railway information: 574-0375/
575-3555
Telephone bill: 177
Telephone directory: 140/141
Telephone service complaints:
16/188
Tourist police: 126
Traffic police: 128
Water service complaints:
575-0059/7416

Travelers' services

American Express: 573-8465
Western Union: 795-7454

Credit card loss

American Express
Nile Tower Building
21-22 Murad St., Giza
Tel: 570-3411/9
Fax: 570-3146/7

Cash Cards (Global Access/Electro Bank/Egyptian British Bank)
3 Abu al-Feda St., Zamalek

Tel: 736-8778/735-4849
Diners' Club
21 Mohammed Mazhar St., Zamalek
Tel: 736-8778
Downtown tel: 333-2628
Master Card/Visa
Bank Misr Tower
153 Mohammed Farid St., fl. 12
Downtown
Tel: 797-1148/9
Fax: 393-1415

Communications

Internet access numbers

No user name or password required. Access numbers starting with (07) are charged LE1.20 per hour, while (09) numbers are charged LE6 per hour.
0777-0444/0555/0666/0777
0707-0505/0707/0808/0909
0707-6666/7777
0908-0444/0505/0908

Computer supplies

Compu Mall
7 al-Sakhawi St., off al-Khalifa al-Mamoun, Heliopolis
Tel: 450-6195/257-7475
Compu Me
17 al-Ahram St., Heliopolis
Tel: 418-6864
Computer City
Gamaat al-Duwal al-Arabiya St.
Mohandessin
Nile Hilton, Downtown

Computer House Mall
13 Damascus St., Roxy, Heliopolis
Computer Market
4 al-Assyouti St., Heliopolis
Nasr Computer Mall
50 Ali Amin St., Mostafa al-Nahas and Abbas al-Aqqad Crossing, Nasr City
Sphinx Computer Mall
3 Sphinx Sq., Mohandessin

PC repair

Computer Center
4 al-Esraa St., Lebanon Sq.
Mohandessin
Tel: 345-2095/96/97
Fax: 303-7459
Compu System
8 Ibn Iyas St., Heliopolis
Tel: 453-7793
Odec
IBM, Compaq & Hewlett Packard dealer
Tel: 414-5994/012-212-7546

Macintosh repair

Apple Line Co.
75 Qasr al-Aini St., Garden City
Tel: 795-1200/792-2614/796-1241
www.appleline.com.eg
Apple Pie
92 Shehab St., Mohandessin
Tel: 747-0328/303-4864/010-156-5330

Mobile phone help

Click Vodafone: 529-2888
From a Click Vodafone mobile: 888
MobiNil: 760-9090
From a MobiNil mobile: 110

Mobile phone hire

Check Abd al-Aziz St. and the Bab al-Louq area for cheap mobiles, accessories, and spare parts. Also, most 5-star hotels rent mobiles.

Parcels and post

National service
Ataba Central Post Office, Ataba Sq.
Open 9-2, closed Friday

International
Ramses Post Office, Ramses Sq., near Railways Museum
Open 9-2, closed Friday
Bring packages open for custom clearance; final wrapping on the premises.

Local road transport (large parcels)
Several companies are found on Port Said St. near Bab al-Khalq courthouse, and Geish St.
Prices charged by volume and weight; avoid fragile items, sturdy packing recommended. Usually departs at night.

Courier services

Aramex
31 Mosaddaq St., Doqqi
Tel: 338-8466
14 Yehya Ibrahim St., Zamalek
Tel: 738-2225

DHL
16 Lebanon St., Mohandessin
Tel: 302-9801

EMS
Branches in all post offices. Round the clock service at Ataba Post Office.
Closed Friday

Federal Express
Hotline: 268-7888

15 Shehab St., Mohandessin
Tel: 760-7922
19 Khaled Ibn al-Walid St.
Masaken Sheraton, Heliopolis
Tel: 268-7888

TNT
33 Doqqi St., Doqqi
Tel: 749-9851

UPS Egypt
7 Hussein Zohdi St., Ard al-Golf
Nasr City
Tel: 415-8445/414-1456

Local courier and parcel service

Egyptian Express
3 Abd al-Hamid Said St.
Downtown
Tel: 576-3711

Kanga
29 Koliyet al-Banat, Nasr City
Tel: 414-6643/414-4279

Middle East Courier Services
118 July 26th St., Zamalek
Tel: 735-6428/737-4253
1 Mahmoud Hafez St., Safir Sq.
Heliopolis
Tel: 635-9281

Area Codes

Alexandria: 03
Arish: 068
Assyout: 088
Aswan: 097
Beheira: 045
Benha: 013
Beni Sueif: 082
Cairo: 02
Damietta: 057

Fayyoum: 084
Ismailiya: 064
Kafr al-Sheikh: 047
Luxor: 095
Mansoura: 050
Marsa Matrouh: 046
Menoufiya: 048
Minya: 086
New Valley: 092
Port Said: 066
Qena: 096
Red Sea Coast: 065
Sinai (south): 069
Sohag: 093
Suez: 062
Tanta: 040
Tenth of Ramadan: 015
Zaqaziq: 055

Cairo Hotels

Cairo Marriott
33 Saraya al-Gezira St., Zamalek
Tel: 735-8888
Fax: 735-6667

Conrad International
1191 Corniche al-Nil, Boulaq
Tel: 580-8000
Fax: 580-8080

Four Seasons Cairo
35 Murad St., Giza
Tel: 573-1212
Fax: 568-1616

Gezira Sheraton
Gezira Island
Tel: 737-3737
Fax: 735-5056

Helnan Shepheard
Corniche al-Nil, Garden City

Tel: 792-1000
Fax: 792-1010
Le Meridien Cairo
Corniche al-Nil, Roda Island
Tel: 362-1717
Fax: 362-1927
Le Meridien Heliopolis
51 Salah Salem St., Heliopolis
Tel: 290-5055
Fax: 290-1819
Le Meridien Pyramids
Alex Desert Rd.
Tel: 383-0383
Fax: 383-1730
Mena House Oberoi
Pyramids Ave.
Tel: 383-3222
Fax: 383-7777
Mövenpick Heliopolis
Cairo International Airport Rd.
Tel: 291-9400
Fax: 418-0761
Mövenpick Pyramids Resort
Alex Desert Rd.
Tel: 385-2555
Fax: 383-5006
Nile Hilton
Corniche al-Nil, Tahrir Sq.
Downtown
Tel: 578-0444
Fax: 578-0475
Pyramids Park Intercontinental Resort
Alex Desert Rd.
Tel: 383-8666
Fax: 383-9000
Pyramisa
60 Murad St., Giza

Tel: 336-9000
Fax: 760-5347
Ramses Hilton
1115 Corniche al-Nil, Downtown
Tel: 577-7444
Fax: 575-7152
Safir Cairo Hotel
Misaha Sq., Doqqi
Tel: 748-2424
Fax: 760-8453
Semiramis Intercontinental
Corniche al-Nil, Downtown
Tel: 795-7171
Fax: 796-3020
Sheraton Cairo
Galaa Sq., Doqqi
Tel: 336-9700
Fax: 336-4602
Sheraton Heliopolis
Salah Salem St., Heliopolis
Tel: 267-7730
Fax: 267-7600
Sofitel Cairo Maadi Towers
29 Corniche al-Nil, Maadi
Tel: 526-0602
Fax: 526-1133
Sofitel le Sphinx
1 Alex Desert Rd.
Tel: 383-7444
Fax: 383-4930
Sonesta Hotel
4 al-Tayaran St., Nasr City
Tel: 262-8111
Fax: 263-5731
Swissotel Cairo
Abd al-Hamid Badawi St., Heliopolis
Tel: 297-4000
Fax: 297-6037

Conference facilities

Conference halls and presentation facilities are found in all 5-star hotels. You can also book space at the CICC and Gezira exhibition grounds as well as various historic palaces from the Ministry of Culture. Leon Momdjian leases audiovisual equipment.

Cairo International Conference Center (CICC)
Nasr St., Nasr City
Tel: 401-8948/402-7370
Fax: 263-4640/401-8950
www.cicc.egnet.net
Leon Momdjian
Tel: 576-3758
Ministry of Culture
2 Shagaret al-Dorr St., Zamalek
Tel: 735-6469

Daily tours

American Express
21 Murad St., Giza
Tel: 573-8465
Misr Travel
1 Talaat Harb St., Downtown
Tel: 393-0010
Thomas Cook
12 Sheikh Ali Youssef Sq., Garden City
Tel: 796-4650

Embassies and consulates

Australia
World Trade Center, Boulaq
Tel: 575-0444
Bahrain
15 Brazil St., Zamalek
Tel: 736-6605

Canada
5 al-Saraya al-Kubra St., Garden City
Tel: 794-3110

France
29 Murad St., Giza
Tel: 570-3916

Germany
8B Hassan Sabri St., Zamalek
Tel: 736-0015

Great Britain
7 Ahmed Ragheb St., Garden City
Tel: 794-0850

Greece
18 Aisha al-Taymouriya St.,
Garden City
Tel: 795-5915

India
5 Aziz Abaza St., Zamalek
Tel: 736-3051

Iran
12 Refaa al-Tahtawi St., Doqqi
Tel: 748-6492

Italy
15 Abd al-Rahman Fahmi St.
Garden City
Tel: 794-0658

Japan
106 Qasr al-Aini St., Downtown
Tel: 795-7553

Jordan
6 al-Guhayni St., Doqqi
Tel: 748-5566

Kuwait
12 Nabil al-Waqqad St., Doqqi
Tel: 760-2661

Lebanon
22 Mansour Mohammed St. Zamalek
Tel: 738-2823

Libya
7 al-Saleh Ayoub St., Zamalek
Tel: 735-1864

Morocco
10 Salah al-Din St., Zamalek
Tel: 735-9849

Netherlands
36 Mohammed Mazhar St., Zamalek
Tel: 735-1936

Oman
52 al-Higaz St., Mohandessin
Tel: 303-6011

Palestine
33 al-Nahda St., Doqqi
Tel: 338-4761

Qatar
10 Simar St., Mohandessin
Tel: 760-4693

Russian Federation
95 Murad St., Giza
Tel: 748-9353

Saudi Arabia
2 Ahmed Nessim St., Giza
Tel: 749-0797

Spain
41 Ismail Mohammed St., Zamalek
Tel: 735-6437

Sudan
3 al-Ibrahim St., Garden City
Tel: 794-5043

Switzerland
10 Abd al-Khaleq Sarwat St., Downtown
Tel: 575-8133

Syria
18 Abd al-Rahim Sabri St., Doqqi
Tel: 335-8806

Tunisia
26 al-Gezira St., Zamalek

Tel: 735-4940

Turkey
25 al-Falaki St., Bab al-Louq
Tel: 794-8364

United Arab Emirates
4 Ibn Sina St., Giza
Tel: 760-9722

United States of America
5 Amrika al-Latiniya St.
Garden City
Tel: 795-7371

Yemen
28 Amin al-Rifai St., Doqqi
Tel: 761-4224

Organizations

Research organizations and learned societies

American Research Center in Egypt (ARCE)
2 Simon Bolivar Sq.
Garden City
Tel: 794-8239
Fax: 795-3052

Bibliotheca Alexandrina (new Alexandria Library)
Corniche, Shatbi
Alexandria
Tel: 03-487-6001/6024/9024
Fax: 03-483-6001
www.bibalex.gov.eg

Centre d'Etudes et de Documentation Economique, Juridique et Sociale (CEDEJ)
2 Sikkat al-Fadl St., off Qasr al-Nil St.
Downtown
Tel: 392-8711/16/39
Fax: 392-8791

Ford Foundation
1 Osiris St., fl. 7, Garden City
Tel: 795-2121
Fax: 795-4018

Fulbright Commission
20 Gamal al-Din Abu al-Mahasen St.
Garden City
Tel: 794-4799/794-8679
Fax: 795-7893

Goethe Institute
5 Bustan St., Downtown
Tel: 575-9877/577-9479

**Institut Francais d'Archeologie
Orientale (IFAO)**
37 Sheikh Ali Youssef St., Mounira
Tel: 797-1600

**Netherlands Institute of
Archaeology and Arabic Studies**
1 Dr. Mahmoud Azmi St., Zamalek
Tel: 338-2522
Fax: 735-4376

International agencies

**American Mideast Educational &
Training Services (AMIDEAST)**
23 Mosaddaq St., Doqqi
Tel: 337-8265
Fax: 795-2946

**Food & Agriculture Organization
(FAO)**
11 al-Islah al-Zerai St., Doqqi
Tel: 337-5029
Fax: 337-8563

**International Finance Corporation
(IFC)**
World Trade Center, Boulaq
Tel: 579-6565
Fax: 579-2211

**International Labor Organization
(ILO)**
9 Taha Hussein St., Zamalek
Tel: 736-9290/735-0123
Fax: 736-0889

**International Monetary Fund
(IMF)**
31 Qasr al-Nil St., Downtown
Tel: 392-4257
Fax: 393-1589

UNDP
World Trade Center, Boulaq
Tel: 578-4840

UNESCO
8 Abd al-Rahman Fahmi St.
Garden City
Tel: 794-3036
Fax: 794-5296

UNICEF
87 Misr-Helwan Agricultural Rd., Maadi
Tel: 526-5083-87/526-5087
Fax: 526-4218

USAID
Off Laselki St., behind the Zahraa al-
Maadi water station, Maadi
Tel: 522-7000
Fax: 516-4628

World Bank
World Trade Center, Boulaq
Tel: 574-1670/1
Fax: 574-1676

Egyptian government

Cairo Stock Exchange
4A al-Sherifein St., Downtown
Tel: 392-1402

Capital Market Authority
20 Emad al-Din St., Downtown
Tel: 579-4176

**Central Agency for Public
Mobilization & Statistics
(CAPMAS)**
Salah Salem St., Nasr City
Tel: 402-4110/402-3191

Egyptian Antiquities Authority
4 Fakhri Abu al-Nour St., Abbasiya
Tel: 685-8643/683-7111
Fax: 683-1117

**Egyptian Environmental Affairs
Agency (EEAA)**
30 Misr-Helwan Agricultural Rd., behind
Sofitel Hotel, Maadi
Tel: 525-6482/52
Fax: 525-6490

Egyptian Tourist Authority
Misr Travel Bldg., Abbasiya Sq.
Tel: 685-4439/3576/4509
Fax: 685-4363

Federation of Egyptian Industries
26A Sherif St., Downtown
Tel: 392-8319

**General Authority for Investment
and Free Zones**
8 Adli St., Downtown
Tel: 390-3776/6163/391-4336
Fax: 390-7315

**Information & Decision Support
Center (IDSC)**
Cabinet Bldg., Maglis al-Shaab St.
Downtown
Tel: 796-1600
Fax: 794-1222

Social Fund for Development:
Hussein Hegazi and Qasr al-Aini Sts.
Downtown
Tel: 794-8339
Fax: 795-0628

Business organizations

Alexandria Businessmen's Association
52 Horriya Ave., Downtown
Alexandria
Tel: 03-483-4062/484-8978
Fax: 03-483-2206/2411

Alexandria Chamber of Commerce
31 al-Ghorfa al-Togariya St.
Downtown, Alexandria
Tel: 03-480-5221/8434/8779
Fax: 03-480-8993

American Chamber of Commerce
33 Soliman Abaza St., Mohandessin
Tel: 338-1050

British Egyptian Businessmen's Association (BEBA)
124 Nile St., Agouza
Tel: 349-1421
Fax: 349-1401

Cairo Chamber of Commerce
4 al-Falaki Sq., Bab al-Louq, Abdin
Tel: 795-8261/2
Fax: 354-4328

Club D'Affaires Franco-Egyptien (CAFE)
5 Shagaret al-Dorr St., fl. 2, apt. 11
Zamalek
Tel: 346-9417/8

Egyptian Businessmen's Association
21 Murad St., Nile Tower, Giza
Tel: 572-3855/573-6030
Fax: 568-1014

German-Arab Chamber of Commerce
3 Abu al-Feda St., Zamalek
Tel: 736-3664

Japanese External Trade Organization (JETRO)
World Trade Center, fl. 7, Boulaq
Tel: 574-1111
Fax: 575-6966

Universities

Ain Shams University
Qasr al-Zaafarani St., Abbasiya
Tel: 684-7818

American University in Cairo
113 Qasr al-Aini St., Tahrir Sq.
Downtown
Tel: 794-2964/9

Azhar University
al-Darrasa
Tel: 510-9243
Nasr City
Tel: 262-8436/263-3070

Cairo University
Orman St., Giza
Fax: 797-3400
Tel: 748-3443/5

Social services

Many of the following organizations need volunteers regularly. For more information on associations and community services, contact the Community Services Association.

Alcoholics Anonymous
Tel: 748-7692

Association for the Protection of the Environment
5 Halim Atallah St., Heliopolis
Tel: 510-2327

Befrienders Cairo
Tel: 344-8200/303-6035/6025

Community Services Association
4 Rd. 21, Maadi
Tel: 358-5284/376-8232

Maadi Environment Rangers
2 Orabi St., Maadi
Tel: 519-9723/358-5959

People's Dispensary for Sick Animals (PDSA)
60 Sikat al-Beida St., Abbasiya
Tel: 482-2294

Sadaka (Refugee Services)
St. Andrew's Church, next to the Ahram building, Downtown
Tel: 575-9451/736-3697

Tree Lovers' Association
Tel: 358-0229/358-0099
zeitouns@aol.com

Women's Association of Cairo
21 Boulos Hanna St., Doqqi
Tel: 760-3457
wac@intouch.com

Culture and Entertainment

Cultural centers

American Cultural Center
5 Amrika al-Latiniya St., Garden City
Tel: 797-3529/795-8927/797-3412
Tel: 337-8277/338-3867

Austrian Cultural Center
Wissa Wassef St.
Riyad Tower, fl. 5, Giza
Tel: 570-2975
Fax: 570-2979

British Council
192 al-Nil St., Agouza
Tel: 303-1514/347-6188/344-8263

4 al-Minya St., off Nazih Khalifa St.
Heliopolis
Tel: 452-3395

Canadian Cultural Center
5 al-Saraya al-Kubra St., Garden City
Tel: 794-3110
Fax: 796-3548

Cervantes Institute
20 Boulos Hanna St., Doqqi
Tel: 760-1746/337-0845/1962

Egyptian Center for International Cultural Cooperation
11 Shagaret al-Dorr St., Zamalek
Tel: 736-5410

French Cultural Center
1 Madrasat al-Huqouq al-Faransiya St.
Mounira
Tel: 795-3725/794-7679/1012
Fax: 795-7136
5 Shafiq al-Dib St., Ard al-Golf
Heliopolis
Tel: 419-3857

Goethe Institute
5 Abd al-Salam Aref St., Downtown
Tel: 577-9479/575-9877
Fax: 577-1140

Greek Cultural Center
18 Aisha al-Taymouriya St.
Garden City
Tel: 795-1871

Indian Cultural Center
23 Talaat Harb St., Downtown
Tel: 393-3396
Fax: 393-6572

Italian Cultural Center
3 al-Sheikh al-Marsafi St., Zamalek
Tel: 735-8791
Fax: 736-5723

Japanese Cultural Center
106 Qasr al-Aini St.
Cairo Center Bldg.
Tel: 795-3962/3/4
Fax: 796-3540

Russian Cultural Center
127 al-Tahrir St., Doqqi
Tel: 760-6371/748-6716
Fax: 749-3714

Swiss Council for the Arts (Pro Helvetia)
10 Abd al-Khaleq Sarwat St., Downtown
Tel: 575-8133/8284
Fax: 574-5236

Sporting and social clubs

Tennis, squash, and swimming pools are found at major clubs. Horseback riding at stables in the Pyramids area, Saqqara Country Club, Shams Club, and the Gezira and Feroussiya Clubs.

Ahli
Gabalaya St., Zamalek
Tel: 735-2114

Automobile and Touring Club of Egypt
Qasr al-Nil St., Downtown
Tel: 574-3176
Fax: 574-3115

Cairo Capital Club
9 Rostom St., Garden City
Tel: 795-3999

Diplomatic Club
12 Abd al-Salam Aref and
Qasr al-Nil Sts.
Tel: 576-7835

Feroussiya Club
In the Gezira Sporting Club; entrance under the flyover.

Tel: 735-6000

Gezira Sporting Club
Gezira St., Zamalek
Tel: 736-5270/735-6000

Greek Club
Talaat Harb Sq., above Groppi
Downtown
Tel: 575-0822

Greek Rowing Club
In front of Cairo Sheraton, Giza

Heliopolis Sporting Club
Merghani St., Heliopolis
Tel: 417-0063

Italian Club
30 July 26th St., Boulaq
Tel: 575-9590

Maadi Sporting Club
8 Palmar St., Maadi
Tel: 380-2066/358-5455

Shooting Club
Nadi al-Seid St., Doqqi
Tel: 749-8479

Swiss Club
90 Gehad St., off Sudan St., Imbaba
Tel: 315-1455

Yacht Club
120 Corniche al-Nil
Beside the State Council, Giza
Tel: 338-3548

Zamalek Club
July 26th St., Mohandessin
Tel: 306-2333

Golf courses

Dreamland Golf and Tennis Resort
Tel: 840-0577/8
Fax: 840-0579
www.dreamlandgolf.com
dreamgolf@ie-eg.com

**JW Marriott Golf Club
at Mirage City**
Tel: 412-5200/300/400
Proshop tel: 409-1464
Fax: 412-5040
**Katameya Heights Golf and Tennis
Resort**
Tel: 758-0512
Fax: 758-0506
www.katameya.com
katameya@egyptonline.com
Mena House Oberoi Golf Course
Tel: 383-3222/3444
Fax: 383-7777
www.oberoihotels.com
obmhobc@oberoi.com.eg
Pyramids Golf and Country Club
Tel and fax: 048-600-953/4/5
Proshop tel: 010-179-9703
acad@soleimania.com

Bowling
Bowling Kingly
Maadi Grand Mall
Tel: 518-1468
Bustan Bowling Center
Bustan Mall, Downtown
Tel: 395-0100
Geneina Mall
Badrawi St., off Abbas al-Aqqad St.
Nasr City
Geroland Obour City
Cairo Ismailiya Rd., Obour City
Tel: 477-1435/33/34
International Bowling Center
Off Salah Salem St., Nasr City
Tel: 336-1637
Nile Bowling
On the Nile near the Yacht Club, Giza

Ramses Hilton Annex
Behind Ramses Hilton Hotel,
Downtown
Tiba Mall
Nasr St., Nasr City

Shopping malls
Arkadia Mall
Corniche al-Nil, Boulaq
City Center
Makram Ebeid St., Nasr City
Digla Mall
11 Hassan Sabri St., Zamalek
First Mall
35 Murad St., annex of
the Four Seasons Hotel, Giza
Florida Mall
Masaken Sheraton, Heliopolis
Geneina Mall
Badrawi St., off Abbas al-Aqqad St.
Nasr City
Horriya Mall
al-Ahram St., Heliopolis
Maadi Grand Mall
Rd. 250, Maadi
Nile Hilton Annex
Tahrir Sq., Downtown
Ramses Hilton Annex
Behind Ramses Hilton
Downtown
Tiba Mall
Nasr St., Nasr City
Wonderland Mall
Abbas al- Aqqad St., Nasr City
World Trade Center
1191 Corniche al-Nil, Boulaq
Yamama Center
3 Taha Hussein St., Zamalek

Amusement and theme parks
Cairo Land
1 Salah Salem St.
Dr. Ragab's Pharaonic Village
Jacob's Island, Saqiet Mekki, Giza
Tel: 571-8675
Dreampark 6th October
October 6th Rd.
Geroland Obour City
Cairo Ismailiya Desert Rd.
Obour City
Tel: 477-1435/33/34
Fax: 840-0887
Magic Land 6th October
Media Production City
Tel: 835-7166
Sindbad
New Nozha, Ismailiya Rd.
**Suzanne Mubarak Children's
Museum**
Abu Bakr al-Sediq St., Heliopolis
13.5-feddan botanical forest
Wonderland Theme Park
Abbas al-Aqqad St.
Behind Wonderland Mall, Nasr City

Museums
Abd al-Wahab Museum
Ramses St., inside the Higher Institute
for Arabic Music
Tel: 561-1034
Open 9-4, closed Friday
Abdin Palace Museum
Abdin Palace, Abdin Sq.
Downtown
Tel: 391-0042
Open 9-3
Includes museum for medals, Mubarak's
presents, weapons, royal paraphernalia.

Agricultural and Cotton Museum
al-Islah al-Zerai St., Doqqi
Tel: 761-4999
Open 9-1, closed Monday

Ahmed Shawqi Museum
6 Ahmed Shawqi St., off Corniche al-Nil
Giza
Tel: 572-9479
Open 10-5, closed Monday

Beit al-Umma Museum
1 Saad Zaghloul St., Mounira
Residence of Saad Zaghloul. Under
renovation, opening soon.

Ceramics Museum
1 al-Sheikh al-Marsafi St., Zamalek
Tel: 390-9930/1520
Open 8:30-4 in winter; 8-1 in summer
Former palace of Prince Amr Ibrahim, a
fine example of neo-Islamic
architecture.

Cheops Boat Museum
Pyramids, next to Cheops' Pyramid
Giza
Open 9-3
Houses the painstakinly restored solar
boat of Cheops.

Citadel
Tel: 512-7135
Open 9-4
Includes police museum, wax museum,
carriage museum, and more.

Coptic Museum
Mari Girgis St., Old Cairo
Tel: 362-8766
Open 9-5

Dar al-Kutub Museum
Corniche al-Nil, Boulaq, inside the
library

Tel: 575-1210/3254
Open 9-9, closed Friday

Egyptian Geological Museum
Maadi Rd.
Tel: 524-0916/7
Open 9-2:30, closed Sunday-Tuesday

Egyptian Museum
Mariette Pasha St., Tahrir Sq.
Downtown
Tel: 575-4319
Open 9-4:30
First housed in Boulaq, flooded and
relocated to Ismail's Giza Palace. The
present neo-classical building was
opened in 1902.

Entomology Museum
14 Ramses St., Downtown
Open 9-1 Sunday-Wednesday; 10-1
Saturday; 5:30-8 Monday and Wednesday

Ethnographic Museum
109 Qasr al-Aini St., at the Geographical
Society
Tel: 794-5450
Open 9:30-2, closed Friday

**Gayer Anderson Museum
(Beit al-Kiritliya)**
4 Ahmed Ibn Tuloun Sq., Sayeda Zeinab
Tel: 364-7822
Open 8-5
Actually made up of two 17th-century
houses stuck together, the complex is
named after the British major-turned-
collector who lived in it.

Islamic Museum
Port Said St., Bab al-Khalq
Downtown
Tel: 390-1520
Open 9-4

Mahmoud Khalil Museum
1 Kafour St., next to the State Council
Giza
Tel: 336-2358
Open 10-5:30, closed Monday
Holds one of Egypt's larger collections
of modern European art; housed in the
collector's neo-classical villa.

Manyal Palace Museum
1 al-Saraya St., Manyal
Tel: 368-7495
Open 9-4:30
Founded in 1938 by Crown Prince
Mohammed Ali in his residence to
house his own collection. Later donated
to the state. Includes rare tropical
gardens.

Mohammed Nagy Museum
9 Mahmoud al-Gindi St.
Hadayeq al-Haram, near the Pyramids
Tel: 383-3484
Open 10-5 in winter, 10-6 summer
Closed Monday

Mostafa Kamel Museum
Salah al-Din Sq., Citadel
Tel: 510-9943
Open 9-3

Museum of Modern Art
Opera House grounds, Zamalek
Tel: 736-6665
Open 10-1, closed Monday

Music Library
Opera House grounds, Zamalek
Tel: 739-8061
Open 9-6, closed Thursday and Friday

Postal Museum
Main Post Office, Ataba Sq., Downtown
Open 9-1, closed Friday

Qasr al-Aini Museum
Qasr al-Aini St., next to Qasr al-Aini
Hospital, Downtown
Tel: 792-1287
Open 9-3
Collection of medical illustrations and
instruments.

Railway Museum
Adjoining the Cairo Railway Station
Ramses Sq., Downtown
Tel: 575-3555
Open 8:30-1, closed Monday

Sixth of October Panorama
Junction of Salah Salem and Ismail al-
Fangari Sts., Heliopolis
Shows at 9:30 am, 11, 12:30, 6, and 7:30
pm; closed Tuesday

Taha Hussein Museum
1 Helmiya al-Ahram St., off Pyramids
Ave.
Tel: 391-0042
Open 10-3, closed Monday

Umm Kulthoum Museum
Monasterly Palace, southern tip of
Manyal Island
Tel: 363-1467
Open 10-2 and 6-10

Art galleries

Atelier du Caire
2 Karim al-Dawla St., Downtown
Tel: 574-6730
Open 10-1 and 5-11, closed Friday

Atelier Palette
25 Rifaa St., off Misaha Sq., Doqqi
Open 11-2 and 5-10

Cairo Opera House Art Gallery
Opera House grounds, Zamalek
Tel: 737-0592

Open 10-2 and 4:30-8:30, closed Friday
Center of Arts, Akhnaton Galleries
1 Maahad al-Swissri St., Zamalek
Tel: 735-8211
Open 10-1:30 and 5:30-9

**Egyptian Center for International
Cultural Cooperation**
11 Shagaret al-Dorr St., Zamalek
Tel: 736-5419
Open 10-3 and 4-9, closed Friday

Espace Karim Francis
1 al-Sharifein St., off Qasr al-Nil St.
Downtown
Tel: 391-6357
Open 10-2 and 6-9

Extra
3 al-Nessim St., Zamalek
Tel: 735-6293
Open 10:30-2 and 5-8, closed Sunday

Gallery Salama
36A Ahmed Orabi St., Mohandessin
Tel: 346-3242/344-8109
Open 10-2:30 and 5-9
Closed Friday

Gamila Gallery
23 Rd. 23, Digla, Maadi
Tel: 521-2294
Open 11-1:30 and 5:30-8:30
Closed Friday and Saturday

Gezira Arts Center
1 al-Sheikh al-Marsafi St., Zamalek
Tel: 736-8672
Open 10-2 and 6-10, Friday 6-9
Closed Monday

Grant Gallery
6 al-Gomhouriya St., Abdin
Tel: 391-6769
Open 12-10, closed Friday

Hanager Arts Center
Opera House grounds, Zamalek
Tel: 735-6861
Open 10-10
Small theater and coffee house on the
premises.

Khan al-Maghraby
18 al-Mansour Mohammed St.
Zamalek
Tel: 735-3349
Open 10:30-9, closed Sunday

Mashrabia
8 Champollion St., Downtown
Tel: 578-4494
Open 11-8, closed Friday

**Orient Express Art Gallery (The
Apartment)**
21 Abd al-Meneim Riyad St.
Mohandessin
Tel: 749-7808
Open 11-6

Palace of Arts
Opera House grounds, Zamalek
Tel: 736-7627
Open 10-2 and 5-9

Safar Khan Art Gallery
6 Brazil St., Zamalek
Tel: 735-3314
Open 9:30-1:30 and 4:30-8:30
Closed Sunday

Sheba Gallery
6 Sri Lanka St., Zamalek
Tel: 735-9192
Open 10-8, closed Sunday

Shomou
12 Rd. 150, Horriya Sq., Maadi
Tel: 358-2073
Open 11-8, closed Friday

Sony Gallery
Adham Center, AUC
113 Qasr al-Aini St., Downtown
Tel: 794-2964
Open 9-12, closed Friday and Saturday

Townhouse Gallery
Hussein Pasha St., off Mahmoud
Bassyouni, Downtown
Tel: 575-5901
Open 10-2 and 6-9; Friday 6-9 only
Closed Thursday

World of Art Gallery
6 Rd. 77C, Maadi
Tel: 359-4362
Open 10-9

Zamalek Art Gallery
11 Brazil St., Zamalek
Tel: 735-1240
Open 10:30-9, closed Friday

Libraries

*Most cultural centers and research
organizations offer library services as well;
please see our listings.*

**American University in Cairo
(AUC) Library**
113 Qasr al-Aini St., Tahrir Sq.
Downtown
Tel: 797-6904
Open 8am-10pm Sunday-Wednesday; 8-
8 Thursday; 10-8 Saturday; closed Friday

AUC Rare Books Library
22 al-Sheikh Rihan St., Bab al-Louq
Tel: 797-5060
Open 8:30-7 Sunday-Thursday, 12-5
Saturday; closed Friday

Dar al-Kutub
Corniche al-Nil, Boulaq
Tel: 575-3254/1210

Open 9-9, closed Friday

Greater Cairo Library
15 Mohammed Mazhar St., Zamalek
Tel: 736-2271
Open 9-5, closed Friday

Mubarak Library
4 al-Tahawiya St., Giza
Tel: 336-0291

Bookstores

Ahram Bookstores
Nile Hilton and most 5-star hotels
Tel: 578-0444/666

**American University in Cairo
Bookstore**
113 Qasr al-Aini St., Tahrir Sq.
Inside Hill House building on the main
campus
Tel: 797-5377/1
Open 8:30-4:30; Saturday 10:30-4:30
Closed Friday and all of August
16 Mohammed Ibn Thaqeb St., Zamalek
Inside AUC Hostel
Tel: 339-7045
Open 10-6:30, closed Friday

Anglo-Egyptian Bookstore
165 Mohammed Farid St., Downtown
Tel: 391-4337
Open 9-1:30 and 4:30-8, closed Sunday

Book House International (BHI)
95 Rd. 9, Maadi
Tel: 750-8517
Open 10-7

Diwan Bookstore
159 July 26th St., Zamalek
Tel: 736-2578

**General Egyptian Bookstore
Organization (GEBO)**
Corniche al-Nil, Boulaq

Tel: 577-5109

Lehnert and Landrock
44 Sherif St., Downtown
Tel: 393-5324/392-7606
Open 9:30-2 and 4-7, closed Sunday

Livres de France
36 Qasr al-Nil St., Downtown
Tel: 393-5512
Open 10-7, Saturday 10-1:30
Closed Sunday

Madbouli
6 Talaat Harb Sq., Downtown
Tel: 575-6421
Open 9-11

Meric
2 Bahgat Ali St., al-Masri Towers, Tower
D, apt. 24, Zamalek
Tel: 736-3826/735-3818
Open 8:30-5:30, closed Friday and
Saturday
Carries specialized publications,
including UN agency reports

Reader's Corner
33 Abd al-Khaleq Tharwat St.
Downtown
Tel: 392-8801

Romansia
32 Shagaret al-Dorr St., Zamalek
Tel: 735-0492

Rose al-Youssef
89 Qasr al-Aini St., Mounira
Tel: 792-0536

Volume 1
17 Rd. 216, Maadi
Tel: 519-6757/8831
3 Abd al-Halim Hussein St., off Thawra
St., Doqqi
Tel: 338-0168

Zamalek Bookshop
19 Shagaret al-Dorr St., Zamalek
Tel: 736-9197
Open 9-8, closed Sunday

Opera and theaters

The historic palaces in the old city are often used as venues. Check the local press for events at Beit al-Harawi, Beit al-Seheimi, Monasterly Palace, and, in the summer, the Citadel open-air theater.

Balloon Theater
Corniche al-Nil, Agouza
Tel: 347-1718/7457

Cairo Opera House
Opera House grounds, Gezira
Tel: 737-0603

Gomhouriya Theater
Gomhouriya St., Downtown
Tel: 390-7707

Hanager Theater
Opera House grounds, Zamalek
Tel: 735-6861

Haram Theater
Pyramids Ave.
Tel: 386-3952

Hosabir Theater
56 Galaa St., Downtown
Tel: 574-0383

Nasr City Theater
52 Youssef Abbas St., Nasr City
Tel: 402-0804

National Theater
Ataba Sq., Downtown
Tel: 591-7783

Puppet Theater
July 26th St., Ezbekiya Gardens
Tel: 591-0954

Qasr al-Nil Theater

6 Qasr al-Nil St., Downtown
Tel: 575-0761

Radio
Talaat Harb St., Downtown
Tel: 578-4910

Ramses
Ramses Hilton Hotel Annex, fl. 7
Tel: 574-7435

Rihani Theater
17 Emad al-Din St., Downtown
Tel: 591-3697

Zamalek Theater
13 Shagaret al-Dorr St., Zamalek
Tel: 736-0660

Cinemas

Cairo Sheraton
Galaa Sq., Doqqi
Tel: 760-6081

Cosmos
12 Emad al-Din St., Downtown
Tel: 574-2177

Diana
17 Alfi St., Downtown
Tel: 592-4727

Geneina
Geneina Mall, al-Batrawi St., off Abbas al-Aqqad St., Nasr City
Tel: 263-0745

Karim
15 Emad al-Din St., Downtown
Tel: 591-6095

Maadi Cinema
1 Palestine St., Bandar 2000
Entertainment Complex
Tel: 519-0770

Metro
35 Talaat Harb St., Downtown
Tel: 393-7566

Miami
38 Talaat Harb St.
Downtown
Tel: 574-5656

Normandy
31 al-Ahram St., Heliopolis
Tel: 258-0254

Odeon
4 Abd al-Hamid Said St.
Downtown
Tel: 575-8797

Radio
24 Talaat Harb St., Downtown
Tel: 575-6562

Ramses Hilton
Ramses Hilton Annex
Tel: 574-7436

Renaissance
World Trade Center
Boulaq
Tel: 580-4039

Renaissance II
Wonderland Mall, end of Abbas al-Aqqad St., Nasr City
Tel: 401-2326

Rivoli
July 26th St., Downtown
Tel: 575-5053

Roxy
Roxy Sq., Heliopolis
Tel: 258-0344

Tahrir
112 Tahrir St., Doqqi
Tel: 335-4726

Tiba
Nasr St., Nasr City
Tel: 262-1084

Websites

Art and culture

www.alazhar.org

www.alwaraq.com
(References in Arabic literature, language, religion, and philosophy)

www.cairoartindex.org
(Contemporary Egyptian art resource)

www.coptic.net
(Coptic Orthodox Church of Egypt)

www.egyptart.org.eg
(Egyptian art resource)

www.egy.com
(Modern history and architecture)

www.guardians.net/hawass
(Egyptology site run by SCA director Zahi Hawass)

www.horus.ics.org.eg
(Egyptology for kids)

www.library.idsc.gov.eg
(Search 140 libraries across Egypt)

www.mazika.com
(Download hundreds of tunes)

www.sakhr.com
(Arabic history and culture, in Arabic)

www.superluminal.com
(Sufism guide with cookbook)

www.thetownhousegallery.com
(Contemporary Egyptian art)

Business and economy

www.arabfinance.com

www.carana.com/pcsu
(Privatization in Egypt)

www.cbe.org.eg
(Central Bank of Egypt)

www.eba.org.eg
(Egyptian Businessmen's Association)

www.eces.org.eg
(Egyptian Center for Economic Studies)

www.economy.gov.eg
(Ministry of Foreign Trade)

www.efg-hermes.com
(Daily stock quotes and news)

www.egyptse.com
(Cairo and Alexandria Stock Exchanges)

www.erf.org.eg
(Economic Research Forum)

www.fei.org.eg
(Federation of Egyptian Industries)

www.kompassbusiness.com

www.mpe-egypt.com
(Ministry of Public Enterprise)

www.sharqfin.com
(Regional Finance Studies)

www.tpegypt.gov.eg
(Egyptian International Trade Point)

www.zawya.com
(Financial news portal)

Egyptian government

www.idsc.gov.eg
(Information Decision Support Center)

www.mcit.gov.eg
(Ministry of Communications and Information Technology)

www.pogar.org
(Info on Egyptian law and judiciary)

www.sis.gov.eg
(State Information Service)

News and portals

www.ahram.org.eg
(Ahram Weekly online)

www.allafrica.com

www.amcham.org.eg/Publications/
BusinessMonthly (Business Monthly)

www.arabia.com

www.arabianbusiness.com

www.arabicnews.com

www.cairolive.com

www.cairotimes.com

www.egyptiansoccer.com

www.egyptinsight.com

www.egypttoday.com

www.planetarabia.com

www.yallabina.com

www.al-bab.com

Real Estate

www.betna.com (Rent and buy)

www.e-dar.com (Rent and buy)

www.misrrealestate.com
(Egypt Real Estate information network)

Services

www.140online.com
(Telephone directory)

www.alhokoma.com
(Government online)

www.careeregypt.com

www.discountegypt.com

www.egyptair.com.eg

www.egyptyellowpages.com.eg

www.otlob.com
(Order food, flowers, and more online)

www.telecomegypt.gov.eg
(Pay phone bills online)

Regional Guide

Useful Numbers

The following numbers work all over Egypt.

Ambulance: 123
Clock: 15
Fire Brigade: 180
National Operator Service: 10
Police: 122
Tourist Police: 126

Accommodation

You can find information and make reservations online at many of Egypt's 5-star hotels at the following websites:

www.intoegypt.com
www.rehalat.com

Central reservation numbers

Hilton: 576-2222
Meridien: 510-0200
(enter 800-288-4614)
Mövenpick: 418-2282
Oberoi: 383-3222
Sheraton: 760-8877
Sofitel: 526-0602

Online travel help

www.alexandriaguide.com
www.aswanguide.com
www.cairoguide.com
www.egyptoffroad.com
www.hurghadaguide.com
www.intoegypt.com
www.luxorguide.com
www.redseadc.com
www.sharmguide.com
www.touregypt.net (Ministry of Tourism)

The Capital (02)

Tourist Office

Misr Travel Tower
Abbasiya Sq.
Tel: 285-4509/284-1970
Fax: 285-4363
Adli St., Downtown
Tel: 391-3454
Pyramids
Tel: 385-0259

Cairo Airport

General Information: 291-4255/66/77
Terminal 1: 244-1460
Terminal 2: 245-9332

Airlines

EgyptAir

Airport office: 244-1460
6 Adli St., Downtown
Tel: 392-7649/80
22 Ibrahim al-Laqani St.
Heliopolis
Tel: 290-8453
July 26th St., Zamalek Club wall
Mohandessin
Tel: 747-5193
Flight information and reservations:
390-3444 (10 am-5 pm)
www.egyptair.com.eg
Air France: 575-8899
Air India: 392-2592/393-4873
Alitalia: 578-5823/5
American Airlines: 345-5707/7-0033
British Airways: 578-0742/6
Emirates: 336-1555/735-1102

Gulf Air: 748-4116/748-4072
Iberia: 579-5800/5700/5600
KLM: 574-7004
Lufthansa: 339-8339
Olympic: 393-1277/1459
TWA: 574-7001/9904

Train station

You can book your ticket at the Ramses central station, or at the following telephone exchange bureaus

Ramses Train Station
Tel: 575-3555/579-0767
Doqqi exchange: 337-4259/761-6200
Maadi exchange: 519-2019
Bab al-Louq exchange: 794-5999

Bus companies

Buses leave from Turgoman Station downtown, Almaza Station in Heliopolis, and the Giza Station in Giza Square. Buses to the Sinai also leave from the Abbasiya Station.

East Delta: 574-2814
Superjet: 579-8181/417-9666
Upper Egypt: 575-2156
West Delta: 575-9751/290-4851

Car rental

Avis: 794-7400/7081
Budget: 735-0070/9474
Hertz: 747-4172/2238

Limousine rental

Limousine Misr: 285-6721
Limousine Nasser: 508-1348/9
Limo One: 735-5920
Rawass Limo: 736-1333

To stay

The five-stars are of a good international standing with the Hiltons, Semiramis, Sheraton, Meridiens, and Marriott conveniently located in the city center. The Four Seasons and the Conrad International

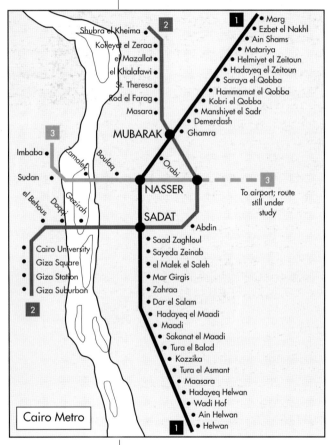

Cairo Metro

have a good reputation for business travelers, while in Maadi the Sofitel stands out. For downtown lovers, we suggest the historic Cosmopolitan or the Carlton, which has an excellent rooftop terrace. In Zamalek, the Mayfair, the Horus, and the Longchamps are fine pensions. Also in Zamalek the Flamenco is a good central four-star choice. Budget-minded travelers can also stay at the Garden City House, a favorite among archaeologists. (For 5-star listings see the Contacts List.)

Carlton (3*)
21 July 26th St., Downtown
Tel: 575-5181/5022/5232
Fax: 575-5323

Cosmpolitan (3*)
11bn Thaalab St., off Qasr al-Nil St. Downtown
Tel: 392-3845/3956/3663
Fax: 393-3531

Flamenco (Golden Tulip) (4*)
2 al-Gezira al-Wosta St., Zamalek
Tel: 735-0815
Fax: 735-0819

Garden City House
1 Ibrahimi St., Garden City
Tel: 794-0527

Horus (3*)
21 Ismail Mohammed St., Zamalek
Tel: 735-3977
Fax: 735-3182

Longchamps (3*)
21 Ismail Mohammed St., Zamalek
Tel: 735-2311
Fax: 735-9644

Mayfair
9 Aziz Osman St., Zamalek
Tel: 735-7315

Eating and drinking

For a comprehensive and up-to-date guide to Cairene eateries and nightlife, pick up a copy of the Cairo Dining Guide. Below are some of the city's favorite eateries and hangouts. Our favorites in Zamalek are the venerable Pub 28, Simmonds for coffee, and Maison Thomas for pizzas, sandwiches, and pork. For books and coffee, try Diwan bookshop. Mohandessin offers everything, but Tia Maria is a long-time favorite, and the Cairo Jazz Club is the only live music venue in town. Maadi boasts two of the best ethnic restaurants in town: Thai Bua Khao and Indian Bukhara. If you're Downtown, Estoril is a must, or try one of the best-kept secrets in town: the unassuming Le Pacha (not the boat), a hole in the wall that caters and delivers Levantine home-cooking. If you've got a big group, check out al-Hati's arabesque upstairs room for atmosphere. In the summer, chill out on the terrace of the Greek Club. For all-night eating, the Rifai kebabgi in Monge Alley and Farahat in Hussein are both Cairo institutions.

Abu el-Sid
157 July 26th St., Zamalek
Tel: 735-9640

Alfi Bey
3 al-Alfi St., Downtown
Tel: 577-1888

Aubergine
5 Sayed al-Bakri St., Zamalek
Tel: 332-0080

Bam-bu
Corniche al-Nil
Casino al-Shagara
In front of World Trade Center
Tel: 579-6512

Bua Khao
9 Rd. 151, Maadi
Tel: 358-0126

Bukhara
43 Misr Helwan Rd., Maadi
Tel: 380-0126

Café Riche
17 Talaat Harb St., Downtown
Tel: 391-8873/392-9793

Cairo Jazz Club
197 July 26th St., opposite the Balloon
Theater, Mohandessin
Tel: 345-9939

Chantilly
11 Baghdad St., Heliopolis
Tel: 290-7303

Chesa
21 Adli St., Downtown
Tel: 393-9360

Cilantro
159 July 26th St., Zamalek
Tel: 736-1115

Diwan Bookstore and Café
159 July 26th St., Zamalek
Tel: 736-2578

Estoril
12 Talaat Harb St., Downtown
Tel: 574-3102

Farahat
Off Azhar St., before Hussein Sq.

Felfela
15 Hoda Shaarawi St., Downtown
Tel: 392-2751

Greek Club
Talaat Harb Sq., above Groppi
Entrance from Mahmoud Bassyouni St.
Downtown
Tel: 575-0822

Harris Café
7 Baghdad St., Heliopolis
Tel: 417-6796

al-Hati
8A July 26th St., entrance from Shariket
Ideal Alley, Downtown
Tel: 391-8829

La Bodega
157 July 26th St., Zamalek
Tel: 735-6761

Le Pacha
15 Mahmoud Bassyouni St.
Downtown
Tel: 575-3130/574-6169

Maison Thomas
157 July 26th St., Zamalek
Tel: 735-7057

Mogul Room
Mena House Hotel, Pyramids Ave.
Giza
Tel: 383-3222

Naguib Mahfouz Café
5 al-Badistan, Khan al-Khalili
Tel: 590-3788

Pub 28
28 Shagaret al-Dorr St., Zamalek
Tel: 735-9200

al-Rifai Kebab
Monge Alley, across from Sayeda Zeinab
mosque
Sayeda Zeinab Sq.

Sangria
Corniche al-Nil, Casino al-Shagara
In front of World Trade Center
Tel: 579-6511

Simmonds
112 July 26th St., Zamalek
Tel: 735-9436

Tabasco
8 Amman Sq., Doqqi
Tel: 336-5583

Tia Maria
32 Jeddah St., Mohandessin
Tel: 335-3273

Daytrips from Cairo

Along the Maryoutiya/Abu Rawash/Dahshour axis, one can spend a day between palm trees and pyramids. Saqqara Country Club and Saqqara Palm Club are favorite rest stops. Sukhna is a beach for Cairenes useable almost all year long, complete with a hot water spring. Further south down the Sinai coast, about three hours from Cairo, Ras Sidr is a windsurfer's paradise. For peaceful gardens, canal-side views, and seafood, Ismailiya and Port Said are also located within a reasonable distance of Cairo. To the west of Cairo, Wadi Natroun features monasteries and some good picnic spots. Sixty kilometers south of Cairo, one enters the Fayyoum depression: lakes, hunting, scenery, and village life. Most of these spots are crowded on Fridays and public holidays.

Pyramids

For a view of the pyramids a drive along the Saqqara Dahshour road is a must. Another way to see the string of pyramids is to take the Upper Egypt Western Desert Road and drive south to Hawara. The name of the game is to recognize the pyramids at a distance against the Nile Valley backdrop. If you come back on the Agricultural Highway, drive carefully. If you just want an outing in the Pyramids area, Christo's fish and seafood can be great, and Andrea's grill is perfect for a day with the kids. For a day

outside the city breathing fresh air and
doing crafts, the Fagnoon Art School is a
delight—also popular with the kids.

Andrea
59-60 Maryoutiya Canal
Tel: 383-1133

Christo
10 Pyramids Ave., Giza
Tel: 383-3582

Fagnoon Art School
Saqqara Rd., 4 km after turnoff to
Saqqara Country Club
Tel: 010-158-6715
Open 10-7 weekends and summer

Saqqara Country Club and Hotel
Zawiet Abu Musalam, Saqqara Rd.
Tel: 381-1415/331-1282
Fax: 381-0571

Saqqara Palm Club
Saqqara Rd., Badrashin
Tel: 286-333
Fax: 286-555

Ras Sidr (069)

Moon Beach (1) (3*)
Tel: 336-5103

Wadi Natroun (045)

*Halfway on the road to Alex sits Wadi
Natroun, famous for natron salts used for
mummification and its monastic tradition.
There are four active monasteries and the
desert is literally scattered with the ruins of
monasteries and kelias buried under the
sands. Close to the old Rest House, a
veritable village of hotels, food, and gas
stations has popped up.*

Rest House
106 km Cairo-Alexandria Rd.

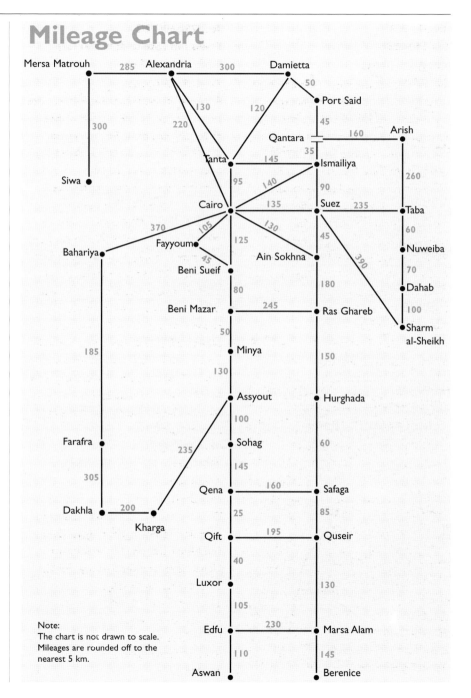

Mileage Chart

Mersa Matrouh — 285 — Alexandria — 300 — Damietta
50
Port Said
130 / 120 / 45
300 / 220 / Qantara — 160 — Arish
35
Siwa / Tanta — 145 — Ismailiya / 260
95 / 140 / 90
Cairo — 135 — Suez — 235 — Taba
370 / 105 / 130 / 45 / 60
Bahariya — Fayyoum / 125 / Ain Sokhna / 390 / Nuweiba
45 / Beni Sueif / 70
180 / Dahab
80 / 100
Beni Mazar — 245 — Ras Ghareb / Sharm al-Sheikh
50
185 / Minya / 150
130
Assyout / Hurghada
100
Farafra / Sohag / 60
235 / 145
305 / Qena — 160 — Safaga
Dakhla — 200 — / 25 / 85
Kharga / Qift — 195 — Quseir
40
Luxor / 130
105
Edfu — 230 — Marsa Alam
110 / 145
Aswan / Berenice

Note:
The chart is not drawn to scale.
Mileages are rounded off to the
nearest 5 km.

Tel: 551-308

Fax: 550-999

Sukhna (062)

Unfortunately, Sukhna beaches are hard to reach. The good beach and the hot spring are at the Ain Sukhna Hotel (2), currently undergoing renovation, so one is forced to use one of the resorts there. To stay overnight, the Swiss Inn (3) at Stella di Mare is a good choice. Also, the Portrait (4) and Palmera Beach Hotel (5) offer day use facilities. There are a couple of fish restaurants located in front of Dolphin Village; the best known is Abu Ali (6). Gas stations at the junction of the Suez and Qatamiya Roads.

Palmera Beach Hotel (4*)

Tel: 410-818/19/20

Portrait Hotel (3*)

59 km Suez Zaafarana Rd.

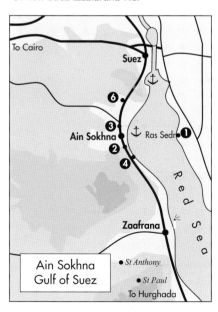

To Cairo

Suez

⑥

③   Ras Sedr ❶

Ain Sokhna ●

②

④

Zaafrana

Red Sea

Ain Sokhna
Gulf of Suez

● St Anthony

● St Paul

To Hurghada

Tel: 325-560/1/2/3

Swiss Inn (Stella di Mare) (5*)

Tel: 250-100/11/12

Port Said (066)

A former shoppers' paradise, Port Said has wooden colonial architecture reminiscent of Bombay and many fish restaurants, though most are a bit heavy-handed. The most well-known are the Borg and al-Castan on the Corniche. Our favorite is the small gambarina near the French market and Galal. You can also have a great lunch at the rooftop Akri Restaurant with a view of the port, while the recently renovated Gianolla is a famous survivor from the good old days. On the eastern side of the canal, there are several nautical clubs and Port Fouad, with the villas of the Suez Canal Company. On the black sands of Port Fouad's beaches there is a string of cafeterias that get very lively at night, the most famous being al-Zaim that sometimes features the Tannoura musical troupe.

Tourist Office

43 Palestine St.

Tel: 235-289

Bus Station

The bus station is located at the city entrance. Several buses daily to Cairo and Alexandria; one bus every day to Upper Egypt and the Red Sea. For the Sinai, transfer at Ismailiya.

Tel (Super Jet): 321-779

American Express

Mena Tours Office

Near al-Gomhouriya St.

Tel: 230-939

Thomas Cook

43 al-Gomhouriya St.

Tel: 227-559

To stay

Akri

24 al-Gomhouriya St.

Tel: 221-013

Sonesta Port Said (4*)

Canal Promenade

Tel: 418-3539

Fax: 418-3548

Eating and drinking

Cecil Bar and Restaurant

Gomhouriya St., in front of Akri Hotel

Tel: 223-911

Galal

Corner of al-Gomhouriya and al-Gabarti Sts.

Gianolla

Gomhouriya St.

To do

Military Museum

July 23rd St.

Tel: 224-657

Open 9-2 in winter, 8-2 in summer

National Museum

Palestine St.

Tel: 237-419

Open 9-4, closed 11-1 Friday

Shooting Club

Close to the tip of the Canal. Enjoy the view of Asia.

Ismailiya (064)

Aside from its vast gardens, Ismailiya is known for its bouri and baklaweez, or clam soup. George Restaurant is itself a reason to go to Ismaililya—try the

calamari sauté. Otherwise Ismailiya features peaceful tree-lined streets, colonial houses, a cathedral, and a neo-Pharaonic-style museum. Check out the Suez Canal Club on the Bitter Lake, or use the brand new bridge at Qantara or the ferry to cross to Sinai.

Tourist office
Governorate Bldg.
Mohammed Ali Quay
Tel: 321-074

Bus Station
Located in front of new university on the Ring Road. Buses daily to all parts of Egypt.

To stay
Mercure Forsan (4*)
P.O. Box 77
Tel: 338-040
Fax: 338-043

Eating and drinking
George Restaurant
Sultan Hussein St.
Tel: 220-494

To do
Ismailiya Museum
Mohammed Ali St., beside the old Governorate Bldg.
Tel: 322-749
Open daily 9-4
Pharaonic and Greco-Roman antiquities

Suez (062)
The southern entrance to the canal, Suez features an immense Corniche, a big port, fish restaurants, oyster sandwiches, and curious shell food. There are several Abu Ali fish restaurants and two fish markets. Stay at the Red Sea Hotel or the Summer Palace (just renovated in pink), a favorite lovers' watering hole looking down the Red Sea. Port Tawfiq has survived two wars with its colonial bearing intact, but Mohammed Ali's Palace is still awaiting renovation.

Tourist Office
al-Marwa St.
Tel: 223-589

Bus Station
Located 7 km outside town. Daily buses to all parts of Egypt.

American Express
3 al-Marwa St., next to the tourist office
Tel: 220-269

To stay
Red Sea Hotel (3*)
13 al-Riyad St., Port Tawfiq
Tel: 334-302/3
Summer Palace
Port Tawfiq
Tel: 224-475

Fayyoum (084)
A hunting heaven famous for its lake, ducks, and sole fish, Fayyoum features stunning scenery and a virtual catalogue of fossil life. But the water wheels, another claim to fame, have disappeared from Fayyoum City. The shores of Lakes Qaroun and Rayan are the most popular spots. Eat fish at Shakshouk if you're not afraid of pollution. The Auberge (1), an old hunting lodge, and the Panorama (2), are the only places to stay. Visit the potters at Ezbat Tunis, an artists' colony.

Tourist Office
Governorate Bldg.
Medinet al-Fayyoum
Tel: 342-313

To stay
Auberge Du Lac (4*)
Lake Qaroun
Tel: 572-001
Fax: 572-003
Panorama Village (4*)
Shakshouk
Lake Qaroun
Tel: 830-757

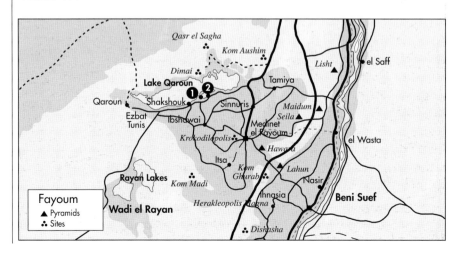

To do
Kom Aushim Museum
Desert Rd. near Karanis
Open 8-4

Second City (03)

Tourist Office
Saad Zaghloul St., Ramleh
Tel: 807985
Nozha Airport, Nozha
Tel: 420-2021

Airports
Borg al-Arab Airport
Tel: 459-1485/86/87

Nozha Airport
Tel: 420-1036

*From Alexandria you can get a local flight
to Hurghada, Sharm al-Sheikh, and Luxor.
There are also direct international flights
from Alexandria to Athens, Frankfurt, Saudi
Arabia, and Dubai.*

Airlines
Air France
22 Salah Salem St.
Tel: 483-8901

British Airways
15 Saad Zaghloul Sq.
Tel: 483-6668

EgyptAir
9 Saad Zaghloul Sq.
Tel: 483-3357

Gulf Air
33 Safiya Zaghloul St.
Tel: 482-1711

KLM
6 Horriya Ave.
482-8547

Lufthansa
6 Talaat Harb St.
Tel: 483-7031

Olympic Airways
19 Saad Zaghloul Sq.
Tel: 482-1014

TWA
2 Horriya Ave.
483-4682

Train station
Central Station (Mahattat Misr)
Tel: 420-7363/322-1133

Sidi Gaber
Tel: 485-1556/427-4423

Bus companies
*The bus station is behind the Sidi Gaber
train station.*
Superjet: 422-8566
West Delta: 420-0916

Travelers' services
American Express
34 al-Moaskar al-Romani St., Rushdi
Tel: 541-0177

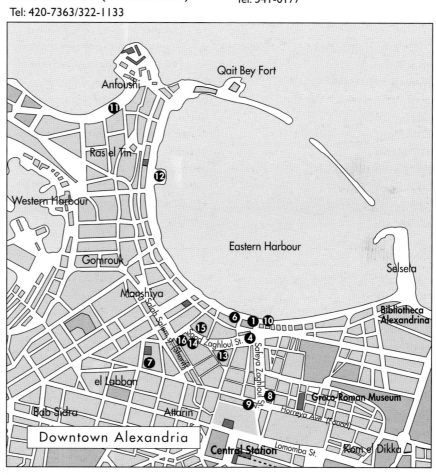

Downtown Alexandria

Thomas Cook
15 Saad Zaghloul Sq.
Tel: 482-7830
Western Union
381 Horriya Ave.
Tel: 427-1654

Courier services

Aramex
37 Ismail Serri St., Semouha
Tel: 426-1770
DHL
18 Tutankhamun St., Sporting
Tel: 427-7141/420-3446
5 Mohammed Baha al-Din St., Semouha
Tel: 425-0001
Federal Express
314 Horriya Ave., Sidi Gaber
Tel: 544-7535/545-3572
TNT Express Worldwide
177 Corniche
Tel: 545-7890/546-4753
UPS Egypt
28 Abdullah al-Gheriani St., Saba Pasha
Tel: 585-7021

Consulates

France
2 Orabi Sq., Manshiya
Tel: 482-7950
Germany
5 Mena St., Rushdi
Tel: 545-7025
Ireland
36 Kafr Abdu St., Rushdi
Tel: 546-4686
Netherlands
18 Horriya Ave.
Tel: 482-9044

Saudi Arabia
9 Ptolemies St.
Tel: 482-9911
United Kingdom
3 Mena St., Rushdi
Tel: 546-7001
United States of America
3 Pharaoh St.
Tel: 472-1009

To stay

All five-star hotels are listed below. Of them. The Cecil (1) is a historical landmark, while the 1960s-era Palestine (2) has a magnificent location and its own beach. Across from it is the Salamlek (3), a former wing of Montazah Palace. Downtown favorites in the upper bracket are the recently renovated Metropole (4) and the Delta. One of the charms of Alex are the many faded pensions of yesteryear. On the Sporting Corniche, the Blue Riveria (5) has great seaside balconies, while the Crillon (6), also on the Corniche, still has its English colonial décor.

Blue Riviera
Corniche, Sporting
Tel: 592-1285
Cecil Hotel (Sofitel) (4*)
16 Saad Zaghloul Sq.
Ramleh
Tel: 480-7055/487-7173
Fax: 485-5655
Crillon
5 Adib Ishaq St., off the Corniche
Tel: 480-0330
Delta Hotel (3*)
14 Champollion St., Mazarita
Tel: 486-5542/188

Helnan Palestine (5*)
Montazah Palace, Montazah
Tel: 547-4033/3500
Fax: 547-3348
Mercure Romance (4*)
303 Corniche, Saba Pasha
Tel: 584-0912/1
Fax: 583-0526
Metropole-Paradise Inn (4*)
52 Saad Zaghloul St.
Ramleh
Tel: 486-1465/6/7
Renaissance (5*)
544 Corniche, Sidi Bishr
Tel: 549- 0935
Salamlek Palace Hotel (5*)
Montazah Palace Gardens
Tel: 547-7999
Fax: 547-3585
San Giovanni (3*)
205 Corniche, Stanley
Tel: 546-7774

Eating and drinking

Another of Alex's charms is its many terraces, cafes, and restaurants, often maintaining their original Durrellian décor. We have many favorites in Alex. Topping the list are the tucked-away Havana Bar (7), the 1950s Elite (8, still masterfully run by Madame Christina), and the pristine Café Delices (4). Don't forget to check out Pastroudis (9), the Athineos Tea Room (10), and the Trianon (4)—if only for the décor. Our school of fish-eating highly recommends Samakmak in Anfoushi (11) and Zephyrion, an institution, or the runner-up, Belavista, both in Abu Qir. More upscale is the seaside Fish Market (12). Both

perfectly preserved Brazilian coffee counters (4, 13) are worth a café glace on the go, while for a 1940s experience of coffee-buying, visit Sofianopoulos (14). Barflies should stop by the Spitfire (15) and have a beer, and fried calamari or barbounya at the Cape d'Or (16).

Athineos
Horriya Ave., Ramleh
Tel: 482-8131

Baqqash (kebab)
Safa Pasha, Ras al-Tin, Anfoushi
Tel: 802-815

Brazilian Coffee Stores
1: Saad Zaghloul St.
2: Corner of Sistotris and Sherif Sts.

Cap D'Or
4 Adib St., south of Saad Zaghloul St.

Delices
Saad Zaghloul Sq.
Tel: 492-5657

Elite
43 Safiya Zaghloul St.
Tel: 482-3592

Fish Market
Kashafa Club, Corniche
Tel: 480-5114

Havana Bar
Corner of Orabi St. and Horriya Ave.
Tel: 483-0661

Khawaga Elias
Place des Syriens, Attarin

L'Ossobuco
14 Horriya Ave.
Tel: 487-2506

Pastroudis
39 Horriya Ave.
Tel: 492-9609

Saber
89 Heliopolis St., Ibrahimiya
Tel: 596-5219

Samakmak
42 Ras al-Tin Palace St.
Tel: 481-1560

Santa Lucia
40 Safiya Zaghloul St.
Tel: 482-1881

Spitfire
7 al-Borsa al-Qadima St.

Manshiya

Trianon
52 Saad Zaghloul St., Ramleh

Zephyrion
Abu Qir
Tel: 560-1319

To do

Cultural venues are listed below. The Mahmoud Said museum—also housing a collection of the brothers' Seif and Adham Wanli—and the Museum of Modern Art are definitely worth a visit. The Greco-Roman Museum and the Villa of the Birds in the amphitheater complex are both a must. The newest in-place for performances is the Garage, run by the Jesuit center. No visit to Alexandria is complete without a stroll in the Attarin antique market. At night, the square in the middle of the flea market is taken over by Khawaga Elias, famous for grilled quail in autumn and pigeon the rest of the year. And, at last, it is again possible to stroll on the Belle Epoque promenade along the shores of the Mahmoudiya Canal now that it has been renovated.

Coast of Alexandria

Golf courses

Alexandria Sporting Club
Tel: 543-3627/8/9
Fax: 546-1413

Cultural centers and performance venues

American Cultural Center
3 Pharaoh St.
Tel: 486-1009

Bibliotheca Alexandrina (Alexandria Library)
Corniche, Shatbi
Tel: 487-6001/6024/9024
Fax: 483-6001
Open daily 9-5

British Council
9 Ptolemies St.
Bab Sharqi
Tel: 482-0199

Conference Center
Port Said St.
Shatbi
Tel: 488-7093

Conservatoire de Musique d'Alexandrie
90 Horriya Ave.
Tel: 483-5086

Foundation for Hellenic Culture
18 Sidi al-Metwalli St., Attarin
Tel: 486-1598

French Cultural Center
30 al-Nabi Daniel St.
Tel: 492-0804/491-8952

The Garage
Jesuit Center, Port Said St., Cleopatra

Goethe Institute
10 Ptolemies St., Azarita
Tel: 483-9870

Italian Cultural Institute
Italian Consulate, Saad Zaghloul Sq.
Tel: 486-0258

L'Atelier
8 Victor Bassili St.
Tel: 482-0526

Roman Amphitheater
Youssef St., at the end of Gomhouriya Sq.

Open daily 9-4

Sayed Darwish Theatre
22 Horriya Ave., facing Cinema Royal
Tel: 486-5106/483-9578
Closed for renovations

Swedish Institute
57 July 26th St., Manshiya
Tel: 485-5113
Fax: 487-3855
institute.alexandria@foreign.ministry.se

Museums

Cavafy Museum
4 Sharm al-Sheikh St., Ramleh
Open 10-3, closed Monday

Greco-Roman Museum
5 al-Mathaf St.
Tel: 486-5820
Open 9-4, closed for Friday prayer

Jewelry Museum
27 Ahmed Yehya St., Gleem
Tel: 586-8348
Open 9-4
Closed for Friday prayer

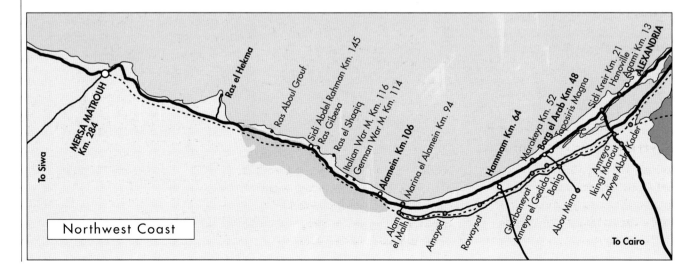

Northwest Coast

Mahmoud Said Museum
60 Mahmoud Pasha Said St., Gianaclis
Tel: 586-1688

Marine Life Museum
Qait Bey Fort, Anfoushi
Open daily 9-2

Montazah Palace Museum
Open daily 9-4

Museum of Fine Arts
18 Menasce St., Moharram Bey
Tel: 493-6616
Open 8-2, closed Friday

Villa of the Birds
Kom al-Dikka, by the Roman
amphitheater

Bookstores

Manshaat al-Maaref
Saad Zaghloul Sq., next to the Brazilian
Coffee Store

Business organizations

**Alexandria Businessmen's
Association**
52 Horriya Ave.
Tel: 484-8978
Fax. 483-2206

**Alexandria Chamber of
Commerce**
31 al-Ghorfa al-Togariya St.
Ramleh
Tel: 488-7093

Daytrips from Alexandria

Swimming in Alex is mission impossible. You
have to resort to either Montazah or
Agami, or further along the North Coast.
There is one public beach in Montazah,
Phoenicia, which tends to get quite

crowded, or you can stay at the Palestine
hotel. You also may be able to access one
of the private beaches—Aida is the
favorite. Further east, Abu Qir is good for a
day out fish-eating. You can take a boat to
Nelson Island or stroll along the sandbar,
the Lisan, or eat in one of the many baladi
fish joints.

Rosetta (Rashid) (03)

This miraculously preserved Ottoman city
has an old bath, mills, mosques, and
merchant homes in the characteristic
Delta brick architecture. Don't miss out on
the little mosque on the sand dune at the
bend of the river at Abu Mandour. The Nile
is extremely wide and blue in Rosetta.
Besides the stone, Rosetta is known for
sardines, when they come, and fisikh, or
salted fish. You can drive back to Cairo via
the Edfina Road. In Edfina, check out the
royal model farm.

Abu Mina (03)

Ancient site of Taposiris Magna and the St.
Menas Monastery, a popular
pilgrimage site during the Roman Empire.
It still boasts a Ptolemaic temple and a
smaller replica of Alexandria's Pharos that
is visible on the coastal highway just before
Borg al-Arab.

North Coast (046)

"One of the finest floras in the world"—
so said EM Forster. Unfortunately
devastated by savage development, it is still
a nice drive along the coastal road and the
parallel Borg al-Arab/al-Hammam Road. Al-
Hammam has turned into a mega-
shopper's paradise. Further west at al-

Alamein stop at the British, German, and
Italian memorials. Nearby is Marina, the
hip resort built on the remains of an
ancient port city, now being excavated. At
Sidi Abd al-Rahman, the Alamein Hotel sits
on a marvelous sandy bay with glowing
white sands. One of the most beautiful
bays on earth is at Marsa Matrouh, again
undergoing over-development; visit
Rommel's cave, now a museum, and stroll
along the white cliffs of Agiba (km 318).
From Marsa Matrouh, you can take the
road to Siwa.

Tourist Office
Governorate Bldg
Marsa Matrouh
Tel: 493-1841

Marsa Matrouh Airport
Near the extension of the Libyan
market
Tel: 493-3751
Flights to and from Cairo on Thursdays,
Fridays, and Sundays. Summer only.

Egypt Air
Galaa St., in front of the Egyptian
National Bank
Marsa Matrouh
Tel: 493-4398

Money Transfer
In Marsa Matrouh, there is Bank Misr at
Galaa St. and a National Bank of Egypt
west of Alexandria St.

To stay

Aida Beach Hotel (4*)
Km 77 Alex Matrouh Rd.
Tel: 410-2818/19/20
Fax: 418-2818

Alamein Hotel (3*)
Sidi Abd al-Rahman, al-Dabaa Center
Tel: 468-0140/0341
Fax: 468-0341
Attic Hotel (3*)
Km 90 Alex Matrouh Rd.
Tel: 410-6183/4/5
Fax: 046-410 6182
Beau Site (3*)
al-Shati St., Corniche
Marsa Matrouh
Tel: 494-4011/12
Fax: 493-3319
Hilton Borg al-Arab (5*)
Tel: 03-990-730/40/50

To do
Alamein War Museum
105 km west of Alexandria, Alamein
Open daily 8-6
Rommel's Cave
Galaa St.
Marsa Matrouh
Tel: 493-5466
Fax: 347-1496

Siwa Oasis (046)
Made famous by Alexander's visit to the oracle of Amun, Siwa has more recently been in the limelight with a project for an airport. Now is the time to see the oasis before it is transformed further. Great hot springs, the most famous being Cleopatra (recently gentrified) and Fatnas. It also has great orchards and palm groves. Home to an expensive, but apparently superb ecolodge.
Tourist Office
Across from Arous al-Waha Hotel

Tel: 460-2338
Ecolodge Adrere Amellal
Tel: 460-2399
Cairo tel: 02-736-7879
Fax: 735-5489
info@eqi.com.eg

Western Desert

Bahariya Oasis' new title to fame are the gilded mummies. It hosts hot springs too. To the northwest, the desert track leads to Siwa, while to the south lies the the White Desert. Farafra is the smallest of the oases, until recently a small fortified village, now a backpackers' hangout. Small uninhabited oases are scattered around the area—check out the great sand dunes. Balat and Qasr in Dakhla are stunning old fortress mudbrick towns, but ancient temples and fortifications line the desert tracks. Bagawat in Kharga is a well-preserved early Coptic necropolis. To the south at Baris is one of Hassan Fathi's pioneering projects, now abandoned. Further down at Dush, the French Mission uncovered a famous gold treasure.

Tour guides
The following guides can be booked from Cairo for safaris all over the Western Desert.
Tareq al-Mahdi
61 Rd. 9, Maadi
Tel: 358-4406
Amr Shannon
11 Rd. 256, Maadi
Tel: 702-0834
Zarzora Expeditions
12B Mahmoud Azmi St., Zamalek

Tel: 736-0350
zarzora@hotmail.com
Bahariya Oasis (018)
Tourist Office
Tel: 802-322
Ahmed Safari Camp
3 km outside of Bawiti
Tel: 902-770/802-090
Located next to a natural hot spring. Camping facilities, huts, and rooms. Safaris to surrounding area also available.
Hotel Alpenblick (1*)
Bawiti
Tel: 802-184
International Health Center
Outside of Bawiti
Tel: 802-322
Hotel with spa facilities.
Farafra Oasis (092)
al-Badawiya Safari Hotel (1*)
Tel: 510-060/1
Cairo Tel: 02-795-8524
Can arrange desert treks.
Dakhla Oasis (092)
Tourist Office
al-Thawra al-Khadra St., Mut
Tel: 821-686
Dakhla Airport
EgyptAir airport office
Tel: 822-453
EgyptAir sales office
Old City Council Bldg.
Tel: 822-853
al-Qasr Hotel
In front of al-Qasr telephone exchange
Tel: 876-013

Mebarez Hotel (1*)
2 al-Tharwa al-Khadra St.
Tel: 821-524
Mut Talata Hotel (3*)
Mut
Tel: 821-530

Kharga Oasis (092)
Tourist Office
Gamal Abd al-Nasser St., near the
Mubarak fountain
Tel: 921-206
Fax: 921-205
Kharga Oasis Hotel
Tel: 901-500
Fax: 927-983
Pioneer Hotel (4*)
Gamal Abd al-Nasser St.
Tel: 927-982
Fax: 927-983
mgg@mggroup.com.eg
New Valley Museum
Near tourist office
Tel: 900-084
Open daily 9-4
Greco-Roman artifacts.

Delta

Accomodation is difficult in the Delta, and so it is better to explore it from either Cairo, Alex, or Port Said. A waterworks tour of the Delta includes the Barrage at Qanater, the Edfina dams, and Zifta, all built or planned by Mohammed Ali Pasha. From Port Said, visit Damietta, Egypt's biggest container port, famous for furniture, home-cooking, dairy products, and Ras al-Bar, a favorite 50s resort. Tanis is reachable via Zaqaziq, known for its Arabian horses. A major Delta site, Tanis has an eerie feel to it. A treasure rivaling that of Tut's was found here in 1939. In the fall, Tanta hosts the huge moulid of al-Sayed Badawi. From there, the moulid circuit goes to Dessouq. Tanta and Mansoura (once a cosmopolitan center) are the two big cities in the middle of the Delta and can be used conveniently as a base. The small, but well-designed museum at Dinsheway is out of the way, but well worth a visit.

Dinsheway Museum
Dinsheway, about 15km west of Shebin al-Kom

Middle Egypt

Though difficult to visit due to severe security measures, the upside is there are no tourists. The scenery here is a stunning array of Egyptian contrasts. Home to the city of Akhenaten, Tell al-Amarna; the rock tombs of Beni Hassan; and a host of monasteries, the most famous being the White and Red Monasteries (important pilgrimage sites in August) and Tuna al-Gebel. Minya is the home of most of these sites, but Assyout has the airport.

Assyout Airport
Tel: 088-315-228/334-486
From Assyout, you can take a domestic flight to Cairo (three flights weekly) and Luxor (two flights weekly).

Egypt Air
Airport office
Tel: 088-315-481
Assyout Governorate Bldg.
Tel: 088-315-228

Minya (086)
Tourist Office
Governorate Bldg.
Tel: 320-150/342-044
Train Station
Saad Zaghloul St.
Next to the Tourist Office
Tel: 363-035
Trains daily to Cairo, Luxor, and Aswan.
Akhenaten Hotel
Corniche al-Nil
Tel: 365-917/18
Dahabia Hotel (houseboat)
Tel: 325-596
Lotus Hotel (2*)
Port Said St.
Tel: 364-500
Fax: 364-576
Mercure Nefertiti and Atun (4*)
Corniche al-Nil
Tel: 341-515/6/7
Fax: 366-467
Mellawi Museum
Mellawi
Collection of artifacts from Tuna al-Gebel and Hermopolis.
Open daily 9-4, Friday until noon
Closed Wednesday

Upper Egypt

Luxor (095)
The place to stay is either the old Winter Palace or on the West Bank. The Marsam, also known as Sheikh Ali (1), is a classic; the rooms on Medinet Habu's terrace (2) overlook the temple; and the new, very upscale Hotel Moudira feels like an orientalist's fantasy. If you feel sportive,

walk the West Bank/Gourna circuit; if you feel less sportive, take a donkey or a horse. All over town, small baladi *restaurants offer*

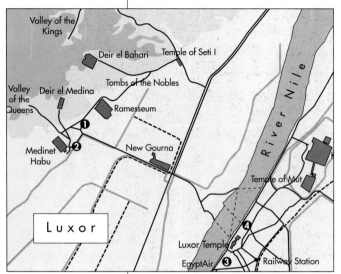

decent local cuisine. The stroll on the Corniche at sunset is, of course, a must. Check out the pool and the terrace of the Winter Palace (3) for a cup of tea with classical music. The Luxor museum (4) is well designed both in terms of architecture and display.

Tourist Office
Corniche al-Nil, Tourist Bazaar
Tel: 372-215/382-215

Luxor Airport
Tel: 374-655
From Luxor, there are flights to Cairo (daily), and Alex, Aswan, and Sharm (three times a week).

EgyptAir
Airport office
Tel: 380-586
Sales office

Corniche al-Nil
Tel: 380-580/1/2/3/4
Karnak office tel: 382-360

Train Station
Mahatta Sq.
Tel: 372-018
Three trains leave to Cairo, one wagon-lit and two others that depart at 8:15 am and 11:30 pm. There are also daily trains to Aswan, Minya, and one every Thursday to Kharga.

Buses
The bus station is behind the Luxor Temple. Buses depart daily to Cairo, Hurghada, Qena, and Aswan, and three times a week to Kharga.

Travelers' services
American Express
Old Winter Palace Hotel
Tel: 372-862

Thomas Cook
Across from the Old Winter Palace
Tel: 372-196

Western Union
Mena Palace Hotel
Corniche al-Nil
Tel: 372-292

To stay
Hotel Moudira (5*)
West Bank
012-325-1307

Marsam (Sheikh Ali Hotel)
West of Memnon Temple
Tel: 372-403

Sofitel Winter Palace (5*)
Corniche al-Nil
Tel: 380-424/2/371-189/94
Fax: 374-087

Eating and drinking
Cafeteria Habu
In front of Medinet Habu Temple

Tutankhamun
By the local ferry dock
Tel: 310-118

To do
Donkey and Horse Rides
Abd al-Nasser Khalifa
Mahmoud Farid St., next to McDonalds
Tel: 372-333/012-317-2411

Hot Air Balloon Rides (at sunrise)
Hod Hod Soliman
Tel: 370-116/012-215-1312

Luxor Museum
Corniche al-Nil
Tel: 380-296
Open daily 9-1 and 4-9

Mummification Museum
Corniche al-Nil, in front of Luxor Temple
Tel: 370-063
Open daily 9-1 and 4-9

Open Museum of Karnak
Karnak Temple
Tel: 380-270
Open daily 6-5:30

Royal Valley Golf Course
Tel: 365-2721/012-246-5017
www.royalvalley.com

Aswan (097)
The city itself hosts no remarkable ruins, but it does boast a few remarkable public buildings built in the colonial style with the famous Nubian sandstone. The beauty of Aswan is in the site, best seen from the Cataract and further south. The places to

stay are the New Cataract (1) with a view of the Old and Amun Island (2), run by Club Med: you can't decide where to look. For the down-at-the-heels, Hathour (3) offers clean, cheap digs with a rooftop pool. Aswan is the home to the annual sculpture symposium, the results of which are scattered in the city or exhibited in the Basma Hotel garden (4). Of course, don't miss out on a felucca ride, a tour of the dams, Philae, the Fatimid cemetery (5), and, if you have time, a game fishing trip on Lake Nasser. There is also Elephantine and Kitchener's Botanical Gardens, and the award-winning Nubian Museum (6). Abu Simbel is a must. Lots of restaurants on the Nile: the latest reported winner was Panorama, near the Cataract.

Tourist Office

Next to the train station
Tel: 312-811

Aswan Airport

Tel: 480-320/333

Abu Simbel Airport

EgyptAir airport office
Tel: 400-317
There are flights daily to Cairo, Luxor, and Abu Simbel.

Egypt Air

Airport office
Tel: 480-307
Abtal al-Tahrir St.
Tel: 315-001/2/3/4

Trains

There are two daily trains to Cairo that leave at 5 am and at 8:45 pm, in addition to daily trains to Luxor and Kom Ombo.
Tel: 314-754

Buses

The bus station is in the middle of the town on Abtal al-Tahrir St. Buses leave daily to Cairo, Marsa Alam, Hurghada, and Abu Simbel.

Travelers' services

American Express

Old Cataract Hotel
Tel: 322-909

Thomas Cook

Corniche al-Nil
Tel: 304-011

Western Union

In front of the Aswan Sporting Club
Tel: 308-040

To stay

Amun Island Hotel (3*)

Amun Island
Tel: 313-800/317-193
Fax: 317-190

Basma Hotel (4*)

Fanadiq St.
Tel: 310-901/2/3
Fax: 310-907

Hathour (1*)

Corniche al-Nil
Tel: 314-580
Fax: 303-462

New Cataract
Abtal al-Tahrir St.
Tel: 316-000/1/2
Fax: 316-011

Sofitel Old Cataract (4*)

Abtal al-Tahrir St.
Tel: 316-000/1/2
Fax: 316-011

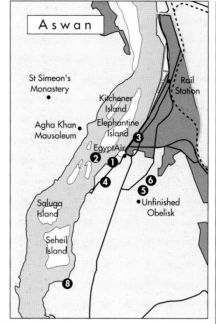

To do

Nubian Museum

Opposite the Basma Hotel
Open daily 9-1 and 4-9

Red Sea (065)

Quseir is an ancient trade port with a picturesque town, an Ottoman fort, and a magnificent bay. It is still almost untouched. The Mövenpick there is one of the most successful attempts to reconcile traditional Nubian architecture with development. A new airport just opened in Marsa Alam, and the whole area is slated for development. Already boat safaris have to go as far south as Halayeb to find any decent fish. Hurghada, to the north, once a sleepy phosphate center, has turned into a thriving discount resort. Fine places in the vicinity

are Soma Bay and Makadi Bay. Club Makadi is a great family resort, complete with babysitters. Gouna is an autonomous republic with its own airport, radio station, art festival, brewery, and bus lines.

Gouna

Airport

There are no commercial flights to Gouna. The small airport is reserved for private aircraft.

Buses

Shuttles leave every 15 minutes to and from Safaga/Hurghada, and they can be rented.

Dawar al-Omda Hotel

Kafr al-Gouna

Tel: 545-060/580-064/5/6

al-Khan Hotel

Kafr al-Gouna

Tel: 549-712/580-052/3

Prototours

Tel: 580-085

Fax: 580-084

www.elgouna.com

Provides information on Gouna hotels.

To do

Steigenberger Golf and Fitness Club

Tel: 580-009

Fax: 580-009

www.elgouna.com

elgouna-golfhotel@steigenberger.de

Hurghada

Tourist office

Bank Misr St., near the top of the main resort strip

Tel: 446-513

Hurghada Airport

Tel: 442-831

Flights to Alex (twice weekly), Cairo (three times weekly), Sharm (four times weekly).

EgyptAir

Airport office

Tel: 443-598/444-365

Sales office

Tel: 447-503/4/5/6/7

You can take a ferry from Hurghada to Sharm weekdays except Wednesday and Friday. The old ferry leaves from the port in Sigala between 9 and 10 am. Tickets can be booked through most hotels. A new high-speed boat departs from the same place on Monday, Tuesday, and Saturday. Tickets can be purchased from Travco (tel: 446-024).

Federal Express

31 Sheraton, Red Cone Mall

Tel: 442-444

Thomas Cook

Sigala, Sheraton St.

Tel: 443-338

Western Union

Sheraton St.

Tel: 442-771

To stay

Club Makadi (5*)

Tel: 590-025

Fax: 590-035

Sofitel Hurghada (4*)

Tel: 442-266

Fax: 442-270

Eating and drinking

Portofino (Italian)

General Hospital St., al-Dahar

Tel: 546-250

To do

The Cascades Golf Resort and Country Club at Soma Bay

Tel: 544-901

Fax: 544-901

www.thecascadessomabay.com

Marine Life Museum

5 km north of town

Open daily 8-8

Quseir

Mövenpick Resort (4*)

7 km north of town, al-Wadim Bay

Tel: 332-000/1/2

Fax: 332-128

Marsa Alam

Marsa Alam Airport

Tel: 700-400

Between Marsa Alam and Port Safaga

Red Sea Diving Safari

Marsa Shaqara

20 km north of Marsa Alam

Tel: 339-9942

Hotel and diving resort.

Sinai

The entire Sinai coast is strewn with resorts and five-star hotels. Sharm is to be avoided unless you speak Italian or are into diving. Great spots at world-famous Ras Mohammed; the best is the Camel Dive Club (1) and its homey hotel. Shark Bay with lodges has the best seafood and snorkeling so good it dispenses with the need to dive. Dahab is a backpackers' favorite and windy and cool in the summer—Nesima is a tasteful five-star hotel. Nuweiba was a favorite among

Israelis, so there is plenty of room now. Tarabin is the spot to stay for basic accommodations, but camps are also scattered up to Taba. The better known are Basata (eco-friendly, reserve in advance) and Ras Shaytan. Ras Abu Gallum, with a nice beach, and Nabaq, with mangroves, are protected areas. Desert safaris are the thing to do in Sinai, whether by camel or jeep. The Colored Canyon, Ain Khudra, Sarabit al-Khadem, and the obscure nawamis (prehistoric structures) are among the favorite spots. St. Katherine's Monastery and Mt. Moses attract many tourists, both religious and otherwise. The climb and the wait for the sunrise are popular.

Tourist Office
Fouad Zikri St., Arish
Tel: 068-340-569
Arish Airport
EgyptAir airport office: 068-321-744
Taba Airport
Egypt Air airport office: 539-367
There are flights from Taba to Cairo once a week.

Sharm al-Sheikh (069)

Sharm al-Sheikh Airport
Tel: 600-314/664

Egypt Air
Airport office
Tel: 600-408
In the Mövenpick Hotel
Tel: 600-100/3
There are flights to Cairo (daily), and Alex, Hurghada, and Luxor (twice a week). The ferry from Sharm to Hurghada runs

on Monday, Thursday, and Saturday. To book a ticket, call Travco (tel: 661-111).

Travelers' services

Tourist Office
Booth next to Marina Sharm Hotel
Tel: 762-704
American Express
Operated through the Egyptian American Bank in the shopping bazaar
Tel: 600-547/601-423/4
Federal Express
al-Zuhour Center, Naama Bey
Tel: 600-200
Thomas Cook
Main Road, Naama Bay
Tel: 601-808
Western Union
Rosita Hotel, Naama Bay
Tel: 602-333

To stay

Camel Dive Club and Hotel
Naama Bay
Tel: 600-581/700/1/2
Sanafir (3*)
Naama Bay
Tel: 600-197
Shark's Bay (3*)
Tel: 600-947
Fax: 600-943

To do

Jolie Ville Golf Resort Sharm al-Sheikh
Tel: 600-635
Fax: 600-642
www.movenpick-sharm.com
golfclub@golf-joliemoven.com

Up the coast (069)

Basata (1*)
22 km north of Nuweiba
Tel: 500-481/530-481
www.basata.com
Nesima Hotel (5*)
Dahab
Tel: 640-320
Centre for Sinai
Dahab
Tel: 640-702/010-938-0267
Offers information on the peninsula and safaris all over the Sinai. Talk to Ahmed al-Sadeq.

St. Katherine's

St. Katherine's Tourist Village (4*)
Wadi al-Raha
Tel: 470-322/3/4
Fax: 470-325
National Parks
Tel: 470-032
Fax: 470-033

Our Sponsors

Cairo Barclays

DaimlerChrysler

GlaxoSmithKline

Siemens

Talaat Mostafa Group

Unilever

Shell

Cairo Barclays

Colin E. McCormack

As Cairo Barclays Managing Director, Colin E. McCormack, puts it: "No bank in Egypt offers the same combination of international corporate banking expertise and extensive personal banking services as Cairo Barclays. We continue to give our customers all the know-how and care they could ever need or ask for... That is our corporate strategy." Through this strategy, Cairo Barclays has gained a reputation over the years for its high quality service, providing full banking services through its four Cairo branches.

Formerly Barclays DCO (Dominion, Colonial and Overseas), Barclays first started trading with Egypt in 1864 in the cotton trade. The company opened its first local branch in 1920 and maintained one of the largest trade networks in Egypt up to the time of nationalization. Later on, with Sadat's open door policy, Barclays re-entered the market in 1975 as an Egyptian joint stock company between Banque Du Caire, one of the largest public sector banks in Egypt, and Barclays Bank PLC, one of Britain's leading financial institutions.

Traditionally, Cairo Barclays is known as a corporate bank with a very diverse portfolio, providing trade finance, project finance, structured finance, bond issues, and finance for industry. The bank also finances infrastructure projects, ranging from pharmaceuticals and the food industry to oil and gas, power stations, cement, and ceramics. But the Banque Du Caire – Barclays Bank PLC combination provides customers with a unique blend of services, going far beyond corporate banking. Cairo Barclays customers have access to all parts of Egypt as well as the international dimension of Barclays top diversified products.

In June 1999, Barclays Bank PLC became the majority shareholder with full management control, increasing its shares to 60% (as compared to Banque Du Caire's 40%) and demonstrating commitment to the market and confidence in the future of the country. Since Barclays assumed its leadership role in Cairo Barclays, the bank has refocused in the market. It recently opened two new Prestige Banking Centers in the Cairo suburb of Maadi and the affluent Alexandria neighborhood of Roushdi, offering personalized banking services to help customers reach their financial goals. Also, Barclays customers can access their accounts 24 hours a day, seven days a week through an extensive network of more than 430 ATM machines. The branch network is expected to grow substantially, extending to other governorates over the next two years.

As a result of its confidence in the potential of the Egyptian market, the bank has brought together some of its most talented and experienced professionals, both local and international, to manage the operation.

Colin E. McCormack, Managing Director since 2002, has had an interesting and varied career within the Barclays Group, spanning over 20 years. His career encompassed both relationship and credit risk management of the biggest and most complex UK/European corporations; project and leveraged debt finance; team leadership; retail banking; change management; and operations. His vast experience led to three board-level executive roles with primary responsibility for risk management in Barclays Bank of Zimbabwe and in Cairo Barclays.

Another corporate officer, Wafaa Zaklama, has worked for Barclays since 1978. In the past 24 years, she has taken on many responsibilities, acquiring hands-on experience in all departments of the bank. As a local employee, she not only has thorough understanding of the banking industry but the local market as well. As such, in March 2002, the bank appointed her Corporate & Business Banking Director, acknowledging her expertise and her lifetime effort contributing to the success of Cairo Barclays.

Retail Banking Director at Cairo Barclays, Garry Marsh, has served as a specialist retail banker for the last 15 years. But his history with Barclays dates back much further than that. In total, he has spent 31 years with Barclays Bank PLC. His last eight years with the bank he worked in management positions for Africa in Country (Zambia) and Africa Regional (encompassing nine countries). The bank brought him to Cairo in July, 2001, as part of its broad initiative to improve retail banking in Egypt.

Cairo Barclays is never content to stand still, no matter how broad the scope of its operations. "In order to meet personal banking needs, we are now in the process of introducing new products and services to extend our retail banking," says Garry Marsh. Cairo Barclays is now implementing a strategy to increase their share of this market, with an emphasis on high value clients. World class service through Prestige Banking is a key element in the strategy. The company plans to open at least four more Prestige Centers, besides the new centers in Maadi and Roushdi, before the end of 2003. Cairo Barclays has excellent links with the wider Barclays Group and also has a dedicated international personal banker to look after customers with funds overseas.

All of the standard banking products are available from Cairo Barclays and new banking products have also been introduced, including High Rate Savings with innovations such as tiered interest rates, daily accrual of interest, monthly payment of interest and no fees. In addition, a USD deferred debit Visa card is also now available.

But the true success of Cairo Barclays Bank S.A.E lies in its customer service, the cornerstone of any successful banking operation. Cairo Barclays performs all banking operations in both foreign and Egyptian currency, in Egypt and abroad, according to the highest customer service standards. "Our customers are our most valuable asset," explains Colin McCormack. "We maintain strong relationships with all our clients, providing complete Banking solutions to suit all types of customer needs."

Yet another dimension of Cairo Barclay's commitment to Egypt, the bank also pursues continuous community service efforts. Most recently, Cairo Barclays made a substantial donation to the SETI Center at College de la Salle in Cairo. In 1987, Caritas Egypt established the SETI Center to provide services for persons with mental disabilities. Cairo Barclays' Colin McCormack was pleased to present the bank's donation to SETI Center supervisor, Naguib Khouzam.

Cairo
BARCLAYS

DaimlerChrysler

George C. Oswald

Euros 152.9 billion of total revenue in 2001; 3,985,600 passenger cars sold in 2001; 492,900 commercial vehicles sold in 2001; 374,059 employees worldwide as of June 30, 2002; products sold in more than 200 countries; manufacturing facilities in 37 countries...Welcome to DaimlerChrysler.

The ability to produce figures like these has made DaimlerChrysler one of the world's leading automotive, transportation and services companies. The company has maintained such figures through a strong research and development program, consistently producing more advanced and more stylish automobiles. Technological expertise, speed and flexibility have made DaimlerChrysler the driving force behind progress in the automotive industry. The company has approximately 28,000 employees working worldwide on the research and development of technical innovations. The company registers around 2,000 patents every year, thus securing its technology and innovation leadership and an important long-term advantage in the face of increasingly tough global competition.

Once the research and development team does its job, DaimlerChrysler Egypt steps in to do its part. A subsidiary of DaimlerChrysler AG, DaimlerChrysler Egypt was formed to handle distribution, sales, marketing and parts and service activities for Mercedes-Benz passenger cars and Chrysler, Jeep, Dodge passenger cars and SUV vehicles throughout Egypt, whether assembled locally or imported.

Hans-Georg Lutz

George C. Oswald, CEO of DaimlerChrysler Egypt, has been heading operations in Egypt since September 17, 2000. Born on September 9, 1951 in Bronxville, NY, Oswald holds a B.S. degree in Business Administration from Ithaca College in Ithaca, NY. He joined Chrysler in 1980 in the domestic sales organization, spending ten years in various sales positions in the New York Zone Office. The New York Office provides sales and service support for 225 dealers in the New York Metropolitan area. In 1990, Chrysler promoted Oswald to Field Operations Manager in the Chicago Zone Office, where he spent six years supervising a sales and service field force of 22 people. He came to Chrysler International in 1996 as Sales Planning and Distribution Manager for Europe, based in Brussels. His most recent position was Sales Operations Manager for Eastern and Central Europe, Middle East and Africa based in Stuttgart, Germany.

After accepting his current post as CEO of DaimlerChrysler Egypt in 2000, Oswald took up residence with his wife, Marion Luidens-Oswald, in Cairo. In this assignment, he takes responsiblity for sales and support of Chrysler, Jeep and Mercedes branded vehicles. He also overseas manufacturing of the two joint venture plants in Egypt, Arab-American Vehicles Company (AAV) and Egyptian-German Automotive Company (EGA).

The AAV, which assembles Jeep Cherokees, is a joint venture initially launched between the Arab Organization for Industrialization and Chrysler Corporation, with 51% and 49% ownership respectively. AAV began assembling Jeep Cherokee sport utility vehicles in 1992 and currently assembles approximately 1,500 units a year, representing roughly 6% of the commercial vehicle market in Egypt. AAV also assembles vehicles for Kia and Peugeot on a contract basis. The factory had an initial capacity of 6,000 vehicles per year using one shift. As of 1998, however, plant capacity increased to 20,000 vehicles per year using one shift.

Established in 1996 the EGA began producing Mercedes-Benz passenger vehicles in October, 1997. Due to the success of the factory's operations in producing the Mercedes-Benz C-class passenger cars over the last five years, DaimlerChrysler selected EGA as the first production facility outside Germany to manufacture the new, "high tech," 6-cylinder E-series models E240 and E320 only six months after the official market introduction in Germany. Proving its commitment to the Egyptian market and production location, DaimlerChrysler and EGA's Egyptian shareholders invested more than 20 million LE in upgrading the factory's facilities to prepare for production of the new E-class vehicles.

The E-class, as a benchmark in safety, requires complete new welding lines and computer controlled equipment. Measuring machines, capable of reaching an accuracy of some microns, are operating in air-conditioned rooms and checking every detail of the welded bodies. Ultrasonic tests, most commonly known from their use in medical procedures, verify the quality of the welding.

The paint shop has also undergone major changes in order to adapt to the 20% aluminum surface of the new product. The wastewater treatment facility and air cleaning equipment, already present in the factory since 1997, serve in production of the E-class as well. Having more than 40 computer control units inside the E240 and E320, ensuring not only luxurious but the utmost safe driving, the assembly process was upgraded with new 100% computer controlled performance and driving tests.

Along with the introduction of its new E-class production facilities, DaimlerChrysler Egypt also introduces its new Managing Director of Mercedes-Benz Passenger Cars, Hans-Georg Lutz. Born in September, 1956, Lutz joined DaimlerChrysler in 1986. Since that time, he spent many years in various sales positions of the Mercedes-Benz branches in German and in the Stuttgart headquarters. His last position before joining the team in Cairo, Lutz served as the Head of the Platform for young used cars. In this department, he oversaw sales of one-year-old employee cars and buybacks from the large rental companies to dealers in Europe. Lutz occupied his current post on August 1, 2002 where he assumes responsibility for all marketing and sales activities. DaimlerChrysler Egypt proudly welcomes to Egypt both Hans-Georg Lutz and the Mercedes-Benz E-class passenger cars.

In yet another strategic move, in order to support the national strategy for the development of exports, EGA decided last year to invest another 25 million LE in automotive components manufacturing and exports. Through close cooperation with Mercedes-Benz in Germany, EGA built up a high tech factory for the production of car axles and brake discs and trained their staff in Mercedes-Benz factories in Stuttgart. More than 90% of the brake discs will be exported to DaimlerChrysler in Germany. Starting with a capacity of 120,000 units, EGA is already preparing for an extension to 250,000 units per year. EGA plans to reach eventually a million brake discs on a medium term basis. The first container of brake discs left for Germany on August 12, 2002.

DAIMLERCHRYSLER

GlaxoSmithKline

After decades of working in the front line of the fight against disease across the world, GlaxoSmithKline and its subsidiaries know that there are no easy solutions to the challenge of providing global access to sustainable healthcare. But when the companies of Glaxo Wellcome and SmithKline Beecham merged on December 27, 2000, they brought together two of the most experienced companies in the pharmaceutical business and produced a single company, GlaxoSmithKline (GSK), dedicated to improving the conditions of healthcare everywhere.

The merger created a world-leading, research-based pharmaceutical company, which has 104 manufacturing sites in 40 countries with over 100,000 employees. Its annual £2.3 billion Research & Development budget ensures a powerful research and development capability, encompassing the application of genetics, genomics and other leading edge technologies.

Under Chairman & Managing Director Maged Gobran, GSK Egypt is the leading pharmaceutical company in the country, with an annual turnover exceeding LE 360 million and a market share of over 8.6%. GlaxoSmithKline has had a presence in Egypt represented by its two legacy companies Glaxo Wellcome and SmithKline Beecham since 1900's. Wellcome had a floating laboratory on the Nile in 1901. The Glaxo Milk was first advertised in the Egyptian media in the 1920's, but in 1990 it officially debued in the Egyptian pharmaceutical market as a shareholder in a local company known as Advanced Biochemical Industries (ABI/Glaxo) with 30 licensors and 10 local products. By 1992, it had acquired controlling interest in ABI and became known as Glaxo Egypt.

The 1995 merger of Glaxo plc and Wellcome plc launched the newly named company, Glaxo Wellcome Egypt, SAE. In 1999 Glaxo Wellcome increased its investment in Egypt by LE 387,202 million through the purchase of Amoun Pharmaceutical Industries Company (APIC).

Parallel to these developments, the Beecham labs had been in business since the early 1970's. The 1980's witnessed a manufacturing agreement with EIPICO and MUP and later SmithKline Beecham partners with VACSERA for the production of its vaccines under license.

The birth of GlaxoSmithKline in December 2000, after the Glaxo Wellcome and SmithKline Beecham merger, brought the two legacy companies into the fold of the newly expanded GSK, with an Egyptian work force of about 1,700 employees, and 5 branches covering the different regions of Egypt.

GSK leads the market, both locally and globally, in four of the five largest therapeutic categories in the pharmaceutical industry: anti-infective, central nervous system, respiratory, and gastro-intestinal/metabolic. The company also holds a leading position in the vaccines' market and has a strong portfolio in consumer healthcare and over-the-counter medicines. With over 100,000 employees worldwide, GSK supplies products to 191 global markets, producing over 1,200 different brands and managing approximately 2,000 new product launches each year. In Egypt over a period of 6 months from January to June 2002, the company launched four new products for Asthma, Diabetes, Hepatitis B and Epilepsy, working in parallel with global launches.

In its El-Salam City facility GSK Egypt produces tablets; syrups; ointments; suppositories; sterile, soft and hard gelatin; aerosol products; and chephalosporins.

While these figures indicate GSK's vast production and distribution capacity, they only tell half the story. One of the greatest contributions of GSK plc to the field of pharmaceuticals is in the field of R & D. Their scientists, using not only their own wide-ranging talents but also the resources of a company devoted to the scientific enterprise, unravel new secrets of health and disease every day. "GSK scientists are fuelled by a sense of urgency. They realize that the highest purpose of their work is to help people around the world enjoy a better quality of life." remarks Gobran.

Far more than a company that produces pharmaceuticals, GSK devotes a great deal of its effort and has vast experience in improving global health, particularly in developing countries. "Our mission is simple…to improve the quality of life for people world-wide," says Gobran. "And we strive to make GlaxoSmithKline a magnet for others who share in our purpose, whether as employees or as collaborators in industry, academia and government."

GSK understands that poverty is the single biggest barrier to improving healthcare in the developing world. They know that only an holistic approach to prevention and treatment will work - one in which medicines play a supporting role in a comprehensive program of prevention, health education, screening diagnosis and treatment, community care and support. GSK believes that tackling the problem is a shared responsibility, involving the country concerned, international governments, non-governmental organizations, the private sector, and affected communities.

GSK is committed to playing a full part by taking an innovative, responsible and, above all, sustainable approach to meeting the healthcare challenges of the developing world. There are three key areas in which GSK contributes in order to achieve real and sustainable results: developing urgently needed medicines and vaccines; making those products available through partnerships; and, ensuring that the necessary products are available to the patients who need them at preferential prices.

To achieve these goals, GSK continues to invest in the research and development of diseases that affect the developing world in particular. The company also offers sustainable preferential pricing arrangements in the least developed countries for the currently available medicines that are needed most. Furthermore, GSK takes a leading role in community activities that promote effective healthcare, on a global and a local level.

Siemens

Werner Von Siemens

Dr. Heinrich v. Pierer

Dr. Henryk Frystacki

"Training and the development of our personnel are the most important elements in the future growth of Siemens in Egypt." Since coming to Egypt four years ago, Dr. Henryk Frystacki, CEO of Siemens Limited and Spokesman of Siemens AG, Germany in Egypt has made training and development his number one priority.

Why this focus on personnel? "Siemens employs nearly 450,000 people worldwide. We are a company of a vast number of products and services and we compete with quality, service, brand excellence, and innovation," Frystacki says. "The only way we can do that is to have the best people addressing our customers' needs, providing service, and manufacturing our products."

Frystacki is also concerned with training and personnel development outside of his office in the sparkling, new Siemens building in Mohandessin. Shortly after arriving in Egypt, Frystacki became the founding chairman of the Human Resource Development Forum of the German Arab Chamber of Industry and Commerce. Siemens sponsors the Training Center for Automation Engineering (TCAE) of the Kohl-Mubarak Project.

Training and personnel development is a personal passion that makes doing his job that much more enjoyable and rewarding. "At Siemens Limited we take our corporate responsibilities seriously by investing in Egypt's greatest potential asset, its trained and talented young people. This engagement is much more important to us and, we believe, valuable to Egypt than simply donating money to worthy causes," says Frystacki.

Since the beginning of 2002, one-third of the Siemens Egypt employees have completed comprehensive professional training programs setting the highest benchmark of educational level in Egypt and the whole Middle East Region. By the end of 2002, Siemens expects this number to reach 45%. Considering attrition and new hiring, this is an exceptional achievement. Making Siemens the "Employer of Choice" in Egypt is the goal of the Human Resources department of the company. In addition to its recruitment programs, training and compensation packages, Siemens also offers a program of student jobs and internships. This program allows potential employees the opportunity to work in the company, while Siemens evaluates their long-term potential.

Siemens Limited has many remarkable attributes. It was established in Egypt in 1901. Its founder, Werner von Siemens came to Egypt more than 140 years ago to lay the telegraph cable under the Suez Canal, connecting Europe with India and the rest of Asia. Last year, the company posted 3.2 billion Egyptian pounds worth of business in Egypt. It is engaged in the communication networks, the electricity generating industry, railway signaling equipment, and medical equipment, to name a few of Siemens' disparate businesses in Egypt.

How does Siemens manage such a broad portfolio? "It's all about communication," says Frystacki. "We have a worldwide Intranet with Siemens that gives us access to the 450,000 minds that Siemens employs. This is a tremendous resource for our clients. An army of the best professionals in every field backs up our local people. It is this interaction of people that makes us so strong."

This year the Corporate Communications department of Siemens Limited launched a new publication, NewsFlash, to improve internal communications. "We are using this publication to keep every employee up-to-date with what all of our businesses are doing. Our employees are not one-dimensional; they have many personal and professional connections outside their own jobs. By knowing what others in the company are doing, we support each other," points out Frystacki.

Dr. Heinrich v. Pierer, the President and CEO of Siemens AG visited Egypt in September 2002 to receive an award from the German Arab Chamber of Industry and Commerce for the century of commitment Siemens has given Egypt and to promote even closer ties in the coming century. In accepting this award, v. Pierer summed up the relationship between Egypt and Siemens: "Our spectrum of activities reflects our strong commitment to Egypt: "we are here to stay!" And with respect to the political crisis in the region he summarized: "We hope along with everyone here today and people throughout the world – that true and lasting peace is found in this region. And that everyone can turn to the task building a better, safer and more just world. We especially trust Egypt as the major peace leader in this region, to play an important role in the process."

SIEMENS

Talaat Mostafa Group

Hisham Talaat Mostafa

Originating in the early 1970's, the Talaat Mostafa Group (TMG) was the brainchild of engineer Talaat Mostafa. The company's prime focus in the early years was in the contracting industry. As TMG grew, through the late 70's and early 80's, it began searching for other business opportunities. The Group has since expanded into a conglomeration of 21 companies, operating in the fields of real estate and tourism, contracting and building materials manufacturing, agriculture and agricultural products, and general investments. TMG is one of Egypt's few integrated organizations, and has an aggregate paid-in capital of approximately 1.5 billion Egyptian pounds.

To become the leading Egyptian enterprise that TMG has become today, it has had to shed its 'family' company image. Hisham Talaat Mostafa, TMG's new chairman and son of Talaat Mostafa, explains: "As we've expanded the business, which is now being publicly traded, we've become more and more open to the market and to our investors.

Hisham Talaat Mostafa is the youngest son of Talaat Mostafa. Hisham, rising from an accounting background, possesses an excellent mix of practical and academic experience. He is the founder and chairman of Alexandria Real Estate Investment Company (AREI), TMG's leading company in the real estate development activity and the marketing arm of all sister companies. Hisham, also continues to participate in numerous public service programs and NGO's, including the Future Foundation, the Real Estate Investment Branch at the Egyptian Federation of Chambers of Commerce and the Media, Communications and Organization Committee of the Egyptian Real Estate Investors' Union.

Speaking of the Group's strategy for future growth and expansion, Hisham points to the fact that contracting is now the company's 'second appetite'. "In order to maximize profitability, we are trying to help the local economy by defining the needs of the community and how to support it. We have found that by raising the standards of the tourism industry and increasing the quality of services provided, we are upgrading the country's tourism prospects and hence its economy. This is our main philosophy. We are also looking very seriously into opportunities outside Egypt. We have the necessary resources, and it's just a matter of identifying the appropriate projects."

Several of the TMG projects – notably Nile Plaza, San Stefano and the Four Seasons Resort in Sharm El Sheikh – have been called Egypt's 'prestige collection'. In reference to this claim, Hisham continues, "The Egyptian tourism industry needs true 5-star services and this is what we are providing. We are trying to satisfy, and exceed the high level of expectation that comes from such a market. If you want to upgrade the community in the direction of tourism, you need to attract the proper management companies and investors to help you reach your objectives."

The Talaat Mostafa Group is not only focused on upgrading the 'prestige' sectors of the community, it also recognizes the needs of the lower income population. Through the Future Foundation, TMG has been working with the government towards providing a new living environment for lower income Egyptians that is in line with the company's high standards.

TMG's work in agriculture and agricultural products also plays a large role in supporting the local economy and lifting its standards of operation. The company has so far reclaimed and cultivated over 4,000 acres of land. It also imports and raises dairy cattle for milk products, with a capacity of 15 tons per day. A factory for high quality fruit juice and milk packaging is currently under construction.

For a company the size of TMG, it is important to protect its interests. Pursuing the country's well being as a whole, and endeavoring to enhance the quality of life for all members of society is certainly taking care of this in a broader sense. But Hisham emphasizes that the key to meeting their global challenges has been investing in the company's people. "One of the most important divisions within the company is our training department", concludes Hisham. "We are constantly looking to modernize our managerial skills and operating methods, even utilizing outside sources in catering for specific needs, such as market research. We are always looking for innovative and creative ways to further develop both ourselves and our products."

مجموعة طلعت مصطفى
Talaat Mostafa Group

Unilever

Rachid M. Rachid

Ray Bremner

Ask any Unilever corporate officer about the Unilever corporate vision and you will undoubtedly get a response much like CEO Ray Bremner's: "Our task is to meet the everyday needs of people everywhere. Whether people are caring for themselves with our food or personal care products, or looking after their homes with our household products it is our responsibility to ensure that the quality of our products meets their needs and adds pleasure to the lives of those who use them."

Unilever was created in 1930 as the result of a merger between the Dutch margarine company Margarine Unie and the British soap maker Lever Brothers. Margarine Unie grew in the 1920's through mergers with other margarine companies. Lever Brothers, founded in 1885 by William Hesketh Lever, developed into much more than a soap company in 1917 when Lever began to diversify into foods. As a result, the Margarine Unie – Lever Brothers merger made perfect sense as the two companies were competing for the same raw materials, were both involved in large-scale marketing of household products and both used similar distribution channels.

Under its parent companies Unilever NV and Unilever PLC, with corporate centers in London and Rotterdam, Unilever today has over 250,000 employees and generates $50 billion a year in revenue. Globally, the company markets over 1,000 brands of washing powders, soaps, shampoos, toothpastes, food products, teas and spreads. As a large, international corporation, the company boasts deep roots in local cultures and markets around the world paralleled by a wealth of knowledge and international expertise to service local consumers. Its products can be found in the largest cities and the smallest, most remote villages. It sells both the most widely recognized international brand names, like Lipton, as well as some that are very local, such as Good Morning soap here in Egypt

Because its products are household products that depend very much on personal taste and customs, Unilever is built upon its local companies. "We recognize that the key to success is to remain as close as possible to our consumers and our customers. If we lose touch with them we lose touch with our markets. Therefore, our business seeks to exploit local knowledge whilst leveraging global resources," says Bremner. In order to accomplish the task of localization, Unilever functions through a conglomeration of local companies. The local companies are predominately run by local people in tune with their communities and who understand their needs and values. In that respect, Unilever calls itself a "truly multi-local multinational."

One such local company is Unilever Mashreq, which employs over 3,000 people within Egypt at its head office in Alexandria and at its factories in Borg El-Arab and Sixth October. The company markets the Unilever brands in Egypt, Sudan, Jordan, Syria, Lebanon, Iraq and the Palestinian Authority. These seven countries have a combined population of 150 million people with a GDP of $180 billion. The company works closely with its distribution partners to satisfy the demands of over 60,000 retail outlets. The Egyptian factories also supply Unilever operations in Kenya, Nigeria, Zimbabwe, Morocco and Russia.

While Unilever internationally markets over 1,000 brands, in each market the company focuses on a portfolio of 'Lead Brands', which best meet the needs of the local consumers. Unilever Mashreq actively markets 15 brands across the region including such powerhouse names as Lipton, Knorr and Dove. Lipton is the number one tea brand in the world. Knorr leads the convenience foods market in over 65 countries. Dove is the world's number one cleansing brand. "The key to our success," says Bremner with pride, "is our winning combination of the best and most recognizable names world-wide with the most popular and highest quality local brands."

Unilever Mashreq results from a long process of mergers and contractual arrangements between local producers and regional suppliers. The company is a joint venture between Unilever and the Rachid Group, founder of Fine Foods. Rachid Mohammed Rachid, Chairman of Rachid Group, also presides as President of Unilever's North Africa, Middle East and Turkey region.

Born in Alexandria, Egypt in 1955, Rachid M. Rachid has a B.Sc. in Mechanical Engineering from Alexandria University. His career with Unilever began in 1991 when the company established a joint venture with Fine Foods of which he was chairman. After the joint venture, Rachid was made chairman of Unilever Egypt with responsibility for new business development in the Middle East.

As chairman of Unilever Egypt, Rachid has been active in social activities related to economic development and art in the region. He is a member of the Egyptian American President's Council and a board member of the Social Fund of Egypt, which has as it main objective the creation of some 500,000 jobs annually. He also serves as a board member of the Future Generation Foundation, founded by Gamal Mubarak, which focuses on young Egyptian graduates. Rachid also chairs the Alexandria Development Center, an NGO for the regional development and revival of Alexandria. He is the Honorary Consul of the Netherlands in Alexandria, chairs the Friends of the Arts Association, established by his father, and is a board member of the Egyptian Center for Economic Studies and the High Institute of Public Health.

CEO of Unilever Mashreq, John Ramsay "Ray" Bremner, received his MA in Literae Humaniores (Classics) at Oxford in 1979. He began his career with Unilever immediately after graduating from Oxford when he joined Unilever PLC as a management trainee and became manager in 1981. Between 1981 and 1990 Bremner served as manager, primarily of marketing, at various Unilever companies in the UK and the US, including Lever Brothers and Thomas J. Lipton. Then, after two years as Marketing Director at Lipton International, he took his first position in the Middle East as Marketing Director of Foods at Unilever Arabia, Dubai, in 1992. In 1996, he moved on to become Chairman of Unilever Israel, where he remained until 2001. In 2001, Bremner assumed his post as CEO of Unilever Mashreq. He has diplomas in grocery marketing and oenology.

While working for Unilever in the Middle East, Bremner has never neglected to serve the communities in which he works. In Dubai, he supported education for women through the Dubai Women's College and contributed $250,000 to children's charities. While serving in Israel, Bremner undertook various projects in the Palestinian autonomous areas, including a water reclamation and recycling project with Arab villages near Bethlehem and the refurbishment of the children's ward in Ramallah Hospital. Here in Egypt, Bremner joined the Association of Friends of the National Cancer Institute (AFNCI), a body dedicated to building a cancer hospital for children, to which Unilever Mashreq donated $250,000 in 2001. The hospital is currently under construction in Cairo.

Unilever
Unilever Mashreq

Shell

Andrew Vaughan

Andrew Vaughan, along with his wife Dominique and their two young children, came to Egypt in 2001 to head Shell's companies. A scientist by training, he spent his first ten years with Shell on the scientific side in the UK before becoming the team leader of Shell's oil production in Syria. Later, from The Hague, he oversaw Shell operations in Egypt, Abu Dhabi and Syria. He became Managing Director of Shell Bangladesh Exploration and Development before coming to Egypt.

"The petroleum industry is a long-term investment requiring a great deal of cooperation between government and industry," Vaughan states. "Egypt is blessed with excellent natural resources, including an enormous reserve of natural gas, the fuel of the future in Egypt and elsewhere in the world." Egypt has more than 50 trillion cubic feet by current estimates, a serious source of foreign currency as Egypt exports through pipelines and tankers carrying LNG to European and US markets. "Given the Egyptian supply there will be multiple options for gas export evolving over the next two to three years," says Vaughan.

At present, Shell explores for and produces enough natural gas to supply 30% of the domestic market, but it is not yet a major player in gas export projects. British Gas and Edison are leading LNG developments. The Spanish firm Union Fenosa is also an important player in this market. Shell also distributes gas to industry and consumers in Fayum and has an 18% interest in Natgas supplying gas to Cairo and Alexandria. "In 20 years, natural gas will supply almost all of Egypt's energy needs," Vaughan predicts.

As part of a long-term investment, Shell has developed methods of converting gas into high quality diesel products and waxes. This project involves the investment of sizable resources realizing returns only after many years.

Investors find Egypt attractive for its large domestic market, political stability, good trade routes, and large workforce. However, Vaughan points out, "in my industry, there are more highly educated Egyptians outside of the country than expatriates living in Egypt. To put it another way, in terms of brain power Egypt is definitely a net exporter." Thus, among its objectives in Egypt, Shell seeks to build a skilled workforce to support its business. The company supports post-graduate scholarships abroad as well as educational programs at the British Council and the American University in Cairo. "Developing the capacity of young Egyptians is something I care about passionately," says Vaughan.

Service is the key to success in this business because the government controls prices and margins. On that account, Shell benefits from a good position in the consumer market and has excellent downstream potential. Over the past ten years the company has developed an effective dealer network marketing fuels and lubricants. Soon to come online, the company will introduce to the market compressed natural gas for cars, a new product in environmentally friendly fuels. A major area of competition is in lubricants and Shell has worked hard to capture market share in its branded lubricant products. Vaughan does not fear competition though. "On the contrary, I welcome it," he says. "Competition improves products and helps the market grow. Everyone benefits, the companies as well as the consumers."

Our Contributors

Contributors

Photo credits

Contributors

Maha Abdelrahman (MA) is an assistant professor of sociology at the American University in Cairo. She has done extensive research on civil society in Egypt.

Tarek Atia is an editor, writer, and the founder of www.cairolive.com, a popular website covering Egyptian news, views, and entertainment since 1996.

Omar Attum is a freelance nature photographer and writer who is completing his PhD in environmental biology.

Véronique Audergon is a Cairo-based Swiss photographer. Her photos have been published in numerous Egyptian and European media and her artwork has been exhibited in Egypt, Switzerland, France, and Germany.

Jean-Claude Aunos is a photographer who has lived and worked in Egypt for more than 15 years. He is a regular contributor to several local and international publications.

Habib Ayeb (HA) is a geographer at Paris VIII University. He is also affiliated with the Centre d'Etudes et Documentation Economique, Juridique and Sociale (CEDEJ) in Cairo.

Paul Ayoub-Geday (PAG) is a publisher and art director with 20 years experience in publishing and concept creation.

Kirsten Bach (KB) is an anthropologist who has conducted research in Egypt on and off for 20 years. She is a research associate at the Center for Development Research in Copenhagen.

Mindy Bahaeddin (MB) is an environmental consultant in Egypt.

Sherif Bahaeddin (SB) is a naturalist and environmental consultant.

Célame Barge (CB) is a researcher at the Centre d'Etudes et Documentation Economique, Juridique and Sociale (CEDEJ). She is working on a PhD on mobility and transportation in Cairo.

Scott Bartot (ScB) is a journalist and is the former deputy editor of *Business Monthly*.

Minha el Batraoui (MeB) is a writer and theater critic for *al-Ahram Hebdo*.

Belleface, Jean-Francois (JFB) is a consultant in performing arts for the Ford Foundation Cairo office. A specialist of the modern history of Arabic music, he worked for several years in Syria and the Sudan as an arts event organizer.

Alaa Chahine (AC) is a sports writer who has contributed to numerous publications on African and Arab football, including the *al-Ahram Weekly* and the London-based *Onefootball* magazine.

Colin Clement (CC) is a writer and translator who has lived in Alexandria for the past ten years.

Mostafa Darwish (MD) has been a cinema critic for 40 years. His articles have appeared in *al-Hilal*, *Rose al-Youssef*, *Sabah al-Kheir*, and *al-Ahram Weekly*.

Khaled Dawoud (KD) has been a reporter and regional affairs editor at the *Ahram Weekly* since 1991. He is also a correspondent for *The Guardian* and the Lebanese daily *Annahar*.

Eric Denis (ED) is an urban geographer with the Centre d'Etudes et de Documentation Economique, Juridique and Sociale (CEDEJ).

Issandr Elamrani (IE) is the editor of the weekly *Cairo Times*. His pieces have appeared in a variety of local and international publications.

Ben Faulks (BF) is a former editor of the *Egypt Almanac*. He now works with the London-based Economist Intelligence Unit.

Hanzada Fikri (HF) worked for 17 years in print and broadcast journalism for organizations like UPI, US News and World Report, and ABC News. She currently teaches at the American University in Cairo.

Aly Gabr (AG) is an assistant professor in the Department of Architecture at Cairo University and an editor and contributor to *Medina*, an architecture and fine arts magazine.

Pierre Gazio (PG) is a teacher in Cairo, where he has lived for over a decade. He is the author of *Fayyoum: une histoire et un guide*.

Mona El-Ghobashy (MG) is working on a PhD on politics and civil society in Egypt. She is a regular contributor on politics to the *Cairo Times*.

Andrew Hammond (AH) is a Cairo-based journalist. He works for Reuters news agency and is a regular contributor to a number of publications.

Malak Helmy is a fine arts student at the American University in Cairo and an amateur photographer.

Salima Ikram (SI) is an Egyptologist who has been working in Egypt since 1986. She has excavatd at East Karnak, Saqqara, Giza, and the Valley of the Kings.

Barry Iverson is a photographer who has been covering the Middle East for *Time* magazine for 20 years.

Richard Jacquemond (RJ) is associate professor of Arabic literature at Université de Provence in France.

Siona Jenkins (SJ) is a freelance journalist and travel writer who has lived in Cairo for over a decade..

Mahmoud Kassem (MK) has worked for Reuters and the Associated Press. He currently writes for the Wall Street Journal, Dow Jones Newswires, and Oster Dow Jones commodity news service.

Ashraf Khalil (AK) is a freelance journalist and the former editor of the weekly *Cairo Times*. He writes for the Chicago Tribune, San Francisco Chronicle, and Philadelphia Inquirer.

Simon Kitchen (SK) worked in as an editor and market analyst for HC Brokerage. He is now pursuing an MA at Columbia University.

Neil MacDonald (NM) is the editor-in-chief of *Business Monthly*, a business and economic journal published by the American Chamber of Commerce in Egypt.

Mandy McClure (MM) is an editor and translator living in Cairo. She is the former editor of the weekly *Cairo Times*.

Amgad Nagib is a collector.

Steve Negus (SN) is a freelance journalist who has lived in Cairo for a decade. He is a regular contributor to a number of local and international publications.

Tom Olson (TO) publishes a number of magazines in Egypt, including *Golf in Egypt*, which appears six times a year.

Susan Postlewaite (SP) is a freelance business writer who covers Egypt for BridgeNews and *Business Week* magazine.

Nicolas Puig (NP) is a researcher at the Centre d'Etudes et de Documentation Economique, Juridique and Sociale (CEDEJ). he is the author of several articles on urban anthropology.

Max Rodenbeck (MR) is the Middle East correspondent for *The Economist*. He is the author of *Cairo: the City Victorious*..

Reem Saad (RS) is an anthropologist. She is a research associate at the Social Research Center, the American University in Cairo.

Ashraf Salama (AS) is an architect and associate professor of architecture at al-Azhar University in Cairo. He also acts as a technical consultant to the Egyptian housing and tourism ministries.

Paul Schemm (PS) is a journalist in Cairo who has worked and contributed to a number of local and international publications. He is currently managing editor of the weekly *Cairo Times*.

Norbert Schiller is an Egypt-based photographer who has covered every major news event in the Middle East for the last two decades. His photographs regularly appear in *Der Spiegel* magazine, the *New York Times*, and other publications.

Randa Shaath is a Palestinian photographer living in Cairo. Her photos regularly appear in *al-Ahram Weekly* and other publications.

Peter Shaw-Smith (PS-S) is a former Cairo-based journalist. He now works in investment research at HC Wainwright and Co. in Boston.

David Sims (DS) is an international consultant, economist, and urban planner with extensive experience in Egypt and Southeast Asia.

Dana Smillie is a Cairo-based photographer and videographer. Her work has appeared in several international publications.

Sherif Sonbol is a staff photographer at *al-Ahram Weekly* and the principal photographer at the Cairo Opera House.

Claude Stemmelin is a photographer who has lived in Egypt for ten years. He is a regular contributor to many local and foreign publications.

Mursi Sultan (MS) is a Port Said-born short story writer and is a co-founder of a collective for the preservation of popular Egyptian culture.

Fouad al-Tohami (FT) is a documentary filmmaker who has worked in Egyptian and Arab cinema for over 20 years.

Sarah Vellozzi (SV) has spent the last three years in Cairo working as an editor for the Egyptian Center for Economic Studies, HC Brokerage, and other economic research institutions. She is now writing at Trans Regional Creative Communication Services (TRACCS), a regional PR agency.

Graham Waite is a Cairo-based photographer.

Nick Warner (NW) is an architect who specializes in the documentation and restoration of Islamic monuments in Egypt.

Richard Woffenden (RW) is a long-time resident of Cairo who has written about the arts in Egypt for a variety of publications. He is currently culture editor of the *Cairo Times*.

Jailan Zayan (JZ) has worked as a freelance journalist in both print and TV journalism.

PHOTO CREDITS

Akhbar Archive: 44, 45L, 50, 65, 70L, 107, 110L, 121, 122, 130, 131, 147, 150, 152, 161, 174, 175, 178, 211, 224R, 235, 236, 252

Nabil Ashour: 48

Tarek Atia: 146, 148

Omar Attum: 36A

Veronique Audergon: 55, 89R, 123, 163, 167, 228

Jean Claude Aunos: 46, 116, 205, 206, 207, 217R, 222, 232m

Sherif Bahaeddin: 32, 36B, 36C, 36R, 38

Courtesy of the Cairo Opera House: 71A, 72L, 80A, 80R, 84A, 84B, 85A, 128

Courtesy of Cairo Theaters: 78, 79A

Cairo Times Archive: 69A, 75A, 75B, 76R, 77, 82B, 85B, 87B, 90B

Centre d'Etudes Alexandrines/CNRS: 96R, 99

Courtesy of the Association for the Development and Enhancement of Women ADEW: 126, 129

Courtesy of Rami El Dahan: 94

Egypt Almanac Archive: 68A, 68B, 68R, 69B, 69D, 70R, 71B, 71C, 72R, 75C, 76A, 76B, 79L, 80B, 82A, 83, 84C, 87L, 87A, 87C, 88, 89L, 90A, 90C, 90D, 91A, 91B, 91C, 91D, 104R, 117, 133, 157, 189B, 192B, 193L, 194, 213B, 215, 216R, 217L, 218, 220, 221R, 227B, 241R, 249, 251, 345, 354

G. Fanfoni/CIERA: 96L

Final Cut: 74

Paul A. Geday: 39, 47, 56, 57, 60, 79B, 95L, 100, 108, 125, 162, 209, 221L, 241L, 242A, 244L, 244R, 245L, 261L, 351, 353, 355, 356. 361, 362, 363, 364, 365, 366, 367. 369. 370, 374

Paul A. Geday Archive: 25, 45R, 67, 68 Center, 85L, 91L, 114, 135, 137, 158, 169, 176, 187, 189A, 195, 200, 219L, 223, 237, 240, 242B, 243, 258, 260, 261R, 347

Malak Helmy: 87R, 93, 141, 160, 180, 190A, 190B, 199, 212, 213A

Ikonos: 41, 103

Barry Iverson: 214, 248

Lehnert and Landrock: 350, 359

Misr International Films: 73

Yousef Nabil: 69C

Amgad Naguib: 191

Amgad Naguib archive: 113, 185, 188, 201, 216L, 224L, 227A, 239L

NARSS/courtesy of N. Amin (EIAS): 102A, 102B, 104L

Nile City Investment Company: 246

Max Rodenbeck archive: 140, 349

Courtesy of Satgolf: 134

Norbert Schiller: 119, 156, 181, 192A, 193R, 198, 210, 229, 256

Courtesy of Semiramis Hotel: 346

Randa Shaath: 138

Dana Smillie: 23, 26, 27, 30, 33, 53, 54, 59, 63, 86, 110R, 111, 145, 173, 225, 245R, 247, 253, 254, 255

Sherif Sonbol: 149, 166

Claude Stemmelin: 35, 37, 51, 61, 92, 98, 105, 112, 143, 203, 204

Yves Tronc: 42

R. Vincent/American Research Center in Egypt: 102C

Graham Waite: 81, 219R, 250

Nick Warner: 95R, 97, 239R

Maps: Condor Productions/ Geday

Graphs & tables: Egypt Almanac

Numbers refer to page numbers. Strips of photos are identified from left to right or top to bottom A, B, C etc.

Abbreviations: R= Right. L= Left.